INSOLVENCY LAW IN SCOTLAND

D1351023

002139

INSOLVENCY LAW IN SCOTLAND

Donna W. McKenzie Skene
Lecturer in Law, University of Aberdeen

T&T CLARK
EDINBURGH
1999

T&T CLARK LTD
59 GEORGE STREET
EDINBURGH EH2 2LQ
SCOTLAND

First published 1999

ISBN 0 567 00541 0

British Library Cataloguing-in-Publication Data
A catalogue record for this book is available from the British Library

Typeset by Waverley Typesetters, Galashiels
Printed and bound by MPG Books, Bodmin

CONTENTS

Part III: Administration of the Insolvent Estate

Part IV: Effect of Insolvency Proceedings on a Debtor and a Company Debtor's Officers

Part V: The End of Insolvency Proceedings

Part VI: Alternatives to Formal Insolvency Proceedings

Part VII: Cross-Border Insolvency

PREFACE

Insolvency law, by which is meant that part of the law which comes into play when a debtor becomes insolvent, is one of the most complex and fascinating areas of the law and an area of increasing importance in the modern economic climate.

When does a debtor become insolvent? Insolvent is the converse of solvent, which generally means capable of meeting financial obligations,[1] and so could be taken to mean incapable of meeting financial obligations. But 'insolvent' and 'insolvency' are not terms of art in Scots law and can have several different meanings. The word 'insolvent' can be used in a financial sense to mean that the debtor is incapable of meeting bills or other financial obligations, but it can also be used in other ways—for example, to mean that a debtor is subject to one of the legal procedures which can follow on from insolvency in the financial sense.[2] Insolvency in any sense raises many economic and social issues and may have important and wide-ranging economic, social and legal consequences not only for the debtor, but also for the debtor's creditors, for third parties such as employees and persons dealing with, or who have dealt with, the debtor, for the debtor's family (where the debtor is an individual), for the state, and for society as a whole. Insolvency law is concerned with all of these matters and is therefore important not only in its own right, but because it impacts on virtually every other area of law including, for example, property law, contract law, delict, employment law, banking law and, if less obviously, environmental law.

Insolvency raises many important policy issues. The most fundamental is the extent to which the law should intervene in cases of insolvency and provide specific mechanisms to cater for it. If such mechanisms are to be provided, the question then arises as to what form they should take. This depends on the function they are to perform, which raises other policy questions, such as how should the law treat an insolvent debtor? Should the law treat different types of insolvent debtor differently? Where should the balance between the rights of creditors, third parties and the debtor be struck? Should it always be struck in the

---

[1] The *Collins English Dictionary* defines 'solvent' as capable of meeting financial obligations and 'solvency' as an ability to pay all debts.

[2] The various meanings of insolvency are discussed in more detail in Chapter 1.

same place, or should it be struck in a different place for different types of debtor? Should it take into account factors such as moral blame? How should the law treat creditors in relation to each other—first come, first served, or on some other basis? The answers to these and other questions not only determine the shape of the law and inform an understanding of it, but give a fascinating insight into the fundamental policies on which the legal system is based.[3]

Scots law distinguishes between different types of debtor in the context of insolvency law. Essentially, the distinction is between company debtors on the one hand and other types of debtor (hereafter referred to collectively as 'non-company debtors') on the other.[4] That part of insolvency law which concerns non-company debtors is commonly referred to as the law of bankruptcy, whereas that part of insolvency law concerning companies is usually referred to simply as company (or corporate) insolvency law. Although both types of debtor are free to seek informal means of dealing with insolvency (in the financial sense),[5] the formal legal procedures which may follow on from such insolvency vary according to the type of debtor involved.[6] Non-company debtors are subject to the judicial procedure known as sequestration. Companies are not subject to sequestration: the formal insolvency procedures potentially applicable to companies are company voluntary arrangements under Part I of the Insolvency Act 1986, compromises or arrangements under s 425 of the Companies Act 1985, administration, receivership and liquidation.[7] Both types of debtor may in certain circumstances have a judicial factor appointed, but the appointment of a judicial factor is not confined to circumstances of insolvency and is only rarely utilised in those circumstances: judicial factories are therefore considered separately in this book and not as formal insolvency proceedings as such.[8] The distinction between company and non-company debtors is partly historical, the law on company insolvency having developed separately from that on non-company insolvency.[9] It is also, however, a result of the fact that, at one level, the question 'Should different types of debtor be treated differently?' has been answered in the affirmative in the context of Scots law: the objectives of insolvency law are not regarded as exactly the same for company and non-company debtors.[10] At another level, however, many of the principles upon which insolvency law is based apply equally to both company and non-company debtors, and this is reflected in the current insolvency legislation which has harmonised the provisions of company and non-company insolvency law in a number of areas.[11]

Most of the Scottish law of insolvency is now statute-based and is contained for the most part in specific insolvency statutes and associated delegated legislation. Some important parts of the law of insolvency are still to be found, however, in

---

[3] The theory and general principles of insolvency law are discussed further in Chapter 3.

[4] Other systems make other distinctions, for example, between trading and non-trading debtors, a distinction which at one time also obtained in Scots law: see Chapter 2.

[5] Extra-judicial alternatives to formal insolvency proceedings are discussed in Chapter 45.

[6] These proceedings are mentioned here by name only: an outline of each can be found in Chapter 4.

[7] Not all of these proceedings apply to all companies: for further details see the chapters relating to the procedure leading to each régime which details the companies to which it applies.

[8] See Chapter 46.

[9] The historical development of Scots law is discussed further in Chapter 2.

[10] See further Chapter 3.

[11] Ibid.

the common law or in other statutory provisions.[12] The impact of devolution on insolvency law in Scotland is yet to be seen. Much of company insolvency law is reserved to the UK Parliament, and although most of non-company insolvency law and the law relating to floating charges and receivers is within the legislative competence of the Scottish Parliament, certain matters relating to those areas are also reserved.[13] In one respect, therefore, the impact of devolution on insolvency law in Scotland may be regarded as limited, but in other respects, it may not be: legislation in devolved areas might have a substantial impact in both Scotland and the other parts of the UK.[14] Much will therefore depend on the extent to which the Scottish Parliament chooses to legislate on devolved matters and, indeed, the extent to which the UK Parliament chooses to legislate on reserved matters.

This book is divided into seven parts. Part I deals with introductory and theoretical matters: the meaning of insolvency, the development of insolvency law in Scotland, the theory and general principles of insolvency law, the current legislation and insolvency proceedings and the insolvency practitioners who administer these. Part II deals with the initiation of formal insolvency proceedings and the subsequent procedure. Part III deals with the administration of the insolvent estate. Part IV deals with the effect of insolvency proceedings on a debtor and on a company debtor's officers. Part V deals with the end of insolvency proceedings. Part VI deals with other procedures available on insolvency and Part VII deals with cross-border insolvency issues.

---

[12] The current legislation and insolvency proceedings are discussed further in Chapter 4.

[13] For a more detailed discussion of the areas which are devolved and reserved respectively, and the impact of devolution on insolvency law generally, see McKenzie Skene, 'Scots Wha' Hae – Insolvency and Devolution', 1999 Recovery 10.

[14] If, for example, the Scottish Parliament chose to abolish floating charges or exclude consumer debtors from the sequestration process—both highly improbable but theoretically possible—this would have a huge impact both in Scotland and in the rest of the UK. Even lesser changes in devolved areas might force changes in practice or influence decisions concerning business planning both in Scotland and other parts of the UK.

ACKNOWLEDGEMENTS

The process of legal research and writing is a complex and difficult as well as a rewarding one, and there are many people without whom this work might never have been written and to whom I therefore owe my thanks. I am grateful to my colleagues, at Aberdeen and elsewhere, and to my family and friends, for support and encouragement over the years as well as in relation to this particular project. In particular, I am grateful to Professor Angelo Forte, who listened to my ideas for this work and not only refrained from pouring cold water on them but contributed invaluable advice and comments, and to Roy Roxburgh of Messrs Iain Smith and Co, Aberdeen, Judith Pearson and Dr Iain MacNeil for invaluable comments and discussions on various points of difficulty. I would also like to thank T&T Clark for their enthusiasm for the project and for their assistance and support. I have benefited greatly from the work of others who have written in this field, in particular Professor McBryde's seminal *Bankruptcy*, St Clair and Drummond Young's *The Law of Corporate Insolvency in Scotland*, Green and Fletcher's *The Law of Receivership in Scotland*, Fletcher, Higham and Trower's *The Law and Practice of Corporate Administrations* and Palmer's *Company Law*, and from the work of the Scottish Law Commission. Last, but not least, I am grateful to my husband for his unfailing patience and support even in the face of what, on many occasions, must have seemed like gross ingratitude when the creative process encountered difficulties of one sort or another.

Donna W. McKenzie Skene
Aberdeen
June 1999

ACKNOWLEDGMENTS

TABLE OF CASES

TABLE OF STATUTES, ETC

STATUTES

STATUTORY INSTRUMENTS

RULES OF THE COURT OF SESSION

Part I

INTRODUCTION AND THEORY

1 : THE MEANING OF INSOLVENCY

I nsolvency is not a term of art in Scots law.[1] It is sometimes used interchangeably with the term bankruptcy,[2] which is not a technical term in Scots law either. Goudy states that '[i]nsolvency and bankruptcy, as general terms in the law of Scotland, do not admit of exact definition'.[3] Both are commonly used to refer to the actual state of any given debtor's financial affairs (for example, a debtor who is unable to pay bills as they fall due may be described as insolvent or bankrupt) and to the fact that a given debtor is subject to one of the legal proceedings which may follow on from such financial difficulties, although strictly speaking the term bankruptcy should not be applied to company debtors at all.

When a debtor is described as insolvent, therefore, this might mean one of several different things. One particular consequence of this is that the use of general terms such as bankruptcy or insolvency, without further definition, in situations where they have legal significance can cause problems—for example, where a contract provides for certain remedies to become available on one party's 'insolvency' without making explicit which type of insolvency is meant.

This chapter examines the different types of insolvency and the consequences of each type for the debtor (and others).

Absolute insolvency

Absolute insolvency occurs where a debtor's total liabilities exceed total assets. It is sometimes referred to as 'balance sheet' insolvency. A debtor who is absolutely insolvent may remain able to pay bills as they fall due and, particularly where this is the case, may continue in a state of absolute insolvency without any immediate consequences. However, certain transactions carried out by an absolutely insolvent debtor may subsequently be open to challenge[4] and, where the debtor is a company, there may be a variety of consequences for the directors and others if trading is carried on in the knowledge that the company is absolutely insolvent.[5]

---

[1] See the Preface.
[2] Being the term usually given to that part of insolvency law relating to non-company debtors: see the Preface.
[3] Goudy, *Bankruptcy* (4th edn), p 15.
[4] See Chapter 30.
[5] See generally Chapter 37.

Practical insolvency

Practical insolvency occurs where a debtor is unable to pay bills as they fall due. A debtor who is insolvent in this sense need not be absolutely insolvent, but has no liquid assets with which to settle current debts. Particularly in a business context, practical insolvency is usually caused by cash-flow problems: it commonly occurs where the debtor's own debtors pay late (or not at all) so that the debtor in turn becomes unable to meet bills on time. Practical insolvency will usually have immediate consequences for a debtor. It may, of itself, entitle a creditor to exercise certain remedies against the debtor. For example, the Sale of Goods Act 1979 (hereafter 'the 1979 Act') specifically provides for an unpaid seller to exercise specified remedies where the debtor is insolvent, and the definition of insolvency adopted is essentially one of practical insolvency. In the absence of such specific provisions, unpaid creditors may resort to one of the remedies available against defaulting debtors under the general law. Most will try informal action first: telephoning or writing to the debtor, perhaps threatening to cut off further supplies or take legal action. If this is unsuccessful, they may resort to court action, followed by diligence. In certain circumstances, a creditor may be entitled to do diligence without first obtaining a court decree—for example, where the document constituting the debt is registered for execution.[6] A creditor may also serve a statutory demand for payment on the debtor in accordance with the relevant statutory provisions,[7] non-compliance with which will render the debtor liable to sequestration (in the case of a non-company debtor) or liquidation (in the case of a company debtor).

Apparent insolvency

Apparent insolvency is a concept introduced by the Bankruptcy (Scotland) Act 1985 (hereafter 'the 1985 Act').[8] Although the provisions relating to apparent insolvency are contained in the 1985 Act, they apply to companies as well.[9] Section 7 of the 1985 Act sets out the ways in which a debtor may become apparently insolvent.[10]

(1)   Where the debtor is sequestrated in Scotland or made bankrupt in England or Wales or Northern Ireland.[11]

---

[6] A detailed discussion of diligence is beyond the scope of this book, but there are a number of useful texts to which the reader may refer. The principal Scottish texts on diligence generally are *Stewart on Diligence* and Maher and Cusine, *The Law and Practice of Diligence*. On inhibitions and adjudications in particular, see Gretton, *The Law of Inhibition and Adjudication* (2nd edn). The Scottish Law Commission has recently published its Report on Diligence on the Dependence and Admiralty Arrestments (Scot Law Com No 164, 1998) which contains proposals for reform in these areas and also a number of general proposals for reform which are of particular relevance to insolvency: see further Chapter 31.

[7] 1985 Act, s 7(1)(d), in the case of non-company debtors, and the Insolvency Act 1986, s 123(1)(a), in the case of company debtors.

[8] It replaced the concept of 'notour bankruptcy', referred to further in Chapter 2, to which references may still sometimes be seen.

[9] 1985 Act, s 7(4), which provides that registered companies and other entities in respect of which sequestration is incompetent may none the less be made apparently insolvent.

[10] Not all the ways listed will in fact be applicable to company debtors.

[11] 1985 Act, s 7(1)(a).

(2) Where the debtor has given *written* notice to creditors of cessation of payment of debts in the normal course of business.[12]

(3) Where the debtor has granted a trust deed for creditors.[13]

(4) Where a charge for payment has been served on the debtor and the debtor has not paid within the time allowed in the charge.[14]

(5) Where a poinding or other seizure of the debtor's moveable property has taken place to enforce a summary warrant for the recovery of rates or taxes and the debtor does not pay within 14 days of the poinding or other seizure.[15] What is covered by 'other seizure of the debtor's moveable property' is not entirely clear. It has been held that it does not include a wages arrestment.[16] There are proposals to amend the definition of apparent insolvency so that it will be constituted on the *service* of a summary warrant.[17]

(6) Where a decree of adjudication in security or for payment of any of the debtor's estate is granted.[18]

(7) Where the debtor's effects are sold as a result of a sequestration for rent.[19]

(8) Where a receiving order is made against the debtor in England or Wales.[20]

(9) Where a creditor has served a statutory demand for payment of debt on the debtor and the debtor has failed, within three weeks of its service, *either* to pay the debt/s due or find security for their payment *or* to intimate to the creditor by recorded delivery post that he denies the existence of the debt or that he denies that it is due at that time.[21] A statutory demand for payment of debt may only be served where the creditor is owed a liquid debt or debts of at least a prescribed amount (currently £750). Evidence of the debt or debts must be attached to the demand.[22] The three-week time-limit is strictly observed.[23]

In situations (3) to (8) inclusive, apparent insolvency will *not* be established where the debtor is willing and able to pay debts as they fall due (or would be but for the existence of specified orders affecting the debtor's property),[24] but the onus of establishing this is on the debtor.

Once constituted, apparent insolvency continues until the debtor becomes able to pay his/its debts and pays them as they fall due, except where it is

---

[12] 1985 Act, s 7(1)(b).

[13] 1985 Act, s 7(1)(c)(i).

[14] 1985 Act, s 7(1)(c)(ii).

[15] 1985 Act, s 7(1)(c)(iii).

[16] *MacKay, Petnr* 1996 SCLR 1091 (Notes). Earnings arrestments, of course, only affect individual debtors.

[17] A new Bill containing this and a number of other amendments to the 1985 Act is being prepared at the time of writing. For details of this and the other amendments which it is proposed to include in the Bill, see The Bankruptcy (Scotland) Act 1985, A Consultation Follow-up: Protected Trust Deeds and Other Issues, issued by the Scottish Office in July 1998. That paper follows on from Apparent Insolvency, A Consultation Paper on Amending the Bankruptcy (Scotland) Act 1985, issued by the Scottish Office in July 1997.

[18] 1985 Act, s 7(1)(c)(iv).

[19] 1985 Act, s 7(1)(c)(v).

[20] 1985 Act, s 7(1)(c)(vi).

[21] 1985 Act, s 7(1)(d).

[22] *Lord Advocate* v *Thomson* (IH) 1994 SCLR 96.

[23] *Guthrie Newspaper Group* v *Morrison* 1992 GWD 22–1244.

[24] 1985 Act, s 7(1)(c).

constituted by the debtor's sequestration, when it continues until the debtor is discharged.[25]

Apparent insolvency may have a number of consequences for any type of debtor. Contracts, leases and other agreements may allow termination of the relevant agreement or the exercise of other remedies in the event of apparent insolvency. Apparent insolvency also affects certain types of diligence done by creditors within specified time-limits.[26] In the case of non-company debtors, it may also render the debtor's estates liable to sequestration:[27] the estates of a debtor who is liable to sequestration may in some cases be sequestrated without the debtor being apparently insolvent,[28] but in other cases apparent insolvency is a necessary prerequisite for sequestration.[29]

Inability to pay debts

The Insolvency Act 1986 (hereafter 'the 1986 Act') uses for certain purposes the concept of a company being unable to pay its debts. In relation to registered companies, this concept is defined in s 123 of the 1986 Act, which deems that a company is unable to pay its debts in the following circumstances.

(1) Where a creditor has served a statutory demand for payment on the company and the company has failed *either* to pay the debt/s due *or* to secure or compound for it/them to the satisfaction of the creditor within three weeks.[30] The debt or debts due must exceed £750 and the statutory demand must be served on the company by leaving it at the company's registered office.[31]

(2) Where, in England and Wales, execution or other process issued on a judgment, decree or order of any court in favour of a creditor of the company is returned unsatisfied in whole or in part.[32]

(3) Where, in Scotland, a charge for payment on an extract decree, extract registered bond or extract registered protest is served on the company and the company fails to make payment within the time allowed in the charge.[33]

(4) Where, in Northern Ireland, a certificate of unenforceability has been granted in respect of a judgment against the company.[34]

(5) If it is proved to the satisfaction of the court that the company is unable to pay its debts as they fall due.[35]

---

[25] 1985 Act, s 7(2).

[26] See Chapter 31.

[27] It is not technically correct to speak of the sequestration of a debtor, only of a debtor's estates, but the former usage is common.

[28] This is why s 7 of the 1985 Act provides that sequestration is one of the events which can make a debtor apparently insolvent.

[29] For a full discussion of the requirements for an award of sequestration, see Chapter 6.

[30] 1986 Act, s 123(1)(a).

[31] Ibid. The minimum amount of the sum due may be altered by order under s 416 of the 1986 Act: 1986 Act, s 123(3).

[32] 1986 Act, s 123(1)(b).

[33] 1986 Act, s 123(1)(c).

[34] 1986 Act, s 123(1)(d).

[35] 1986 Act, s 123(1)(e).

(6) If it is proved to the satisfaction of the court that the value of the company's assets is less than its liabilities, including contingent and prospective liabilities.[36]

This definition incorporates elements of what is in effect both practical and absolute insolvency. The fact that a registered company is unable to pay its debts within the meaning of this section may not of itself have any immediate consequences for the company unless contracts, leases or other agreements contain provisions related to the fact that the company is insolvent in this way, but it may enable a petition for administration or liquidation of the company to be presented. The fact that a company is, or is likely to be, unable to pay its debts within the meaning of s 123 of the 1986 Act is a prerequisite for presentation of an administration petition, which may be presented by creditors or others,[37] and it is one of the grounds on which a company may be wound up by the court.[38]

In relation to unregistered companies, the concept is defined in ss 222–224 of the 1986 Act, which deems that an unregistered company is unable to pay its debts for the purposes of s 221 of the 1986 Act in the following circumstances.

(1) Where a creditor has served a statutory demand for payment on the company and the company has failed *either* to pay the debt/s due *or* to secure or compound for it/them to the satisfaction of the creditor within three weeks.[39] The debt or debts due must exceed £750 and the statutory demand must be served on the company by leaving it at the company's principal place of business *or* by delivering it to the secretary or a director, manager or principal officer of the company *or* otherwise as the court approves or directs.[40]

(2) Where notice in writing of an action or other proceeding which has been instituted against any member of the company for any debt or demand due or claimed to be due from the company or from him *qua* member has been served on the company and the company has not, within three weeks of that service, *either* paid the debt or demand *or* secured or compounded for it *or* procured a sist of the proceedings *or* indemnified the defender against all costs and other specified items.[41]

(3) Where, in England and Wales, execution or other process issued on a judgment, decree or order of any court in favour of a creditor against the company or other specified persons is returned unsatisfied in whole or in part.[42]

(4) Where, in Scotland, a charge for payment on an extract decree, extract registered bond or extract registered protest is served on the company and the company fails to make payment within the time allowed in the charge.[43]

---

[36] 1986 Act, s 123(2).
[37] See further Chapter 10.
[38] See further Chapter 16.
[39] 1986 Act, s 222(1).
[40] Ibid. The minimum amount of the sum due may be altered by regulations under s 417 of the 1986 Act: 1986 Act, s 222(2).
[41] 1986 Act, s 223.
[42] 1986 Act, s 224(1)(a).
[43] 1986 Act, s 224(1)(b).

(5) Where, in Northern Ireland, a certificate of unenforceability has been granted in respect of a judgment against the company.[44]

(6) If it is proved to the satisfaction of the court that the company is unable to pay its debts as they fall due.[45]

(7) If it is proved to the satisfaction of the court that the value of the company's assets is less than its liabilities, including contingent and prospective liabilities.[46]

Again, this definition incorporates elements of what is in effect both practical and absolute insolvency. As for registered companies, the fact that an unregistered company is unable to pay its debts within the meaning of these sections may not have any immediate consequences for the company unless contracts, leases or other agreements contain provisions related to the fact that the company is insolvent in this way, but it may enable a petition for liquidation of the company to be presented. The fact that a company is unable to pay its debts as defined is one of the grounds on which an unregistered company may be wound up.[47]

Other types of insolvency

Insolvency may be used to mean that a debtor has entered into some form of extra-judicial arrangement with creditors[48] or is subject to formal insolvency proceedings. An example of the latter type of usage can be found in the 1986 Act where, for the purpose of interpretation of the first group of Parts of that Act, insolvency in relation to a company is defined as including, except where the context otherwise requires, the approval of a voluntary arrangement under Part I of that Act, the making of an administration order or the appointment of an administrative receiver.[49] This particular example is also an example of insolvency being defined in a particular way by a particular statute for the purpose(s) specified in that statute. The provisions of the 1979 Act allowing an unpaid seller to exercise specified remedies where the debtor is insolvent, referred to above, are another example of this usage: as noted, the 1979 Act provides a specific definition of insolvency for that purpose.[50]

---

[44] 1986 Act, s 224(1)(c).

[45] 1986 Act, s 224(1)(d).

[46] 1986 Act, s 224(2).

[47] 1986 Act, s 225(1)(b), and see further Chapter 17.

[48] For extra-judicial arrangements with creditors, see Chapter 45.

[49] 1986 Act, s 247(1).

[50] See above in connection with practical insolvency, the definition in this case essentially being one of practical insolvency.

2 : THE DEVELOPMENT OF INSOLVENCY LAW
IN SCOTLAND

Historically, the law on company insolvency developed later than, and continued to develop separately from, the law relating to non-company debtors. This chapter outlines the development of both non-company and company insolvency law.

Non-company insolvency law[1]

Goudy states that 'prior to the eighteenth century, the law of bankruptcy presents itself in a comparatively rude and undeveloped form'.[2] The law provided, as it does today, a number of remedies whereby unpaid creditors could make the debtor's assets available for payment of their debts: adjudication (formerly 'comprising')[3] in relation to the heritable estate; poinding and arrestment in relation to the moveable estate; and imprisonment.[4] This last remedy was exerciseable in addition to the other remedies described and did not amount to satisfaction of the debt: it was meant to act as a compulsitor to make the debtor disclose any hidden assets against which the creditor might then exercise any of the other remedies.[5] A debtor could try to negotiate with his creditors, but this depended on agreement in each case. There was no collective procedure whereby a debtor could surrender his assets to his creditors and receive in return a discharge from his debts. He could avoid (or be released from) imprisonment by utilising the procedure known as *cessio bonorum*, whereby he surrendered all his assets to his creditors, but he remained liable for any unpaid balance of his debts. Thus, he was likely both to remain destitute (having given over all his assets to his creditors) and to be unable to make any sort of fresh start (because any assets he subsequently acquired remained subject to diligence by creditors with any part of their debts still unpaid). Further, not only was the law thus unsympathetic to debtors, but it allowed individual creditors to pursue such remedies as were open to them

---

[1] For a detailed history of non-company insolvency law, see the Introduction to Goudy, *Bankruptcy*. See also McBryde, *Bankruptcy* (2nd edn), para 1–08 et seq.
[2] Goudy, p 1.
[3] See further below.
[4] See Bell's *Commentaries*.
[5] See Lord Dunedin in *Caldwell* v *Hamilton* 1919 SC (HL) 100 at 106.

without regard to other creditors, so that 'he who outstripped his fellows in the race of diligence enjoyed the fruits thereof'.[6]

Perhaps unsurprisingly, many debtors facing financial difficulties seem to have responded by trying to put their assets beyond the reach of their creditors—for example, by transferring them to others. The common law, which still exists today, provided remedies for such fraudulent conduct on the part of debtors, but seems to have been regarded as inadequate to deal with it without statutory assistance. Accordingly, the first bankruptcy legislation was enacted in the form of the Bankruptcy Act 1621, which dealt with gratuitous alienations by debtors to 'conjunct and confident' persons and other voluntary alienations after the commencement of diligence. That Act was followed in due course by the Bankruptcy Act 1696, which dealt with the problem of debtors favouring particular creditors at the expense of the general body of creditors within a short period prior to the debtor's 'notour bankruptcy'.[7]

In the period between those two Acts, the first legislation to regulate competing diligence was enacted, although it affected only diligence against the debtor's heritable property. The Diligence Act 1661 made provision for the *pari passu* ranking of 'comprisings' (replaced, in the Adjudications Act 1672, by adjudications) and the Judicial Sale Act 1681 subsequently introduced the process of ranking and sale by virtue of which land which was the subject of competing adjudications could be sequestrated, that is, put into the hands of the court, which then arranged for the land to be factored if necessary, sold, and for the creditors to be ranked on the proceeds.

In 1772 a similar form of process was introduced in relation to moveable property by the Bills of Exchange (Scotland) Act 1772. That Act provided for sequestration of a debtor's moveable estate, its management by a factor, its subsequent sale and the distribution of the proceeds among the debtor's creditors, all under the supervision of the court. The Act expired after 10 years and a new statute was then enacted in the form of the Payment of Creditors (Scotland) Act 1783, which extended the procedure to include the debtor's heritable property but limited the availability of the procedure to traders. This Act also expired after 10 years and was replaced by the Payment of Creditors (Scotland) Act 1793, in turn replaced by the Bankruptcy Act 1814, which was renewed annually until the Bankruptcy (Scotland) Act 1839 was enacted as a permanent measure. The 1839 Act was replaced by the Bankruptcy (Scotland) Act 1856, which acted as a consolidating statute but also made various amendments to the law, including removal of the restriction limiting the procedure to traders. The Debtors (Scotland) Act 1880 abolished civil imprisonment for debt, with some exceptions, and introduced a new form of the *cessio bonorum* procedure, which was in turn abolished by the Bankruptcy (Scotland) Act 1913, which also replaced the 1856 Act. The 1913 Act was itself replaced, following an extensive review of bankruptcy law and related matters by the Scottish Law Commission,[8] by the 1985 Act which, as amended, now contains most of the modern Scots law of bankruptcy.

---

[6] Ibid.

[7] The Act laid down a number of criteria by which it could be determined that the debtor was publicly or 'notoriously' bankrupt, the appropriate consequences then flowing from that state. The concept has now been replaced by that of apparent insolvency: see Chapter 1.

[8] Discussed in Chapter 3.

Company insolvency law[9]

The history of company insolvency law goes hand in hand with the history of the company itself. The original methods of incorporating a company in Scots law were by Act of Parliament or by Royal Charter (or its equivalent, ie, Letters Patent from the sovereign). Companies also came to be formed by voluntary association, investors subscribing a specific sum of money and the company's business being carried on by directors. Such 'joint stock' companies were intended to trade with the advantages of companies incorporated by the more traditional methods, that is a separate legal personality and with it limited liability for the investors (who did not wish to be liable for the debts of the company beyond the sum they had already contributed) and transferability of their interest in the company.

From the point of view of insolvency law, separate legal personality and limited liability are crucial, because they determine against whom the creditors can have recourse in the event of the company failing to pay its debts. The South Sea Company Act of 1720 (commonly referred to as the Bubble Act), which extended to Scotland, made all companies other than those incorporated by Act of Parliament or Royal Charter illegal. It was ultimately repealed in 1825[10] but joint stock companies not incorporated in these ways continued to flourish in the intervening period, despite the fact that the logical corollary of the fact that they were illegal was that the investors (contrary to their desires) remained personally liable for all the debts of the company. The position of investors was for some time unsettled, however. In 1757, in *Stevenson & Co v MacNair*[11] the court effectively held that joint stock companies did have limited liability when it held that the 'partners' in the Arran Fishing Company were not liable for the company's debts beyond the funds subscribed by them. In 1778, however, in *Douglas, Heron & Co v Alexander Hair*[12] the 'partners' of a company trading as a bank were held liable to contribute further sums to the company in an action at the instance of the company itself, such contributions being sought to enable it to settle indebtedness beyond the sums subscribed by those involved, and this later case seems to have been regarded as settling the point that a joint stock company did *not* have limited liability and investors did remain liable for the company's debts.

Limited liability for joint stock companies was finally introduced by statute in the form of the Companies Act 1856, and with the acceptance of the concept of limited liability came the necessity to make proper provision for the insolvency of the company, since creditors would no longer be able to pursue subscribers to the company for its unpaid debts. The Companies Act 1862 introduced the 'modern' company, providing for the first time for incorporation of a company with limited liability on registration in accordance with the appropriate statutory formalities. At the same time, it introduced provisions for the winding up of such a company in the event, *inter alia*, of its insolvency. Provisions relating to winding up continued to appear in succeeding companies statutes, and the current provisions are now contained in the 1986 Act.

---

[9] For a detailed history, see particularly St Clair and Drummond Young, *The Law of Corporate Insolvency in Scotland* (2nd edn), p 1 et seq.

[10] By 6 Geo 4 c 91.

[11] (1757) Mor 14560 and 14467.

[12] (1778) Mor 14605.

The Companies Act 1870 introduced a procedure whereby a company in liquidation could reach a compromise with its creditors. The Companies Act 1900 extended the procedure to allow compromises with members. The Companies Act 1907 further extended the procedure to companies which were not in liquidation, thus allowing companies which were not insolvent at all, or which were insolvent but not yet in liquidation, to take advantage of the procedure. Similar provision was made in succeeding companies statutes and the current provision is now contained in s 425 of the Companies Act 1985 (hereafter 'CA 1985'). It provides for a company, whether solvent or insolvent and, in the latter case, whether or not it is subject to any other formal insolvency proceedings, to reach a compromise or arrangement with its members and/or creditors and/or any class or classes of either.

The Companies (Floating Charges) (Scotland) Act 1961 introduced the floating charge into Scots law to address the problem that it was virtually impossible in Scots law to create a security over moveable property without possession. The floating charge allowed a company (and only a company) to grant security over all or any part of its undertaking, including heritable and moveable property, while retaining possession of that property and the ability to dispose of it and acquire new property without the need to discharge the security over the property disposed of and/or create a new security over the property acquired every time. Initially, a floating chargeholder who wished to enforce his security against his defaulting debtor had to petition for the winding up of the company, at which point the charge would attach to whatever assets the company had at that time which came within its terms. However, the Companies (Floating Charges and Receivers) (Scotland) Act 1972 introduced the concept of receivership into Scots law by providing for the floating chargeholder to be able to appoint, or obtain the appointment of, a receiver to enforce the security outwith liquidation. The current provisions on receivership are contained in the 1986 Act.

Following the Report of the Review Committee on Insolvency Law and Practice chaired by Sir Kenneth Cork in 1982[13] (hereafter 'the Cork Report' and 'the Cork Committee' respectively), two further corporate insolvency procedures were introduced: company voluntary arrangements (CVAs) and administration. The current provisions relating to these procedures are also contained in the 1986 Act.

---

[13] Cmnd 8558 (1982).

3 : THE THEORY AND GENERAL PRINCIPLES
OF INSOLVENCY LAW

It was noted earlier that insolvency raises many economic and social issues and that these issues arise at different levels.[1] The most fundamental question is whether and, if so, to what extent, the law should intervene in cases of insolvency and provide specific procedures to cater for it. In other words, should there be special rules (insolvency law) which come into operation on insolvency and displace the normal rules of law at all? If so, to what extent should they do so and thereby interfere with the rights and expectations otherwise protected by the normal rules?

If special insolvency rules and procedures are to be provided, the question arises as to the form these should take. This depends on the function which they are to perform, which in turn depends on the answers to other important policy questions, such as the attitude to be adopted towards an insolvent debtor and the appropriate balance between the respective rights of the various parties who may be affected by the insolvency. The answers to these questions provide the underlying principles on which the law is based and determine its shape and form. The law itself can therefore only be properly understood if the principles on which it is based are understood. Accordingly, this chapter examines briefly the justifications for insolvency law itself and the general principles on which the current insolvency law of Scotland is based.[2]

Justifications for insolvency law

What are the justifications for insolvency law itself? It might be supposed that, since the law of Scotland clearly does incorporate specific rules and legal procedures to cater for insolvency, these must have been thought to be justifiable in some way. However, it is not merely an academic exercise to consider what the possible justifications are. The justifications for insolvency law itself provide

---

[1] See the Preface.
[2] Space precludes a detailed examination of all the issues, which are complex, but the chapter aims to give a basic understanding of the issues involved. There are a number of excellent texts which give a more detailed treatment: see, in particular, Rajak, *Insolvency Law Theory and Practice*, and also Goode, *Principles of Corporate Insolvency Law*.

the framework, or context, for the principles on which that law is based. It is therefore appropriate to examine them before embarking on an examination of the principles themselves.

Goudy stated:

> '[B]ankruptcy law is based on the principle that, so soon as man becomes insolvent, his estate becomes the property of his creditors, and ought to be distributed among them according to their several rights and preferences. And it seems a legitimate extension of this principle that the debtor, upon surrendering his estate, should receive a discharge from the creditors' claims. *But these are legal conceptions by no means self evident.* The natural and immediate view ... is that the creditor should be allowed to enforce payment of his debt by all lawful means, and that he has no concern with claims by other creditors. If he can obtain payment or security by means of diligence, or through his debtor's voluntary act, why should he have to give up his advantage, and be compelled to share with more dilatory or less fortunate creditors?'[3] (emphasis supplied).

More recently it has been said in relation to company insolvency law:

> 'It cannot be assumed that since corporate managerial power in a going concern requires legitimation, insolvency regimes and powers automatically require legitimation. Insolvency processes do, however, impinge strongly upon the public interest in so far as decisions are made about the lives or deaths of enterprises and those decisions affect livelihoods and communities. Insolvency processes also have dramatic import for private rights in so far as, for instance, pre-insolvency property rights and securities can be frozen and individual efforts to enforce other legal rights constrained. On both public and private interest grounds, accordingly, the powers involved in insolvency processes can be seen as requiring strong justification.'[4]

Does such justification exist? Finch identifies four rationales for justifying insolvency processes, namely efficiency, accountability, fairness and expertise.[5] The reader may come to his or her own conclusion as to whether the insolvency law of Scotland is justified in the light of these rationales after studying it further. But Goudy at least was in no doubt that the principles of bankruptcy law as identified by him in the quotation above were justified, on the basis of their utility and fundamental equity:

> 'It is not until the matter is examined by the light of experience—the experience especially, which mercantile affairs and commercial intercourse with other nations afford—that the fundamental equity of the bankrupt laws is fully perceived.'[6]

---

[3] *Bankruptcy*, p 1.

[4] Finch, 'The Measures of Insolvency Law' 1997 OJLS 227 at 246.

[5] Ibid at 247, 250. She makes it clear, however, that assessing the legitimacy of individual rules is different from assessing the legitimacy of insolvency law as a whole (at 249) and that assessing legitimacy is also different from expressing a political view on the topic (at 248).

[6] *Bankruptcy*, p 1.

The functions and general principles of insolvency law

It was stated above that the form of the rules and procedures of insolvency law depends on the function or functions the law is to perform and that this in turn depends on policy issues such as the attitude to be taken to the debtor and the correct balance between the rights of the parties potentially affected by the insolvency.[7] The relevant policy issues were canvassed extensively by the Scottish Law Commission in its Report on Bankruptcy and Related Aspects of Insolvency and Liquidation[8] (hereafter 'the Scottish Law Commission Report') and by the Cork Committee, which examined insolvency law and practice in England and Wales.

Basic policy issues

One very basic issue is the way in which insolvent debtors are to be regarded. It has already been noted that historically, insolvent (non-company) debtors in Scotland were regarded in a very unsympathetic light,[9] but as bankruptcy law has evolved, it has reflected a steadily more liberal attitude to insolvent debtors generally. There has been a recognition that, particularly in our modern, credit-based society, debtors can become insolvent through misfortune or unwisdom, and that such debtors at least may deserve to be treated with a greater degree of sympathy.[10] Company debtors raise different issues to a certain extent. The Cork Committee stated:

> 'Society is concerned to relieve and protect the individual insolvent from the harassment of his creditors, and to enable him to regain financial stability and to make a fresh start'[11] whereas '[i]n the case of an insolvent company, society has no interest in the preservation or rehabilitation of the company as such, though it may have a legitimate concern in the preservation of the commercial enterprise'.[12]

However, as the Scottish Law Commission had correctly identified in the Memorandum which preceded its Report,[13] in the case of a trading debtor, the form of the business might be quite fortuitous, and the arrangements for dissolving a business should therefore proceed as far as possible on the same principles, irrespective of whether bankruptcy or liquidation is involved.[14] That point was reiterated in its Report, where it stated that despite differences between bankruptcy and liquidation, there were certain areas in which substantially the same rules ought to apply, as had indeed already been recognised in the then applicable law.[15] The Cork Committee too ultimately took the view that reform should lead to 'the harmonisation and integration, wherever possible, of the law and

---

[7] See also the Preface.
[8] Scot Law Com No 68; 1982.
[9] See Chapter 2.
[10] See, for example, Cmnd 8558, para 1980.
[11] Ibid, para 192.
[12] Ibid, para 193.
[13] Scot Law Com Memorandum No 16, Insolvency, Bankruptcy and Liquidation in Scotland, 1971.
[14] Ibid, para 13.
[15] Report No 68, para 1.6.

practice relating to the individual and the corporate debtor alike'.[16] The form of the debtor is therefore relevant to, but not exclusively determinative of, the form of the insolvency rules.

Another issue is the correct balance to be adopted between the rights of the various parties who may be affected by the insolvency. The most obvious issue here is the correct balance between the rights of the debtor and those of the creditors, but there are also issues involving the correct balance between the rights of the creditors *inter se* and between the rights of the creditors and those of third parties including, where applicable, the rights of the debtor's family.

A third, interrelated, issue is that of public interest. Society as a whole is affected by the insolvency of any of its members in a variety of ways. For example, a business insolvency may result in employees of that business becoming unemployed; others dependent on the debtor, such as family members, may lose their source of support; there may be loss of revenue by the state in the form of irrecoverable taxes; the insolvency of one debtor may have a 'domino effect' resulting in other insolvencies, affecting the economy overall. These matters must be taken into account in determining the correct insolvency rules and procedures to select. Public interest also has other aspects. First, there is the public interest in efficient administration of whatever system is chosen, so the system must be devised in such a way as to be able to be administered efficiently. Secondly, there is the public interest in ensuring that the system will operate to deter those who would take advantage of it to the detriment of others (such as those engaged in deliberate fraud), but will also allow those deserving of relief to obtain it. This is connected to another important issue, that of moral blame and the weight to be attached to it.

Once a view has been taken on the relevant policy matters, the functions of the law and the principles on which it will be based will be identified, and suitable rules and systems can be created to implement these.

The functions of insolvency law generally

There are a number of different theories about the proper functions and purposes of insolvency law. Finch[17] classifies those relating to company insolvency law under six headings: creditor wealth maximisation and the creditors' bargain; contractarian approach; communitarian vision; forum vision; ethical vision; and multiple values/eclectic approach. Many of these are equally applicable to non-company insolvency, particularly where a business is involved, notwithstanding the different issues which can arise in some areas.[18]

These different theories represent a variety of responses to the types of policy issues discussed above.[19] The creditor wealth maximisation theory, for example, as its name suggests, sees the proper function of insolvency law solely in terms of maximising the return to creditors.[20] It follows from this that it sees the proper form of insolvency procedure as a compulsory, collective procedure for gathering

---

[16] Cmnd 8558, para 1980.
[17] Note 4 above.
[18] See above.
[19] Finch provides an excellent summary and critique of the basic elements of each theory.
[20] The principal proponent of this theory is the US commentator Thomas H. Jackson: see his book *The Logic and Limits of Bankruptcy Law* and earlier works referred to therein.

in the assets of the debtor for distribution to the creditors. It also advocates, however, that insolvency should not create any new rights, and accordingly that that distribution to the creditors should be in accordance with their existing pre-insolvency rights. This theory emphasises creditors' rights and rejects the rights of others affected by the insolvency and the public interest (except insofar as it is served by the maximisation of returns to creditors) to the extent that they have not already been taken into account by allocation of rights prior to insolvency which can still be enforced on insolvency. In contrast, the communitarian approach emphasises community rights, ie, the public interest, above all else. It follows from this that this approach allows for insolvency procedures designed to rehabilitate commercial enterprises where this would have a better result for the community—for example by preserving jobs, even at the expense of some other rights. It allows for the alteration of pre-insolvency rights on insolvency. A different type of response altogether is exemplified by the multiple values/eclectic approach, which sees the proper function of insolvency law as being to reflect a variety of values and policies such as those discussed above. It sees insolvency law as being multi-purpose, providing rules and procedures which reflect different values and policies, as opposed to only one (such as in the creditor wealth maximisation approach).

Insolvency law as a whole in Scotland can probably best be seen as an example of the multiple values/eclectic approach. This is discussed further below.

The functions/principles of insolvency law in Scotland

It was noted above that Goudy saw the basic principle of bankruptcy law as the principle that when a man becomes insolvent, his estate becomes the property of his creditors and should be distributed among them according to their several rights and preferences, the debtor receiving a discharge from the creditors' claims in return for surrendering his estate. That formulation encapsulates some of the different aspects of the policy issues discussed above, such as the balance between the rights of the creditor and the debtor and the attitude which the law ought to take to the debtor (eventual discharge), but even in the early stages of bankruptcy law there were other principles at work. It has already been noted that the earliest bankruptcy legislation dealt with gratuitous alienations by the debtor and that further legislation on fraudulent preferences followed in due course.[21] That legislation reflected a policy decision which related not only to the balance between the rights of the debtor and the creditors, but also to the balance between the rights of creditors and third parties and, in the case of the legislation on fraudulent preferences, the rights of creditors *inter se*. Similarly, the early provisions regulating competing diligences reflected a policy decision on the rights of creditors *inter se*.

In 1971, the Scottish Law Commission in its memorandum on Insolvency, Bankruptcy and Liquidation in Scotland[22] set out four objectives which it thought the law of bankruptcy should and did seek to attain.

'(1) To promote commercial morality by providing, in a situation of insolvency, adequate safeguards against alienation of the debtor's property

---

[21] See Chapter 2.
[22] Note 13 above.

to the disadvantage of his creditors or the creation of preferences for particular creditors, and by making information as to undischarged bankrupts available for the protection of persons who might otherwise enter into transactions with them.

(2) To provide efficient machinery, available in all circumstances of insolvency, whereby a debtor or his creditors may secure the transfer of the debtor's assets to an impartial person for realisation and distribution among his creditors.

(3) To adjudicate fairly amongst the creditors *inter se* by providing for equalisation of diligences, the protection of security and other rights and preferences lawfully obtained or created and the recognition of claims which may properly be treated as preferential and, subject thereto, the distribution of any remaining assets amongst the general creditors in proportion to the amounts of their respective claims.

(4) To enable a bankrupt who has made a full disclosure of the state of his affairs to obtain, with the minimum of humiliation and delay, a discharge of his liabilities and the opportunity to make a fresh start.'[23]

When it published its Report[24] 11 years later in 1982, it set out an extended list of the objectives behind its recommendations for reform:

'1. To preserve the rights of creditors to come to voluntary arrangements with insolvent debtors for resolving their indebtedness.

2. To preserve, where voluntary arrangements are not made, and so far as consistent with the humane treatment of the debtor, the effectiveness of the system of sequestration as a support for the system of commercial credit.

3. To ensure that, in so far as the law does not otherwise direct, sequestration should be available in all cases of insolvency.

4. To protect creditors by ensuring that the bankrupt makes a full disclosure of his estate, wherever situated, and by providing procedures by which the extent of that estate may be verified.

5. To ensure that the estate may be rapidly recovered and distributed among the creditors.

6. To protect creditors, also, by retaining those rules of bankruptcy law designed to ensure that disposals of property made by the debtor before the sequestration and likely to have been made in contemplation of it may be reduced for the benefit of the creditors.

7. To promote equality among the creditors as a class by reducing the categories of preferential creditors, by retaining provision for cutting down preferences to individual creditors, by ensuring that diligences effected within a short period prior to the sequestration are cut down, and by providing appropriate rules for the valuation of debts and appropriate machinery for adjudication upon them.

8. To protect the interests of the debtor so far as the fulfilment of the preceding objectives allows. In particular, the law should not discourage the bankrupt from earning his living during the sequestration or prevent him retaining sufficient income to aliment himself and his family.

---

[23] Ibid, para 5.
[24] Note 8 above.

9. To facilitate the discharge of the bankrupt and to ensure that bankrupt debtors do not remain indefinitely subject to the disqualifications of a bankrupt.

10. To strengthen the law relating to bankruptcy offences, but to ensure, also, that the civil law of bankruptcy is not used as an instrument of penal policy.

11. To provide an efficient and expeditious machinery for attaining the preceding objects; to ensure, also, that this machinery is adaptable to the circumstances of particular cases.

12. To provide a clear and comprehensive statement of the relevant law.'[25]

Both of these formulations concentrate on the law of bankruptcy because both Memorandum and Report, although containing some recommendations in relation to liquidation, were primarily concerned with bankruptcy law. It was noted above, however, that many of the responses to the policy issues raised by insolvency are in fact the same regardless of the type of debtor involved, and that both the Scottish Law Commission and the Cork Committee emphasised the need for the law to be based, so far as possible, on the same principles. Much of what the Scottish Law Commission says can therefore be treated as equally applicable to companies, and this is borne out by the approach adopted by the Cork Committee. The Cork Committee examined company and non-company insolvency in England and Wales and dealt with both together in its formulation of the aims of a good modern insolvency law. It emphasised that a basic objective of the law of insolvency was to support the maintenance of commercial morality and encourage the fulfilment of financial obligations[26] and, although recognising that insolvency law was not an exact science, felt that there were certain general principles to which the law should strive to give effect.[27] It set out the aims, or principles, of a good modern insolvency law as being

'(a) to recognise that the world in which we live and the creation of wealth depend upon a system founded on credit and that such a system requires, as a correlative, an insolvency procedure to cope with its casualties;

(b) to diagnose and treat an imminent insolvency at an early rather than a late stage;

(c) to relieve and protect where necessary the insolvent, and particularly the individual insolvent, from any harassment and undue demands by his creditors, whilst taking into consideration the rights which the insolvent (and, where an individual, his family) should legitimately continue to enjoy; at the same time to have regard to the rights of creditors whose own position may be at risk as a result of the insolvency;

(d) to prevent conflicts between individual creditors;

(e) to realise the assets of the insolvent which should properly be taken to satisfy his debts, with the minimum of delay and expense;

(f) to distribute the proceeds of the realisations amongst the creditors in a fair and equitable manner, returning any surplus to the debtor;

---

[25] Ibid, para 2.49.
[26] Cork Report, para 191.
[27] Ibid, para 196.

(g) to ensure that the process of realisation and distribution is administered in an honest and competent manner;

(h) to ascertain the causes of the insolvent's failure and, if and insofar as his conduct or, in the case of a company, the conduct of its officers and agents, merits criticism or punishment, to decide what measures, if any, require to be taken against him or his associates, or such officers or agents;

(i) to recognise that the effects of the insolvency are not limited to the private interests of the insolvent and his creditors, but that other interests of society or other groups in society are vitally affected by the insolvency and its outcome, and to ensure that these public interests are recognised and safe-guarded;

(j) to provide means for the preservation of viable commercial enterprises capable of making a useful contribution to the economic life of the country;

(k) to devise a framework of law for the governing of insolvency matters which commands universal respect and observance, and yet is sufficient to adapt to and deal with the rapidly changing conditions of our modern world; in particular, to achieve a system that:

    (i) is seen to produce practical solutions to financial and commercial problems,

    (ii) is simple and easily understood,

    (iii) is free from anomalies and inconsistencies,

    (iv) is capable of being administered efficiently and economically;

(l) to ensure due recognition and respect abroad for English insolvency pro-ceedings.'[28]

The formulations of the Cork Committee and the Scottish Law Commission have much in common and it will be demonstrated in the following chapters how these principles have been reflected in the law of Scotland as it stands today.

It must be pointed out, however, that the Cork Committee's formulation at least has not been without criticism. Finch says that its 'statement of multiple and concurrent objectives, some of which are incompatible in various degrees, is of very limited assistance in guiding judges or others ... on the direction in which insolvency law and processes should be developed'.[29] Justice,[30] while accepting that the Cork Committee's principles were and remained valid, expressed concern that because the principles had been so widely formulated, there was a risk that the true essence of the insolvency process might be lost and insufficient attention given to the proper priorities. It felt that insufficient attention might have been given to formulating a more limited number of core principles to which the others might be regarded as ancillary.[31]

---

[28] Ibid, para 198. It should be noted that although, as is obvious from the last sub-paragraph, the Committee were primarily concerned with England and Wales, what is said undoubtedly holds true for Scotland also, and is not widely discrepant from the views of the Scottish Law Commission discussed above.

[29] Finch, note 4 above, at 230.

[30] Justice, *Insolvency Law: An Agenda for Reform*, 1994.

[31] Ibid, paras 3.7 – 3.8.

It is undoubtedly true that some of these multiple objectives or principles do conflict to a greater or lesser degree, and that this is an almost inevitable consequence of adopting such a broad formulation. To that extent, the more concise statement of objectives or principles set out by the Scottish Law Commission in 1971, with the addition of some further, similarly concisely expressed, principles to take account of the differences between bankruptcy and corporate insolvency, might be regarded as a good starting-point for the formulation of more limited core principles such as Justice suggests. It is difficult, however, to see how tensions between some of these objectives could ever be entirely eliminated, and it is suggested that this does not necessarily make the multiple approach invalid, so long as a clear decision is made between conflicting principles when the issue arises and the resulting legislation is similarly clear. Whether this has actually been achieved in practice is another matter, and some of the difficulties encountered in that respect will be highlighted in the treatment of particular aspects of the law.

The Reports of the Scottish Law Commission and the Cork Committee led to new, revised insolvency legislation in both Scotland and England and Wales. An outline of the current legislation and the current insolvency procedures available in Scots law is contained in the next chapter.

4 : CURRENT LEGISLATION AND INSOLVENCY PROCEEDINGS

Following the reports of the Scottish Law Commission and the Cork Committee, new revised insolvency legislation was introduced in both Scotland and England and Wales. The 1985 Act implemented most of the Scottish Law Commission's recommendations relating to bankruptcy and represented a major restatement of the Scottish law of bankruptcy. The 1986 Act and associated legislation[1] ultimately implemented many of the recommendations of the Cork Committee and represented a radical revision of the law on company insolvency in both Scotland and England and Wales and the law of bankruptcy in England and Wales.[2]

Bankruptcy law in Scotland remains quite distinct from that in England and Wales. The new provisions of the 1986 Act relating to company insolvency mostly apply throughout the UK, although there still are a number of important substantive as well as procedural differences in the two jurisdictions.[3] The provisions of bankruptcy and company insolvency law within Scotland have been harmonised where possible.[4]

This chapter outlines the current legislation relating to insolvency law in Scotland and the current insolvency proceedings.

The current legislation

The law relating to non-company insolvency is now contained for the most part in the 1985 Act, as amended, supplemented by the Bankruptcy (Scotland) Regulations 1985,[5] as amended (hereafter 'the Bankruptcy Regulations'). Purely

---

[1] Described below.
[2] The 1986 Act and associated legislation replaced, on the day it came into force, the Insolvency Act 1985 which had initially been promulgated to implement most of the changes accepted following the Cork Report.
[3] For example, the statutory provisions on gratuitous alienations and unfair preferences in Scotland differ in important respects from the corresponding provisions on transactions at an undervalue and preferences in England and Wales.
[4] See Chapter 3. Again, one example of this is the statutory provisions on gratuitous alienations and unfair preferences, which are discussed further in Chapter 30.
[5] SI 1985/1925.

consequential amendments to the 1985 Act are not generally separately discussed, but substantial amendments, such as the extensive amendments resulting from the Bankruptcy (Scotland) Act 1993 (hereafter 'the 1993 Act'), which have resulted in major changes to the law, are highlighted where relevant.

The law relating to company insolvency is now contained principally in the 1986 Act, as amended, supplemented by the Insolvency (Scotland) Rules 1986,[6] as amended (hereafter 'the Scottish Rules'). Important parts of the law relating to company insolvency are, however, to be found in other legislation, most notably in the Companies Act 1985 (hereafter 'CA 1985'), which contains, *inter alia*, the provisions relating to the procedure whereby a company may reach a compromise or arrangement with some or all of its creditors and/or members; the Company Directors (Disqualification) Act 1986 (hereafter 'CDDA 1986'), which deals with the important area of disqualification;[7] the 1985 Act, parts of which affect companies[8] and certain provisions of which are imported directly into company insolvency law;[9] the Industrial and Provident Societies Act 1965, which makes special provision for the winding up of such societies; the Insurance Companies Act 1982 and the Insurance Companies (Winding-Up) Rules 1985,[10] which make special provision for the winding up of insurance companies; the Building Societies Act 1986, which makes special provision for the winding up of building societies and the application of other insolvency proceedings to them; the Financial Services Act 1986, which makes special provision for the winding up of authorised persons and their representatives; the Banking Act 1987 and the Banks (Administration Proceedings) Order 1989,[11] which alter certain provisions of the normal insolvency procedures in relation to authorised and former authorised institutions; the Companies Act 1989 and the Financial Markets and Insolvency Regulations 1991,[12] which affect transactions on a recognised stock exchange, making these immune from normal insolvency law rules; the Friendly Societies Act 1992, which makes special provision for the winding up of such societies; and the Receivers (Scotland) Regulations 1986,[13] which supplement the Scottish Rules in relation to receivers.

These provisions do not contain all the bankruptcy and company insolvency law of Scotland. Some important parts of the law are still to be found in the common law,[14] and only the major legislation of relevance to insolvency has been mentioned here: other legislation is referred to where relevant. There are, in addition, a variety of other statutory instruments and Acts of Sederunt regulating various aspects of procedure which are too numerous to list separately, but which are referred to where appropriate.

---

[6] SI 1986/1915.

[7] Disqualification is discussed in detail in Chapter 39.

[8] For example, the provisions in terms of which a company may be made apparently insolvent (see Chapter 1) and the provisions relating to equalisation of diligence on apparent insolvency (see Chapter 31).

[9] For example, the liquidator in a compulsory liquidation is given the powers of a trustee in sequestration in addition to those set out in the 1986 Act itself: see Chapter 28.

[10] SI 1985/95.

[11] SI 1989/1276.

[12] SI 1991/880.

[13] SI 1986/1917.

[14] For example, the common law provisions relating to the challenge of certain pre-insolvency transactions by a debtor remain alongside the new statutory provisions: see Chapter 30.

Outline of different types of formal insolvency proceedings

Non-company debtors

Sequestration is the only type of formal insolvency proceedings applicable to non-company debtors. It is the judicial procedure whereby such a debtor's assets are taken away and put into the hands of a trustee to be realised and distributed among the creditors.[15] The procedure is initiated by a petition to the appropriate court. Where sequestration is awarded, an interim trustee is appointed by the court. The interim trustee administers the sequestration until a permanent trustee is put in place. The permanent trustee gathers in the debtor's assets, sells or otherwise realises them and distributes them among the creditors according to their rights. The trustee may be supervised and assisted in these functions by creditors known as commissioners elected for the purpose. In some cases, principally those where there are few or no assets, the normal sequestration procedures are modified to save time and money. There are two types of modified procedure: Schedule 2 procedure and summary administration. When administration of the debtor's estate is complete, the sequestration is brought to an end. The debtor receives a discharge in respect of most pre-sequestration debts and the trustee also receives a discharge in respect of his conduct of the sequestration.

Company debtors

There are essentially five types of formal insolvency proceedings which are potentially applicable to company debtors:[16] company voluntary arrangements under Part I of the 1986 Act (hereafter 'CVAs'), compromises or arrangements under s 425 of CA 1985 (hereafter 'section 425 arrangements'); administration; receivership; and liquidation.

A CVA is a binding composition or scheme of arrangement concluded by a company with its creditors. The proceedings may be initiated by the directors or, where the company is already in administration or liquidation, by the administrator or liquidator as appropriate. A proposal is drawn up setting out the details of the proposed composition or arrangement and nominating a qualified insolvency practitioner[17] as nominee to oversee the procedure. Meetings of the company's members and creditors are then called to consider the proposal. Provided any necessary consents are obtained and the specified majorities of the members and creditors respectively accept the proposal, it takes effect immediately and binds all the creditors who received notice of, and were entitled to vote at, the meetings. Its implementation is overseen by the nominee or his replacement, now known as the supervisor. There is, designedly, very little court involvement in this procedure, although the court does have a minimal role in the early stages of the procedure in some cases, and various applications may be made to the court in defined circumstances.

---

[15] The extra-judicial alternatives to sequestration, some of which are equally applicable to corporate debtors as an alternative to the formal insolvency proceedings applicable to them, are discussed in Chapter 45; judicial factories, which as noted in Chapter 1 may also form an alternative to specific insolvency proceedings, are discussed in Chapter 46.

[16] See also the Preface.

[17] Insolvency practitioners and their qualifications are discussed in the next chapter.

A section 425 arrangement is a compromise or arrangement concluded by a company with its creditors and/or members or any class of its creditors and/or members. The procedure is not specifically designed for or restricted to insolvency, but may be utilised on insolvency, including where the company is in administration, receivership or liquidation. The process is initiated by a petition to the appropriate court seeking an order to call a meeting or meetings of the members and/or creditors or such classes of either with whom the company wishes to conclude a compromise or arrangement. Where the court orders the calling of the appropriate meetings, they will then be called to consider the proposed compromise or arrangement. Where the compromise or arrangement is accepted by the requisite majority at each meeting the matter is referred back to the court, whose sanction is also required. Where such sanction is granted, the compromise or arrangement takes effect and binds all creditors or all creditors of the appropriate class or classes with whom it was concluded, and is duly implemented by the company.

Administration is designed to give a company a breathing space to reorganise its affairs with a view to either rehabilitating the company or enabling a more advantageous realisation of its assets than would be available on a winding up. There are four purposes for which an administration order may be made: survival of the company and the whole or part of its undertaking; approval of a CVA; the sanctioning of a section 425 arrangement; and a more advantageous realisation of assets than would be available on a winding up. The process is initiated by a petition to the appropriate court specifying the purpose(s) for which the administration order is sought. The company is protected from specified actions of creditors from the time of presentation of the petition.[18] Where an administration order is made, an administrator is appointed by the court to manage the affairs, business and property of the company and the statutory moratorium against creditor actions is continued and extended. The administrator takes over the running of the company and formulates proposals for achieving the purpose(s) for which the order was granted. He then calls a meeting of creditors to consider those proposals. If the proposals are approved, they are then carried through by the administrator; if not, the administration will usually be brought to an end.

Receivership is somewhat different from the other corporate insolvency régimes because it is essentially about the enforcement of one creditor's security, namely the floating charge under which the receiver is appointed. The receiver may be appointed by the floating chargeholder directly or by the court on the application of the floating chargeholder.[19] The receiver takes control of all the company's assets affected by the floating charge. Where all or substantially all of the company's assets are affected by the charge,[20] the receiver is known as an administrative receiver. Otherwise, he is simply known as a receiver. In this book, the term 'receiver' will be used as a generic term referring to both types of receiver, and where there is a distinction between the different types of receiver, this will be made clear. Although a receiver who has control of all the assets necessary to continue running the company's business may do so with a view to turning it round and making it profitable, thus paying the chargeholder from

---

[18] This does not include the appointment of a receiver by a floating chargeholder, however: see below.

[19] Receivers are, in practice, almost invariably appointed by the former method.

[20] This is almost invariably the case in practice.

profits, in the great majority of cases either the business will be sold as a going concern or the assets affected by the charge will be realised separately with a view to paying the chargeholder as quickly as possible. The receiver then pays the monies realised to the floating chargeholder in satisfaction of the chargeholder's debt after first paying certain other specified creditors. The receiver is not, however, obliged to deal with the claims of other creditors, any surplus monies falling to be returned to the company or otherwise disposed of as provided for in the 1986 Act.

Liquidation (or winding up—the terms may be used interchangeably) is the company equivalent of sequestration, where the company's assets are placed in the hands of a liquidator solely with a view to distributing them among the creditors. It is the most drastic of the insolvency procedures because it ends with the dissolution of the company. There are two types of liquidation: voluntary liquidation and compulsory liquidation (also referred to as winding up by the court—the terms are interchangeable). Voluntary liquidation is initiated by the members of the company and may be conducted without any court involvement at all, although the court may be applied to in defined circumstances if required. There are two types of voluntary liquidation: members' voluntary liquidation, where the directors of the company have made a statutory declaration of solvency confirming that the company will be able to pay all its debts with appropriate interest within a period not exceeding 12 months; and creditors' voluntary liquidation, where no such statutory declaration of solvency has been made. A members' voluntary liquidation is, therefore, normally a solvent liquidation. It may, however, be converted into a creditors' voluntary liquidation if the liquidator is of the view that the company will not be able to pay its debts and interest in the period stated in the statutory declaration.[21] Compulsory liquidation is initiated by a petition to the appropriate court. A company may be wound up by the court for a variety of reasons, not only because it is insolvent. Where a winding-up order is made, the court appoints an interim liquidator to administer the liquidation process until a liquidator is put in place. There is no interim liquidator in a voluntary liquidation because there is no court procedure. In all types of liquidation, once a liquidator has been put in place, he gathers in the company's assets and realises them. In a members' voluntary liquidation, because the company is (usually) solvent, the liquidator then pays the creditors and distributes the remaining assets to the members according to their rights. In a creditors' voluntary liquidation or compulsory liquidation where the company is insolvent, the assets are distributed among the creditors according to their rights. Where the company turns out not to be insolvent, however, or where the company has been wound up by the court on grounds other than insolvency, any assets remaining after all the creditors have been paid will be distributed among the members according to their rights. The company will then be dissolved.

Interrelationship of insolvency proceedings

Some types of insolvency proceedings may, in certain circumstances, co-exist with others. This is most likely to occur with certain types of company insolvency proceedings, and so an overview of the potential interrelationship of these proceedings is given here.

---

[21] See further below.

A CVA may be approved even where the company is already in administration or liquidation.[22] It is unlikely that a CVA could be concluded after a company has gone into receivership: only the directors may propose a CVA where the company is not in administration or liquidation and the receivership is likely effectively to deprive them of the power to do so.[23] In theory a CVA may continue after the appointment of a receiver, although in practice the receiver's appointment may result in it being brought to an end.[24] It appears that a CVA may also continue after liquidation in some circumstances, but the authorities are somewhat unclear[25] and there is no direct authority on the effect of a subsequent administration.

A section 425 arrangement can be entered into where the company is in administration, receivership or liquidation.[26]

Administration may co-exist with a receivership which is not an administrative receivership, although the administrator may require a receiver other than an administrative receiver to vacate office if he so wishes.[27] It cannot, however, co-exist with administrative receivership. A floating chargeholder is entitled to notice of an administration petition, and so has an opportunity to appoint a receiver prior to the court's decision on the application.[28] Where there is an administrative receiver in place, whether as a result of the chargeholder receiving such notice or not, the court must dismiss the administration petition unless it is satisfied that the floating chargeholder who appointed him consents to the making of the administration order or that the charge under which the administrative receiver is appointed is open to challenge on specified grounds.[29] Conversely, where an administration order is made, any administrative receiver must vacate office.[30] Administration cannot co-exist with liquidation.[31]

Receiverships may co-exist with each other. Multiple receiverships can occur because a company may grant more than one floating charge, and it is competent for a receiver or receivers to be appointed in respect of each charge.[32] All the receivers cannot necessarily act at once, however. Where receivers have been

---

[22] As noted above, where the company is in administration or liquidation, the administrator or liquidator may propose a CVA (see further Chapter 8) and the approval of a CVA is one of the purposes for which an administration order may be granted (see further Chapter 10).

[23] The effect of insolvency proceedings on the ability of the directors of a company to affect its property generally, as making a proposal on behalf of the company to enter into a CVA would do, is discussed in detail in Chapter 23.

[24] See further Chapter 41.

[25] Ibid.

[26] Where the company is in administration or liquidation, only the administrator or liquidator may initiate the section 425 procedure: CA 1985, s 425(1). Conclusion of a section 425 arrangement is, of course, one of the purposes for which an administration order may be granted: 1986 Act, s 9(3)(c). Where the company is in receivership the floating chargeholder could initiate the procedure in his capacity as a creditor, or it could be initiated by any other competent person: see Chapter 9. It is thought that it could not be initiated by the directors, however, as they would have no power to do so. For the effect of insolvency proceedings on the ability of the directors of a company to affect its property generally, see Chapter 23.

[27] 1986 Act, s 11(2).

[28] See further Chapter 10.

[29] 1986 Act, s 9(3), and see Chapter 10.

[30] 1986 Act, s 11(1)(b).

[31] 1986 Act, s 8(4).

[32] 1986 Act, s 56(1). Indeed, the same receiver may be appointed under two or more floating charges: 1986 Act, s 56(7).

appointed under floating charges which rank equally with each other, the receivers are deemed to have been appointed as joint receivers[33] and will generally act jointly.[34] Where receivers are appointed under floating charges which do not rank equally, the receiver appointed under the highest ranking of the floating charges in respect of which receivers have been appointed takes precedence and is entitled to exercise the powers conferred on him by that charge and by the 1986 Act itself to the exclusion of such other receivers;[35] but where a particular receiver (receiver A) is acting, and another receiver (receiver B) is subsequently appointed under a charge which has priority over the charge under which receiver A is acting, receiver A's powers are suspended in favour of receiver B.[36] On the conclusion of whichever receivership has priority, the outgoing receiver will hand over any remaining assets to the receiver who next has precedence in terms of the provisions discussed.[37] Receivership may also co-exist with liquidation.[38] Where this happens, however, the receiver takes precedence over the liquidator in relation to the assets attached by the charge[39] and will hand over any remaining assets to the liquidator at the completion of the receivership.[40] Where there are multiple receiverships and the company is in liquidation at the same time, the acting receiver will hand over any remaining assets to the receiver who next has precedence, as described above, until all the receiverships are complete, when any remaining assets will be handed on to the liquidator by the last receiver.[41]

A members' voluntary liquidation may be converted into a creditors' voluntary liquidation where the liquidator is of the opinion that the company will be unable to pay its debts in full, together with interest at the official rate, within the period stated in the statutory declaration of solvency.[42] Either a members' or creditors' voluntary liquidation may be superseded by a compulsory liquidation.

---

[33] 1986 Act, s 56(2).

[34] 1986 Act, s 56(3).

[35] 1986 Act, s 56(1).

[36] 1986 Act, s 56(4). Receiver A's powers will, however, come back into effect when the charge under which receiver B is acting ceases to attach to the company's property.

[37] 1986 Act, s 60(2).

[38] This may come to pass in two ways: the company may go into liquidation at a time when a receivership is already in operation, or the floating chargeholder may appoint a receiver after liquidation has commenced.

[39] This is the result of the statutory powers granted to the receiver under the 1986 Act, which are discussed further in Chapter 27: see also *Manley, Petnr* 1985 SLT 42. In the vast majority of cases, all the assets of the company will be attached by the charge.

[40] 1986 Act, s 60(2).

[41] Ibid.

[42] 1986 Act, ss 95, 96, and see Chapter 15.

5 : INSOLVENCY PRACTITIONERS

A mong the aims or principles of a good modern insolvency law identified by the Cork Committee is the necessity to ensure that the process of realisation and distribution of the debtor's estate is administered in an honest and competent manner.[1] The Cork Committee took the view that the success of any insolvency system was very largely dependent on those who administered it[2] and made recommendations as to regulation of those persons. This chapter considers the law relating to those administering the assets of insolvent debtors (hereafter referred to as 'insolvency practitioners').

Historically, Scots law did not have any public official with a role in the actual administration of insolvent estates equivalent to the Official Receiver in England and Wales. The office of the Accountant in Bankruptcy was created in 1856, and has undergone a number of changes since then, but until 1993 his role in relation to insolvencies was confined to certain supervisory functions and record-keeping in relation to non-company insolvency. Insolvency proceedings were administered by private individuals selected by the creditors or, in default of such selection, appointed by the court. The Scottish Law Commission Report No 68 considered whether the office of Official Receiver should be adopted into Scots law,[3] but rejected it in favour of an improved system of administration of insolvent estates which remained based on the appointment of private insolvency practitioners.

Administration of the estates of insolvent companies continues to be based solely on the appointment of private insolvency practitioners to the relevant office (ie, liquidator, administrator, receiver, etc). In relation to non-company debtors, however, the 1993 Act extended the role of the Accountant in Bankruptcy to include actual administration of sequestrated estates in certain circumstances. Private insolvency practitioners continue to play an important part in the administration of sequestrated estates, however, since they may still act as interim or permanent trustees in many cases.[4] All private insolvency practitioners are now, however, subject to specific regulation as such.

---

[1] See Chapter 3.
[2] Cmnd 8558, para 732.
[3] See Scot Law Com No 68, especially para 2.25 et seq.
[4] They also have a role to play in relation to extra-judicial alternatives to sequestration in the form of trust deeds for creditors: see Chapter 45.

Regulation of insolvency practitioners

Prior to the coming into force of the 1986 Act, there was virtually no regulation of insolvency practitioners as such. Insolvency practitioners who were solicitors, accountants, etc, were subject to regulation by their own professional bodies but might have little or no practical experience in insolvency matters, and there was no statutory requirement for insolvency practitioners generally to have any professional qualifications or expertise. The Cork Committee, while accepting that the majority of insolvency practitioners carried out their duties perfectly adequately, found this to be 'alarming'.[5] They felt that insolvency practitioners required a certain degree of knowledge and experience in order to be able to carry out their functions adequately[6] and that the then system was too open to abuse to command public confidence.[7] Undoubtedly, abuse of the insolvency procedures did exist, particularly in relation to companies. Cases involving the appointment of 'cowboy' liquidators, 'often people with no practical experience or relevant qualifications, who engaged in dubious practices to the detriment of creditors, sometimes in league with the controllers of the defunct company whose irresponsibility (and perhaps fraud) had brought about its collapse'[8] were not uncommon. The Cork Committee identified one of the major areas of dissatisfaction with the then insolvency procedures as being cases of what is now known as the phoenix syndrome, where the directors of an insolvent company would set up a new company and acquire the assets of the insolvent company at a very low price, thereby enabling them to do the same thing all over again, free of the debts of the insolvent company and leaving its creditors with little or nothing.

The Cork Committee took the view that in order to deal with such abuses some minimum professional qualification and control was necessary and that measures which would ensure 'a high standard of competence as well as integrity' in insolvency practitioners should be introduced.[9] They recommended that insolvency practitioners should be required to be members of a professional body approved by the Department of Trade, laid out the criteria they felt such a body should satisfy before being so approved, further recommended that practitioners should have five years' experience before being allowed to act as insolvency practitioners[10] and made recommendations for transitional provisions for dealing with practitioners who had been competently practising for many years but could not meet the qualification requirements under which they could be authorised to act as insolvency practitioners by the Department of Trade.[11] They also recommended that compulsory insurance and caution should be a qualifying requirement for all insolvency practitioners.[12] Finally, they recommended that control over insolvency practitioners should be exercised by their professional bodies.[13] The main points of their recommendations were accepted and the statutory provisions dealing with insolvency practitioners and their qualifications are now

---

[5] Cmnd 8558, paras 735, 736.
[6] Ibid, para 736.
[7] Ibid, para 756.
[8] Sealy and Milman, *Annotated Guide to the 1986 Insolvency Legislation* (3rd edn), p 424.
[9] Cmnd 8558, Ch 15, para 756.
[10] Ibid, para 758.
[11] Ibid, para 762.
[12] Ibid, paras 763 and 766.
[13] Ibid, para 769.

contained in Part XIII of the 1986 Act, as supplemented by various statutory instruments.[14]

Qualifications

All insolvency office holders with the exception of receivers who are not administrative receivers now require to be persons qualified to act as insolvency practitioners in relation to the debtor,[15] and the 1986 Act provides that it is an offence for a person to act as an insolvency practitioner in relation to a debtor at a time when that person is not qualified to do so.[16] The meaning of 'act as an insolvency practitioner' in this context is set out in s 388 of the 1986 Act. It means, in the case of a company, to act as its liquidator (which would include an interim liquidator), provisional liquidator, administrator, administrative receiver or supervisor of a company voluntary arrangement.[17] In the case of non-company debtors, it means (in Scotland) to act as interim or permanent trustee in a sequestration or as trustee under a trust deed for creditors.[18] The Accountant in Bankruptcy, however, need not be a qualified insolvency practitioner, and it is not an offence for him to act as interim or permanent trustee in a sequestration, notwithstanding that he is not a qualified insolvency practitioner.[19]

To be qualified to act as an insolvency practitioner, a person must fulfil a complex set of requirements which are not restricted to educational or professional qualifications. These may be divided into three categories. Only if the requirements in relation to all three categories are satisfied will an insolvency practitioner be regarded as qualified. The categories are as follows.

(1) Status of the insolvency practitioner.

    Only individuals may be qualified insolvency practitioners.[20] Further, a person cannot be a qualified insolvency practitioner at any time at which

---

[14] The principal statutory instrument is the Insolvency Practitioners Regulations 1990 (SI 1990/439), as amended. See also the Insolvency Practitioners (Recognised Professional Bodies) Order 1986 (SI 1986/1764) and the Insolvency Practitioners Tribunal (Conduct of Investigations) Rules 1986 (SI 1986/952).

[15] The relevant provisions relating to the original appointment are: interim trustee in sequestration, 1985 Act, s 2(3)(b); permanent trustee in sequestration, 1985 Act, s 24(2)(b); nominee in CVA, 1986 Act, s 1(2); supervisor of CVA—no specific provision, but will be the nominee (or his replacement), so will in fact be a qualified insolvency practitioner; administrator, administrative receiver, provisional liquidator and liquidator (including an interim liquidator who is a liquidator albeit an interim one), 1986 Act, s 230. The legislation also makes appropriate provision for all replacement office holders to be qualified insolvency practitioners: reference should be made to the relevant provisions dealing with replacement office holders, which are discussed in Chapter 19. It is not known why receivers who are not administrative receivers have escaped, but this seems to be the result of the 1986 Act, s 230, which only requires administrative receivers to be qualified insolvency practitioners. Nor is it an offence to act as a receiver other than an administrative receiver without being a qualified insolvency practitioner: see below. It should also be noted that the requirements in relation to liquidators apply irrespective of the type of liquidation: a liquidator in a members' voluntary liquidation (or for that matter a compulsory liquidation on grounds other than insolvency) must be a qualified insolvency practitioner even though the company is solvent.

[16] 1986 Act, s 389.

[17] 1986 Act, s 388(1). 'Company' in this context means a company within the meaning of s 735 of the Companies Act 1985 (ie, a registered company) or an unregistered company which may be wound up under Part V of the 1986 Act: 1986 Act, s 388(4).

[18] 1986 Act, s 388(2).

[19] 1986 Act, ss 388(5) and 389(2).

[20] 1986 Act, s 390(1).

he is an undischarged bankrupt,[21] is subject to a disqualification order under the CDDA 1986[22] or is a patient within the meaning of Part VII of the Mental Health Act 1983 or s 125(1) of the Mental Health (Scotland) Act 1984.[23]

(2) Requirement for authorisation (incorporating educational and experiential requirements).

A qualified insolvency practitioner must be authorised to act as such. Authorisation may be gained in one of two ways.[24] These are:

(a) Authorisation by recognised professional body.

An insolvency practitioner may be authorised to act as such by a recognised professional body (hereafter 'RPB') of which he is a member.[25] RPBs are bodies declared to be such by the Secretary of State for Trade and Industry where he is satisfied that they meet the requirements of s 391(2).[26] These are that the body regulates a profession and maintains and enforces rules ensuring that members acting as insolvency practitioners are fit and proper persons and meet acceptable requirements as to education and practical training and experience. These rules vary from RPB to RPB (there are currently seven[27]), but each RPB has a Memorandum of Understanding with the Secretary of State setting out the conditions on which the latter is prepared to accord them the status of RPB. These conditions, which are broadly similar in most cases, include matters such as minimum educational and experiential requirements which the body must require its members to satisfy before authorising them (or renewing their authorisation) to act as insolvency practitioners. At the time of writing, the Law Society of Scotland, unlike most of the other RPBs, is not required to impose any specific requirements in relation to the number of cases handled or time spent on insolvency cases as part of its conditions for the granting of authorisation. However, the Memoranda of Understanding with all RPBs are currently under review with respect to this and other matters.

(b) Authorisation by a competent authority.[28]

The Cork Committee's recommendation for authorisation by a competent authority was intended to be a purely transitional measure, but the 1986 Act provides this a free-standing alternative. Competent authorities for this purpose are the Secretary of State himself and any

---

[21] 1986 Act, s 390(4)(a).

[22] 1986 Act, s 390(4)(b).

[23] 1986 Act, s 390(4)(c).

[24] 1986 Act, s 390(2).

[25] 1986 Act, s 390(2)(a). The term 'member' includes those who are subject to its rules in the practice of their profession, whether they are actually members of the body or not: 1986 Act, s 390(3).

[26] 1986 Act, s 391.

[27] The Chartered Association of Certified Accountants, the Insolvency Practitioners Association, the Institute of Chartered Accountants in England and Wales, the Institute of Chartered Accountants in Ireland, the Institute of Chartered Accountants in Scotland, the Law Society and the Law Society of Scotland: the Insolvency Practitioners (Recognised Professional Bodies) Order 1986, note 14 above.

[28] 1986 Act, s 391(2)(b).

other body or person designated by him.[29] At the time of writing no other persons or bodies have been so designated and the Secretary of State is therefore the only competent authority. The competent authority must be satisfied that the applicant is a fit and proper person to act as an insolvency practitioner and meets prescribed educational and experiential requirements before granting the application.[30] Part II of the Insolvency Practitioners Regulations (hereafter 'the IP Regulations') relates to authorisation by competent authorities and contains provisions, *inter alia*, on the matters to be taken into account in determining whether a person is fit and proper[31] and the education, training and experience which they are required to possess.[32]

Each RPB has its own procedures for dealing with applications, including those for dealing with cases where authorisation is, or is proposed to be, refused. In the case of applications to the Secretary of State, he himself determines the form of the application and the information to be provided in support of it[33] and the 1986 Act itself prescribes the procedures for dealing with cases where it is proposed to refuse an application. In such cases, a notice is served on the applicant[34] who has the right to make written representations[35] and further to refer the matter to the Insolvency Practitioners Tribunal established under the Act.[36]

(3) Requirement for caution.

A person can only act as a qualified insolvency practitioner in relation to a particular debtor if there is in force caution for the proper performance of his functions which meets the prescribed requirements in relation to that particular debtor.[37] These requirements are set out in Part III of the IP Regulations. In essence, the insolvency practitioner must have caution for a general penalty of £250,000[38] together with caution for a specific penalty for each debtor in respect of whom he has been appointed insolvency practitioner equivalent to the value of that debtor's assets calculated in accordance with Part II of Sched 2 to the IP Regulations.[39] The asset value according to Part II of Sched 2 varies according to the circumstances, including the type of appointment, but the minimum value of the assets for the purpose of caution is deemed to be £5,000. The maximum value is deemed to be £5,000,000.

Control

The Cork Committee's recommendation that control of insolvency practitioners should be a matter for their professional bodies has largely been followed, in

---

[29] 1986 Act, s 392(1).
[30] 1986 Act, s 393(2).
[31] IP Regulations, reg 4.
[32] Ibid, regs 6, 7 and 8.
[33] 1986 Act s 392(3).
[34] 1986 Act, s 394(2).
[35] 1986 Act, s 395.
[36] 1986 Act, s 396.
[37] 1986 Act, s 390(3).
[38] IP Regulations, reg 1(a) and Sched 2, Part I.
[39] Ibid, reg 12(1)(b).

respect that where an insolvency practitioner is authorised by an RPB, control over his activities is maintained through the mechanism of the disciplinary procedures of that RPB. However, the Memoranda of Understanding between the Secretary of State and the RPBs impose certain conditions as to how the RPBs must exercise that control. Where the insolvency practitioner is authorised by a competent authority, the legislation itself lays down the mechanisms of control of insolvency practitioners. These are discussed further below.

The legislation imposes certain direct obligations on insolvency practitioners. In the sederunt book relating to the relevant proceedings,[40] they are required to keep evidence that the necessary caution in relation to each set of insolvency proceedings has been obtained by them and, on a regular basis, to submit particulars of the caution obtained in respect of each new appointment to their authorising body.[41] They are also required to keep prescribed records in respect of every case in which they are appointed in a capacity which requires them to be a qualified insolvency practitioner[42] and to notify their authorising body of where these records are kept and the form in which they can be produced.[43] Such records are subject to inspection by the authorising body and, in the case of an insolvency practitioner authorised by an RPB, by the Secretary of State as well.[44] The records must be kept for a period of 10 years after the insolvency practitioner has been discharged or released as the case may be.[45] Failure to comply with these obligations may lead to disciplinary action by the RPB or the competent authority.

There are also indirect controls. Authorisation to act as an insolvency practitioner is not granted for an indefinite period of time. Where insolvency practitioners are authorised by a competent authority, the maximum period for which authorisation can be granted is laid down by the legislation and is currently three years.[46] The same effect is achieved in the case of authorisation by RPBs through the imposition of a condition in the Memoranda of Understanding between the RPBs and the Secretary of State to the effect that authorisations shall not be granted for any period exceeding three years. After expiry of the period of time for which authorisation was originally granted, the insolvency practitioner must apply to have his authorisation renewed. Further, authorisation to act as an insolvency practitioner may be withdrawn at any time in appropriate cases. In the case of an insolvency practitioner authorised by a competent authority, the grounds on which authorisation may be withdrawn are set out in s 393(4) of the 1986 Act. These are that the holder is no longer a fit and proper person *or* that he has failed to comply with any provisions of Part XIII of the 1986 Act or any of the regulations made under that part or Part XV of the 1986 Act or, in purporting to comply with them, has supplied misleading or false information to the competent authority. The procedures for dealing with a case where it is proposed to withdraw authorisation are the same as for proposed refusal of an application.[47] In the case of an insolvency practitioner authorised by an RPB, the grounds on

[40] Ibid, reg 15.
[41] Ibid, reg 15A.
[42] Ibid, reg 17 and Sched 3.
[43] Ibid, reg 19.
[44] Ibid, reg 18.
[45] Ibid, reg 20.
[46] 1986 Act, s 393(3), and IP Regulations, reg 10.
[47] See above.

which disciplinary action may be taken and the nature of that action, up to and including withdrawal of authorisation, as well as the procedures for dealing with such cases, are determined by the body itself (subject to any conditions imposed in the Memorandum of Understanding).

Review of regulation of the profession

The current system is essentially one of self-regulation. The majority of insolvency practitioners are authorised by RPBs, who are also responsible for discipline. Recently, the system has been the subject of criticism, particularly regarding perceived differences in regulatory standards, given that each RPB has its own rules for authorisation, monitoring and discipline subject to any minimum standards imposed by the Memoranda of Understanding, and it has been questioned whether self-regulation is appropriate for the profession.

In 1997 the Department of Trade issued a Consultation Document prepared by a working party comprising members of the Insolvency Service and the RPBs seeking views on a number of matters connected with regulation of the insolvency profession,[48] including whether the profession should continue effectively to be self-regulated; if so, whether that regulation should continue in its current form or be carried out by a single regulator; the role of the Insolvency Service as regulator; the possibility of granting limited authorisations enabling, for example, a practitioner to carry out non-company insolvency work only; whether firms as well as individuals should be regulated; and the possibility of firms acting as insolvency practitioners. The document also mooted the idea of an Insolvency Board and ombudsman, although it did not favour the latter. The Report of the Working Party was issued in February 1999. It rejects both the creation of a single regulator and any reduction in the current number of RPBs in favour of retaining the current approach to regulation with the addition of a proposed new Insolvency Practices Council which would have a majority of lay members and a minority of members representing insolvency interests and which would provide input reflecting public interest concerns into the setting of ethical and professional standards. It also rejects the creation of an Insolvency Ombudsman (on the basis that it would be unlikely to bring practical benefits because it would not be coherent with the particular nature of insolvency processes), the regulation of firms as well as individuals, the possibility of the appointment of firms as insolvency practitioners and the possibility of limited authorisations. With regard to the role of the Insolvency Service, the report recognises that it will require to retain a residual role in licensing insolvency practitioners, if only because of the position in relation to EU applicants, but recommends that this should not be used for the benefit of applicants who could be authorised by an RPB. It also makes a number of other recommendations, including that adequate professional indemnity cover be a condition of authorisation.

---

[48] Insolvency Practitioner Regulation Ten Years On.

Part II

THE INITIATION OF FORMAL INSOLVENCY PROCEEDINGS AND SUBSEQUENT PROCEDURE

6 : PROCEDURE LEADING TO AN AWARD OF SEQUESTRATION

S equestration is the judicial procedure for dealing with the affairs of insolvent non-company debtors. It has been described as 'a judicial process for attaching and rendering litigious the whole estate, heritable and moveable, real and personal, of the bankrupt, wherever situated, in order that it may be vested in a trustee elected by the creditors, to be recovered, managed, sold and divided by him, according to certain rules of distribution'.[1] That process may be initiated by the debtor himself or by a creditor or creditors. This chapter deals with the procedure up to the award of sequestration itself, including the procedure for recall of an award of sequestration.

Applying for sequestration

An award of sequestration is obtained as a result of a petition to the relevant court. This section deals with various aspects of applying for sequestration.

Whose estate may be sequestrated?

It has already been said that sequestration is the procedure applicable to non-company debtors. The 1985 Act sets out in detail exactly which debtors are and are not liable to have their estates sequestrated.

Section 5(1) of the 1985 Act provides that the estate of 'a debtor' may be sequestrated in accordance with the Act. 'Debtor' is defined in s 73(1) of the 1985 Act as including, without prejudice to the generality of the expression, an entity whose estate may be sequestrated by virtue of s 6 of the Act, a deceased debtor, his executor or a person entitled to be appointed the executor of a deceased debtor. The entities whose estate may be sequestrated by virtue of s 6 are: trusts; partnerships, including dissolved partnerships; bodies corporate or unincorporated bodies; and limited partnerships, including dissolved partnerships, within the meaning of the Limited Partnerships Act 1907. The combined effect of these provisions is that it is competent to sequestrate the estate of any of the following types of debtor.

(1) A living individual.
(2) A deceased individual, his executor or a person entitled to be appointed as his executor.

[1] Bell, *Commentaries*, ii (7th edn), p 283.

(3) A trust.

(4) A partnership or limited partnership within the meaning of the Limited. Partnerships Act 1907, including, in either case, a dissolved partnership.[2]

(5) A body corporate or an unincorporated body.

Where sequestration of the estates of a partnership is applied for by a creditor,[3] it is competent to combine the petition with a petition for sequestration of the estates of any of the partners.[4] The sequestrations remain distinct, however, and the different estates must be administered separately: the court cannot make a joint award of sequestration.[5] This is currently the only situation in which it is competent to combine petitions for sequestration: it is not competent, for example, to have a combined petition for sequestration of the estates of a husband and wife, unless they are actually in partnership.[6] There are, however, proposals to amend the law to allow one petition to be presented jointly in relation to two or more persons resident at the same address.[7]

Section 6(2) of the 1985 Act specifically states that it is incompetent to sequestrate the estate of a registered company[8] or any entity in respect of which an enactment provides, expressly or by implication, that sequestration is incompetent.[9] Such companies and entities may, however, be made apparently insolvent.[10]

Who may apply?

Section 5 of the 1985 Act prescribes who may petition for sequestration of the estates of a living or deceased debtor, and s 6 prescribes who may do so in the case of a trust, partnership, body corporate or unincorporated body. The effect of these sections is as follows:

(1) In all cases the debtor[11] may petition for sequestration with the concurrence of a qualified creditor or creditors.

(2) In all cases a qualified creditor or creditors may petition for sequestration if the debtor is apparently insolvent.[12]

---

[2] For ease of reference, the word partnership will hereafter be used to include limited partnerships, dissolved partnerships and dissolved limited partnerships unless otherwise stated or the context otherwise requires.

[3] For the circumstances in which a creditor may apply for sequestration, see further below.

[4] 1985 Act, s 6(5).

[5] *The Royal Bank of Scotland plc* v *J. & J. Messenger* 1991 SLT 492.

[6] *Campbell* v *Dunbar* 1989 SLT (Sh Ct) 29.

[7] A new Bill containing this and a number of other amendments to the 1985 Act is being prepared at the time of writing. For details of this and the other amendments which it is proposed to include in the Bill, see The Bankruptcy (Scotland) Act 1985, A Consultation Follow-up: Protected Trust Deeds and Other Issues, issued by the Scottish Office in July 1998. That paper follows on from Apparent Insolvency, A Consultation Paper on Amending the Bankruptcy (Scotland) Act 1985, issued by the Scottish Office in July 1997. The awards of sequestration would still be separate, however, as would the administration of the different estates.

[8] That is, companies registered under the Companies Act 1985 or the former Companies Acts within the meaning of that Act: 1985 Act, s 6(2).

[9] See, for example, the Insurance Companies Act 1982, s 55(1), which provides that no insurance company to which Part II of that Act applies and which is an unincorporated body carrying on long-term business may be sequestrated.

[10] 1985 Act, s 7(4), and see Chapter 1.

[11] In the case of a trust, this means the majority of the trustees (1985 Act, s 6(3)(a)) and in the case of a body corporate or an unincorporated body, a person authorised to act on behalf of the body (1985 Act, s 6(6)(a)).

[12] See Chapter 1.

(3) A living individual may petition for sequestration of his own estates without the concurrence of a qualified creditor or creditors on certain conditions. These are:

(a) the total amount of his debts (including interest) at the date of presentation of the petition is not less than £1,500; and

(b) there has been no award of sequestration made against him in the period of five years prior to the presentation of the petition;[13] and

(c) *either* he is apparently insolvent[14] *or* he has granted a trust deed which has failed to become protected.[15]

(4) In the case of a living individual, the trustee acting under a trust deed may petition for sequestration if one or more of the following conditions is satisfied:

(a) the debtor has failed to comply with an obligation imposed on him by the trust deed with which he could reasonably have complied; or

(b) the debtor has failed to comply with any instruction or requirement reasonably imposed by the trustee; or

(c) the trustee avers that it is in the best interests of the creditors that an award of sequestration be made.[16]

'Qualified creditor' is defined in s 5(4) of the 1985 Act and means a creditor who is owed by the debtor a debt or debts[17] amounting to not less than £1,500[18] at the date of presentation of the petition. Qualified creditors means creditors who have debts amounting to that sum between them.[19] In calculating the amount of a creditor's debt or debts for this purpose, broadly the same principles as those which govern the amount he would be entitled to claim in the sequestration are applied.[20] Section 11 of the 1985 Act requires a petitioning or concurring creditor to produce an oath in prescribed form,[21] which must have attached to it evidence of the creditor's debt or debts.[22]

---

[13] The five-year period is calculated back from the day preceding the day of presentation of the petition.

[14] For this purpose, however, the debtor is not regarded as being apparently insolvent by reason only of having granted a trust deed or given notice to his creditors that he has ceased to pay his debts in the ordinary course of business under s 7(1)(b): 1985 Act, s 5(2B).

[15] 1985 Act, s 5(2), s 5(2B). For trust deeds generally, including the conditions for a trust deed to become protected, see Chapter 45.

[16] 1985 Act, s 5(2), s 5(2C).

[17] 'Debts' includes liquid or illiquid debts, but not future or contingent debts.

[18] This is the figure at the time of writing: it may be altered from time to time by statutory instrument. The Scottish Office is currently consulting on whether the figure should be lowered to £750: see The Bankruptcy (Scotland) Act 1985, A Consultation Follow-up: Protected Trust Deeds and Other Issues, note 7 above.

[19] 1985 Act, s 73(1) and s 5(4).

[20] 1985 Act, s 5(5), applying paras 1(1), 1(3), 2(1)(a), 2(2) and 6 of Sched 1 to the 1985 Act. See also *Arthur* v *SMT Sales & Service Co Ltd* (IH) 14th October 1998 (unreported). For a full discussion of the rules relating to the amount of a creditor's claim generally, see Chapter 32.

[21] 1985 Act, s 11(1).

[22] 1985 Act, s 11(5). The requirement to produce evidence of the debt or debts along with the oath is a separate requirement from that to attach such evidence to a statutory demand for payment of debt if that is relevant: *Lord Advocate* v *Thomson* (IH) 1994 SCLR 96.

Time-limits

Section 8 of the 1985 Act sets out certain time-limits for presentation of a petition. In the case of debtors other than deceased debtors, a petition by the debtor or by the trustee acting under a trust deed may be presented at any time, but a creditor's petition must be presented within four months of the constitution of the debtor's apparent insolvency.[23] In the case of deceased debtors, a petition by an executor or person entitled to be appointed executor may be presented at any time;[24] a petition by a creditor may also be presented at any time where the debtor's apparent insolvency was constituted within four months before his death, but in any other circumstances must be presented within six months of the death.[25]

Which court?

Section 9 of the 1985 Act sets out the requirements relating to jurisdiction. Sequestration is competent in both the sheriff court and the Court of Session. The majority of petitions are, however, presented in the sheriff court and where an award of sequestration is made in the Court of Session it will be remitted to the appropriate sheriff court.[26] In the case of a living or deceased debtor, jurisdiction is established if the debtor either had an established place of business[27] or was habitually resident[28] within Scotland (in the case of a Court of Session petition) or the sheriffdom in which the petition is presented (in the case of a sheriff court petition) at any time in the year immediately preceding the presentation of the petition or date of death.[29] In addition, both the Court of Session and the sheriff court have jurisdiction to deal with a petition for sequestration of the estates of a partner of a firm if there is a current sequestration in relation to that firm, even if the grounds of jurisdiction discussed above are not established in relation to the partner.[30] In the case of an entity which may be sequestrated by virtue of s 6 of the 1985 Act, jurisdiction is established if the entity either had an established place of business within Scotland or the sheriffdom in which the petition is presented (as appropriate) at any time in the year immediately preceding the presentation of the petition[31] *or* was constituted or formed under Scots law and at any time carried on business[32] within Scotland or the sheriffdom within which the petition was presented (as appropriate).

---

[23] 1985 Act, s 8(1). In effect, the same time-limits apply in the case of limited partnerships by virtue of the 1985 Act, s 8(2), and the Bankruptcy Regulations, reg 12(4).

[24] 1985 Act, s 8(3)(a).

[25] 1985 Act, s 8(3)(b).

[26] 1985 Act, s 15(1).

[27] This concept is not defined, but means something more than temporary or transitory.

[28] Again, this concept is not defined, but it implies something more than temporary, and probably even something more than ordinary, residence: see Professor McBryde's annotations to the 1985 Act.

[29] Note that it is *at any time* within that year: this is to cater for the situation where the debtor has ceased carrying on business or has ceased to be habitually resident prior to presentation of the petition.

[30] 1985 Act, s 9(3).

[31] The comments made in relation to individuals apply *mutatis mutandis*.

[32] Carrying on business is different from having an established, or indeed any, place of business. This test may therefore be satisfied where the other would not.

Form of petition

A petition in the sheriff court must be in the prescribed form.[33] Sequestration petitions in the Court of Session are in the normal form.[34]

The award of sequestration

This section deals with the procedure from presentation of the petition to the award of sequestration.

Conditions for award

Where the petition is presented by the debtor and the court is satisfied of certain specified procedural matters,[35] it must award sequestration 'forthwith' unless cause is shown why sequestration cannot competently be awarded.[36] Debtor petitions do not usually involve an actual hearing in court. Where the petition is presented by someone other than the debtor, a warrant is granted to cite the debtor to appear before the court on a specified date to put forward any reason why sequestration should not be awarded.[37] Although service by post is competent, because service of the petition on the debtor must take place not more than 14 and not less than six days before the date fixed by the court,[38] the petition will usually be served by sheriff officers[39] or Messengers-at-Arms[40] to ensure that service does take place within that period. If service within that period fails, the petitioner may ask for a fresh warrant to cite the debtor when the petition calls in court on the date fixed in the original warrant. When the petition calls in court and the court is satisfied of specified procedural matters,[41] it must award sequestration 'forthwith' unless s 12(3A) applies.[42] Section 12(3A) states that sequestration shall not be awarded if *either* cause is shown why sequestration is incompetent *or* the debtor forthwith pays or satisfies, or produces written evidence of payment or satisfaction of, or gives or shows that there is sufficient security for the payment of, both the debt which gave rise to his apparent insolvency and any other debts due to the petitioning and any concurring creditor.[43]

Non-discretionary and summary nature of sequestration

The court has no discretion in deciding whether to award sequestration or not. The 1985 Act provides that if the court is satisfied of the relevant procedural matters relating to the type of petition before it, it *shall* award sequestration unless one of the relevant grounds specified above applies.[44] Sequestration is also

---

[33] Act of Sederunt (Sheriff Court Bankruptcy Rules) 1996 (SI 1996/2507), rule 3.

[34] That is, Form 14.4: there are no special requirements for sequestration petitions.

[35] These are discussed further below.

[36] 1985 Act, s 12(1). The circumstances in which sequestration cannot competently be awarded are discussed further below.

[37] 1985 Act, s 12(2).

[38] Ibid.

[39] In the case of a sheriff court petition.

[40] In the case of a Court of Session petition.

[41] Discussed further below.

[42] 1985 Act, s 12(3).

[43] These concepts are discussed further below.

[44] See, for example, *Sales Lease Ltd* v *Minty* (Sh Ct) 1993 SCLR 130 (Notes).

a summary remedy.[45] The court is directed to award sequestration *forthwith*. Forthwith means immediately.[46] The court should not normally sist or continue a petition unless a relevant ground of objection as specified in the 1985 Act is raised at the hearing;[47] even then, it should not do so unless the matter cannot be dealt with at the hearing but requires further inquiry.[48] In some cases a sist or continuation has been granted for other reasons—for example, where the pursuers were interdicted from proceeding with sequestration[49]—but it is thought that a sist or continuation to allow the debtor time to pay, to allow a cheque to clear or for any other reason except in the most exceptional circumstances is incompetent.[50]

Grounds for refusing sequestration

There are a number of situations in which the court may refuse to award sequestration. These have been mentioned briefly above and will now be discussed in greater detail.

(1) The court must be satisfied of certain procedural matters before awarding sequestration. The procedural matters of which the court must be satisfied in the case of a debtor petition are set out in s 12(1) of the 1985 Act which requires the court to be satisfied that:

(a) the petition has been presented in accordance with the provisions of the 1985 Act;

(b) *either* the petition is presented with the concurrence of a qualified creditor *or* the debtor, if a living individual, satisfies the conditions for petitioning without the concurrence of a qualified creditor; and

(c) the requirements of s 5(6) and s 5(6A) have been complied with. Section 5(6) requires the petitioner to send a copy of the petition to the Accountant in Bankruptcy on the day the petition is presented.[51] Section 5(6A) requires the debtor to lodge with the petition a statement of assets and liabilities[52] and send a copy to the Accountant in Bankruptcy.

In the case of a non-debtor petition, s 12(3) of the 1985 Act requires the court to be satisfied that:

(a) proper citation has been made of the debtor;

(b) the petition has been presented in accordance with the provisions of the Act;

---

[45] *Scottish Milk Marketing Board* v *Wood* 1936 SC 604. See also *Royal Bank of Scotland plc* v *Aitken* 1985 SLT (Sh Ct) 13; *Campbell* v *Sheriff* 1991 SLT (Sh Ct) 37; *Sales Lease Ltd* v *Minty*, note 44 above.

[46] Although the contrary argument has been advanced: see Stewart, '"Forthwith" and Avoiding Sequestration' 1995 SLT (News) 19 and the reply by McKenzie, '"Forthwith" and Avoiding Sequestration: Some Observations' 1995 SLT (News) 151.

[47] *Royal Bank of Scotland plc* v *Forbes* 1988 SLT 73; *Sales Lease Ltd* v *Minty*, note 44 above. The actual grounds are discussed further below.

[48] *Royal Bank of Scotland plc* v *Forbes*, note 47 above; *Racal Vodac* v *Hislop* 1992 SLT (Sh Ct) 21; *Sales Lease Ltd* v *Minty*, note 44 above.

[49] *Hart (Chris) (Business Sales) Ltd* v *Campbell* (Sh Ct) 1993 SCLR 383 (Notes).

[50] Again, the contrary argument has been advanced by Stewart, and see the response by McKenzie, note 46 above.

[51] See *Scottish and Newcastle Breweries plc* v *Harvey-Rutherford* (Sh Ct) 1994 SCLR 131.

[52] The statement must be in the prescribed form: see further Chapter 7 and, for statements of affairs generally, Chapter 29.

(c) the provisions of s 5(6) of the Act have been complied with;[53] and
(d) *either* the debtor is apparently insolvent[54] (if the petition is by a creditor) *or* the averments of the trustee under the trust deed in relation to the debtor's failure/s under s 5(2C) are true (if the petition is by the trustee under a trust deed).

Where the court is not satisfied in relation to any of the matters specified, it will not necessarily refuse to award sequestration. For example, if the petition was by a creditor and the court was not satisfied that there had been proper citation of the debtor, it might order re-service rather than refusing the petition outright.

(2) The court may refuse to award sequestration in either a debtor or non-debtor petition if cause is shown why sequestration cannot competently be awarded.[55] This concept is not defined in the 1985 Act, but case-law provides some examples. In *Unity Trust Bank plc* v *Ahmed*[56] the creditor averred that the debtor was apparently insolvent as a result of the expiry of a charge for payment served on him without payment having been made. The creditor had also served a statutory demand on the debtor, however, and the period allowed for payment under the statutory demand had not expired at the time the petition was presented. The court held that the creditor had presented the debtor with 'directly contradictory ultimata' and refused the petition as incompetent. In *Racal Vodac Ltd* v *Hislop*[57] there was a dispute over the identity of the debtor and it held that this was a matter which, if proved, would affect the competence of any award of sequestration.

(3) The court may refuse to award sequestration in a non-debtor petition if the debtor *forthwith* pays or satisfies specified debts, produces written evidence of payment or satisfaction of these debts or gives or shows that there is sufficient security for the payment of these debts. The debts in question are those which gave rise to his apparent insolvency *and* any other debts due to the petitioning and any concurring creditor.[58]

It is important to note that the debtor is required to act *forthwith* in order to escape sequestration on any of the specified alternatives. It is suggested, therefore, that to escape sequestration by paying the relevant debts, the debtor would require to make payment at the hearing in cash or by banker's draft. It is not uncommon for the debtor to appear at the hearing and *either* tender a cheque *or* offer to make payment within a specified period of time or by instalments. A creditor would not, however, be obliged to accept a cheque tendered to him at the hearing and, since sequestration is a summary remedy, the court will (or should) not continue the petition to allow the debtor further time to pay. If payment in an

---

[53] See above.
[54] Where it is averred that the debtor is apparently insolvent as a result of s 7(1)(d) (unsatisfied statutory demand for payment of debt), the requirements of *Lord Advocate* v *Thomson* (note 22 above) that evidence of the debt or debts should have been attached to the statutory demand before it will be held to be competent to constitute apparent insolvency should be noted.
[55] 1985 Act, s 12(1) (debtor petitions) and s 12(3A) (non-debtor petitions).
[56] (Sh Ct) 1993 SCLR 53.
[57] See note 48 above.
[58] 1985 Act, s 12(3A)(b).

acceptable form is made, the court may dismiss the petition but award expenses against the debtor. Similarly, if the debtor states to the court that he has already paid or otherwise satisfied the debt, it is suggested that he must produce the necessary written evidence of this at the hearing. The court should not continue the petition to allow it to be produced at a later stage (unless perhaps there is a good reason why it cannot be produced immediately). If the debtor wishes to escape sequestration by offering to give sufficient security for payment of the debt or to demonstrate that this already exists, the requirement that this must be done at the hearing is especially problematic. Depending on the type of security involved, it would almost invariably be virtually impossible for the debtor to produce a security at the hearing. It may not be possible to determine the validity or sufficiency of any security without further evidence. It has been held that notwithstanding this, the court should be able to be satisfied of any necessary points at the hearing if it is to refuse sequestration, but in certain circumstances it may be permissible to allow further procedure to resolve any outstanding points.[59]

(4) The court may dismiss a sequestration petition if there are concurrent proceedings for sequestration or an analogous remedy pending before another court or there has already been an award of sequestration or an analogous remedy.[60] The court will not necessarily do so, however. It may allow the petition to proceed or sist it.[61] The Court of Session may direct any of the courts before which concurrent sequestration petitions are pending to sist or dismiss them, or to hear them together.[62]

A decision to refuse sequestration is subject to appeal.[63]

Date of sequestration

Where sequestration is awarded, the date of sequestration is the date of the *award* of sequestration in the case of a debtor petition[64] and the date on which the *original* warrant to cite the debtor was granted in the case of a non-debtor petition.[65]

Registration of court order

The clerk of court must send a certified copy of the 'relevant order' to the Keeper of the Register of Inhibitions and Adjudications forthwith after the date

---

[59] See *Royal Bank of Scotland plc* v *Forbes*, note 47 above; also *National Westminster Bank plc* v *W. J. Elrick & Co* 1991 SLT 709. For a full discussion of the difficulties with this provision, see McKenzie, 'Avoiding Sequestration by Provision of Sufficient Security' 1993 SLT (News) 269.

[60] 1985 Act, s 10(3)(a) and s 10(4).

[61] Ibid.

[62] 1985 Act, s 10(3)(b).

[63] 1985 Act, s 15(3).

[64] 1985 Act, s 12(4)(a).

[65] 1985 Act, s 12(4)(b). Prior to the 1993 Act there was conflicting authority about the correct date of sequestration where more than one warrant to cite was granted, and the 1993 Act accordingly amended this subsection to make it clear that the correct date of sequestration in such cases was the date of the original warrant to cite. The amendment was not retrospective, but it has now been confirmed that in pre-1993 Act cases also the correct date of sequestration where more than one warrant to cite was issued is the date of the original warrant: see *Sutherland* v *Lord Advocate* (IH) 14th October 1998 (unreported).

of sequestration.[66] In the case of a debtor petition, this is the order making the award; in the case of a non-debtor petition, it is the original warrant to cite.[67] The order or warrant to cite, as the case may be, is then registered in the Register of Inhibitions and Adjudications and has the effect of an inhibition against the debtor.[68] This effect lasts for three years, unless a certified copy of an order refusing the sequestration,[69] recalling the sequestration[70] or granting discharge on composition[71] is recorded before then. The initial three-year period can be extended for further periods of three years if the trustee records a memorandum to that effect.[72]

The clerk of court must also send a copy of the relevant order to the Accountant in Bankruptcy forthwith after the date of sequestration.[73]

Recall of sequestration

There is no provision for an appeal against a decision to award sequestration. Instead, the 1985 Act provides for recall of an award of sequestration by the Court of Session in certain circumstances.

Sections 16 and 17 of the 1985 Act contain the general rules governing recall of sequestration. Section 41 of the 1985 Act contains special rules where recall is sought by a non-entitled spouse of the debtor seeking to protect his occupancy rights in the matrimonial home. Where recall is competent in terms of these sections, it should be sought in preference to any other remedy which might otherwise be available, such as reduction of the award.[74]

Grounds for recall

The debtor, any creditor, the interim or permanent trustee, the Accountant in Bankruptcy or any other person having an interest may apply for recall of the award.[75] The court has a general power to recall the sequestration if it is satisfied in all the circumstances, including those arising after the date of sequestration, that it is appropriate to do so.[76] The court's discretion is very wide.[77] Without

---

[66] 1985 Act, s 14(1).

[67] 1985 Act, s 14(5).

[68] As provided for under the 1985 Act, s 14(2).

[69] As provided for under the 1985 Act, s 15(5)(a).

[70] As provided for under the 1985 Act, s 17(8)(a). Recall of sequestration is discussed further below.

[71] As provided for under the 1985 Act, Sched 4, para 11. Discharge on composition is discussed further in Chapter 36.

[72] 1985 Act, s 14(4).

[73] 1985 Act, s 14(1).

[74] *Spence* v *Davie* 1993 SLT 217. Where the time-limit for recall has passed, the debtor may attempt to have the sequestration reduced, but reduction is not available as of right and will depend on the circumstances of the particular case, lapse of time since the sequestration and the fact that the debtor had other remedies such as recall which went unused being important factors: see *Arthur* v *SMT Sales & Service Co Ltd* (IH) 14th October 1998 (unreported).

[75] 1985 Act, s 16(1).

[76] 1985 Act, s 17(a).

[77] See, for example, *Button* v *Royal Bank of Scotland* 1987 GWD 27–1019 (recall refused as debtor's proposed scheme too uncertain); *Royal Bank of Scotland* v *Gillies* 1987 SLT 54; *Wright* v *Tenant Caledonian Breweries Ltd* 1991 SLT 823; *Archer Car Sales (Airdrie) Ltd* v *Gregory's Tr* 1993 SLT 223; *McGee*, Petnr, 7th June 1996 (unreported); *Murray* v *Valentine*, 14th January 1998 (unreported).

prejudice to that general power, there are three specific grounds, as follows, on which the court may recall the sequestration.

(1) That the debtor has paid his debts in full or provided sufficient security for their payment.[78] Because the debtor's assets will have vested in the permanent trustee as at the date of sequestration and the debtor will not thereafter be in a position to deal with them,[79] the money or security must have come from a source other than assets of the debtor which have vested in the trustee—for example, a third party.

(2) That the majority in value of the creditors reside in a country other than Scotland and it is more appropriate to have the sequestration there.[80]

(3) That one or more other awards of sequestration or analogous awards have been made.[81] Although the grounds of jurisdiction for sequestration proceedings[82] are designed to minimise the risk of more than one award of sequestration being made and the court may sist or dismiss sequestration proceedings if the existence of another award or pending proceedings is known to the court before an award of sequestration is made,[83] it may sometimes happen that more than one award of sequestration is made. The court is given discretion to recall either the award in respect of which the petition for recall has been presented or any other award which has been made.[84] It may be appropriate, for example, to recall a different award of sequestration if the administration of the estate in that case is less advanced.

Time-limits

Where the petition for recall is based on any of the three specific grounds discussed above, it may be presented at any time, but the court will take into account the stage the administration of the estate has reached in exercising its discretion as to whether or not to recall. In any other case, the petition must be presented within 10 weeks of the award of sequestration.[85]

Effect of recall

Recall of the sequestration has the effect, so far as possible, of putting the debtor and anyone else affected by it back in the same position as they would have been in had the sequestration not been granted.[86] Recall will not, however, affect any interruption of the running of prescription which resulted from the sequestration, or invalidate any transaction by the interim or permanent trustee, provided the other party to that transaction was in good faith.[87] The court has power to make

---

[78] 1985 Act, s 17(1)(a), and see *Martin v Martin's Tr* 1994 SLT 261.
[79] See Chapters 21 and 23.
[80] 1985 Act, s 17(1)(b).
[81] 1985 Act, s 17(1)(c).
[82] Discussed above.
[83] Ibid.
[84] 1985 Act, s 17(2).
[85] 1985 Act, s 16(4).
[86] 1985 Act, s 17(4).
[87] 1985 Act, s 17(5).

any orders which it considers necessary or reasonable as a result of the recall[88] and will also make provision for payment of the interim and, if appropriate, permanent trustee.[89] It may also make various orders in relation to expenses.[90]

Refusal of recall

The court may refuse outright to recall an award of sequestration or it may make an order that the sequestration continue subject to such conditions as it thinks fit.[91]

Recall by non-entitled spouse

Where the debtor's estate includes a property which is a matrimonial home in which the debtor's spouse has occupancy rights under the Matrimonial Homes (Family Protection) (Scotland) Act 1981, the spouse who has such occupancy rights may apply to the court for recall of the debtor's sequestration on the ground that the purpose of the sequestration was wholly or mainly to defeat the spouse's occupancy rights.[92] Where the permanent trustee is aware of the existence and whereabouts of a non-entitled spouse, he has an obligation to inform him of the sequestration and his right to petition for recall of it on this ground.[93] Where the spouse wishes to petition for recall, the petition must be presented within 40 days of the trustee's intimation to him or within 10 weeks from the date of sequestration.[94] The court may recall the sequestration or make any other order it thinks appropriate to protect the occupancy rights.[95]

---

[88] 1985 Act, s 17(3).
[89] 1985 Act, s 17(3)(a).
[90] 1985 Act, s 17(3)(b) and s 17(7).
[91] 1985 Act, s 17(6).
[92] 1985 Act, s 41(1).
[93] 1985 Act, s 41(1)(a).
[94] 1985 Act, s 41(1)(b).
[95] Ibid.

7 : PROCEDURE FOLLOWING AN AWARD
OF SEQUESTRATION

This chapter deals with the procedure from the award of sequestration to the putting in place of the permanent trustee who takes over from the interim trustee and administers the sequestration process.

Notification of award of sequestration and appointment of interim trustee

It has already been noted that the relevant court order will be registered in the Register of Inhibitions and Adjudications, and a copy sent to the Accountant in Bankruptcy by the clerk of court.[1] The interim trustee will be advised of his appointment by the petitioner's solicitor. Where the award of sequestration follows on from a petition other than a debtor petition, the interim trustee has a duty to notify the debtor of his appointment.[2] The interim trustee must also advertise his appointment in all cases.[3]

Interim preservation of the debtor's estate

The interim trustee must take the necessary steps to preserve the debtor's estate in the interim and he will do so as soon as he is notified of his appointment. The functions and powers of the interim trustee are discussed more fully in Chapter 20.

Preparation of statement of affairs

The debtor is obliged to provide the interim trustee with a statement of assets and liabilities, a document in prescribed form containing details of the debtor's assets, liabilities, income and expenditure and other prescribed information.[4] In

---

[1] See Chapter 6.
[2] 1985 Act, s 2(7).
[3] 1985 Act, s 15(6).
[4] 1985 Act, s 73(1), as amended. The relevant form is Form 4 in the Schedule to the Bankruptcy Regulations. See also Chapter 29.

the case of a debtor petition, this document will already have been lodged with the court,[5] and the debtor is only required to send a copy of it to the interim trustee;[6] in other cases, the debtor must prepare the document and send it to the trustee.[7] On receipt of the statement of assets and liabilities, the interim trustee must prepare a 'statement of affairs' detailing what he knows about the debtor's financial position and giving a view on whether he thinks any of the debtor's unsecured creditors will receive any money from the sequestration.[8] Where the interim trustee is a private insolvency practitioner, he must send a copy of the debtor's statement of assets and liabilities and his own statement of affairs to the Accountant in Bankruptcy, together with his comments on what he believes caused the insolvency and the debtor's role in bringing it about.[9]

Statutory meeting

The statutory meeting is the first meeting of creditors in the sequestration.[10] It is an opportunity for the creditors to get together, to exchange information and, if appropriate, to choose the permanent trustee who will administer the debtor's estate. This section deals with the calling of, and procedure at, the statutory meeting.

Calling of statutory meeting

Where the interim trustee is a private insolvency practitioner, he must call the statutory meeting.[11] He must notify all known creditors and the Accountant in Bankruptcy of the details of the meeting and invite creditors to submit claims in the sequestration.[12]

Where the interim trustee is the Accountant in Bankruptcy, he may choose whether or not to call the statutory meeting, but he must advise the creditors of what he intends to do.[13] If he decides not to call the statutory meeting, any creditor may request him to do so[14] and if creditors representing at least one quarter of the value of the debts make such a request, he must then call it.[15] Where no statutory meeting is called, the Accountant in Bankruptcy submits a report to the sheriff and provides the sheriff with a copy of the trustee's statement of affairs, whereupon the sheriff will appoint the Accountant in Bankruptcy or his nominee to be permanent trustee.[16] Where the statutory meeting is called, the procedure is substantially the same as where the interim trustee is a private insolvency practitioner.[17]

---

[5] See the preceding chapter.
[6] 1985 Act, s 19(1).
[7] 1985 Act, s 19(2).
[8] 1985 Act, s 20(1).
[9] 1985 Act, s 20(2).
[10] 1985 Act, s 20A.
[11] 1985 Act, s 21(1).
[12] 1985 Act, s 21(2).
[13] 1985 Act, s 21A(2).
[14] 1985 Act, s 21A(4).
[15] 1985 Act, s 21A(5).
[16] See further Chapter 19, which deals with appointment of insolvency office holders generally.
[17] 1985 Act, s 21A(6), (7) and (8).

Procedure at statutory meeting

The statutory meeting commences with the interim trustee in the chair; the creditors may elect a new chairman later in the proceedings, but if they do not, the interim trustee remains chairman throughout.[18]

The interim trustee's first task is to decide whether to accept or reject claims already submitted by creditors:[19] only creditors whose claims have been accepted, and who are not otherwise disqualified,[20] can vote in any election to choose the permanent trustee. The interim trustee makes available the debtor's statement of assets and liabilities and his own statement of affairs[21] (which most creditors will already have received with the notice of the meeting), answers questions,[22] gives his opinion on the likelihood of the unsecured creditors receiving any payment[23] and, if necessary as a result of further information disclosed at the meeting, prepares (or indicates he will prepare) a revised statement of affairs.[24]

The meeting then moves on to the election of the permanent trustee.[25] This is discussed further in Chapter 19, which deals with the appointment and re-placement of insolvency office holders generally.

---

[18] 1985 Act, s 23(1).
[19] 1985 Act, s 23(1)(a). Claims are dealt with in Chapters 32 and 33.
[20] 1985 Act, s 24(3).
[21] 1985 Act, s 23(3)(a).
[22] 1985 Act, s 23(3)(b).
[23] 1985 Act, s 23(3)(c).
[24] 1985 Act, s 23(3)(d). Any such revised statement must thereafter be sent to the creditors: 1985 Act, s 23(5).
[25] 1985 Act, s 24(1).

8 : PROCEDURE LEADING TO A COMPANY VOLUNTARY ARRANGEMENT UNDER PART I OF THE INSOLVENCY ACT 1986

The CVA is one of the new procedures introduced on the recommendation of the Cork Committee to facilitate the rescue of companies in financial difficulties. It is designed to provide a simple procedure whereby a company can conclude a binding 'composition in satisfaction of its debts or ... scheme of arrangement of its affairs'[1] with its creditors. This chapter deals with the procedure for putting a CVA in place.

Initiating a company voluntary arrangement

Unlike most other formal insolvency proceedings, CVAs are not initiated by an application to the court. Indeed, one of the features of CVAs is that they have comparatively little court involvement. Rather, CVAs are initiated by a proposal to the company and its creditors which, although reported to the court in some cases, is then carried forward by a qualified insolvency practitioner. This section deals with the various aspects of initiating a CVA.

Which companies may be subject to a company voluntary arrangement?

Part I of the 1986 Act does not define the companies to which the CVA procedure applies. Reference must be made to s 251 of the 1986 Act, which states that, except insofar as the context otherwise requires, any expression other than one specifically defined in the section for whose interpretation provision is made by Part XXVI of the Companies Act 1985 (hereafter 'CA 1985') is to be construed in accordance with that statute. This leads to s 735 of CA 1985 which defines 'company' as a company registered under that Act or under any former Companies Acts as defined by the section.[2] It has been argued that the CVA procedure should be regarded as open to companies other than registered companies,[3] but this must be regarded as a matter of debate, although it would appear to be open to a company other than a registered company if that company

---

[1] 1986 Act, s 1(1).
[2] CA1985, s 735(1).
[3] Preece, 'The United Kingdom Insolvency Act and International Corporate Rescue', *Newsletter of the EIPA*, Issue 7, September 1995.

is in liquidation.[4] A modified form of the CVA procedure is open to building societies incorporated or deemed to be incorporated under the Building Societies Act 1986.[5]

Who may propose a company voluntary arrangement?

A proposal for a CVA may be made by the directors of a company which is not in administration or liquidation.[6] Where a company is in administration or liquidation, any proposal must be made by the administrator or liquidator.[7]

A proposal cannot be made by the company itself, or by creditors.

Which court?

Although a CVA is not initiated by an application to the court, the court still has a role to play in relation to certain aspects of the CVA procedure.

Part I of the 1986 Act simply refers to 'the court' without defining that term. Again, therefore, reference must be made to s 251 of the 1986 Act. This leads to s 744 of CA 1985 which provides that the court, in relation to a company, is the court having jurisdiction to wind up the company.[8]

Form and content of the proposal

The proposal will name a 'nominee' to act as trustee or otherwise in relation to the voluntary arrangement for the purpose of supervising its implementation.[9] The nominee must be a qualified insolvency practitioner.[10] Where the proposal is made by an administrator or liquidator of the company, he may act as nominee himself, or nominate another qualified insolvency practitioner to be the nominee.

The terms of the proposed arrangement will obviously depend on the precise circumstances of the company and its creditors. However, the Scottish Rules prescribe a number of matters which must be dealt with in the proposal.[11] These are as follows.

(1) A short statement as to why a voluntary arrangement is desirable and why the company's creditors might be expected to concur with it.[12]

(2) So far as within the knowledge of the proposer(s), the company's assets and their value, any security over these assets and the extent to which any assets are to be excluded from the voluntary arrangement.[13]

---

[4] 1986 Act, s 229(1), which provides that the liquidator in the winding up of an unregistered company may exercise any powers which he would have in the case of the liquidation of a registered company. This would include proposing a CVA: see further below.

[5] Building Societies Act 1986, s 90A. The relevant modifications are contained in Sched 15A to that Act.

[6] 1986 Act, s 1(1).

[7] 1986 Act, s 1(3).

[8] See further Chapter 16 (registered companies) and Chapter 17 (unregistered companies).

[9] 1986 Act, s 1(2).

[10] Ibid.

[11] Rule 1.3 of the Scottish Rules sets out the specific matters which must be dealt with in a proposal by the directors. The same matters must be dealt with in a proposal by an administrator or liquidator by virtue of rule 1.10 (where the administrator or liquidator is himself acting as nominee) and rule 1.12(3) (where the administrator or liquidator nominates another insolvency practitioner to act as nominee). Further references will be to the provisions of rule 1.3 as applied by those rules.

[12] Scottish Rules, rule 3.1(1).

[13] Scottish Rules, rule 3.1(2)(a).

(3) Details of any property other than that belonging to the company itself which is to be included in the voluntary arrangement, including its source and the terms on which it is to be made available.[14]

(4) Details of the company's liabilities and the way in which it is proposed that these are to be met, modified, postponed or otherwise dealt with by the voluntary arrangement.[15] Specific reference must be made to the way in which preferred creditors and creditors connected with the company are to be dealt with.[16] Specific reference must also be made to whether there are any circumstances which would give rise to challenge of any prior transactions under ss 242–245 of the 1986 Act by a liquidator and, if so, whether and how it is proposed to make provision for this in the voluntary arrangement.[17]

(5) Details of cautionary obligations undertaken to the company and whether any of the persons who have granted such obligations are connected persons.[18]

(6) The proposed duration of the voluntary arrangement.[19]

(7) Details of the proposed dates and amounts of distributions to creditors.[20]

(8) Details of the nominee's proposed remuneration and expenses.[21]

(9) Details of the supervisor's proposed remuneration and expenses.[22]

(10) Whether any (further) cautionary obligations are to be undertaken in pursuance of the voluntary arrangement and whether any security is to be given for these.[23]

(11) Details of how funds are to be dealt with pending distribution to creditors.[24]

(12) Details of how any unpaid dividends are to be dealt with.[25]

(13) How the business of the company is to be conducted during the course of the voluntary arrangement.[26]

(14) Details of any additional credit facilities to be arranged for the purposes of the voluntary arrangement and how these are to be repaid.[27]

(15) The proposed functions of the supervisor.[28]

---

[14] Scottish Rules, rule 3.1(2)(b).
[15] Scottish Rules, rule 3.1(2)(c).
[16] Scottish Rules, rule 3.1(2)(c)(i),(ii). 'Connected with' is defined in s 249 of the 1986 Act.
[17] Scottish Rules, rule 3.1(2)(c)(iii). Curiously, this provision does not seem to require disclosure of whether a transaction might be challengeable at common law: it is possible that a transaction may not be challengeable under any of the statutory provisions but be challengeable at common law. Challengeable transactions are discussed in Chapter 30.
[18] Scottish Rules, rule 3.1(2)(d).
[19] Scottish Rules, rule 3.1(2)(e).
[20] Scottish Rules, rule 3.1(2)(f).
[21] Scottish Rules, rule 3.1(2)(g).
[22] Scottish Rules, rule 3.1(2)(h). The supervisor is the nominee or his replacement who becomes known as the nominee on the CVA taking effect: see further below.
[23] Scottish Rules, rule 3.1(2)(i).
[24] Scottish Rules, rule 3.1(2)(j).
[25] Scottish Rules, rule 3.1(2)(k).
[26] Scottish Rules, rule 3.1(2)(l).
[27] Scottish Rules, rule 3.1(2)(m).
[28] Scottish Rules, rule 3.1(2)(n).

(16) Details of the proposed supervisor and confirmation that he is, so far as the proposer(s) are aware, a qualified insolvency practitioner.[29]

Where the proposal is being made by an administrator or liquidator of the company, he must, in addition to the matters detailed above, specify such other matters, if any, as he considers are necessary to enable the members and creditors of the company to reach an informed decision on the proposal.[30] Where the proposal is being made by an administrator, he must further specify the names and addresses of the preferential creditors and the amounts owing to them.[31]

Procedure following the preparation of the proposal

The procedure which follows the preparation of the proposal depends on who has prepared it.

(1) Proposal prepared by directors *or* by administrator or liquidator where another qualified insolvency practitioner is to act as nominee.

In these cases, written notice of the proposal together with a copy of it is delivered to the nominee[32] who must decide whether to agree to act. If he does, he endorses a copy of the notice with the date it was received by him and returns it to the proposer(s).[33] The nominee must thereafter submit, within 28 days of that date or such longer period as the court may allow, a report to the court stating whether he thinks meetings of the company and its creditors should be called to consider the proposal and, if so, the proposed date and time for these meetings.[34]

The person(s) making the proposal must submit to the nominee a document setting out the terms of the proposed voluntary arrangement and a statement of affairs containing prescribed information in order to enable the nominee to prepare his report.[35] In the case of a proposal by the directors, rule 1.5 of the Scottish Rules requires the directors to submit a statement of affairs to the nominee within seven days or such longer period as the nominee may allow and prescribes the information to be contained in the statement of affairs;[36] in the case of a proposal by the administrator or liquidator, rule 1.12(5) requires him to submit a copy of the company's statement of affairs, which will have been prepared in connection with the relevant proceedings, to the nominee along with the proposal.[37] The nominee may also call on the directors, administrator or

---

[29] Scottish Rules, rule 3.1(2)(o).

[30] Scottish Rules, rule 1.10(b), where the administrator or liquidator is himself acting as nominee, as applied to cases where another insolvency practitioner is nominated to act as nominee by rule 1.12(3).

[31] Scottish Rules, rule 1.10, where the administrator or liquidator is himself acting as nominee, as applied to cases where another insolvency practitioner is nominated to act as nominee by rule 1.12(3).

[32] Scottish Rules, rule 1.4(1), (2) (directors' proposal); rule 1.12(1) (administrator's or liquidator's proposal).

[33] Scottish Rules, rule 1.4(3), (4), as applied to the administrator's or liquidator's proposal by rule 1.12(2).

[34] 1986 Act, s 2(2). The court to which the report is made is any court with jurisdiction to wind up the company.

[35] 1986 Act, s 2(3).

[36] See further Chapter 29.

[37] For statements of affairs in administration and liquidation, see ibid.

liquidator for further information as to the circumstances of the company's insolvency (or threatened insolvency), any previous proposals for a CVA and any other information about the company's affairs he feels is necessary to enable him to prepare his report.[38] He may also ask for certain further information about current or certain former directors or officers of the company,[39] and he is entitled to have access to the company's accounts and records.[40]

If the nominee recommends that meetings of the company and its creditors should be called, he must annex his comments on the proposal to his report.[41] He will then call the meetings for the time, date and place specified in the report, unless the court directs otherwise.[42] The meetings must be held not less than 14 days and not more than 28 days after the lodging of the nominee's report with the court.[43]

If the nominee takes the view that meetings of the company and its creditors should not be called, he must give reasons for this view,[44] but that would appear to be the end of the matter. If the proposer(s) still wished to proceed with a CVA, they would have to start again with a fresh proposal.

Whatever the nominee recommends, he must send a copy of his report (together with a copy of his comments on the proposal, if applicable) to the company.[45] Any director, member or creditor of the company is entitled to inspect his report and, if applicable, comments.[46]

(2) Proposal prepared by administrator or liquidator where he himself acts as nominee.

In this case, the administrator or liquidator in his capacity as nominee will already have decided that the proposal is viable and will simply summon the requisite meetings of the company and its creditors.[47] There is no report to the court at this stage. The nominee must give at least 14 days' notice of the meetings.[48]

The decision on the proposal

The decision on the proposal is made by the meetings of the company and its creditors. This section deals with the procedure from the calling of the meetings to the decision.

---

[38] Scottish Rules, rule 1.6(1), as applied to the administrator's or liquidator's proposal by rule 1.12(4).
[39] Scottish Rules, rule 1.6(2), as applied to the administrator's or liquidator's proposal by rule 1.12(4). The sub-paragraph applies to former directors or officers of the company who have been such within the period of two years preceding the proposal.
[40] Scottish Rules, rule 1.6(3), as applied to the administrator's or liquidator's proposal by rule 1.12(4).
[41] Scottish Rules, rule 1.7(2), as applied to the administrator's or liquidator's proposal by rule 1.12(6).
[42] 1986 Act, s 3(1).
[43] Scottish Rules, rule 1.9(1).
[44] Ibid.
[45] Scottish Rules, rule 1.7(3), as applied to the administrator's or liquidator's proposal by rule 1.12(6).
[46] Ibid.
[47] 1986 Act, s 3(2).
[48] Scottish Rules, rule 1.11(1).

The meetings of the company and its creditors

The general rules on meetings contained in Chapter 1 of Part 7 of the Scottish Rules apply to the meetings of the company and its creditors, subject to the provisions of rules 1.9, 1.11 and 1.12(6) and the rules specifically dealing with these meetings contained in Chapter 5 of Part I of the Scottish Rules.[49]

All creditors of the company of whose claims and addresses the nominee is aware must be summoned to the creditors' meeting.[50] There is no corresponding provision specifying the persons who are to be summoned to the meeting of the company, but it is presumed that every member known to the nominee should be given the requisite notice.[51] The nominee must also give at least 14 days' notice of the meetings to all directors of the company and any other person whom the nominee thinks should be present as an officer of the company *or* as a former director or officer of the company who has been such within the two years preceding the date of the notice.[52]

In fixing the date, time and place for the meetings, the nominee must have regard primarily to the convenience of the creditors.[53] The meetings must be held on the same day and in the same place, but the creditors' meeting must take place in advance of the company meeting.[54]

The decision

The meetings must decide whether to approve the proposal placed before them, with or without modifications.[55] Where the proposal is modified, both meetings must agree on the same modifications.[56] There is provision for the meetings to be adjourned from time to time on the day of the meetings itself and for further adjournments if agreement cannot be reached in the course of the day, and if the chairman thinks fit for the purpose of obtaining the simultaneous agreement of both meetings to the proposal (with the same modifications, if any), the meetings may be held together.[57] This makes the obtaining of agreement easier—especially where there are proposed modifications.

At the creditors' meeting, a majority of at least 75 per cent in value of those present in person or represented and voting, in person or by proxy, is required to approve any proposal or modification.[58] A creditor's entitlement to vote is determined in accordance with the Scottish Rules.[59] The amount of a creditor's debt for the purposes of voting is calculated in accordance with the rules applicable to the calculation of the amount of a creditor's claim in a sequestration, as modified

---

[49] Scottish Rules, rule 1.13.
[50] 1986 Act, s 3(3).
[51] Cf the corresponding provisions in England and Wales, which specify who is to be given notice of the members' meeting : Insolvency Rules 1986 (SI 1986/1925), rule 1.11.
[52] Scottish Rules, rule 1.15(1).
[53] Scottish Rules, rule 1.14(1).
[54] Scottish Rules, rule 1.14(2).
[55] 1986 Act, s 4(1).
[56] 1986 Act, s 5(1).
[57] Scottish Rules, rule 1.16. Any adjournment to a later date requires to be reported to the court in the case of a directors' proposal: Scottish Rules, rule 1.16(5).
[58] Scottish Rules, rule 7.12(2).
[59] See Scottish Rules, rule 7.9, which applies to creditors' meetings in any insolvency proceedings and cross-applies the provisions of Chapter 5 of Part 4 of the Scottish Rules, which deals with claims in a liquidation, subject to specified modifications in respect of terminology and other necessary modifications.

in its application to CVAs,[60] and is calculated as at the date of the meeting or, where the company is in administration or liquidation, the date of the administration order or the company's going into liquidation, under deduction of any sums paid subsequent to that date.[61]

In contrast, at the company meeting, only a simple majority in value of those present in person or represented and voting, in person or by proxy, is required to approve any proposal or modification.[62] Members vote according to the rights attaching to their shares respectively in accordance with the articles of association,[63] but are entitled to vote on any proposal or modification, notwithstanding that no voting rights attach to their shares.[64]

It should be noted, however, that the meetings cannot approve any proposal or modification which affects the right of any secured creditor to enforce his security without his specific consent.[65] Secured creditors are, except where the context otherwise requires, those who hold 'any security (whether heritable or moveable), any floating charge and any right of lien or preference and any right of retention (other than a right of compensation or set off)'.[66] Similarly, the meetings cannot approve any proposal or modification which either alters the priority of any preferential debt or provides for payment of a smaller proportion of any preferential debt than is to be paid in respect of any other preferential debt without the specific consent of the creditor so affected.[67] Preferential debts are those defined in accordance with s 386 of the 1986 Act.[68]

Report to the court

The chairman of each meeting must report the outcome of the meeting to the court.[69] The report must contain certain prescribed information and be lodged with the court within four days of the conclusion of the meeting.[70] Where the CVA is approved, he must also send a copy of his report to the Registrar of Companies.[71]

---

[60] Scottish Rules, rule 4.16, as applied to voluntary arrangements by virtue of rules 1.13 and 7.9 of the Scottish Rules. For the rules applicable to the calculation of the amount of a creditor's claim in sequestration, see Chapter 32. It should be noted that the amount of the creditor's debt for this purpose is not necessarily the amount which he will be able to claim in any CVA which is agreed: see further Chapters 32 and 33.

[61] Scottish Rules, rule 4.15(5), as modified by rule 7.9(4)(c) and applied to voluntary arrangements by rule 1.13.

[62] Scottish Rules, rule 7.12(1), as applied to voluntary arrangements by rule 1.13 of the Scottish Rules.

[63] Scottish Rules, rule 7.10(1), as applied to voluntary arrangements by rule 1.13 of the Scottish Rules. The term 'shares' includes any other interests which the member may have as a member of the company: rule 7.10(3).

[64] Scottish Rules, rule 7.10(2).

[65] 1986 Act, s 4(3).

[66] 1986 Act, s 248(b)(ii). See further Chapter 32, in particular as to whether security may, for this purpose, include diligence.

[67] 1986 Act, s 4(4).

[68] 1986 Act, s 4(7). Preferential debts are those contained in Sched 6 to the 1986 Act read with Sched 4 to the Pension Schemes Act 1993: 1986 Act, s 386, and see further Chapter 33.

[69] 1986 Act, s 4(6).

[70] Scottish Rules, rule 1.17.

[71] Scottish Rules, rule 1.17(5).

Immediately after the report has been lodged in court, the chairman must also give notice of the result of the meetings to all those who received notice of them.[72]

Date of the company voluntary arrangement

Where the CVA is approved, it takes effect as if made by the company at the creditors' meeting,[73] subject to any subsequent challenge under s 6 of the 1986 Act.[74]

Effect of the company voluntary arrangement

The CVA binds every creditor who, in accordance with the Scottish Rules had notice of, and was entitled to vote at, the creditors' meeting as if he were a party to the arrangement.[75]

Challenge of decisions

Although the CVA takes effect from the date of the creditors' meeting,[76] the decisions of the meetings may be challenged in the circumstances set out in s 6 of the 1986 Act. This section considers the circumstances in which such a challenge may be made.

Who may challenge?

An application under s 6 of the 1986 Act may be made by any person who was entitled to vote at the company or creditors' meeting, the nominee or any person who has replaced him and, if the company is in administration or liquidation, the administrator or liquidator (if different from the nominee).[77]

Grounds for challenge

The application may be made on either or both of the following grounds.

(1) The CVA approved at the meetings unfairly prejudices the interests of a creditor, member or contributory of the company.[78]

The 1986 Act gives no guidance as to what is meant by the interests of a creditor or member being unfairly prejudiced.[79] In *Re Primlaks (UK) Ltd (No 2)*[80] Harman J said:

---

[72] 1986 Act, s 4(6), and Scottish Rules, rule 1.17(4).
[73] 1986 Act, s 5(2)(a).
[74] See below.
[75] 1986 Act, s 5(2)(b).
[76] See above.
[77] 1986 Act, s 6(2).
[78] 1986 Act, s 6(1)(a).
[79] The concept of unfair prejudice is used elsewhere in the law, notably in s 429 of CA 1985 which affords a remedy to members of a company where it is established that the company's affairs are being conducted in a manner which is unfairly prejudicial to some or all of the members or that some act or omission of the company would be so prejudicial, but that is not to say it has exactly the same meaning in this context. Indeed, in the case of *Doorbar v Alltime Securities Ltd (Nos 1 and 2)* [1996] 1 BCLC 487, a case involving an English individual voluntary arrangement, the grounds for challenge of which are exactly the same as the grounds for challenge of a CVA, the court said that it did not find references to s 459 of much assistance in this very different context, although the fact that it was an individual rather than a company which was involved may have had something to do with that. The concept of unfair prejudice is also used in s 27 of the 1986 Act in relation to administrations: see further Chapters 11 and 26.
[80] [1990] BCLC 234.

'[W]hat is unfair prejudice is a question which nobody could attempt to define in advance. It must always be a question of looking at the facts and finding out, first, has there been prejudice, and second, is it unfair to that particular creditor that he should be so prejudiced, presumably in comparison with the prejudice suffered by others in a like position to him, but that may be open to argument. . . . The words are plainly very wide.'[81]

Clearly, therefore, while each case will turn on its own facts, there must be prejudice, it must be unfair and it must relate to the particular applicant. Where the application is made by a creditor, the prejudice must be to his interests as a creditor (and not in some other capacity).[82] The prejudice must also arise from the terms of the CVA itself,[83] and the fact that other creditors of the same type are also prejudiced by the terms of the CVA does not necessarily mean that it is not unfairly prejudicial to the creditor in question.[84] It has been suggested that the principles to be applied in considering whether to sanction a section 425 arrangement should be referred to for the purpose of interpreting unfair prejudice, since both types of arrangement are justifying purposes for an administration order and it would be anomalous if different principles were utilised for judging the acceptability of each.[85] However, in *Re Primlaks (UK) Ltd (No 2)* Harman J, in making the point that the fact that other creditors of the same type are also prejudiced by the terms of the CVA did not necessarily mean that it was not unfairly prejudicial to the creditor in question, specifically stated that he was avoiding the use of the word 'class' (of creditor) to show that he had not slipped into considering a section 425 arrangement. This tends to suggest that he viewed the 'looser and wider voluntary arrangement under the 1986 Act' as being a different type of arrangement, with different principles applying.

(2) There was some material irregularity at or in relation to either of the meetings.[86]

This ground would not appear to be confined merely to procedural irregularities, although they are the most likely kind to have occurred. The irregularity must have been material, which implies something which was capable of influencing the outcome of the decision of the meeting. In *Re a Debtor (No 259 of 1990)*,[87] a case relating to an individual voluntary arrangement, it was held that where the vote of a creditor could not have made any difference to the outcome, there was no material irregularity in the fact that he had not received notice of the creditors' meeting.

---

[81] [1990] BCLC 234 at 239–240.
[82] *Doorbar v Alltime Securities Ltd (Nos 1 and 2)*, note 79 above.
[83] See *Re a Debtor (No 259 of 1990)* [1992] 1 WLR 226. Again this is an English case dealing with an individual voluntary arrangement under the 1986 Act, but as the grounds for challenging an individual voluntary arrangement are identical to those for challenging a CVA, it is relevant to interpretation of s 6 of the 1986 Act.
[84] Harman J in *Re Primlaks (UK) Ltd (No 2)* (note 80 above) at 236.
[85] St Clair and Drummond Young, *The Law of Corporate Insolvency in Scotland* (2nd edn), p 172. The principles to be applied in considering whether to sanction a section 425 arrangement are considered in Chapter 9.
[86] 1986 Act, s 6(1)(b).
[87] See note 83 above.

Unless an irregularity is successfully challenged under this provision, it will not affect the validity of any approval given at the meeting to which it relates.[88]

Time-limits

The application must be made within 28 days of the date on which the report of the meetings was lodged in court.[89]

Powers of the court

If the court is satisfied that either of the grounds of challenge has been made out, it may do one or both of the following.

(1) Revoke or suspend the approval given by the meetings.

The court may revoke or suspend the approval of both meetings or, where it has found material irregularity in relation to one of the meetings, revoke or suspend the approval of that meeting.[90] The applicant must serve a copy of the court's order on the supervisor of the CVA and the original proposer(s) of the CVA[91] and deliver a copy of it to the Registrar of Companies within seven days.[92] The original proposer(s) must thereafter give notice of the court's order to all persons who received notice of the meetings and anyone else who appears to be affected by it.[93]

The court may also give any supplementary directions it thinks necessary in connection with such revocation or suspension, including directions in relation to things already done under the approved CVA.[94]

Unless such revocation or suspension is combined with an order directing the calling of fresh meetings,[95] this would seem effectively to bring the CVA to an end. There would be nothing to prevent a fresh proposal being drawn up, but the chances of success of such a proposal would normally, in practice, be slim.

(2) Direct the calling of further meetings.

The court may *either* direct the calling of further meetings of both the creditors and the company to consider any revised proposal which the original proposer(s) may wish to make *or*, where it has found material irregularity in relation to one of the meetings, direct the calling of a further such meeting to reconsider the original proposal.[96] Where such a direction is included in an order for revocation or suspension of the approval of one or both meetings, the applicant is required, in addition to serving and delivering copies of the order as described above, to give notice of this fact to the person who is directed to summon the meeting or meetings.[97]

---

[88] 1986 Act, s 6(7).
[89] 1986 Act, s 6(3).
[90] 1986 Act, s 6(4)(a).
[91] Scottish Rules, rule 1.20(2).
[92] Scottish Rules, rule 1.20(5).
[93] Scottish Rules, rule 1.20(4)(a).
[94] 1986 Act, s 6(6).
[95] See below.
[96] 1986 Act, s 6(4)(b).
[97] Scottish Rules, rule 1.20(3). The person directed to summon the meetings need not be the original nominee: s 6(4)(b) of the 1986 Act allows the court to direct 'any person' to call the meeting or meetings.

The original proposer(s) must thereafter give notice to the court of whether it is intended to make a revised proposal or invite reconsideration of the original proposal, as appropriate.[98] Curiously, the Scottish Rules make no provision for such steps where the court simply directs the calling of further meetings without suspending or revoking the approval of the meetings,[99] despite the fact that such an option is clearly envisaged by s 6 of the 1986 Act. Presumably, it would be open to the court to make supplementary directions regarding service and notice in such a case: the court has power to give any supplementary directions it thinks necessary in connection with a direction to call further meetings.[100]

Where the court has directed the calling of further meetings of both the company and the creditors to consider a revised proposal and it is subsequently satisfied that no revised proposal is to be submitted, it must revoke the direction and revoke or suspend the approval given at the previous meetings (if this has not already been done).[101] This will effectively bring the CVA to an end. The court may give any supplementary directions it thinks necessary in connection with such revocation or suspension of approval, including directions in relation to things already done under the approved CVA.[102] Once again, there is nothing to stop a fresh proposal being drawn up, but the chances of its success would normally, in practice, be slim.

---

[98] Scottish Rules, rule 1.20(4)(b). The notice must be given within seven days or such longer period as the court may allow.

[99] Rule 1.20 of the Scottish Rules applies only where there is revocation or suspension of the arrangement.

[100] 1986 Act, s 6(6).

[101] 1986 Act, s 6(5).

[102] 1986 Act, s 6(6).

9 : PROCEDURE LEADING TO COMPROMISE OR ARRANGEMENT UNDER SECTION 425 OF THE COMPANIES ACT 1985

Section 425 of CA 1985 provides a procedure whereby a company may conclude a binding 'compromise or arrangement'[1] with its members or creditors, or any class of its members or creditors. It appears in Part XIII of CA 1985, which deals with arrangements and reconstructions, and is more frequently used in the context of reconstructions, takeovers or mergers in the normal course of business than on insolvency, but it is open to a company which is insolvent or in financial difficulties. Until the introduction of CVAs, it was the only means by which a company could achieve an arrangement which was binding on all its creditors without their unanimous consent. Although the CVA procedure was designed to provide a simpler means for a company which was insolvent or in financial difficulties to reach a binding agreement with its creditors than s 425 provided,[2] a section 425 arrangement remains an option for such a company and is one of the justifying purposes for the making of an administration order.[3] It is therefore included here as a formal insolvency procedure open to a company.

This chapter deals with the procedure for concluding a section 425 arrangement.

Initiating a section 425 arrangement

A section 425 arrangement is initiated by a petition to the court.

Which companies may be the subject of a section 425 arrangement?

Section 425(6) of CA 1985 defines company for the purpose of the section as 'a company liable to be wound up under this Act'.[4] CA 1985, as originally enacted, contained provisions relating to winding up, but no longer does so: these are now contained in the 1986 Act. One approach to this problem would be to ignore s 425(6), on the basis that it does not make sense (there are now no winding-up provisions in CA 1985 and no company is therefore liable to be

---

[1] CA 1985, s 425(1).
[2] Cork Report, Chapter 7, Part II, and see Chapter 8.
[3] See Chapter 10.
[4] Including a company or body corporate which would be so liable but for the Water Industry Act 1991, s 25: see the Water Consolidation (Consequential Provisions) Act 1991, Sched 1, para 40(1).

wound up under that Act), and to interpret 'company' according to the general definition of the word in s 735 of CA 1985. This would confine the application of s 425 to registered companies. However, the definitions in s 735 apply 'unless the contrary intention appears' and it is clear that s 425(6) shows a contrary intention because it intends the provision to apply to companies which are liable to be wound up, even if the reference to the Act under which that takes place is now inept. The provisions of CA 1985 as originally enacted included provisions for the winding up of registered and unregistered companies, as the 1986 Act does now. It is thought, therefore, that the better view is that a section 425 arrangement should be regarded as being open to any company liable to be wound up (under the 1986 Act), not just registered companies.

A section 425 arrangement is open to such a company even if it is in liquidation, administration or receivership.[5]

Who may apply?

The following may apply to the court to initiate a section 425 arrangement.[6]

(1) The company.

(2) Any creditor.

(3) Any member.

(4) Where the company is in liquidation, the liquidator only.

(5) Where the company is in administration, the administrator only.

A petition by the company would usually be presented by the directors, who are the agents of the company and would usually have power to present an application in its name. Where the petition is presented by a member or creditor rather than the company, the company must also approve of the application.[7] There is no requirement, however, in the case of a petition by a creditor for the sum owed to that creditor to be of a minimum amount.[8] A petition by a receiver is not specifically provided for, but a receiver is deemed to be an agent of the company[9] and so might be thought to have power to present a petition in its name; even if this is not the case, the creditor in the obligation secured by the charge under which he was appointed would be able to apply *qua* creditor during the course of the receivership.

Which court?

The court is the court having jurisdiction to wind up the company.[10]

Form of petition

The petition will seek an order that a meeting of the members, the creditors or such classes of either with whom it proposed to reach a compromise or arrangement be called in such manner as the court directs.[11]

---

[5] See further below.

[6] CA 1985, s 425(1).

[7] *Re Savoy Hotel Ltd* [1981] Ch 351.

[8] With respect to the definition of creditor, see further below.

[9] See Chapter 27.

[10] CA 1985, s 744, and see further Chapter 16 (registered companies) and Chapter 17 (unregistered companies).

[11] CA 1985, s 425(1).

In a case where the company is insolvent or in financial difficulties, the proposed section 425 arrangement will usually be between the company and its creditors as a whole. The term 'creditor' is not defined for this purpose by CA 1985, but it has been said in relation to the use of the term in the equivalent section of an earlier Act[12] that it is used in the widest sense and includes all persons having any pecuniary claim against the company.[13] It has been held to include contingent creditors,[14] a creditor who had an illiquid claim for damages,[15] secured creditors[16] and foreign creditors.[17] The petition will normally seek an order for the calling of separate meetings of different classes of creditors (and, if appropriate, members).[18] The court does not, however, give directions as to what the appropriate classes of creditors and members should be when ordering the calling of the meetings. That decision rests with the applicant, together with the attendant risk that if the decision is wrongly made, the whole arrangement may ultimately fail.[19] Classes must be determined according to the interests of those proposed to be included in the class. In relation to creditors, obvious divisions are those such as secured and unsecured creditors and financial and trade creditors, but even then it may be necessary to subdivide such categories. The underlying interests of the creditors must be looked at to ensure that all creditors in any particular class have common interests and are not affected by different matters which may affect their judgment on the proposal: a class 'must be confined to those persons whose rights are not so dissimilar as to make it impossible for them to consult together with a view to their common interests'.[20] The same applies to classes of members, if relevant. 'Classes' in this context will not necessarily equate with 'classes' identified for other purposes within the companies legislation. For example, even where the memorandum itself divides shares into separate classes, the shares within any one such class may still need to be divided into separate classes for the purposes of considering a section 425 arrangement if some are fully paid up and others are not.

The decision on the proposed section 425 arrangement

The court has a discretion as to whether to order that the relevant meetings be called. Where it does so, the decision on the proposed section 425 arrangement is made by these meetings, subject to the sanction of the court. This section deals with the procedure from the calling of the meetings to the final decision on the proposed section 425 arrangement.

---

[12] The Joint Stock Companies Arrangements Act 1870.
[13] *Re Midland Coal, Coke and Iron Co* [1895] 1 Ch 267.
[14] Ibid.
[15] *Re R.L. Child & Co Pty Ltd* (1986) 4 ACLC 312; cf *Trocko v Renlita Products Pty Ltd* (1973) 5 SASR 207, where it was held that a person having such a claim was not a creditor. The apparently contradictory decisions have been explained on the basis that whether any particular person is a creditor for this purpose may depend on the terms of the scheme itself: see *CCH Law and Practice*, para 67–200.
[16] *In Re Alabama, New Orleans, Texas and Pacific Junction Ry Co* [1891] 1 Ch 213.
[17] *New Zealand Loan and Mercantile Agency Co Ltd v Morrison* [1898] AC 349.
[18] *Tritonia* 1948 SN 11.
[19] The court may refuse to sanction the scheme even if the meetings as called approved the proposed s 425 arrangement by the requisite majority: in relation to these requirements, see further below.
[20] *Sovereign Life Assurance Co v Dodd* [1892] 2 QB 573 at 583.

The meetings

The meetings will be called in such manner as the court has specified in the order directing that they should be called. Normally, notice will require to be given to each individual creditor and/or member concerned and advertisement will also be ordered.

Where the court orders individual notices to be sent to creditors and/or members, they must be accompanied by a statement explaining the effect of the proposed section 425 arrangement.[21] This statement must disclose, in particular, any material interests of the directors in whatever capacity these arise and the effect of the proposed section 425 arrangement on those interests so far as it differs from its effect on the like interests of other persons.[22] The statement must also disclose the same information in relation to the trustees of the deed for securing the issue of debentures where the proposed section 425 arrangement affects the interests of debenture holders.[23]

Where notice is given by advertisement, the former statutory requirement to include such a statement or details of how and where it could be obtained in the advertisement itself has been repealed,[24] but the court may make a specific direction to similar effect. Where a notice by advertisement states that such a statement can be obtained by those entitled to attend the meeting, it must be supplied free of charge to those applying for it in the manner specified in the advertisement.[25]

Failure to comply with the requirements of s 426 of CA 1985 not only leads to the company and its officers becoming liable to a default fine,[26] but the meetings, if held, will be invalid and will require to be reconvened.[27]

The decision of the meetings

A majority of 75 per cent in value of those present and voting either in person or by proxy is required to approve the proposed section 425 arrangement.[28] Unlike the position in relation to the other formal insolvency régimes, there are no specific provisions detailing how the interests of those voting are to be valued for this purpose. In the case of members, valuation will usually be unproblematic, at least in the case of a company limited by shares where the calculation will be based on the value of the shares of those voting. It was held, where a company was limited by guarantee and each member had an equal stake in the company, that a numerical majority of 75 per cent of those voting satisfied the statutory requirements because it was as if each member had a single share of the same value in the company.[29] In the case of creditors, valuation may be more problematic, yet is obviously crucial. In *Re Exchange Securities & Commodities Ltd (No 3)*,[30] the liquidator of two companies sought directions from

---

[21] CA 1985, s 426(2).
[22] Ibid.
[23] CA 1985, s 426(4).
[24] The requirement was contained in s 426(3) of CA 1985, which was repealed by the Requirements of Writing (Scotland) Act 1995, s 14(2), s 15 and Sched 5, as from 1st August 1995.
[25] CA 1985, s 426(5).
[26] CA 1985, s 426(7). The subsection gives an extended definition of officers of the company for this purpose.
[27] See, eg, *Scottish Eastern Investment Trust* 1966 SLT 285.
[28] CA 1985, s 425(2).
[29] *Re NFU Development Trust Ltd* [1972] 1 WLR 1548.
[30] [1987] BCLC 425.

the court as to how the claims of certain creditors should be valued in connection with a proposed section 425 arrangement. The creditors in question were investors in the company who had been advised by the company that certain profits had been made and credited to them. The reported profits were in fact false. The creditors none the less claimed that for the purposes of voting on the arrangement, their claims should be valued based on the information they had been given. The court disagreed and held that their claims should be valued at their true value. There may still, however, be difficult problems in deciding on the true value of certain types of claims—for example, contingent claims.

Where the requisite majorities are not achieved, the matter will end there. Even if the requisite majorities are achieved, however, the sanction of the court is still required before the section 425 arrangement can take effect.

Sanction of the court

The criteria to be applied by the court in deciding whether to sanction the agreement were established in the case of *Shandon Hydropathic Co Ltd*,[31] where Lord President Dunedin adopted as authoritative the observations of Lindley LJ in the case of *In Re Alabama, New Orleans, Texas and Pacific Junction Ry Co*[32] to the effect that:

> 'What the court has to do is to see first of all that the statutory provisions have been complied with; and secondly, that the majority have been acting bona fide. The court also has to see that the minority is not being overridden by a majority, having interests of its own clashing with those of the minority whom they seek to coerce. Further than that, the court has to look at the scheme and see whether it is one as to which persons, acting honestly and viewing the scheme laid before them in the interests of those whom they represent, take a view which can be reasonably taken by business men. The court must look at the scheme and see whether the Act has been complied with, whether the majority are acting bona fide, and whether they are coercing the minority in order to promote interests adverse to those of the class whom they purport to represent; and then see whether the scheme is a reasonable one, or whether there is any reasonable objection to it, or such an objection to it as that any reasonable man might say that he could not approve of it.'[33]

The court is therefore concerned with both the procedural fairness and the reasonableness of the scheme in question.

It has already been noted that the court may refuse to sanction a section 425 arrangement if the classes into which those voting have been divided are not appropriate,[34] and other examples of circumstances where the court has refused to sanction an arrangement may be found in the case-law.[35] The court may

---

[31] 1911 SC 1153.
[32] See note 16 above.
[33] 1911 SC 1153 at 1155.
[34] See, for example, *Re Hellenic & General Trust Ltd* [1976] 1 WLR 123 (shareholder in subsidiary company should have formed separate class).
[35] See, for example, *Lainière de Roubaix v Glen Glove and Hosiery Co Ltd* 1926 SC 91 (scheme not sanctioned *inter alia* as preferential treatment given to one creditor); *Re Holders Investment Trust Ltd* [1976] 1 WLR 583 (scheme not sanctioned as class had not voted bona fide in the interests of

sanction the section 425 arrangement subject to conditions or restrictions rather than refuse sanction outright.

Date of section 425 arrangement

The section 425 arrangement takes effect only once an office copy of the order of the court sanctioning the arrangement has been delivered to the Registrar of Companies for registration.[36]

Effect of section 425 arrangement

A section 425 arrangement binds all creditors affected by it, including any dissenting minority.

Registration of the order

As indicated above, an office copy of the order sanctioning the agreement must be delivered to the Registrar of Companies for registration before the section 425 arrangement can take effect. A copy of the order must also be annexed to all copies of the company's memorandum or other instrument constituting the company or defining its constitution issued after the making of the order.[37] It is the company's responsibility to attend to these matters and failure to do so renders the company and its officers liable to a default fine.[38]

Appeals

An order that meetings should be called under s 425(1) of CA 1985 is not subject to review, reduction, suspension or stay of execution when pronounced by the judge acting as vacation judge.[39] Any other order will be appealable in the normal way.

---

that class); *Re Minster Assets plc* (1985) 1 BCC 99 (directors had not disclosed share dealings subsequent to issuing of original circular: scheme sanctioned as court satisfied no reasonable shareholder would have acted differently if information disclosed, but stated if satisfied would have acted differently, sanction would have been refused).

[36] CA 1985, s 425(3).
[37] Ibid.
[38] CA 1985, s 425(4).
[39] CA 1985, s 425(5).

10 : PROCEDURE LEADING TO THE MAKING OF AN ADMINISTRATION ORDER

Administration was one of the new insolvency régimes introduced on the recommendation of the Cork Committee. It may be utilised to facilitate the rescue of companies in financial difficulties or to achieve a more advantageous realisation of a company's assets than could be achieved on winding up. Part II of the 1986 Act permits the court, in certain defined circumstances, to make an administration order, which is 'an order directing that, during the period for which the order is in force, the affairs, business and property of the company shall be managed by a person ("the administrator") appointed for the purpose by the court'.[1] This chapter deals with the procedure up to the making of an administration order.

Applying for an administration order

An administration order is obtained as a result of a petition to the relevant court. This section deals with various aspects of applying for an administration order.

Which companies may be subject to an administration order?

Part II of the 1986 Act does not define the companies to which administration applies. Reference must be made to s 251 of the 1986 Act, which states that, except insofar as the context otherwise requires, any expression other than one specifically defined in the section for whose interpretation provision is made by Part XXVI of CA 1985 is to be construed in accordance with that statute. This leads to s 735 of CA 1985, which defines 'company' as a company registered under that Act or under any former Companies Acts as defined by the section.[2] It has been argued that administration proceedings should be regarded as open to companies other than registered companies,[3] but this must be regarded as a matter of debate. An administration order has been made in respect of a foreign company

---

[1] 1986 Act, s 8(2).
[2] CA 1985, s 735(1).
[3] Preece, 'The United Kingdom Insolvency Act and International Corporate Rescue', *Newsletter of the EIPA*, Issue 7, September 1995.

where this was requested pursuant to an application under s 426 of the 1986 Act[4] and the conditions for the granting of an administration order, discussed further below, were fulfilled,[5] but it is thought that that is the only situation where an administration order may be made in relation to a company other than a registered company.[6] A modified form of administration is open to building societies incorporated or deemed to be incorporated under the Building Societies Act 1986.[7]

Section 8(4) of the 1986 Act specifically states that an administration order shall not be made in relation to a company which has gone into liquidation, a company which is an insurance company within the meaning of the Insurance Companies Act 1982 or a company which is an authorised institution or former authorised institution under the Banking Act 1987. In relation to the last of these, however, the Banks (Administration Proceedings) Order 1989[8] applies Part II of the 1986 Act to authorised institutions or former authorised institutions under the Banking Act 1987 which are companies within the meaning of s 735 of CA 1985 with various modifications including the omission of the reference to their exclusion in s 8(4). Authorised or former authorised institutions under the Banking Act 1987 which are companies within the meaning of s 735 of CA 1985 *are* therefore subject to a modified version of the administration procedure by virtue of the Banks (Administration Proceedings) Order 1989.

Who may apply?

A petition for an administration order in Scotland may be presented by:

(1) The company itself.[9]

(2) The directors.[10]

(3) A creditor or creditors.[11]

(4) In the case of authorised institutions or former authorised institutions under the Banking Act 1987 which are companies within the meaning of s 735 of CA 1985 only, the Financial Services Authority.[12]

(5) In the case of a building society incorporated or deemed to be incorporated under the Building Societies Act 1986 only, the Building Societies Commission or a shareholding member entitled to petition for the winding up of the society under s 89(3) of the Building Societies Act 1986.[13]

(6) Any combination of the parties listed above.[14]

---

[4] That section relates, *inter alia*, to the assistance to be granted to the insolvency courts of certain foreign jurisdictions by the insolvency courts of the UK: see further Chapter 48.

[5] *Re Dallhold Estates (UK) Pty Ltd* [1992] BCLC 621.

[6] For a full and reasoned discussion of this point, which reaches this conclusion, see Fletcher, Higham and Trower, *The Law and Practice of Corporate Administrations*, paras 18.25 – 18.33.

[7] Building Societies Act 1986, s 90A. The relevant modifications are contained in Sched 15A to that Act.

[8] SI 1989/1276.

[9] 1986 Act, s 9(1).

[10] Ibid.

[11] Ibid. Creditors are defined by that subsection as including contingent or prospective creditors.

[12] Banks (Administration Proceedings) Order 1989, as amended by the Bank of England Act 1998 (Consequential Amendments to Subordinate Legislation) Order 1998 (SI 1998/1129).

[13] Building Societies Act 1986, s 90A and Sched 15A. The circumstances in which a shareholding member may petition for the winding up of a building society are discussed in Chapter 16.

[14] 1986 Act, s 9(1).

(7) The supervisor of a CVA.[15]

(8) In the case of authorised persons under the Financial Services Act 1986, including their representatives and authorised persons who are suspended or subject to a direction under s 33(1)(b) of that Act, who are companies to which administration proceedings apply, the Secretary of State *or* the relevant self-regulating organisation or recognised professional body by virtue of membership of which the person is authorised, as appropriate.[16]

In the case of a petition by the directors, the use of the term 'the directors' in the 1986 Act seems to exclude the possibility of a petition by only one or some of them.[17] However, where a board decision is taken to petition for an administration order, all the directors would be bound to implement it even if they had dissented from the decision, and accordingly a petition could be presented on behalf of all the directors by any one of them.[18] In the case of a petition by a creditor or creditors, there is no requirement that the debt or debts owed to the creditor or creditors be of any minimum amount, although in practice it is only major creditors who would be likely to wish, or be in a position, to petition for administration.

Which court?

Part II of the 1986 Act simply refers to 'the court' without defining that term. Again, therefore, reference must be made to s 251 of the 1986 Act. This leads to s 744 of CA 1985 which provides that the court, in relation to a company, is the court having jurisdiction to wind up the company.[19]

Form of petition and supporting documentation

A Court of Session petition must be in Form 14.4 and must contain certain prescribed information.[20] There is no prescribed form of petition in the sheriff court, but the petition must contain certain prescribed information[21] and there must be produced with it any document instructing the facts relied upon or otherwise founded upon by the petitioner.[22] In both sheriff court and Court of Session petitions any independent report prepared under rule 2.1 of the Scottish Rules must also be produced.[23]

Rule 2.1 of the Scottish Rules provides that a report to the effect that the appointment of an administrator to the company would be expedient may be prepared by the proposed administrator or any other independent person having adequate knowledge of the company's affairs.[24] Such a report must specify which

---

[15] 1986 Act, s 7(4).

[16] Financial Services Act 1986, s 74.

[17] *Re Instrumentational Electrical Services Ltd* (1988) 4 BCC 301.

[18] *Re Equiticorp International plc* [1989] BCLC 597.

[19] See further Chapter 16 (registered companies) and Chapter 17 (unregistered companies).

[20] Act of Sederunt (Rules of the Court of Session) 1994 (SI 1994/1443) (hereafter 'the Court of Session Rules'), rules 14.4 and 74.10(1).

[21] Act of Sederunt (Sheriff Court Company Insolvency Rules) 1986 (SI 1986/2297) (hereafter 'the Sheriff Court Rules'), rule 10(1).

[22] Sheriff Court Rules, rule 10(2)(a). Documents founded on or adopted in a Court of Session petition must also be produced with it by virtue of rule 27.1 of the Court of Session Rules.

[23] Sheriff Court Rules, rule 10(2)(b); Court of Session Rules, rule 74.10(2).

[24] Except the company secretary and any director, manager, member or employee of the company: Scottish Rules, rule 2.1(2).

of the purposes for which an administration order may be made its writer thinks might be achieved if an order were made.[25] The report is not compulsory and unlike the courts in England and Wales, which have made the equivalent report in that jurisdiction virtually compulsory, the Scottish courts have not insisted on such a report being produced in every case. Provided that there is sufficient information in the petition and it is accompanied by a statement of affairs showing the position of the company, the court may be prepared to proceed without it, although where no report has been prepared, the petition must say why.[26]

The making of an administration order

This section deals with the procedure from the presentation of the petition to the making of the order.

Effect of presentation of petition

In most cases, the company is protected from specified actions by creditors immediately on presentation of the petition and this protection continues until a decision on the petition is made.[27] The exception to this is where there is an administrative receiver already in place at the time of presentation of the petition and the chargeholder has not consented to the making of the administration order. In such cases, the period of protection does not begin until the chargeholder so consents.[28] The specific actions from which the company is protected are as follows.

(1) No resolution to wind up the company may be passed and no winding-up order may be made.[29]

A petition for winding up may still be presented during this period[30] because many of the important consequences of liquidation are linked to the date of presentation of the petition, and if an administration order is ultimately refused and a winding-up order is then made, the date of presentation of the liquidation petition may be crucial. However, the winding-up petition will not be dealt with until after a decision has been made on the petition for the administration order and advertisement of the former may be delayed until that time.[31]

(2) No steps to enforce any security over the company's property or to repossess goods under a hire-purchase agreement may be taken except with the leave of the court and on such conditions as it sees fit.[32]

Security is defined as 'any security (whether heritable or moveable), any floating charge and any right of lien or preference and any right of retention (other than a right of compensation or set-off)'.[33] Because it is only security over the company's property which is affected, a creditor

---

[25] The purposes for which an administration order may be made are discussed further below.
[26] Court of Session Rules, rule 74.10(2); Sheriff Court Rules, rule 10(1)(h).
[27] 1986 Act, s 10.
[28] 1986 Act, s 10(3).
[29] 1986 Act, s 10(1)(a).
[30] 1986 Act, s 10(2)(a).
[31] *Re a Company (No 001992 of 1988)* [1989] BCLC 9.
[32] 1986 Act, s 10(1)(b).
[33] 1986 Act, s 248.

may still enforce other security interests which are not over the company's property as such—for example, cautionary obligations. Hire-purchase agreement is given an extended meaning and includes conditional sale agreements, chattel leasing agreements and retention of title agreements.[34] The interpretation of this provision and the question of when and on what conditions leave to take the steps referred to will be granted are discussed more fully below in connection with the effect of the administration order itself.

(3) No other proceedings, no execution or diligence and no other legal process may be commenced or continued against the company or its property except with the leave of the court and on such conditions as it sees fit.[35]

The interpretation of this provision and the question of when and on what conditions leave to take the steps referred to will be granted is discussed more fully below in connection with the effect of the administration order itself.

It should be noted that an administrative receiver may still be appointed during this period and any administrative receiver (whenever appointed) may carry out his functions unimpeded within this period.[36] Furthermore, the statutory moratorium does not prevent the enforcement of market charges as defined by s 173(1) of the Companies Act 1989.[37]

Procedure following presentation

Once the petition has been presented, it cannot be withdrawn except with the leave of the court.[38] Following presentation, the court will pronounce a first order for intimation, notice and service. The petitioner is required to give notice of the petition to any person who has appointed, or is or may be entitled to appoint, an administrative receiver[39] and also to any administrative receiver who has been appointed, the petitioner in any pending liquidation petition, any provisional liquidator, the proposed administrator, the Registrar of Companies, the Keeper of the Register of Inhibitions and Adjudications, the company (if the administration petition is presented by the directors or a creditor or creditors) and any other person whom the court directs.[40] If the company in respect of which the petition is presented is an authorised or former authorised institution under the Banking Act 1987 in respect of which an administration order may be made by virtue of the Banks (Administration Proceedings) Order 1989, notice

---

[34] 1986 Act, s 10(4). For the meaning of each of these expressions see, in the case of conditional sale agreements, the Consumer Credit Act 1974, s 189(1), as applied by the 1986 Act, s 251, and CA 1985, s 744, and, in the case of chattel leasing agreements and retention of title agreements, 1986 Act, s 251. Retention of title is discussed further in Chapter 22.

[35] 1986 Act, s (10)(1)(c), as modified in its application to Scotland by s 10(5).

[36] 1986 Act, s 10(2).

[37] Companies Act 1989, s 175(1)(a). Part VII of that Act is specifically designed to ensure that the operation of the financial markets is not affected by the insolvency of those participating in those markets.

[38] 1986 Act, s 9(2)(b).

[39] 1986 Act, s 9(2)(a). In the case of a building society, this is to be read as a reference to the Building Societies Commission unless it is itself a petitioner: Building Societies Act 1986, s 90A and Sched 15A.

[40] 1986 Scottish Rules, rule 2.2.

must also be given to the Financial Services Authority unless it is itself the petitioner in terms of that order.

The court may also at this stage make any interim orders which it thinks fit,[41] including an order restricting the powers of the directors of the company *either* by reference to the consent of the court or a person qualified to act as an insolvency practitioner in relation to the company *or* otherwise.[42] It became common practice to make, where sought, an interim administration order and an order appointing an administrator *ad interim* (usually the proposed administrator) on presentation of the petition. This practice was called into question and has been discontinued, although the proposed administrator or, presumably, some other suitable person may still be appointed to manage the company *ad interim* if this is required.[43]

Any person who has received notice or service of the petition and any other person claiming an interest may lodge answers within the period allowed. There are no special rules regarding procedure in relation to the hearing of an administration petition, and so the normal procedure for dealing with petitions will apply. Where answers are lodged, normal procedure would be for there to be a period of adjustment of the petition and answers and then a proof, but in view of the nature of the application, the normal procedure may be abridged. Where, as in the usual case, no answers are lodged, the petition will call in court. The court may dismiss the petition, adjourn it conditionally—for example, to allow further information to be produced—or unconditionally, make an interim order or make any other order that it thinks fit including, obviously, an administration order.[44]

Discretionary nature of administration

Although the powers of the court to deal with the petition are very wide, they must be read subject to the general requirements of the 1986 Act as to the circumstances in which an administration order may be made. An administration order may only be made if the court is satisfied of the matters specified in s 8(1) of the 1986 Act. Conversely, the court must dismiss the petition if it is satisfied that there is an administrative receiver of the company *unless* it is satisfied *either* that the chargeholder has consented to the appointment *or* that the security by virtue of which the receiver was appointed is challengeable on any of the grounds specified in s 9(3)(b).[45]

Subject to these requirements, the making of an administration order is a matter for the court's discretion. Section 8(1) of the 1986 Act states that if the court is satisfied of the matters specified therein, it *may* make an administration order. In *Re Consumer & Industrial Press Ltd*[46] this discretion was said to be a complete discretion, in which all material factors would be taken into account, and was not limited to taking into account the matters specified in s 8(1). The

---

[41] 1986 Act, s 9(4).

[42] 1986 Act, s 9(5). This power is specifically stated to be without prejudice to the general power contained in s 9(4).

[43] This is discussed further in Chapter 19 which deals with appointment and replacement of office holders generally.

[44] Ibid.

[45] 1986 Act, s 9(3). These requirements are discussed more fully below.

[46] (1988) 4 BCC 68.

court will consider, among other factors, exactly *how* likely it is that the purposes for which the administration order are to be granted will be achieved. It will also consider matters such as the availability of funding to finance the administration and the interests of those who are interested in the fate of the company, including creditors and, where applicable, members. The interests of all creditors will not necessarily be the same, however, and the court will also take that into account. In the case of *Re Imperial Motors (UK) Ltd*,[47] for example, the court held that the interests of secured creditors should be weighed more lightly than those of the unsecured creditors, since the former had less to lose, and in *Cornhill Insurance plc v Cornhill Financial Services Ltd*[48] it was held that an administration order would not be granted if this resulted in unfair prejudice to individual creditors or groups of creditors. The court will also weigh up the relative advantages and disadvantages of administration and any alternative, such as liquidation. It will also consider practical matters: in the case of *Re Business Properties Ltd*[49] it was held that it would not normally be appropriate to appoint an administrator in a case where there had been a breakdown of trust within the management of the company, a winding up being more appropriate in such a case. Nor will the court make an administration order if it is clear that the extent of creditor opposition is such that any proposals made by the administrator will be rejected.[50]

Conditions for the making of an administration order

Section 8(1) of the 1986 Act sets out two matters of which the court must be satisfied before it can make an administration order. These are:

(1) The company is or is likely to become unable to pay its debts.[51]

 The meaning of the phrase 'unable to pay its debts' is that set out in s 123 of the 1986 Act.[52]

(2) The making of an administration order must be likely to achieve one or more of the purposes specified in s 8(3) of the 1986 Act.[53]

 The meaning of the phrase 'likely to achieve' is crucial. It was the subject of differing judicial interpretation in the early days of administration, but the accepted interpretation now seems to be that it means that there is a 'real prospect' of the specified purpose or purposes being

---

[47] (1989) 5 BCC 214.
[48] (1992) BCC 818.
[49] (1988) 4 BCC 684.
[50] See *Re Arrows Ltd (No 3)* [1992] BCLC 555; *Re Land and Property Trust Co plc (No 2)* [1991] BCLC 849. The administrator's proposals are discussed in the following chapter.
[51] 1986 Act, s 8(1)(a).
[52] Ibid. This is fully discussed in Chapter 1. For the purposes of a petition presented by the Building Societies Commission (alone or in conjunction with other parties), a building society is deemed to be unable to pay its debts within the meaning of the section if it has defaulted in an obligation to pay any sum due and payable in respect of any deposit or share: Building Societies Act 1986, s 90A and Sched 15A. Similarly, for the purposes of a petition presented by the Bank of England (alone or in conjunction with other parties), an authorised institution or former authorised institution is deemed to be unable to pay its debts within the meaning of the section if it has defaulted in an obligation to pay any sum due and payable in respect of a deposit within the meaning of s 92 of the Banking Act 1987: Banks (Administration Proceedings) Order 1989, as amended by the Bank of England Act 1998 (Consequential Amendments to Subordinate Legislation) Order 1998 (SI 1998/1129).
[53] 1986 Act, s 8(1)(b).

achieved.[54] The purposes for which an administration order may be made are:

(a) The survival of the company and the whole or any part of its undertaking as a going concern.

This purpose seems not to allow for the situation where the intention is to save (all or part of) the business only—for example by hiving it down—because the purpose requires the survival of the company as a going concern as well. This may be seen as unduly restrictive, but if the company is not to survive as a going concern, the same result can be achieved by specifying the purpose in s 8(3)(d) as the relevant purpose.[55]

(b) The approval of a CVA.

The use of administration to achieve a CVA obviously involves two sets of proceedings and is consequently cumbersome and expensive. However, the advantage administration has over a proposed CVA is that the company is protected from creditors as soon as an administration petition is presented, whereas in a CVA creditors are free to carry on with independent action until the arrangement is actually approved. The immediate protection from creditors gained by invoking administration proceedings may therefore make the successful conclusion of a CVA more likely.[56]

(c) The sanctioning of a section 425 arrangement.[57]

Again, this involves a double procedure, but may be worthwhile for the same reasons as discussed in relation to the preceding purpose.

(d) A more advantageous realisation of the company's assets than would be achieved on a winding up.

On the passing of a resolution that the company be wound up or the making of a winding-up order by the court, the company must cease trading except insofar as necessary for the beneficial winding up of the company.[58] An administrator, however, may continue to trade, protected from creditors, for much longer than would be acceptable in a liquidation, notwithstanding that administration is meant to be a temporary régime.

---

[54] Hoffmann J in *Re Harris Simons Construction Ltd* [1989] BCLC 202. Given the nature of language, it might be questioned whether this is any more precise a text than the original words of the statute.

[55] See below.

[56] The lack of a statutory moratorium similar to that available in administration is one of the reasons which has been identified for a lack of use of CVAs generally. The Insolvency Service consulted on both CVAs and administrations some time ago (see Company Voluntary Arrangements and Administration Orders: A Consultation Document, 1993, and Revised Proposals for a New Company Voluntary Arrangement Procedure: A Consultative Document, 1995) and the last government brought forward proposals to enact a statutory moratorium for CVAs, but no legislation was enacted before the last election. The present government has indicated an intention to review business-rescue procedures generally and to legislate for a stay of up to three months on creditor actions to allow a business in difficulties time to come to an arrangement with its creditors: White Paper on Competitiveness, 1998, para 2.13.

[57] This purpose is not available in the case of a building society: Building Societies Act 1986, s 90A and Sched 15A.

[58] See Chapter 28.

He also has the advantage of being able to deal with secured property as if it was not subject to the security concerned, subject only to the consent of the court in the case of securities other than floating charges.[59] These and other advantages, including tax advantages, mean that the administrator will usually be able to obtain a better price for (all or part of) the business and/or its component assets than a liquidator would be able to achieve. The monies so realised will usually be distributed in the subsequent liquidation of the company.[60]

Where the court makes an administration order, it must specify in the order the purpose or purposes for which it is made. An administration order may only be made for the purposes specified in s 8(3), but it is clear from s 8(1) that it may be made for more than one purpose. It is also possible to amend the purpose or purposes for which the order is sought prior to its being made[61] and to vary the purpose or purposes for which the order was granted by adding an additional purpose on the application of the administrator.[62] So if, for example, an order is made for the purpose of a better realisation of assets and it subsequently becomes clear that the company may be able to survive, this change of purpose can be accommodated. It is, however, common to specify multiple purposes in the initial petition, with the result that variation is not often required in practice.[63]

Dismissal of petition where there is an administrative receiver

It has already been stated that the court must dismiss a petition for an administration order if it is satisfied that there is an administrative receiver of the company *unless* it is also satisfied that *either* the chargeholder has consented to the appointment *or* the security by virtue of which the receiver was appointed is challengeable on any of the grounds specified in s 9(3)(b).[64] So far as applicable in Scotland, these are:

(1) That the security would be avoided under s 245 of the 1986 Act (avoidance of certain floating charges).

(2) That the security would be challengeable under s 242 of the 1986 Act (gratuitous alienations) or s 243 of that Act (unfair preferences) or under any Scottish rule of law.[65]

This provision effectively gives the person who has appointed an administrative receiver the right to veto the making of an administration order by refusing to consent to it, unless his security is open to challenge on any of the grounds specified. Because the provision requires the court to dismiss the petition *unless it is satisfied* that the chargeholder has consented to the order or his security is open to challenge, the administration petition will be dismissed unless there is positive

---

[59] For the meaning of security in this context, see further Chapter 22. For the administrator's powers in this respect, see further Chapter 26.

[60] Ibid.

[61] By amending the petition in the normal way.

[62] 1986 Act, s 18(1).

[63] For an example of where such a variation was approved in practice, see *Re St Ives Windings Ltd* (1987) 3 BCC 634 (order varied to specify additional purpose of approval of CVA).

[64] See above.

[65] For a discussion of the various types of challengeable transactions, see Chapter 30.

evidence of such consent or grounds for challenge. It will be up to the petitioner to produce this. It is not enough, for example, to rely on lack of active objection by the chargeholder.[66]

Date of administration

Administration commences with the making of the administration order itself, even where interim orders have been made prior to that date.[67]

Effect of administration order

On the making of the administration order, any liquidation petition is dismissed and any administrative receiver must vacate office.[68] During the administration, no resolution may be passed, or order made, for the winding up of the company[69] and the protection from creditors' actions afforded to the company on presentation of the petition is continued and extended as follows:

(1) No administrative receiver may be appointed.[70]

This stops a chargeholder who consented to the administration order, or decided not to appoint a receiver before the order was made, from changing his mind and appointing such a receiver during the administration.

(2) No steps to enforce any security over the company's property or to re-possess goods under a hire-purchase agreement may be taken except with the consent of the administrator or the leave of the court, in the latter case on such conditions as it sees fit.[71]

The definition of 'security' and the meaning of 'hire-purchase agreement' have already been considered in the context of the equivalent provision applicable on presentation of the petition.[72] The interpretation of this provision, the administrator's consent and leave are discussed further below.

(3) No other proceedings and no execution, diligence or other legal process may be commenced or continued against the company or its property except with the consent of the administrator or the leave of the court, in the latter case on such conditions as it sees fit.[73]

The interpretation of this and the preceding provision and their equivalents where a petition for an administration order has been presented[74] will now be discussed, together with the related matter of the administrator's consent/leave of the court.

---

[66] Note that these provisions apply only where an administrative receiver has actually been appointed. Where no administrative receiver has been appointed, there is no requirement to produce the chargeholder's consent or to show that his security is open to challenge.

[67] *Secretary of State for Trade and Industry v Palmer* 1995 SLT 188.

[68] 1986 Act, s 11(1)(a) and (b) respectively. The administrator may require any receiver who is not an administrative receiver to vacate office also: 1986 Act, s 11(2), and see Chapter 26.

[69] 1986 Act, s 11(3)(a).

[70] 1986 Act, s 11(3)(b).

[71] 1986 Act, s 11(3)(c).

[72] See above. The extended definition of 'hire-purchase agreement' applies to this provision also by virtue of 1986 Act, s 10(4).

[73] 1986 Act, s (11)(3)(d), as modified in its application to Scotland by s 10(5).

[74] See above.

The question of exactly what actions are caught by these provisions, and therefore require the appropriate consent or leave, has been considered in a number of cases. In relation to enforcement of a security, it has been held, for example, that retaining goods after the administrator had requested their delivery amounted to enforcement of a lien;[75] similarly, the exercise of a statutory right to detain aircraft in security of landing fees and dues has been held to require leave,[76] and the exercise of a landlord's right of re-entry has been held to come within the definition of security in England, with the result that it could not be exercised without the relevant consent or leave.[77] In relation to 'other proceedings', it has been held that this phrase in s 11(3)(d) of the 1986 Act must be given a restricted construction *eiusdem generis* with s 11(3)(a)-(c), and accordingly a hearing conducted by the Civil Aviation Authority on an application to have the air transport licences of the company in administration revoked did not constitute other proceedings;[78] similarly, it has been held that an application for leave to register a charge out of time does not amount to proceedings which require consent or leave.[79] In relation to 'other legal process', it has been held that this does not include the service of a notice of irritancy under a lease, on the basis that it is a non-judicial step required by the contract of lease,[80] nor the service of a notice to make time of the essence or treat a contract with the company as terminated on the ground of the company's repudiatory breach, again on the basis that this was a non-judicial step and that 'legal process' was a well-understood concept which embraced all steps from the commencement of legal proceedings to the final judgment but not such non-judicial steps.[81]

Where the consent of the administrator or the leave of the court is required for any particular action, guidelines to be followed by the administrator in deciding whether or not to give consent and by the court in deciding whether or not to grant leave were laid down by the Court of Appeal in the English case of *Re Atlantic Computer Systems plc*.[82] The court emphasised, however, that these were guidelines only and pointed out that the circumstances in which leave was sought would vary almost infinitely because of the wide range of steps and proceedings which could be the subject of an application. It is up to the person applying for leave to make out his case.[83] The guidelines have been applied in Scotland in a case where landlords were granted leave to bring irritancy proceedings against the company in administration.[84] Leave was granted in that case on the basis that

---

[75] *Re Sabre International Products Ltd* [1991] BCLC 470.
[76] *Bristol Airport plc and Another v Powdrill and Others* [1990] BCLC 585.
[77] *Exchange Travel Agency Ltd v Triton Property Trust plc* [1991] BCLC 396. It should be noted that the definition of security applicable to England and Wales is slightly different from that applicable to Scotland (discussed above) but, for practical purposes, it is thought that English cases can none the less be referred to as a guide to interpretation of the relevant provision.
[78] *Air Ecosse Ltd v Civil Aviation Authority* 1987 SLT 751.
[79] *Re Barrow Borough Transport Ltd* [1990] Ch 227.
[80] *Scottish Exhibition Centre Ltd v Mirestop Ltd (No 2)* 1996 SLT 8.
[81] *Re Olympia & York Canary Wharf Ltd; American Express Europe Ltd v Adamson* (1993) BCC 154. Cf *Exchange Travel Agency Ltd v Triton Property Trust plc* (note 77 above), where it was held that the exercise of a landlord's right of re-entry also amounted to 'other legal process'.
[82] [1992] Ch 505. Considerations of space prevent a recitation of the guidelines, which are extensive, but they should be read carefully where any application for the administrator's consent or the leave of the court is to be made.
[83] *Re Atlantic Computer Systems plc*, note 82 above.
[84] See *Scottish Exhibition Centre Ltd v Mirestop Ltd* 1993 SLT 1034.

the landlords had a seriously arguable case, that administration was meant to be an interim and temporary measure and the administrators had been in position for over 18 months and had not been able to dispose of the business and that allowing any further period to elapse before leave to bring proceedings was granted would achieve nothing.

As noted above, the statutory moratorium does not prevent the enforcement of market charges as defined by s 173(1) of the Companies Act 1989.[85]

Registration of court order

There is no provision in administration equivalent to that in sequestration where the clerk of court is charged with sending a copy or certified copy, as appropriate, of the relevant order to specified parties.

Where an administration order is made, the court is required to notify the administrator of the making of the order forthwith,[86] but further notifications are the responsibility of the administrator.[87] Where the petition is dismissed, notification of this is the responsibility of the petitioner or otherwise as the court may direct.[88]

Appeals

In the case of an administration petition in the sheriff court, the Sheriff Court Rules prescribe the procedure for an appeal to the Sheriff Principal or the Court of Session in company insolvency cases generally 'where such an appeal is competent'[89] but do not specify the circumstances in which an appeal may be made. In the absence of any specific provisions in the 1986 Act or the Scottish Rules or the Sheriff Court Rules themselves, the normal rules regarding appeals in the sheriff court will apply. In the case of an administration petition in the Court of Session, the Court of Session Rules do not contain any special procedural rules relating to appeals in insolvency proceedings, nor any rules as to when appeals in such cases are competent. Again, therefore, in the absence of any specific provisions in the 1986 Act or the Scottish Rules, the normal rules regarding appeals in the Court of Session will apply.

---

[85] Companies Act 1989, s 175(1)(a).
[86] 1986 Scottish Rules, rule 2.3(1).
[87] 1986 Scottish Rules, rule 2.3(2) and (3). See further Chapter 11.
[88] 1986 Scottish Rules, rule 2.3(4) and (5).
[89] Sheriff Court Rules, Part VI.

11 : PROCEDURE FOLLOWING THE MAKING OF AN ADMINISTRATION ORDER

This chapter deals with the procedure following the making of an administration order.

Notification of order

Immediately on the making of an administration order, the administrator must send a copy of it to the company[1] and advertise it.[2] Within 14 days of the making of the order, he must send a notice, together with a certified copy of the order, to the Registrar of Companies, and a copy of the order to other prescribed persons.[3] Within 28 days of the administration order, unless the court otherwise directs, he must send notice of the order to all creditors of the company whose addresses are known to him.[4]

Obtaining statement of affairs

Immediately on the making of an administration order, the administrator must require the production of a statement of affairs from some or all of the persons obliged to provide such a statement.[5] Statements of affairs are discussed in Chapter 29.

Taking possession of the company's property and management of the company's affairs

The administrator is required, on his appointment, to take into his custody or under his control all the property to which the company is or appears to be

---

[1] 1986 Act, s 21(1)(a).
[2] Ibid, and Scottish Rules, rule 2.3(2).
[3] 1986 Act, s 21(2), and Scottish Rules, rule 2.3(3). The prescribed persons are: any person who has appointed, or may be entitled to appoint, an administrative receiver; any administrative receiver; any petitioner in a pending liquidation petition; any provisional liquidator of the company; and the Keeper of the Register of Inhibitions and Adjudications.
[4] 1986 Act, s 21(1)(b).
[5] 1986 Act, s 22(1).

entitled.[6] Thereafter, he will manage the affairs, business and property of the company in accordance with any directions of the court until his proposals for achieving the purpose or purposes specified in the administration order are approved.[7] The powers of the administrator in this connection are discussed further in Chapter 26.

Statement of proposals

The administrator is required to prepare a statement of his proposals for achieving the purpose or purposes specified in the administration order. He must, within three months of the making of the administration order or such longer period as the court may allow, send a copy of his statement of proposals to the Registrar of Companies and all creditors of the company, and lay a copy of it before a meeting of the company's creditors called for the purpose of considering it.[8] The copy sent to the Registrar of Companies and laid before the creditors' meeting must have a statement annexed to it containing details of the administration order and the history of the application for the order; the names of the directors and secretary of the company; a copy or summary of any statement of affairs and the administrator's comments thereon or, if there is no statement of affairs, details of the financial position of the company; details of the administrator's management of the company in the interim; his proposals for its management after approval of his proposals; and any other information he considers relevant.[9] The administrator must also either send a copy of his statement of proposals to all members of the company or publish details of where members can obtain a copy of it.[10]

The creditors' meeting

The creditors' meeting decides whether to approve the administrator's proposals.[11] A simple majority is required for approval. A creditor's entitlement to vote is determined in accordance with the Scottish Rules.[12] The amount of a creditor's debt for the purposes of voting is calculated in accordance with the rules applicable to the calculation of the amount of a creditor's claim in a sequestration, as modified in their application to administration,[13] and is calculated as at the date of the administration order, under deduction of any sums paid subsequent to that date.[14]

---

[6] 1986 Act, s 17(1).
[7] 1986 Act, s 17(2)(a). The administrator's proposals are discussed below.
[8] 1986 Act, s 23(1).
[9] Scottish Rules, rule 2.7.
[10] 1986 Act, s 23(2).
[11] 1986 Act, s 24(1).
[12] See Scottish Rules, rule 7.9, which applies to creditors' meetings in any insolvency proceedings and cross-applies the provisions of Chapter 5 of Part 4 of the Scottish Rules, which deals with claims in a liquidation, subject to specified modifications in respect of terminology and other necessary modifications.
[13] Scottish Rules, rule 4.16, as applied to administration by virtue of rules 2.9 and 7.9 of the Scottish Rules and as further modified by rules 2.11 and 2.12. For the rules applicable to the calculation of the amount of a creditor's claim in sequestration, see Chapter 32. It should be noted that the amount of the creditor's debt for this purpose is not necessarily the amount to which he will be entitled in terms of any distribution which takes place within the administration proceedings: see further Chapters 32 and 33.
[14] Scottish Rules, rule 4.15(5), as modified by rule 7.9(4)(c) and applied to administration by rule 2.9.

The meeting may approve the proposals with or without modifications, but where modifications are proposed, the administrator must consent to them.[15] The meeting may, of course, reject the proposals out of hand, or it may prove to be impossible to obtain agreement on proposed modifications.

Procedure following meeting

The administrator must report the outcome of the meeting to the court.[16] If the proposals, with or without modifications, have not been approved, the court has a wide discretion as to how it proceeds, including discharging the administration order.[17] If the proposals are approved, with or without modifications, the administrator will continue to manage the affairs, business and property of the company in accordance with the proposals.[18]

Challenge of proposals

Any creditor or member of the company may challenge the implementation of the proposals under s 27 of the 1986 Act within 28 days of the approval of the proposals.[19] The section allows any creditor or member to apply to the court on the ground that *either* the company's affairs, business and property are being or have been managed by the administrator in a way which is unfairly prejudicial to the interests of the creditors or members generally, or to some part of its creditors or members including at least himself/herself, *or* any actual or proposed act or omission of the administrator is or would be so prejudicial. A creditor or member could therefore challenge the approved proposals on the grounds that they would be unfairly prejudicial to his interests. This section is discussed further in Chapter 26.

Revision of proposals

Where the administrator proposes to make 'substantial' revisions to the proposals, he must put his proposed revisions to a meeting of creditors for approval.[20] It would seem to be implicit from the statutory language that the administrator may make revisions which are not substantial without utilising this or any other procedure. The term 'substantial' is not defined in the legislation, and whether any proposed revisions fall within that term will be a question of fact in each case, depending on the original terms of the proposals. The meeting may approve the proposed revisions with or without modifications, but the administrator must consent to any proposed modifications.[21] The result of the meeting must be notified to the Registrar of Companies and other prescribed persons.[22]

---

[15] 1986 Act, s 24(2).

[16] 1986 Act, s 24(4). The subsection also requires him to notify the Registrar of Companies and other prescribed persons of the result of the meeting, but no further persons are in fact prescribed by the Scottish Rules.

[17] 1986 Act, s 24(5).

[18] 1986 Act, s 17(2)(b). The powers of the administrator are discussed in Chapter 26.

[19] 1986 Act, s 27(3). Outwith that period the court may not make any order which would prevent or prejudice the implementation of the proposals.

[20] 1986 Act, s 25(1), (2). He must also send a copy of his proposed revisions to the members of the company or publish details of how they may obtain a copy of them: 1986 Act, s 25(3).

[21] 1986 Act, s 25(4).

[22] 1986 Act, s 25(6). No other persons are currently prescribed.

Where the proposed revisions are approved, the administrator will continue to manage the affairs, business and property of the company in accordance with the revised proposals.[23] Where the proposed revisions are not approved and the administrator takes the view that, without them, the administration could not achieve its purpose, he must apply for discharge of the administration order;[24] otherwise, he will continue to manage the company in accordance with the original proposals.

---

[23] 1986 Act, s 17(2)(b), and see Chapter 26 in relation to the powers of the administrator in this respect.
[24] 1986 Act, s 18(2).

12 : PROCEDURE LEADING TO RECEIVERSHIP

Receivership is different from the other formal insolvency régimes because it is instituted by the holder of a particular type of security (the floating charge) for the purpose of enforcing that security.[1] The receiver is, however, obliged to deal with the claims of certain specified creditors other than the floating chargeholder, and receivership is therefore treated as a formal insolvency proceeding.

The Cork Committee believed that the power to appoint a receiver had been of outstanding benefit to the public and society as a whole, receivers being able in some cases to return a business to profit and to its original owners and in others to dispose of the whole or part of a business as a going concern, thus preserving viable businesses to the benefit of the community.[2] Receivership may be used in appropriate circumstances as a means of turning round companies which are in financial difficulty, so that the security holder is repaid by a restored company able to meet its debt in the way originally envisaged rather than through the realisation of its assets and the application of the proceeds to discharge the debt. In practice, however, the more likely result of receivership is that a company's assets will be sold off to meet the chargeholder's debt and the company will then go into liquidation. The business of the company will often be sold as a going concern, however, and thereby be preserved in a new incarnation. Receiverships are dealt with in Part III of the 1986 Act: Chapter I applies to England and Wales, Chapter II to Scotland and Chapter III to both jurisdictions.

This chapter deals with the procedure for initiating receivership.

Initiating receivership

Receivership is initiated by the appointment of a receiver under a floating charge. The appointment may be made directly by the holder of the floating charge or

---

[1] See Chapter 24.
[2] See Cmnd 8558, ch 9. Indeed, they thought that many companies had been forced into liquidation and potentially viable businesses closed down for want of a floating charge under which a receiver could have been appointed, and the administration procedure was devised so that a similar régime would be available to a company whether or not there was a floating charge.

by the court on his application. This section deals with various aspects of the appointment of a receiver.

Which debtors may be put into receivership?

Receivership is created by the appointment of a receiver under a floating charge. Floating charges may only be created by certain defined companies. It is competent in Scots law for an incorporated company, whether a company within the meaning of CA 1985 or not, to create a charge, known as a floating charge, over all or part of its property and undertaking, in favour of the creditor in any debt or obligation of the company or any other person, as security therefor.[3] The ability to *create* a floating charge under the law of Scotland is not, therefore, confined to companies registered in Scotland, but extends to any company which is an incorporated company. However, a receiver may only be appointed under a floating charge which is created by any such company which the Court of Session has jurisdiction to wind up.[4]

Appointment of receiver by chargeholder

A receiver may be appointed by the holder of a floating charge created by an incorporated company (whether a company within the meaning of CA 1985 or not) which the Court of Session has jurisdiction to wind up.[5]

Such an appointment may be made in the circumstances provided for in the floating charge itself or, unless the floating charge itself provides otherwise, in the following circumstances:[6]

(1) Where a period of 21 days expires after the making of a demand for payment of the whole or any part of the principal sum secured by the charge without payment.[7]

(2) Where a period of two months expires during the whole of which interest due under the charge has been in arrears.[8]

(3) Where a resolution to wind up the company has been passed or a winding-up order has been made.[9]

(4) Where a receiver has been appointed under any other floating charge created by the company.[10]

The appointment must be made by a validly executed instrument of appointment.[11] The instrument of appointment must be endorsed by the appointee or on his behalf, with a written docquet confirming the date and time that it was received by him or on his behalf.[12] For the appointment to be effective, it must

---

[3] CA 1985, s 462(1).

[4] 1986 Act, s 51. For the jurisdiction of the Court of Session to wind up companies, see Chapter 16 (registered companies) and Chapter 17 (unregistered companies).

[5] 1986 Act, s 51(1).

[6] 1986 Act, s 52(1).

[7] 1986 Act, s 52(1)(a).

[8] 1986 Act, s 52(1)(b).

[9] 1986 Act, s 52(1)(c).

[10] 1986 Act, s 52(1)(d).

[11] 1986 Act, s 53(1). The instrument may be executed on behalf of the floating chargeholder in accordance with the provisions of s 53(4) of the 1986 Act.

[12] 1986 Act, s 53(6)(b), and Scottish Rules, rule 3.1(2).

be accepted by the appointee before the end of the next business day following that on which the instrument was received by him or on his behalf.[13] The acceptance need not be in writing, but it must be communicated to the floating chargeholder or his agent before the end of the next business day following that on which the instrument was received by the appointee or on his behalf, and a docquet to that effect must be endorsed on the instrument of appointment as soon as possible after acceptance.[14] In the case of the appointment of joint receivers, such an appointment is only effective if all the joint receivers accept appointment in the way described.[15] The receiver or, if there is a joint appointment with more than one receiver endorsing the same instrument of appointment, the last receiver so to endorse it, must then deliver a copy of the endorsed instrument of appointment to the floating chargeholder or his agent as soon as possible.[16]

Appointment of a receiver by the court

A receiver may be appointed by the court on the application of the holder of a floating charge created by an incorporated company (whether a company within the meaning of CA 1985 or not) which the Court of Session has jurisdiction to wind up.[17] Part III of the 1986 Act refers simply to 'the court' without defining that term. Reference must therefore be made to s 251 of the 1986 Act. This leads to s 744 of CA 1985 which provides that the court, in relation to a company, is the court having jurisdiction to wind up the company.[18]

The appointment of a receiver by the court may be made in any circumstances in which the floating charge itself provides that the holder may appoint a receiver or, unless the floating charge itself provides otherwise, in the following circumstances.[19]

(1) Where the court is satisfied that the position of the chargeholder is likely to be prejudiced if no such appointment is made.[20]

(2) Where a period of 21 days expires after the making of a demand for payment of the whole or any part of the principal sum secured by the charge without payment.[21]

(3) Where a period of two months expires during the whole of which interest due under the charge has been in arrears.[22]

(4) Where a resolution to wind up the company has been passed or a winding-up order has been made.[23]

The application is made by petition to the court.[24] The petition must contain averments relating to any floating charge created by the company and the property

---

[13] 1986 Act, s 53(6)(a). For the definition of the term 'business day' see 1986 Act, s 251.
[14] Scottish Rules, rule 3.1.
[15] Receivers (Scotland) Regulations 1986 (SI 1986/1917), reg 5(a).
[16] Scottish Rules, rule 3.1(3) and (4).
[17] 1986 Act, s 51(2).
[18] See further Chapter 16 (registered companies) and Chapter 17 (unregistered companies).
[19] 1986 Act, s 52(2).
[20] 1986 Act, s 52(2)(a).
[21] 1986 Act, s 52(2)(b), applying paragraph (a) of 1986 Act, s 52(1).
[22] 1986 Act, s 52(2)(b), applying paragraph (b) of 1986 Act, s 52(1).
[23] 1986 Act, s 52(2)(b), applying paragraph (c) of 1986 Act, s 52(1).
[24] 1986 Act, s 54(1).

over which it is secured; whether to the petitioner's knowledge there is any petition for an administration order pending and, if so, details of it; the name and address of the proposed receiver and his qualification to act as receiver and any other matters which the petitioner thinks will assist the court in deciding to appoint a receiver.[25] Where the petition is in the sheriff court, it is specifically provided that any documents instructing the facts relied on or which are founded on in the petition must be produced with the petition.[26] Following presentation of the petition, the court will pronounce an order for intimation, service and advertisement. The petition must be served on the company[27] and, unless the court otherwise directs, on any person who has petitioned for an administration order and any respondent to that petition[28] and advertised once in the Edinburgh Gazette and once in one or more such newspapers as the court directs.[29] The period of notice within which answers must be lodged if so advised is eight days, subject to the court's power to lengthen or shorten that period.[30] There are no special rules relating to procedure for the hearing of a petition to appoint a receiver and so the normal petition procedure will apply. Although s 54(7) of the 1986 Act requires the Court of Session to have regard to the need to make special provision for dealing with urgent cases when making rules of court for the purposes of regulating matters relating to petitions for the appointment of a receiver, neither the Sheriff Court Rules nor the Court of Session Rules contain any special provisions for urgent cases. The court's decision as to whether to appoint a receiver is discretionary.[31]

Date of appointment

In the case of a receiver appointed by the chargeholder, the appointment is deemed to be made on the day and at the time that the instrument of appointment was received by him or on his behalf as evidenced by the written docquet to that effect endorsed on the instrument.[32] Where joint receivers have been appointed by the chargeholder, the appointment is deemed to be made on the day and at the time that the instrument of appointment was received by the last of them to receive it, as evidenced by the written docquet to that effect endorsed on the instrument.[33]

In the case of a receiver appointed by the court, the receiver is to be regarded as being appointed on the date of his appointment by the court.[34]

Effect of receivership

On the appointment of a receiver, the floating charge by virtue of which he was appointed crystallises and attaches to the property then subject to the charge.[35]

---

[25] Sheriff Court Rules, rule 15(1); Court of Session Rules, rule 74.17.
[26] Sheriff Court Rules, rule 15(1). Documents founded on or adopted in a Court of Session petition must also be produced with it by virtue of rule 27.1 of the Court of Session Rules.
[27] 1986 Act, s 54(2); Sheriff Court Rules, rule 16(2)(a); Court of Session Rules, rule 74.18(1)(a)(i).
[28] Sheriff Court Rules, rule 16(2)(b); Court of Session Rules, rule 74.18(1)(a)(ii).
[29] Sheriff Court Rules, rule 16(6); Court of Session Rules, rule 74.18(1)(b).
[30] Sheriff Court Rules, rule 16(8); Court of Session Rules, rule 74.18(2).
[31] 1986 Act, s 54(2), which provides that the court shall appoint a receiver 'if it thinks fit'.
[32] 1986 Act, s 53(6)(b). In relation to the docquet, see above.
[33] Ibid, as modified by reg 5(b) of the Receivers (Scotland) Regulations 1986, note 15 above.
[34] 1986 Act, s 54(5).
[35] 1986 Act, s 53(7) (receiver appointed by chargeholder) and s 54(6) (receiver appointed by the court), and see further Chapter 21.

Registration of appointment of receiver

Where a receiver is appointed by the chargeholder, a certified copy of the instrument of appointment, together with a notice in prescribed form, must be delivered by or on behalf of the chargeholder to the Registrar of Companies for registration within seven days of its execution.[36] Where a receiver is appointed by the court, a certified copy of the interlocutor making the appointment, together with a notice in the prescribed form, must be delivered by or on behalf of the petitioner to the Registrar of Companies for registration within seven days of its date or such longer period as the court may allow.[37]

In either case, on receipt of the relevant documents, the Registrar enters the particulars of the appointment in the Register of Charges.[38] Any person who fails to comply with the requirement to deliver the prescribed documents to the Registrar of Companies without reasonable excuse is liable to a fine and to a daily default fine for continued contravention.[39]

Challenge of appointment

The appointment of a receiver by a chargeholder might be challenged in appropriate circumstances by anyone with an interest to do so, such as the company itself[40] or another creditor. For example, it might be alleged that grounds on which the appointment was based were not in fact established or that the charge was invalid.

In the case of a receiver appointed by the court, the normal rules in relation to appeals will apply.[41]

---

[36] 1986 Act, s 53(1). For the mode of certification of the copy of the instrument of appointment and the form of the prescribed notice, see reg 4 of the Receivers (Scotland) Regulations 1986 (note 15 above) and the Schedule thereto respectively.

[37] 1986 Act, s 54(3). For the form of the prescribed notice, see the Schedule to the Receivers (Scotland) Regulations 1986, note 15 above.

[38] 1986 Act, s 53(5) (appointment by chargeholder) and s 54(4) (appointment by the court).

[39] 1986 Act, s 53(2) (appointment by chargeholder) and s 54(3) (appointment by the court).

[40] Although the powers of the directors to deal with the company's property attached by the charge are effectively suspended on the appointment of a receiver, they retain certain residual powers which would enable them to do this: see further Chapter 23.

[41] In the case of a sheriff court petition, the procedure for appeals is prescribed by rule 36 of the Sheriff Court Rules.

13 : PROCEDURE FOLLOWING THE APPOINTMENT OF A RECEIVER

This chapter deals with the procedure following the appointment of a receiver.

Notification of appointment

Immediately on his appointment, the receiver must send notice of his appointment to the company and advertise it.[1] He must also, unless the court directs otherwise, send notice of his appointment to all the creditors of whose addresses he is aware within 28 days of his appointment.[2]

Obtaining a statement of affairs

Immediately on his appointment, the receiver must require the production of a statement of affairs from some or all of the persons obliged to provide such a statement.[3] Statements of affairs are discussed in Chapter 29.

Taking possession of property attached by the floating charge

The receiver has power to take possession of, collect and get in the property attached by the floating charge from the company, the company's liquidator or any other person[4] and he will do so as soon as possible after his appointment. Thereafter, he will take the necessary steps to procure payment of the floating chargeholder's debt. Usually, this will be realisation of the assets attached by the floating charge, which may include sale of the company's business as a going concern in appropriate cases, and payment of the proceeds to the floating chargeholder after payment of the claims specified by the 1986 Act.[5] It may, however, take the form of trading with a view to turning the business around so that it is returned to prosperity, allowing payment of the floating chargeholder's

---

[1] 1986 Act, s 65(1)(a). The notice is Form 4 (Scot) in the Schedule to the Receivers (Scotland) Regulations 1986: see 1986 Act, s 71 and reg 3 of said regulations.
[2] 1986 Act, s 65(1)(b).
[3] 1986 Act, s 66(1).
[4] 1986 Act, s 55 and Sched 2. The charge will usually confer this power also.
[5] See further Chapter 27.

debt from future profit. The receiver's functions and powers are discussed further in Chapter 27.

Report by the receiver

The receiver must, within three months of his appointment or such longer period as the court may allow, prepare and send to specified persons a report containing details of the events leading to his appointment (so far as he is aware of them); the disposal or proposed disposal of any of the company's property and the carrying on or proposed carrying on of the company's business; the sums due to the floating chargeholder and preferential creditors; a summary of the statement of affairs and the receiver's comments on it; and the amount, if any, likely to be available for payment of other creditors.[6] The report must be sent to the Registrar of Companies, the holder of the floating charge by virtue of which he was appointed, any trustees for secured creditors of the company and all secured creditors of the company of whose addresses he is aware.[7]

The receiver must also, within the same time-limit, *either* send a copy of the report to all unsecured creditors of the company of whose addresses he is aware *or* publish details of where they should apply to obtain a copy.[8] In addition, unless the court directs otherwise, he must lay a copy of the report before a meeting of the unsecured creditors called to receive it.[9] If he intends to apply to the court for a direction that he can dispense with the meeting, he must say so in the report and ensure that the copy report is sent to the unsecured creditors or the appropriate notice published at least 14 days before the application is heard.[10]

Where the company has gone or goes into liquidation, the receiver must also send a copy of the report to the liquidator.[11] Where this is done before the receiver has complied with the requirements relating to the company's unsecured creditors described in the preceding paragraph, he is relieved of the obligation of complying with these requirements.[12]

The receivership may, of course, continue for some time after the submission of the report. There is no provision for any further reports in the legislation itself, although the receiver will in practice report regularly to the floating chargeholder.

---

[6] 1986 Act, s 67(1), (5). The report, however, is not required to disclose anything which would seriously prejudice the carrying out of the receiver's functions: 1986 Act, s 67(6).

[7] Ibid.

[8] 1986 Act, s 67(2).

[9] Ibid. The meeting must be called on at least 14 days' notice.

[10] 1986 Act, s 67(3).

[11] 1986 Act, s 67(4). The receiver must send the report to the liquidator within seven days of submitting it to the Registrar of Companies, chargeholder, secured creditors and trustees for secured creditors or within seven days of the liquidator's appointment if later.

[12] Ibid.

14 : PROCEDURE LEADING TO A VOLUNTARY WINDING UP

A voluntary winding up (or liquidation: the terms may be used interchangeably) is initiated by the members of the company. The court plays no part in the decision to wind up the company and the whole liquidation may be conducted without any court involvement, although the court may be called upon in particular circumstances if required. There are two types of voluntary liquidation: members' voluntary liquidation and creditors' voluntary liquidation. If the directors have made a declaration of solvency under s 89 of the 1986 Act, the liquidation is a members' voluntary liquidation; if they have not done so, the liquidation is a creditors' voluntary liquidation.[1] In the latter case, the company will usually, although not invariably, be insolvent. There is provision for converting a members' voluntary liquidation into a creditors' voluntary liquidation if the company in fact proves to be insolvent as the liquidation proceeds.[2]

Voluntary liquidations are dealt with mainly in Part IV of the 1986 Act, which deals with the winding up of companies registered under the Companies Acts generally. Chapters II, III, IV and V of Part IV of the 1986 Act relate specifically to voluntary liquidations: Chapter III relates to members' voluntary liquidation only, Chapter IV to creditors' voluntary liquidation only and Chapters II and V to both. The remainder of the chapters in Part IV of the 1986 Act, with the exception of Chapter VI which relates specifically to winding up by the court, relate to the winding up of registered companies generally and so apply equally to voluntary liquidations.[3]

This chapter deals with the procedure leading up to the commencement of a voluntary winding up.

Initiating a voluntary winding up

A voluntary winding up is initiated by a resolution of the members. This section deals with the various aspects of initiating a voluntary liquidation.

---

[1] 1986 Act, s 90.
[2] 1986 Act, s 96. For the relevant procedure, see Chapter 15.
[3] It should be noted that although Chapter VI of Part IV of the 1986 Act relates to compulsory liquidations, some of its provisions may also be utilised in a voluntary liquidation by virtue of s 112 of the 1986 Act, which provides for applications to the court, *inter alia*, to exercise all or any of the powers which it might exercise in a compulsory liquidation.

Which companies may be wound up voluntarily?

Companies formed and registered under CA 1985 or under any former Companies Acts, as defined by s 735(1) of CA 1985, may be wound up voluntarily,[4] with the exception of such companies which are insurance companies to which Part II of the Insurance Companies Act 1982 applies and which carry on long-term business as defined by that Act.[5] Section 221(4) of the 1986 Act specifically states that no unregistered company may be wound up voluntarily, but such a company may register under CA 1985 and then be wound up voluntarily. A registered society under the Industrial and Provident Societies Acts may be also wound up voluntarily under Part IV of the 1986 Act,[6] as may a European Economic Interest Grouping (hereafter 'an EEIG').[7] A building society incorporated or deemed to be incorporated under the Building Societies Act 1986 may be wound up voluntarily under Part IV of the 1986 Act, as modified by the Building Societies Act 1986,[8] and an incorporated friendly society may also be wound up voluntarily under Part IV of the 1986 Act, as modified by the Friendly Societies Act 1992.[9]

The resolution to wind up voluntarily

The resolution of the members to wind up a company[10] voluntarily may be:

(1) An ordinary resolution, where any fixed period for the duration of the company has come to an end or an event whereby it is provided the company will be dissolved has happened.[11]

(2) An extraordinary resolution, where the company decides that it can no longer continue because of its liabilities and it is advisable to wind up.[12]

(3) A special resolution, in any other case, no particular reason being required.[13]

In the case of a building society and an incorporated friendly society, however, any resolution to wind up must be a special resolution.[14]

---

[4] 1986 Act, s 73(1).

[5] Insurance Companies Act 1982, s 55(2). Insurance companies are treated differently from other companies on insolvency generally: it has already been noted, for example, that an administration order may not be made in relation to an insurance company: see Chapter 10.

[6] Industrial and Provident Societies Act 1965, s 55(a).

[7] Council Regulation (EEC) No 2137/85, art 31, as implemented by the European Economic Interest Grouping Regulations 1989 (SI 1989/638).

[8] Building Societies Act 1986, s 86(1)(b). The relevant modifications are contained in Sched 15 to that Act. This chapter describes the normal procedures under Part IV of the 1986 Act unless otherwise stated and reference should be made to the Schedule for the relevant modifications.

[9] Friendly Societies Act 1992, s 19(1)(b). The relevant modifications are contained in Sched 10 to that Act. This chapter describes the normal procedures under Part IV of the 1986 Act unless otherwise stated and reference should be made to the Schedule for the relevant modifications.

[10] Including a registered society under the Industrial and Provident Societies Acts: Industrial and Provident Societies Act 1965, s 55(a).

[11] 1986 Act, s 84(1)(a).

[12] 1986 Act, s 84(1)(c).

[13] 1986 Act, s 84(1)(b).

[14] Building Societies Act 1986, s 88(1) and Sched 15, and Friendly Societies Act 1992, s 21(1) and Sched 10.

Procedure leading to resolution for voluntary winding up

A meeting of the company's members to consider the proposed resolution to wind up voluntarily will be called by the directors in the normal way. The normal rules concerning matters such as notice must be followed. Where the company is an authorised institution or former authorised institution within the meaning of the Banking Act 1987, the directors must give notice of the meeting to the Bank of England and the Deposit Protection Board.[15] If the winding up is to proceed as a creditors' voluntary winding up, a meeting of creditors will also require to be called,[16] but the creditors have no say in the decision to wind up voluntarily: that is a matter solely for the members.

Members' or creditors' voluntary winding up?

If the liquidation is to proceed as a members' voluntary liquidation, the directors must have made a declaration of solvency under s 89 of the 1986 Act within the five weeks preceding the date of the resolution or on that date but before the passing of the resolution.[17] Such a declaration may be made at a directors' meeting and the decision to make it may be made by the majority of the directors.[18] The declaration must state that the directors have made a full investigation of the company's affairs and that, having done so, they are of the opinion that the company will be able to pay its debts in full, together with interest at the official rate, within the period specified in the declaration (which must not exceed 12 months).[19] It must also contain a statement of the company's assets and liabilities as at the latest practicable date before the date of the declaration.[20] The declaration must be delivered to the Registrar of Companies within 15 days of the passing of the resolution to wind up the company:[21] failure to do so renders the company and every officer in default liable to a default fine and daily default fine[22] but does not appear to affect the validity of the declaration or the status of the subsequent liquidation as a members' voluntary winding up.

The directors must think carefully before making a statutory declaration under s 89. If a director who is party to the making of the declaration does not have reasonable grounds for his opinion that the company will be able to pay its debts and interest within the period stated in the declaration, he is liable to a fine or imprisonment or both.[23] It is presumed that the director had no reasonable grounds

---

[15] Scottish Rules, rule 7.4(2). It is thought that the reference to the Bank of England ought to have been amended to a reference to the Financial Services Authority following the transfer of the former's supervisory functions to the latter under the Bank of England Act 1998. Although the equivalent rules in England and Wales (the Insolvency Rules 1986) were amended by the Bank of England Act 1998 (Consequential Amendments to Subordinate Legislation) Order 1998 (SI 1998/1129) to take account of the change, the Scottish Rules have not been so amended. It is thought that this was an oversight and should be rectified.

[16] See further below.

[17] 1986 Act, s 89(2)(a).

[18] 1986 Act, s 89(1).

[19] Ibid. The subsection defines the official rate of interest by reference to s 251, which in turn refers to s 189(4). The latter subsection, as modified in its application to Scotland by s 189(5), provides that the official rate of interest is the higher of that prescribed in the Scottish Rules or applicable to the debt other than on winding up.

[20] 1986 Act, s 89(2)(b).

[21] 1986 Act, s 89(3).

[22] 1986 Act, s 89(6).

[23] 1986 Act, s 89(4).

for his opinion if it transpires that the company is not in fact able to meet its debts and interest within the specified period, although the presumption is rebuttable.[24]

Where no valid statutory declaration under s 89 is made, the liquidation will proceed as a creditors' voluntary liquidation. In such a case, a meeting of creditors must be called to take place no later than 14 days after the date on which the members' meeting is to be held.[25] Notice of the meeting must be sent to creditors by post at least seven days before the date of the creditors' meeting[26] and also advertised in the Edinburgh Gazette and two local newspapers.[27] The notice must contain *either* the name and address of a qualified insolvency practitioner who will furnish creditors free of charge with such information about the company's affairs as they reasonably request in the period before the meeting[28] *or* details of a place where the creditors may inspect, free of charge, a list of the names and addresses of the company's creditors on the two business days immediately preceding the date of the meeting.[29] Failure to comply with these requirements is an offence and renders the company liable to a fine.[30] Subject to these specific requirements, the rules in Chapter 7 of the Scottish Rules, which deal with meetings generally, also apply to the creditors' meeting.[31] This means, for example, that the date, time and place of the meeting must be fixed with the convenience of the creditors in mind[32] and the notice sent to the creditors must contain the information prescribed by Chapter 7 as well as the information specified above.

The directors must also prepare a statement of affairs of the company to be placed before the creditors' meeting and appoint one director to preside at it.[33] The statement of affairs must be verified by affidavit by some or all of the directors and give details of the company's assets, debts and liabilities; the names and addresses of the creditors and any security held by them, including the date on which any such security was given; and such other information as may be prescribed.[34] It must be made up to the later of the nearest practicable date before

---

[24] 1986 Act, s 89(5).

[25] 1986 Act, s 98(1)(a).

[26] 1986 Act, s 98(1)(b).

[27] 1986 Act, s 98(1)(c). The two newspapers must circulate within the locality in which the company had its principal place of business in Great Britain within the six months preceding the sending of the notices: 1986 Act, s 98(1)(c) and (5). Where the principal place of business in Great Britain changed within the period, advertisement in all the relevant localities is required: 1986 Act, s 98(3). Where the company did not have a place of business in Great Britain within that period at all, the newspapers must be those circulating in the locality of any registered office of the company within that period: 1986 Act, s 98(4).

[28] 1986 Act, s 98(2)(a). The exact length of the period before the meeting during which the creditors can obtain the relevant information is not specified.

[29] 1986 Act, s 98(2)(b). The place must be within the locality in which the company had its principal place of business in Great Britain within the six months preceding the sending of the notices and, as in the case of newspaper advertisements, where the principal place of business in Great Britain changed within the period, a place in all the relevant localities is required under this alternative: 1986 Act, s 98(3). Similarly, where the company did not have a place of business in Great Britain within that period at all, a place where the list may be inspected is required in the locality of any registered office of the company within that period: 1986 Act, s 98(4). 'Business day' is defined by s 251 of the 1986 Act.

[30] 1986 Act, s 98(6).

[31] Scottish Rules, rule 7.1.

[32] Scottish Rules, rule 7.2.

[33] 1986 Act, s 99(1).

[34] 1986 Act, s 99(2). Statements of affairs are discussed further in Chapter 29.

the creditors' meeting or a date not more than 14 days before the passing of the resolution by the company.[35] Where it is not made up to the date of the meeting, the director presiding at the meeting or some other person with the relevant knowledge must make an oral or written report to the meeting updating the statement in relation to any material transactions since the date of the statement.[36] Failure to make up the statement of affairs, to lay it before the creditors' meeting or to appoint a director to preside at the creditors' meeting, and failure by the director so appointed to attend the creditors' meeting and preside over it, are all offences.[37]

The role of the creditors' meeting is discussed in Chapters 19 and 33.[38]

The decision on the resolution to wind up voluntarily

The members' meeting will decide whether to pass the resolution to wind up voluntarily. The requisite majority is that appropriate to the type of resolution being proposed: in the case of an ordinary resolution, a simple majority, and in the case of a special or extraordinary resolution, a majority of not less than 75 per cent of those present and voting in person or by proxy.[39]

If the resolution to wind up the company voluntarily is not passed by the members' meeting with the requisite majority, that will be the end of the matter.

Date of commencement of a voluntary winding up

Both members' and creditors' voluntary liquidations commence on the date of the passing of the appropriate resolution.[40]

Publication of resolution

A copy of the resolution must be sent to the Registrar of Companies within 15 days of its being passed.[41] Failure to do so renders the company and every officer of it who is in default liable to a fine and a daily default fine.[42] The resolution must also be advertised in the Edinburgh Gazette within 14 days of its being passed.[43] Again, failure to do so renders the company and every officer of it who is in default liable to a fine and a daily default fine.[44]

---

[35] Scottish Rules, rule 4.7(5), as substituted in relation to voluntary liquidations by Scottish Rules, rule 4 and Sched 1, para 4.

[36] Scottish Rules, rule 4.7(6), as substituted in relation to voluntary liquidations by Scottish Rules, rule 4 and Sched 1, para 4.

[37] 1986 Act, s 99(3).

[38] Chapter 19 (appointment of liquidator); Chapter 33 (establishing creditors' committee).

[39] Companies Act 1985, s 378.

[40] 1986 Act, s 86.

[41] 1986 Act, s 84(3), applying s 380 of CA 1985. The sidenote to the subsection says 'copy of resolution to registrar', and the text of the subsection itself states that the resolution 'is subject to section 380 of the Companies Act [1985] (copy of resolution to be forwarded to registrar of companies within 15 days)'. However, s 380 of CA 1985 imposes other requirements in relation to the resolution which would also seem to apply in this case, because notwithstanding the references to copying the resolution to the Registrar of Companies, s 380 is applied in its entirety, and not only in relation to that part of the section which deals with such copying.

[42] Companies Act 1985, s 380(5), as applied by 1986 Act, s 84(3). 'Officer of the company' includes the liquidator: Companies Act 1985, s 380(7).

[43] 1986 Act, s 85(1).

[44] 1986 Act, s 85(2). Again, the subsection extends the meaning of 'officer of the company' to include the liquidator.

15 : PROCEDURE FOLLOWING A RESOLUTION
TO WIND UP

This chapter deals with the procedure following the passing of a resolution to wind up.

Appointment of a liquidator

Following the passing of a resolution to wind up, a liquidator will be appointed. The procedure is discussed in Chapter 19, which deals with the appointment and replacement of office holders generally.

Notification of appointment

The liquidator must, within 14 days of his appointment, deliver notice of it in the prescribed form to the Registrar of Companies and advertise it.[1]

Taking possession of a company's property

As soon as possible after his appointment, the liquidator must take possession of the whole assets of the company and any property, books, papers or records in the possession or control of the company or to which the company appears to be entitled.[2] The functions and powers of the liquidator are discussed more fully in Chapter 28.

Conversion of members' voluntary liquidation to creditors' voluntary liquidation

Where a voluntary winding up commences as a members' winding up but it subsequently becomes clear that the company is insolvent,[3] the winding up will be converted to a creditors' voluntary winding up. This section deals with the relevant procedure.

---

[1] 1986 Act, s 109(1). The prescribed form is Form 4.9 (Scot) in Sched 5 to the Scottish Rules.

[2] Scottish Rules, rule 4.22, applied to creditors' and members' voluntary liquidations by rules 5 and 6 respectively of the Scottish Rules.

[3] For the meaning of 'insolvent' in this context, see further below.

Circumstances in which conversion will take place

Where the liquidator in a members' voluntary liquidation forms the opinion that the company will not be able to pay its debts in full, together with interest at the official rate, within the period stated in the directors' statutory declaration of solvency under s 89 of the 1986 Act, he must invoke the procedure for converting the liquidation to a creditors' voluntary liquidation.[4]

It should be noted that although the headnote of s 95 of the 1986 Act refers to the effect of the company's insolvency, the company may not ultimately prove to be insolvent: all that is required is that the company will not be able to meet its debts and interest within the period specified in the statutory declaration. It is probably rare, however, for the company ultimately to be proved solvent.

Procedure for conversion

The liquidator must call a meeting of creditors to take place not later than 28 days after he has formed the view that the company is insolvent in the sense described above.[5] The provisions regulating the calling of the meeting are similar to those applying to a creditors' meeting called by the directors where the winding up commenced as a creditors' winding up. The liquidator must send notice of the meeting to the creditors by post at least seven days before the date of the meeting[6] and advertise it in the Edinburgh Gazette and two local newspapers.[7] Where the company is an authorised institution or a former authorised institution within the meaning of the Banking Act 1987, the liquidator must also give notice of the meeting to the Bank of England and the Deposit Protection Board.[8] The liquidator must supply the creditors free of charge with such information as they may reasonably require in the period prior to the meeting[9] and the notice of the meeting must contain a statement to that effect.[10] Subject to these specific require-ments, the rules in Chapter 7 of the Scottish Rules, which deal with meetings

---

[4] 1986 Act, s 95(1), (2). The statutory declaration of solvency is discussed in the preceding chapter. Conversion to a creditors' voluntary liquidation is compulsory: s 95(2) of the 1986 Act states that the liquidator 'shall' do the various things specified in the section, and failure to comply renders the liquidator liable to a fine: 1986 Act, s 95(8).

[5] 1986 Act, s 95(2)(a).

[6] 1986 Act, s 95(2)(b).

[7] 1986 Act, s 95(2)(c). The requirements in relation to newspaper advertisements apropos the calling of a creditors' meeting by the directors in a winding up which commenced as a creditors' winding up apply *mutatis mutandis*. Thus, the newspapers must circulate within the locality in which the company had its principal place of business in Great Britain within the six months preceding the sending of the notices: 1986 Act, s 95(2)(c) and (5). Where the principal place of business in Great Britain changed within the period, advertisement in all the relevant localities is required: 1986 Act, s 95(5). Where the company did not have a place of business within Great Britain within that period at all, the newspapers must be those circulating in the locality of any registered office of the company within that period: 1986 Act, s 95(6).

[8] Scottish Rules, rule 7.4(3). It is thought that the reference to the Bank of England ought to have been amended to a reference to the Financial Services Authority following the transfer of the former's supervisory functions to the latter under the Bank of England Act 1998. Although the equivalent rules in England and Wales (the Insolvency Rules 1986) were amended by the Bank of England Act 1998 (Consequential Amendments to Subordinate Legislation) Order 1998 (SI 1998/1129) to take account of the change, the Scottish Rules have not been so amended. It is thought that this was an oversight and should be rectified.

[9] 1986 Act, s 95(2)(d).

[10] 1986 Act, s 95(2). Failure to comply with that duty without reasonable excuse, as with failure to comply with any other requirement of the section, would render the liquidator liable to a fine: 1986 Act, s 95(8).

generally, also apply to this meeting.[11] This means, for example, that the date, time and place of the meeting must be fixed with the convenience of the creditors in mind[12] and the notice sent to the creditors must contain the information prescribed by Chapter 7 as well as the information specified above.

The liquidator must prepare a statement of affairs to be laid before the meeting and attend and preside at it.[13] As with the statement of affairs to be prepared by the directors where the winding up commenced as a creditors' voluntary winding up, the statement of affairs must be verified by affidavit by the liquidator and give details of the company's assets, debts and liabilities; the names and addresses of the creditors and any security held by them, including the date on which any such security was given; and such other information as may be prescribed.[14] It must be inserted in the sederunt book for the liquidation.[15] The date to which it must be made up, however, is not prescribed.[16] Failure to prepare the statement of affairs, to place it before the meeting or to attend and preside over the meeting without reasonable excuse renders the liquidator liable to a fine.[17]

Date of conversion

The conversion is effective from the date on which the creditors' meeting called by the liquidator is held.[18]

Effect of conversion

As from the date of conversion, the 1986 Act will have effect as if the declaration of solvency under s 89 of the 1986 Act had not been made and as if the members' and creditors' meetings were those which would have taken place had the liquidation commenced as a creditors' voluntary liquidation.[19] The liquidation then continues in all respects as a creditors' voluntary liquidation.

---

[11] Scottish Rules, rule 7.1.
[12] Scottish Rules, rule 7.2.
[13] 1986 Act, s 95(3).
[14] Statements of affairs are dealt with in Chapter 29.
[15] Scottish Rules, rule 4.7(4), as substituted in relation to voluntary liquidations by Scottish Rules, Sched 1, para 4.
[16] The provisions of the Scottish Rules discussed in relation to the statement of affairs by directors apply only to such statements of affairs, unlike the other provisions of rule 4.7(4), as substituted in relation to voluntary liquidations by Scottish Rules, Sched 1, para 4, referred to above.
[17] 1986 Act, s 95(8).
[18] 1986 Act, s 96.
[19] Ibid.

16 : PROCEDURE LEADING TO A WINDING-UP ORDER: REGISTERED COMPANIES

Winding up by the court (or compulsory winding up or liquidation: the terms may be used interchangeably) may be initiated by the company itself but is usually forced on the company from outside.

Compulsory liquidation is mainly dealt with in Parts IV and V of the 1986 Act. As already noted,[1] Part IV of the 1986 Act deals with the winding up of registered companies generally. Chapters II, III, IV and V of Part IV apply specifically to voluntary liquidations. Chapter VI applies specifically to compulsory liquidations and the remainder of the chapters apply to both types of liquidation. Part V of the 1986 Act deals with the winding up of unregistered companies. This chapter deals with the procedure leading to the making of a winding-up order in relation to companies registered in Scotland and the following chapter deals with the procedure leading to the making of a winding-up order in relation to unregistered companies.

Applying for a winding-up order

A winding-up order is obtained as a result of a petition to the relevant court. This section deals with various aspects of applying for a winding-up order.

Which companies are liable to be wound up by the court under Part IV of the 1986 Act?
A company formed and registered under CA 1985 or under any former Companies Acts, as defined by s 735(1) of that Act, may be wound up by the court under Chapter VI of Part IV of the 1986 Act.[2] In addition, any company registered in Scotland, even though not formed under the relevant legislation, may be wound up by the court.[3]

A company registered under the Industrial and Provident Societies Acts may also be wound up by the court under Part IV of the 1986 Act.[4] A building society incorporated or deemed to be incorporated under the Building Societies Act 1986 may be wound up under Part IV of the 1986 Act, as modified by the

---

[1] See Chapter 14.
[2] 1986 Act, s 73(1), and CA 1985, s 735.
[3] See the 1986 Act, s 120(1).
[4] Industrial and Provident Societies Act 1965, s 55(a).

Building Societies Act 1986,[5] and an incorporated friendly society may also be wound up under Part IV of the 1986 Act, as modified by the Friendly Societies Act 1992.[6]

Who may apply?

A petition for a winding-up order in Scotland may be presented by:

(1) The company itself.[7]

(2) The directors.[8]

(3) Any creditor or creditors.[9]

(4) A contributory or contributories.[10]

(5) Any combination of the parties listed above.[11]

(6) A receiver.[12]

(7) An administrator.[13]

(8) The supervisor of a company voluntary arrangement (CVA).[14]

(9) In the case of a company which is an authorised institution or former authorised institution under the Banking Act 1987 only, the Financial Services Authority.[15]

(10) In the case of a company which is an insurance company within the meaning of Part II of the Insurance Companies Act 1982, 10 or more policyholders owning policies of an aggregate value of not less than £10,000.[16]

(11) In the case of a society to which s 4 of the Industrial and Provident Societies Act 1965 and certain other conditions apply, the appropriate registrar.[17]

(12) In the case of a building society incorporated or deemed to be incorporated under the Building Societies Act 1986, the Building Societies Commission, the building society or its directors, any creditor or creditors, any contributory or contributories or any combination of these parties.[18]

---

[5] Building Societies Act 1986, s 86(1)(b). The relevant modifications are contained in Sched 15 to the Building Societies Act 1986. This chapter describes the provisions of Part VI of the 1986 Act as they normally apply to companies except where otherwise stated and the Schedule should therefore be consulted for any necessary modifications to that procedure.

[6] Friendly Societies Act 1992, s 19(1)(b). The relevant modifications are contained in Sched 10 to the Friendly Societies Act 1992. This chapter describes the provisions of Part VI of the 1986 Act as they normally apply to companies except where otherwise stated and the Schedule should therefore be consulted for any necessary modifications to that procedure.

[7] 1986 Act, s 124(1).

[8] Ibid.

[9] Ibid. 'Creditors' are defined by the subsection as including contingent or prospective creditors.

[10] Ibid. 'Contributory' is defined by s 79 of the 1986 Act.

[11] Ibid.

[12] 1986 Act, s 55 and Sched 2, para 21. It should be noted that this provision is not confined to administrative receivers.

[13] 1986 Act, Sched 1, para 21.

[14] 1986 Act, s 7(4)(b).

[15] Banking Act 1987, s 92(1).

[16] Insurance Companies Act 1982, s 53.

[17] Industrial and Provident Societies Act 1965, s 56.

[18] Building Societies Act 1986, s 89(2). The provisions of s 124 of the 1986 Act are disapplied: Building Societies Act 1986, Sched 15. 'Creditor' includes a contingent or prospective creditor and 'contributory' is defined in Sched 15.

(13) In the case of an incorporated friendly society, the Friendly Societies Commission, the society or its committee of management, any creditor or creditors, any contributory or contributories or any combination of these parties.[19]

(14) The Secretary of State.[20]

A company may resolve by special resolution that it be wound up by the court[21] and present a petition on that basis. Such a petition will normally be presented by the directors in the name of the company, but the directors also have a separate right to petition for the liquidation of the company. A creditor need not be owed any minimum amount in order to be able to present a petition for the compulsory liquidation of the company.[22] A contributory may only petition for liquidation in certain circumstances. He may petition if he is a contributory by virtue of s 76 of the 1986 Act (which deals with the liability of past directors and shareholders), but only on certain limited grounds.[23] He may also petition, on any of the available grounds, if he is a contributory otherwise than by virtue of s 76 of the 1986 Act, but only if *either* the number of members is reduced below two *or* he was the original allottee of the shares (or some of them) in respect of which he is a contributory, he has had such shares registered in his name for at least six of the 18 months preceding the winding up or he has had such shares devolved on him by virtue of the death of the previous holder.[24] A shareholder's trustee in sequestration is a contributory of the company[25] and may therefore petition for its liquidation as such, and he may petition in his own name even where he has not registered the debtor's shares in his own name.[26] In the case of a building society, a contributory may only petition if the number of members is reduced below 10 *or* the share in respect of which he is a contributory has been held by him for at least six months or he has inherited it on death and it has been held by him and the deceased for at least six months between them.[27] In the case of a friendly society, a contributory may only petition if the number of members is reduced below seven *or* he has been a contributory for at least six months.[28]

The Financial Services Authority and the appropriate registrar in relation to an industrial and provident society may only petition on limited grounds. The grounds for a winding-up petition are discussed further below.

---

[19] Friendly Societies Act 1992, s 22(2). The provisions of s 124 of the 1986 Act are disapplied: Friendly Societies Act 1992, Sched 10. 'Creditor' includes a contingent or prospective creditor and 'contributory' is defined in Sched 10.

[20] Under a number of different provisions. These are discussed further below.

[21] 1986 Act, s 122(1)(a). For building societies, see the Building Societies Act 1986, s 89(1)(a); for friendly societies, see the Friendly Societies Act 1992, s 22(1)(a).

[22] If, however, the ground on which liquidation is sought is that the company cannot pay its debts, this will need to be established and one of the most common ways of doing so is to show that the company has not responded to a statutory demand for payment of debt. This can only be used where the amount of the debt is at least £750. The grounds for liquidation are discussed more fully below.

[23] 1986 Act, s 124(3). The grounds on which such a contributory may petition are those set out in s 122(1)(f) and (g) of the 1986 Act. The grounds for liquidation are discussed more fully below.

[24] 1986 Act, s 124(2).

[25] See ss 74 and 82(2) of the 1986 Act.

[26] *Cumming's Tr v Glenrinnes Farms Ltd* 1993 SLT 904.

[27] Building Societies Act 1986, s 89(3).

[28] Friendly Societies Act 1992, s 22(3).

The Secretary of State may petition for a winding up by the court in the following circumstances only.

(1) If the ground for the petition is *either* that under s 122(1)(b) (the company in question was registered as a public company but no certificate under s 117 of CA 1985 has been issued and more than a year has expired since it was so registered) *or* that under s 122(1)(c) (the company is an old public company within the meaning of the Companies Consolidation (Consequential Provisions) Act 1985).[29]

(2) If he considers it expedient that the company be wound up as a result of any report made or information obtained under the provisions specified in s 124A of the 1986 Act.[30]

(3) If the company is an insurance company to which Part II of the Insurance Companies Act 1982 applies, but only on the following grounds: that the company is unable to pay its debts within the meaning of s 123 of the 1986 Act *or* that the company has failed to satisfy an obligation to which it is or was subject by virtue of the Insurance Companies Act 1982 or other defined legislation *or* that the company has failed to satisfy an obligation to which it is subject by virtue of the laws of another EU member state implementing specified EU insurance legislation *or* that the company has failed to comply with ss 221 and 222 of CA 1985 with the result that the Secretary of State is unable to ascertain its financial position[31] *or* he thinks it is expedient in the public interest that the company should be wound up.[32]

(4) If the company is an authorised person or appointed representative under the Financial Services Act 1986, but only on the ground *either* that the company is unable to pay its debts within the meaning of s 123 of the 1986 Act or by virtue of having defaulted in an obligation to pay any sum due and payable under any investment agreement *or* that it is just and equitable to wind it up[33] and only with the relevant consent in specified cases.[34]

Which court?

Section 120 of the 1986 Act sets out the requirements in relation to jurisdiction. The Court of Session has jurisdiction to wind up any company registered in Scotland.[35] In practice, liquidation petitions are dealt with in the Outer House by a Lord Ordinary nominated as the insolvency judge.[36] The sheriff court of the

---

[29] 1986 Act, s 124(4)(a).
[30] 1986 Act, s 124(4)(b).
[31] Insurance Companies Act 1982, s 54(1).
[32] Insurance Companies Act 1982, s 54(4).
[33] Financial Services Act 1986, s 72(1), (3). 'Authorised persons' includes authorised persons whose authorisations are suspended under s 28 of that Act or who are the subject of a direction under s 33(1)(b) of that Act: Financial Services Act 1986, s 72(2).
[34] See the Financial Services Act 1986, s 72(5).
[35] 1986 Act, s 120(1).
[36] See the 1986 Act, s 121 and Court of Session Rules, rule 74.2. If the insolvency judge is not available, the petition may come before any other judge, including the vacation judge: Court of Session Rules, rule 74.2. Where the Court of Session is in vacation, the petition will be dealt with by the vacation judge: 1986 Act, s 120(2).

sheriffdom where the company's registered office is situated has concurrent jurisdiction to wind up any such company which is limited by shares and whose share capital, paid up or credited as paid up, does not exceed £120,000.[37] The Court of Session may, however, remit a liquidation petition presented in the Court of Session to the sheriff court or require a petition presented in the sheriff court to be remitted to the Court of Session if it thinks it is appropriate having regard to the amount of the company's assets;[38] it may also require a petition presented in one sheriff court to be remitted to another.[39]

There is special provision for jurisdiction to wind up a registered society within the meaning of the Industrial and Provident Societies Act 1965. Where such a society is wound up in Scotland, the sheriff court within whose jurisdiction the registered office of the society is situated has exclusive jurisdiction in relation to the winding up.[40]

Form of petition and supporting documentation

Court of Session petitions must be in Form 14.1,[41] but there is no prescribed form of petition in the sheriff court. All petitions must contain certain prescribed information including details of the petitioner, if other than the company; prescribed details of the company; the grounds on which the petition is presented;[42] and details of the proposed interim liquidator.[43] The Sheriff Court Rules also specifically require any document instructing the title of the petitioner or any other fact relied on, or otherwise founded on, to be lodged with the petition.[44]

The petition must specify the orders applied for, including intimation, service and advertisement.[45]

Grounds for winding up

Section 122 of the 1986 Act, so far as relevant to Scotland, sets out the following grounds for winding up.

(1) The company has resolved by special resolution that it should be wound up by the court.[46]

---

[37] 1986 Act, s 120(3). Where there has been a change of registered office, the registered office for this purpose means the place which has been the registered office for the longest period in the six months preceding presentation of the petition: 1986 Act, s 120(4). The monetary limit is subject to change by statutory instrument: 1986 Act, s 120(5).

[38] 1986 Act, s 120(3)(a).

[39] 1986 Act, s 120(3)(b).

[40] Industrial and Provident Societies Act 1965, s 59(a)(ii).

[41] Court of Session Rules, rule 14.1.

[42] See below.

[43] See the Sheriff Court Rules, rule 18.1, and the Court of Session Rules, rule 74.21(1). The appropriate rules should be consulted in each case, as the terms of the two sets of rules are not identical—for example, a Court of Session petition specifically requires an averment as to whether a receiver, or a liquidator in a voluntary liquidation, has been appointed and a sheriff court petition does not.

[44] Sheriff Court Rules, rule 18.1(2). Documents founded on or adopted in a Court of Session petition must be produced with it by virtue of rule 27.1 of the Court of Session Rules.

[45] Sheriff Court Rules, rule 18.1(1), and the Court of Session Rules, rule 14.4.

[46] 1986 Act, s 122(1)(a).

(2) The company was registered as a public company, but no certificate under s 117 of CA 1985 has been issued and more than a year has expired since it was so registered.[47]

(3) The company is an old public company within the meaning of the Companies Consolidation (Consequential Provisions) Act 1985.[48]

(4) The company has not commenced business within a year from its incorporation, or has suspended business for a whole year.[49]

(5) The number of members has fallen below two (except in the case of a private company limited by shares or guarantee).[50]

(6) The company is unable to pay its debts.[51] The meaning of the phrase 'unable to pay its debts' is set out in s 123 of the 1986 Act and is discussed in detail in Chapter 1 above.

(7) It is just and equitable that the company should be wound up.[52] This covers a wide variety of circumstances,[53] usually not related to insolvency. It has been said, however, that it could apply where a business is unsuccessful and, although not yet insolvent, would become so.[54]

(8) The security of the holder of a floating charge is in jeopardy.[55] The chargeholder's security is defined as being in jeopardy if events have occurred or are about to occur which would make it unreasonable in the interests of the chargeholder for the company to retain the right to dispose of the property which is the subject of the floating charge.[56]

In some cases, the grounds on which a petition may be presented are limited or are other than the general grounds described above. The particular grounds and limitations applicable to a petition by a contributory and a petition by the Secretary of State are discussed above. The Financial Services Authority is only entitled to petition for the winding up of an authorised or former authorised institution where the institution in question is *either* unable to pay its debts within the meaning of s 123 of the 1986 Act *or* it is just and equitable that the institution should be wound up.[57] The appropriate registrar may only petition for the winding up of an industrial and provident society if neither of the conditions specified in s 1(2) of that Act is fulfilled in relation to it *and* it would be in the interests of the society's investors or depositors or any other person that the society should be wound up.[58]

---

[47] 1986 Act, s 122(1)(b).

[48] 1986 Act, s 122(1)(c).

[49] 1986 Act, s 122(1)(d).

[50] 1986 Act, s 122(1)(e).

[51] 1986 Act, s 122(1)(f).

[52] 1986 Act, s 122(1)(g).

[53] See *Ebrahami* v *Westbourne Galleries Ltd* [1973] AC 360.

[54] St Clair and Drummond Young, *The Law of Corporate Insolvency in Scotland* (2nd edn) at p 80.

[55] 1986 Act, s 122(2).

[56] Ibid.

[57] Banking Act 1987, s 92(1). The subsection deems for this purpose that an institution is unable to pay its debts within the meaning of s 123 if it defaults on an obligation to pay any sum due and payable in respect of a deposit. 'Deposit' is in turn defined by s 5 of the Banking Act 1987.

[58] Industrial and Provident Societies Act 1965, s 56.

A petition in respect of a building society may be presented by the Building Societies Commission on the ground that it has reason to believe that its purpose or principal purpose has ceased to be that required by the Building Societies Act 1986[59] or by anyone entitled to petition[60] on any of the following grounds.

(1) It has resolved by special resolution to be wound up by the court.[61]

(2) The number of members is reduced below 10.[62]

(3) The number of directors is reduced below two.[63]

(4) It has not been granted specified authorisations more than three years after its registration as a building society.[64]

(5) It has had its authorisation revoked and not renewed.[65]

(6) It exists for an illegal purpose.[66]

(7) It cannot pay its debts.[67]

(8) It is just and equitable to wind it up.[68]

A petition in respect of a friendly society may be presented on any of the following grounds.

(1) It has resolved by special resolution to be wound up by the court.[69]

(2) The number of members is reduced below seven.[70]

(3) The number of members of the committee of management is reduced below two.[71]

(4) It has not commenced business within a year from its incorporation or has suspended its business for a whole year.[72]

(5) It exists for an illegal purpose.[73]

(6) It cannot pay its debts.[74]

(7) It is just and equitable to wind it up.[75]

The making of a winding-up order

This section deals with the procedure from presentation of the petition to the making of a winding-up order.

---

[59] Building Societies Act 1986, s 37(1).
[60] See above.
[61] Building Societies Act 1986, s 89(1)(a).
[62] Building Societies Act 1986, s 89(1)(b).
[63] Building Societies Act 1986, s 89(1)(c).
[64] Building Societies Act 1986, s 89(1)(d).
[65] Building Societies Act 1986, s 89(1)(e).
[66] Building Societies Act 1986, s 89(1)(f). See also s 89(4)(b).
[67] Building Societies Act 1986, s 89(1)(g).
[68] Building Societies Act 1986, s 89(1)(h).
[69] Friendly Societies Act 1992, s 22(1)(a).
[70] Friendly Societies Act 1992, s 22(1)(b).
[71] Friendly Societies Act 1992, s 22(1)(c).
[72] Friendly Societies Act 1992, s 22(1)(d).
[73] Friendly Societies Act 1992, s 22(1)(e).
[74] Friendly Societies Act 1992, s 22(1)(g).
[75] Friendly Societies Act 1992, s 89(1)(h).

Procedure following presentation

Unless the court summarily dismisses the petition, the first order following presentation will normally be for intimation, service and advertisement. In the case of a Court of Session petition, service will normally be required on the company, if it is not a company petition; on the liquidator if the company is already in voluntary liquidation; and on any receiver or administrator who has been appointed.[76] Provision is also made for service on the Bank of England where the company is an authorised or former authorised institution under the Banking Act 1987 and the Bank of England is not the petitioner.[77] Clearly, the reference to the Bank of England ought to have been amended to a reference to the Financial Services Authority following the transfer of the Bank of England's supervisory functions to the Financial Services Authority under the Bank of England Act 1998, given that, as set out above, it is now the Financial Services Authority who may present a petition for the liquidation of such an institution, but although certain consequential amendments have been made by the Bank of England Act 1998 itself and by the Bank of England Act 1998 (Consequential Amendments to Subordinate Legislation) Order 1998[78] to take account of the change, the Court of Session Rules have not been so amended, and it is thought that the position is not covered by the provisions of s 23(3) of the Bank of England Act 1998 which deals with references to the Bank of England in 'relevant provisions'. It is thought that this is an oversight and should be rectified. In the case of a sheriff court petition, rule 19.2 of the Sheriff Court Rules is similar in its terms except that it does not require service on an administrator.[79] Where a petition for the winding up of an insurance company to which Part II of the Insurance Companies Act 1982 applies is presented by someone other than the Secretary of State, a copy of the petition must be served on him and he is entitled to be heard in the petition.[80]

Unless advertisement is dispensed with,[81] the petition is advertised once in the Edinburgh Gazette and once in one or more newspapers chosen to ensure that the matter comes to the attention of the company's creditors.[82]

The court may also make any other orders sought at this stage,[83] including an order to sist any proceedings pending against the company (or, in certain circumstances, a contributory)[84] and for the appointment of a provisional liquidator.[85]

Answers to the petition may be lodged within the period allowed—normally eight days after the appropriate service, intimation and advertisement.[86] Normal

---

[76] Court of Session Rules, rule 74.22(1).

[77] Ibid.

[78] SI 1998/1129.

[79] The points made with reference to the Bank of England in the Court of Session Rules apply equally here.

[80] Insurance Companies Act 1982, s 54(4).

[81] Which may be allowed where it is really unnecessary—for example, in the case of a contributory's petition where the company is solvent.

[82] Sheriff Court Rules, rule 19(6), and the Court of Session Rules, rule 74.22(1)(c).

[83] 1986 Act, s 125(1).

[84] 1986 Act, s 126.

[85] 1986 Act, s 135(1). The appointment of a provisional liquidator is discussed further in Chapter 19.

[86] Sheriff Court Rules, rule 19(8), and the Court of Session Rules, rule 74.22(2). The period of notice may be shortened or extended on application.

petition procedure applies. This means that where answers are lodged, there would normally be a period of adjustment of the petition and answers followed by a proof, but in view of the nature of the application, the normal procedure may be abridged. Where, as in the usual case, no answers are lodged, the petition will usually be dealt with in chambers. In either case the court may dismiss the petition, adjourn it conditionally—for example, to allow further information to be produced—or unconditionally, make an interim order or make any other order that it thinks fit including, obviously, a winding-up order.[87]

Discretionary nature of winding up

Where the petition is a contributories' petition on the ground that it is just and equitable that the company be wound up, and the court is of the view that the petitioners are entitled to relief and in the absence of any other remedy it would be just and equitable that the company be wound up, the court *must* make a winding-up order, except where it is also of the view that the petitioners have another remedy open to them and they are being unreasonable in seeking a winding-up order rather than pursuing such an alternative remedy.[88] Subject to this stricture, the making of a winding-up order is essentially a matter for the discretion of the court, although it must not refuse to make a winding-up order solely on the basis that the company has no assets or that its assets have been mortgaged to an amount equal to or in excess of its assets.[89]

In the case of a creditor petition, where it is established that the debt is due and that the company is unable to pay its debts, the creditor is prima facie entitled to a winding-up order,[90] but where the debt on which the petition is based is genuinely disputed, a petition for liquidation is not appropriate and may be dismissed.[91] Liquidation will not necessarily be refused, however, if only part of the debt is disputed.[92] Opposition to the petition by the company will not result in the petition being refused,[93] but where there is opposition by other creditors, the court will have regard to the wishes of all the creditors in making its decision.[94] In the case of a contributory petition where winding up is sought on the just and equitable ground, the petitioner must show that the constitutional methods of resolving the company's difficulties have been exhausted,[95] but this is not necessary where the petition is on the ground that the company cannot pay its debts.[96] Whatever the ground, the contributory must show an interest in bringing the petition, but so long as it is a tangible interest of some sort, it need

---

[87] 1986 Act, s 125(1).
[88] 1986 Act, s 125(2).
[89] 1986 Act, s 125(1).
[90] See, for example, *Rocks v Brae Hotel (Shetland) Ltd*; sub nom *Morrice v Brae Hotel (Shetland) Ltd* 1997 SLT 474.
[91] See *Pollock v Gaeta Pioneer Mining Co Ltd* 1907 SC 182. Expenses may be awarded against the petitioner: see, for example, *Re Cannon Screen Entertainment Ltd* [1989] BCLC 660.
[92] See *Blue Star Security Services (Scotland) Ltd*, Petnrs, 1992 SLT (Sh Ct) 80.
[93] See, for example, *Rocks v Brae Hotel (Shetland) Ltd*, note 90 above.
[94] It will normally have regard to the wishes of the majority in value of the creditors, but this is not invariable: see *Palmer's Company Law*, para 15.623 and cases there cited.
[95] See *Cox v The Gosford Ship Co* (1894) 21 R 334; *Scobie and Ors v Atlas Steel Works Ltd* (1906) 8F 1052.
[96] *O'Connor v Atlantis Fisheries Ltd*, 28th January 1998 (unreported).

not necessarily be an interest in a potential surplus or, indeed, a pecuniary interest at all.[97]

Date of commencement of winding up

The date of commencement of the liquidation is the date on which the petition is presented, except where there has been an earlier resolution to wind up the company voluntarily, in which case it is the date of the resolution.[98]

Publication of a winding-up order

There is no provision equivalent to that in sequestration where the clerk of court is charged with sending a copy or certified copy, as appropriate, of the relevant order to specified parties. However, the company must forward a copy of the order forthwith to the Registrar of Companies for entry into the company's record[99] The order is accompanied by Form 4.2 (Scot).[100]

Appeals

Section 162 of the 1986 Act provides that, subject to the provisions of the section itself, an appeal from any order or decision made or given in the winding up of a company lies in the same manner and subject to such conditions as in any other type of case. A winding-up order or a decision to refuse a winding-up order made by a sheriff would therefore be appealable either to the Sheriff Principal and thereafter to the Inner House of the Court of Session or directly to the Inner House, and such an order made by a Lord Ordinary would be appealable to the Inner House. Any such appeal from the decision or order of a vacation judge or Lord Ordinary is made to the Inner House by way of a reclaiming motion to be enrolled within 14 days of the date of the decision or order.[101]

---

[97] Ibid. In that case, the petitioner was a fully paid-up shareholder and so could have had no pecuniary interest in a liquidation on the grounds that the company was unable to pay its debts. Where the contributory's interest *is* pecuniary, is it not necessarily restricted to there being a surplus in which he will participate: in the case of a shareholder whose shares are only partly paid up, it may be in minimising his loss.

[98] 1986 Act, s 129.

[99] 1986 Act , s 130(1).

[100] See the Scottish Rules, Sched 5.

[101] 1986 Act, s 162(2)(b) and (4).

17 : PROCEDURE LEADING TO A WINDING-UP ORDER: UNREGISTERED COMPANIES

This chapter deals with the procedure leading to the making of a winding-up order in relation to unregistered companies.

Applying for a winding-up order

A winding-up order is obtained as a result of a petition to the relevant court. This section deals with various aspects of applying for a winding-up order.

Which companies are liable to be wound up under Part V of the 1986 Act?

Section 221 of the 1986 Act states that, subject to the provisions of Part V of the Act, any unregistered company may be wound up under the 1986 Act. An unregistered company is defined as *including* 'any association and any company', with the exception of a company registered in any part of the United Kingdom under the Joint Stock Companies Acts or under any other legislation, past or present, relating to companies in Great Britain.[1] This definition is very wide. It includes foreign companies,[2] and a company incorporated in Northern Ireland may be wound up by a British court under Part V of the 1986 Act as an unregistered company.[3] An open-ended investment company which has its head office in Scotland may be wound up as an unregistered company by the Court of Session[4] and an EEIG may also be wound up as an unregistered company.[5] A Scottish partnership is generally liable to sequestration[6] and may not generally be wound up under Part V of the 1986 Act,[7] but partnerships which are authorised

---

[1] 1986 Act, s 220. The Joint Stock Companies Acts are the Joint Stock Companies Act 1856, the Joint Stock Companies Acts 1857, the Joint Stock Banking Companies Act 1857, and the Act to enable joint stock banking companies to be formed on the principle of limited liability, but not the Joint Stock Companies Act 1844: 1986 Act, s 251, and the Companies Act 1985, s 735(3).

[2] *Marshall* (1895) 22 R 697.

[3] *Re Normandy Marketing Ltd* (1993) BCC 879.

[4] See the Open-Ended Investment Companies (Investment Companies with Variable Capital) Regulations 1996 (SI 1996/2827).

[5] See the European Economic Interest Grouping Regulations 1989 (SI 1989/638).

[6] See Chapter 6.

[7] *Smith* v *Smith*, Dumfries Sheriff Court, 19th January 1998 (unreported).

or former authorised institutions under the Banking Act 1987 *or* authorised persons or appointed representatives under the Financial Services Act 1986 will in certain circumstances fall to be wound up under Part V of the 1986 Act.[8] An unregistered company which has a principal place of business in Northern Ireland may not be wound up in Scotland under Part V of the 1986 Act unless it also has a principal place of business in Scotland.[9]

It is specifically provided that a company incorporated outside Great Britain which carried on business in Great Britain and then ceased to do so may be wound up as an unregistered company under the 1986 Act, even if it has been dissolved or otherwise ceased to exist as a company in terms of the law of the country of its incorporation.[10]

Who may apply?

Section 221(1) of the 1986 Act provides that all the provisions of the 1986 Act and CA 1985 concerning winding up apply to an unregistered company, with the exceptions and additions specified in the remainder of the section. Accordingly, anyone who is entitled to apply for the compulsory liquidation of a company registered in Scotland by virtue of the 1986 Act could apply for the winding up of an unregistered company: that is, the company itself; the directors; any creditor or creditors; a contributory or contributories;[11] any combination of those parties; a receiver; an administrator;[12] the supervisor of a CVA;[13] and the Secretary of State, insofar as the circumstances in which he may petition under the 1986 Act are relevant to unregistered companies.[14]

The following persons may also apply for the winding up of particular types of unregistered company by virtue of the specified statutory provisions:

(1) In the case of a company which is an authorised institution or former authorised institution under the Banking Act 1987,[15] the Financial Services Authority (on certain limited grounds).[16]

(2) In the case of a company which is an insurance company within the meaning of Part II of the Insurance Companies Act 1982, 10 or more policyholders owning policies of an aggregate value of not less than £10,000[17] *or* the Secretary of State, on the following grounds only, namely: the company is unable to pay its debts within the meaning of s 221 of the

---

[8] See the Banking Act 1987, s 92(2), and the Financial Services Act 1986, s 72(4), respectively. 'Authorised persons' under the Financial Services Act 1986 include authorised persons whose authorisations are suspended under s 28 of that Act or who are the subject of a direction under s 33(1)(b) of that Act: Financial Services Act 1986, s 72(2).

[9] 1986 Act, s 221(2).

[10] 1986 Act, s 225.

[11] 'Contributory' in relation to an unregistered company is defined in s 226 of the 1986 Act.

[12] For a discussion of when an administration order may be made in relation to an unregistered company, see Chapter 10.

[13] For a discussion of when a CVA may be made in relation to an unregistered company, see Chapter 8.

[14] See further the preceding chapter in relation to those who may petition for the compulsory liquidation of a registered company.

[15] Including, in certain circumstances, a partnership: see above.

[16] Banking Act 1987, s 92(1). The grounds are discussed further below.

[17] Insurance Companies Act 1982, s 53. Such a petition may only be presented with the leave of the court, which will not be granted until a prima facie case has been established and security for costs for such amount as the court may think reasonable has been given.

1986 Act;[18] the company has failed to satisfy an obligation to which it is or was subject by virtue of the Insurance Companies Act 1982 or other defined legislation;[19] the company has failed to satisfy an obligation to which it is subject by virtue of the laws of another EU member state implementing specified EU insurance legislation;[20] the company has failed to comply with ss 221 and 222 of CA 1985, with the result that the Secretary of State is unable to ascertain its financial position[21] or he thinks it is expedient in the public interest that the company should be wound up.[22]

(3) In the case of a company which is an authorised person or appointed representative under the Financial Services Act 1986,[23] the Secretary of State, but only on the ground *either* that the company is unable to pay its debts within the meaning of s 221 of the 1986 Act or by virtue of having defaulted in an obligation to pay any sum due and payable under any investment agreement *or* that it is just and equitable to wind it up[24] and only where he has the necessary consent if required.[25]

Which court?

As a result of s 221(1) of the 1986 Act the rules for determining jurisdiction to wind up registered companies[26] also apply to unregistered companies, and for this purpose an unregistered company which has a principal place of business in Scotland is deemed to be registered in Scotland, and that place of business is deemed to be the registered office of the company for all purposes of the winding up.[27] It is specifically provided that an EEIG is to be treated as if it were a company having a paid-up share capital of less than £120,000, and is therefore liable to be wound up by either the Court of Session or the appropriate sheriff court.[28]

Form of petition and supporting documentation

This will follow, so far as appropriate, the style of petition for the compulsory winding up of a company registered in Scotland.[29]

Grounds for winding up

Section 221(5) sets out the following grounds for winding up.

---

[18] Insurance Companies Act 1982, s 54(1).
[19] Ibid.
[20] Ibid.
[21] Ibid.
[22] Insurance Companies Act 1982, s 54(4).
[23] Including, in certain circumstances, a partnership: see above.
[24] Financial Services Act 1986, s 72(1), (3). 'Authorised persons' include authorised persons whose authorisations are suspended under s 28 of that Act or who are the subject of a direction under s 33(1)(b) of that Act: Financial Services Act 1986, s 72(2).
[25] See the Financial Services Act 1986, s 72(5).
[26] See the preceding chapter.
[27] 1986 Act, s 221(3).
[28] European Economic Interest Grouping Regulations 1989, reg 19(2).
[29] 1986 Act, s 221(1). The requirements in relation to the form of the petition and supporting documentation in relation to a petition for the winding up by the court of a company registered in Scotland are discussed in the preceding chapter.

(1) The company is dissolved, or has ceased to carry on business, or is carrying on business only for the purpose of winding up its affairs.[30]

(2) The company is unable to pay its debts.[31] Sections 222–224 of the 1986 Act set out the various circumstances in which an unregistered company is deemed to be unable to pay its debts. These are discussed fully in Chapter 1 above.

(3) It is just and equitable that the company be wound up.[32]

(4) The security of the holder of a floating charge is in jeopardy.[33] The chargeholder's security is defined as being in jeopardy if events have occurred or are about to occur which would make it unreasonable in the interests of the chargeholder for the company to retain the right to dispose of the property which is the subject of the floating charge.[34]

In some cases the grounds on which a petition may be presented are limited or are other than the general grounds described above. The Financial Services Authority is only entitled to petition for the winding up of an authorised or former authorised institution where the institution in question is *either* unable to pay its debts within the meaning of s 221 of the 1986 Act *or* it is just and equitable that the institution should be wound up.[35] The particular grounds and limitations applicable to a petition by the Secretary of State are discussed above.

The making of a winding-up order

This section deals with the procedure from presentation of the petition to the making of a winding-up order.

Procedure following presentation

The procedure following presentation of the petition will be the same as for compulsory liquidation of a company registered in Scotland.[36]

Discretionary nature of winding up

As in the case of the compulsory liquidation of a company registered in Scotland, the making of a winding-up order is essentially a matter for the discretion of the court, and the same kinds of issues which are relevant to the exercise of that discretion in the case of a company registered in Scotland will generally be relevant in the case of an unregistered company also.[37] In the case of a foreign company, the court will wish to be satisfied that there is some relevant connection with

---

[30] 1986 Act, s 221(1)(5)(a).

[31] 1986 Act, s 221(1)(5)(b).

[32] 1986 Act, s 221(1)(5)(c).

[33] 1986 Act, s 221(7).

[34] Ibid.

[35] Banking Act 1987, s 92(1). The subsection deems for this purpose that an institution is unable to pay its debts within the meaning of s 221 if it defaults on an obligation to pay any sum due and payable in respect of a deposit. 'Deposit' is in turn defined by s 5 of the Banking Act 1987.

[36] 1986 Act, s 221(1). The procedure following presentation of the petition in relation to a petition for the winding up by the court of a company registered in Scotland is discussed in the preceding chapter.

[37] Some of these issues are discussed in the preceding chapter.

Scotland—for example, the presence of assets within the jurisdiction, before making a winding-up order.[38]

Date of commencement of liquidation

The date of commencement of the liquidation is the date on which the petition is presented.[39]

Publication of a winding-up order

The requirements in relation to the publication of a winding-up order will be the same as those pertaining to the publication of a winding-up order in the compulsory liquidation of a company registered in Scotland.[40]

Appeals

Appeals will be dealt with in the same way as in relation to a petition for the compulsory liquidation of a company registered in Scotland.[41]

---

[38] *Inland Revenue v Highland Engineering Ltd* 1975 SLT 203. In England, a relevant connection with the jurisdiction seems to have been regarded as an additional requirement, over and above the relevant statutory provisions, for establishing the jurisdiction of the court to wind up a foreign company in the first place: see *Re Lloyd General Italiano* [1885] 29 Ch 219; *Banque des Marchands de Moscou (Koupetschesky) v Kindersley* [1951] Ch 112; *Re Eloc Electro-Optieck and Communicatie BV* [1982] Ch 43; *Re a Company (No 00359 of 1987)* [1988] Ch 210, the last two cases having reduced the test to be applied by the court in this regard. It is thought that the Scottish approach is the correct one: the statutory criteria in the 1986 Act must be regarded as the only criteria for establishing the jurisdiction of the Scottish court, and any decision to refuse a winding up on the grounds of lack of a sufficient connection with Scotland is merely an exercise of the court's discretion as to whether to make a winding-up order.

[39] 1986 Act, s 129, as applied by 1986 Act, s 221(1). The alternative provision relating to the prior passing of a resolution to wind up the company voluntarily is, of course, inapplicable, since an unregistered company may not be wound up voluntarily under the 1986 Act: 1986 Act, s 221(4), and see Chapter 14.

[40] 1986 Act, s 221(1). The requirements for the publication of a winding-up order in the compulsory liquidation of a company registered in Scotland are discussed in the preceding chapter.

[41] 1986 Act, s 221(1). Appeals in relation to a petition for the compulsory liquidation of a company registered in Scotland are discussed in the preceding chapter.

18 : PROCEDURE FOLLOWING THE MAKING OF A WINDING-UP ORDER

This chapter considers the procedure from the making of a winding-up order to the appointment of the liquidator who will take over from the interim liquidator for the purpose of realising and distributing the company's assets.

Notification of appointment of the interim liquidator

Within seven days of his appointment the interim liquidator must give notice of it to the Registrar of Companies.[1] Within 28 days he must also give notice of it to the creditors and contributories or advertise it in accordance with the directions of the court.[2]

Taking possession of the company's property

On the making of the winding-up order the interim liquidator is required to take into his custody or under his control all the property or things in action to which the company appears to be entitled.[3] The functions and powers of the interim liquidator are discussed more fully in Chapter 20.

Obtaining a statement of affairs

The interim liquidator may, but is not obliged to, obtain a statement of affairs.[4]

First meetings in the liquidation

As soon as practicable within the 28 days after his appointment, or such longer period as the court may allow, the interim liquidator must call meetings of the creditors and contributories of the company to choose a liquidator of the

---

[1] Scottish Rules, rule 4.18(4)(a).
[2] Scottish Rules, rule 4.18(4)(b). Advertisement is the usual practice and will have been craved in the petition.
[3] 1986 Act, s 144(1), and Scottish Rules, rule 4.22(1).
[4] 1986 Act, s 131. Statements of affairs are discussed further in Chapter 29.

company.[5] Where the company is being wound up on grounds which include its inability to pay its debts and the interim liquidator is of the view that it would be inappropriate to call a meeting of contributories, he may call only a meeting of creditors.[6] These meetings are known as the first meeting of creditors and (where called) first meeting of contributories and, collectively, as the first meetings in the liquidation.[7] This section deals with the calling of, and procedure at, the first meetings in the liquidation.

Calling of first meetings in liquidation

The first meetings in the liquidation must be called to take place within 42 days of the date of the winding-up order or such longer period as the court may allow.[8] As indicated above, in certain cases only a meeting of creditors will be called.

Procedure at first meetings in liquidation

The first meetings are chaired by the interim liquidator, although where it is proposed to appoint the interim liquidator to be liquidator, the meeting may elect another person to act as chairman for the purpose of choosing the liquidator.[9] In the case of the creditors' meeting, the interim liquidator will require to accept or reject claims which have already been submitted to him or which are submitted at the meeting for the purpose of determining the respective creditors' entitlement to vote on the resolutions to be proposed at the meeting. The business of the meetings is limited:[10] the only resolutions which may be passed at these first meetings are resolutions to nominate the liquidator or liquidators to take over from the interim liquidator;[11] in the case of a nomination of joint liquidators, to determine whether they must act together or can act independently; to establish a liquidation committee;[12] to adjourn the meeting for up to three weeks; to resolve on any other matter which the chairman is prepared to allow for a special reason; and, in the case of the creditors' meeting only, where no liquidation committee is to be established, to establish the terms on which the liquidator is to be remunerated or defer consideration of that matter.

---

[5] 1986 Act, s 138(3).
[6] 1986 Act, s 138(4).
[7] Scottish Rules, rule 4.12(2).
[8] Scottish Rules, rule 4.12(2A). There must be 14 days' notice of the meeting: Scottish Rules, rule 7.3(2).
[9] Scottish Rules, rule 7.5(4).
[10] Scottish Rules, rule 4.12(3), (4).
[11] The appointment of the liquidator is discussed further in the following chapter.
[12] Liquidation committees are discussed in Chapter 34.

19 : APPOINTMENT AND REPLACEMENT
OF OFFICE HOLDERS

This chapter deals with the appointment and replacement of office holders in the various insolvency proceedings.

Sequestration

The sequestration process is administered by a trustee in sequestration. An *interim trustee* is appointed by the court in every sequestration. The appointment is normally made when the court awards sequestration,[1] but in certain circumstances an interim trustee may be appointed at an earlier stage.[2] Thereafter, a *permanent trustee* is either elected at the statutory meeting (if held)[3] or appointed by the sheriff.

Appointment of interim trustee

The petitioner may nominate a person to act as interim trustee in the petition.[4] The person so nominated must be resident within the jurisdiction of the Court of Session, be qualified to act as an insolvency practitioner and have given an undertaking to act as interim and, if necessary, permanent trustee.[5] (In practice, a private insolvency practitioner will normally only give such an undertaking if it appears that there will be at least sufficient assets in the estate to pay his fees and outlays.[6]) If the court is satisfied that the person nominated meets these conditions,

---

[1] See 1985 Act, s 2(1), (2).

[2] See 1985 Act, s 2(5).

[3] The statutory meeting is the first meeting of creditors in the sequestration. It will always be held where the interim trustee is a private insolvency practitioner, but where the interim trustee is the Accountant in Bankruptcy, it is possible for the statutory meeting to be dispensed with. For a full discussion, see Chapter 7.

[4] 1985 Act, s 2(1).

[5] 1985 Act, s 2(3). These facts must be averred in the petition: 1985 Act, s 2(1)(b). See also Chapter 5 which deals with the qualifications of insolvency practitioners.

[6] The 1985 Act introduced what was in effect public funding of sequestrations where there were insufficient assets to pay a dividend by providing for the fees and outlays of the trustee administering the sequestration to be payable from public funds to the extent that there were insufficient assets in the estate to meet them. However, combined with new provisions making access to the sequestration process by the debtor easier, this resulted in a massive increase in the number of sequestrations, many of which were cases attracting public funding. The government

it may appoint that person to be interim trustee.[7] Where no interim trustee is nominated in the petition, or the court declines to appoint the person nominated, the Accountant in Bankruptcy will be appointed as interim trustee.[8]

In non–debtor petitions, an interim trustee may be appointed before the award of sequestration is made where the debtor consents or cause is shown.[9] Common reasons for seeking the appointment of an interim trustee before the award of sequestration include the necessity to ensure that the debtor's business is looked after in the interim period, the danger of the debtor destroying records or disposing of assets and the danger of the debtor absconding.

Replacement of interim trustee

There are a number of reasons why an interim trustee may require to be replaced.

(1) Death. If the interim trustee dies in office, a new interim trustee will be appointed by the court.[10]

(2) Resignation. A private insolvency practitioner who wishes to resign as interim trustee must apply to the court for permission to do so.[11] The court must permit him to resign where *either* he is unable to continue to act—for example, because he no longer qualifies as an insolvency practitioner or because he is seriously ill—*or* the court is satisfied that he has behaved in such a way that he should no longer be interim trustee.[12] In such a case, the court will appoint a new interim trustee.[13]

(3) Removal. An interim trustee may be removed by the court on the application of the debtor, a creditor or the Accountant in Bankruptcy on the same grounds as those on which the court will permit his resignation.[14] He may also be removed following a report to the court by the Accountant in Bankruptcy that he has failed to perform any of his duties without reasonable excuse.[15] In either case, the court will appoint a new interim trustee.[16]

Selection of permanent trustee

There must be a permanent trustee in every sequestration.[17] The permanent trustee must be qualified to act as an insolvency practitioner in relation to the

---

regarded the consequent increase in public expenditure as unacceptable and the 1993 Act, *inter alia*, amended the law so that the fees and outlays of the trustee administering the sequestration in such cases are no longer met by the state if the debtor's estate is insufficient to meet them. Hence, a private insolvency practitioner is only likely to agree to act as permanent trustee if there will be sufficient funds in the estate to meet his fees and outlays.

[7] 1985 Act, s 2(1).

[8] 1985 Act, s 2(2).

[9] 1985 Act, s 2(5).

[10] 1985 Act, s 13(5).

[11] 1985 Act, s 13(3).

[12] Ibid, referring to paras (a) and (b) of s 13(2) respectively.

[13] 1985 Act, s 13(4).

[14] 1985 Act, s 13(2).

[15] 1985 Act, s 1A(2). The court may, however, simply censure the interim trustee or make some other appropriate order.

[16] 1985 Act, s 13(2) and s 13(1) respectively.

[17] 1985 Act, s 3(1).

debtor[18] and may be elected at the statutory meeting, if held, or appointed by the sheriff. There may not be joint permanent trustees.[19]

Where a permanent trustee is elected at the statutory meeting, a report to that effect is made to the sheriff by the interim trustee.[20] There is a procedure for objecting to any matter connected with the permanent trustee's election.[21] Where such an objection is made and sustained, a new meeting to hold another election will be ordered;[22] where no objection is made or is rejected, the permanent trustee's appointment is confirmed by the sheriff.[23] The Accountant in Bankruptcy may not be elected as permanent trustee,[24] although he may become permanent trustee by other means.[25]

Where no permanent trustee is elected, the procedure which follows depends on the circumstances. Where no permanent trustee is elected because the Accountant in Bankruptcy is interim trustee and there has been no statutory meeting, the Accountant in Bankruptcy in his capacity as interim trustee reports the circumstances of the sequestration to the sheriff[26] and he or his nominee will be appointed permanent trustee.[27] Where the statutory meeting is held but no permanent trustee is elected because no creditors who were eligible to vote attended, or for some other reason, the interim trustee will report the outcome of the statutory meeting to the sheriff.[28] If the interim trustee is a private insolvency practitioner, he will be appointed as permanent trustee[29] and may apply for a certificate of summary administration.[30] If the interim trustee is the Accountant in Bankruptcy, he or his nominee will be appointed as permanent trustee[31] and he may also apply for a certificate of summary administration.[32]

In any case where the Accountant in Bankruptcy is interim trustee and applies for and is granted a certificate of summary administration, he or his nominee will be appointed as permanent trustee.[33]

---

[18] 1985 Act, s 24(2)(b), and see Chapter 5 which deals with the qualifications of insolvency practitioners.

[19] *Inland Revenue Commissioners* v *MacDonald* 1988 SLT (Sh Ct) 7.

[20] 1985 Act, s 25(1)(a). The interim trustee may also apply for a certificate of summary administration at the same time: 1985 Act, s 25(2A). Summary administrations are discussed in Chapter 35.

[21] 1985 Act, s 25(1)(b).

[22] 1985 Act, s 25(4)(b).

[23] 1985 Act, s 25(2) and s 25(4)(a).

[24] 1985 Act, s 24(2).

[25] See below.

[26] 1985 Act, s 21B(1).

[27] 1985 Act, s 21B(2) and s 25A. The Accountant in Bankruptcy may also apply for a certificate of summary administration: 1985 Act, s 21B(2)(b). Where this is not applied for or not granted, the sequestration will proceed as a Schedule 2 case: 1985 Act, s 25A(3). Schedule 2 cases are discussed together with summary administration in Chapter 35.

[28] 1985 Act, s 24(3A) (where the interim trustee is the Accountant in Bankruptcy) and s 23(4) (where he is a private insolvency practitioner). Where the interim trustee is a private insolvency practitioner, he must also notify the Accountant in Bankruptcy: 1985 Act, s 23(4).

[29] 1985 Act, s 23(4).

[30] 1985 Act, s 23(4A). Where this is not applied for or not granted, the sequestration will proceed as a Schedule 2 case: 1985 Act, s 24(5).

[31] 1985 Act, s 24(3A), applying s 25A.

[32] 1985 Act, s 23(3B). Again, where this is not applied for or not granted, the sequestration will proceed as a Schedule 2 case: 1985 Act, s 25A(3).

[33] 1985 Act, ss 23A(4) and 25A.

Replacement of permanent trustee

There are a number of reasons why a permanent trustee may require to be replaced.

(1) Death. If the permanent trustee dies in office, the commissioners or, if there are no commissioners, the Accountant in Bankruptcy, must call a meeting of the creditors for the election of a new permanent trustee.[34]

(2) Resignation. If the permanent trustee wishes to resign, he must apply to the court for permission to do so. The court will permit his resignation in the same circumstances in which it will permit the resignation of an interim trustee.[35] If the application is granted unconditionally, the commissioners or, if there are no commissioners, the Accountant in Bankruptcy, must call a meeting of the creditors for the election of a new permanent trustee.[36] Alternatively, the application may be granted subject to election of a new permanent trustee,[37] in which case the resigning permanent trustee must call the appropriate meeting of creditors.[38] If no new permanent trustee is elected at any such meeting, the Accountant in Bankruptcy or his nominee is appointed by the court and the sequestration thereafter proceeds as a Schedule 2 case.[39]

(3) Removal. The permanent trustee may be removed in several ways on different grounds. He may be removed by the creditors at a creditors' meeting called for that purpose if they also elect a new permanent trustee,[40] without any reason being given. He may be removed following on a report to the court by the Accountant in Bankruptcy that he has failed to perform any of his duties without reasonable excuse.[41] He may be removed by the court on the application of a commissioner, the debtor, a creditor or the Accountant in Bankruptcy on substantially the same grounds as those on which the court will permit him to resign.[42] Finally, he may be removed by the court on the application of the commissioners, the Accountant in Bankruptcy or a person representing at least a quarter in value of the creditors on cause shown other than those grounds.[43] In the last three cases, the commissioners or, if there are no commissioners, the Accountant in Bankruptcy, must call a meeting of the creditors for the election of a new permanent trustee.[44] If no new permanent trustee is elected at any such meeting, the Accountant in Bankruptcy or his nominee is appointed by the court and the sequestration thereafter proceeds as a Schedule 2 case.[45]

[34] 1985 Act, s 28(3). Commissioners are discussed in Chapter 34.
[35] 1985 Act, s 28(1), referring to the grounds set out in s 13(2)(a) and (b) and discussed above.
[36] 1985 Act, s 28(2)(a).
[37] 1985 Act, s 28(1A).
[38] 1985 Act, s 28(2)(b).
[39] 1985 Act, s 28(5), applying s 25A.
[40] 1985 Act, s 29(1)(a).
[41] 1985 Act, s 1A(2). Alternatively, the court may simply censure him or make some other appropriate order.
[42] 1985 Act, s 28(6), (9).
[43] 1985 Act, s 29(1)(b).
[44] 1985 Act, s 29(5) and (6).
[45] 1985 Act, s 29(8), applying, *inter alia*, s 28(5) above.

Company voluntary arrangements

The initial stages of the procedure leading to a CVA are in the hands of a *nominee*. Once the CVA has taken effect, its implementation is overseen by a *supervisor*.

Appointment of nominee

The proposal for a CVA names a nominee to act as trustee or otherwise in relation to the arrangement for the purpose of supervising its implementation.[46] The nominee must agree to act[47] and, if he refuses, the proposer(s) will require to substitute the name of a fresh nominee in the proposal and start again. The nominee must be qualified to act as an insolvency practitioner in relation to the company.[48]

Replacement of nominee

A nominee who is not himself the administrator or liquidator of the company may be replaced by the court on the application of the person(s) making the proposal if he has failed to submit to the court the report required under s 2 of the 1986 Act.[49]

A nominee may also be replaced as a result of a modification made to the proposal by the meetings of the company and its creditors called to consider the proposal: the meetings may resolve that someone else should take on the nominee's functions in supervising the arrangement.[50] Where such a modification is proposed at the meetings, written confirmation that the proposed replacement is qualified to act as an insolvency practitioner in relation to the company must be produced and the replacement must be personally present and consent to act or written confirmation of his consent to act must be produced.[51]

There are no specific provisions dealing with the death or resignation of the nominee as such.

Appointment of supervisor

When the CVA takes effect, the nominee or his replacement automatically becomes the supervisor of the arrangement.[52] There may be more than one supervisor, and where this is the case, the meetings may resolve that acts in connection with the arrangement may be carried out by any supervisor alone, or require to be done by all together.[53]

Replacement of supervisor

The arrangement itself may contain provisions relating to the replacement of the supervisor and the circumstances in which they will operate.

---

[46] 1986 Act, s 1(2).
[47] Where he does agree to act, he must endorse a copy of the notice received by him to that effect and return it to the proposer(s): Scottish Rules, rule 1.4(3), (4) (as applied by rule 1.12(2) where the proposer is the administrator or liquidator).
[48] 1986 Act, s 1(2), and see Chapter 5 which deals with the qualifications of insolvency practitioners.
[49] 1986 Act, s 2(4).
[50] 1986 Act, s 4(2). The new nominee must also be a person qualified to act as an insolvency practitioner in relation to the company.
[51] Scottish Rules, rule 1.18(3).
[52] 1986 Act, s 7(2).
[53] Scottish Rules, rule 1.18(1).

Section 7(3) of the 1986 Act provides that if any creditor or any other person is dissatisfied by any act, omission or decision of the supervisor, he may apply to the court. The court is empowered to do a number of things—including make any order it thinks fit—which could include replacing the supervisor.

Further, s 7(5) of the 1986 Act empowers the court to appoint a supervisor where it is expedient to do so and it is inexpedient, difficult or impracticable for an appointment to be made without the assistance of the court. Such an appointment might be made to replace an existing supervisor or to fill a vacancy.

Administration

The administrator is appointed by the court in the administration order[54] and the petition will name the person(s) proposed. The proposed administrator or another suitable person may also be appointed to manage the company prior to the making of the administration order.[55]

Interim appointment

The court may appoint the proposed administrator or some other suitable person to manage the company in the period between presentation of the petition and a final decision on it.[56] In Scotland the courts initially interpreted the power to make an interim order in s 9(4) of the 1986 Act as enabling them to appoint an interim administrator prior to a final decision on the petition.[57] In contrast, the courts in England and Wales took the view that although it was competent to appoint a suitable person to take control of the company and manage its affairs if the proceedings had to be adjourned to allow a person entitled to appoint an administrative receiver to decide whether to do so, it was not competent to appoint an interim administrator as such.[58] The competence of the Scottish procedure was put into doubt in *Secretary of State for Trade and Industry* v *Palmer*[59] and in *Care Scotland plc*, Petnrs,[60] the court held on the basis of that case that it could not appoint an administrator *ad interim* as such. The court did go on to appoint the proposed administrators to manage the company in the interim period, however, and it would therefore seem that, in appropriate

---

[54] 1986 Act, s 13(1).

[55] 1986 Act, s 9(4).

[56] Ibid.

[57] In the first case in which such an order was made, *Air Ecosse Ltd* (1987, unreported in relation to the initial decision to make an interim order), its competence was not disputed. The competence of such an order was disputed in the subsequent case of *Avenel Hotel Ltd*, March 1987 (unreported), but the order was held to be competent. It was also the practice to make an interim administration order at the same time.

[58] *Re a Company (No 00175 of 1987)* [1987] BCLC 467. In that case the period of notice was also abridged, and although the practice of shortening the period of notice—sometimes to the extent of making an administration order on a mere undertaking that a petition will be presented—has been described as undesirable (see Harman J in *Re Rowbotham Baxter Ltd* [1990] BCLC 397 at 399), it seems to remain the favoured method in England and Wales for dealing with urgent cases, notwithstanding that the appointment of interim managers is competent: see, for example, *Re Cavco Floors Ltd* [1990] BCLC 940; *Re Shearing and Loader Ltd* [1991] BCLC 764; *Re Gallidoro Trawlers Ltd* [1991] BCLC 411; *Re Chancery plc* [1991] BCLC 712.

[59] 1995 SLT 188.

[60] 6th June 1996 (OH) (unreported).

circumstances, an interim appointment to manage the company may still be made prior to the making of an administration order.[61]

Replacement of interim appointee

There are no specific provisions relating to the replacement of an interim appointee, but should an interim appointee require to be replaced for any reason, the court would be able to make an appropriate order under s 9(4).

Appointment of administrator

The administrator is appointed in the administration order.[62] He must be qualified to act as an insolvency practitioner in relation to the company.[63] There may be joint administrators, in which case the appointment must specify whether acts are to be done by all the administrators or by one or more of them.[64]

Replacement of administrator

There may be a number of reasons why an administrator requires to be replaced.

(1) Death. Where an administrator has died, notice of the death must be given to the court.[65]

(2) Resignation. An administrator may resign on the following grounds: ill-health; an intention to cease being in practice as an insolvency practitioner; a conflict of interest; or a change of personal circumstances which precludes him from carrying on as an administrator or makes it impracticable for him to do so.[66] He may also resign on any other ground on which the court has given him leave to resign.[67] He must give notice to specified persons of his intention to resign or his intention to apply for leave to resign.[68]

(3) Other vacation of office. An administrator is required to vacate office if he ceases to be qualified as an insolvency practitioner in relation to the company.[69] He may also be removed from office at any time by the order of the court.[70]

Where, for any reason, a vacancy occurs in the office of administrator, the court may appoint a new administrator.[71] Such an appointment may be made on the application of: any continuing administrator; where there is no such

---

[61] The exact nature of this appointment, any difference between it and previous appointments of administrators *ad interim* and the status and powers of the interim appointee are perhaps less than clear. For a detailed discussion, see McKenzie Skene and Enoch, 'Petitions for Administration Orders where there is a Need for Interim Measures: A Comparative Study of the Approach of the Courts in Scotland and in England and Wales', to be published in a forthcoming issue of the *Journal of Business Law*.

[62] 1986 Act, s 13(1).

[63] 1986 Act, s 230(1), and see Chapter 5 which deals with the qualifications of insolvency practitioners.

[64] 1986 Act, s 231(2).

[65] Scottish Rules, rule 2.19.

[66] Scottish Rules, rule 2.18(1).

[67] Scottish Rules, rule 2.18(2).

[68] Scottish Rules, rule 2.18(3).

[69] 1986 Act, s 19(1).

[70] Ibid.

[71] 1986 Act, s 13(2).

administrator, the creditors' committee; where there is no continuing administrator or creditors' committee, the company, the directors or any creditor or creditors of the company; where the company is an authorised institution or former authorised institution within the meaning of the Banking Act 1987, the Financial Services Authority.[72] Any new administrator must give notice of and advertise his appointment in the same way as an administrator appointed in the administration order itself.[73]

Receivership

Appointment of receiver

A receiver may be appointed by the chargeholder or the court.[74] A receiver may not be a body corporate, an undischarged bankrupt or a firm,[75] and an administrative receiver must be qualified to act as an insolvency practitioner in relation to the company.[76] Joint receivers may be appointed.[77] Where joint administrative receivers are appointed, the appointment must specify whether acts are to be done by all of them or by one or more of them.[78]

Where the appointment is made by the chargeholder, it must be made by a validly executed instrument of appointment.[79] For the appointment to be effective, it must be accepted by the appointee before the end of the next business day following that on which the instrument was received by him or on his behalf,[80] and in order to facilitate proof of this, the instrument of appointment must be endorsed by the appointee or on his behalf with a written docquet confirming the date and time that it was received by him or on his behalf.[81] The acceptance of the appointment need not be in writing, but it must be communicated to the floating chargeholder or his agent before the end of the next business day following that on which the instrument was received by the appointee or on his behalf, and a docquet to that effect must be endorsed on the instrument of appointment as soon as possible after acceptance.[82] An appointment of joint receivers is only effective if all the joint receivers accept appointment in the way described.[83] The receiver or, if there is a joint appointment with more than one receiver endorsing the same instrument of appointment, the last receiver so to endorse it, must then deliver a copy of the endorsed instrument of appointment to the floating chargeholder or his agent as soon as possible.[84]

---

[72] 1986 Act, s 13(3), as modified by art 2 and para 5 of the Schedule to the Banks (Administration Proceedings) Order 1989 (SI 1989/1276), as amended by the Bank of England Act 1998 (Consequential Amendments to Subordinate Legislation) Order 1998 (SI 1998/1129).

[73] Scottish Rules, rule 2.20.

[74] See Chapter 12.

[75] 1986 Act, s 51(3). A body corporate or a firm which acts as a receiver is liable to a fine and an undischarged bankrupt who does so is liable to a fine or imprisonment or both: 1986 Act, s 51(4) and (5) respectively.

[76] 1986 Act, s 230(2), and see further Chapter 5 which deals with the qualifications of insolvency practitioners.

[77] See 1986 Act, ss 51(6), 231.

[78] 1986 Act, s 231(2).

[79] 1986 Act, s 53(1). The instrument may be executed on behalf of the floating chargeholder in accordance with the provisions of s 53(4) of the 1986 Act.

[80] 1986 Act, s 53(6)(a). For the definition of the term 'business day', see the 1986 Act, s 251.

[81] 1986 Act, s 53(6)(b), and the Scottish Rules, rule 3.1(2).

[82] Scottish Rules, rule 3.1.

[83] Receivers (Scotland) Regulations (SI 1986/1917), reg 5(a).

[84] Scottish Rules, rule 3.1(3) and (4).

Where the appointment is made by the court, the receiver is appointed by an interlocutor issued by the court.[85]

Replacement of receivers

A receiver may require to be replaced for a variety of reasons.

(1) Death. Where the receiver dies, the holder of the floating charge must give notice to specified persons on becoming aware of the death.[86] A new receiver may be appointed in the normal way.

(2) Resignation. A receiver may resign for any reason at any time by giving notice of his resignation in the prescribed way to specified persons.[87] A new receiver may be appointed in the normal way.

(3) Removal. A receiver may be removed by the court on the application of the floating charge holder on cause shown.[88] A new receiver may be appointed in the normal way.

(4) Other vacation of office. An administrative receiver must vacate office if he ceases to be qualified to act as an insolvency practitioner in relation to the company.[89] A new receiver may be appointed in the normal way.

Liquidation

In all types of liquidation, the process is administered by a liquidator, who must be a qualified insolvency practitioner.[90] In a compulsory liquidation, however, he is preceded by an *interim liquidator*, appointed by the court when the winding-up order is made,[91] who may in turn be preceded by a *provisional liquidator* appointed at an earlier stage.[92] The provisions relating to voluntary and compulsory liquidations are therefore dealt with separately.

Appointment of liquidator in voluntary winding up

In a members' voluntary winding up, the liquidator is appointed by the company in general meeting.[93] Joint liquidators may be appointed;[94] and where such an appointment is made, it must specify whether acts are to be done by all of them or by one or more of them.[95]

---

[85] 1986 Act, s 54(2).

[86] Scottish Rules, rule 3.10.

[87] 1986 Act, s 62(1). For details of the manner of giving notice and the persons to whom it must be given, see the Receivers (Scotland) Regulations 1986, reg 6. The receiver must also give notice of his ceasing to act after his resignation in accordance with the 1986 Act, s 62(5).

[88] 1986 Act, s 62(1), (3). The floating chargeholder must give notice of the removal in accordance with the 1986 Act, s 62(5).

[89] 1986 Act, s 62(2). The section in fact refers to 'a receiver', which would include a receiver who was not an administrative receiver, but only an administrative receiver requires to be a qualified insolvency practitioner, and it suggested that this section must be read accordingly. Again, the receiver must give notice of his ceasing to act in accordance with the 1986 Act, s 62(5), and in addition must give further notice in accordance with the Scottish Rules, rule 3.11, to the persons prescribed therein.

[90] 1986 Act, s 230(3), and see further Chapter 5 which deals with the qualifications of insolvency practitioners.

[91] 1986 Act, s 138(1).

[92] 1986 Act, s 135(1), (3).

[93] 1986 Act, s 91.

[94] Ibid.

[95] 1986 Act, s 231(2).

In a creditors' voluntary liquidation, the creditors and the company may each nominate a liquidator at their respective meetings called under s 98 of the 1986 Act.[96] Where the creditors nominate a liquidator, that person will become liquidator,[97] but if the company has nominated a different person as liquidator, an application may be made to the court to have the company's nominee appointed liquidator in place of, or to act jointly with, the liquidator chosen by the creditors *or* to have someone else entirely appointed as liquidator.[98] Where the creditors do not nominate a liquidator but the company does, that company's nominee becomes the liquidator.[99] Where there is no nomination for liquidator by either the creditors or the company, a liquidator will be appointed by the court.[100] Joint liquidators are competent, but the appointment must specify whether acts are to be done by all of them or by one or more of them.[101]

Replacement of liquidator in voluntary winding up

The liquidator may require to be replaced for a variety of reasons.

(1) Death. Where the liquidator dies in office, notice of this must be given to specified parties.[102] In the case of a members' voluntary liquidation, a new liquidator may be appointed by the company in general meeting.[103] In the case of a creditors' voluntary liquidation, a new liquidator may be appointed by the creditors where the deceased liquidator was not appointed by the court;[104] where the deceased liquidator was appointed by the court, a new liquidator will require to be appointed by the court under s 108(1) of the 1986 Act, which allows the court to appoint a new liquidator where there is no liquidator acting for any reason.[105]

(2) Resignation. A liquidator may normally only resign on the grounds of ill-health, an intention to cease being in practice as an insolvency practitioner *or* a conflict of interest or a change of personal circumstances which precludes him from carrying on as liquidator or makes it impracticable for him to do so.[106] Where there are joint liquidators, any one of them may also resign on the ground that, in the opinion of all of them, it is no

---

[96] 1986 Act, s 100(1).
[97] 1986 Act, s 100(2).
[98] 1986 Act, s 100(3). The application may be made by any director, member or creditor of the company within seven days of the date on which the creditors' nomination was made.
[99] 1986 Act, s 100(2).
[100] 1986 Act, s 108(1). This section provides in relation to *both* a members' and a creditors' voluntary winding up that if there is no liquidator acting for any reason whatever, the court may appoint a liquidator, and would thus cover this and any other exceptional situation where no liquidator was acting.
[101] 1986 Act, s 231(2).
[102] Scottish Rules, rule 4.36, as applied to a members' voluntary liquidation by rule 6 and Sched 2, para 10, and to a creditors' voluntary liquidation by rule 5 and Sched 1, para 19.
[103] 1986 Act, s 92(1). The meeting may be convened by any contributory or any continuing liquidator and will be held in accordance with the rules laid down in the 1986 Act, the articles or any directions of the court obtained on application for same: 1986 Act, s 91(2) and (3) respectively.
[104] 1986 Act, s 104. The meeting may be convened by any creditor or any continuing liquidator: Scottish Rules, rule 4.19(7), as applied to a creditors' voluntary liquidation by rule 5 and Sched 1, para 12.
[105] This is because the 1986 Act, s 104, only allows the creditors to fill a vacancy where the liquidator was not appointed by the court.
[106] Scottish Rules, rule 4.28(3), as applied to a members' voluntary liquidation by rule 6 and Sched 2, para 9, and to a creditors' voluntary liquidation by rule 5 and Sched 1, para 16.

longer expedient for there to be the current number of joint liquidators.[107] The liquidator must call the appropriate meeting (a meeting of the creditors in the case of a creditors' voluntary liquidation and a meeting of the company in the case of a members' voluntary liquidation) to receive his resignation.[108]

In the case of a creditors' voluntary liquidation, the meeting can decide to accept or reject the liquidators' resignation.[109] Where it accepts his resignation, it may appoint a new liquidator;[110] where it rejects his resignation, the liquidator may apply to the court for leave to resign.[111] Where the court grants leave for the liquidator to resign, it may appoint a new liquidator.[112]

In the case of a members' voluntary liquidation, there is no option for the meeting of the company to refuse to accept the liquidator's resignation. The meeting may, however, appoint a new liquidator.[113]

(3) Removal. A liquidator in a voluntary liquidation may be removed by the court on cause shown[114] and a new liquidator will be appointed by the court.[115] A liquidator may also be removed by a meeting (in the case of a creditors' voluntary liquidation, a meeting of the creditors and, in the case of a members' voluntary liquidation, a meeting of the company) summoned specifically for that purpose,[116] although where the liquidator is one who has been appointed by the court under s 108 of the 1986 Act, such a meeting may only be called in specific circumstances.[117] The meeting may appoint a new liquidator to replace the one so removed in the normal way.

(4) Other vacation of office. A liquidator must vacate office if he ceases to be qualified to act as an insolvency practitioner in relation to the company.[118] A new liquidator may then be appointed in the case of a members' voluntary liquidation, by the company in general meeting[119] and, in the case of a creditors' voluntary liquidation, by the creditors.[120]

---

[107] Scottish Rules, rule 4.28(4), as applied to a members' voluntary liquidation by rule 6 and Sched 2, para 9, and to a creditors' voluntary liquidation by rule 5 and Sched 1, para 16.

[108] Scottish Rules, rule 4.28(1), as applied to a members' voluntary liquidation by rule 6 and Sched 2, para 9, and to a creditors' voluntary liquidation by rule 5 and Sched 1, para 16.

[109] If there is no quorum at the meeting, it is deemed to have been held and the liquidator's resignation accepted: Scottish Rules, rule 4.29(6), as applied to a creditors' voluntary liquidation by rule 5 and Sched 1, para 17.

[110] Assuming the resigning liquidator was not appointed by the court: 1986 Act, s 104. Where the resigning liquidator was appointed by the court, the matter would need to be dealt with under the 1986 Act, s 108(1), as discussed above in relation to death. Where an appointment is made by the meeting, the same rules apply as where a liquidator is initially so appointed: Scottish Rules, rule 4.29(5), as applied to a creditors' voluntary liquidation by rule 5 and Sched 1, para 17.

[111] Scottish Rules, rule 4.30.

[112] This could be done under the 1986 Act, s 108(1).

[113] 1986 Act, s 92(1). If no liquidator was appointed, one could be appointed by the court under the 1986 Act, s 108(1), if appropriate.

[114] 1986 Act, s 108(2).

[115] Ibid.

[116] 1986 Act, s 171(2).

[117] 1986 Act, s 171(3).

[118] 1986 Act, s 171(4).

[119] 1986 Act, s 92(1).

[120] Assuming the liquidator is not one appointed by the court: 1986 Act, s 104. Where the liquidator was appointed by the court, the matter would need to be dealt with under the 1986 Act, s 108(1), as discussed above in relation to death.

Section 108(1) of the 1986 Act[121] gives the court a general power to appoint a liquidator if, for any reason, there is no liquidator acting.

Appointment of provisional liquidator in compulsory liquidation

The court may appoint a provisional liquidator at any time between the presentation of the petition for liquidation and the first appointment of liquidators.[122] The provisional liquidator must be qualified to act as an insolvency practitioner in relation to the company.[123] An application for the appointment of a provisional liquidator may be made by the petitioner, any creditor, a contributory, the company itself or any person entitled to petition for the liquidation of the company.[124] Although the 1986 Act does not limit or define the circumstances in which such an appointment may be made, the grounds on which the appointment is sought must be averred in the application[125] and in practice the court will only make an appointment if it is satisfied that there are sufficient grounds to justify it.[126] Such grounds would include a need for someone to take control of the company's business immediately or to take action to prevent the danger of records being destroyed, assets being disposed of or directors or others absconding.

Replacement of provisional liquidator in compulsory liquidation

Provisional liquidators may require to be replaced for a number of reasons.

(1) Death. There are no specific provisions dealing with the death of a provisional liquidator in office, but the court would be able to appoint a new provisional liquidator on an application under s 135 of the 1986 Act.

(2) Resignation. A provisional liquidator may apply to the court for termination of his appointment.[127] The court has a discretion whether to grant this.[128]

(3) Removal. A provisional liquidator may be removed from office only by the court.[129] An application for termination of his appointment may be made by any person entitled to make an application for his appointment.[130]

---

[121] Referred to above.

[122] 1986 Act, s 135(1), (3). The first appointment of liquidators will be the appointment of the interim liquidator when the winding-up order is made: see the 1986 Act, s 138(1), and further below.

[123] 1986 Act, s 230(4), and see further Chapter 5 which deals with the qualifications of insolvency practitioners.

[124] Scottish Rules, rule 4.1(1). An application by the petitioner may be made either as part of the petition itself or subsequently by note in the process; any other application is made by note in the process: Sheriff Court Rules, rule 23(1); Court of Session Rules, rule 74.25(1).

[125] Sheriff Court Rules, rule 23(2)(a); Court of Session Rules, rule 74.25(2)(a).

[126] Sheriff Court Rules, rule 23(3), actually implies that an appointment can only be made in such circumstances, for it states: '[W]here the court is satisfied that sufficient grounds exist for the appointment of a provisional liquidator . . .'. In contrast, the Court of Session Rules merely state '[W]here the court decides to appoint a provisional liquidator . . .' (rule 74.25(3)). The latter is more consistent with the terms of the 1986 Act which, as indicated, does not limit or define the circumstances in which a provisional liquidator may be appointed, but in practice a provisional liquidator will only be appointed in any case if there is a justifiable reason for this.

[127] Scottish Rules, rule 4.6(1).

[128] Ibid: the rule states that the court *may* terminate the appointment.

[129] 1986 Act, s 172(2).

[130] Scottish Rules, rule 4.6(1). Those who may apply for the appointment of a provisional liquidator are listed above.

(4) Dismissal of petition. A provisional liquidator's appointment will terminate on dismissal of the liquidation petition.[131]

(5) Other vacation of office. A provisional liquidator must vacate office if he ceases to be qualified to act as an insolvency practitioner in relation to the company.[132]

Appointment of interim liquidator in compulsory liquidation

An interim liquidator is appointed by the court when the winding-up order is made.[133] He must be qualified to act as an insolvency practitioner in relation to the company.[134] The petition will usually nominate a person to act as interim liquidator, and a statement that the proposed interim liquidator is an insolvency practitioner, is duly qualified under the Act to be liquidator of the company and consents to so act, must be lodged with the court.[135]

Replacement of interim liquidator

Section 138(2) of the 1986 Act states that an interim liquidator shall continue in office until he is replaced by a liquidator appointed under ss 138 or 139,[136] but this does not cater for situations such as the death of an interim liquidator or his ceasing to be qualified as an insolvency practitioner in relation to the company, where the appointment of a new interim liquidator as such will be required. The various provisions governing replacement of liquidators generally[137] do not sit well with the provisions of s 138(2) and the correct procedure is therefore somewhat unclear.

Appointment of liquidator in compulsory winding up

The liquidator is appointed either as a result of the first meetings in the liquidation or by the court. The first meetings in the liquidation are the meetings of the creditors and contributories called by the interim liquidator specifically for the purpose of choosing a liquidator.[138] Each meeting may nominate a liquidator,[139] who may or may not be the interim liquidator, and where the creditors nominate a liquidator, that person will become liquidator.[140] If, however, the contributories have nominated a different person as liquidator, an application may be made to the court to have the contributories' nominee appointed liquidator in place of, or to act jointly with, the liquidator chosen by the creditors *or* to have someone else entirely appointed as liquidator.[141] Where the creditors do not nominate a liquidator but the contributories do, the contributories' nominee becomes the

---

[131] The court will make an appropriate order when dismissing the petition.

[132] 1986 Act, s 172(5).

[133] 1986 Act, s 138(1). See also s 138(2) which confirms that the liquidator so appointed is to be known as an interim liquidator.

[134] 1986 Act, s 230(3), and see further Chapter 5 which deals with the qualifications of insolvency practitioners.

[135] Scottish Rules, rule 4.18(2). The court will not make the appointment without such a statement.

[136] See below.

[137] Discussed further below.

[138] 1986 Act, s 138(3), and see Chapter 18.

[139] 1986 Act, s 139(2).

[140] 1986 Act, s 139(3).

[141] 1986 Act, s 139(4). The application may be made by any contributory or creditor of the company within seven days of the date on which the creditors' nomination was made.

liquidator.[142] Where neither the creditors nor the contributories nominate a liquidator, the interim liquidator must make a report to the court, which will appoint either the interim liquidator or some other person to be liquidator.[143] Where the company is being wound up on grounds which include being unable to pay its debts, the meeting of contributories may be dispensed with and only a meeting of creditors called.[144] If that meeting of creditors fails to nominate a liquidator, the interim liquidator must make a report to the court, which will appoint either the interim liquidator or some other person to be liquidator.[145] Joint liquidators are competent but the appointment must specify whether acts are to be done by all of them or by one or more of them.[146]

It should be noted that where a compulsory liquidation follows immediately upon a CVA or an administration, there are special provisions regarding the appointment of a liquidator. Where compulsory liquidation follows immediately on the discharge of an administration order, the court may appoint the (former) administrator to be the liquidator of the company.[147] Similarly, where a winding-up order is made when a CVA is in force, the court may appoint the supervisor of the CVA to be the liquidator of the company.[148]

Replacement of liquidator in compulsory liquidation

The liquidator may require to be replaced for a number of reasons.

(1) Death. Where the liquidator dies in office, notice of this must be given to the court and the Registrar of Companies.[149] There are no general provisions relating to the filling of a vacancy in the office of liquidator in a compulsory liquidation equivalent to those in ss 92, 104 and 108 of the 1986 Act relating to voluntary liquidations,[150] and those relating to resignation or removal of the liquidator are obviously not applicable to this situation, but it is thought that the liquidator might be replaced either by a meeting of the creditors or by the court.

(2) Resignation. A liquidator may resign in certain prescribed circumstances by giving notice of his resignation to the court.[151] He may normally only resign on the grounds of ill-health, an intention to cease being in practice as an insolvency practitioner *or* a conflict of interest or a change of personal circumstances which precludes him from carrying on as liquidator or makes it impracticable for him to do so.[152] Where there are joint liquidators, any one of them may also resign on the ground that, in the opinion of all of them, it is no longer expedient for there to be the current number of joint liquidators.[153] The Scottish Rules provide that a liquidator who wishes to

---

[142] 1986 Act, s 139(3).
[143] 1986 Act, s 138(5).
[144] 1986 Act, s 138(4).
[145] 1986 Act, s 138(5).
[146] 1986 Act, s 231(2).
[147] 1986 Act, s 140(1).
[148] 1986 Act, s 140(2).
[149] Scottish Rules, rule 4.36.
[150] See above.
[151] 1986 Act, s 172(6).
[152] Scottish Rules, rule 4.28(3).
[153] Scottish Rules, rule 4.28(4).

resign must call a meeting of creditors to receive his resignation[154] and the meeting must decide whether to accept or reject it.[155] Where it accepts it, it may appoint a new liquidator;[156] where it rejects it, the liquidator may apply to the court for leave to resign.[157] Where leave to resign is granted, there again arises the issue of how the liquidator is to be replaced, for no specific provision is made for this and, as indicated in the preceding paragraph, there are no general provisions relating to the filling of a vacancy in the office of liquidator in a compulsory liquidation.[158] It is thought that the liquidator might be replaced either by a subsequent meeting of the creditors or by the court.

(3) Removal. A liquidator may be removed by the court.[159] Those who may apply to the court for the removal of the liquidator are not specified, and so it must be presumed that anyone who can demonstrate sufficient title and interest in the normal way may do so.[160] Where the court removes the liquidator on such an application, it may appoint a new one.[161] A liquidator may also be removed by a meeting of creditors specifically called for that purpose,[162] although, in the majority of cases, where the liquidator was appointed by the court, a meeting of creditors for the purpose of removing the liquidator may only be summoned in specified circumstances.[163] Where the liquidator is removed, the meeting may appoint a new liquidator to replace him.[164]

(4) Other vacation of office. A liquidator must vacate office if he ceases to be qualified to act as an insolvency practitioner in relation to the company.[165]

---

[154] Scottish Rules, rule 4.28(1). It has been held in England that a liquidator may apply to the court directly under s 172(2) for his own removal and replacement where he wishes to resign, rather than go through the procedure just described: see *Re Sankey Furniture Ltd, ex parte Harding* [1995] 2 BCLC 594; *Re Sutton (Removal of Liquidator), The Times,* 3rd November 1997. This certainly seems to be consistent with the terms of s 172(2).

[155] If there is no quorum at the meeting, it is deemed to have been held and the liquidator's resignation accepted: Scottish Rules, rule 4.29(6).

[156] Where an appointment is made by the meeting, the same rules apply as where a liquidator is initially so appointed: Scottish Rules, rule 4.29(5).

[157] Scottish Rules, rule 4.30.

[158] See above.

[159] 1986 Act, s 172(2).

[160] Curiously, the Court of Session Rules in specifying the procedure for applications to the court for removal of a liquidator under s 172 refer only to applications by a creditor (rule 74.29), but this cannot be read as restricting applicants to that category. The Sheriff Court Company Insolvency Rules specify the procedure for such an application without any such restriction (rule 27).

[161] This is implicit from rule 4.26(4).

[162] 1986 Act, s 172(2).

[163] See the 1986 Act, s 172(3). The exceptions are where the liquidator appointed by the court is either a contributories' nominee appointed under s 139(4)(a) or a former administrator appointed where liquidation followed immediately on discharge of an administration order under s 140(1).

[164] This is implicit from rule 4.24(1)(a) of the Scottish Rules.

[165] 1986 Act, s 172(5).

Part III

ADMINISTRATION OF THE INSOLVENT ESTATE

20 : FUNCTIONS AND POWERS OF INTERIM APPOINTEES

It has already been noted that, in sequestration, administration and compulsory liquidation, an interim appointment may be made by the court to preserve the position pending a final decision on whether or not to make the relevant order and that, in sequestration and compulsory liquidation, an interim appointment is made when the award of sequestration/winding-up order is made.[1]

This chapter considers the functions and powers of such interim appointees.

Interim trustee in sequestration

An interim trustee appointed before the award of sequestration and an interim trustee appointed when the award of sequestration is made have the same functions and powers.

Functions of interim trustee

The general functions of an interim trustee are set out in s 2 of the 1985 Act. They are:

(1) To safeguard the debtor's estate pending the appointment of a permanent trustee.[2]

(2) To ascertain the reasons for the debtor's insolvency.[3]

(3) To ascertain what the debtor's assets and liabilities are.[4]

(4) To administer the sequestration process pending the appointment of a permanent trustee.[5]

(5) In the case of an interim trustee who is a private insolvency practitioner, to supply various information to the Accountant in Bankruptcy.[6]

---

[1] See, in particular, the preceding chapter for details of these appointments.
[2] 1985 Act, s 2(4)(a).
[3] 1985 Act, s 2(4)(b).
[4] 1985 Act, s 2(4)(c).
[5] 1985 Act, s 2(4)(d).
[6] 1985 Act, s 2(4)(e). This requirement remains even after the interim trustee has ceased to act in the sequestration.

Powers of interim trustee

The interim trustee is essentially a caretaker, but has extensive powers. These are contained for the most part in s 18 of the 1985 Act, which deals with interim preservation of the estate. In terms of that section, the interim trustee may give the debtor directions about the management of his estate.[7] In addition, in carrying out the functions described above, he may do the following things.

(1) Recover from the debtor money, valuables or documents relating to his business or financial affairs[8] and place them in safe custody.[9]

(2) Sell or otherwise dispose of perishable goods.[10] Normally, disposal of the estate would be a matter for the permanent trustee, but in the case of perishable goods, it may be necessary to act immediately so that the value of the goods, if not the goods themselves, is retained for the estate.

(3) Inventory the debtor's property.[11]

(4) Require the debtor to carry through any transaction which he has already entered[12]—for example, a contract of sale of the debtor's property.

(5) Take out or maintain insurance policies for the debtor's business or property.[13] This is essential in case it should be stolen or otherwise damaged or destroyed.

(6) Borrow money where necessary to safeguard the debtor's estate.[14] For example, the trustee may wish to borrow money to complete the purchase of an asset so as to preserve it as part of the estate.

(7) Carry on the debtor's business[15] or close it down.[16]

In addition, the interim trustee may apply to the court for the following.

(1) A warrant to enter and search the debtor's house or business premises.[17] A warrant is necessary because of the invasion of the debtor's privacy.

(2) Any other order for the purpose of safeguarding the debtor's estate.[18] This is a catch-all provision. An example of the type of order which can be made under this subsection can be seen in the case of *Scottish & Newcastle plc*, Petnrs,[19] where the court authorised the interim trustee to sell licensed premises in the special circumstances of that case.

The interim trustee also has the power to request the debtor, the debtor's spouse or any other person the trustee thinks can give him information about the

---

[7] 1985 Act, s 18(1). The debtor may appeal against any such directions if he thinks they are unreasonable, but must comply with them in the meantime: 1985 Act, s 18(4).
[8] 1985 Act, s 18(2)(a).
[9] 1985 Act, s 18(2)(b).
[10] 1985 Act, s 18(2)(c).
[11] 1985 Act, s 18(2)(d).
[12] 1985 Act, s 18(2)(e).
[13] 1985 Act, s 18(2)(f).
[14] 1985 Act, s 18(2)(h).
[15] Ibid.
[16] 1985 Act, s 18(2)(g).
[17] 1985 Act, s 18(3)(b).
[18] 1985 Act, s 18(2)(c).
[19] (OH) 1992 SCLR 540 (Notes).

debtor's financial affairs to appear before him and give him such information.[20] He also has the power to apply to the court for an order for a private examination of any of these persons.[21]

Interim appointment in administration

The functions and powers of an interim appointee in administration are at present somewhat unclear. The 1986 Act does not specify what functions and powers such an interim appointee should have. Until relatively recently, it was the practice of the court to appoint an administrator *ad interim* in appropriate cases,[22] without further specification of that appointee's functions and powers. There appears to have been a general consensus among such appointees that their function was to perform a holding operation pending the final decision on the administration petition, but less consensus on the powers attached to the appointment, some believing that they had the powers of a full administrator, others that their powers were more restricted.[23] The practice of appointing interim administrators as such has been discontinued, but the court may still make interim appointments to manage the company pending a final decision on the petition.[24] In the case of *Care (Scotland) plc*[25] the court specifically refused to specify the functions and powers which the appointees should have and doubt therefore remains as to what these are. It is thought that such appointees should not be regarded as having the functions and powers of full administrators but rather as being the equivalent of a provisional liquidator.[26] It is suggested that the 1986 Act requires to be amended to clarify the functions and powers of such appointees; in the meantime, confusion might be avoided if specific functions and powers were sought in the application for appointment and spelt out in the interlocutor.

Provisional and interim liquidator

Functions and powers of provisional liquidator

Where a provisional liquidator is appointed, he has the functions conferred on him by the court.[27] In addition, he is required to take into his custody and control all the property to which the company is, or appears to be, entitled.[28] Technically, because he is a liquidator, albeit a provisional one, a provisional liquidator appears to have all the powers of a liquidator,[29] and s 135(5) of the 1986 Act appears to support this interpretation by providing that the provisional liquidator's powers may be *limited* by the court.[30] In practice, however, specific

---

[20] 1985 Act, s 20(4).
[21] Ibid. Recovery of information generally is discussed further in Chapter 29.
[22] See the preceding chapter.
[23] This information was gained as a result of a research project carried out in 1996, the findings of which will be published in an article by the author and Yvonne Enoch entitled 'Petitions for Administration Orders where there is a Need for Interim Measures: A Comparative Study of the Approach of the Courts in Scotland and in England and Wales' in a forthcoming issue of the *Journal of Business Law*.
[24] *Care (Scotland) plc* (OH) 6th June 1996 (unreported) and see the preceding chapter.
[25] Ibid.
[26] See below.
[27] 1986 Act, s 135(4).
[28] 1986 Act, s 144(1).
[29] The powers of a liquidator are discussed in Chapter 28.
[30] 1986 Act, s 135(5).

powers are usually sought in the application for the provisional liquidator's appointment and only such powers are conferred on the provisional liquidator by the court. The powers sought are usually limited to the power conferred on a liquidator by para 5 of Part II of Sched 4 to the 1986 Act (ie, the power to carry on the business of the company),[31] although further powers may be sought and conferred as appropriate in the circumstances. Separately from this, a provisional liquidator has a statutory power to require any of the persons subject to an obligation to provide a statement of affairs to provide him with such a statement[32] and to apply for the appointment of a special manager where it appears to him that the nature of the company's business or property, or the interests of the company's creditors, contributories or members generally, require such an appointment.[33]

Functions and powers of interim liquidator

An interim liquidator is a liquidator, albeit an interim one, and technically therefore has all the functions and powers of a liquidator.[34] In practice, however, the interim liquidator's main function is to call the meetings of the company and its creditors for the purpose of electing a liquidator.[35] In the meantime, he will take into his custody and control all the property to which the company is, or appears to be, entitled[36] and may, with the requisite sanction, run the business and do such other things as are necessary in order to preserve the position pending his replacement by the liquidator.[37]

---

[31] The powers of a liquidator are discussed in Chapter 28.
[32] 1986 Act, s 131. Statements of affairs are discussed further in Chapter 29.
[33] 1986 Act, s 177. The provisions of this section are discussed further in Chapter 28 in the context of the powers of a liquidator.
[34] See Chapter 28.
[35] 1986 Act, s 138(3), and see Chapter 18.
[36] 1986 Act, s 144(1), and Scottish Rules, rule 4.22(1).
[37] See Chapter 28 in relation to the liquidator's powers generally.

21 : THE EFFECT OF INSOLVENCY PROCEEDINGS ON THE DEBTOR'S PROPERTY: PROPERTY AFFECTED AND THE NATURE OF THE OFFICE HOLDER'S RIGHT

The effect of particular insolvency proceedings on the debtor's property and the nature of the office holder's right to the property vary according to the proceedings in question.

This chapter considers the effects of the different insolvency proceedings on the debtor's property and the nature of the office holder's right in each case; Chapter 22 discusses types of property which raise special issues on insolvency.

Sequestration

Following confirmation of the permanent trustee's election or his appointment by the court, he is issued with his act and warrant by the sheriff clerk. The act and warrant has the effect of vesting, as at the date of sequestration, the whole estate of the debtor in the permanent trustee for the benefit of the creditors.[1]

The concept of vesting

In broad terms, vesting means that ownership of the property in question is transferred from the debtor to the permanent trustee. This is the effect of s 31 of the 1985 Act, which provides that:

(1) In relation to heritable property, the act and warrant has the effect of a decree in an action of adjudication in implement of sale as well as in such an action for payment and in security of debt.[2]

(2) In relation to moveable property, where delivery, possession or intimation of its assignation would normally be required to transfer title, the act and warrant vests the property in the permanent trustee as if delivery, possession or intimation had taken place at the date of sequestration.[3]

(3) Any non-vested contingent interest vests in the permanent trustee as if it had been assigned by the debtor and intimated to the permanent trustee on the date of sequestration.[4]

---

[1] 1985 Act, s 31(1).
[2] 1985 Act, s 31(1)(b).
[3] 1985 Act, s 31(4).
[4] 1985 Act, s 31(5).

The nature of the trustee's right to the debtor's property

The trustee generally acquires a real right to the debtor's moveable property, but in some cases further steps are necessary to complete title to the property and to give him a real right to it—for example, registration of shares in a company. It has traditionally been accepted that if this is not done, there is a danger that a prior transferee of the debtor may obtain a title preferable to that of the trustee by completing his own right to the property in question before the trustee does so.[5] The trustee's position may have changed, however, as a result of the decision of the House of Lords in *Sharp v Woolwich Building Society*.[6]

The trustee does not acquire a real right to heritage. In order to obtain a real right to heritage the trustee must take the necessary steps to complete his title, usually by recording a title to the heritage in his own name, as trustee, in the Register of Sasines or registering such a title in the Land Register.[7] The trustee will not invariably go to the trouble of doing so, since he may deal with the property without completing title in this way.[8] Again, it has traditionally been accepted that if he does not do so, or if he delays in doing so, there is a risk that someone else to whom the debtor has granted a title prior to the sequestration will be able to complete title first and so obtain a real right to the property which will be preferred to that of the trustee: the so-called 'Race to the Register'. Once again, however, the trustee's position may have changed as a result of the decision in *Sharp v Woolwich Building Society*.[9]

The trustee does not, in general, acquire any better right to the estate which has vested in him than the debtor had, and his title is therefore generally subject to any limitations which affected the debtor's title.[10] The trustee is said to take the property *tantum et tale*. This principle is part of the common law[11] and is not explicitly mentioned in the 1985 Act, although s 33(3) of the 1985 Act, which provides that the vesting of property in the trustee under the Act is without prejudice to the rights of secured creditors which are preferable to the right of the trustee, is effectively an example of its operation.[12] Rather, it continues to exist alongside the provisions of the 1985 Act. There are, however, some circumstances in which the trustee may be said to be in a better position than the debtor in relation to property vesting in him. The trustee may deal with heritable property despite any inhibitions against the debtor[13] and in certain circumstances diligence will be ineffective to secure a preference over the trustee;[14] further, the

---

[5] *Morrison v Harrison* (1876) 3 R 406, which concerned shares in a company.

[6] 1997 SC (HL) 66, sub nom *Sharp v Thomson*. The decision and its implications are discussed in the following chapter.

[7] Where the debtor himself has only an uncompleted right to the heritage, the trustee may complete title in his own or the debtor's name: 1985 Act, s 31(3).

[8] See further Chapter 24.

[9] Note 6 above and see further the following chapter.

[10] Although it is not clear whether his right to the debtor's home is affected by the occupancy rights of a non-entitled spouse under the Matrimonial Homes Act 1981: see McBryde, *Bankruptcy*, pp 204–207, and further sources there cited.

[11] The leading case is *Heritable Reversionary Co. Ltd v Millar* (1892) 19 R (HL) 43.

[12] Property subject to security is discussed further in the following chapter. See also the 1985 Act, s 51(6), and Chapter 32 in relation to the effect of this principle on the ranking of creditors' claims.

[13] 1985 Act, s 31(2).

[14] See Chapter 31.

trustee may challenge certain transactions of the debtor which the debtor would not have been in a position to reverse.[15]

Property affected by the sequestration

Section 31(1) of the 1985 Act vests 'the whole estate of the debtor' in the permanent trustee. This in turn is defined in s 31(8) as the whole estate of the debtor as at the date of sequestration, wherever situated, including any income or estate vesting in the debtor on that date, and any rights which the debtor was entitled to exercise in relation to his property.[16] It does not, however, include the debtor's interest in certain specified types of tenancies (although such an interest may vest in the trustee following service of an appropriate notice by him),[17] and certain property is specifically excluded from vesting in the trustee, namely property which is exempt from poinding for the purposes of protecting the debtor and his family[18] and property which the debtor holds in trust for another.[19]

Section 31 of the 1985 Act deals only with the estate held by the debtor at the date of sequestration. Income or property acquired by the debtor after that date, generally referred to as *acquirenda*, is dealt with in s 32 of the 1985 Act. Income which derives from the estate vested in the permanent trustee vests in the permanent trustee, but any other income received by the debtor—for example from employment—vests in the debtor.[20] The trustee may, however, apply to the court for an order requiring a debtor to pay to the trustee any income which is in excess of the sum the court considers suitable for the debtor's own aliment and any 'relevant obligations' which he may have.[21] 'Relevant obligations' are aliment,[22] periodical allowance and child support under the Child Support Act 1991.[23] In deciding how much should be allowed for any relevant obligation, the court is not bound by any prior decree or agreement fixing the amount of aliment or periodical allowance. So if, for example, a debtor was obliged to pay his wife aliment of £250 per month under a separation agreement, the court fixing the amount allowable as a relevant obligation for this purpose would not be bound to allow all of the £250 as a relevant obligation. The Act does not contain any guidelines as to how the court should decide what is a suitable amount for the debtor's aliment and his relevant obligations. In the case of *Brown's Tr v Brown*[24] the court made clear that there is no 'formula' for calculating the sum which is to be paid over to the trustee, but set out a number of principles to be applied by the court in deciding the appropriate amount. These included balancing the interests of the creditors and the debtor; considering the total amount of debts and how much the creditors are likely to receive in the sequestration; and that the debtor should not have much free income after the payment to the trustee. The debtor, the permanent trustee or any other interested person may apply

---

[15] Challengeable transactions are dealt with in Chapter 30.
[16] 1985 Act, s 31(8).
[17] 1985 Act, s 31(9), (10).
[18] 1985 Act, s 33(1)(a). The property so exempted is defined in s 16 of the Debtors (Scotland) Act 1987.
[19] 1985 Act, s 33(1)(b). See *Council of the Law Society of Scotland v McKinnie* (IH) 1991 SCLR 850.
[20] 1985 Act, s 32(1).
[21] 1985 Act, s 32(2).
[22] As defined in the Family Law (Scotland) Act 1985: 1985 Act, s 32(3)(a).
[23] 1985 Act, s 32(3).
[24] 1995 SLT (Sh Ct) 2.

to the court to have any order varied or recalled if circumstances change.[25] It should be noted that creditors of the debtor cannot use diligence to attach post-sequestration income to satisfy pre-sequestration debts.[26] They can, however, attach it in relation to debts which arose after the sequestration and which are not included in the sequestration. It would appear, however, that if the debtor is entitled to benefits, the Secretary of State for Social Security may make deductions from them in relation to pre-sequestration debts in the form of loans to the debtor from the Social Fund, on the grounds, *inter alia*, that the deductions are not diligence.[27]

Property which is acquired by the debtor after the date of sequestration but before his discharge, and which would have vested in the trustee if it had belonged to the debtor on the date of sequestration, vests in the trustee.[28] Thus if the debtor receives, for example, an inheritance or gift, this will vest in the trustee and not the debtor. The debtor is not free to deal with the property in any way[29] and must notify the permanent trustee of any assets he acquires.[30]

Company insolvency proceedings

All company insolvency proceedings differ from sequestration because the company's property does not generally vest in the office holder concerned.[31] There is provision for the court in a compulsory liquidation to vest specific property in the liquidator on his application,[32] and this provision may also be invoked in a voluntary liquidation by virtue of s 112(1) of the 1986 Act,[33] but this is relatively rare. Title to the company's property therefore remains with the company although the relevant office holder is given appropriate powers to ingather and deal with it.

The property affected by the proceedings and the extent of the office holder's right vary according to the proceedings concerned. Each is now considered individually.

Company voluntary arrangements

The property which is affected by a CVA depends on the terms of the particular arrangement. The proposal must contain details of any assets of the company which are to be excluded from the arrangement and also any assets other than those belonging to the company which are to be included in the arrangement.[34]

---

[25] 1985 Act, s 32(5). For instance, the debtor may lose the job which gave rise to the income, or he may obtain a better-paid job allowing the amount payable to the trustee to be increased. The debtor is under an obligation to notify the permanent trustee of any change in his financial circumstances, failure to do so being an offence: 1985 Act, s 32(7).

[26] 1985 Act, s 32(5).

[27] *Mulvey* v *Secretary of State for Social Security* 1997 SC (HL)105.

[28] 1985 Act, s 32(6).

[29] See, for example, *Alliance & Leicester Building Society* v *Murray's Tr* 1995 SLT (Sh Ct) 77; cf *Royal Bank of Scotland plc* v *Lamb's Tr* (OH) 1998 SCLR 923; and see further Chapter 23.

[30] 1985 Act, s 32(7). Failure to do so is an offence.

[31] Indeed, in the case of a section 425 arrangement, there is no office holder as such at all, unless the company is also in administration, liquidation or receivership.

[32] 1986 Act, s 145(1).

[33] Which empowers the liquidator, any contributory or any creditor to apply to the court, *inter alia*, to exercise any of the powers which the court might exercise if the company were being wound up by the court.

[34] Scottish Rules, rule 1.3(2) (directors' proposal); the provisions of this rule are also applied to proposals by administrators or liquidators by rule 1.10.

Once the arrangement has been approved, the supervisor will be put in possession of all the assets included in the arrangement.[35] The supervisor has no higher or better right to the property included in the arrangement than the company has; except to the extent to which it is competent for the CVA to confer this and it in fact does so—for example, property subject to a security remains subject to that security except to the extent that the secured creditor's rights are altered by the CVA.[36] The supervisor's dealings with the property will therefore be constrained by any third-party rights and interests and any other limitations on the company's rights to the property which is included in the CVA in the same way as the company's own dealings would be except to the extent provided for in the agreement.

Section 425 arrangements

The property to be included in a section 425 arrangement will depend on the terms of the arrangement itself.

Administration

An administration order places the 'affairs, business and property' of the company in the hands of an administrator.[37] 'Property' is defined in s 436 of the 1986 Act as *including* 'money, goods, things in action, land and every description of property wherever situated and also obligations and every description of interest, whether present or future or vested or contingent, arising out of, or incidental to, property'.

Since title to the property remains with the company, it continues to be affected by third-party rights and interests and other limitations on the company's rights to the property—for example, securities,[38] diligence,[39] leases—and the administrator is constrained accordingly in his dealings with the property. The administrator is, however, in a better position than the company in some respects. For example, although the rights of creditors remain valid and cannot be overridden by the administrator, the statutory moratorium prevents most creditors from enforcing their rights against the company's property without the leave of the court;[40] the administrator has certain powers in relation to the disposal of secured property and property which is subject to hire-purchase agreements, conditional sale agreements, chattel leasing agreements and retention of title agreements;[41] and the administrator may challenge certain transactions of the company which the company itself would not have been in a position to reverse.[42]

Receivership

On the appointment of a receiver, the floating charge by virtue of which he was appointed crystallises and attaches to 'the property then subject to the

---

[35] Scottish Rules, rule 1.19(1).
[36] Any such alteration would have had to have been specifically consented to by the security holder: see Chapter 8.
[37] 1986 Act, s 8(2).
[38] See further the following chapter and Chapter 32.
[39] See further Chapter 31.
[40] The effect of the statutory moratorium is discussed in Chapter 10.
[41] 1986 Act, s 15, and see further Chapter 26.
[42] Challengeable transactions are dealt with in Chapter 30.

charge'.[43] The property affected by the receivership therefore depends on the wording of the charge. Most modern charges are granted over all of the company's property.

On crystallisation, the charge has effect as if it were a fixed security over the property to which it has attached[44]—for example, it will have effect in relation to heritable property as if it was a standard security.

The property which is subject to the charge may also be affected by third-party rights and interests and other limitations. The 1986 Act provides that the powers of the receiver are subject to the rights of the holder of any fixed security or floating charge which has priority over, or ranks *pari passu* with, the floating charge under which the receiver is appointed[45] and to the rights of any person who has 'effectually executed diligence' on all or any part of the company's property prior to the receiver's appointment.[46] The receiver is, however, in certain respects in a better position than the company, since he need not concern himself with diligence other than effectually executed diligence, and he has certain powers in relation to the disposal of secured property and property subject to effectually executed diligence.[47] He does not, however, have the power to challenge prior transactions of the company.[48]

Liquidation

The 1986 Act refers variously to the assets, the property and the funds from the assets of the company in liquidation. In relation to voluntary liquidations, s 107 of the 1986 Act provides, *inter alia*, for the application of 'the company's property' in payment of its liabilities in accordance with the section. There is no directly equivalent section in relation to compulsory liquidations, but s 143 of the 1986 Act speaks of the assets of the company being got in, realised and distributed to the company's creditors, and s 144 of the 1986 Act provides that where a winding-up order is made or a provisional liquidator is appointed, the liquidator or provisional liquidator must take charge of 'all the property or things in action to which the company is or appears to be entitled'.[49] 'Property' is defined in s 436 of the

---

[43] 1986 Act, s 53(7) (receiver appointed by chargeholder) and s 54(6) (receiver appointed by the court). It should be noted that where a floating charge crystallises on liquidation, rather than on the appointment of a receiver, the statutory wording is slightly different in that the charge is said to attach to 'the property then comprised in the company's property and undertaking or, as the case may be, in part of that property and undertaking': Companies Act 1985, s 463(4). It is thought, however, that in *The Law of Corporate Insolvency in Scotland* (2nd edn) St Clair and Drummond Young are correct in stating, at p 139, that the different wording has no legal import.

[44] 1986 Act, s 53(7) (receiver appointed by chargeholder) and s 54(6) (receiver appointed by the court). Where the charge crystallises on liquidation, the relevant provision is s 436(2) of CA 1985.

[45] 1986 Act, s 55(3)(b). Where the floating charge has crystallised on liquidation, the equivalent provision is s 463(1)(b) of CA 1985.

[46] 1986 Act, s 55(3)(a). Where the floating charge has crystallised on liquidation, the equivalent provision is s 463(1)(c) of CA 1985. For the meaning of 'effectually executed diligence', see Chapter 31 which deals with diligence and insolvency generally.

[47] 1986 Act, s 61, and see further Chapter 27.

[48] See further Chapter 27.

[49] See also rule 4.22 of the Scottish Rules which requires the liquidator to take possession of 'the whole assets of the company and any property . . . in the possession or control of the company or to which the company appears to be entitled'. The rule applies to both creditors' and members' voluntary liquidations by virtue, respectively, of rule 5 and Sched 1 and rule 6 and Sched 2 to the Scottish Rules.

1986 Act as *including* 'money, goods, things in action, land and every description of property wherever situated and also obligations and every description of interest, whether present or future or vested or contingent, arising out of, or incidental to, property'.

Since title to the property remains with the company, it continues to be affected by third-party rights and interests and other limitations on the company's rights to the property—for example, securities,[50] diligence,[51] leases. In certain respects, however, the liquidator is in a better position than the company itself: certain diligences will not be effective to secure a preference over the liquidation[52] and a liquidator may challenge certain transactions of the company which the company itself would not have been in a position to reverse.[53]

---

[50] See further the following chapter and Chapter 32.
[51] See further Chapter 31.
[52] Ibid.
[53] Challengeable transactions are dealt with in Chapter 30.

22 : THE EFFECT OF INSOLVENCY PROCEEDINGS ON THE DEBTOR'S PROPERTY: TYPES OF PROPERTY RAISING SPECIAL ISSUES

S ome types of property raise special issues in the context of insolvency, whether in relation to some or all types of debtor and/or some or all types of insolvency proceedings. This chapter examines the types of property which raise such issues.

Property subject to a security

The concept of security and its role on insolvency

The classic definition of security is 'any right which a creditor may hold for ensuring the payment or satisfaction of his debt, distinct from, and in addition to, his right of action and execution against the debtor under the latter's personal obligation'.[1] Security rights are important in the context of insolvency law because their very purpose is to protect the creditor in the event of the debtor's insolvency by putting that creditor in a better position than the debtor's other, unsecured, creditors. A secured creditor is, in general terms, effectively insulated from the effect of any insolvency proceedings affecting the debtor, because he is entitled to enforce his security and thereby receive payment of his debt regardless of the existence of such proceedings.[2]

A security may be over the property of the debtor, over the property of a third party or in the form of a cautionary obligation where the creditor has the right to proceed against another for payment of his debt,[3] but insolvency proceedings are generally concerned solely with security over the debtor's property. This is reflected in the definitions of security and secured creditor in the relevant insolvency legislation. For the purposes of the 1985 Act, a secured creditor is defined as 'a creditor who holds *a security for his debt over any part of the debtor's*

---

[1] Gloag and Irvine, *Law of Rights in Security and Cautionary Obligations* (1897), pp 1–2.
[2] It should be noted that receivership, which is the means of enforcing the particular type of security known as a floating charge, is also separately regarded as insolvency proceedings of itself.
[3] A security over heritable or moveable property is generally referred to as a real right in security because it confers rights against the specific property which is the subject of the security allowing the creditor first claim on that property for the purposes of payment of his debt. A cautionary obligation, however, is generally referred to as a personal security right, because it does not confer rights against property, but against another person.

estate' and security is defined as 'any security, heritable or moveable, or any right of lien, retention or preference'[4] and, for the purpose of the various insolvency proceedings under the 1986 Act, a secured creditor is defined as 'except in so far as the context otherwise requires . . . a creditor of the company who holds in respect of his debt *a security over property of the company*' and security is defined as 'except in so far as the context otherwise requires . . . any security (whether heritable or moveable), any floating charge and any right of lien or preference and any right of retention (other than a right of compensation or set off)'[5] (emphases added). In the following discussion, references to secured creditors and to security are to those terms as defined by the 1985 and 1986 Acts unless the contrary is stated.

The effect of a security over the debtor's property on insolvency

Insolvency is the 'acid test' of a security. It was noted in the preceding chapter that, on sequestration, the debtor's property vests in the trustee subject to the right of any secured creditor which is preferable to the rights of the permanent trustee.[6] It was also noted that in company insolvency proceedings, the property affected by the relevant proceedings does not generally vest in the office holder and title to it remains with the company while the relevant office holder is given appropriate powers to deal with it, and the property remains subject to any valid security over it. This has two main effects. First, all insolvency office holders are constrained in their dealings with property subject to a security by the rights of the security holder,[7] except in the circumstances and to the extent provided for by the legislation itself.[8] Secondly, the ranking of claims in those proceedings where this applies is subject to the rights of secured creditors.[9]

Restrictions on the rights of secured creditors on insolvency

The legislation imposes a number of restrictions on the rights of secured creditors in the context of particular insolvency proceedings. These are:

(1) Certain restrictions are placed on the enforcement of a security over a company's property by the presentation of a petition for an administration order and by any subsequent administration order.[10]

(2) A trustee in sequestration and a liquidator may sell heritable property which is subject to a heritable security or securities where the rights of the secured creditor(s) are preferable to those of the trustee or liquidator, although the consent of the creditor(s) concerned will be required unless a sufficiently high price is obtained to discharge every security in full.[11] A trustee or liquidator who wishes to sell must intimate his intention to do so to the heritable creditor(s), but once he has done so the heritable

---

[4] 1985 Act, s 73(1). What exactly is encompassed within that definition is discussed further below.
[5] 1986 Act, s 248.
[6] The definition of secured creditor is discussed above.
[7] There is, of course, no office holder in section 425 proceedings unless the company is also in administration, receivership or liquidation. The company's property, however, remains subject to any security over it except to the extent modified by the arrangement itself, which will affect the implementation of the arrangement: see the preceding chapter.
[8] See below.
[9] Ranking of claims is dealt with in Chapter 33.
[10] See further Chapter 10.
[11] 1985 Act, s 39(4), applied to liquidations by 1986 Act, s 185(1). See also Chapters 24 and 28.

creditor(s) are precluded from enforcing their security or securities unless the trustee or liquidator delays unreasonably.[12]

(3) An administrator and a receiver have certain powers in relation to the disposal of property which is subject to a security.[13]

(4) In sequestration and all types of insolvency proceedings under the 1986 Act, a secured creditor must deduct the value of his security, as estimated by him, from the amount of his claim, unless he surrenders it or undertakes in writing to surrender it for the benefit of the debtor's estate/the company's assets.[14]

(5) In sequestration and liquidation, the trustee or liquidator may require a secured creditor to discharge his security or convey or assign it to him on payment of its value as estimated by the creditor and, where this has been done, the creditor must deduct the payment received by him from the amount of his claim.[15] A creditor whose security has been realised must also deduct the net proceeds of the security (ie, the proceeds of the security less the expenses of realisation) from his claim.[16]

It should be noted, however, that although a CVA may be approved by the specified majority of creditors and thereby bind dissenting creditors,[17] it is specifically provided that it may *not* affect the right of a secured creditor of the company to enforce his security except with his specific consent.[18]

Diligence as a security

It is generally accepted that one of the ways of acquiring a right of security over property is by the use of diligence.[19] Whether diligence can be said to be a security within the definitions contained within the 1985 and 1986 Acts, however, is an issue which is not free from difficulty. This is discussed further in the next section.

Property affected by diligence

Where a debtor is insolvent, the law regulates diligence carried out by creditors in order to ensure that some creditors do not gain an advantage over others. Currently, there are rules regulating diligence both outwith formal insolvency proceedings and in the context of such proceedings. The result of these rules is that certain diligence is ineffectual to secure any preference over other creditors or subsequent insolvency proceedings. These rules are discussed in detail in Chapter 31.

Where diligence is not affected by these rules, the question arises as to what effect it has in the context of any formal insolvency proceedings. It was noted in the preceding section that in general terms the use of diligence is regarded as

---

[12] Ibid.
[13] See Chapters 26 and 27 respectively.
[14] See further Chapter 32.
[15] Ibid.
[16] Ibid.
[17] See Chapter 8.
[18] 1986 Act, s 4(3), and see ibid.
[19] Gloag and Henderson, *Introduction to the Law of Scotland* (10th edn), para 19.1.

creating a security over the property affected by the diligence, but the question of whether it was a security within the definitions contained in the 1985 and 1986 Acts was not free from doubt. If valid diligence *is* a security for the purpose of any formal insolvency proceedings under the 1985 and 1986 Acts, the result of this would be as described in the preceding section. If it is not, this would leave the question as to what effect it did have. This issue is explored further in Chapter 31.

Property subject to retention of title

The concept of retention of title and its role in insolvency proceedings

It is very common for suppliers of goods to commercial buyers to include in their contracts a provision, generally referred to as a retention (or reservation) of title clause, to the effect that ownership in the goods remains with the seller until certain conditions, usually relating to payment, are satisfied. Where property has been purchased by a debtor subject to a valid retention of title,[20] it continues to belong to the seller until the conditions under which title is to pass are satisfied. The importance of such clauses in the context of insolvency is that because title remains with the seller, the property does not form part of the debtor's property for the purposes of the insolvency proceedings. Such property does not vest in a trustee in sequestration and, except in certain circumstances where there is specific statutory provision to the contrary,[21] cannot be dealt with by the relevant office holder in company insolvency proceedings as part of the company's property, unless the conditions on which property is to pass are satisfied. Retention of title clauses raise a variety of issues.[22]

Forms of retention of title clauses

Retention of title clauses are found in a variety of forms, some of which are very complex, and questions may arise as to the validity of a clause or parts of it. There are two main types of retention of title clause, 'simple' and 'all sums'. Simple retention of title clauses provide for title to goods to be retained by the seller only until the price of those particular goods has been paid. Such clauses are valid retentions of title. Section 17(1) of the Sale of Goods Act 1979 provides that in a sale of specific or ascertained goods, property passes when the parties intend it to pass, which may be before or after delivery, and s 19(1) of that Act provides that in a sale of specific goods, or where goods are subsequently appropriated to a contract, the seller has the right to reserve the right to dispose of the goods pending fulfilment of conditions imposed by him and, where he does impose

---

[20] Validity is discussed further below.

[21] Such statutory provision exists only in relation to administration. The administrator may apply to the court for authority to sell or otherwise dispose of property subject to a valid retention of title: 1986 Act, s 15, discussed further in Chapter 26.

[22] The discussion which follows outlines some of the most important of these. Retention of title clauses have been the subject of extensive debate in academic circles: see, in particular, Cusine, 'The Romalpa Family Visits Scotland' (1982) 27 JLSS 147, 221; Gretton and Reid, 'Retention of Title and Romalpa Clauses' 1983 SLT (News) 77, 'Retention of Title for All Sums: A Reply' 1983 SLT (News) 165, 'Romalpa Clauses: The Current Position' 1985 SLT (News) 329 and 'All Sums Retention of Title' 1989 SLT (News) 185; Wilson, 'Retention of Title: Lord Watson's Legacy' 1983 SLT (News) 106; Reid, 'Constitution of Trusts' 1986 SLT (News) 177; and Clark, 'All Sums Retention of Title: A Comment' 1991 SLT (News) 155.

such conditions, title will not pass until they are fulfilled.[23] Clearly, therefore, a simple retention of title is valid as an expression of the intention of the parties as to when property should pass or as a condition of property passing and it has been recognised as such in a number of cases.[24] All sums retention of title clauses, where title is retained by the seller until all sums (usually of any nature) due to the seller are paid, were initially rejected as invalid by the Scottish courts, but in *Armour v Thyssen Edelstahlwerke AG*[25] the House of Lords held that they are valid, for the same reason that simple retention title clauses were valid: the clause is simply an expression of the intention of the parties as to when property should pass. It was recognised that such a clause 'does in a sense give the seller security for the unpaid debts of the buyer',[26] but held that it was not the creation of a right of security as such and so was perfectly valid.

Other provisions in retention of title clauses

Retention of title clauses often contain a variety of other provisions designed to deal with the common situation where the property to which title is retained is to be (or may be) sold on or used in a manufacturing process by the debtor. Such provisions can give rise to difficult issues.

Dealing first with sales by the debtor, the difficulty for the seller is that provided the provisions of s 25(1) of the 1979 Act are satisfied, a purchaser from the debtor will obtain a good title to the goods, leaving the seller with only a claim against the debtor for the price—exactly the situation he was trying to prevent. Section 25(1) of the 1979 Act provides, in essence, that where someone buys or agrees to buy goods and subsequently obtains possession of either the goods or the documents of title to them with the consent of the seller, and then sells them to another person who is in good faith and has no notice of the original seller's right, that person will obtain a good title to the goods.[27] Even where the provisions of s 25(1) are not satisfied, the debtor may have express authority to resell the goods or such authority might be implied, and again the seller will lose the benefit of the retention of title clause on a resale. The retention of title clause may therefore attempt to make provision for this situation. A common device employed in this connection is an attempt to create a trust in relation to the proceeds of any such sales, with the debtor being regarded as trustee of the seller in relation to such proceeds, since property held in trust does not form part of the assets of the debtor on insolvency. Such a provision was not given effect to in the leading Scottish case, *Clark Taylor & Co Ltd v Quality Site Development (Edinburgh) Ltd*,[28] where it was held, in essence, that the clause merely created an obligation to set up a trust and could not of itself create it as it failed to comply with the requirements of Scots law in relation to the creation of trusts. The case is generally

---

[23] The legislation reflects the common law, which presumed that title would pass on delivery, but gave effect to suspensive conditions in contracts of sale which had the effect of delaying the passing of property pending fulfilment of the condition(s).

[24] See, for example, *Archivent Sales & Development Ltd v Strathclyde Regional Council* 1985 SLT 154; *Glen v Gilbey Vintners Ltd* 1986 SLT 553.

[25] 1990 SLT 891.

[26] Lord Keith, ibid, at 895.

[27] The requirements of the section were discussed in detail in *Archivent Sales & Development Ltd v Strathclyde Regional Council*, note 24 above.

[28] 1981 SC 111.

regarded as precluding the success of a trust provision in a retention of title clause in Scots law,[29] but where a trust which complied with the requirements of Scots law in relation to the creation of trusts was actually established, it is thought this should be given effect to. A trust clause was given effect to in the case of *Tay Valley Joinery Ltd* v *CF Financial Services Ltd*,[30] but this seems to have been principally on the basis that the contract was governed by English law, which does recognise such trusts. Another device which may be employed to circumvent the problem of resales is to make the debtor the agent of the seller. If the debtor is merely an agent, both unsold goods and, generally speaking, the proceeds of goods which have been sold belong to the seller/principal and would therefore not be affected by the debtor/agent's insolvency. The courts will examine the terms of the contract carefully, however, to determine whether the contract is genuinely an agency or in reality a sale.[31]

Turning to goods subject to a retention of title being used in a manufacturing process by the debtor, the difficulty for the seller is in the operation of the doctrines of accession and specification. In broad terms, where an article is attached to a larger article in such a way as to become part of it, and cannot be removed without damage—for example, where gold foil is applied to a decorative panel—ownership of the smaller article will pass to the owner of the larger by virtue of the doctrine of accession. Similarly, where a number of components are combined so as to create a totally new article which cannot be reduced again to its component parts—for example, where flour, yeast, fat and water are combined to make bread—the new article is owned by the manufacturer and ownership of the separate components is lost by the original owners. It may be difficult to determine exactly when accession or specification has taken place,[32] but where it has, the seller will have lost ownership of the articles and be left with only a claim against the debtor for the price—exactly the situation he was trying to prevent. One device which may be employed to circumvent this is to provide in the clause for common ownership of any new articles manufactured using the goods, but it has been argued that such a provision would not be effective in Scots law.[33] The trust and agency devices already discussed in connection with resales may also be employed in this context and the points already made in relation to these devices apply *mutatis mutandis*.

Severability

Where a clause contains some provisions which are valid and others which are not, the valid parts of the clause may be given effect to if it is possible to sever the invalid parts of the clause without destroying the sense of the valid parts.[34] Most

---

[29] Indeed, it was thus interpreted in the subsequent cases of *Emerald Stainless Steel Ltd* v *South Side Distribution Ltd* 1983 SLT 162 and *Deutz Engines Ltd* v *Terex Ltd*, 1984 SLT 273.

[30] (IH) 1987 SCLR 117.

[31] For a discussion of the differences, see *Michelin Tyre Co Ltd* v *Macfarlane (Glasgow) Ltd* 1917, 2 SLT 205.

[32] See, in the particular context of retention of title, *Zahnrad Fabrik Passau GmbH* v *Terex Ltd* 1986 SLT 84 (whether ownership of axles and transmissions incorporated into earth-moving equipment was lost by accession) and *Armour* v *Thyssen Edelstahlwerke AG* (note 25 above) (whether ownership of coils of steel which had been cut into strips was lost as a result of specification).

[33] See St Clair and Drummond Young, *The Law of Corporate Insolvency in Scotland* (2nd edn), p 275.

[34] *Glen* v *Gilbey Vintners Ltd* (note 24 above); cf *Emerald Stainless Steel Ltd* v *South Side Distribution Ltd* (note 29 above). This is often referred to as 'the blue-pencil rule'.

clauses which contain multiple provisions have an express provision relating to severability.[35]

Identification of goods subject to retention of title clause

A practical difficulty with retention of title is that of identification of the goods which are subject to the retention of title. The goods in respect of which retention of title is claimed must be identifiable as those belonging to the seller, and it is generally up to the seller to prove which goods are his in order to reclaim them.[36] The office holder must, however, carefully investigate any claim that there is a valid retention of title, otherwise he might find himself liable to the seller if he disposes of the goods and it is subsequently established that there was a valid retention of title.[37] If the seller cannot establish his ownership, he will be in the same position as any other creditor with a claim for the price.

Usually, the clause will require the debtor to keep the goods separate and clearly labelled so that they can be identified as the seller's goods, but this requirement may not be complied with or it may be inappropriate. One situation which requires special mention in this connection is where goods are mixed with other goods of the same nature and cannot be separated out again—for example, grain or milk.[38] The general rule is that the owners of the goods which have been mixed together become owners of the whole in the appropriate proportions,[39] so that where 100 tons of grain in a store containing 1,000 tons of grain came from one seller, he would own one-tenth of the grain. Where there has been a series of additions to and removals from the bulk, however, the relative proportions may be difficult to establish.

Identification of the goods is important also in the context of payments or part payments by the debtor. Where the clause is a simple retention of title, it will be important to identify which goods have been paid for and which have not: the seller will only retain ownership of those which have not been paid for. Where it is possible to identify which goods have been paid for—for example, by means of serial numbers on specific invoices—there is no difficulty; where it is possible to identify the seller's goods but not exactly which ones have been paid for, the normal rules concerning ascription of payments will apply to part payments made by the debtor[40] and this may have important consequences for the effectiveness of the retention of title clause.[41] Where the clause is an all sums retention of title, it will be important to check whether there was any time at which there was no

---

[35] As did the clause in *Glen* v *Gilbey Vintners Ltd.*

[36] In relation to sequestration, see the 1985 Act, s 31(6), which makes specific provision for an application to the court by a person claiming property which is also claimed by the permanent trustee.

[37] See *Vale Sewing Machines Ltd* v *Robb* (Sh Ct) 1997 SCLR 797 (Notes).

[38] This is known as commixtion in the case of solids, confusion in the case of liquids.

[39] Erskine, *Institute*, II, i, 17.

[40] In brief, these are that the debtor may ascribe the payments to any debt which he chooses; if he fails to do so, the seller may so ascribe them; where there is an account current and no ascription has taken place, the rule in *Clayton's Case* (1816) 1 Mor 572, to the effect that payments made extinguish the earliest debts, will apply: see the major texts on contract, such as McBryde, *The Law of Contract in Scotland*, paras 22–26 – 22–29.

[41] For example, the retention of title may not apply to goods still in the debtor's possession and only apply to goods which have, for example, been sold on and which the seller cannot therefore effectively reclaim.

outstanding balance due to the seller: where this is so, property in goods supplied up to that time will have passed in terms of the clause.[42]

Property situated outwith Scotland

Sequestration, liquidation and administration all claim to affect the company's property 'wherever situated'[43] and a floating charge may be worded to apply to property of the company outwith Scotland. However, whether the trustee, administrator, liquidator or receiver will be able to enforce his right to property outwith Scotland, and recover and/or realise it for the benefit of the creditors, depends in practice on whether his right is recognised by the legal system of the country where the property is situated.[44]

Where a CVA affects property of the company situated outwith Scotland, the problem may be less acute, at least where the implementation of the CVA is wholly or partly in the hands of the directors: the foreign system may not classify the company as being subject to an insolvency régime as such and allow the company to deal with its property in the normal way. The position may be more problematic where the implementation of the CVA is in the hands of the supervisor, however, and where the company is also in administration or liquidation, the same issues as to the right of the office holder to enforce his claim to the property will arise as where the company is subject to one of those régimes without also being subject to a CVA. Similarly, where the company has concluded a section 425 arrangement which includes property situated outwith Scotland, few problems are likely to arise where the section 425 arrangement is being implemented by the directors, but where the company is in administration, receivership or liquidation, the same issues will arise as where the company is subject to those régimes without also being subject to a section 425 arrangement.[45]

Property to which the debtor has title but no beneficial interest

A situation may arise where a debtor has transferred property to another prior to the commencement of insolvency proceedings, but the transferee has not completed title prior to the commencement of such proceedings—for example, where the debtor has transferred shares to another but the transfer has not been registered, or where the debtor has transferred heritage to another but the title has not been recorded or registered.

Until recently, it had generally been accepted that in such a situation, since the title to the property remained with the debtor, it was part of the debtor's property for the purpose of insolvency proceedings.[46] Following the decision of the House of Lords in *Sharp* v *Woolwich Building Society*,[47] however, it is clear that

---

[42] Although if goods supplied after that were also subject to a retention of title, title to those goods will not have passed so long as any new balance remained outstanding.

[43] See the preceding chapter.

[44] See further Chapter 47.

[45] Ibid.

[46] This resulted in a race to complete title to the property between the person to whom the property had been conveyed and the appropriate office holder which, in the case of heritable property, was generally referred to as the 'Race to the Register', the first to record their title obtaining the preferable right to the property.

[47] 1997 SC (HL) 66, sub nom *Sharp* v *Thomson*.

this is not the position in relation to receivership. In that case, a company sold a flat to purchasers. After the price had been paid and the title deed delivered to the purchasers, but before the deed had been recorded by them, a receiver was appointed to the company. The question was whether the flat, to which the company still had title, was part of the company's 'property and undertaking' and so caught by the receivership. The House of Lords held that although title remained with the company, it had no beneficial interest in the flat, which could not, therefore, be regarded as part of the company's 'property and undertaking' so as to be caught by the receivership.

The implications of the decision are a matter of considerable debate.[48] If the concept of beneficial interest on which the decision was based extends beyond receivership, property which the debtor has conveyed away prior to sequestration, administration or liquidation will not be affected by these proceedings and it could not be included in a CVA or section 425 arrangement. Further case-law or legislation will, however, be required to clarify the position.[49]

Consigned funds

It has been held that sums consigned in court to await the outcome of a pending litigation are not affected by the sequestration of the consigning party,[50] nor are they attached by a floating charge on the appointment of a receiver under the charge.[51] The basis for these decisions is that the sums were no longer the property of the debtor and logically, therefore, consigned sums in other company insolvency proceedings will also remain unaffected by such proceedings. It has also been held that money placed in the hands of a third party pending the outcome of a dispute was not affected by the sequestration of the party whose funds they were,[52] and again this would logically apply to such sums in company insolvency proceedings also. It is thought the same would apply to funds placed on deposit receipt pending the outcome of a dispute—at least where the effect of the agreement to place the funds on deposit receipt was to divest the debtor of the funds and any power and control over them.[53]

---

[48] See, for example, Reid, 'Jam Today: *Sharp* in the House of Lords' 1997 SLT (News) 79; Reid, 'Equity Triumphant: *Sharp* v *Thomson*' (1997) 1 ELR 464; Rennie, '*Sharp* v *Thomson*: The Final Act' (1997) 42 JLSS 130; Birrell, '*Sharp* v *Thomson*: The Impact on Banking and Insolvency Law' 1997 SLT (News) 151; Cusine, '*Sharp* v *Thomson*: The House of Lords Strikes Back' (1997) 26 *Greens Property Law Bulletin* 5; Guild, '*Sharp* v *Thomson*: A Practitioner's View' (1997) 42 JLSS 274; Sellar 'Commercial Law Update' (1997) 42 JLSS 181. See also the Scottish Law Commission Discussion Paper on Diligence Against Land (No 107, 1998).

[49] At the time of writing, the author is aware of one case in which the applicability of the *Sharp* v *Thomson* decision in sequestration is an issue, that of *Reid* v *Granger*, heard in Aberdeen Sheriff Court on 9th June 1998. A decision is awaited. The Scottish Law Commission has also considered the difficulties raised by the decision and put forward four possible options for reform of the law insofar as it relates to heritable property, the preferred option being to introduce measures which would preserve a race to the Register while ensuring that if good conveyancing practice is followed, the race will always be won by the debtor's disponee: see the Scottish Law Commission Discussion Paper on Diligence Against Land, note 48 above.

[50] See, for example, *Gordon* v *Brock* (1838) 1 D 1, especially Lord President Hope at 9.

[51] *Hawking* v *Hafton House Ltd* 1990 SC 198.

[52] *Dixon & Wilson* v *McIntyre* 1898, 6 SLT 188.

[53] *Craiglaw Developments* v *Wilson* (IH) 1997 SCLR 1157 (Notes). The case involved a company in liquidation and the matter was being examined from a slightly different perspective, but it is thought that the principle employed leads to this result in this context also.

Damages for personal injury (non-company debtors)

Generally, any damages which have been paid to a debtor prior to sequestration form part of the estate and vest in the trustee under s 31(8) of the 1985 Act. Damages paid to a debtor during the sequestration will also vest in the trustee, with the exception of those which are in the nature of income.[54] These rules apply equally to damages in the form of solatium for personal injury. Where the debtor's right to damages has not yet been realised, however, the matter is more complicated. The right to damages for patrimonial loss of any description vests in the trustee, and the trustee can raise an action for that patrimonial loss.[55] The right to raise an action for solatium is personal to the debtor, however, and the trustee cannot therefore raise an action for solatium due to the debtor.[56] Where the debtor has himself raised an action, whether before or after sequestration, the trustee may sist himself in that action and thereby obtain payment of any damages ultimately awarded, including solatium. It has also been held that the trustee may apply for deferral of the debtor's discharge in order to secure payment of damages due to the debtor.[57] In a recent Inner House decision, however, it was held that the trustee could claim damages, including solatium, where the relevant action was raised by the debtor during the sequestration, even though he had not adopted either of the courses just described and even though the damages were paid after the debtor's discharge and as a result of an extra-judicial settlement.[58] The court held that the personal right of the debtor to raise an action for solatium was transformed into a right which was capable of vesting in the trustee at the time the action was raised, and vested in the trustee at that time.

Pension rights (non-company debtors)

Pension rights raise difficult issues on insolvency.[59] This section outlines briefly the general rules at the present time and current proposals for reform.

At present, whether a debtor's pension rights vest in his trustee in sequestration depends on the type of pension involved. Generally, where the debtor is a member of an occupational pension scheme, his rights under the scheme will not vest in the trustee,[60] although he may be required to make a contribution to the estate

---

[54] For property acquired during sequestration generally, see the preceding chapter.

[55] *Muir's Tr v Braidwood* 1958 SC 169.

[56] See *Muir's Tr v Braidwood* above; *Watson v Thompson* (IH) 1992 SCLR 78.

[57] *Watson v Henderson* (Sh Ct) 1988 SCLR 439. The issue of the treatment of damages for personal injury in sequestration was considered by the Scottish Law Commission in 1988, but following consultation, it recommended no change in the present law: Consultation Paper on the Law of Bankruptcy: Solatium for Personal Injury/Future Wage Loss (February 1994).

[58] *Coutts' Tr v Coutts*, 3rd June 1998 (unreported), discussed in *Greens Business Law Bulletin*, 34–35.

[59] A full discussion of the complexities of the law in this area is beyond the scope of this work, and reference should be made to specialist texts for further details.

[60] The Pensions Act 1995, s 91(3) makes specific provision to the effect that rights under an occupational pension scheme are excluded from a person's estate for the purposes of the 1985 Act, but this subsection has not been brought into force ss 91–95, which deal with various aspects of assignation, forfeiture and bankruptcy came into force on 6th April 1996 for the purpose of making regulations only (Pensions Act 1995 (Commencement No 3) Order 1996 (SI 1996/778) and s 91(1), (2) and (4)–(7) and ss 92–94 came fully into force on 6th April 1997 (Pensions Act 1995 (Commencement No 10) Order 1996 (SI 1997/664), but s 91(3) has not been brought into force. However, it is generally accepted that rights under occupational pension schemes will not usually form part of the debtor's estate under the present law. For a contrary view, see Gordon, 'The Effect of Bankruptcy on Personal Pensions' (1997) 42 JLSS 329.

out of pension income.[61] With respect to pensions other than occupational pensions prior to 1st July 1988, self-employed persons or employed persons with no other pension provision could take out a retirement annuity contract (RAC). Although no new RAC could be taken out after that date, existing RACs could be continued. Unless such an RAC has been transferred into a trust, which would be unusual, it will vest in the trustee. All new private pensions from 1st July 1988 take the form of personal pension policies, and a debtor's rights under such a policy will generally vest in the trustee, unless there is a valid forfeiture clause.[62] Where pension rights do vest in a trustee, he will generally be unable to obtain payment of sums due under the RAC or personal pension policy until they become payable in terms thereof (usually on retirement),[63] but once they have so vested he will be entitled to all sums due under the contract or policy,[64] even if paid after the debtor's discharge.

At the time of writing, the Welfare Reform and Pensions Bill is currently before Parliament. It contains provisions designed to end the different treatment of personal and occupational pensions on bankruptcy by excluding pension rights under all approved pension schemes from a debtor's sequestration. It also contains a power to make regulations providing for a debtor's rights under an unapproved scheme to be excluded from his sequestration in prescribed circumstances and a provision to make forfeiture of pension rights on bankruptcy incompetent.

Property or money recovered, or contribution ordered, under certain sections of the 1986 Act (company debtors)

Under s 212 of the 1986 Act (summary remedy against delinquent directors and others), in defined circumstances property or money which has been misapplied or retained by persons to whom the section applies may be recovered as a result of an action under the section and the court may also order a contribution to be made to the assets of the company where any fiduciary or other duty owed to the company by such a person has been breached.[65] Similarly, under ss 213 and 214 of the 1986 Act (fraudulent trading and wrongful trading respectively), certain persons may be ordered to make a contribution to the assets of the company in defined circumstances.[66] Where this happens, an issue arises as to how the property, money or contribution is to be dealt with in the relevant insolvency proceedings—in particular, whether it is attached by an appropriately worded floating charge. This question will only arise in the context of liquidation, since

---

[61] 1985 Act, s 32(4). Contributions out of income are discussed in the preceding chapter.

[62] Many policies now contain clauses providing for forfeiture of the benefits under the policy, *inter alia*, on sequestration or other defined insolvency events. Such clauses often also allow the pension fund trustees to make discretionary payments notwithstanding that the debtor's rights have been forfeited. The Pensions Act 1995, s 92 provides that, in general, rights under an *occupational* pension scheme cannot be forfeited, but permits forfeiture, *inter alia*, on the bankruptcy of the person entitled under the scheme and the making of discretionary payments by the pension trustees where rights are forfeited on bankruptcy, but the position regarding the validity of forfeiture clauses in personal pensions is less clear: see Gordon, note 60 above.

[63] He may, however, be able to exercise any right of the debtor to elect to have early payment.

[64] 1985 Act, s 32(1).

[65] See further Chapter 38.

[66] Ibid.

actions under these sections can only be brought by a liquidator, but the answer may vary depending on the section involved. The issue is discussed fully in Chapter 38, which deals in detail with these sections.

Under ss 242, 243 and 244 of the 1986 Act (gratuitous alienations, unfair preferences and extortionate credit transactions respectively), property disposed of by the company prior to the commencement of certain insolvency proceedings, or its value, may be recovered following a successful challenge of the relevant transactions in defined circumstances.[67] Similarly, property disposed of by the company, or its value, may be recovered in certain circumstances if the transaction amounted to a gratuitous alienation or fraudulent preference at common law.[68] Where this happens, an issue arises as to how the property or money recovered is to be dealt with in the relevant insolvency proceedings—in particular, whether it is attached by an appropriately worded floating charge. In the case of anything recovered under the statutory provisions, this question will only arise where the company is either in liquidation or in administration,[69] because actions under these sections can only be brought where the company is in liquidation or administration, but in the case of property or money recovered following the successful challenge of a transaction at common law, the issue may arise even where the company is not in liquidation or administration, because an action at common law can be brought by a creditor at any time after the trans-action in question took place, as well as following liquidation or administration. The issue is discussed fully in Chapter 30, which deals in detail with challengeable transactions.

Rights of commercial value and significance

In *Independent Pension Trustee Ltd* v *LAW Construction Co*[70] it was held that the assets of a company which were attached by a floating charge included not only its property in the narrow sense but its rights and powers insofar as they have commercial value and significance. The case was concerned with the exercise of a company's right, *inter alia*, to appoint trustees to a pension scheme. It was held that if the rights, powers and obligations of the company under the pension scheme were of commercial value and significance, and in this case they were, then they were to be regarded as part of the company's property and undertaking and therefore within the scope of the charge. Such rights would, presumably, form part of a company's, or indeed any other debtor's, property for the purposes of other insolvency proceedings also.

Acquirenda

It has already been noted that property (although not income) acquired by the debtor between the date of sequestration and his discharge, being property which

---

[67] See further Chapter 30.
[68] Ibid.
[69] In the case of an overlap between administration and receivership, the receivership would have to be a receivership other than an administrative receivership because administration cannot coexist with an administrative receivership: see Chapter 4. Since receiverships other than administrative receiverships are, however, extremely rare, this particular conjunction of events is very unlikely to arise.
[70] 1997 SLT 1105.

would have vested in the trustee in sequestration had it been owned by the debtor at the date of sequestration, will vest in a trustee in sequestration.[71] Similarly, property acquired by a company in administration or liquidation will be affected by the administration or liquidation because these affect the property of the company as it is at any given time. Property acquired by a company during the currency of a CVA or section 425 arrangement, however, will only fall within that arrangement if provision is made in the arrangement to that effect. It has been held that an appropriately worded floating charge can attach to property which comes into the hands of the company after the appointment of the receiver.[72] Where the floating charge has crystallised on the appointment of a receiver but property acquired subsequent to the receiver's appointment is not covered by the charge, it has also been held that property acquired between the appointment of the receiver and a subsequent liquidation was attached by the 'recrystallisation' of the charge on liquidation,[73] but this decision must be treated with some caution: it was decided under the Companies (Floating Charges and Receivers) (Scotland) Act 1972 and it is not clear whether the same result would be reached under the current legislation.

---

[71] See Chapter 21.
[72] *Ross* v *Taylor* 1985 SLT 387, which concerned goods reacquired by the receiver.
[73] Ibid.

23 : THE EFFECT OF INSOLVENCY PROCEEDINGS ON THE DEBTOR'S POWER TO DEAL WITH THE PROPERTY AFFECTED

This chapter considers the effect of insolvency proceedings on the power of the debtor[1] to deal with the property affected.

Sequestration

The debtor has no power to deal with property which has vested in the permanent trustee: this is the logical corollary of the fact that such property has vested in the trustee. Section 32(8) of the 1985 Act provides that any dealing of, or with, the debtor relating to any of the property which has vested in the permanent trustee under s 31 of the 1985 Act[2] is invalid in a question with the trustee, subject to a number of exceptions. These are:

(1) Where the permanent trustee has abandoned the property to the debtor.[3] The permanent trustee may, for example, consider that it is not worth the expense of recovering a particular piece of property. He may abandon property expressly or impliedly.

(2) Where the permanent trustee has expressly or impliedly authorised the dealing.[4]

(3) Where the trustee has otherwise acted in such a way as to be personally barred from challenging the debtor's action.[5]

(4) Where the third party was obligated to the debtor and carried out his obligation[6]—for example, by paying him a debt which was due to him.

(5) Where the debtor has sold goods and the purchaser has paid the debtor for them or is willing to pay the trustee.[7]

---

[1] In the case of a debtor other than an individual, this must be read as the debtor acting through its agents—for example, in the case of a company, its directors.
[2] See Chapter 21.
[3] 1985 Act, s 32(9)(a)(i).
[4] 1985 Act, s 32(9)(a)(ii).
[5] 1985 Act, s 32(9)(a)(iii).
[6] 1985 Act, s 32(9)(b)(i).
[7] 1985 Act, s 32(9)(b)(ii).

(6) Where the transaction is a banking transaction in the ordinary course of business[8]—for example, honouring a cheque or allowing a withdrawal from an account.

In all cases, the party dealing with the debtor must have been unaware of the sequestration and have had no reason to believe that the debtor's estate had been sequestrated.[9] Otherwise, the transaction will not be protected.

Section 32(8) of the 1985 Act applies only to dealings with property vesting in the trustee under s 31, but an attempt by the debtor to deal with property vesting in the trustee under s 32 of the 1985 Act has also been held to be invalid.[10]

Company insolvency proceedings

There are few specific statutory provisions governing dealings with the company's property during insolvency proceedings. Sections 88 and 127 of the 1986 Act deal with defined transactions after the commencement of voluntary and compulsory liquidation respectively,[11] but in all other cases, including cases in liquidation not covered by ss 88 and 127, the matter must be considered from first principles by examining the effect of the relevant proceedings on the ability of the directors, as its agents, to bind the company.

CVAs

There are no statutory provisions dealing with the validity of transactions by the directors of a company after conclusion of a CVA. The validity of any such transactions will therefore depend on the terms of the CVA itself. Particularly where the company is not in administration or liquidation, the CVA may provide for the directors to have a role in its implementation, and in such a case any transactions carried out by them within the terms of the CVA will be perfectly valid. It is more common, however, for the implementation of the CVA to be carried out by the supervisor, particularly where the company is in administration or liquidation. Where the directors attempt to deal with the company's property without having a right to do so in terms of the CVA itself, they will be doing so without the necessary power or authority. The logical corollary of this is that any such transaction entered into by the directors is void insofar as it purports to bind the company, and any property disposed of may be recovered, even from a third party who has acquired it in good faith and for value.[12]

---

[8] 1985 Act, s 32(9)(b)(iii).

[9] Note that it is the knowledge of the *party to the transaction* which is relevant, not that of any agent actually carrying out the transaction on the party's behalf: *Minhas's Tr* v *Bank of Scotland* 1990 SLT 23, sub nom *Watt* v *Bank of Scotland* (OH) 1989 SCLR 548.

[10] See *Alliance & Leicester Building Society* v *Murray's Tr* 1995 SLT (Sh Ct) 77, which involved a standard security over a property purchased after the date of sequestration. It was held that the security was invalid as the debtor had no power to grant it, the property having vested in the trustee in sequestration under s 32. Cf, however, *Royal Bank of Scotland plc* v *Lamb's Tr* (OH) 1998 SCLR 923, where such a security was held to be valid as a result of the debtor's fraud.

[11] See further below.

[12] Unless the directors, as agents of the company, can be held to have apparent authority even though their actual authority has been restricted or terminated by the CVA. This point raises difficult issues which are beyond the scope of this work, but see McKenzie and O'Donnell, 'Intervening Insolvency: How Can You Know?' (1996) 1 SLPQ 173, which discusses these issues in relation to administration, receivership and liquidation (which raise the same issues) in a

Section 425 arrangements

There are no statutory provisions dealing with the validity of transactions by the directors of a company after conclusion of a section 425 arrangement. As in CVAs, the validity of any transactions carried out by the directors will be governed by the terms of the arrangement itself. Where the company is not in administration, liquidation or receivership, the arrangement will usually be carried out by the directors on behalf of the company, and any transactions carried out within the terms of the arrangement will be valid. Where the company is in administration, liquidation or receivership, however, it is unlikely that the directors will have an unfettered role, if any, in implementing the arrangement. Any purported transaction by the directors outwith the terms of the arrangement will therefore be one which they have no authority to make. The logical corollary of this is that any such transaction entered into by the directors is void insofar as it purports to bind the company, and any property disposed of may be recovered, even from a third party who has acquired it in good faith and for value.[13]

Administration

There are no specific statutory provisions governing dealings with the company's property during administration. The presentation of the administration petition and the administration order itself must be registered in the Register of Inhibitions and Adjudications,[14] but it is thought that this of itself does not have any effect on transactions by the company.[15] The matter must therefore be considered from first principles by examining the effect of administration on the directors' ability to bind the company.

Prior to the making of the administration order, the court may make an interim order restricting the exercise of any powers of the directors or of the company.[16] Such an order may provide that any such powers be exercised only with the consent of the court or an insolvency practitioner, or otherwise.[17] Once an administration order is made, the directors' powers are effectively suspended for the duration of the administration order. This results from the operation of s 14(4) of the 1986 Act, which provides that any power conferred on the company or its officers which could interfere with the exercise of the administrator's functions is not exercisable except with the consent of the administrator, and

---

slightly different context. It should be noted, however, that the article refers to the Inner House decision in the case of *Sharp* v *Woolwich* 1997 SCLR 328, sub nom *Sharp* v *Thomson*, and since the House of Lords reached a different decision from the Inner House, the article insofar as it relies on the Inner House decision in that case must be read with caution.

[13] Unless, in the same way as discussed in relation to CVAs, the directors, as agents of the company, can be held to have apparent authority even though their actual authority has been restricted or terminated by the section 425 arrangement: see further note 12 above.

[14] 1986 Act, s 9(2)(a), and rule 2.2(1) of the Scottish Rules (presentation); rule 2.2(3) of the Scottish Rules (order).

[15] Cf s 14(2) of the 1985 Act, which clearly states that the effect of registration of the appropriate order in the Register of Inhibitions and Adjudications is that of an inhibition and citation in an action of adjudication at the instance of all the creditors. There is no such provision in the case of administration. It is thought, therefore, that the registration is simply another form of notice rather than having any effect on transactions by the company.

[16] 1986 Act, s 9(5).

[17] Ibid. 'Otherwise' might include a complete suspension of powers (for example, where an insolvency practitioner has been appointed to manage the company in the interim period) or a restriction to exercising only certain limited powers such as taking ordinary day-to-day decisions.

generally from the fact that control of the affairs, business and property of the company has been transferred to the administrator. Where, therefore, the directors purport to deal with the company's property *either* in breach of an order under s 9(5) *or* at any time after the making of the administration order without the consent of the administrator, they will be doing so without the necessary power or authority. The logical corollary of this is that any such transaction entered into by the directors is void insofar as it purports to bind the company, and any property disposed of may be recovered by the administrator, even from a third party who has acquired it in good faith and for value.[18]

Receivership

There are no statutory provisions governing dealings with the company's property during receivership. The matter must be looked at from first principles by examining the effect of the receivership on the directors' powers in relation to the company and its property.

The directors may continue to exercise their powers in relation to any part of the company's property which is not attached by the floating charge in the normal way.[19] In relation to such property as is attached by the floating charge, however, the directors are effectively superseded by the receiver and, during the currency of the receivership, have no power over the assets falling under the charge.[20] Where, therefore, the directors purport to deal with such property at any time after the appointment of a receiver, they will be doing so without the necessary power or authority. The logical corollary of this is that any such transaction entered into by the directors is void insofar as it purports to bind the company, and any property disposed of may be recovered by the receiver even from a third party who has acquired it in good faith and for value.[21]

Liquidation

In the case of voluntary liquidations, s 88 of the 1986 Act provides that any transfer of shares other than to or with the consent of the liquidator and any alteration in the status of members after the commencement of the winding up is void.[22]

In the case of compulsory liquidations, s 127 of the 1986 Act provides that any transfer of shares or alteration in the status of the company's members *and* any

---

[18] Unless, as discussed above in relation to CVAs, the directors, as agents of the company, can be held to have apparent authority even though their actual authority has been restricted or terminated: see note 12 above.

[19] In practice, the charge will almost invariably attach to all of the company's property.

[20] *Independent Pension Trustee Ltd* v *LAW Construction Co Ltd* 1997 SLT 1105; see also *Imperial Hotel (Aberdeen) Ltd* v *Vaux Breweries* 1978 SC 86, in which Lord Grieve held that the directors' powers in relation to the property attached by a floating charge were entirely in abeyance during the currency of the receivership. In *Shanks* v *Central Regional Council* 1987 SLT 410, however, Lord Weir held that although that might be applicable to most situations where a receiver was appointed, it was not necessarily the case that the directors of a company were completely disempowered from dealing in any way with the assets attached by a floating charge during the currency of a receivership (including raising proceedings in relation to them). This decision may, however, be doubted. For a fuller discussion of the issues in a slightly different context, see McKenzie and O'Donnell, 'Intervening Insolvency: How Can You Know?', note 12 above.

[21] Unless, as discussed in the context of CVAs, the directors, as agents of the company, can be held to have apparent authority even though their actual authority has been restricted or terminated: see note 12 above.

[22] Voluntary liquidation commences with the passing of the resolution to wind up: 1986 Act, s 86.

disposition of the company's property made after the commencement of the winding up is void unless the court orders otherwise.[23] 'Disposition' is not used in a narrow conveyancing sense, but means dealing with, settling or transferring a company's property to another.[24] The section therefore applies to a wide variety of transactions concerning all types of property: for example, the granting of a floating charge has been held to be a disposition within the meaning of the section,[25] as has the making of payments into and out of a company's bank account.[26] Sometimes a transaction takes place in a number of stages: for example, a conveyancing transaction normally involves missives followed by delivery of a disposition followed by recording of the disposition. In such cases, it is the time at which the disposition within the meaning of s 127 takes place which is crucial. It has been suggested in one English case that once a binding contract for the sale of an interest in land, or probably any other specifically enforceable contract for the alienation of property, has been concluded, the company has effectively disposed of the property because it no longer has a beneficial interest in it and the subsequent completion of the conveyancing formalities after the commencement of the liquidation would not amount to a 'disposition' within the meaning of the section.[27] If this is correct, a similar result *might* be reached in Scotland if the decision in *Sharp v Woolwich Building Society*[28] can be regarded as being of general application,[29] but since there is still much uncertainty regarding the effect of that decision,[30] the position must be regarded as remaining unclear in Scotland if not in England. Since any transaction caught by the section is void unless the court orders the contrary, the liquidator may recover any property disposed of even if the holder is a purchaser in good faith and for value. It is thought that there would be little difficulty in obtaining an order from the court to the effect that the transaction is not void where that was the case, but the onus to obtain such an order would be on the party wishing to retain the property.

Some dealings with the company's property will not be caught by either s 88 or s 127 of the 1986 Act.[31] In relation to such transactions, the matter must be looked at from first principles by examining the effect of the liquidation on the directors' powers in relation to the company and its property. In a voluntary liquidation, it is specifically provided that the powers of the directors cease on the appointment of a liquidator except insofar as their continuance is given the

---

[23] A compulsory liquidation is deemed to commence at the time of presentation of the petition or, if a resolution for the voluntary winding up of the company was passed prior to the presentation of the petition, the time of the passing of that resolution: 1986 Act, s 129.

[24] Lord Ross in *Site Preparations Ltd v Buchan Development Co Ltd* 1983 SLT 317 at 319.

[25] Ibid.

[26] *Re Gray's Inn Construction Co Ltd* [1980] 1 WLR 711.

[27] *Re French's Wine Bar Ltd* (1987) 3 BCC 173. The case is somewhat unsatisfactory, however, because it suggested that it would none the less be prudent to make an application for an order that the transaction was not void insofar as it did involve a disposition within the meaning of s 127.

[28] Note 12 above and discussed in Chapter 22.

[29] The reasoning would be that since it also regards beneficial interest and not title as being the crucial factor, where the beneficial interest in the property has been disposed of prior to the commencement of the liquidation, any subsequent part of the transaction would be unimportant.

[30] See Chapter 22.

[31] In fact, in voluntary liquidations, most transactions will not be caught by s 88 because of its rather narrow application.

appropriate sanction,[32] and where no liquidator is appointed or nominated by the company when the resolution to wind up is passed, the directors' powers are restricted until a liquidator is appointed or nominated.[33] In that situation, the directors' powers may only be exercised with the sanction of the court, with two exceptions: the directors are allowed to dispose of perishable goods or other goods whose value is likely to diminish if not immediately disposed of, and to do all other such things as may be necessary for the protection of the company's assets, without such sanction.[34] There are no equivalent provisions relating to compulsory liquidation, but it has been said that, 'on principle, the directors' powers must cease. The liquidator's powers are inconsistent with the concurrent exercise of those powers by directors. Even if there is no liquidator, the property of the company is deemed to be in the custody of the court'.[35] The powers of the directors seem to cease on the appointment of a provisional liquidator, if any;[36] otherwise, they would cease on the making of the winding-up order and appointment of the interim liquidator. Where, therefore, directors purport to deal with the company's property after their powers have ceased, they will be doing so without the necessary power or authority. The logical corollary of this is that any such transaction, even if not struck at by s 88 or s 127 of the 1986 Act, is void insofar as it purports to bind the company, and any such dealing with the company's property will not be upheld in a question with the liquidator, even where the other party acted in good faith and gave value.[37]

---

[32] 1986 Act, s 91 (members' voluntary liquidation) and s 103 (creditors' voluntary liquidation). The sanction required in the former case is that of the company in general meeting or the liquidator; in the latter, it is the sanction of the liquidation committee or, if there is no such committee, the creditors.

[33] 1986 Act, s 114.

[34] Ibid.

[35] McBryde, *Contract*, p 168.

[36] *Re Mawcon Ltd* [1969] 1 WLR 78.

[37] Unless, as discussed in the context of CVAs, the directors, as agents of the company, can be held to have apparent authority even though their actual authority has been restricted or terminated: see note 12 above.

24 : ADMINISTRATION OF THE DEBTOR'S ESTATE ON SEQUESTRATION

The permanent trustee takes over from the interim trustee for the purpose of managing and realising the estate which has vested in him and distributing it to the creditors.

This chapter sets out the functions of the permanent trustee and describes how he recovers, manages and realises the debtor's estate for distribution to the creditors. In certain cases, the normal procedures for administration of the estate are modified: these cases, and the relevant modifications, are discussed in Chapter 35 below.

Functions of the permanent trustee

The principal functions of the permanent trustee are recovery, management and realisation of the debtor's estate[1] and distribution of the estate among the debtor's creditors according to their respective entitlements.[2] In addition, he must ascertain the debtor's assets and liabilities[3] and the reasons for the debtor's insolvency[4]— tasks which he has in common with, and which will have been begun by, the interim trustee—keep a record of the progress of the sequestration by means of a sederunt book,[5] into which important documents are inserted, and keep regular accounts,[6] which can be inspected by the debtor, the creditors and the commissioners, if any.[7] Where the permanent trustee is a private insolvency practitioner, he must also provide information to the Accountant in Bankruptcy, even when he has ceased to act as permanent trustee.[8]

---

[1] 1985 Act, s 3(1)(a).
[2] 1985 Act, s 3(1)(b).
[3] 1985 Act, s 3(1)(d).
[4] 1985 Act, s 3(1)(c).
[5] 1985 Act, s 3(1)(e).
[6] 1985 Act, s 3(1)(f).
[7] Commissioners are discussed in Chapter 34.
[8] 1985 Act, s 3(1)(g), s 3(5).

Recovery of estate

Recovery of estate generally

Once the permanent trustee has been issued with his act and warrant,[9] he must take possession of the debtor's property. He must consult with the commissioners or, if there are no commissioners, the Accountant in Bankruptcy, about recovery of the estate,[10] and he must comply with any directions given to him by the creditors,[11] the court[12] or the Accountant in Bankruptcy[13] in this respect.

The permanent trustee must take possession of all the estate which has vested in him as soon as possible after his confirmation in office.[14] He may, if necessary, take legal proceedings to recover such property.[15] He must also take possession of any documents relating to the debtor's assets, business or finances which are in the debtor's possession or control[16] and he has the right to have access to, and to copy, such documents in the hands of third parties.[17] He also has a right to delivery of title deeds and other documents of the debtor, even where a lien is claimed over the documents.[18] Recovery of documents and other information generally is discussed in Chapter 29.

Challengeable transactions

The permanent trustee may challenge certain transactions by the debtor prior to insolvency with a view to recovering assets disposed of as result of such transactions, or their value, for distribution to the creditors through the mechanism of the sequestration. The types of transaction which may be challenged and the conditions which require to be satisfied for a successful challenge are discussed in Chapter 30.

Management and realisation of the estate

Management of the estate generally

The permanent trustee is given extensive powers to manage the debtor's estate pending its realisation and distribution to the creditors. He must, however, consult with the commissioners or, if there are no commissioners, the Accountant in Bankruptcy, about the management and realisation of the estate[19] and he must comply with any directions given to him by the creditors,[20] the court[21] or the Accountant in Bankruptcy in this respect,[22] with one exception: he need not

---

[9] See Chapter 21.

[10] 1985 Act, s 39(1).

[11] 1985 Act, s 39(1)(a).

[12] On application of the commissioners: 1985 Act, s 39(1)(b).

[13] If there are no commissioners: 1985 Act, s 39(1)(c).

[14] 1985 Act, s 38(1). For the property which vests in the permanent trustee, see Chapter 21.

[15] 1985 Act, s 39(2)(b). If there are commissioners, however, the trustee will need their consent or that of the creditors or the court to this course of action.

[16] 1985 Act, s 38(1).

[17] 1985 Act, s 38(2).

[18] 1985 Act, s 38(4).

[19] 1985 Act, s 39(1).

[20] 1985 Act, s 39(1)(a).

[21] On application of the commissioners: 1985 Act, s 39(1)(b).

[22] If there are no commissioners: 1985 Act, s 39(1)(c).

comply with any directions given to him by the creditors or the Accountant in Bankruptcy where he has to sell perishable goods and believes the directions will adversely affect the sale price.[23]

Powers of permanent trustee

The permanent trustee may do the following things if they would benefit the estate.

(1) Carry on the business of the debtor.[24] The trustee may wish to continue trading in order to preserve goodwill and enable the business to be sold as a going concern, which will usually realise more than selling the assets individually.

(2) Raise, defend or continue any court actions concerning the estate.[25]

(3) Create a security over any part of the estate.[26] This may be necessary if the trustee requires, for example, to borrow money for some reason, such as to complete contracts of the debtor.

(4) Make payments or incur other liabilities in order to obtain property under a right or option which is part of the estate.[27] For example, if the debtor had an option to purchase shares, the trustee might wish to exercise it and then sell the shares at a profit for the benefit of the creditors.

As indicated above, the exercise of these powers requires the consent of the commissioners, the creditors or the court.

Contracts

Particularly where the debtor is running a business, there may be existing contracts to consider. The permanent trustee may adopt any of the debtor's pre-sequestration contracts where he considers this would be beneficial to the estate, unless such adoption is precluded by the express or implied terms of the contract itself.[28] He must decide whether to adopt a contract within a reasonable time, otherwise he will be held to have abandoned it.[29] Any other party to the contract may force the issue by making a written request for a decision. In such a case, the trustee must make a decision within 28 days of receipt of the request, or such longer period as the court may allow:[30] if he does not respond in writing to the request within that period, he is deemed to have refused to adopt the contract.[31] Where a contract is not adopted, the other party or parties to the contract may have a claim for damages for breach of contract in the sequestration.[32] A contract

---

[23] 1985 Act, s 39(6).
[24] 1985 Act, s 39(2)(a).
[25] 1985 Act, s 39(2)(b).
[26] 1985 Act, s 39(2)(c).
[27] 1985 Act, s 39(2)(d).
[28] 1985 Act, s 42(1).
[29] *Crown Estate Commrs* v *Liquidator of Highland Engineering Ltd* 1975 SLT 58. What is reasonable will depend on the circumstances of the case: a decision on a construction contract might reasonably be expected to take longer than a decision on whether to continue having papers delivered!
[30] 1985 Act, s 42(2).
[31] 1985 Act, s 42(3).
[32] *Crown Estate Commrs* v *Liquidator of Highland Engineering Ltd*, note 29 above.

may give any party other than the sequestrated debtor the option to terminate the contract or exercise other remedies on the sequestration.

The trustee may also enter into new contracts where they would be beneficial to the administration of the estate.[33] This may be necessary, for example, where the trustee is running the debtor's business prior to selling it.

There are special provisions regarding contracts for the supply of gas, electricity, water and telecommunications services. Where the supply is for the purposes of carrying on the debtor's business, the suppliers of these utilities may not make it a condition of continued supply that pre-sequestration debts are paid, although they may make it a condition of continued supply that the trustee personally guarantees payment for future supplies.[34]

The trustee is personally liable on pre-sequestration contracts adopted by him[35] and on new contracts entered into by him,[36] unless such liability is specifically excluded. He is, however, entitled to a right of relief against the estate.

Sale of estate

The trustee may sell the debtor's heritable or moveable property by public sale or private bargain,[37] subject to special rules where heritable property is subject to a security and/or is a family home as defined by the 1985 Act. He may sell heritable property notwithstanding that there is an inhibition against the debtor, although the inhibitor's preference will be preserved and given effect to in the ranking of claims where the inhibition remains otherwise unaffected by the sequestration.[38]

It is specifically provided that the trustee's failure to comply with procedural requirements relating to realisation, such as the need to consult with the commissioners or the Accountant in Bankruptcy or to follow their directions, will not affect the validity of the purchaser's title.[39]

Heritable property subject to a security

Where heritable property is subject to a valid prior security or securities, s 39(4) sets out special rules regarding the sale of the property. In broad terms, either the trustee or the heritable creditor may intimate his intention to sell the property to the other, and once he has done so, the other is precluded from taking steps to sell the property himself.[40] If, however, either the trustee or the heritable creditor, having intimated his intention to sell, then delays unduly in doing so, the other may obtain the authority of the court to sell the property himself.[41] Where the trustee is selling the property, he requires the concurrence of any heritable creditor or creditors *unless* he obtains a sufficiently high price to discharge all the securities.[42]

---

[33] 1985 Act, s 42(4).
[34] 1985 Act, s 70. This provision also applies to trustees under trust deeds. Trust deeds are discussed in Chapter 45.
[35] *Dundas* v *Morrison* (1857) 20 D 225 (rent arrears due under a lease adopted by the trustee).
[36] *Mackessack* v *Molleson* (1886) 13 R 445 (charterparty).
[37] 1985 Act, s 39(3).
[38] 1985 Act, s 31(2). An inhibition within 60 days prior to the sequestration will not be effective to secure a preference: see Chapter 31. For the ranking of the inhibiting creditor's claim where the inhibition is effective to secure a preference, see Chapter 33.
[39] 1985 Act, s 39(7).
[40] 1985 Act, s 39(4)(b).
[41] 1985 Act, s 39(4)(c).
[42] 1985 Act, s 39(4)(a).

The family home

Section 40 of the 1985 Act puts some limitations on the trustee's power to dispose of the debtor's right or interest in his 'family home'. The provision is designed to prevent undue hardship to the debtor's family.

'Family home' is defined as a home which was occupied *immediately before the date of sequestration* by (1) the debtor and spouse; or (2) the debtor and a child of the family; or (3) the debtor's spouse or former spouse.[43]

Where the property is not a family home, there are no restrictions on the trustee's right to deal with the debtor's interest in it and the debtor, and any other occupants (unless they have proprietorial rights of their own in the property—for example, as co-owners) may be evicted at the trustee's instance in order to allow him to dispose of the debtor's interest. Where the property is a family home, however, the trustee must obtain *either* the relevant consent *or* the authority of the court before selling or disposing of the debtor's interest in the home.

Relevant consent is defined in s 40(4). Where a family home is occupied by a spouse or former spouse of the debtor, it is the consent of the spouse or former spouse which is required, irrespective of who else is living there. Where there is no spouse or former spouse occupying the family home, and it is occupied by the debtor and a child of the family, it is the debtor's consent which is required.

Where the trustee does not obtain the relevant consent, he must apply to the court for authority to sell or otherwise dispose of the family home. The court may refuse the application, postpone it for up to 12 months to allow the family time to find alternative accommodation or grant it subject to any conditions which it thinks fit.[44] The court has a very wide discretion as to the nature of any conditions which it may attach to the grant of the application.[45] In reaching its decision the court must have regard to all the circumstances of the case, including the needs and financial resources of the debtor's spouse or former spouse and any child of the family, the interests of the creditors and the length of time the home has been occupied by the debtor's spouse, former spouse or child of the family before and after the sequestration.[46] These factors must also be taken into account where the trustee is seeking a division and sale of the family home or an order for vacant possession.[47] The way in which the court balances these factors can be seen in the case-law,[48] but each case will ultimately turn on its own facts.

It should be noted that s 40 applies only where the family home is being disposed of by the trustee: where a heritable creditor is selling the property, the section does not apply even if the property falls within the definition of family home.[49]

---

[43] 1985 Act, s 40(4). 'Child of the family' is defined as including any child or grandchild of the debtor or his spouse or former spouse, and any person who has been brought up or accepted by either the debtor or his spouse or former spouse as if he or she were a child of the debtor or his spouse or former spouse, whatever their age.

[44] 1985 Act, s 40(2).

[45] *McMahon's Tr* v *McMahon* (IH) 1997 SCLR 439.

[46] Ibid.

[47] 1985 Act, s 40(3).

[48] See, for example, *Salmon's Tr* v *Salmon* 1989 SLT (Sh Ct) 49; *Gourlay's Tr, Petnrs* 1995 SLT (Sh Ct) 7. See also *McMahon's Tr* v *McMahon*, note 45 above.

[49] This might be a factor in the trustee's mind when he is deciding whether to intimate to the heritable creditor that he intends to sell the property himself or whether to wait and allow the heritable creditor to sell if he wishes to do so.

Distribution of the estate

Ultimately, the permanent trustee must distribute the debtor's estate to the creditors in accordance with their respective rights. Claims are submitted to the trustee by the creditors for this purpose among others. The valuation and procedural aspects of creditors' claims are dealt with in Chapter 32, and the distribution of the estate is dealt with in Chapter 33.

Defects in procedure

The procedure involved in all aspects of sequestration is complex and it is inevitable that, on occasion, matters will be overlooked, time-limits will not be complied with and generally mistakes will be made. Section 63 of the 1985 Act allows the sheriff to make a variety of orders which can effectively cure most problems, including failure to comply with time-limits.

25 : ADMINISTRATION OF COMPANY VOLUNTARY ARRANGEMENTS AND SECTION 425 ARRANGEMENTS

The way in which CVAs and section 425 arrangements are administered depends largely on the nature and terms of the arrangement and whether the company is also subject to any other formal insolvency proceedings. This chapter considers various aspects of the administration of CVAs and section 425 arrangements.

Company voluntary arrangements

Administration of company voluntary arrangements generally

The implementation of a CVA is overseen by the supervisor(s) named in the proposal. The CVA itself will set out the role and powers of the supervisor(s) in relation to the arrangement. These will vary according to what the CVA is trying to achieve. The directors may have a role to play in the implementation of the CVA or this may be a matter solely for the supervisor(s).[1]

Joint supervisors

Where joint supervisors are appointed, the creditors may pass a resolution determining whether acts to be done in connection with the CVA may be done by one of the supervisors or must be done by all of them.[2]

Handover of property to supervisor(s)

Immediately after approval of the CVA, the supervisor(s) must be put in possession of all the assets included in the arrangement.[3] Where the company is in

---

[1] The directors are more likely to have a role in the implementation of the CVA where the company is not already in administration or liquidation, although this is not inevitable.

[2] Scottish Rules, rule 1.18(1). The arrangement itself will usually make an appropriate provision where it is proposed to appoint more than one supervisor, usually to the effect that acts may be done by either one or all of the supervisors and that by approving the proposals the creditors are deemed to have passed the appropriate resolution under this rule.

[3] Scottish Rules, rule 1.19(1). Where the company is not in administration or liquidation, it is up to the directors to do whatever is necessary to put the supervisor(s) in possession of the appropriate assets; where the company is in administration or liquidation, it is up to the administrator or liquidator to do this where he is not himself acting as supervisor.

administration or liquidation and the administrator or liquidator is not himself acting as supervisor, the supervisor must either make payment of certain specified balances due to the administrator or liquidator on taking possession of the assets,[4] or give a written undertaking to pay them out of the first realisation of assets before taking possession of the assets.[5] The balances in question are any balance due to the administrator or liquidator in respect of his remuneration, any outstanding fees, costs, charges and expenses properly incurred under the 1986 Act or the Scottish Rules, and any advances made in respect of the company, together with interest at the official rate.[6] These sums have priority over all other payments to be made out of the assets with the exception of the properly incurred expenses of realisation of the assets.[7]

Contracts

The CVA itself will regulate what is to happen to existing contracts and the power to enter new contracts. There are, however, statutory provisions regarding contracts for the supply of gas, electricity, water and telecommunications services. The suppliers of these utilities may make it a condition of continued supply that the supervisor personally guarantees payment with respect to future supplies, but may not make it a condition of continued supply that prior outstanding charges are paid.[8]

Accounts of the administration of the company voluntary arrangement

Where, in terms of the CVA, the supervisor is to run the company's business, realise assets of the company or otherwise administer or dispose of any of its funds, he must keep accounts of all his dealings in connection with the arrangement, including records of all receipts and payments of money.[9] At least once a year, commencing with the date of his appointment, he must prepare an abstract of these receipts and payments, and comments on the progress and efficiency of the arrangement, and send a copy of them to the court, the Registrar of Companies, the company, all the creditors bound by the arrangement, the company's auditors (where the company is not in liquidation) and, unless this requirement has been dispensed with altogether by the court or the court has authorised the supervisor to advertise details of the availability of the abstract and comments instead, to the members of the company who are bound by the arrangement.[10] Where there have been no payments and receipts, a report to that effect must be sent instead to those indicated.[11]

Fees, costs, charges and expenses of the company voluntary arrangement

Rule 1.22 of the Scottish Rules specifies the fees, costs, charges and expenses that may be incurred for any of the purposes of the CVA. These fall into two categories. The first is disbursements made by the nominee prior to the approval of the CVA and any remuneration for his services agreed between himself and

---

[4] Scottish Rules, rule 1.19(2).
[5] Scottish Rules, rule 1.19(3).
[6] Scottish Rules, rule 1.19(2).
[7] Scottish Rules, rule 1.19(4).
[8] 1986 Act, s 233.
[9] Scottish Rules, rule 1.21(1).
[10] Scottish Rules, rule 1.21(2) and (5).
[11] Scottish Rules, rule 1.21(2).

the company or the administrator or liquidator as appropriate.[12] The second is any fees, costs or charges which are provided for in the CVA itself or which (or the equivalent of which) would be payable in an administration or liquidation.[13]

Applications to the court for directions

The supervisor may himself apply to the court for directions in relation to any matter arising under the CVA.[14]

In addition, any creditor or other person who is dissatisfied by any act, omission or decision of the supervisor in relation to his administration of the CVA may apply to the court, and the court may confirm, reverse or modify any of the supervisor's acts or decisions, give him directions or make any other order that it thinks fit.[15]

Section 425 arrangements

Where the company is not also subject to other formal insolvency proceedings, the section 425 arrangement will generally be implemented by the directors utilising their normal powers, subject to the terms of the arrangement itself. Where the company is also subject to administration, receivership or liquidation, the arrangement will be carried out by the office holder on behalf of the company utilising his usual powers, again subject to the specific terms of the agreement.

There are no specific statutory provisions regulating particular aspects of the administration of a section 425 arrangement such as those discussed above in relation to CVAs.

---

[12] Scottish Rules, rule 1.22(a)
[13] Scottish Rules, rule 1.22(b). The arrangement will usually make detailed provision in this respect.
[14] 1986 Act, s 7(4)(a).
[15] 1986 Act, s 7(3).

26 : MANAGEMENT OF THE AFFAIRS, BUSINESS AND PROPERTY OF THE COMPANY IN ADMINISTRATION

The administrator is appointed to manage the affairs, business and property of the company during the period for which the administration order is in force.[1] This chapter sets out the functions and powers of the administrator.

Functions of the administrator

The administrator's principal function is to manage the affairs, business and property of the company during the period for which the administration order is in force.[2]

Recovery of the company's property

Recovery of property generally

The administrator is entitled, indeed has a duty, to take possession or control of all the property to which the company is or appears to be entitled[3] and he may take any proceedings which he thinks are expedient to recover the company's property.[4] He may apply to the court for an order under s 234 of the 1986 Act in terms of which the court may order any person who has in his possession or control any property, books, papers or records to which the company appears to be entitled to pay, deliver, convey, surrender or transfer (as appropriate) any such items to the administrator and thereby recover not only property but the company's books, papers and records. He may also apply to the court for an order under s 237 of the 1986 Act, in terms of which the court has power to order any person who appears to the court as a result of evidence obtained under s 236 or s 237 of the 1986 Act *either* to have in his possession property of the company *or* to owe a debt to the company to deliver the whole or part of such property to the administrator or pay the whole or any part of the debt due to the administrator as appropriate. These sections are discussed further in Chapter 29 which deals with the recovery of documents and other information generally.

---

[1] 1986 Act, s 8(2).
[2] Ibid.
[3] 1986 Act, Sched 1, para 1, and see also the 1986 Act, s 17(1).
[4] 1986 Act, Sched 1, para 1.

Challengeable transactions

The administrator may challenge certain transactions by the company prior to the administration with a view *either* to recovering assets disposed of as a result of such transactions, or their value, to be utilised in the context of the administration *or* avoiding certain securities. The types of transaction which may be challenged and the conditions which require to be satisfied for a successful challenge are discussed in Chapter 30.

Management of the company's business, property and affairs and realisation of its property

Management of the company's affairs, business and property generally

The administrator must manage the affairs, business and property of the company in accordance with the directions of the court until his proposals for achieving the purpose or purposes for which the administration order was made are approved and in accordance with the terms of the approved proposals thereafter.[5] The powers which he exercises and the way in which he exercises them will therefore depend initially on any directions he is given by the court and, after approval of his proposals, on the terms of these proposals. Any directions of the court and the terms of the proposals will, in turn, reflect the purpose or purposes for which the order was made. In addition, the court may give the administrator directions about any particular matter on his own application[6] or on an application under s 27 of the 1986 Act[7] and, where the purpose or one of the purposes for which the administration order was made is the approval of a CVA and a CVA is subsequently approved, it may give him directions as to the conduct of the administration in order to facilitate the implementation of the CVA.[8] The following description of the administrator's powers must therefore be read in the light of these provisos.

Powers of the administrator

The administrator is given extensive powers to enable him to manage the company's business, property and affairs and to realise its property, and he effectively supersedes the directors of the company.[9]

Section 14(1) of the 1986 Act states that the administrator 'may do all such things as may be necessary for the management of the affairs, business and property of the company'. In addition, he is given the specific powers contained in Sched 1 to the 1986 Act, which are identical to the statutory powers given to an administrative receiver in England and Wales and to a Scottish receiver.[10] They include:

---

[5] 1986 Act, s 17(2). For the procedure relating to the approval of the administrator's proposals, see Chapter 11.

[6] 1986 Act, s 14(3), and see further below.

[7] See Chapter 11 and also further below.

[8] 1986 Act, s 5(3)(b).

[9] See Chapter 23 in connection with the director's powers to deal with the company's property post-administration.

[10] In addition to the powers contained in the charge, an administrative receiver in England and Wales is given the powers contained in Sched 1 to the 1986 Act, and a Scottish receiver (whether or not an administrative receiver) is given the virtually identical powers contained in Sched 2 to the 1986 Act. The powers of a Scottish receiver are discussed in the following chapter.

(1) Power to get in the company's property and take any necessary proceedings to that end.

(2) Power to sell, feu, hire or otherwise dispose of the company's property by public roup or private bargain.

(3) Power to borrow money and grant security.

(4) Power to appoint a solicitor or other professionally qualified person to assist him in performing his functions.

(5) Power to bring or defend legal proceedings on behalf of the company or to refer matters to arbitration.

(6) Power to effect and maintain insurance.

(7) Power to appoint an agent to carry out tasks which the administrator cannot do or could more conveniently be done by the agent, and power to employ and dismiss employees.

(8) Power to do everything necessary for the realisation of the company's property.

(9) Power to make payments incidental to his functions.

(10) Power to carry on the business of the company.

(11) Power to establish subsidiaries of the company and transfer all or part of the company's business or property to those subsidiaries.

(12) Power to grant or take a lease on behalf of the company or accept a surrender of a lease of the company.

(13) Power to make arrangements or compromises on behalf of the company.

(14) Power to call up uncalled capital.

(15) Power to participate in the insolvency proceedings of any debtor of the company.

(16) Power to present or defend a liquidation petition.

(17) Power to do all things incidental to the exercise of his powers.

In addition, the administrator has power to remove and appoint directors of the company,[11] to call meetings of the members or creditors of the company[12] and to apply to the court for directions in relation to any matter relating to the carrying out of his functions.[13]

The administrator is an agent of the company[14] and he cannot utilise his powers to do acts which are *ultra vires* of the company—for example, to run a business which is not within the objects of the company.[15] It is specifically provided, however, that a person dealing with the administrator in good faith and for value is not obliged to inquire whether the administrator is acting within his powers.[16]

---

[11] 1986 Act, s 14(2)(a).
[12] 1986 Act, s 14(2)(b).
[13] 1986 Act, s 14(3).
[14] 1986 Act, s 14(5).
[15] See *Re Home Treat Ltd* [1991] BCLC 705.
[16] 1986 Act, s 14(6).

Contracts

Existing contracts of the company will continue after the appointment of the administrator, although the contract may contain provisions allowing any of the other parties to the contract to terminate it or exercise other specified remedies on administration. It has been held in England that in general an administrator is not entitled to break the company's contracts at will and that another party to the contract may obtain an injunction to prevent the termination of a contract by the administrator.[17] Where the administrator chooses not to continue with a contract, any other party to it will have a claim for damages for breach of contract against the company.[18]

Existing contracts of employment also continue after the making of an administration order.[19] The administrator may wish to terminate or adopt such contracts of employment depending on the circumstances—for example, whether or not it is intended to continue the company's business. It is specifically provided that nothing done (or omitted to be done) by the administrator within the 14 days after his appointment will be taken to mean that he has adopted the contract,[20] but if the administrator does not take steps to terminate the contract within that time, he will be held to have adopted it.[21] Where a contract of employment is terminated, the employee will have a claim against the company for any sums due to him as a result of the termination in the normal way.

The administrator may also enter new contracts on behalf of the company. His ability to enter some types of contract is expressly spelt out: for example, Sched 1 to the 1986 Act specifically empowers the administrator, *inter alia*, to borrow money and grant security in return, to appoint a solicitor or accountant or other professionally qualified person to assist him in the administration, to effect and maintain insurance, to employ employees and so on. His ability to enter other types of contract not specifically mentioned in Sched 1 to the 1986 Act is implied in his power to run the business[22] and to do all things incidental to his other powers,[23] although the contract would, it is suggested, have to be for and in accordance with the purposes of the administration.

There are special provisions regarding contracts for the supply of gas, electricity, water and telecommunications services. The suppliers of these utilities may make it a condition of continued supply that the administrator personally guarantees payment in respect to future supplies, but may not make it a condition of continued supply that pre-administration debts are paid.[24]

Debts or liabilities incurred under contracts entered into by an administrator, and qualifying liabilities incurred under contracts of employment adopted by an administrator, form a first charge on the company's assets and fall to be paid even before the administrator's own remuneration and expenses,[25] but an administrator is not personally liable in respect of such contracts except where this is specifically provided for. 'Qualifying liabilities' under a contract of employment are those

---

[17] See *Astor Chemicals Ltd* v *Synthetic Technology Ltd* [1990] BCLC 1.
[18] This is because the administrator is acting as agent for the company: 1986 Act, s 14(5).
[19] *Re Paramount Airways Ltd (No 3)* (1995) BCC 319.
[20] 1986 Act, s 19(10).
[21] *Re Paramount Airways Ltd (No 3)*, note 19 above.
[22] 1986 Act, Sched 1, para 14.
[23] 1986 Act, Sched 1, para 23.
[24] 1986 Act, s 233.
[25] 1986 Act, s 19(5) and (6).

sums representing wages or salary or contributions to an occupational pension scheme which are due in respect of services rendered wholly or partly after the adoption of the contract by the administrator,[26] but excluding any part of such sum which represents payment for services rendered before the adoption of the contract.[27] The terms 'wages' and 'salary' include certain holiday pay, sick pay and payments in lieu of holiday.[28]

Sale of the company's property

The administrator has power to sell the company's heritable or moveable property by public roup or private bargain,[29] subject to special rules which apply to the sale or other disposal of property subject to a security or a hire-purchase agreement.[30] There is some doubt about the administrator's power to sell property which is affected by diligence: although the carrying out of diligence and the completion of diligence already commenced is prevented by the statutory moratorium,[31] there are no provisions for the cutting down of existing diligence on administration, and such diligence therefore remains effective. If such diligence can be said to be a security within the meaning of the 1986 Act, the provisions just mentioned on sale or other disposal of property subject to a security will apply, but if not, the administrator would seem to require to procure the consent of the relevant creditor before dealing with the property. This issue was mentioned in Chapter 22 and is explored further in Chapter 31.

Property subject to a security or hire-purchase agreement

The administrator may dispose of, or otherwise exercise his powers in relation to, any property which is subject to a security which, as created, was a floating charge, as if the property was not subject to the security.[32] However, the holder of the security is given the same priority over the proceeds of the property so disposed of, or any other property directly or indirectly representing the property disposed of—for example, goods bought with the proceeds—as he had in relation to the property disposed of.[33]

The administrator may also dispose of, or otherwise exercise his powers in relation to, property subject to a security other than a floating charge as if it was not subject to the security, and may dispose of, or otherwise exercise his powers in relation to, property subject to a hire-purchase agreement as if the rights of the owner were vested in the company, but in both of these cases, may only do so with the sanction of the court.[34] For this purpose, 'hire-purchase agreement' is given an extended meaning to include conditional sale agreements, chattel leasing agreements and retention of title agreements.[35] Before giving the administrator sanction, the court will require to be satisfied that the disposal or other proposed exercise of power is likely to promote the purpose, or one or more of the

[26] 1986 Act, s 19(7).
[27] 1986 Act, s 19(8).
[28] 1986 Act, s 19(9) and (10).
[29] See above.
[30] See further below.
[31] See Chapter 10.
[32] 1986 Act, s 15(1), (3).
[33] 1986 Act, s 15(4).
[34] 1986 Act, s 15(2), (3).
[35] 1986 Act, s 15(9).

purposes, for which the administration order was granted.[36] The administrator must apply the net proceeds of the disposal towards discharging the security or paying the sums due under the hire-purchase agreement as appropriate; and where those proceeds are less than would have been expected from an open-market sale between a willing buyer and seller, the administrator must also make up the difference out of general funds.[37] The administrator must send an office copy of any order made under this section to the Registrar of Companies within 14 days of its date.[38]

The administrator must give the disponee a conveyance or other appropriate document of transfer.[39] Where property subject to a security is involved and recording, registration or intimation of the document is required to complete title, such recording, registration or intimation will have the effect of dis-encumbering or freeing the property from the security; otherwise, that effect is achieved by the document itself.[40] In the case of goods subject to a hire-purchase agreement, conditional sale agreement, chattel leasing agreement or retention of title agreement, the disposal extinguishes the owner's rights as against any third party,[41] though not against the company itself, except to the extent that the goods could have been repossessed.

Applications to the court concerning the administrator's management of the company's affairs

It has already been noted that the administrator may himself apply to the court for directions in relation to any particular matter arising out of the administration.[42]

In addition, any creditor or member of the company may apply to the court on the ground that the company's business, affairs and property are being, or have been, managed in a way which is unfairly prejudicial to all or part of the creditors or members, including at least himself, or that any actual or proposed act or omission of the administrator is so prejudicial.[43] It has already been noted that this provision may be used to challenge the approved proposals themselves,[44] but it is obviously much wider and applies to the administrator's management both prior to and after the approval of the proposals. The concept of unfair prejudice utilised here is also used as one of the grounds on which an approved CVA may be challenged and has already been discussed in that connection.[45] It is noted by Fletcher, Higham and Trower[46] that the courts have derived assistance from the reported cases on s 459 of CA 1985 in interpreting s 27 of the 1986 Act

---

[36] 1986 Act, s 15(2).
[37] 1986 Act, s 15(5). Where there are two or more securities involved, the proceeds and any additional sums which the administrator is required to make up are distributed to the security holders in order of priority of the securities: 1986 Act, s 15(6).
[38] 1986 Act, s 15(7).
[39] 1986 Act, s 16(1).
[40] Ibid.
[41] 1986 Act, s 16(2).
[42] 1986 Act, s 14(3).
[43] 1986 Act, s 27(1).
[44] See Chapter 11.
[45] See Chapter 8. See also *Re Charnley Davies Ltd (No 2)* [1990] BCLC 760, where it was held that a petition which was essentially based on negligence, rather than mismanagement, was not within s 27 of the 1986 Act.
[46] *The Law and Practice of Corporate Administration*, p 187.

and they conclude from this that the interests of a company's creditor(s) may be wider than their interests *qua* creditor, but this does not seem to accord with the way in which the identical provision in s 6 of the 1986 Act has been interpreted.[47] Of course, as noted, s 27 of the 1986 Act is wider than s 6 of the 1986 Act, but this would not seem to provide an adequate reason for a different interpretation of the two provisions. The court has a very wide discretion in dealing with an application under s 27[48] and it is specifically provided that it may in particular, *inter alia*, regulate the administrator's future management of the company, or require the administrator to do, or refrain from doing, particular acts.[49]

Distribution of the company's property

Distribution of the company's property to creditors is dealt with in Chapter 33.

Defects in procedure

Rule 7.32 of the Scottish Rules applies s 63 of the 1985 Act, subject to appropriate modifications, to all company insolvency proceedings under the 1986 Act. The section allows the court to make a variety of orders which can effectively cure most problems, including failure to comply with time-limits.

[47] See Chapter 8.
[48] 1986 Act, s 27(2).
[49] 1986 Act, s 27(4)(a) and (b) respectively.

27 : ADMINISTRATION OF THE COMPANY'S PROPERTY ON RECEIVERSHIP

The receiver is appointed to enforce the floating chargeholder's security.[1] He is therefore concerned only with that part of the company's property which is subject to the charge under which he is appointed. In practice, however, this will almost invariably be the whole of the company's property.

This chapter sets out the functions of the receiver and his powers in relation to the property attached by the charge.

Functions of the receiver

The receiver's principal function is to enforce the floating chargeholder's security, which he will do by paying sums received by him to the floating chargeholder in or towards satisfaction of the chargeholder's debt, after first paying certain other specified debts.[2]

Recovery of the company's property

Recovery of property generally

A receiver has the powers which are conferred on him by the floating charge under which he was appointed[3] and, where these are not inconsistent with the powers conferred by the charge, the powers set out in Sched 2 to the 1986 Act.[4] Paragraph 1 of Sched 2 to the 1986 Act entitles the receiver to ingather the property attached by the charge from the company, the liquidator or any other person, and to take such proceedings as are expedient to that end. An administrative receiver may apply to the court for an order under s 234 of the 1986 Act, in terms of which the court may order any person who has any property, books, papers or records to which the company appears to be entitled in his possession or control to pay, deliver, convey, surrender or transfer (as appropriate) any such

---

[1] As already noted, this makes receivership somewhat different from the other company insolvency régimes: see Chapter 4.
[2] See 1986 Act, s 60(1).
[3] 1986 Act, s 55(1).
[4] 1986 Act, s 55(2).

items to the administrative receiver and thereby recover not only property but the company's books, papers and records. An administrative receiver may also apply to the court for an order under s 237 of the 1986 Act, in terms of which the court has power to order any person who appears to the court as a result of evidence obtained under s 236 or s 237 of the 1986 Act *either* to have in his possession property of the company *or* to owe a debt to the company to deliver the whole or part of such property to the administrative receiver or pay the whole or any part of the debt due to the administrative receiver as appropriate. These sections are discussed further in Chapter 29 which deals with the recovery of documents and other information generally.

Challengeable transactions

Certain types of transaction by a company prior to insolvency may subsequently be challenged in certain circumstances,[5] but the statutory powers to challenge such transactions do not extend to a receiver, nor does a receiver have the power to challenge such transactions at common law. The creditor in the obligation secured by the charge under which he is appointed may however be in a position to challenge prior transactions *qua* creditor. The rights of a creditor in this respect are discussed further in Chapter 30.

Management of the company's business and property and realisation of its property

Management of the company's business and property generally

Where, as in most cases, the floating charge extends to the whole of the company's property and undertaking, the receiver will effectively supersede the directors of the company in the management of the company's business and property; even where it does not, he will supersede them in relation to the management of that part of the company's property which is attached by the floating charge.[6] A receiver also takes precedence over a liquidator of the company and may manage the company's business in preference to the liquidator and without the restriction applicable to the liquidator that he must only continue the company's business so far as is necessary for the beneficial winding up of the company.[7]

Statutory powers of the receiver

As noted above, a receiver has the powers which are conferred on him by the floating charge under which he was appointed[8] and, where these are not inconsistent with the powers conferred by the charge, the powers set out in Sched 2 to the 1986 Act.[9] The statutory powers conferred on the receiver are virtually identical to those conferred on an administrator, and include the following.

(1) Power to get in the company's property and take any necessary proceedings to that end.

---

[5] See Chapter 30.
[6] See Chapter 23.
[7] See Chapter 28.
[8] 1986 Act, s 55(1).
[9] 1986 Act, s 55(2).

(2) Power to sell, feu, hire or otherwise dispose of the company's property by public roup or private bargain, with or without advertisement.

(3) Power to borrow money and grant security.

(4) Power to appoint a solicitor or other professionally qualified person to assist him in performing his functions.

(5) Power to bring or defend legal proceedings on behalf of the company or to refer matters to arbitration.

(6) Power to effect and maintain insurance.

(7) Power to appoint an agent to carry out tasks which the administrator cannot do or could more conveniently be done by the agent, and power to employ and dismiss employees.

(8) Power to do everything necessary for the realisation of the company's property.

(9) Power to make payments incidental to his functions.

(10) Power to carry on the business of the company or any part of it.

(11) Power to establish subsidiaries of the company and transfer all or part of the company's business or property to those subsidiaries.

(12) Power to grant or take a lease on behalf of the company or accept a surrender of a lease of the company.

(13) Power to make arrangements or compromises on behalf of the company.

(14) Power to call up uncalled capital.

(15) Power to participate in the insolvency proceedings of any debtor of the company.

(16) Power to present or defend a liquidation petition.

(17) Power to do all things incidental to the exercise of his powers.

In addition, the receiver has the power to apply to the court for directions in respect of any matter arising out of the receivership.[10]

The receiver is an agent of the company in relation to the property attached by the charge.[11] He should not, therefore, utilise his powers to act in a way which is *ultra vires* of the company, although it is specifically provided that a person dealing with a receiver in good faith and for value is not obliged to inquire whether the receiver is acting within his powers.[12]

It should be noted that the powers of the receiver are subject to the rights of any person who has effectually executed diligence[13] and to the rights of any person who has a fixed security or floating charge which ranks prior to or *pari passu* with the floating charge in respect of which the receiver was appointed.[14]

---

[10] 1986 Act, s 63(1).

[11] 1986 Act, s 57(1).

[12] 1986 Act, s 55(4). However, such a person may wish to check whether the receiver has been validly appointed; if there is any defect in the appointment, the third party may only look to the receiver for performance of the contract, not to the company itself: the provisions of this sub-section apply only to the situation where the receiver is acting *ultra vires*.

[13] The meaning of effectually executed diligence is discussed in Chapter 31.

[14] 1986 Act, s 55(3).

Contracts

Existing contracts continue in force after the appointment of the receiver[15] but the receiver may choose whether or not to continue with any particular contract. Where he chooses not to continue with a contract, any other party to it will have a claim for damages for breach of contract against the company.[16]

Existing contracts of employment will also continue in force after the appointment of the receiver and again the receiver may choose to terminate or adopt such contracts depending on the circumstances—for example, whether or not it is intended to continue the company's business. It is specifically provided that nothing done (or omitted to be done) by the receiver within the 14 days after his appointment will be taken to mean that he has adopted the contract,[17] but if the receiver does not take steps to terminate the contract within that time, he will be held to have adopted it.[18] Where a contract of employment is terminated, the employee will have a claim against the company for any sums due to him as a result of the termination in the normal way.

The receiver may also enter new contracts on behalf of the company. Schedule 2 to the 1986 Act confers on the receiver powers to enter specific types of contract (such as borrowing money and granting security in return, appointing a solicitor or accountant or other professionally qualified person to assist him in the receivership, effecting and maintaining insurance, employing employees and so on) and, by implication from his power to run the business[19] and to do all things incidental to his other powers,[20] power to enter other contracts related to the business or his other powers which are not specifically mentioned in Sched 2 or elsewhere.

There are special provisions regarding contracts for the supply of gas, electricity, water and telecommunications services. The suppliers of these utilities may make it a condition of continued supply that the receiver personally guarantees payment in respect to future supplies, but may not make it a condition of continued supply that pre-receivership debts are paid.[21]

The receiver is personally liable on any contract entered into by him, unless such personal liability is specifically excluded, and he is also personally liable on any contract of employment adopted by him to the extent of any 'qualifying liability' under the contract.[22] 'Qualifying liabilities' are wages or salary or contributions to an occupational pension scheme which become due while the receiver is in office and which relate to services rendered wholly or partly after the adoption of the contract,[23] excluding any part of such sums which represents payment for services rendered before the adoption of the

---

[15] 1986 Act, s 57(4).
[16] Since the receiver is the agent of the company: 1986 Act, s 57(1).
[17] 1986 Act, s 57(5).
[18] *Re Paramount Airways Ltd (No 3)* (1995) BCC 319.
[19] 1986 Act, Sched 2, para 14.
[20] 1986 Act, Sched 2, para 23.
[21] 1986 Act, s 233.
[22] 1986 Act, s 57(2). The way in which the subsection is worded suggests that the receiver cannot contract out of personal liability for qualifying liabilities under any contract of employment adopted by him, although it would appear that there is nothing to stop him terminating a contract of employment and then re-employing the employee on a new contract with different terms, excluding personal liability, provided the terms are sufficiently different for him to be able to say that it really is a new contract.
[23] 1986 Act, s 57(2A).

contract.[24] The terms 'wages' and 'salary' include certain holiday pay, sick pay and payments in lieu of holiday.[25] Where the receiver does incur personal liability, however, he is entitled to be indemnified out of the assets of the company which are subject to the charge,[26] unless he has entered into or adopted the contract without authority.[27]

It should be noted that creditors in respect of all liabilities, charges and expenses incurred by or on behalf of the receiver require to be paid before the floating chargeholder, and indeed before the receiver's own liabilities, expenses, remuneration and any indemnity to which he is entitled.[28] This category does not, however, include liabilities incurred by the receiver to employees whose contract of employment he has adopted which are *not* qualifying liabilities as defined above.[29]

Sale of the company's property

The receiver has power to sell any of the company's property by public roup or private bargain, with or without advertisement,[30] subject to the special rules which apply to the sale or other disposal of property or any interest in property which is subject to another security or effectually executed diligence.[31]

Property subject to a security or effectually executed diligence

Section 61 of the 1986 Act provides that where property is subject to a security or effectually executed diligence and the receiver cannot obtain the consent of the creditor concerned to the disposal of the property, he may apply to the court for authority to sell or otherwise dispose of the property in question free of the security or diligence.[32] The court may authorise the disposal if it thinks fit and on such conditions (if any) as it thinks fit.[33] However, where the application relates to property subject to a fixed security which ranks prior to the floating charge, the court will not authorise any sale or disposal where the debt to which the security relates has not been met or provided for in full, unless it is satisfied that the sale or disposal would provide a more advantageous realisation than would otherwise be effected;[34] where it does authorise the disposal, the receiver must apply the net proceeds of the disposal towards discharging the fixed security and where those proceeds are less than would have been expected from an open-market sale between a willing buyer and seller, the receiver must also make up the difference out of general funds.[35] The receiver must send an office copy of

---

[24] 1986 Act, s 57(2B).

[25] 1986 Act, s 57(2C) and (2D).

[26] 1986 Act, s 57(3).

[27] 1986 Act, s 57(6). As noted above, the receiver is deemed to be the agent of the company, and must therefore act *intra vires* of the company's powers: if he does not, he will not be entitled to indemnity for any personal liability he incurs.

[28] 1986 Act, s 60(1).

[29] *Lindop v Stuart Noble & Sons Ltd* (OH) 7th April 1998 (unreported).

[30] 1986 Act, Sched 2, para 2.

[31] 1986 Act, s 61, discussed further below.

[32] 1986 Act, s 61(1).

[33] 1986 Act, s 61(2).

[34] 1986 Act, s 61(3). An example might be where the receiver intended to dispose of, say, a factory as part of the business, and the factory on its own and the business without the factory would be worth less than selling them both together as a going concern.

[35] 1986 Act, s 61(4). Where there are two or more securities involved, the proceeds and any additional sums which the receiver is required to make up are distributed to the security holders in order of priority of the securities: 1986 Act, s 61(5).

any order made under this section to the Registrar of Companies within 14 days of its date.[36]

The receiver must give the disponee a conveyance or other appropriate document of transfer on disposal of the property.[37] Where recording, registration or intimation of the document is required to complete title to the property disposed of, such recording, registration or intimation will have the effect of disencumbering or freeing the property from the security or diligence as appropriate; otherwise that effect is achieved by the document itself.[38]

It is specifically provided that nothing in the section prejudices the right of any creditor to rank for his debt on the liquidation of the company.[39]

Applications to the court concerning the receiver's management of the company's business and property

It has already been noted that the receiver has the power to apply to the court for directions in respect of any matter arising out of the receivership.[40]

The holder of the floating charge may similarly apply to the court to give directions to the receiver in relation to any matter arising from the receivership.[41]

Distribution of the company's property to creditors

Receivership involves only a partial distribution of the company's assets to creditors. The distribution of assets in a receivership is dealt with in more detail in Chapter 33.

Defects in procedure

Rule 7.32 of the Scottish Rules applies s 63 of the 1985 Act, subject to appropriate modifications, to all company insolvency proceedings under the 1986 Act. The section allows the court to make a variety of orders which can effectively cure most problems, including failure to comply with time-limits.

---

[36] 1986 Act, s 61(6).
[37] 1986 Act, s 61(8).
[38] Ibid.
[39] 1986 Act, s 61(9).
[40] 1986 Act, s 63(1).
[41] Ibid.

28 : ADMINISTRATION OF THE COMPANY'S ASSETS ON LIQUIDATION

The liquidator is appointed to wind up the company and distribute its assets prior to its dissolution.

This chapter sets out the liquidator's functions and describes how he recovers, manages and realises the company's assets for distribution to those entitled to them.

Functions of the liquidator

In a voluntary liquidation, the liquidator is appointed 'for the purpose of winding up the company's affairs and distributing its assets'.[1] In a compulsory liquidation, the functions of the liquidator are specifically set out as being 'to secure that the assets of the company are got in, realised and distributed to the company's creditors and, if there is a surplus, to the persons entitled to it'.[2]

Recovery of the company's property

Recovery of property generally

The liquidator has the right, indeed a duty, to take possession of the whole assets of the company and any property, books, papers or records in the possession or control of the company or to which the company is or appears to be entitled.[3] The liquidator may apply for an order under s 234 of the 1986 Act, in terms of which the court has power to order any person who has any property, books, papers or records to which the company appears to be entitled in his possession or control to pay, deliver, convey, surrender or transfer (as appropriate) any such items to the liquidator and thereby recover any property and any papers, books and records of the company. He may also apply to the court for an order under s 237 of the 1986 Act, in terms of which the court has power to order any person who appears to the court as a result of evidence obtained under s 236 or s 237 of

---

[1] 1986 Act, s 91(1) (members' voluntary liquidation) and s 100(1) (creditors' voluntary liquidation).
[2] 1986 Act, s 143(1).
[3] Scottish Rules, rule 4.22 (compulsory liquidations), applied to creditors' and members' voluntary liquidations by rule 5 and Sched 1, and rule 6 and Sched 2, respectively. See also the 1986 Act, s 144(1), in relation to compulsory liquidations.

the 1986 Act *either* to have in his possession property of the company *or* to owe a debt to the company to deliver the whole or part of such property to the administrator or pay the whole or any part of the debt due to the administrator as appropriate. In addition, he has the right to have access to, and to copy, any documents relating to the company's assets, business or finances which are in the hands of third parties[4] and a right to delivery of title deeds and other documents and records of the company even where a lien is claimed over them.[5] These provisions are discussed further in the next chapter, which deals with the recovery of documents and other information generally.

Challengeable transactions

The liquidator may challenge certain transactions by the company prior to the liquidation with a view *either* to recovering assets disposed of as result of such transactions, or their value, for distribution to the creditors through the mechanism of the liquidation process *or* to avoiding certain securities. The types of transaction which may be challenged and the conditions which require to be satisfied for a successful challenge are discussed in Chapter 30.

Money or property of the company which has been misapplied or retained by directors or others

Where, *inter alia*, money or property of the company has been misapplied or retained by directors, other officers of the company or other specified persons, the liquidator may apply to the court for an order under s 212 of the 1986 Act. The court may order the person concerned to repay, restore or otherwise account for the money or property or any part of it.[6] This section is discussed further in Chapter 38, which deals with the personal liability of directors and others.

Management of the company's business, property and affairs and realisation of its assets

Management of the company's business, property and affairs generally

In all liquidations the liquidator is given extensive powers to manage the company's business, property and affairs pending realisation and distribution of the company's assets to the creditors, but he may only carry on the business of the company so far as is necessary for the beneficial winding up of the company:[7] he cannot take it on and try to make it viable again. In addition, it is specifically provided that the exercise of certain powers conferred on a liquidator in a compulsory liquidation is subject to the control of the court,[8] and where a CVA is approved while the company is in liquidation, the court may give the liquidator directions as to the conduct of the liquidation in order to facilitate the

---

[4] Scottish Rules, rule 4.22(2) (compulsory liquidations), applied to creditors' and members' voluntary liquidations by rule 5 and Sched 1, and rule 6 and Sched 2, respectively.
[5] Scottish Rules, rule 4.22(4) (compulsory liquidations), applied to creditors' and members' voluntary liquidations by rule 5 and Sched 1, and rule 6 and Sched 2, respectively.
[6] 1986 Act, s 212(3)(a).
[7] See further below.
[8] 1986 Act, s 167(3), which states that the powers conferred by s 167 are so subject. These powers are the powers contained in Sched 4 to the 1986 Act: see further below.

implementation of the CVA.[9] The following description of the liquidator's powers must be read in the light of these provisos.

Powers of liquidator

The powers available to a liquidator in a compulsory liquidation are broadly similar, but not identical, to those available to a liquidator in a voluntary liquidation, and a liquidator in a compulsory liquidation requires sanction to exercise certain powers which a liquidator in a voluntary liquidation is able to exercise without such sanction. Powers which may be exercised without sanction are usually referred to as ordinary powers; those which require sanction as extraordinary powers. In the following discussion, all liquidations are treated together, and differences between voluntary and compulsory liquidations are identified where appropriate. It is not intended to list every power which a liquidator has, but rather to outline the most important general powers relating to management and realisation of the company's assets; where appropriate, reference is made to other powers discussed elsewhere.

Schedule 4 to the 1986 Act contains general powers available to a liquidator in a winding up. It is divided into three parts. Part I contains those powers which may be exercised in any winding up only with sanction.[10] In the case of a members' voluntary liquidation, that sanction is an extraordinary resolution of the company;[11] in the case of a creditors' voluntary liquidation, it is the sanction of the court or the liquidation committee or, if there is no liquidation committee, a meeting of the company's creditors;[12] and in the case of a compulsory liquidation, it is the sanction of the court or the liquidation committee.[13] The powers contained in Part I are:

(1) Power to pay any class of creditors in full.

(2) Power to make compromises or arrangements with creditors or those claiming to be creditors or to have claims against the company.

(3) Power to compromise any calls, debts or claims of the company and any questions relating to the company's assets or the winding up, and to take security for the discharge of any such call, debt or claim and give a complete discharge in respect of it.

Part II of Sched 4 contains powers which may be exercised by a liquidator in a compulsory liquidation with sanction,[14] and by a liquidator in a voluntary liquidation without sanction.[15] The powers contained in Part II are:

(1) Power to bring or defend any legal proceedings on behalf of the company.

(2) Power to carry on the business of the company, but only insofar as necessary for its beneficial winding up.

---

[9] 1986 Act, s 5(3)(b).

[10] 1986 Act, s 165(2) (voluntary liquidation) and s 167(1)(a) (compulsory liquidation).

[11] 1986 Act, s 165(2)(a).

[12] 1986 Act, s 165(2)(b).

[13] 1986 Act, s 167(1)(a).

[14] 1986 Act, s 167(1)(a). Where there is no liquidation committee, the liquidator may be authorised by the court to exercise these powers without the sanction or intervention of the court: 1986 Act, s 169(1).

[15] 1986 Act, s 165(3).

Part III of Sched 4 contains powers which may be exercised by all liquidators without sanction.[16] The powers contained in Part III include:

(1) Power to sell the company's property by public roup or private bargain, in parcels or otherwise.

(2) Power to participate in the insolvency proceedings of debtors of the company.

(3) Power to borrow money on the security of the company's assets.

(4) Power to do all things necessary for obtaining payment of money due from a contributory or a deceased contributory's estate.

(5) Power to appoint an agent to carry out tasks the liquidator cannot do himself.

(6) A general power to do all such things as are necessary for winding up the company's affairs and distributing its assets.

In addition, in a voluntary winding up, the liquidator has power to settle the list of contributories, make calls, summon general meetings of the company for the purpose of obtaining any necessary sanction or otherwise, pay the company's debts and adjust the rights of contributories among themselves.[17] It should be noted, however, that with some exceptions, a liquidator nominated by the company in a creditors' voluntary liquidation may only exercise these powers and the powers contained in Sched 4 with the sanction of the court before the creditors' meeting.[18] The exceptions are that the liquidator is allowed to take the company's property into his custody, to dispose of perishable goods and other goods whose value is likely to diminish if not disposed of immediately and to do whatever is necessary to safeguard the company's assets without such sanction.[19] The liquidator in a voluntary liquidation also has the power to sell or transfer all or part of the company's property to another company in exchange or part exchange for shares or other similar interests in the transferee company[20] and to apply to the court to exercise any of the powers which the court could exercise in a compulsory liquidation.[21]

In a compulsory liquidation, the liquidator has, in addition to the powers in Sched 4, and subject to the Scottish Rules, the same powers as a trustee in sequestration.[22]

In all liquidations, the liquidator may also apply for the appointment of a special manager where it appears to him that the nature of the company's business or property, or the interests of the creditors, contributories or members, require the appointment of another person to manage the business or property.[23] This

---

[16] 1986 Act, s 165(3) (voluntary liquidation) and s 167(1)(b) (compulsory liquidation).

[17] 1986 Act, s 165(4) and (5). The power to settle the list of contributories, make calls and adjust the rights of contributories is exercised by the court in a compulsory liquidation, albeit on the initiative of the liquidator: see the 1986 Act, ss 148, 150 and 154 respectively and further below.

[18] 1986 Act, s 166(1), (2).

[19] 1986 Act, s 166(3).

[20] 1986 Act, s 110. There is some dubiety over whether the liquidator in a compulsory liquidation also has this power: the matter is discussed further below in connection with the sale of the company's property.

[21] 1986 Act, s 112(1).

[22] 1986 Act, s 169(2). For the powers of a trustee in sequestration, see Chapter 24.

[23] 1986 Act, s 177(1), (2). The appointment of a special manager may also be applied for by a provisional liquidator in a compulsory liquidation, if appointed: see further Chapter 19.

allows the liquidator to obtain assistance where the company's business or property is in an area where he does not have the requisite expertise to deal with matters himself. The special manager is given any necessary powers by the court.[24] A liquidator also has power to apply to the court for an order for a contribution to the company's assets under ss 212, 213 and 214 of the 1986 Act (summary remedy against delinquent directors and others, fraudulent trading and wrongful trading respectively). These provisions are discussed further in Chapter 38, which deals with the personal liability of directors and others.

Contracts

Existing contracts of the company will continue after liquidation, although a contract may contain provisions allowing any of the other parties to the contract to terminate it or exercise other specified remedies on liquidation. The liquidator may choose whether or not to adopt any existing contract,[25] but since he may only carry on the company's business so far as is necessary for its beneficial winding up,[26] he should only adopt contracts for that purpose. He must decide whether to adopt the contract within a reasonable time, otherwise he will be held to have abandoned it.[27] What is reasonable will vary according to the circumstances and the contract involved, and where a contract is not adopted, the other party or parties to it may have a claim for damages for breach of contract in the liquidation. There is no provision such as exists in sequestration for another party to the contract to force the liquidator to decide within a set period,[28] but any other party to the contract may apply to the court to have it rescinded.[29] Where the court rescinds the contract, it may impose conditions as to the payment of damages by either the company or the other party, and where damages are to be paid by the company, these are claimed as a debt in the liquidation.[30]

In relation to contracts of employment, liquidation acts as constructive notice of termination of the contract, entitling the employee to regard himself as no longer bound by it.[31] He may leave immediately and claim damages; alternatively, the liquidator may adopt the contract or terminate it by actually dismissing the employee.

The liquidator may also enter new contracts: he is specifically empowered to enter the types of contract specified in Sched 4 to the 1986 Act (such as raising money on security and appointing an agent to do business which he is unable to

---

[24] 1986 Act, s 177(3).
[25] See, for example, *Asphaltic Limestone Concrete Co Ltd* v *Glasgow Corporation* 1907 SC 463; *Turnbull* v *Liquidator of Scottish County Investment Co* 1939 SC 5.
[26] 1986 Act, Sched 4, para 5: this power may be exercised without sanction in a voluntary winding up (1986 Act, s 165(3)), but requires the sanction of the court or the liquidation committee in a compulsory liquidation (1986 Act, s 167(1)).
[27] *Crown Estate Commissioners* v *Liquidators of Highland Engineering Ltd* 1975 SLT 58.
[28] See above.
[29] 1986 Act, s 186.
[30] Ibid.
[31] *Day* v *Tait* (1900) 8 SLT 40. Cf *Smith* v *Lord Advocate* 1978 SC 259, where the terminology employed by the court suggested that liquidation automatically terminated the employment contract, an entirely different matter. The generally accepted view, however, is that liquidation does not automatically terminate the contract but acts only as constructive notice of dismissal, which entitles the employee to treat himself as no longer bound by the contract and to leave and claim damages: see St Clair and Drummond Young, *The Law of Corporate Insolvency in Scotland* (2nd edn), pp 26–28; *Palmer's Company Law*, para 15.695.

do himself) and, by implication from his power to carry on the company's business so far as is necessary for the beneficial winding up of the company and his general power to do all such things as may be necessary for winding up the company's affairs and distributing its assets,[32] to enter other types of contract not specifically mentioned in Sched 4 or elsewhere so long as the contracts are for those purposes.

There are special provisions regarding contracts for the supply of gas, electricity, water and telecommunications services. Where the supply is for the purposes of carrying on the company's business, the suppliers of these utilities may make it a condition of continued supply that the liquidator personally guarantees payment in respect of future supplies, but may not make it a condition of continued supply that pre-liquidation debts are paid.[33]

The liquidator is not personally liable on any contract unless this has specifically been agreed.[34]

Sale of the company's property

All liquidators have power to sell the company's property by public roup or private bargain, in parcels or otherwise, without the sanction of the court,[35] subject to special rules where heritable property is subject to a security. A liquidator may sell heritable property free from any inhibition against the company although the inhibitor's preference will be preserved and given effect to in the ranking of claims where the inhibition remains otherwise unaffected by the liquidation.[36]

Where the whole of the company's business or property is to be sold or transferred to another company, the liquidator in a voluntary winding up has an express power to accept shares, policies or similar interests in the purchasing company for distribution among the members as the whole or part of the consideration for that sale or transfer,[37] or alternatively to agree that the members of the company in liquidation will participate in the profits of, or get some other benefit from, the purchasing company instead of receiving shares, policies or similar interests in the purchasing company.[38] The exercise of this power requires sanction, however:[39] in the case of a members' voluntary liquidation, the sanction of a special resolution of the company (which may confer a general sanction or one particular to a proposed arrangement) and in the case of a creditors' voluntary liquidation, the sanction of the liquidation committee or the court.[40] There is no equivalent provision in relation to compulsory liquidation. There is old authority to the effect that such an arrangement is not possible in a compulsory liquidation,[41]

---

[32] 1986 Act, Sched 4, para 5, and Sched 4, para 13, respectively: the latter power may be exercised by the liquidator without sanction in both voluntary and compulsory liquidations.

[33] 1986 Act, s 233.

[34] See *Stead Hazel & Co* v *Cooper* [1933] 1 KB 840.

[35] See above.

[36] 1986 Act, s 169(2), which gives the liquidator the powers of a trustee in sequestration, one of which is the power to sell heritable property free from an inhibition: see further Chapter 24. An inhibition within 60 days prior to the liquidation will not be effective to secure a preference: see Chapter 31. For the ranking of the inhibiting creditor's claim where the inhibition is effective to secure a preference, see Chapter 33.

[37] 1986 Act, s 110(1), (2).

[38] 1986 Act, s 110(4).

[39] 1986 Act, s 110(2), (4).

[40] 1986 Act, s 110(3).

[41] *Re London and Exchange Bank* (1867) 16 LT 340.

but it is thought that such an arrangement could in fact be effected utilising the general powers of the liquidator in a compulsory liquidation.

Where the liquidator sells or otherwise disposes of property to a person who is connected with the company (within the meaning of s 249 of the 1986 Act), and there is a liquidation committee, he must notify the committee.[42] There are also special rules about disposal of the company's property to members of the liquidation committee or other persons associated with it.[43]

Heritable property subject to a security

Where heritable property is subject to a valid prior security or securities, there are special rules regarding the sale of the property. In broad terms, either the liquidator or the heritable creditor may intimate his intention to sell the property to the other, and once he has done so, the other is precluded from taking steps to sell the property himself.[44] If, however, either the liquidator or the heritable creditor, having intimated his intention to sell, then delays unduly in doing so, the other may obtain the authority of the court to sell the property himself.[45] Where the liquidator is selling the property, he requires the concurrence of any heritable creditor or creditors *unless* he obtains a sufficiently high price to discharge all the securities.[46] It is specifically provided, however, that failure to comply with any of these formalities will not affect the title of the purchaser.[47]

Applications to the court concerning the liquidator's administration •of the liquidation

In a voluntary liquidation the liquidator himself, or any creditor or contributory, may apply to the court to determine any question arising in the liquidation, and if the court is satisfied that the determination of the question is just and beneficial, it may make any order which it thinks fit.[48]

As noted above, in a compulsory liquidation the liquidator's exercise of the powers contained in Sched 4 to the 1986 Act is specifically stated to be subject to the control of the court, and any creditor or contributory may apply to the court with respect to any exercise or proposed exercise of these powers.[49]

Other powers of the court in relation to the administration of the liquidation

Control of proceedings against the company

In a voluntary liquidation the court has power, on the application of the liquidator, to make a direction that no proceedings be commenced or continued against the

---

[42] 1986 Act, s 165(6) (voluntary liquidations) and s 167(2)(a) (compulsory liquidations).

[43] See Chapter 34, which deals with creditors' committees.

[44] 1985 Act, s 39(4)(b), as applied to liquidations of companies registered in Scotland by the 1986 Act, s 185(1)(b); see also the Scottish Rules, rule 4.22(5) (compulsory liquidations), applied to creditors' and members' voluntary liquidations by rule 5 and Sched 1, and rule 6 and Sched 2, respectively.

[45] 1985 Act, s 39(4)(c), applied to liquidations as noted ibid.

[46] 1985 Act, s 39(4)(a), applied to liquidations as noted in note 44 above.

[47] 1985 Act, s 39(7), applied to liquidations as noted in note 44 above.

[48] 1986 Act, s 112.

[49] 1986 Act, s 167(3).

company except with the leave of the court and on such terms as the court may direct.[50] In a compulsory liquidation this effect on proceedings against the company follows automatically as a consequence of the appointment of a provisional liquidator or the making of the winding-up order,[51] but the court also has power to sist proceedings against a company on the application of the company itself or any creditor or contributory at any time between presentation of the petition and the making of the winding-up order.[52]

Power of the court to sist liquidation proceedings

In a compulsory liquidation, the court has power to sist the liquidation proceedings if satisfied that, in the circumstances, the liquidation ought to be sisted.[53]

Settlement of the list of contributories and related matters

It has already been noted that in a voluntary liquidation the liquidator has power to settle the list of contributories, make calls and adjust the rights of contributories among themselves,[54] but in a compulsory liquidation these powers are exercised by the court. The list of contributories will in fact be drawn up by the liquidator and the court must then settle the list as soon as possible after the making of the winding-up order.[55] The court may then make calls on any or all of the contributories on the list to make payment of such sums as the court thinks necessary for payment of the company's debts and the liquidation expenses and for any adjustment of the rights of the contributories themselves, up to the extent of their liability.[56] The court may also order a contributory to make payment of any sums due to the company other than by way of calls,[57] and may adjust the rights of contributories among themselves.[58]

Power to arrest absconding contributory

Where there is probable cause for believing that a contributory is about to leave the UK or otherwise abscond, or remove or conceal property to avoid paying calls, the court may order the arrest of the contributory and the seizure of books, papers and moveable property.[59]

Power to order the inspection of books

The court may make an order setting out the extent to which creditors and contributories may inspect the company's books and papers.[60]

---

[50] 1986 Act, s 113.
[51] 1986 Act, s 130(2).
[52] 1986 Act, s 126.
[53] 1986 Act, s 147.
[54] See above.
[55] 1986 Act, s 148(1).
[56] 1986 Act, s 150(1).
[57] 1986 Act, s 149(1).
[58] 1986 Act, s 154.
[59] 1986 Act, s 158 (compulsory liquidation); this power would also be available in a voluntary liquidation by virtue of s 112 of the 1986 Act.
[60] 1986 Act, s 155(1) (compulsory liquidation); this power would also be available in a voluntary liquidation by virtue of s 112 of the 1986 Act.

Power to order attendance at meetings

The court may make an order requiring any officer of the company to attend any meeting of creditors, contributories or the liquidation committee to give information about the company's trade, dealings, affairs or property.[61]

The court also has extensive powers to assist the liquidator in the recovery of information. These are discussed in the following chapter.

Distribution of the company's assets

Ultimately the liquidator must distribute the company's assets to those who are entitled to them, in accordance with their respective rights. Claims are submitted to the liquidator by the creditors for this purpose among others. The valuation and procedural aspects of creditors' claims are dealt with in Chapter 32 and the distribution of the estate is dealt with in Chapter 33.

Defects in procedure

Rule 7.32 of the Scottish Rules applies s 63 of the 1985 Act, subject to appropriate modifications, to all company insolvency proceedings under the 1986 Act. The section allows the court to make a variety of orders which can effectively cure most problems, including failure to comply with time-limits.

---

[61] 1986 Act, s 157 (compulsory liquidation); this power would also be available in a voluntary liquidation by virtue of s 112 of the 1986 Act.

29 : RECOVERY OF DOCUMENTS AND OTHER INFORMATION

The efficient administration of insolvency proceedings depends greatly on all the relevant documents and other information being available to the office holder. He must have detailed information about the debtor's assets, liabilities, financial affairs and, where relevant, business affairs in order to administer the proceedings properly. Such information is essential to ensure, so far as appropriate to the particular proceedings, that all the assets to which he is or may be entitled have been identified and can be ingathered and realised properly and efficiently; that any prior transactions which can be challenged are identified and challenged; that the reasons for the insolvency and the conduct of the debtor or the directors and other officers of the company can be investigated and any appropriate contribution to the estate or the company's assets sought; and that the assets are distributed properly according to the respective rights and entitlements of those who have a right to them.

This chapter deals with the ways in which the insolvency practitioner may obtain documents and other information, including the examination of persons.

Recovery of documents

This section deals with the specific issue of recovery of documents.

Sequestration

An interim trustee may require the debtor to deliver to him, *inter alia*, any document relating to the debtor's business or financial affairs belonging to or in the possession of the debtor or in his control.[1] A permanent trustee is similarly empowered, indeed required, as soon as may be after his confirmation in office, to take possession of any document in the debtor's possession or control which relates to the latter's assets or business or financial affairs.[2] A permanent trustee is also empowered to have access to and to copy such documents in the hands of third parties[3] and may require delivery of any title deeds or other documents of

---

[1] 1985 Act, s 18(2)(a).
[2] 1985 Act, s 38(1)(a).
[3] 1985 Act, s 38(2).

the debtor even where their holder claims a lien over them—for example, a solicitor claiming a lien over title deeds pending payment of his account.[4] The holder of the deeds or documents will, however, remain entitled to any preference to which he would have been entitled as a result of his lien, notwithstanding that he has had to hand the title deeds or documents over to the permanent trustee.[5]

Anyone who obstructs the permanent trustee in exercising the power to have access to and to copy documents outlined above may be ordered to cease obstructing him by the court.[6] Apart from this provision, the 1985 Act does not make any specific provision for the situation where an interim or permanent trustee meets with a lack of co-operation in taking possession of documents to which he is entitled. However, a permanent trustee is empowered to bring proceedings in relation to the estate of the debtor[7] and can therefore utilise that power to recover any documents to which he is entitled. He can also simply request the debtor either to hand over any relevant documents in his possession or to co-operate in retrieving any such documents from third parties: the debtor is required to co-operate with the permanent trustee in terms of s 64 of the 1985 Act and a debtor who fails to do so may be ordered to do so by the court.[8] The court may also, in the context of a private or public examination, order the debtor or any relevant person to produce for inspection any document in his custody and control which relates to the debtor's assets, his dealings with his assets or his conduct in relation to his business or financial affairs and to deliver any such document or a copy of it to the permanent trustee.[9]

Liquidation

A liquidator's powers to take possession of, and to have access to and copy, documents are essentially identical to those of a permanent trustee.[10] A liquidator is required, as soon as possible after his appointment, to take possession of any books, papers or records which are either in the possession or control of the company or to which the company otherwise appears to be entitled.[11] He is also empowered to have access to and to copy such documents in the hands of third parties[12] and to require delivery of any title deeds or other documents of the debtor even where the holder of the deeds or documents claims a lien over them.[13] As in sequestration, however, the holder of the deeds or documents will remain entitled to any preference to which he would otherwise have been entitled as a result of the lien, notwithstanding that he has had to hand the title deeds or documents over to the liquidator.[14]

---

[4] 1985 Act, s 38(4).
[5] Ibid, and see *Findlay* v *Waddell* 1910 SC 670.
[6] 1985 Act, s 38(3). Failure to comply with such an order would amount to contempt of court.
[7] 1985 Act, s 39(2), and see Chapter 24.
[8] 1985 Act, s 64(2), and see Chapter 35. Failure to comply with the court order is an offence: 1985 Act, s 64(3).
[9] 1985 Act, s 46(4). Examination of persons is discussed further below.
[10] See above.
[11] Scottish Rules, rule 4.22(1)(a) (compulsory liquidations), rule 5 (creditors' voluntary liquidations), and rule 6 and Sched 2 (members' voluntary liquidations).
[12] Scottish Rules, rule 4.22(2) (compulsory liquidations), rule 5 (creditors' voluntary liquidations), and rule 6 and Sched 2 (members' voluntary liquidations).
[13] Scottish Rules, rule 4.22(4) (compulsory liquidations), rule 5 (creditors' voluntary liquidations), and rule 6 and Sched 2 (members' voluntary liquidations).
[14] Ibid, and see *Findlay* v *Waddell*, note 5 above.

Anyone obstructing the liquidator in exercising his power to have access to and to copy documents may be ordered to cease so obstructing him by the court.[15] In addition, s 234 of the 1986 Act provides that where the company, *inter alia*, goes into liquidation, or a provisional liquidator is appointed, the court may require anyone who has in his possession or control, *inter alia*, any books, papers or records to which the company appears to be entitled to hand them over to the liquidator or provisional liquidator. There are also two separate provisions similar to that relating to production of documents in the context of a private or public examination in a sequestration. Section 236 of the 1986 Act, which makes provision for the examination of specified persons about the company's dealings where the company, *inter alia*, goes into liquidation, or a provisional liquidator is appointed,[16] also provides that the court may require any such person, *inter alia*, to produce any books, papers or other records in his possession or under his control relating to the company or its promotion, formation, business, dealings, affairs or property.[17] Section 198 of the 1986 Act, which makes provision for the examination of certain persons regarding the trade, dealings, affairs or property of a company which is in the course of being wound up,[18] also provides that such a person may be ordered to produce any books or papers called for by the court which are in his possession or power.[19]

Administration and receivership

There are no specific provisions empowering or requiring an administrator or receiver to take possession of, or to have access to and copy, documents comparable to those available on sequestration or liquidation,[20] although it is arguable that either would be able to obtain, at the very least, access to documents on the basis of his general powers. However, ss 234 and 236 of the 1986 Act, discussed above in the context of liquidation, also apply where a company has gone into administration or an administrative receiver has been appointed, and an administrator or administrative receiver would therefore be able to utilise those provisions in the same way as a liquidator or provisional liquidator.[21]

Company voluntary arrangements and section 425 arrangements

There is very little provision for recovery of documents in CVAs. Where a proposal for a CVA is made by the directors, or by the administrator or liquidator of a company where he is not acting himself as nominee, the directors, or the administrator or liquidator as the case may be, must give the nominee access to

---

[15] Scottish Rules, rule 4.22(3) (compulsory liquidations), rule 5 (creditors' voluntary liquidations), and rule 6 and Sched 2 (members' voluntary liquidations). Failure to comply with such an order would amount to contempt of court.

[16] See further below.

[17] 1986 Act, s 236(3). For a more detailed discussion of the operation of s 236 of the 1986 Act in relation to examination of persons, many aspects of which are equally relevant to production of documents under that section, see Recovery of information: examination of persons, p 222 below.

[18] See further below.

[19] 1986 Act, s 198(3). For a more detailed discussion of the operation of s 198 of the 1986 Act, including the production of documents under that section, see Recovery of information: examination of persons, p 222 below.

[20] See above.

[21] See above.

the company's accounts and records.[22] Once the CVA has been approved, however, while the directors or, if he himself is not the supervisor, the administrator or liquidator, must put the supervisor into possession of all the assets included in the arrangement,[23] no separate mention is made of records or documents. This lack of provision may simply be because it was regarded as unnecessary: where the proposal is being made by the administrator or liquidator, he will already have all the relevant documents or will be able to obtain them using his powers as administrator or liquidator[24] and will have no reason not to co-operate with the nominee and subsequent supervisor where he is not occupying those roles himself, and where the proposal is made by the directors, they will also be co-operative. Third parties may not be so co-operative, however, and neither a nominee nor a supervisor who is not an administrator or liquidator would appear to have any power to force them to co-operate. Although the supervisor of a CVA has the power to apply to the court for directions, this provision would not seem to be wide enough to entitle him to an order against an unco-operative third party, and any provision in the arrangement itself would be of no use against a third party not bound by the arrangement.

The position in relation to section 425 arrangements would appear to be somewhat better. Where the company is already in administration, receivership or liquidation, the relevant office holder, who will be implementing the arrangement, will be able to utilise the powers he has in relation to documents in his capacity as administrator, receiver or liquidator. Where it is not, the company itself will be administering the arrangement and will be able to recover any documents belonging to it from third parties in the normal way.

Recovery of information: statements of affairs

This section deals with the obligation of the debtor or other prescribed persons to provide the relevant office holder with information in the form of a formal statement, referred to here as a statement of affairs.[25]

Sequestration

Where a petition for sequestration is presented by an individual debtor himself, he must lodge with the petition a statement of assets and liabilities[26] and send a copy of it to the Accountant in Bankruptcy on the day the petition is presented.[27]

---

[22] Scottish Rules, rule 1.6(3) (proposal by directors), and rule 1.12(4) (proposal by administrator or liquidator not acting himself as nominee).

[23] Scottish Rules, rule 1.19(1).

[24] See above.

[25] Strictly speaking, this term is slightly inaccurate in relation to the statement to be produced by the debtor in a sequestration, because although the 1986 Act uses the term 'statement of [the company's] affairs' to describe the statement to be produced in the relevant company insolvency proceedings, the 1985 Act uses the term 'statement of assets and liabilities'. However, for ease of reference the general term 'statement of affairs' will be used here to include all such statements. They must not be confused, however, with the 'statement of the debtor's affairs' which the interim trustee is required to produce in a sequestration and which, although based partly on the statement of assets and liabilities provided by the debtor, is quite distinct from it: see further in this connection Chapter 7.

[26] 1985 Act, s 5(6A)(a).

[27] 1985 Act, s 5(6A)(b). Failure to comply with this requirement without reasonable excuse is an offence: 1985 Act, s 5(9), (10).

Where the Accountant in Bankruptcy is not appointed interim trustee, the debtor must also send a copy of the statement to the interim trustee within seven days of the latter's appointment.[28]

Where a petition for sequestration is presented by a creditor or a trustee acting under a trust deed, the debtor must send a statement of assets and liabilities to the interim trustee within seven days of receiving notification of his appointment under s 2(7) of the 1985 Act.[29] 'Debtor' in this context would not appear to be confined to a living individual: the term is used generally and s 73(1) of the 1985 Act defines debtor as including, without prejudice to the expression's generality, an entity whose estate may be sequestrated by virtue of s 6 of the 1985 Act, a deceased debtor or his executor or a person entitled to be appointed as his executor. The Act obviously cannot mean that a deceased debtor must provide a statement of assets and liabilities, since this is physically impossible, but Professor McBryde takes the view that as a result of the definition in s 73(1) of the 1985 Act, an executor or person entitled to be appointed as executor would be required to provide one.[30]

The 1985 Act defines a statement of assets and liabilities as a document (including a copy of a document) in such form as may be prescribed containing a list of the debtor's assets and liabilities, a list of income and expenditure and such other information as is prescribed.[31]

If the debtor without reasonable excuse fails to disclose any material fact, or makes a material misstatement, in the statement, he is guilty of an offence.[32]

Where a certificate of summary administration has been granted, the permanent trustee must require the debtor to produce a written account of his affairs every six months.[33] Where the debtor fails to produce the required account, the permanent trustee could apply for an order under s 64 of the 1985 Act ordaining the debtor to produce it on the grounds that the latter had failed to co-operate with him.[34]

Liquidation

There is no provision for statements of affairs in a members' voluntary liquidation. Where a members' voluntary liquidation is converted to a creditors' voluntary liquidation, however, the liquidator must prepare a statement of affairs in the prescribed form to be laid before the creditors' meeting.[35] Here, the function of the statement of affairs is not to give the office holder information, but to give information to the creditors. Section 95(4) of the 1986 Act states that the statement of affairs must be verified by affidavit by the liquidator and must contain the following.

---

[28] 1985 Act, s 19(1). Failure to do so without reasonable excuse is an offence: 1985 Act, s 19(3), (4).
[29] 1985 Act, s 19(2). Failure to do so without reasonable excuse is an offence: 1985 Act, s 19(3), (4).
[30] *Bankruptcy*, p 142.
[31] 1985 Act, s 73(1). The prescribed form is Form 4 in the Schedule to the Bankruptcy (Scotland) Regulations 1985 (SI 1985/1925), as amended.
[32] 1985 Act, ss 5(9), (10) and 19(3), (4).
[33] 1985 Act, Sched 2A, para 2.
[34] Section 64 of the 1985 Act has already been mentioned above in connection with recovery of documents. Failure to comply with any such order would amount to contempt of court.
[35] 1986 Act, s 95(3).

(1) Particulars of the company's assets, debts and liabilities.[36]

(2) The names and addresses of its creditors.[37]

(3) The securities held by such creditors[38] and the dates they were given.[39]

(4) Such other information as may be prescribed.[40]

The prescribed form for the statement of affairs is Form 4.4 (Scot) in Sched 5 to the Scottish Rules.[41]

In a creditors' voluntary liquidation the directors must make up a statement of affairs in the prescribed form to be laid before the creditors' meeting.[42] The statement of affairs must also be sent to the liquidator when appointed.[43] It must be verified by affidavit by some or all of the directors[44] and again must show:

(1) Particulars of the company's assets, debts and liabilities.[45]

(2) The names and addresses of its creditors.[46]

(3) The securities held by such creditors[47] and the dates they were given.[48]

(4) Such other information as may be prescribed.[49]

Again, the prescribed form for the statement of affairs is Form 4.4 (Scot) in Sched 5 to the Scottish Rules.[50] It must be made up to the later of the nearest practicable date before the meeting of creditors *or* a date not more than 14 days before the passing of the winding-up resolution,[51] and where it is not made up to the date of the creditors' meeting, the directors must cause a report of any material transactions between the date of the statement of affairs and the date of the meeting to be given to the meeting.[52] If the directors fail without reasonable excuse to comply with their obligations under s 99(1) or (2) of the 1986 Act in relation to the statement of affairs, they will be guilty of an offence.[53] However,

---

[36] 1986 Act, s 95(4)(a).

[37] 1986 Act, s 95(4)(b).

[38] 1986 Act, s 95(4)(c).

[39] 1986 Act, s 95(4)(d).

[40] 1986 Act, s 95(4)(e).

[41] Scottish Rules, rule 7.30.

[42] 1986 Act, s 99(1).

[43] Scottish Rules, rule 4.7(3), as substituted in its application to creditors' voluntary liquidations by the Scottish Rules, rule 5 and Sched 2. See also the Scottish Rules, rule 4.7(3A), which imposes a similar obligation on the directors to send a copy of the statement of affairs to the liquidator nominated by the company where the company meeting takes place on a day prior to the creditors' meeting.

[44] 1986 Act, s 99(2).

[45] 1986 Act, s 99(2)(a).

[46] 1986 Act, s 99(2)(b).

[47] 1986 Act, s 99(2)(c).

[48] 1986 Act, s 99(2)(d).

[49] 1986 Act, s 99(2)(e).

[50] Scottish Rules, rule 4.7(2), as substituted in its application to creditors' voluntary liquidations by the Scottish Rules, rule 5 and Sched 2.

[51] Scottish Rules, rule 4.7(5), as substituted in its application to creditors' voluntary liquidations by the Scottish Rules, rule 5 and Sched 2.

[52] Scottish Rules, rule 4.7(6), as substituted in its application to creditors' voluntary liquidations by the Scottish Rules, rule 5 and Sched 2.

[53] 1986 Act, s 99(3).

they may be able to obtain payment of any reasonable and necessary expenses of preparing the statement of affairs.[54]

In a compulsory liquidation, where a winding-up order has been made or a provisional liquidator appointed, the liquidator or provisional liquidator may require some or all of a number of specified persons to make out and submit to him a statement of affairs in the prescribed form.[55]

The statement of affairs must be verified by affidavit by the persons required to submit it[56] and must contain the following.

(1) Particulars of the company's assets, debts and liabilities.[57]

(2) The names and addresses of its creditors.[58]

(3) The securities held by such creditors[59] and the dates they were given.[60]

(4) Such other information as may be prescribed or as the liquidator or provisional liquidator may require.[61]

The prescribed form for the statement of affairs is Form 4.4 (Scot) in Sched 5 to the Scottish Rules.[62]

The persons who are liable to be called upon to submit such a statement of affairs are prescribed by s 131(3) of the 1986 Act as follows.

(1) Anyone who is or has been an officer of the company.[63]

(2) Anyone who took part in the formation of the company within the year preceding the relevant date.[64]

(3) Anyone employed by the company or who was employed by the company within the year preceding the relevant date whom the liquidator or provisional liquidator believes to be capable of giving the information required.[65]

(4) Anyone who is, or was within the year preceding the relevant date, an officer or employee of another company which itself is, or within that year was, an officer of the company in liquidation.[66]

The relevant date is the date of the winding-up order or, where a provisional liquidator was appointed, the date of his appointment.[67]

---

[54] Scottish Rules, rule 4.9, as substituted in its application to creditors' voluntary liquidations by the Scottish Rules, rule 5 and Sched 2. If such a payment is made, it counts as an expense of the liquidation.
[55] 1986 Act, s 131(1), as modified in its application to Scotland by s 131(8).
[56] 1986 Act, s 131(2).
[57] 1986 Act, s 131(2)(a).
[58] 1986 Act, s 131(2)(b).
[59] 1986 Act, s 131(2)(c).
[60] 1986 Act, s 131(2)(d).
[61] 1986 Act, s 131(2)(e).
[62] Scottish Rules, rule 4.8(1).
[63] 1986 Act, s 131(3)(a).
[64] 1986 Act, s 131(3)(b).
[65] 1986 Act, s 131(3)(c). 'Employed' includes employed under a contract for services: 1986 Act, s 131(6).
[66] 1986 Act, s 131(3)(d). 'Employed' includes employed under a contract for services: 1986 Act, s 131(6).
[67] 1986 Act, s 131(6).

Where the liquidator or provisional liquidator decides that he will require some or all of the specified persons to submit a statement of affairs, he must send to any such person a notice in the appropriate form requiring him to do so.[68] Persons notified to submit a statement of affairs must do so within 21 days of the day following the day on which the prescribed notice is given,[69] unless *either* the liquidator or provisional liquidator releases the person concerned from the requirement to submit the statement or extends the time-limit[70] *or* the court decides to do either of these things where the liquidator or provisional liquidator has refused to do so.[71] Anyone who fails without reasonable excuse to comply with any obligation imposed under s 131 of the 1986 Act is liable to a fine and a daily default fine for continued contravention.[72] However, a person required to submit a statement of affairs may apply to the liquidator or provisional liquidator for an allowance towards the expenses of preparing it on the grounds that he cannot do so properly himself and the liquidator or provisional liquidator may authorise such an allowance.[73] His decision as to whether to authorise the allowance is subject to appeal.[74]

Administration

Once an administration order has been made, the administrator must forthwith require some or all of a number of specified persons to make out and submit to him a statement of affairs in the prescribed form.[75]

Section 22(2) of the 1986 Act states that the statement of affairs must be verified by affidavit by the persons required to submit it and must contain the following.

(1) Particulars of the company's assets, debts and liabilities.[76]

(2) The names and addresses of its creditors.[77]

(3) The securities held by such creditors[78] and the dates they were given.[79]

(4) Such other information as may be prescribed.[80]

The prescribed form for the statement of affairs is Form 2.6 (Scot) in Sched 5 to the Scottish Rules.[81]

The persons who are liable to be called upon to submit such a statement of affairs are prescribed by s 22(3) of the 1986 Act as follows.

---

[68] Scottish Rules, rule 4.7(3). The appropriate form is Form 4.3 (Scot) in Sched 5 to the Scottish Rules.

[69] 1986 Act, s 131(4).

[70] 1986 Act, s 131(5). The time-limit may be extended in the original notice or subsequently.

[71] Ibid.

[72] 1986 Act, s 131(7).

[73] Scottish Rules, rule 4.9(1). If the allowance is authorised, it forms an expense of the liquidation: Scottish Rules, rule 4.9(5).

[74] Scottish Rules, rule 4.9(6).

[75] 1986 Act, s 22(1).

[76] 1986 Act, s 22(2)(a).

[77] 1986 Act, s 22(2)(b).

[78] 1986 Act, s 22(2)(c).

[79] 1986 Act, s 22(2)(d).

[80] 1986 Act, s 22(2)(e).

[81] Scottish Rules, rule 2.5(1).

(1) Anyone who is or has been an officer of the company.[82]

(2) Anyone who took part in the formation of the company within the year preceding the date of the administration order.[83]

(3) Anyone employed by the company or who was employed by the company within the year preceding the date of the administration order whom the administrator believes to be capable of giving the information required.[84]

(4) Anyone who is, or was within the year preceding the date of the administration order, an officer or employee of another company which itself is, or within that year was, an officer of the company in administration.[85]

Once the administrator has decided whom he will require to submit a statement of affairs, he must send to such persons a notice in the appropriate form requiring them to do so.[86] Persons notified to submit a statement of affairs must do so within 21 days of the day following the day on which the prescribed notice is given,[87] unless *either* the administrator releases the person concerned from the requirement to submit the statement or extends the time-limit[88] *or* the court decides to do either of these things where the administrator has refused to do so.[89] Anyone who fails to comply with any obligation imposed under s 22 without reasonable excuse is liable to a fine and a daily default fine for continued contravention.[90] However, a person required to submit a statement of affairs may be paid any expenses incurred in doing so which the administrator considers reasonable,[91] his decision on that matter being subject to appeal.[92]

Receivership

On his appointment a receiver must forthwith require some or all of a number of specified persons to make out and submit to him a statement of affairs in the prescribed form.[93]

The statement of affairs must be verified by affidavit by those required to submit it[94] and must contain:

(1) Particulars of the company's assets, debts and liabilities.[95]

(2) The names and addresses of its creditors.[96]

---

[82] 1986 Act, s 22(3)(a).

[83] 1986 Act, s 22(3)(b).

[84] 1986 Act, s 22(3)(c). 'Employed' includes employed under a contract for services: 1986 Act, s 22(3).

[85] 1986 Act, s 22(3)(d). 'Employed' includes employed under a contract for services: 1986 Act, s 22(3).

[86] Scottish Rules, rule 2.4(2). The appropriate form is Form 2.5 (Scot) in Sched 5 to the Scottish Rules.

[87] 1986 Act, s 22(4).

[88] 1986 Act, s 22(5). The time-limit may be extended in the original notice or subsequently.

[89] Ibid.

[90] 1986 Act, s 22(6).

[91] Scottish Rules, rule 2.6(1). The administrator is not, however, personally liable for such expenses: they fall to be paid from the administrator's receipts.

[92] Scottish Rules, rule 2.6(2).

[93] 1986 Act, s 66(1).

[94] 1986 Act, s 66(2).

[95] 1986 Act, s 66(2)(a).

[96] 1986 Act, s 66(2)(b).

(3) The securities held by such creditors[97] and the dates they were given.[98]

(4) Such other information as may be prescribed.[99]

The prescribed form for the statement of affairs is Form 5 (Scot) in the Schedule to the Receivers (Scotland) Regulations 1986.[100]

The persons who are liable to be called on to submit a statement of affairs are prescribed by s 66(2) of the 1986 Act and are:

(1) Anyone who is or has been an officer of the company.[101]

(2) Anyone who took part in the formation of the company within the year preceding the date of the appointment of the receiver.[102]

(3) Anyone employed by the company or who was employed by the company within the year preceding the date of the appointment of the receiver whom the receiver believes to be capable of giving the information required.[103]

(4) Anyone who is, or was within the year preceding the date of the appointment of the receiver, an officer or employee of another company which itself is, or within that year was, an officer of the company in receivership.[104]

Once the receiver has decided whom he will require to submit a statement of affairs, he must send to such persons a notice in the appropriate form requiring them to do so.[105] Persons notified to submit a statement of affairs must do so within 21 days of the day following the day on which the prescribed notice is given,[106] unless *either* the receiver releases the person concerned from the requirement to submit the statement or extends the time-limit[107] *or* the court decides to do either of these things where the receiver has refused to do so.[108] Anyone who fails to comply with any obligation imposed under s 66 without reasonable excuse is liable to a fine and a daily default fine for continued contravention.[109] However, a person required to submit a statement of affairs may be paid any expenses incurred in doing so which the receiver considers reasonable,[110] his decision on that matter being subject to appeal.[111]

---

[97] 1986 Act, s 66(2)(c).

[98] 1986 Act, s 66(2)(d).

[99] 1986 Act, s 66(2)(e).

[100] SI 1986/1917; Scottish Rules, rule 3.2(1).

[101] 1986 Act, s 66(3)(a).

[102] 1986 Act, s 66(3)(b).

[103] 1986 Act, s 66(3)(c). 'Employed' includes employed under a contract for services: 1986 Act, s 66(3).

[104] 1986 Act, s 66(3)(d). 'Employed' includes employed under a contract for services: 1986 Act, s 66(3).

[105] Scottish Rules, rule 3.2(1). The appropriate form is Form 3.1 (Scot) in Sched 5 to the Scottish Rules.

[106] 1986 Act, s 66(4).

[107] 1986 Act, s 66(5). The time-limit may be extended in the original notice or subsequently.

[108] Ibid.

[109] 1986 Act, s 66(6).

[110] Scottish Rules, rule 3.3(1). Such expenses are treated an expense of the receivership.

[111] Scottish Rules, rule 3.3(2).

Company voluntary arrangements

Where a proposal for a CVA is made by the directors of a company, they are required to deliver a statement of the company's affairs to the nominee within seven days after the delivery of their proposal to him or such longer period as he allows.[112] The content of the statement of affairs is prescribed by rule 1.5(2) of the Scottish Rules, which states that it must contain details of the following matters, supplementing or amplifying the particulars already given in the directors' proposal.[113]

(1) A list of the company's assets, divided into categories for easy identification, with estimated values.[114]

(2) Particulars of any secured claim, including its amount and how and when the security was created.[115]

(3) The names and addresses of the preferential creditors and the amounts of their claims.[116]

(4) The names and addresses of the unsecured creditors and the amounts of their claims.[117]

(5) Details of any debts owed to the company by persons connected with it and debts owed by the company to persons connected with it.[118]

(6) The names and addresses of the company's members and details of their shareholdings.[119]

(7) Any other particulars which the nominee has requested in writing be provided.[120]

The statement of affairs must be made up to a date within the period of two weeks prior to the notice of the proposal given to the nominee, unless the nominee permits it to be made up to an earlier date, which must be the nearest practical date and must not in any event be any earlier than two months prior to the date of the notice.[121] The statement must be certified by two or more directors (or the company secretary and at least one director other than the company secretary) as being correct to the best of the knowledge and belief of those so certifying it.[122]

Where the proposal for a CVA is made by an administrator or liquidator but he himself is not acting as nominee, he must give the nominee a copy of the company's statement of affairs along with his proposal.[123]

---

[112] 1986 Act, s 2(3), and Scottish Rules, rule 1.5(1).
[113] The directors' proposal must contain certain prescribed information: for details of this, see Chapter 8.
[114] Scottish Rules, rule 1.5(2)(a).
[115] Scottish Rules, rule 1.5(2)(b).
[116] Scottish Rules, rule 1.5(2)(c). For preferential claims, see Chapter 33.
[117] Scottish Rules, rule 1.5(2)(d).
[118] Scottish Rules, rule 1.5(2)(e). 'Connected persons' are defined in s 249 of the 1986 Act.
[119] Scottish Rules, rule 1.5(2)(f).
[120] Scottish Rules, rule 1.5(2)(g).
[121] Scottish Rules, rule 1.5(3).
[122] Scottish Rules, rule 1.5(4).
[123] Scottish Rules, rule 1.12(5). Statements of affairs in administration or liquidation are discussed above.

Curiously, although the directors or, if he himself is not the supervisor, the administrator or liquidator must put the supervisor into possession of all the assets included in the arrangement once the arrangement has been approved,[124] there appears to be no requirement for a nominee who has not become supervisor to hand over records and documents, including the statement of affairs, to the supervisor, although in practice this will in fact be done.[125]

Recovery of information: examination of persons

This section deals with the recovery of information through the examination of persons.

Sequestration

There are three ways in which a trustee in sequestration may seek to recover information directly from the debtor or others.

(1) Appearance before trustee.

Although not an examination as such, both an interim and a permanent trustee may request a debtor to appear before him and give information on his assets, his dealings with them, or his conduct in relation to his business or financial affairs.[126] Where the debtor is an entity rather than an individual, there is a curious discrepancy between the powers of an interim and a permanent trustee in relation to this provision. Section 44(4) of the 1985 Act states that where the debtor is an entity rather than an individual, references in the section to the debtor are to be construed as references to a person representing the entity.[127] A permanent trustee on the sequestrated estates of an entity is therefore able to request a person representing the entity to appear before him and give information in the same way as a permanent trustee on the sequestrated estates of an individual debtor can request the debtor to appear and give information. It would appear, however, that an interim trustee on the sequestrated estates of an entity cannot request a person representing the entity to appear before him in the same way. Section 20 of the 1985 Act contains no provision equivalent to s 44(4), and s 20(5) applies the provisions of s 44(4) to a private examination by the interim trustee only, and not to a request for an appearance before him.[128]

Both an interim and a permanent trustee may also request a debtor's spouse, or any other person whom the interim or permanent trustee believes has relevant information about the debtor's assets, his dealings with them, or his conduct in relation to his business or financial affairs, to appear before him and divulge any such information to him.[129]

There is no sanction for failing to comply with a request to appear before the trustee or for failing to give information. Since, however, both an interim and a permanent trustee may apply for a private examination

---

[124] Scottish Rules, rule 1.19(1).
[125] See also discussion on CVAs in relation to recovery of documents above.
[126] 1985 Act, s 20(4) (interim trustee) and s 44(1) (permanent trustee).
[127] This provision also applies to references to the debtor in ss 45 to 47 of the 1985 Act, discussed further below.
[128] Private examinations are discussed below.
[129] 1985 Act, s 20(4) (interim trustee) and s 44(1) (permanent trustee).

and a permanent trustee may, in addition, apply for a public examination, failure to co-operate is likely to result in an application for such an examination.

(2) Private examination.

Both an interim and a permanent trustee may apply to the sheriff for a private examination of the debtor, his spouse or any other person whom the trustee believes can give him the required information.[130] Where the debtor is an entity, rather than an individual, 'debtor' is construed as a person representing the entity, with the result that a private examination of such a person may be sought: unlike the situation in relation to a request to appear before the trustee, this is the case whether the examination is sought by an interim or permanent trustee.[131] The decision whether to order a private examination is a matter for the sheriff's discretion. Where a private examination is ordered, the person to be examined is cited to attend before the sheriff in private[132] and failure to appear without reasonable excuse is an offence.[133] The examination is conducted on oath[134] and a charge of perjury may therefore result if it is subsequently discovered that the examinee has not told the truth. The trustee or his legal representative may question the examinee about the debtor's assets, his dealings with them and his conduct in relation to his business or financial affairs. Where the examinee is someone other than the debtor, the debtor may also ask questions.[135] The examinee is obliged to answer any questions put to him relating to the matters specified and may not refuse to answer questions on the ground that his answers may be incriminating or on the ground of confidentiality, but the answer to a question is not admissible in evidence in any subsequent criminal proceedings except those for perjury, and a person need not disclose any information received from a person who is not also called for examination if the information is confidential between them.[136] The examinee may be ordered to produce any relevant documents in his custody or control and to deliver such documents or copies thereof to the interim or permanent trustee as appropriate.[137]

(3) Public examination.

The permanent trustee may apply to the sheriff for a public examination of the debtor, his spouse or any other person whom the trustee believes

---

[130] 1985 Act, s 20(4) (interim trustee) and s 44(1), (2) (permanent trustee).

[131] 1985 Act, s 20(5), applying s 44(4) (interim trustee) and s 44(4) (permanent trustee).

[132] On a date not less than eight and not more than 16 days after the date of the order: 1985 Act, s 44(2) (private examination at the request of the permanent trustee; also applied to private examinations at the request of the interim trustee by s 20(5)).

[133] 1985 Act, s 44(3) (private examination at the request of the permanent trustee; also applied to private examinations at the request of the interim trustee by s 20(5)).

[134] 1985 Act, s 47(1) (applied to private examinations at the request of the interim trustee by s 20(5)).

[135] 1985 Act, s 47(2) (applied to private examinations at the request of the interim trustee by s 20(5)).

[136] 1985 Act, s 47(3) (applied to private examinations at the request of the interim trustee by s 20(5)).

[137] 1985 Act, s 46(4) (applied to private examinations at the request of the interim trustee by s 20(5)): see also above in relation to recovery of documents.

can give him the required information.[138] As in relation to a private examination, where the debtor is an entity, rather than an individual, 'debtor' is construed as a person representing the entity, with the result that a public examination of such a person may be sought.[139] Where the Accountant in Bankruptcy, the commissioners or at least one-quarter in value of the creditors request him to do so, the permanent trustee must apply for a public examination.[140] The sheriff has no discretion as to whether or not to order a public examination: he must do so.[141] The person or persons to be examined are cited to attend for examination in open court[142] and there is an elaborate procedure for publicising the examination.[143] Failure on the part of the person ordered to attend the examination to do so without reasonable excuse is an offence.[144] Apart from the fact that it takes place in open court rather than in private and the fact that creditors may also attend and ask questions at a public examination, the examination is conducted in the same way as a private examination and the same rules as discussed above in that context apply.[145] As in a private examination, the examinee may be ordered to produce any relevant documents in his custody or control and to deliver them or copies thereof to the interim or permanent trustee as appropriate.[146]

If the court is satisfied that such a step is necessary to secure the attendance of the debtor or any other person ordered to attend a private or public examination, it may grant a warrant to arrest the individual concerned and to have him taken to the place of examination.[147] If, however, the debtor or other examinee cannot attend the examination for a good reason (for example, illness), a commission may be granted to take his examination.[148]

---

[138] Such a request may only be made not less than eight weeks before the end of the first accounting period unless cause is shown, when it may be permitted at any other time: 1985 Act, s 45(1).

[139] 1985 Act, s 44(4).

[140] 1985 Act, s 45(1)(b).

[141] 1985 Act, s 45(2).

[142] On a date not less than eight and not more than 16 days after the date of the order: 1985 Act, s 45(2).

[143] 1985 Act, s 45(3). The permanent trustee is required to publish a notice in the Edinburgh Gazette and to send a notice to all known creditors and advise them of their right to participate in the examination, although he does not appear to be obliged to inform the debtor. Where the examination is of someone other than the debtor, he must also inform the debtor and advise him of his right to participate in the examination.

[144] 1985 Act, s 45(4).

[145] 1985 Act, s 47.

[146] 1985 Act, s 46(4) (applied to private examinations at the request of the interim trustee by s 20(5)): see also above in relation to recovery of documents.

[147] 1985 Act, s 46(1). In the case of a debtor residing in Scotland, the warrant is granted by the sheriff; in the case of a debtor residing in another part of the UK, the warrant may be granted by either the sheriff or the Court of Session, and may be enforced throughout the UK. In the case of a private or public examination applied for by a permanent trustee, the warrant is granted on his application: s 46(1). In the case of a private examination applied for by an interim trustee, the warrant is granted on his application: s 46(1), as applied to private examinations on the application of the interim trustee by s 20(5).

[148] 1985 Act, s 46(2); the subsection is also applied to private examinations on the application of the interim trustee by s 20(5).

Liquidation

There are a number of ways in which the liquidator may seek to recover information directly from those concerned with the company and its affairs.

(1) Attendance on the liquidator.

Section 235 of the 1986 Act which applies, *inter alia*, where the company goes into liquidation or a provisional liquidator is appointed, provides that specified persons must provide to the liquidator or provisional liquidator such information concerning the company and its promotion, formation, business, dealings, affairs or property as he may reasonably require and must attend on him at such times as he may reasonably require.[149] The persons who are liable to give such information and attend on the liquidator or provisional liquidator are:

(a) anyone who is or has been an officer of the company;[150]

(b) anyone who took part in the formation of the company within the year preceding the effective date;[151]

(c) anyone employed by the company or who was employed by the company within the year preceding the effective date whom the liquidator or provisional liquidator believes to be capable of giving the information required;[152]

(d) anyone who is, or was within the year preceding the effective date, an officer or employee of another company which itself is, or within that year was an officer of the company in liquidation or provisional liquidation;[153]

(e) in the case of a company being wound up by the court, any person who has acted as administrator, administrative receiver or liquidator of the company.[154]

The effective date, where the company has gone into liquidation, is the date on which the company went into liquidation; where a provisional liquidator has been appointed, it is the date of his appointment.[155] In contrast to the position in sequestration where there is no sanction for failing to appear before the trustee at his request or give him information at such a meeting, anyone who fails without reasonable excuse to comply with the obligation to attend on the liquidator or provisional liquidator and/or give him the necessary information is liable to a fine and, for continued contravention, a daily default fine.[156]

(2) Private examination.

Section 236 of the 1986 Act which applies, *inter alia*, where the company goes into liquidation or a provisional liquidator is appointed, provides that on the application of the liquidator or provisional liquidator the court

---

[149] 1986 Act, s 235(2).
[150] 1986 Act, s 235(3)(a).
[151] 1986 Act, s 235(3)(b).
[152] 1986 Act, s 235(3)(c). 'Employed' includes employed under a contract for services.
[153] 1986 Act, s 235(3)(d). 'Employee' includes an employee under a contract for services.
[154] 1986 Act, s 235(3)(e).
[155] 1986 Act, s 235(4).
[156] 1986 Act, s 235(5).

may summon to appear before it any officer of the company, any person known or suspected to have in his possession any property of the company or to be indebted to the company, or any person whom the court thinks capable of providing information concerning the promotion, formation, business, dealings, affairs or property of the company.[157] The court may also require such a person to submit an affidavit to the court detailing his dealings with the company or to produce any relevant books, papers or other records in his possession or under his control.[158] In addition, the court may order that any person who would be liable to be summoned to appear before it if he were within the jurisdiction of the court be examined in any part of the United Kingdom where he is for the time being or in a place outwith the United Kingdom.[159] It has also been held that the court may order the examination of a person resident outwith the jurisdiction altogether, although whether the court will actually do so will depend on whether the order would be enforceable with the co-operation of the foreign court.[160]

The court always has a discretion as to whether or not to order an examination (or, indeed, the production of documents). Guidelines as to the factors which might influence the court in exercising that discretion generally were set out in the case of *Cloverbay Ltd (Joint Administrators)* v *Bank of Credit and Commerce International SA*,[161] where the court identified factors such as the purpose of an examination (to get sufficient information to reconstitute the state of knowledge the company should possess), the reasonableness of the requirement for the information in that context, the position of the proposed examinee (there would generally be a stronger case for an order in the case of a company officer as opposed to a third party), possible oppression in relation to the examinee (an order to produce documents, for example, would generally be less oppressive than an examination) and the balancing of that oppression against the legitimate requirements of the liquidator. It was subsequently held by the House of Lords in *Re British and Commonwealth Holdings (Nos 1 and 2)*[162] that the discretion of the court is not restricted to making an order only for the purpose of allowing reconstitution of the state of knowledge the company should possess, but should be exercised so as to allow the office holder to obtain what was reasonably required by him to carry out his functions, without placing an unreasonable burden on those required to comply with the order.[163] The court said that neither the fact that the request was

---

[157] 1986 Act, s 236(2).

[158] 1986 Act, s 235(3). In relation to the latter, see also the section on recovery of documents above.

[159] 1986 Act, s 237(3).

[160] See *McIsaac and Wilson, Petnrs* 1995 SLT 498, although the court in that case in fact made an error as to the basis on which the foreign court might have been expected to extend co-operation.

[161] [1991] BCLC 135.

[162] [1992] 3 WLR 853.

[163] See also *First Tokyo Index Trust Ltd* v *Gould* (1994) BCC 410; *Re Bishopsgate Investment Management Ltd (No 2)* (1994) BCC 732; *Homan & Ors* v *Vogel & Ors* (1994) BCC 741; *Re Barlow Clowes Gilt Managers Ltd* [1991] 4 All ER 385. The case-law on various aspects of the exercise of the discretion is extensive and considerations of space prevent a full review; however, a useful review of the authorities preceding *Cloverbay Ltd (Joint Administrators)* v *Bank of Credit and Commerce International SA* (note 161 above) is contained in that case.

inconvenient for the addressee or caused him considerable work or made him vulnerable to future claims, nor the fact that he was not an officer, employee or contractor of the company made the application unreasonable, although they were factors to be taken into account. The matter is, however, for the court to decide in each case, applying these principles, taking into account the particular circumstances and weighing the relevant factors.

Where an examination is ordered, the examinee will be cited to attend before the insolvency judge for examination.[164] There are virtually no provisions regulating the conduct of the examination. It is provided that the examination may be on oath,[165] and this is the normal practice, so that an examinee who does not tell the truth will expose himself to a charge of perjury. There is, however, no specific requirement in the legislation to answer questions and in the absence of specific provisions such as those applying in sequestrations,[166] the issue of whether an examinee must answer questions, or whether he may refuse to do so (either altogether or only those which would or might incriminate him or would involve the disclosure of confidential information), is a difficult one. In the English case of *Bishopsgate Investment Management Ltd (In Provisional Liquidation) v Maxwell*[167] it was held that an examinee was not entitled to refuse to answer questions on the ground that the answers might incriminate him. One of the reasons for this decision was that an individual bankrupt in England and Wales could not do so, and that Parliament could not have intended a company director to be in any better a position. Indeed, the court thought that to allow an examinee to refuse to answer questions on this ground would defeat the whole purpose of the section. The difficulty in simply applying this decision to Scotland is that the analogy with bankruptcy will not work in a Scottish context: although a bankrupt cannot refuse to answer questions on the ground that the answers may incriminate him, it is expressly provided that such answers will not be admissible in any subsequent criminal proceedings except those for perjury in relation to the statement itself.[168] In the absence of any express provision to this effect in the 1986 Act, and in the light of the fact that it is extremely doubtful that the court could competently impose a condition that any answers should not be used in subsequent criminal proceedings,[169] following the decision in *Bishopsgate* not to allow examinees to refuse to answer questions on the grounds that they might incriminate themselves would mean that examinees under s 236 and bankrupts were in fact in a different position from each other in Scotland. On the other hand, refusing to follow it would mean that examinees in Scotland and in England and Wales were in a different position from each other, which may be an even bigger anomaly, given that the statutory provision in question is the

---

[164] There are, surprisingly, no specific provisions for notification of persons required to attend an examination under s 236.

[165] 1986 Act, s 237(4).

[166] See above.

[167] [1992] 2 WLR 991.

[168] 1985 Act, s 47(3), and see above.

[169] In the light of the decision in *Re Arrows plc (No 4)* [1994] 3 All ER 814.

same.[170] The position in Scotland will only be clarified by a decision in an appropriate case or by legislation.

If it appears to the court from the information obtained at an examination that any person is in possession of any of the company's property, or is indebted to the company, then on the application of the liquidator or provisional liquidator, the court may order that person to deliver the whole or any part of such property to the liquidator or provisional liquidator, or to pay the whole or part of any amount due to the liquidator or provisional liquidator as appropriate.[171] The court may attach such conditions as it sees fit to such orders.[172]

Where a person who is summoned to appear before the court fails to do so without reasonable excuse, or where there are reasonable grounds for believing that a person so summoned has absconded, or is about to abscond, in order to avoid appearing as summoned, the court may cause a warrant to be issued to a constable or an appropriate officer of the court for the arrest of the person and the seizure of any books, papers, records, money or goods in that person's possession.[173] A person arrested under such a warrant may be kept in custody until he is brought before the court or until such other time as the court may order; similarly, anything seized under such a warrant may be kept until such time.[174]

(3) Public examination.

The liquidator in a compulsory winding up may apply for a public examination of any person who is or has been an officer of the company, any person who has acted as liquidator, administrator or receiver of the company or any other person who is or has been concerned in, or has taken part in, the promotion, formation or management of the company[175] and, where he is requested to do so by one-half in value of the company's creditors or three-quarters in value of the company's contributories, he must do so, unless the court orders otherwise.[176] An application for a public examination may also be made in a voluntary liquidation by virtue of s 112 of the 1986 Act. In a compulsory liquidation, the court has no discretion in dealing with an application for a public examination: it must order the public examination of the person or persons to whom the application relates.[177] It will have a discretion as to whether to order a

---

[170] For a full discussion of the issues and, in some cases, expression of differing views on this point, see *Palmer's Company Law*, para 15.720; St Clair and Drummond Young, *The Law of Corporate Insolvency in Scotland* (2nd edn), p 64 et seq; and Taylor, 'Insolvency Act Office Holders' Powers of Investigation: Self-Incrimination, Disclosure and the Potential Effects of Saunders *v* The United Kingdom' (1997) 2 SLPQ 297.

[171] 1986 Act, s 237(1) and (2) respectively. The provision applies to any person, not just the examinee.

[172] Ibid.

[173] 1986 Act, s 236(4) and (5).

[174] 1986 Act, s 236(6).

[175] 1986 Act, s 133(1).

[176] 1986 Act, s 133(2). Rule 4.75 of the Scottish Rules requires that the request must contain certain specified information, be made in writing and be accompanied by certain prescribed documents. A sum determined by the liquidator as appropriate caution for the expenses of the examination must be deposited with him prior to his making the application, which he must do within 28 days of receiving the request unless he is of the opinion that it is unreasonable. In the latter case, he may apply to the court for an order relieving him of the obligation to apply.

[177] 1986 Act, s 133(3).

public examination in a voluntary liquidation, however, since it has a discretion in dealing with an application to exercise any of its powers under s 112.

The examinee(s) will be cited to attend on a specified date to be publicly examined as to the promotion, formation or management of the company or the conduct of its business and affairs or their conduct or dealings in relation to the company.[178] There are also provisions for notification to various parties who have the right to attend the examination and ask questions, and for advertisement.[179] The examination takes place in open court and the liquidator, any special manager, any creditor who has submitted a claim in the liquidation and any contributory may attend and ask questions. There are no other specific provisions regulating the conduct of the examination. The issue of whether an examinee must answer questions or may refuse to do so (either altogether or on limited grounds), discussed above in relation to private examinations, arises in this context also and the comments made in relation to private examinations apply *mutatis mutandis*.[180]

If a person fails to attend his public examination without reasonable excuse, he is guilty of contempt of court[181] and the court may cause a warrant to be issued to a constable or an appropriate officer of the court for the arrest of the person and the seizure of any books, papers, records, money or goods in that person's possession.[182] Such a warrant may also be issued where there are reasonable grounds for believing that a person has absconded or is about to abscond in order to avoid or delay his examination.[183] A person arrested under such a warrant may be kept in custody until such time as the court may order; similarly, anything seized under such a warrant may be held, in accordance with the rules, until such time.[184]

(4) Examination under s 198 of the 1986 Act.

Under s 198 of the 1986 Act the court has power to order the examination in Scotland of any person for the time being in Scotland regarding the trade, dealings, affairs or property of any company in the course of being wound up or any contributory of such a company. The order is directed to the Sheriff Principal of the sheriffdom where the person is residing or happens to be at the time, and the Sheriff Principal must then summon the person to appear before him at a specified time and place for examination on oath.[185] The person may also be ordered to produce any books or papers called for by the court which are in his possession or power.[186] After the examination the Sheriff Principal must report back to

---

178 Ibid.
179 See the Scottish Rules, rule 4.75.
180 In *Bishopsgate Investment Management Ltd (In Provisional Liquidation)* v *Maxwell* (note 167 above) the court treated examinations under s 236 and s 133 of the 1986 Act in the same way, and this seems logical.
181 1986 Act, s 134(1).
182 1986 Act, s 134(2).
183 Ibid.
184 1986 Act, s 134(3).
185 1986 Act, s 198(2).
186 Ibid.

the court together with any books and papers produced or, if the original order did not call for the originals, copies or authenticated extracts.[187]

If the examinee fails to attend the examination, refuses to be examined or refuses to produce the documents called for, the Sheriff Principal is directed to proceed against him as a witness or haver duly cited.[188]

Administration and receivership

There are no provisions for examination of persons particular to administration or receivership. However, s 236 of the 1986 Act applies where the company has gone into administration or an administrative receiver has been appointed, as well as where the company has gone into liquidation or a provisional liquidator has been appointed. An administrator or administrative receiver will therefore be able to apply for the private examination of any officer of the company, any person known or suspected to have in his possession any property of the company or to be indebted to the company, or any person whom the court thinks capable of providing information concerning the promotion, formation, business, dealings, affairs or property of the company under this section in the same way as a liquidator or provisional liquidator, and what is said above in relation to private examinations under this section in a liquidation applies equally where such an examination is sought by an administrator or administrative receiver.

Company voluntary arrangements and section 425 arrangements

Where a proposal for a CVA is made by the directors of a company, the nominee may call on them to produce certain specified information in addition to that which has already been provided to him.[189] Similarly, where a proposal for a CVA is made by an administrator or a liquidator who is not intending to act as nominee himself, the nominee may call on the administrator or liquidator to provide such additional information.[190] There are, however, no provisions for examination of persons as such by either the nominee or the supervisor, although where the proposal for the CVA is being made by an administrator or a liquidator, he will be able to utilise the powers available to him in that capacity where appropriate.[191]

There are no provisions for examination of persons in connection with a section 425 agreement as such, but where the company is in administration, administrative receivership or liquidation, the administrator, administrative receiver or liquidator will be able to utilise the powers available to him in that capacity where appropriate.

Recovery of information: miscellaneous provisions

This section discusses briefly a number of miscellaneous provisions which allow the recovery of information in various circumstances.

---

[187] 1986 Act, s 198(3).
[188] 1986 Act, s 198(4).
[189] Scottish Rules, rule 1.6(1), (2). See also Chapter 8.
[190] Scottish Rules, rule 1.12(4), applying rule 1.6.
[191] For the powers of administrators and liquidators in relation to examination of persons, see above.

(1) Inspection of books by creditors and contributories in a liquidation.

At any time after the making of a winding-up order, the court may make an order for inspection of the company's books and papers by creditors or contributories.[192] The making of an order is discretionary, and should be exercised for the benefit of the liquidation rather than to assist individual shareholders or creditors in pursuing a course of action beneficial to themselves.[193] A creditor or a contributory in a voluntary liquidation would also be able to apply to the court for an order for inspection of the company's books and papers in an appropriate case by virtue of s 112 of the 1986 Act, and the court may make such an order, on such terms and conditions as it thinks fit, if it is satisfied that the exercise of the power would be just and beneficial.[194]

(2) Attendance at meetings in various proceedings.

The director nominated to do so must attend and preside at the meeting of creditors called under s 98 of the 1986 Act in a creditors' voluntary winding up[195] and he or some other person with the relevant knowledge must present a report of any material transactions of the company occurring after the date of the statement of affairs laid before the meeting where this is not made up to the date of the meeting.[196] Failure to attend and preside at the meeting is an offence.[197]

A liquidator in a compulsory or creditors' voluntary winding up may give notice to any of the company's personnel that they are required to attend any meeting of the company or of contributories.[198] Such questions as the chairman of the meeting allows may be put to such a person at such a meeting.

In a compulsory liquidation, the court has power to require any officer of the company to attend any meeting of creditors, contributories or the liquidation committee for the purposes of giving information about the trade, dealings, affairs or property of the company.[199] Such an order might also be made in a voluntary liquidation by virtue of s 112 of the 1986 Act.

Directors and any other persons whose attendance the convener thinks is required as being officers of the company or as having been directors or officers of it within the preceding two years are given notice to attend the meetings of the company and the creditors called to consider a proposal for a CVA.[200]

---

[192] 1986 Act, s 155.
[193] See, for example, *Re Embassy Art Products* [1988] BCLC 1: *Halden v Liquidator of the Scottish Heritable Security Co Ltd* (1887) 14 R 633.
[194] 1986 Act, s 112(2).
[195] 1986 Act, s 99(1).
[196] Scottish Rules, rule 4.7(6), as amended, in its application to creditors' voluntary liquidations by rule 5 of and Sched 1 to the said rules.
[197] 1986 Act, s 99(3).
[198] Scottish Rules, rule 4.14. This rule applies directly to compulsory liquidations, and is also applied to creditors' voluntary liquidations by rule 5 of the Scottish Rules. The personnel who may be required to attend such meetings are those who have a duty to co-operate with the liquidator under s 235(3) of the 1986 Act, for which see above.
[199] 1986 Act, s 157.
[200] Scottish Rules, rule 1.15.

(3) Arrest of absconding contributory in liquidation.

Section 158 of the 1986 Act provides that at any time either before or after the making of a winding-up order, the court may order a contributory to be arrested and his books, papers and moveable property seized and kept until such time as the court orders. The court will require proof that there is probable cause for believing that the contributory is about to leave the United Kingdom or otherwise abscond or remove or conceal his assets so as to avoid paying calls before it will make such an order.

Such an order might also be made in a voluntary liquidation by virtue of s 112 of the 1986 Act.

30 : CHALLENGE OF PRIOR TRANSACTIONS

Certain transactions by a debtor prior to insolvency may be challenged with a view to *either* returning the assets disposed of as a result of these transactions, or their value, to the debtor's estate *or*, in some cases, avoiding a security. This chapter considers the types of transaction which are open to challenge and the circumstances in which a challenge may be made.

The 1985 and 1986 Acts make provision for the challenge of defined types of transaction by non-company and company debtors respectively. This is one area where there has been harmonisation of company and non-company insolvency law and some of the statutory provisions are therefore common to both kinds of debtor and in virtually identical terms. In addition, the provisions for the challenge of transactions at common law remain alongside the statutory provisions. The transactions which can be challenged at common law have traditionally been divided into two types corresponding with two of the types of transaction challengeable under statute, namely gratuitous alienations and fraudulent preferences.[1] In the leading modern textbook on bankruptcy, Professor McBryde argues that this categorisation does not accurately reflect the principles involved and that a proper analysis of the cases discloses rather a general principle of striking at any transaction which is a fraud on the creditors.[2] His argument is persuasive, but since he himself states that, in most cases, his approach will not have an appreciably different result from the traditional approach in practice, the more traditional analysis of the common law is adopted in this text. The common law applies to transactions (however classified) by both company and non-company debtors.

The relevant provisions may conveniently be discussed under the following headings.

(1) Provisions applying to company and non-company debtors.

(2) Provisions applying to company debtors only.

(3) Provisions applying to non-company debtors only.

---

[1] Goudy, *Bankruptcy*. His treatment has been followed by most other writers in the field. The current statutory provisions on gratuitous alienations and (as they are now known) unfair preferences supersede those contained in the Bankruptcy Act 1621 and the Bankruptcy Act 1696, which dealt with gratuitous alienations and fraudulent preferences respectively.

[2] *Bankruptcy* (2nd edn, 1995).

Provisions applying to company and non-company debtors

Gratuitous alienations

The relevant statutory provisions are contained in s 34 of the 1985 Act and s 242 of the 1986 Act respectively. They are identical except for the differences in terminology necessary to reflect the different types of debtor, and cases and examples relating to different types of debtor are therefore used interchangeably.

A statutory challenge is only available in certain circumstances. In the case of a non-company debtor, these are where the debtor's estate has been sequestrated, the debtor has granted a trust deed which has become protected, the estate of a deceased debtor has been sequestrated within 12 months of his death, or a judicial factor has been appointed to the estate of a deceased debtor under s 11A of the Judicial Factors (Scotland) Act 1889 within 12 months of the debtor's death.[3] In the case of a company debtor, these are where winding up has commenced or an administration order has been made.[4]

The challenge may be made by the relevant office holder, ie, the permanent trustee, the trustee under the trust deed, the judicial factor, the liquidator or the administrator.[5] In all cases except administration, it may also be made by any creditor whose debt was incurred before the relevant event.[6]

The challenge is available where 'any of the debtor's property has been transferred or any claim of the debtor has been discharged or renounced'.[7] This is very wide. Some examples of the types of transaction which would fall within that definition would be a debtor gifting his house to his wife[8] or giving her money,[9] discharging his right to claim legal rights in a deceased relative's estate or renouncing rights under a contract.[10]

The statutory challenge is only available if the transaction took place within certain time-limits. If the alienation was made to an 'associate' of the debtor, it must have been made 'completely effectual' within the five years preceding the sequestration, trust deed, death, liquidation or administration.[11] If it was made to someone other than an associate, it must have been made completely effectual within the two years preceding the relevant event.[12] This can be illustrated diagrammatically.

five years (associate)

I.. ⎫ date of sequestration, granting
                                                ⎪ of trust deed or death, or date
        two years (non-associate) ⎬ of administration order or
I.................................... ⎭ commencement of liquidation

---

[3] 1985 Act, s 34(2). In the case of the appointment of a judicial factor, the estate must also have been absolutely insolvent at the date of death. Judicial factors are discussed in Chapter 45.

[4] 1986 Act, s 242(1).

[5] 1985 Act, s 34(1); 1986 Act, s 242(1).

[6] Ibid.

[7] 1985 Act, s 34(2)(a); 1986 Act, s 242(2)(a).

[8] See, for example, *Matheson's Tr* v *Matheson* 1992 SLT 685.

[9] See, for example, *Cay's Tr* v *Cay* (IH) 1998 SCLR 456.

[10] See, for example, *Ahmed's Tr* v *Ahmed (No 2)* 1993 SLT 651.

[11] 1985 Act, s 34(3)(a); 1986 Act, s 242(3)(a).

[12] 1985 Act, s 34(3)(b); 1986 Act, s 242(3)(b).

'Associate' is defined in s 74 of the 1985 Act[13] and the 1986 Act specifically adopts that definition for this purpose.[14] The definition is complex and
encompasses a variety of relatives and business relationships. An individual is
associated with his or her spouse, with defined categories of relatives and the
spouse of any of these relatives and also with defined categories of relatives of
his or her spouse and their spouses.[15] 'Spouse' includes former and reputed
spouses.[16] The categories of relatives are brother, sister, uncle, aunt, nephew,
niece, lineal ancestors and lineal descendants, including relationships of the half
blood.[17] Step, adopted and illegitimate children are also included.[18] (Business)
partners are associates of each other and also of anyone with whom their partner
is associated, and a firm is an associate of anyone who is member of it.[19] Employers
and employees are associated with each other, and directors and other officers of
a company are treated as employed by it for this purpose.[20] A company is an
associate of another person if that person, or that person together with his
associates, has control of it[21] and it is an associate of another company if *either* the
same person has control of both companies *or* a person has control of one company
and he, or he and his associates, have control of the other *or* a group of two or
more persons who are essentially the same people or their associates have control
of both companies.[22]

The time at which any particular transaction becomes 'completely effectual'
depends on the type of transaction and the particular circumstances of the case.
For example, a transaction involving heritage will become completely effectual
on the recording of the title deed, and a gift of moveables will normally become
completely effectual on delivery.[23]

In order to succeed, the challenger need only show that an alienation has
taken place within the relevant time-limits, but the challenge may be defeated by
the defender if he is able to establish any of the following grounds.

(1) That the debtor was absolutely solvent immediately or at any other time
    after making the alienation.[24] Assume, for example, that an individual
    debtor transfers his house to his wife on 1st January. His estates are
    subsequently sequestrated, the date of sequestration being 1st May. If on
    2nd January his assets exceeded his liabilities, the defender would be able
    to defeat any challenge of the transfer even if the debtor became absolutely
    insolvent thereafter. Similarly, a challenge would be defeated if the debtor's
    assets were less than his liabilities on 2nd January, but exceeded them on
    any date between then and 1st May.

---

[13] As amended by the Bankruptcy (Scotland) Regulations 1985 (SI 1985/1925), reg 11.

[14] 1986 Act, s 242(3)(a).

[15] 1985 Act, s 74(2).

[16] 1985 Act, s 74(4).

[17] Ibid. Lineal ancestors would encompass parents, grandparents, etc; lineal descendants children,
grandchildren, etc.

[18] 1985 Act, s 74(4).

[19] 1985 Act, s 74(3).

[20] 1985 Act, s 74(5).

[21] 1985 Act, s 74(5B).

[22] 1985 Act, s 74(5A). The concept of control is defined in s 74(5C).

[23] See also *Masson's Tr* v *W. & J. Bruce (Builders) Ltd* 20th April 1998 (unreported) (mandates);
Craiglaw Developments Ltd v *Wilson* (IH) 1997 SCLR 1157 (Notes) (deposit receipts).

[24] 1985 Act, s 34(4)(a); 1986 Act, s 242(4)(a).

(2) That the alienation was made for adequate consideration.[25] There are two issues here: what amounts to consideration and what is adequate. Consideration in this context generally means money or money's worth, although it may take a variety of forms.[26] In *MacFadyen's Tr* v *MacFadyen*[27] the court said that in the absence of a statutory definition, consideration must be given its ordinary meaning 'as something which is given or surrendered in return for something else'[28] and that it must be 'something of material or patrimonial value which could be vindicated in a legal process'.[29] Something which was not intended to be consideration at the time it was given—for example, something which was intended as a gift or loan—cannot later be said to be consideration.[30] In order to be adequate, the consideration need not necessarily represent the best value that could have been obtained—for example, on a sale[31]—but it has been held that the term 'adequate' implies an objective assessment, and the consideration should be 'not less than would reasonably be expected in the circumstances, assuming that persons ... were acting in good faith and at arm's length from each other'.[32] Where it is argued that the alienation is for adequate consideration because it is being undertaken to implement a prior obligation, this will only be established if the prior obligation itself was undertaken for adequate consideration.[33]

(3) That the alienation was a permitted gift.[34] There are two categories of permitted gift. The first is a birthday, Christmas or other conventional gift[35]—for example, a wedding gift or a retirement gift to an employee. The second is a charitable gift, provided that it was not made to an associate of the debtor.[36] Two points arise in relation to the second category. First, 'charitable' is given a wide meaning. It covers any gift which has a 'charitable, benevolent or philanthropic purpose', and is not restricted to gifts which are charitable within the meaning of any rule of law.[37] Secondly, there may be some doubt over the meaning of the term 'associate' in relation to company debtors in this context. It was noted above that for the purpose of deciding whether someone was an associate

---

[25] 1985 Act, s 34(4)(b); 1986 Act, s 242(4)(b).

[26] For example, in *John E. Rae (Electrical Services) Linlithgow Ltd* v *Lord Advocate* 1994 SLT 788 the issue of an exemption certificate by the Inland Revenue was held to be capable of amounting to adequate consideration; in *Cay's Tr* v *Cay* (note 9 above) the assumption of responsibility for another's debts was similarly held to be capable in principle of amounting to adequate consideration.

[27] 1994 SLT 1245.

[28] Ibid at 1248I.

[29] Ibid at 1248J–K. See also *Cay's Tr* v *Cay* (note 9 above), where it was held that an undertaking to fulfil an obligation of aliment did not fall within this definition.

[30] *MacFadyen's Tr* v *MacFadyen*, note 27 above. See also *Matheson's Tr* v *Matheson*, note 8 above.

[31] *Short's Tr* v *Chung* 1991 SLT 472 at 475A–B. See also *Lafferty Construction Ltd* v *McCombe* 1994 SLT 858 and *McLuckie Brothers Ltd* v *Newhouse Contracts Ltd* 1993 SLT 641.

[32] *Lafferty Construction Ltd* v *McCombe*, above, at 861D–E. See also *Cay's Tr* v *Cay* (note 9 above), where it was held that a consideration which amounted to less than 60 per cent of the value of the property transferred could not be adequate.

[33] 1985 Act, s 34(6); 1986 Act, s 242(6).

[34] 1985 Act, s 34(4)(c); 1986 Act, s 242(4)(c).

[35] 1985 Act, s 34(4)(c)(i); 1986 Act, s 242(4)(c)(i).

[36] 1985 Act, s 34(4)(c)(ii); 1986 Act, s 242(4)(c)(ii).

[37] 1985 Act, s 34(5); 1986 Act, s 242(5).

for the purposes of determining the relevant time-limit, s 242(3) of the 1986 Act specifically adopted the definition of associate contained in s 74 of the 1985 Act, thus ensuring that the provisions are identical in relation to this point. Section 242(4), however, simply uses the word 'associate' without any further reference to s 74 of the 1985 Act. *Palmer*[38] argues that, absent such a reference, the definition of 'associate' for the purposes of s 242(4) must be the definition provided in the 1986 Act itself. This is contained in s 435 of the 1986 Act, and differs in certain respects from the definition in s 74 of the 1985 Act. Section 435 provides, insofar as relevant for the purposes of this discussion, that a person is an associate of any person with whom that person is in partnership, and also the spouse or relative of any such person,[39] any person whom he employs or by whom he is employed,[40] any director or other officer of a company being treated as an employee of it;[41] a trustee of a trust (with some exceptions) is an associate of any beneficiary, potential beneficiary or any person associated with such beneficiary or potential beneficiary;[42] a company is an associate of another company if *either* the same person has control of both, a person has control of one and he and his associates have control of the other or he has control of one and his associates have control of the other *or* a group of two or more persons who are essentially the same people or their associates have control of both companies,[43] and a company is an associate of another person if that person has control of it either alone or with his associates.[44] If *Palmer* is correct, the result is rather strange: s 242 not only contains two different definitions of associate, but the meaning of associate in relation to the provision on charitable gifts is different from that in the same provision in s 34 of the 1985 Act. Such a result must presumably have been unintentional and should be remedied.

Permitted gifts falling within either category must have been reasonable in all the circumstances. It would probably not be reasonable, for example, for a small family company to give an ex-employee a gift of his company car on his retirement, but such a gift might be perfectly reasonable from a large company.

Unless one of these grounds is established, the court must grant decree of reduction, restoration of the property or such other redress as appropriate.[45] Reduction would normally be appropriate, for example, where the alienation involved the transfer of heritable property. An order for restoration of the property would normally be appropriate, for example, where the alienation was of moveable property transferred by delivery, there being no deed to reduce. If property has been transferred on by the original transferee, the challenger may

---

[38] *Palmer's Company Law*, para 15.708.
[39] 1986 Act, s 435(2). 'Spouse' and 'relatives' have the same meaning assigned to them as in s 74 of the 1985 Act: 1986 Act, s 435(8).
[40] 1986 Act, s 435(4).
[41] 1986 Act, s 435(9).
[42] 1986 Act, s 435(5).
[43] 1986 Act, s 435(6).
[44] 1986 Act, s 435(7). The concept of 'control' for the purposes of the section is defined in s 435(10).
[45] 1985 Act, s 34(4); 1986 Act, s 242(4).

not be able to recover the property itself, since a third party who has acquired the property from or through the original transferee in good faith and for value is protected from challenge.[46] In such a situation, 'other redress' would be appropriate—for example, payment of the value of the property by the original transferee.

In *Short's Tr* v *Chung*, referred to above, it was held that reduction was the principal remedy if applicable. Only if reduction was not applicable would restoration of the property be ordered, and only if neither of these was applicable would 'other redress' be granted. It was held that 'other redress' was not a licence to the court to fashion an equitable solution, and this approach was followed in the case of *Cay's Tr* v *Cay*: see above. This may in some cases cause difficulty. Assume, for example, a transfer of property for inadequate consideration and a subsequent challenge against the transferee. The result of the decision is that the challenger is restricted to seeking reduction or restoration as appropriate, and cannot simply seek payment of the difference in value between the inadequate consideration and the true value, even where this might be a more desirable solution for both parties. In such a case there is also an unfair benefit to the insolvent estate and corresponding disadvantage to the transferee: the latter will be left with a probably worthless claim in the relevant proceedings for such consideration as was paid, while the former has had the benefit of that consideration and has now recovered the property. Another difficulty was highlighted in the case of *Short's Tr* v *Keeper of the Registers of Scotland*,[47] which involved reduction of dispositions of heritable property under s 34 of the 1985 Act. Where the title to property is registered in the Register of Sasines, the effect of reduction, in simple terms, is to restore the property to the debtor's estate. *Short's Tr* v *The Keeper of the Registers of Scotland* shows that where property is registered in the Land Register, however, reduction may, and in many cases will, not have this effect.[48] The decision of the House of Lords in that case resulted in further litigation, and in *Short's Tr* v *Chung (No 2)*[49] the trustee finally obtained an order for the transfer of the disputed properties to him.[50] Although it was not necessary to address the issue directly, the decision tends to suggest that a challenger may no longer be constrained to bring an action of reduction where heritable property is registered in the Land Register, but further litigation may be required to clarify this point.[51]

As noted above, the common law provisions for the challenge of gratuitous alienations continue to be available alongside the statutory provisions. The types of transaction which will be challengeable at common law are similar to those which are challengeable under statute.[52] However, the matters which have to be established by the challenger in order to succeed in a challenge at common law are somewhat different. Whereas the statutory provisions only require the challenger to show that there has been an alienation within the relevant time-limit and it is then up to the defender, if he wishes to resist the challenge, to

---

[46] 1985 Act, s 34(4); 1986 Act, s 242(4).

[47] 1996 SLT 166.

[48] See McKenzie, 'Short's Tr *v* The Keeper of the Registers' 1996 JR 217.

[49] (OH) 1997 SCLR 1181.

[50] The reasoning in the decision may, however, be open to question in some respects: see the case note in 1998 *Greens Business Law Bulletin* 31–7.

[51] This approach would also leave discrepancies between property registered in the Register of Sasines and that registered in the Land Register.

[52] See, for example, Goudy, p 23.

establish that the transaction is not challengeable because it falls within one of the specified grounds, at common law it is up to the challenger to establish both that the alienation was gratuitous (ie, for nothing or for inadequate consideration) *and* that the debtor was absolutely insolvent at the time of the alienation (or was made so by it) and remained so up to the date of challenge. This is disadvantageous from the challenger's point of view. The challenger must also show that the transaction was to the prejudice of lawful creditors. Since, however, it is not necessary to show that the debtor intended to defraud the creditors by his actions, the conjunction of insolvency and the gratuitous nature of the transaction being sufficient to infer the necessary fraud, this requirement will not usually be problematic.

The advantage of the common law provisions, however, is that there is no requirement that the transaction must have taken place within specific time-limits. This means that a challenge at common law might be possible where a statutory challenge was impossible because the alienation took place outwith the statutory time-limits.

A challenge at common law may be brought by a permanent trustee, a trustee acting under a protected trust deed, a judicial factor, a liquidator or an administrator.[53] A creditor may also challenge a transaction at common law *at any time* after the alienation has taken place, without waiting for the debtor's sequestration, liquidation, etc. A creditor may be reluctant to incur the expense of doing so since the result of any successful challenge is to restore any assets recovered (or their value) to the debtor's estate, where it is subject to the diligence of all creditors, rather than transfer them to the challenging creditor.[54] An early challenge might, however, be worthwhile if it results, for example, in recovery of the actual asset disposed of, which might be a better outcome than later trying to recover its value from a recipient who has subsequently disposed of it.

Unfair preferences

The relevant statutory provisions are contained in s 36 of the 1985 Act and s 243 of the 1986 Act. As with the statutory provisions on gratuitous alienations, they are identical except for the differences in terminology necessary to reflect the different types of debtor, and cases and examples relevant to different types of debtor are therefore used interchangeably. They have also been harmonised so far as possible with the statutory provisions on gratuitous alienations.

A statutory challenge is only available in certain circumstances. In the case of a non-company debtor, these are where the debtor's estate has been sequestrated, the debtor has granted a trust deed which has become protected, the estate of a deceased debtor has been sequestrated within 12 months of his death or a judicial factor has been appointed to the estate of a deceased debtor under s 11A of the Judicial Factors (Scotland) Act 1889 within 12 months of the debtor's death.[55] In the case of a company debtor, these are where winding up has commenced or an administration order has been made.[56]

---

[53] 1985 Act, s 34(8); 1986 Act, s 242(7).
[54] This is logical, since otherwise the effect would simply be to give the challenging creditor an unfair advantage over the other creditors in place of the person from whom the assets (or their value) were recovered.
[55] 1985 Act, s 36(1).
[56] 1986 Act, s 243(1).

The challenge may be made by the relevant office holder, ie, the permanent trustee, the trustee under the trust deed, the judicial factor, the liquidator or the administrator as appropriate.[57] In all cases except administration, it may also be made by any creditor whose debt was incurred before the relevant event.[58]

Transactions which may be challenged are those entered into by the debtor which have 'the effect of creating a preference in favour of a creditor to the prejudice of the general body of creditors'.[59] There are two separate elements within this definition. The first is that the transaction must favour one creditor. The second is that it must create a disadvantage to the general body of creditors. Both elements are necessary. If one is present without the other, the transaction will not be challengeable. An example of the type of transaction which would fall within the provisions would be the granting of a security for an unsecured debt.[60] Both elements are present in such a case, because the creditor to whom the security is granted is thereafter in a more favourable position (instead of having to take a share of the debtor's assets along with other unsecured creditors, he now has a priority claim on the assets over which the security is granted) while the other (unsecured) creditors are prejudiced because the pool of assets on which they have a claim has been reduced to the extent of the new security.

The statutory challenge is only available in respect of transactions which become 'completely effectual' within the period of six months prior to the date of sequestration, granting of the trust deed, death, administration order or liquidation.[61] This concept is discussed above in the context of gratuitous alienations. It has been suggested that where the original agreement to carry out a transaction was made outwith the six-month period referred to, a transaction which is made completely effectual within that period none the less escapes challenge because it is not a 'voluntary' transaction.[62] The statutory predecessor of the current provision[63] specifically required a transaction to be voluntary, but the current provisions do not contain any reference to such a requirement. It is thought, therefore, that the better view is that such a transaction is challengeable, notwithstanding that it is not voluntary.[64] The time-limit is obviously very short.

Some types of transaction are specifically stated not to be challengeable.[65] These are:

(1) Transactions in the ordinary course of trade or business.[66] Whether or not a transaction falls into this category depends on the particular circumstances of each case. It may be necessary to consider the specific practices in the particular trade or profession in question to determine if a transaction falls within this category.

---

[57] 1985 Act, s 36(4); 1986 Act, s 243(4).
[58] Ibid.
[59] 1985 Act, s 36(1); 1986 Act, s 243(1).
[60] See *McCowan* v *Wright* (1853) 15 D 494.
[61] 1985 Act, s 36(1); 1986 Act, s 243(1).
[62] 'Voluntary' in this context means that it could not be legally compelled: see *Nordic Travel Ltd* v *Scotprint Ltd* 1980 SC 1.
[63] The Bankruptcy Act 1696.
[64] See McKenzie, 'Gratuitous Alienations and Unfair Preferences on Insolvency' (1993) 41 JLSS 141 and the letter in response by Sellar (1993) 41 JLSS 215. See also McBryde, *Bankruptcy* (note 2 above), p 317 and Palmer (note 38 above), para 15.711.
[65] 1985 Act, s 36(2); 1986 Act, s 243(2).
[66] 1985 Act, s 36(2)(a); 1986 Act, s 243(2)(a).

(2) Payments in cash for debts actually due.[67] Such a payment will usually also be a payment in the ordinary course of trade, but need not be. Cash includes coins and banknotes and probably also cheques, banker's drafts and bills.[68]

(3) Transactions involving reciprocal obligations.[69] Such transactions are commonly referred to as '*nova debita*'. The obligations undertaken can be performed at different times so long as they are undertaken at the same time. For example, a security for a loan may be granted after the loan has been advanced provided the original agreement provided for the granting of the security for the loan. The obligations undertaken must, however, be of a strictly equivalent value in order to fall within this category.[70]

(4) The granting of a mandate authorising payment of arrested funds to the arresting creditor.[71] The arresting creditor must, however, have a decree or summary warrant, and the arrestment must have been made on the dependence, or in execution, of this.[72]

It should be noted, however, that transactions falling within the terms of (2) or (3) above will not be exempted from challenge where they are collusive with the purpose of prejudicing the general body of creditors.[73] The creditor's knowledge of the debtor's insolvency is necessary, but not sufficient, for collusion.[74]

Where the court is satisfied that a transaction is an unfair preference it must grant decree of reduction, restoration of the property or such other redress as appropriate,[75] but a third party acquiring property in good faith *and* for value from or through the creditor in whose favour the preference was created is protected from challenge.[76] It is thought that the principles laid down in *Short's Tr v Chung*, and the problems arising from that decision and the subsequent decisions relating to that sequestration, discussed above in relation to gratuitous alienations, apply equally to unfair preferences.

The common law provisions for the challenge of certain preferences continue to be available alongside the statutory provisions. Such preferences are known at common law as fraudulent preferences. The same types of transaction will generally be challengeable at common law as under statute, with two important qualifications. First, at common law, the transaction must be voluntary.[77] Secondly, the categories of exempt transactions at common law may not correspond directly with those set out in statute. Professor McBryde[78] argues that the

---

[67] 1985 Act, s 36(2)(b); 1986 Act, s 243(2)(b).

[68] The authoritative exposition of this and the preceding exception is to be found in *Whatmough's Tr v British Linen Bank* 1932 SC 525; on appeal, 1934 SC (HL) 51.

[69] 1985 Act, s 36(2)(c); 1986 Act, s 243(2)(c).

[70] *Nicoll v Steelpress (Supplies) Ltd* (IH) 1992 SCLR 332.

[71] 1985 Act, s 36(2)(d); 1986 Act, s 243(2)(d).

[72] Ibid.

[73] 1985 Act, s 36(2)(b) and (c) respectively; 1986 Act, s 243(2)(b) and (c) respectively.

[74] *Nordic Travel Ltd v Scotprint Ltd* 1980 SC 1, note 62 above. See also *Secretary of State for Trade and Industry v Burn*, 30th September 1997 (unreported).

[75] 1985 Act, s 36(5); 1986 Act, s 243(5).

[76] Ibid.

[77] This concept is discussed above in connection with its applicability in the context of the statutory provisions, to which discussion reference should be made.

[78] Note 2 above.

types of transaction excepted under statute and, with the exception of mandates, commonly listed as the exceptions at common law also, can only be regarded as examples and not definitive categories. If that is so, a transaction exempted under statute might in fact be challengeable at common law.

As with gratuitous alienations, it will be up to the challenger to establish all the necessary elements for a successful challenge: the voluntary nature of the transaction; that the debtor was absolutely insolvent at the time of the preference (or was made so by it); that he remained so up to the date of challenge; and that he was aware of his insolvency. Once again, however, it is not necessary to prove that he intended to defraud the creditors by his actions, the conjunction of insolvency and the preferential nature of the transaction being sufficient to infer the necessary fraud.

The advantage of the common law is that there is no requirement that the transaction must have taken place within specific time-limits. A challenge at common law would therefore be possible where a statutory challenge was impossible because the preference took place outwith the relevant time-limit.

A challenge at common law may be brought by a permanent trustee, a trustee acting under a protected trust deed, a judicial factor, a liquidator or an administrator.[79] It may also be brought by a creditor at any time after the preference has taken place.[80]

Extortionate credit transactions

The relevant statutory provisions are contained in s 61 of the 1985 Act and s 244 of the 1986 Act. Although s 244(1) states that the section applies 'as does s 238', which applies only in England and Wales, s 244(5) contains provisions relating to Scotland which would not make sense unless the whole section is meant to apply in Scotland.[81] Section 244(1) is therefore generally accepted as meaning that the section 'applies as does s 238' only insofar as s 238 restricts its application to specified types of insolvency proceedings rather than insofar as it restricts its application only to England and Wales, and the section will therefore be treated as applying in Scotland. The sections are not so nearly identical in their terms as the respective provisions on gratuitous alienations and unfair preferences: the structure of the sections is slightly different and there are a number of additional provisions in s 61 of the 1985 Act which are necessary to reflect the different type of debtor. In substantive terms, however, the sections are virtually identical in their effect.

The provisions apply to non-company debtors only where the debtor's estate has been sequestrated[82] and to company debtors on liquidation or administration.[83] The challenge may be made only by the relevant office holder, ie, the permanent trustee, administrator or liquidator.[84]

The provisions apply to transactions for or involving the provision of credit to the debtor. 'Credit' is not defined in s 244, but for the purposes of s 61 it is

---

[79] 1985 Act, s 36(6); 1986 Act, s 243(6).
[80] The issues for a creditor who is considering bringing a challenge at common law are discussed in connection with gratuitous alienations above, to which discussion reference should be made, the issues being the same in the context of fraudulent preferences.
[81] See further below.
[82] 1985 Act, s 61(1).
[83] 1986 Act, s 244(1), (2).
[84] 1985 Act, s 61(2); 1986 Act, s 244(2).

defined by that section as having the same meaning as it does in the Consumer Credit Act 1974.[85]

Credit transactions entered into by the debtor within the three-year period prior to sequestration, administration or liquidation may be challenged where they are or were extortionate.[86] 'Extortionate' means the agreement required 'grossly exorbitant' payments or otherwise 'grossly contravened the ordinary principles of fair dealing'.[87] These concepts are not further defined. A transaction is presumed to be extortionate unless the contrary is proved,[88] thus putting the onus on the defender to establish that the transaction was not extortionate in the event of a challenge being made. Where the court is satisfied that the transaction was extortionate, it has very wide powers to reopen the transaction: it may order all or part of the agreement to be set aside, vary the terms of the agreement, require repayment of money paid under the agreement to the challenger, order any property taken as security to be surrendered to the challenger and/or order an accounting.[89] Any sums or property returned to a permanent trustee under s 61 vest in the trustee.[90]

Provisions applying to company debtors only

Avoidance of certain floating charges

Section 245 of the 1986 Act contains provisions relating to the avoidance of certain floating charges created by a company. Like s 244, it is stated to apply 'as does s 238',[91] but unlike s 244 it specifically states that the section applies to Scotland as well as to England and Wales.[92] The effect of this is to restrict the application of the section to the situation where the company has gone into administration or liquidation.

The section applies to render invalid, except to the extent provided for in the section, any floating charge[93] created[94] by the company within certain time periods. The relevant time periods are, in the case of a charge created in favour of a person 'connected with' the company, a period of two years prior to the date of presentation of the petition for administration or the date of commencement of the liquidation as appropriate[95] and, in the case of a charge created in favour of any other person, a period of 12 months prior to the date of presentation of the petition for administration or the date of commencement of the liquidation as appropriate.[96] A person is 'connected with' the company if he is a director or

---

[85] 1985 Act, s 61(7). The Consumer Credit Act 1974 defines 'credit' as including a cash loan and any other form of financial accommodation: 1974 Act, s 9(1).

[86] 1985 Act, s 61(2); 1986 Act, s 244(2).

[87] 1985 Act, s 61(3); 1986 Act, s 244(3).

[88] Ibid.

[89] 1985 Act, s 61(4); 1986 Act, s 244(4).

[90] 1985 Act, s 61(5).

[91] 1986 Act, s 245(1).

[92] Ibid.

[93] This includes any charge which was created as a floating charge, and Scottish floating charges: 1986 Act, s 251.

[94] A floating charge is created on the date that the instrument creating the charge is executed by the company: Companies Act 1985, s 410(5), and see also *AIB Finance Ltd v Bank of Scotland* 1995 SLT 2.

[95] 1986 Act, s 245(3)(a) and (5).

[96] 1986 Act, s 245(3)(b) and (5).

shadow director of the company or an associate of such a director or shadow director[97] or is an associate of the company,[98] 'associate' having the meaning given by s 435 of the 1986 Act.[99] It is the status of the person at the time of creation of the charge which is relevant: the fact that a connected person has ceased to be so by the time of challenge, or vice versa, is not relevant.

There are two situations in which a floating charge will not be rendered invalid, even if created within the periods described.

(1) A charge will not be rendered invalid to the extent that it was created in exchange for 'new money' or other specified types of consideration. These are: money advanced to the company, goods or services supplied to the company, the discharge or reduction of any debt of the company and interest on any of these items, provided that the advances, supplies or reductions in question were made at the same time as or after the creation of the charge.[100] 'At the same time as' should probably be taken to mean on the same day as creation of the charge, even if slightly before the actual execution of the charge, but not on any earlier date.[101] There is a proviso in relation to the supply of goods or services to the company to the effect that the charge will only be valid to the extent of the true value of the goods or services supplied, rather than any inflated value which has been put on them.[102]

(2) A charge created in favour of a person who is not connected with the company will only be rendered invalid if the company was unable to pay its debts within the meaning of s 123 of the 1986 Act at the time the charge was created, or was rendered unable to pay its debts within the meaning of that section by the creation of the charge.[103] Accordingly, where a charge is created in favour of a person not connected with the company, and the company was solvent in the sense provided for by s 123 at the time of the creation of the charge and was not rendered insolvent in that sense by its creation, the charge is not rendered invalid.

Section 245 speaks only of the charge being 'rendered invalid'. Unlike the provisions for challenge of other types of transaction, there is no provision for the court to do anything in particular, such as reducing the charge or making orders. Where a charge is declared to be either wholly or partly invalid under the section, therefore, the effect is simply that the chargeholder is not entitled to rely on the charge as security for his debt in the administration or liquidation to the extent that it has been declared invalid. The debt itself is not affected; it simply ranks as unsecured. It follows from this that if the debt in respect of which the charge was granted has already been paid off, the fact that the charge is subsequently

---

[97] 1986 Act, s 249(a).

[98] 1986 Act, s 249(b).

[99] This definition of associate is discussed above in connection with gratuitous alienations.

[100] 1986 Act, s 245(1).

[101] See the Companies Act 1985, s 410(5), and in particular, Palmer (note 38 above), para 15.714, where a convincing argument based on that section is put forward. See also the English case of *Re Shoe Lace Ltd* (1993) BCC 609.

[102] 1986 Act, s 245(6).

[103] 1986 Act, s 245(4). The meaning of 'unable to pay its debts' in s 123 of the 1986 Act is discussed in Chapter 1 above.

held to have been invalid under s 245 is irrelevant, and the administrator or liquidator, as the case may be, is not entitled to reclaim any monies paid to the chargeholder. The effect of the case of *Mace Builders (Glasgow) Ltd v Lunn*,[104] decided under s 322 of the Companies Act 1948, appears to be that this same result applies even if the debt in respect of which the charge subsequently held to be invalid was granted was paid off as a result of the appointment of a receiver under that charge, although doubts have been cast on the extent to which the case can be regarded as a reliable authority.[105]

Provisions applying to non-company debtors only

Orders on divorce

Section 35 of the 1985 Act applies where a debtor has been ordered to make payment of a capital sum and/or transfer property to his ex-spouse on divorce. By its nature, this section applies only to individual debtors.

A trustee in sequestration, trustee under a protected trust deed for creditors or a judicial factor appointed to the estate of a deceased debtor under s 11A of the Judicial Factors (Scotland) Act 1889 within 12 months of the debtor's death can apply to the court to have any such order recalled. The section applies only where the relevant order was made within the period of five years prior to certain specified events, namely the debtor's sequestration, his granting of a trust deed which subsequently became protected, or the sequestration of, or appointment of a judicial factor to, the estate of a deceased debtor.[106] The applicant must show that the debtor was either absolutely insolvent when the order was made or was made absolutely insolvent by the order.[107]

If the court is satisfied that the section applies, it may recall the order made on divorce and *either* order the ex-spouse to repay all or part of the money paid to him under that order *or* order him to return all or part of the property transferred to him under that order *or*, if property transferred under that order has been sold, order him to pay over all or part of the proceeds of sale.[108] The court is directed, however, to have regard to all the circumstances, including the financial and other circumstances of the ex-spouse before making an order under the section.[109]

The section clearly and intentionally puts the interests of creditors before the interests of the debtor's ex-spouse, despite the fact that this might clearly, in some cases, cause hardship to the ex-spouse. The section appears, however, to be seldom used.[110]

Payments into occupational pension schemes

Section 95(2) of the Pensions Act 1995 provides for the addition of three new sections dealing with the recovery of excessive pension contributions to the 1985 Act, ss 36A, 36B and 36C. Section 95 was partially brought into force (for the

---

[104] [1986] Ch 459; affd [1987] Ch 191.
[105] See Palmer (note 38 above), para 15.716.
[106] 1985 Act, s 35(1).
[107] Ibid.
[108] 1985 Act, s 35(2).
[109] Ibid.
[110] For a good discussion of financial provision on divorce and sequestration, see McBryde, 'Financial Provision on Divorce and Sequestration' 1996 SLT (News) 389.

purposes of making regulations only) on 6th April 1996[110a] but has not yet been fully brought into force. The provisions are, however, discussed here for the sake of completeness.

The sections will apply only on sequestration of the debtor,[111] and in effect are relevant only to individual debtors. They allow the permanent trustee to apply to the court for an order where the debtor has made contributions to an occupational pension scheme, or such contributions have been made on his behalf, within the five years preceding the date of sequestration.[112] If the court is satisfied that 'excessive contributions', defined as contributions which have unfairly prejudiced the debtor's creditors, have been made, it may make any order it thinks fit for restoring the position to what it would have been if the excessive contributions had not been made.[113] In deciding whether excessive contributions have been made, the court must consider in particular (but not exclusively) whether any of the contributions were made for the purpose of putting assets beyond the reach of creditors; whether the total contributions made during the five-year period were excessive in view of the debtor's circumstances at the time they were made; and whether the level of benefits under this and any other occupational pension scheme was excessive in all the circumstances.[114]

The court has an unfettered discretion as to the type of order it can make, but it is specifically provided that an order may require the trustees or managers of the pension scheme to make a payment to the permanent trustee and/or make specified provisions for reduction of the benefits available under the scheme or other adjustments to it.[115] The court is not affected by the fact that the benefits under the scheme are unassignable.[116] Orders may subsequently be varied, rescinded or reviewed on the application of interested persons.[117]

Overlap of provisions for the challenge of transactions

The provisions described above operate in addition to any existing grounds of challenge. For example, a floating charge may be void in a question with the administrator, liquidator or any creditor of a company for want of registration.[118]

A transaction may also be challengeable under more than one of the provisions described above. The scheme of the statutory provisions allows for overlapping challenges. Section 61 of the 1985 Act and s 244 of the 1986 Act (the provisions relating to challenge of extortionate credit transactions) specifically provide that the powers conferred under those sections are exercisable, in the case of s 61 of the 1985 Act, concurrently with any powers exercisable in relation to that transaction as a gratuitous alienation or unfair preference[119] and in the case of s 244 of the 1986 Act, concurrently with any powers exercisable in relation to that

---

[110a] Pensions Act 1995 (Commencement No 3) Order 1996 (SI 1996/778).
[111] 1985 Act, s 36A(1).
[112] Ibid. 'Occupational pension scheme' means an occupational pension scheme as defined by s 1 of the Pension Schemes Act 1993: 1985 Act, s 36C(5).
[113] 1985 Act, s 36A(2).
[114] 1985 Act, s 36A(3).
[115] 1985 Act, s 36B(1).
[116] 1985 Act, s 36C(1).
[117] 1985 Act, s 36B(7).
[118] Companies Act 1985, s 410(2).
[119] 1985 Act, s 61(6).

transaction under s 242 of the 1986 Act (gratuitous alienations).[120] Section 245 of the 1986 Act does not contain a specific provision of similar effect, but it appears that the power to challenge under that section should be regarded as being available concurrently with the power to challenge the floating charge under any other applicable statutory provision[121] or at common law. The statutory predecessor of s 245, s 613 of CA 1985, contained a provision to the effect that a floating charge could *only* be challenged under that section, and not as an alienation or preference at statute or common law, but that provision has not been re-enacted, and it would therefore appear that concurrent challenges would be possible. It is also clear that a challenge may be made at common law or under statute or under both if the circumstances are such that both would apply. The effect of the availability of overlapping challenges is to allow those wishing to challenge a transaction a great deal of flexibility.

Destination of property recovered on the successful challenge of transactions

Where a successful challenge has resulted in the recovery of assets or their value, these will fall to be distributed, to the extent that the proceedings provide, to those who have a right to them. In the case of an insolvent company which has created a valid floating charge or charges, however, there may be some difficulty in determining who has a right to them. The issue is essentially whether what is recovered is attached by a floating charge which is drawn in sufficiently wide terms and can therefore be claimed by the chargeholder to the exclusion of the general body of creditors.

In the English case of *Re Yagerphone Ltd*[122] it was held that sums which had allegedly been paid out by the company as a fraudulent preference and were subsequently recovered by the liquidators were not subject to a floating charge and the debenture holders were not entitled to payment of the monies recovered. The decision was based on two grounds. The first was that the monies were not part of the company's property (present or future) at the date of crystallisation of the charge. The second was that the right to recover monies from a creditor fraudulently preferred by the debtor was one which was conferred for the benefit of the general body of creditors, and any sums so recovered did not form part of the general assets of the company but were impressed with a trust for the general body of creditors among whom they fell to be distributed. The decision has, however, been subjected to criticism, and it has been suggested that it ought not to be followed in Scotland.[123] In the case of *Ross v Taylor*[124] the court held that certain assets, which had been 'sold' by the company prior to the appointment of a receiver but returned to the receiver voluntarily after he had pointed out to the creditor that the transaction was a potential fraudulent preference if the company had been in liquidation, were attached by the charge in respect of which the receiver had been appointed. The case is not directly in point: the assets had been

---

[120] 1986 Act, s 244(5). It is not clear, however, why the provision contained in s 244 appears to be more restrictive than that in s 61.

[121] That is, ss 242, 243 and 244 of the 1986 Act.

[122] [1935] Ch 392.

[123] See Sellar, 'Floating Charges and Fraudulent Preferences' 1983 SLT (News) 253; St Clair and Drummond Young, *The Law of Corporate Insolvency in Scotland* (2nd edn), pp 140–142.

[124] 1985 SLT 387.

returned voluntarily rather than as a result of a statutory challenge,[125] and the court itself pointed out that there was no agreement that the transaction, which had not been reduced, was an unfair preference or that the creditor had ever agreed that it was, and that the references to unfair preferences were simply a distraction. However the court, although holding that *Re Yagerphone Ltd* was not in fact of any assistance to it in these circumstances, commented that it was a case which had been decided on its own particular facts and on the terms of the debenture involved. The approach taken in this case may therefore suggest that a different decision might be reached in Scotland.

Whatever approach is to be regarded as correct in Scotland in relation to the proceeds of a successful challenge of an unfair or fraudulent preference, the same approach would logically apply to the proceeds of the successful challenge of a gratuitous alienation or extortionate credit transaction.

---

[125] Which the receiver would not, of course, have had title to make: see the conditions for challenge of different types of transactions discussed above.

31 : INSOLVENCY AND DILIGENCE

Diligence is the legal means by which creditors may attach the assets of their debtors *inter alia* in payment, or in security for payment, of their debts.[1] A creditor who carries out diligence generally gains an advantage over other creditors and since, as a general rule, diligences affecting a particular asset rank in date order, the creditor who is quickest in carrying out diligence will usually gain the greatest advantage. This can result in a 'race of diligence', with creditors trying to seize the assets of the debtor as quickly as possible, and creditors who are not quick enough losing out to those who have managed to carry out diligence more quickly. The Bills of Exchange (Scotland) Act 1772 summed the matter up thus:

> '[T]he personal estates of such debtors as become insolvent are generally carried off by the diligences . . . executed by a few creditors who . . . get the earliest notice of their insolvency, to the great prejudice of creditors more remote and unconnected.'

Such a race of diligence operates 'to the disappointment of that equality which ought to take place in the distribution of estates of insolvent debtors amongst their creditors'.[2] The law therefore regulates diligence carried out by creditors in certain circumstances in order to ensure that some do not gain an unfair advantage over others. Currently, there are rules regulating diligence both outwith formal insolvency proceedings and in the context of such proceedings.[3]

Regulation of diligence outwith formal insolvency proceedings

Certain types of diligence are regulated even where no formal insolvency proceedings have commenced. There are two sets of rules to be considered here: those relating to arrestments and poindings and those relating to adjudications for debt.

Arrestments and poindings
Regulation of arrestments and poindings outwith formal insolvency proceedings is linked to the apparent insolvency of the debtor. 'Arrestments' in this context

---

[1] Diligence may also be used to found jurisdiction, but this is not of concern in the context of insolvency proceedings.

[2] Bills of Exchange (Scotland) Act 1772. See also Chapter 3.

[3] The Scottish Law Commission has recommended the abolition of the rules regulating diligence outwith formal insolvency proceedings: see further below.

would appear to include arrestments of ships,[4] but the rules discussed here do not apply to earnings arrestments, current maintenance arrestments or conjoined arrestment orders.[5] The relevant provisions are contained in para 24 of Sched 7 to the 1985 Act (which re-enacts certain provisions of the Bankruptcy (Scotland) Act 1913) and apply to companies and other entities in respect of which seques-tration is not competent.[6]

All arrestments and poindings within the period 60 days prior to and four months after apparent insolvency are treated as if they had taken place on the same date, subject to the proviso that any arrestment which was executed on the dependence of an action is followed up without undue delay.[7] This is commonly referred to as equalisation of diligence, and can be illustrated diagramatically as follows.

arrestments and poindings equalised

<··>

I ···································· I ··· I

sixty days   apparent insolvency   four months

Any creditor producing liquid grounds of debt or a decree for payment within that period in any judicial process relating to the arrestments or poindings—for example, an action of multiplepoinding—is also entitled to share equally in the assets affected by the diligence as if they had arrested or poinded.[8] The result is that no creditor gains any advantage over the others.

A debtor may be made apparently insolvent more than once, and the periods within which diligences are equalised in relation to each apparent insolvency may overlap. This may cause difficult problems in determining the correct ranking of the respective diligences.[9]

The Scottish Law Commission has recommended that these rules be repealed.[10]

---

[4] See the Scottish Law Commission Report on Bankruptcy and Related Aspects of Insolvency and Liquidation, 1982, para 13.2, and the cases cited therein which describe the position prior to the 1985 Act. There is no reason to suppose that there is any change from that position.

[5] 1985 Act, Sched 7, para 24(8). Earnings arrestments, current maintenance arrestments and conjoined arrestment orders are, of course, only relevant to individual debtors.

[6] 1985 Act, Sched 7, para 24(5). The sub-paragraph states that references to a debtor include references to an entity whose apparent insolvency may be constituted under s 7(1) of the 1985 Act by virtue of s 7(5) of that Act. There is in fact no s 7(5) in the 1985 Act, but s 7(4) provides that the apparent insolvency of any entity mentioned in 6(2)(a) or (b) of the 1985 Act (being companies registered under CA 1985 or the former Companies Acts as defined by that Act *and* any entity in respect of which sequestration is explicitly or impliedly incompetent respectively) may be constituted under s 7(1) of the 1985 Act. It is assumed that the reference to s 7(5) is an error and should be read as a reference to s 7(4), otherwise para 24(5) would not make sense. It was certainly the case that the rules applied to companies prior to the 1985 Act: see *Clark* v *Hinde Milne & Co* (1884) 12 R 347.

[7] 1985 Act, Sched 7, para 24(2). The Scottish Law Commission has recommended various changes to the law relating to diligence on the dependence: Report on Diligence on the Dependence and Admiralty Arrestments (Scot Law Com No 164).

[8] 1985 Act, Sched 7, para 24(3).

[9] For more detailed discussion, see McBryde, *Bankruptcy*, pp 330–331; Gretton, 'Multiple Notour Bankruptcy' (1983) 28 JLSS 18; the Scottish Law Commission's Discussion Paper on Equalisation of Diligences (1988) No 79; and the Report on Diligence on the Dependence and Admiralty Arrestments, note 7 above.

[10] Report on Diligence on the Dependence and Admiralty Arrestments, note 7 above.

Adjudications

The rule is that all adjudications before, or within one year and a day after, an effectual adjudication are equalised with each other.[11] In practice, this type of diligence is now rare. The Scottish Law Commission has proposed that adjudication as a diligence against heritable property be replaced with a new type of diligence to be known as a land attachment[12] and that adjudication as a residual diligence be replaced with a new type of diligence to be known as an attachment order.[13] It has also proposed that the rule relating to equalisation of adjudications outwith formal insolvency proceedings should be repealed and that the new land attachments should not be subject to equalisation outwith formal insolvency proceedings;[14] rather, land attachments and attachment orders should only be affected by a subsequent sequestration or liquidation taking place within a defined period.[15]

Regulation of diligence in the context of formal insolvency procedures

Regulation of certain diligences on sequestration or liquidation

The position on sequestration and liquidation is regulated principally by s 37 of the 1985 Act, the majority of the provisions of which are applied to liquidations by s 185 of the 1986 Act, with the modifications necessary to reflect the different type of debtor.

For ease of reference, this chapter will refer only to s 37 of the 1985 Act as such: this should be read as meaning that section as modified by s 185 of the 1986 Act in its application to company debtors unless the contrary is stated.

Section 37 of the 1985 Act affects inhibitions, arrestments, poindings, poindings of the ground and adjudications. 'Arrestments' would appear to include arrestments of ships,[16] but the section does not apply to earnings arrestments, current maintenance arrestments, conjoined arrestment orders or deductions from earnings orders under the Child Support Act.[17]

Inhibitions, arrestments and poindings which take place within the period 60 days prior to the date of sequestration[18] or date of commencement of the liquidation[19] *or* at any time thereafter do not secure any preference for the

---

[11] Diligence Act 1661 and the Adjudications Act 1672. There is no link to the apparent insolvency of the debtor.

[12] Scottish Law Commission Discussion Paper on Diligence Against Land (No 107, 1998) and see further below.

[13] Scottish Law Commission Discussion Paper on Attachment Orders and Money Attachment (No 108, 1998).

[14] Scottish Law Commission Discussion Paper on Diligence Against Land, note 12 above.

[15] See the Scottish Law Commission Discussion Papers on Diligence Against Land and on Attachment Orders and Money Attachment.

[16] See above.

[17] 1985 Act, s 37(5A). These are, none the less, effectively terminated on sequestration of the debtor: Debtors (Scotland) Act 1987, s 72, as amended; see also s 66 of that Act. As indicated above, these diligences are relevant only to individual debtors.

[18] In the case of a deceased debtor, this should be read as the date of death: 1985 Act, s 37(7).

[19] For the date of commencement of the liquidation in the case of a voluntary liquidation, see Chapter 14 above. In the case of a winding up by the court, the normal meaning of the date of commencement of the liquidation is the date of presentation of the petition or an earlier resolution for winding up: 1986 Act, s 129, and see Chapter 16; but, for this purpose, the commencement of the liquidation means the date on which the winding-up order is made: 1986 Act, s 185(3). For ease of reference, this will be referred to hereafter as 'the date of liquidation'.

creditor.[20] It is generally said that the diligence in question is 'cut down'. The effect of the provisions can again be illustrated diagramatically.

inhibitions, arrestments and poindings cut down

<···>

I ·· I ·· I

       sixty days   date of   at any time
                   sequestration/
              commencement of
                   liquidation

Where an arrestment or poinding is cut down, any arrested or poinded estate, or the proceeds of sale thereof, must be handed over to the permanent trustee or liquidator.[21] This would appear to be the case even where the assets are held by third parties and even where such third parties have taken them in good faith and for value. There is no corresponding provision for inhibitions because they do not attach to specific assets, but any right which the inhibitor would have had to challenge a subsequent deed of the debtor or to receive payment for the discharge of the inhibition is transferred to the trustee or liquidator at the date of sequestration or liquidation.[22] There is some dispute as to whether, or in what precise circumstances, monies paid to an arresting or poinding creditor as a result of an arrestment or poinding carried out within the 60 days prior to the date of sequestration or liquidation must be returned to the trustee or liquidator. In *Johnston* v *Cluny Estates Trs*,[23] a case decided under the statutory predecessor of s 37, the court held that a creditor who had arrested within the 60-day period prior to sequestration and had thereafter obtained a decree of furthcoming as a result of which he had been paid before the sequestration could keep the monies received by him. However, s 37(4) now applies to poindings and arrestments carried out within the prescribed period 'whether subsisting or not' at the date of sequestration or liquidation. Most commentators take the view that the addition of the phrase 'whether subsisting or not' alters the effect of *Johnston* v *Cluny Estates Trs*, with the result that even where the diligence has been withdrawn or otherwise falls, money which has been paid to the creditor as a result of it has to be returned to the trustee or liquidator.[24] It has been argued, however, that this is incorrect, and *Johnston* v *Cluny Estates Trs* remains good law.[25] In relation to inhibitions, it is specifically provided that the trustee or liquidator cannot recover any money paid to the inhibiting creditor before the date of sequestration or liquidation, and the validity of anything done in consideration of such a payment cannot be challenged.[26]

[20] 1985 Act, s 37(2) (inhibitions) and s 37(4) (arrestments and poindings).
[21] 1985 Act, s 37(4).
[22] 1985 Act, s 37(2) and (3).
[23] 1957 SLT 293.
[24] This view is taken, for example, in McBryde, *Bankruptcy*, p 332, and in Maher and Cusine, *The Law and Practice of Diligence*, p 287.
[25] *Palmer's Company Law*, para 15.699. St Clair and Drummond Young, *The Law of Corporate Insolvency in Scotland* (2nd edn), pp 218–219, take the view that the effect of *Johnston* v *Cluny Estates Trs* has been altered where monies are paid over as a result of a furthcoming or sale, but may not be in other circumstances where the diligence is merely followed by a payment.
[26] 1985 Act, s 37(2).

A creditor carrying out an arrestment or poinding within the 60-day period prior to sequestration or liquidation is entitled to payment of certain expenses out of any assets or money which have had to be handed over to the trustee as a result of s 37(4).[27] There is no corresponding provision in relation to inhibitions because they do not attach to specific assets out of which payment could be made.

A poinding of the ground[28] carried out within the 60-day period prior to sequestration or at any time thereafter is not effectual in a question with the trustee or liquidator, except in relation to certain interest.[29] There is no provision for payment of the expenses of the ineffectual diligence.

An adjudication after the date of sequestration or liquidation is incompetent.[30] As noted above, the Scottish Law Commission has proposed that adjudications against heritable property be replaced by land attachments and adjudications as residual diligence be replaced by attachment orders and that any such land attachment or attachment order within a defined period prior to sequestration or liquidation should not be effectual to create a preference for the attacher in a question with the trustee or liquidator. It is also proposed that a creditor carrying out a land attachment or attachment order within the relevant period prior to the sequestration or liquidation be entitled to payment of certain expenses out of the assets affected by the land attachment or attachment order in the same way as creditors whose arrestments and poindings are cut down by sequestration or liquidation are at present.[31]

The effect of sequestration or liquidation on diligence may, in certain cases, extend beyond that provided for in s 37 as a result of the operation of the rules regulating diligence outwith formal insolvency proceedings. This occurs because although neither sequestration nor liquidation is a diligence of itself,[32] each has the effect, in relation to diligence done, of a duly recorded decree of adjudication of the debtor's heritable estate, an arrestment in execution and decree of furthcoming, an arrestment in execution and warrant of sale and a completed poinding.[33] This results in the effect of sequestration or liquidation on prior diligence being extended beyond that provided for directly in s 37 in the following circumstances.

(1) Where there is an adjudication within one year and a day prior to the date of sequestration or liquidation. It was noted in the preceding section that all adjudications before, or within one year and a day after, an effectual adjudication are equalised with each other. An adjudication within one

[27] 1985 Act, s 37(5).
[28] A diligence available to the creditor in any real security entitling him to attach and sell corporeal moveables on the ground belonging to the debtor.
[29] 1985 Act, s 37(6).
[30] 1985 Act, s 37(8).
[31] See the Scottish Law Commission Papers, notes 12 and 13 above.
[32] In relation to sequestration, see *Sinclair v Edinburgh Parish Council* 1909 SC 1353; *G. & A. Barnie v Stevenson* (Sh Ct) 1993 SCLR 318. The position would be the same for liquidation.
[33] 1985 Act, s 37(1). The Scottish Law Commission has recommended, consequent on its recommendation for the abolition of the rules relating to equalisation of diligence around apparent insolvency, that the provisions equating sequestration to an arrestment and a completed poinding be repealed: Report on Diligence on the Dependence and Admiralty Arrestments, note 7 above. It has also proposed, consequent on its proposals relating to adjudications, that the provision equating sequestration to a duly recorded decree of adjudication be repealed: Discussion Paper on Diligence Against Land, note 12 above.

year and a day prior to the date of sequestration or liquidation will therefore effectively be cut down because that adjudication and the sequestration or liquidation in its capacity as an adjudication are equalised, leaving the prior adjudication with no preference over the sequestration or liquidation. This effect will, of course, disappear if the proposals of the Scottish Law Commission in relation to adjudications, discussed above, are accepted.

(2)　Where sequestration or liquidation is preceded by the debtor's apparent insolvency and occurs within four months of it.[34] In such a situation, not only will arrestments and poindings within the period provided for in s 37(4) be cut down, but all arrestments and poindings within the entire period from 60 days prior to apparent insolvency up to and after the date of sequestration or liquidation will also be cut down. This is because where sequestration or liquidation occurs within the equalisation period around apparent insolvency, it will, in its capacity as an arrestment or poinding, be equalised with all the other arrestments or poindings carried out within that equalisation period. Such arrestments and poindings are therefore effectively cut down even though they are outwith the 60 days prior to the sequestration or liquidation itself.[35] This can be illustrated diagrammatically.

arrestments and poindings cut down

<···>

I ······················ I ··························· I

sixty days　apparent　　four months
　　　　　　insolvency

I ······················ I ··························· I

sixty days　date of　　at any time
　　　　　sequestration/
　　　　　liquidation

It is the overlap of the date of sequestration or liquidation and the period surrounding apparent insolvency which is important. If the date of sequestration or liquidation is after the end of the four-month period following apparent insolvency, then the diligences affected by the apparent insolvency will be equalised with each other, but will not be cut down by the sequestration or liquidation. This effect will, of course, disappear if the recommendations of the Scottish Law Commission are accepted and the rules relating to equalisation of diligence on apparent insolvency are repealed.[36]

---

[34] This will in practice be quite common, particularly in the case of non-company debtors, where apparent insolvency is a prerequisite of applying for sequestration in a number of cases. It is, for example, a prerequisite of a creditor petition, which must be presented within four months of apparent insolvency: see Chapter 6.

[35] See *Stewart v Jarvie* 1938 SC 309.

[36] See above.

Actions for mails and duties and sequestration for rent remain unaffected by sequestration or liquidation.

Finally under this heading, it should be noted that the Scottish Law Commission has recommended the introduction of a new diligence against cash and negotiable instruments in the debtor's possession, to be known as a money attachment.[37] It proposes that any such money attachments coming into effect within the period of 60 days prior to the debtor's sequestration or liquidation should be ineffectual in a question with the trustee or liquidator, except as to the expenses of the attachment.[38]

Regulation of diligence in the context of company voluntary arrangements and section 425 arrangements

There are no specific statutory provisions regulating diligence carried out either before or after a CVA or section 425 arrangement, but the agreement itself will generally make provision for how valid diligence carried out prior to the arrangement is to be treated and for the regulation of future diligence.[39]

Regulation of diligence on administration

No diligence may be begun or continued in the period from presentation of the petition for administration to the making of the administration order or dismissal of the petition, except with the leave of the court and on such conditions as the court thinks fit,[40] and no diligence may be begun or continued while an administration order is in force, except with the consent of the administrator or the leave of the court, subject, in the latter case, to such conditions as the court thinks fit.[41] There are, however, no provisions regulating diligence prior to the administration. It has been argued that administration itself constitutes apparent insolvency, and that accordingly the rules relating to equalisation of diligence on apparent insolvency will apply,[42] but this has been disputed[43] and remains an open question.[44]

Regulation of diligence on receivership

Section 55(3)(a) of the 1986 Act provides that the powers of a receiver are subject to the rights of any person who has effectually executed diligence on any of the company's property.[45] Any diligence which is *not* effectually executed diligence is effectively 'cut down' by the receivership because the receiver may ignore it.

---

[37] Scottish Law Commission Discussion Paper on Attachment Orders and Money Attachment, note 13 above.

[38] Ibid.

[39] The position with regard to valid diligence carried out prior to the arrangement is discussed further below.

[40] 1986 Act, s 10(1), as modified in its application in Scotland by s 10(5).

[41] 1986 Act, s 11(3), as modified in its application in Scotland by s 10(5).

[42] St Clair and Drummond Young (note 22 above), p 211.

[43] Wilson, *The Law of Scotland Relating to Debt* (2nd edn), p 282.

[44] It is thought, however, that Professor Wilson's view is the better one. The matter will become academic if the Scottish Law Commission's recommendation to abolish these rules is accepted.

[45] Where the floating charge crystallises as a result of winding up rather than the appointment of a receiver, it does so subject to the rights of any person with effectually executed diligence: CA 1985, s 463(1)(c).

'Effectually executed diligence' is not defined in the 1986 Act but has been the subject of case-law. In *Lord Advocate v Royal Bank of Scotland Ltd*[46] it was held that a bare arrestment which had not been followed up by furthcoming before the receiver's appointment was an inchoate diligence and was not therefore effectually executed diligence. In that case the arrestment had been executed after creation of the floating charge. In the subsequent case of *Iona Hotels Ltd (In Receivership)* Petnrs,[47] an arrestment had been executed prior to the registration of the floating charge and it was held that the arrestment prevailed in a question with the receiver, not on the basis that it was effectually executed diligence (on the basis of *Lord Advocate v Royal Bank of Scotland Ltd* it was not), but on the basis that arrestment renders the arrested subjects litigious and the floating chargeholder must take the property subject to the rights of the arrester. It has been argued that the court's selection of *registration* of the floating charge as the relevant reference point is neither logical nor supported by authority[48] and that logically the arrestment should prevail where it is executed at any time prior to crystallisation, because it is only at that time that the floating charge takes effect.[49] This approach is precluded, however, by the decision in *Lord Advocate v Royal Bank of Scotland Ltd*.

The approach taken in *Lord Advocate v Royal Bank of Scotland Ltd* would tend to suggest that a poinding which has not been followed by a sale prior to the appointment of the receiver will not be effectually executed diligence either, and so will be cut down by the receivership. Following the logic of *Iona Hotels Ltd*, however, a poinding executed before creation of the floating charge would not be cut down. Similarly, an inhibition not followed up by an adjudication before the appointment of a receiver would appear not to be effectually executed diligence and therefore to be cut down by the receivership.[50] However, an inhibition prior to the *creation* of a floating charge would prevail over it insofar as it affected heritage because an inhibition strikes at subsequent voluntary deeds by the debtor.[51]

The decision in *Lord Advocate v Royal Bank of Scotland Ltd* has been severely criticised.[52] It is difficult to reconcile with other provisions relating to effectually

---

[46] 1977 SC 155.

[47] 1991 SC 330.

[48] See St Clair and Drummond Young (note 25 above), pp 213–217, particularly p 215, and Palmer (note 25 above), para 14–221.

[49] St Clair and Drummond Young.

[50] *Armour and Mycroft*, Petnrs, 1983 SLT 453. Lord Kincraig specifically stated that it was unnecessary for him to decide the question of whether an inhibition was effectually executed diligence or not, but the point was conceded by counsel for the inhibitors and the remainder of the judgment appears to proceed on the basis that it is not. This would be consistent with the reasoning in *Lord Advocate v Royal Bank of Scotland Ltd*, note 46 above, but the conclusion that inhibition is an inchoate diligence is disputed by Professor Gretton: see the references in note 52.

[51] Of course, if the charge was created in terms of an enforceable obligation which existed before the inhibition, it would not be voluntary.

[52] For both sides of the debate, see St Clair and Drummond Young, pp 213–217; Palmer, para 14–221; Wilson (note 43 above), p 203; Maher and Cusine (note 24 above), para 10.21; Greene and Fletcher, *The Law and Practice of Receivership in Scotland* (2nd edn), p 34; Wilson, 'Effectually Executed Diligence' 1978 JR 253; Gretton, 'Diligence, Trusts and Floating Charges' (1981) 26 JLSS 57 and 102, 'Inhibitions and Company Insolvencies' 1983 SLT (News) 145 and 'Receivers and Arresters' 1984 SLT (News) 177; JADH, 'Inhibitions and Company Insolvencies: A Contrary View' 1983 SLT 177; Sim, 'The Receiver and Effectually Executed Diligence' 1984 SLT (News) 25. See also the Scottish Law Commission Report on Diligence on the Dependence and Admiralty Arrestments, note 7 above.

executed diligence in receivership[53] and has resulted in confusion in this area of the law. Unfortunately, the opportunity to rectify the difficulties created by the decision in this area by amending legislation has not been taken.[54] Where diligence is cut down by receivership, there is no provision comparable to that in sequestration and liquidation for any expenses of such diligence to be met by the receiver.

Sequestrations for rent should be regarded as unaffected by receivership. It was held in *Cumbernauld Development Corporation* v *Mustone*[55] that a sequestration for rent was not competent against a company in receivership, but the decision was the subject of criticism[56] and in *Grampian Regional Council* v *Drill Stem (Inspection Services) Ltd (In Receivership)*[57] it was held that a landlord's hypothec gave the landlord a real right in security which prevailed over receivership, and a sequestration for rent enforcing that security was therefore competent. The sheriff in the latter case referred to the academic criticism of the former, and on examination of the relevant authorities concluded that it was wrong. Both are decisions of a single judge, but it is suggested that the *Grampian Regional Council* case should be regarded as the correct authority on the matter.

A poinding of the ground and an action of maills and duties should also be regarded as unaffected by receivership, for the same reason, namely that they are means of enforcing an existing security.

Diligence unaffected by formal insolvency proceedings

This section considers the effect of diligence which is not cut down by the rules considered in the preceding sections.

Sequestration and liquidation

Diligence which is not cut down as a result of the rules discussed in the preceding sections remains valid and takes precedence over the sequestration or liquidation.

In the case of sequestration, an asset which is affected by valid diligence but remains part of the debtor's estate at the date of sequestration vests in the permanent trustee and must therefore be handed over to him.[58] However, it has been held that an arrestment not cut down by the sequestration amounts to a security[59] and it is thought that the same would apply to a completed poinding.

---

[53] Namely 1986 Act, ss 60 and 61: see further below.

[54] The Scottish Law Commission recommended in its Report on Diligence on the Dependence and Admiralty Arrestments (note 7 above), that the basis on which an arrestment operates, which is at the root of this problem at least insofar as the decisions in *Lord Advocate* v *Royal Bank of Scotland Ltd* (note 46 above) and *Iona Hotels Ltd* (note 47 above) are concerned, should be spelt out in properly formulated principles, but that this should be achieved through judicial development rather than through legislation. It is thought by the author, however, that the provisions relating to the relationship between receivership and pre-existing diligence should be amended by legislation to clarify this important area of the law.

[55] 1983 SLT (Sh Ct) 55.

[56] Gretton, 'Receivership and Sequestration for Rent' 1983 SLT (News) 277; Halliday, *Conveyancing Law and Practice In Scotland*, Vol I, para 2–114, and Vol II, para 41–24; Greene and Fletcher (note 52 above), p 35; Simmons, 'A Legal Black Hole' (1983) 28 JLSS 352; Wilson (note 43 above), p 112.

[57] (Sh Ct) 1994 SCLR 36.

[58] *Berry* v *Taylor* 1993 SLT 718.

[59] *Gibson* v *Greig* (1853) 16 D 233; and see McBryde (note 24 above), pp 338–339, who takes the view that such diligence is a security within the meaning of the 1985 Act.

The affected asset(s) therefore vest in the trustee subject to that security.[60] This means, *inter alia*, that the creditor obtains a right to be paid first out of the proceeds of the asset affected by the valid diligence.[61] It has been held in the context of liquidation that where diligence is not cut down by the liquidation, the liquidator is not entitled to insist on the asset affected being handed over to him[62] and that the creditor may proceed to complete his diligence and obtain payment.[63] The rationale for this decision was that the property of the company does not vest in the liquidator as it does in a trustee in sequestration,[64] but the competence of a creditor proceeding in this way has been doubted[65] and it is thought that the decision is wrong in principle. The liquidator is entitled to take possession of all the company's property[66] and while diligence is incomplete, the property affected by it remains the property of the company, notwithstanding the diligence. Nor would the creditor be disadvantaged, because the liquidator would take the property subject to the rights of the diligence creditor who, as in sequestration, would be treated as a secured creditor and, *inter alia*, effectively obtain a right to be paid first out of the proceeds of the asset affected by the valid diligence as a result of the security conferred by it.[67]

An inhibition which is not cut down by a sequestration or liquidation may also be regarded as conferring a security on the inhibiting creditor to the extent that it gives the inhibiting creditor a preference over the sequestration or liquidation, but of course an inhibition does not attach to specific assets. In both sequestration and liquidation, the preference created by a valid inhibition is given effect to by ranking the inhibition on the debtor's heritable estate[68] as if post-inhibition creditors did not exist. This is achieved by the application of certain canons of ranking.[69] All creditors are ranked according to their rights but without reference to the inhibition in the first instance, then the same exercise is carried out again with only the inhibiting creditor and creditors whose debts were prior to the inhibition. Pre-inhibition creditors receive only what they achieved in the first exercise, because they are not affected by the inhibition, and the inhibitor

---

[60] 1985 Act, s 33(3).

[61] See further Chapter 33. The fact that the diligence is treated as a security also has other implications, such as the requirement to value the security for the purposes of calculating the creditor's claim: these are discussed in Chapter 22.

[62] *Commercial Aluminium Windows Ltd* v *Cumbernauld Development Corporation* 1987 SLT (Sh Ct) 91.

[63] Ibid. In that case the question of whether the arrested funds required to be handed over to the liquidator arose in the context of an action of furthcoming by the arresting creditor and, as indicated, it was held that the liquidator was not entitled to the funds and the creditor obtained decree of furthcoming.

[64] Ibid.

[65] McBryde (note 24 above), p 339.

[66] See Chapter 28.

[67] See *Liquidators of Benhar Coal Co* v *Turnbull* (1883) 10 R 558. In that case arrested funds were in the hands of the liquidator because the court had recalled the arrestments under reservation of the arresting creditor's rights. The court were of the view that the creditor's preference was secured by the diligence which he had used and the funds must therefore be devoted in the first instance to payment of the arresting creditor's debt. The fact that the diligence is treated as a security also has other implications, such as the requirement to value the security for the purposes of calculating the creditor's claim: see Chapter 22. The classification of diligence as a security in the context of company insolvency proceedings also raises other issues: see further below.

[68] An inhibition only affects heritable estate. The creditors will rank on the moveable estate in the normal way.

[69] Bell, *Commentaries*, ii 413 (7th edn); *Baird & Brown* v *Stirrat's Tr* (1872) 10 M 414. See also *Stewart on Diligence*; Gretton, *The Law of Inhibition and Adjudication* (2nd edn).

receives what he achieved in the second exercise, the money to make up this larger amount being taken away from the post-inhibition creditors, who receive correspondingly less. The Scottish Law Commission has sought views on whether inhibitions should be abolished or retained in the event of its proposed new diligence of land attachment being introduced and has made several proposals for reform of the law relating to inhibitions in the event of their being retained.[70] One of these is that an inhibition should continue to prohibit the debtor from granting future voluntary deeds affecting his heritable property but should no longer prohibit him from incurring debts after the date of the inhibition, with the result that the inhibitor's preference in relation to post-inhibition debts as described here would disappear.

Receivership

Diligence which is 'effectually executed diligence' takes precedence over the receivership and the receiver's powers are subject to the rights of creditors who have effectually executed diligence. The receiver is entitled to ingather the property of the company which is subject to such diligence,[71] but if he cannot obtain the consent of the creditor, he can only sell or dispose of such property with the consent of the court.[72] Where the court authorises any sale or disposal, it may impose such conditions as it thinks fit[73] but, unlike the situation where the court authorises the sale or disposal of property subject to a prior ranking fixed security, there is no *obligation* to impose a condition that the proceeds of sale be applied to discharge the debt of the creditor who carried out the diligence.[74] However, the receiver is bound to pay, *inter alia*, creditors with effectually executed diligence prior to the floating chargeholder[75] and the creditor's right to rank in a subsequent liquidation is preserved.[76]

It has been held that a receiver could obtain the consent of the court to the disposal of property subject to an inhibition under the statutory predecessor of s 61 of the 1986 Act even though it was not effectually executed diligence.[77] The section was invoked on the basis that the inhibition was a 'security or interest of, or encumbrance in favour of, a creditor'.[78] The court noted that the parties had agreed that the inhibition came within the scope of that provision, 'the most apposite [provision] being an encumbrance',[79] but also talked of the inhibition in terms which showed that it was regarded as a security. The decision is somewhat doubtful because, *inter alia*, as the court itself recognised, if the inhibition was not

---

[70] Scottish Law Commission Discussion Paper on Diligence Against Land, note 12 above.
[71] 1986 Act, s 55 and Sched 1.
[72] 1986 Act, s 61(1). This section is discussed in Chapter 27.
[73] 1986 Act, s 61(2).
[74] The obligation to impose such a condition in relation to a prior-ranking fixed security arises from s 61(3), (4) and (5).
[75] 1986 Act, s 60(1).
[76] 1986 Act, s 61(9).
[77] *Armour and Mycroft*, Petnrs, note 50 above. The application under the section was necessary because although the receiver could dispose of the property without reference to the inhibition if it was not effectually executed diligence, he had bound himself to deliver clear searches to the purchaser and the inhibiting creditors refused to consent to the sale: the receiver therefore required to obtain the consent of the court in order to be able to deliver the clear searches.
[78] Companies (Floating Charges and Receivers) (Scotland) Act 1972, s 21(1)(a), the terms of which are identical to the current provision in this respect.
[79] *Armour and Mycroft*, Petnrs (note 50 above) at 455.

effectually executed diligence, it should not be able to acquire an equivalent status because it fell within the other part of the section. If such diligence is to be regarded as a security, however, this would have other implications.[80]

It has already been noted that it is difficult to reconcile the way that 'effectually executed diligence' has been interpreted with the other provisions relating to effectually executed diligence in receivership. These provisions, as has just been seen, envisage the receiver ingathering property subject to effectually executed diligence and require him to obtain consent before disposing of such property and to pay creditors who have effectually executed diligence before the floating chargeholder. It is virtually impossible to reconcile these provisions with an interpretation of effectually executed diligence which equates that concept with completed diligence. Completion of a diligence transfers the property affected by it to the creditor. The property is thereby removed from the company's ownership. If the property is no longer in the company's ownership, it could not be affected by the receivership. If it is not affected by the receivership, the provisions on consent and payment are unnecessary. Palmer,[81] recognising this, suggests that it must therefore be open to argument that a diligence becomes effectual for the purposes of these provisions at some point between the initial step (such as arrestment or poinding) and completion, but it is difficult to see at what point this could be held to happen. The solution will only be found in clarification of the meaning of effectually executed diligence as suggested above.

Effectually executed diligence may be cut down by a subsequent liquidation.

Administration

Although the provisions of ss 10 and 11 of the 1986 Act prevent creditors continuing with diligence which has already begun, such diligence remains valid. Even if the argument that diligence taking place within 60 days prior to the administration is cut down because the administration itself constitutes apparent insolvency were correct,[82] diligences outside that period would remain valid.

The position of the administrator in relation to property under his control which is affected by such diligence is uncertain. If the creditor consents to withdraw the diligence or give up his preference, there is no difficulty. If the creditor refuses to do so, however, there is some doubt as to what powers the administrator has in relation to the property. It has already been seen that s 15 of the 1986 Act gives the administrator the power to dispose of property subject to a floating charge as if the charge did not exist and to apply to the court for authority to dispose of, *inter alia*, property subject to a security other than a floating charge.[83] Unlike the corresponding provisions in receivership,[84] however, property subject to (valid) diligence is not specifically mentioned in s 15. The administrator will therefore only be able to apply to the court for authority to dispose of the property affected by the diligence under s 15 if the diligence can be regarded as a security. 'Security' is defined in s 248(b)(ii) of the 1986 Act as being, 'except where the context otherwise requires . . . any security (whether heritable or moveable), any floating charge and any right of lien or preference

---

[80] See Chapter 22.
[81] Para 14.221.
[82] See above and note 42.
[83] See Chapter 26.
[84] See above and Chapter 27.

and any right of retention (other than a right of compensation or set off)'. Professor Wilson[85] doubts whether diligence can be said to be a security within that definition, particularly since the provisions in relation to administrations deal with securities and diligence separately in other contexts.[86] However, as noted above, valid diligence is treated as a security in the context of both sequestration and liquidation: indeed, it is only because it is classified as a security that it has a preference over the sequestration or liquidation when it comes to the ranking of claims.[87] Furthermore, as noted above, it has been held in the context of receivership that a receiver could obtain the consent of the court to the disposal of property subject to an inhibition under the statutory predecessor of s 61 of the 1986 Act, not because it was effectually executed diligence, which it was not, but on the basis that it was a 'security or interest of, or encumbrance in favour of, a creditor'.[88] As noted, the decision may be somewhat doubtful,[89] but it suggests that it is not impossible to regard diligence as a security even where diligence is separately dealt with in other contexts in relation to the same type of proceedings. It is therefore arguable that Professor Wilson is wrong and diligence should be regarded as falling within the definition of security in the 1986 Act for the purposes of s 15 of that Act. It must also be recalled that the definition in the 1986 Act only applies *except insofar as the context requires*, although this may cut two ways: it could be argued on that basis that even if Professor Wilson is correct, security may be taken to include diligence for the purpose of s 15, on the basis that it would be odd if the administrator had no means of disposing of property subject to valid diligence given the nature of the régime; on the other hand, it could be said that even if diligence is a security for the purpose of classifying a creditor's claim, it does not follow that is so for other purposes such as the purpose of s 15. If valid diligence is to be regarded as security, this also has other implications, such as the need to value the security for the purposes of calculating the creditor's claim.[90] The issue therefore remains one of difficulty and should, perhaps, be clarified by statute.

Company voluntary arrangements and section 425 arrangements
The rights of those who have carried out diligence against the company will only be affected by a CVA or section 425 arrangement to the extent provided for in the arrangement itself.

In the context of CVAs, a question arises as to whether the arrangement may affect the rights of creditors who have carried out diligence without their specific consent. It has been noted that s 4(3) of the 1986 Act provides that the specific consent of any secured creditor must be obtained if his right to enforce his security is to be affected.[91] If diligence is a security within the definition contained in the 1986 Act, the specific consent of the creditor would be required to any alteration of his rights.[92] If it is not, his rights can be affected by the arrangement without

---

[85] At pp 281–282.
[86] He refers in particular to the 1986 Act, s 11.
[87] See further Chapter 33.
[88] *Armour and Mycroft, Petnrs*, note 50 above.
[89] See above.
[90] See Chapter 22.
[91] See Chapter 8.
[92] It would also have other implications, such as the need to value the security for the purposes of calculating the value of the creditor's claim: see Chapter 22.

his consent and even, if the requisite majorities are achieved,[93] against his will: he could, for example, be required to withdraw his diligence or give up its preference. The arguments regarding the interpretation of the definition of security have already been rehearsed above and the issue is no less difficult in this context. It is thought that the matter should be clarified by statute.

[93] Ibid.

32 : CREDITORS' CLAIMS: PROCEDURE AND VALUATION

In sequestration, creditors' voluntary liquidation and compulsory liquidation, creditors must submit claims to the trustee or liquidator in order to determine their entitlement to vote at creditors' meetings and to receive payment of a dividend.[1] In CVAs, administration and receivership, creditors submit such claims for the purpose of determining their entitlement to vote at creditors' meetings.[2]

This chapter deals with the submission and calculation of creditors' claims for these purposes in sequestration, creditors' voluntary and compulsory liquidation, CVAs, administration and receivership,[3] the liabilities and rights of co-obligants and the balancing of accounts in bankruptcy. The distribution of the debtor's assets is discussed in the following chapter.

Submission of claims

The procedure for submission of claims in sequestration is set out in the 1985 Act. The rules relating to claims generally, including the procedure for the submission of claims, in compulsory liquidation are set out in rules 4.15 and 4.16 of the Scottish Rules and, insofar as they relate to the procedure for submission of claims, are virtually identical to those applying in sequestration: indeed, some

---

[1] 1985 Act, s 22(1) (submission of claims to interim trustee for purposes of voting at statutory meeting) and s 48(1) (submission of claims to permanent trustee for purposes of voting at meetings other than statutory meeting and drawing a dividend); the Scottish Rules, rule 4.15 (compulsory liquidation), applied to creditors' voluntary liquidation by rule 5. The rules relating to submission of claims do not apply to members' voluntary liquidation: Scottish Rules, rule 6 and Sched 2. The issue of entitlement to vote at creditors' meetings does not arise in relation to a members' voluntary liquidation so long as the liquidation continues as such, because there are no creditors' meetings, and because the company is solvent, the creditors will be paid in full.

[2] Scottish Rules, rule 7.9. The value of a creditor's claim for the purposes of voting in these régimes will not necessarily be the value of his claim for the purpose of any distribution: see, for example, *Re Cranley Mansions Ltd* (1994) BCC 576, a case involving a CVA. Distribution of the debtor's assets is discussed in the following chapter.

[3] It has already been noted that the rules on submission of claims do not apply to members' voluntary liquidation: see note 1 above. The provisions relating to submission of claims described here do not extend to section 425 arrangements either: the position with respect to valuing creditors' claims for the purpose of voting in section 425 arrangements has been touched on in Chapter 9.

263

of the rules relating to the submission of claims in sequestration are applied, subject to appropriate modifications, directly to compulsory liquidation by rule 4.16 of the Scottish Rules. The rules relating to compulsory liquidation, including those relating to sequestration which are applied to compulsory liquidations by rule 4.16 of the Scottish Rules, are in turn applied, subject to specified and any other necessary modifications, to creditors' voluntary liquidation by rule 5 of the Scottish Rules and to CVAs, administration and receivership by rule 7.9(3) of the Scottish Rules.[4] References will therefore be to the rules relating to compulsory liquidations, as applied to those other procedures by the rules referred to. References to liquidation in this section are to compulsory and creditors' voluntary liquidation only.

Claim to be on the prescribed form

Creditors must submit their claims on the prescribed form,[5] which requires details of the debt (or debts) due and of any security for the debt and which must be accompanied by appropriate accounts or vouchers which are prima facie evidence of the debt—for example, invoices or a court decree.[6] The person to whom the claim is to be submitted[7] may, however, dispense with these requirements in relation to any debt or class of debts,[8] and in relation to sequestration it is specifically provided that the interim or permanent trustee may allow foreign creditors to submit claims informally in writing.[9]

The lodging of claims

In sequestration, claims may be submitted to the interim trustee or to the permanent trustee. If a claim has been submitted to the interim trustee and wholly or partly accepted by him, the creditor does not need to submit it again to the permanent trustee,[10] but the permanent trustee is not bound by the interim trustee's decision on the claim.[11] In liquidation, the claim is submitted to the liquidator[12] or, if appropriate, the chairman of a meeting if other than the liquidator.[13] In CVAs, administrations and receiverships, the claim is submitted to the supervisor of the CVA, the administrator or the receiver as appropriate[14] or to the chairman of a meeting if other than the supervisor, administrator or receiver.[15]

---

[4] Which applies the rules on claims in compulsory liquidations, subject to the specified and any other necessary modifications, for the purposes of determining a creditor's right to vote at any creditors' meeting in any insolvency proceedings in the same way as they apply in a liquidation.

[5] 1985 Act, ss 22(2)(a), 48(3) (sequestration) and the Scottish Rules, rule 4.15(2)(a) (all insolvency proceedings under the 1986 Act). The prescribed form in relation to sequestration is Form 5, in the Schedule to the Bankruptcy (Scotland) Regulations 1985, and in relation to insolvency proceedings under the 1986 Act it is Form 5 in Sched 5 to the Scottish Rules.

[6] 1985 Act, ss 22(2)(b), 48(3) and the Scottish Rules, rule 4.15(2)(b).

[7] See the next section.

[8] 1985 Act, s 22(2), and the Scottish Rules, rule 4.15(2).

[9] 1985 Act, ss 22(3)(b) and 48(3). There is no specific equivalent provision in relation to insolvency proceedings under the 1986 Act, but it is thought that the general provision allowing for formalities to be dispensed with could be used to achieve the same effect. Claims in foreign currency are discussed further below.

[10] 1985 Act, s 48(2).

[11] Ibid.

[12] Scottish Rules, rule 4.15(1).

[13] Scottish Rules, rule 4.15(6).

[14] Scottish Rules, rule 4.15(1), as modified in relation to such proceedings by rule 7.9(4)(a).

[15] Scottish Rules, rule 4.15(6), as modified in relation to such proceedings by rule 7.9(4)(a).

Only one claim need be submitted in order to be able to vote at meetings and, where applicable, claim payment of a dividend. To be entitled to vote at any particular meeting, a creditor must submit his claim at or prior to that meeting[16] and to be entitled to claim payment of a dividend in sequestration or liquidation, a creditor must submit his claim at least eight weeks before the end of the relevant accounting period.[17] Once a claim has been submitted, however, it is deemed to be resubmitted for the purposes of future meetings[18] and, in sequestration and liquidation, for the purpose of claiming payment of dividend in subsequent accounting periods.[19]

In a compulsory liquidation, the court may fix a time or times within which creditors must prove their debts or claims or be excluded from the benefit of any distribution made before those debts are proved.[20] This may also happen in a creditors' voluntary liquidation by virtue of s 112 of the 1986 Act. A strict reading of the section would suggest that a creditor who fails to submit his claim within the time fixed by the court will not be entitled to receive anything in respect of dividends already paid in accounting periods prior to the submission of his claim. This would conflict with the principle that all creditors should be treated equally, however, and it is generally accepted that the section does not have such an effect but is merely procedural, so that a creditor lodging his claim late will, in fact, be entitled to have any dividends he has thereby missed made up to him if funds permit.[21]

Claims in foreign currency

A creditor may state his claim in a foreign currency where *either* his claim is constituted by a decree or other court order for payment in such foreign currency *or*, where that is not the case, his claim arises from a contract or bill of exchange in terms of which payment is or may be required to be made in such foreign currency.[22] Such claims are converted into sterling at a rate of exchange equivalent to the average of the buying and selling spot rates for exchange of that currency prevailing in the London market at close of business on the appropriate date.[23]

---

[16] For sequestrations, see the 1985 Act, s 22(1) (voting at statutory meeting) and s 48(1) (voting at any meeting other than the statutory meeting); for the relevant procedures under the 1986 Act, see rule 4.15(1) which applies directly to compulsory liquidations and to all other relevant procedures by virtue of rule 7.9(3) of the Scottish Rules.

[17] 1985 Act, s 48(1) (sequestrations); the Scottish Rules, rule 4.15(1) (which applies directly to compulsory liquidations and to creditors' voluntary liquidations by virtue of rule 5 of the Scottish Rules). Accounting periods are the periods into which the administration of sequestrations and liquidations are divided: see further Chapter 33.

[18] 1985 Act, s 48(2) (sequestrations); the Scottish Rules, rule 4.15(3) (which applies directly to compulsory liquidations and to all other relevant procedures by virtue of rule 7.9(3) of the Scottish Rules).

[19] 1985 Act, s 48(2) (sequestrations); the Scottish Rules, rule 4.15(3) (which applies directly to compulsory liquidations and to creditors' voluntary liquidations by virtue of rule 5 of the Scottish Rules).

[20] 1986 Act, s 153.

[21] See St Clair and Drummond Young, *The Law of Corporate Insolvency in Scotland* (2nd edn), pp 290–291; *Palmer's Company Law*, para 15.671. The way in which the estate is distributed is discussed in the following chapter.

[22] 1985 Act, ss 22(6) and 48(7), and the Bankruptcy (Scotland) Regulations 1985, reg 6 (sequestration), and the Scottish Rules, rule 4.17(1) (all insolvency proceedings under the 1986 Act).

[23] 1985 Act, ss 23(1)(a) and 49(3), and the Bankruptcy (Scotland) Regulations 1985, reg 7 (sequestration), and the Scottish Rules, rule 4.17(2) (all insolvency proceedings under the 1986 Act).

The appropriate date is, in the case of sequestration, the date of sequestration;[24] in the case of liquidation, the date of commencement of the liquidation;[25] in the case of a CVA, the date of the meeting or, if the company is in liquidation or administration, the date of the company going into liquidation or the date of the administration order as appropriate;[26] in the case of administration, the date of the administration order;[27] and in the case of receivership, the date of the appointment of the receiver.[28]

Submission of a different claim

A creditor who has already submitted a claim may submit a different claim at a later stage.[29] In sequestration and liquidation, however, a secured creditor may not submit a new claim specifying a different value for his security at any time after he has been required to discharge, convey or assign the security under the provisions of para 5(2) of the 1985 Act.[30]

Submission of a false claim

It is an offence for a creditor to submit a false statement of claim or supporting account or voucher, although it is a defence for the creditor to show that he neither knew nor had reason to believe that the offending item was false.[31] It is also an offence for the debtor to fail to report knowledge of such a false statement of claim, supporting account or voucher to the relevant office holder as soon as practicable after acquiring the knowledge.[32]

Effect of the submission of a claim on prescription and limitation

The lodging of a claim in a sequestration or liquidation is the equivalent of an effective acknowledgement of a creditor's claim for the purpose of any enactment or rule of law relating to the limitation of actions in any part of the United Kingdom, with the exception of an enactment which implements or gives effect to an international agreement.[33] It also interrupts the running of prescription.[34]

---

[24] 1985 Act, ss 23(1)(a) and 49(3). For the date of sequestration, see Chapter 6.

[25] Scottish Rules, rule 4.17(2). For the date of commencement of the liquidation, see Chapter 14 in relation to voluntary liquidations and Chapters 16 and 17 in relation to compulsory liquidations.

[26] Scottish Rules, rule 4.17(2), as modified by rule 7.9(4)(c)(i).

[27] Scottish Rules, rule 4.17(2), as modified by rule 7.9(4)(c)(ii).

[28] Ibid.

[29] 1985 Act, s 48(4), and the Scottish Rules, rule 4.15(4).

[30] Ibid. The provisions of para 5(2) of the 1985 Act, *inter alia*, are disapplied in the case of claims in company insolvency proceedings other than liquidation by rule 7.9(5) of the Scottish Rules. The provisions relating to the requirement for a secured creditor to value his security and the circumstances in which he may be required to discharge, convey or assign it are discussed further below.

[31] 1985 Act, s 22(5), 48(7) (sequestrations). The provisions of s 22(5) of the 1985 Act are applied to compulsory liquidations by the Scottish Rules, rule 4.16(1), and thence to all other relevant company insolvency proceedings under the 1986 Act, as discussed at the beginning of this section.

[32] Ibid.

[33] For sequestration, see the 1985 Act, ss 22(8) and 48(7), as interpreted by s 73(5); for liquidation, see the Scottish Rules, rule 4.76 (which applies these provisions of the 1985 Act to compulsory liquidations subject to specified and any other necessary modifications) and rule 5 of the Scottish Rules (which applies, *inter alia*, rule 4.76 of the Scottish Rules to creditors' voluntary liquidations). The presentation of, or concurrence in, a petition for sequestration or compulsory liquidation has the same effect: see the 1985 Act, s 8(5), as interpreted by s 73(5), and rule 4.76 of the Scottish Rules, which applies these provisions of the 1985 Act to compulsory liquidations, respectively.

[34] Prescription and Limitation (Scotland) Act 1973, s 9. That section also provides that the presentation of, or concurrence in, a petition for sequestration or compulsory liquidation has the

Adjudication

Adjudication is the process whereby creditors' claims are accepted or rejected.

The rules on adjudication in sequestration (other than for the purposes of voting at the statutory meeting, where the rules are set out separately[35]) are contained principally in s 49 of the 1985 Act. These rules, subject to specified modifications, are applied directly to compulsory liquidation by rule 4.16(1) of the Scottish Rules and thence, subject to further specified and any other necessary modifications, to creditors' voluntary liquidation[36] and to CVAs, administration and receivership.[37] References in this section are to s 49 of the 1985 Act, as applied to the relevant company insolvency proceedings under the 1986 Act by the rules referred to. References to liquidation relate to compulsory and creditors' voluntary liquidation only.

The appropriate office holder or, in some cases, the chairman of a meeting if other than the office holder, must accept or reject each claim submitted to him in whole or in part. For the purpose of voting at meetings, the claim is accepted or rejected at the commencement of every meeting;[38] for the purpose of determining entitlement to dividend in sequestration and liquidation, it is accepted or rejected at least four weeks before the end of the relevant accounting period.[39] To satisfy himself about the amount or validity of the claim, the appropriate office holder may ask the creditor or any other person whom he believes to have it to produce further evidence relating to the claim, and where the person refuses or delays in doing so, the office holder may apply for an order for him to be privately examined.[40] The procedure is essentially the same as for a private examination under s 44 of the 1985 Act.[41]

---

same effect. In the case of sequestration, it should be noted that the subsequent recall of the sequestration will not affect the interruption of prescription caused by the presentation of the petition for sequestration or the submission of a claim: 1985 Act, s 17(5).

[35] In the 1985 Act, s 23(1).

[36] Rule 5 of the Scottish Rules, which applies the rules on compulsory liquidation subject to the specified and other necessary modifications.

[37] Rule 7.9(3) of the Scottish Rules, which applies the rules on claims in compulsory liquidations, subject to the specified and any other necessary modifications, for the purposes of determining a creditor's right to vote at any creditors' meeting in any insolvency proceedings in the same way as they apply in a liquidation.

[38] For sequestrations, see the 1985 Act, s 23(1) (statutory meeting) and s 49(1) (all other creditors' meetings); for company insolvency proceedings, see s 49 of the 1985 Act, as applied to such proceedings as described at the beginning of this section.

[39] 1985 Act, s 49(2).

[40] 1985 Act, s 48(5), applied subject to specified and other necessary modifications to compulsory liquidations by rule 4.16(1) of the Scottish Rules and thence to creditors' voluntary liquidations by rule 5 and, for the purposes of determining entitlement to vote, to all other relevant company insolvency proceedings by rule 7.9(3). Where the creditor is an entity rather than an individual, the examination will be of a representative of the entity: 1985 Act, s 48(6).

[41] 1985 Act, s 48(6), applying ss 44(2) and (3) and 47(1) of the 1985 Act, subject to any necessary modifications. These provisions, subject to such other specified and any necessary modifications, are applied to compulsory liquidations by rule 4.16(1) of the Scottish Rules and thence to creditors' voluntary liquidations by rule 5 and, for the purposes of determining entitlement to vote, to all other relevant company insolvency proceedings by rule 7.9(3). For a discussion of private examinations in sequestrations, see Chapter 29.

Depending on the type of claim and whether or not it is disputed, adjudication may be more or less straightforward.[42] Once he has made a decision, however, the office holder must record the amount of the claim accepted by him (if any), the category of the debt (for example, secured), the value of any security and, where the claim has been rejected, the reasons for rejection.[43] Where the claim has been rejected in whole or in part, he must also notify the creditor of the reasons for rejection.[44] The creditor or the debtor can appeal against the office holder's decision in relation to acceptance or rejection of the claim, the amount of the claim accepted, the categorisation of the debt or the value placed on any security.[45]

Calculation of claims

A creditor's claim is calculated principally according to the rules laid down in Sched 1 to the 1985 Act. These rules, subject to specified modifications, are applied directly to compulsory liquidation by rule 4.16(1) of the Scottish Rules and thence, subject to further specified and any other necessary modifications, to creditors' voluntary liquidation[46] and to CVAs, administration and receivership.[47] References in this section are to the rules laid down in Sched 1 to the 1985 Act as applied to the relevant company insolvency proceedings under the 1986 Act by the rules referred to. References to liquidation relate to compulsory and creditors' voluntary liquidations only.

The basic rule

The basic rule is that a creditor may claim the total amount of principal and interest due at the appropriate date.[48] In the case of sequestration, this is the date of sequestration; in the case of liquidation, the date of commencement of the liquidation;[49] in the case of a CVA, the date of the meeting or, if the company is in liquidation or administration, the date of its going into liquidation or the date of the administration order as appropriate;[50] in the case of administration, the date of the administration order;[51] and in the case of receivership, the date of appointment of the receiver.[52]

---

[42] For a discussion of the mechanics of adjudication and some of the problems which can arise, see Aird, 'The Liquidator, the Permanent Trustee and the Adjudication of Complicated Claims' (1997) 42 JLSS 229.

[43] 1985 Act, s 49(5).

[44] 1985 Act, s 49(4).

[45] 1985 Act, s 49(6).

[46] Rule 5 of the Scottish Rules, which applies the rules on compulsory liquidation subject to specified and other necessary modifications.

[47] Rule 7.9(3) of the Scottish Rules, which applies the rules on claims in compulsory liquidations, subject to the specified and any other necessary modifications, for the purposes of determining a creditor's right to vote at any creditors' meeting in any insolvency proceedings in the same way as they apply in a liquidation.

[48] 1985 Act, Sched 1, para 1.

[49] Within the meaning of s 129 of the 1986 Act in the case of a compulsory liquidation (Scottish Rules, rule 4.16(2)) and s 88 of the 1986 Act in the case of a creditors' voluntary liquidation (Scottish Rules, rule 4.16(2) as modified by rule 5 and Sched 1, para 10, to the Scottish Rules).

[50] Scottish Rules, rule 4.16(2), as applied and modified by rules 7.9(3) and 7.9(4)(c)(i) of the Scottish Rules respectively.

[51] Scottish Rules, rule 4.16(2), as applied and modified by rules 7.9(3) and 7.9(4)(c)(ii) of the Scottish Rules, respectively.

[52] Ibid.

Only interest which is legally due—for example, in terms of a contract or by virtue of a court decree—may be claimed: a creditor cannot claim interest to which he is not otherwise entitled. The creditor must deduct any discount (other than discount for payment in cash) to which the debtor was entitled by virtue of a contract, course of dealing or trade usage.[53]

Special rules relating to certain types of debt

Schedule 1 to the 1985 Act sets out a number of special rules relating to particular types of debt or claim.

(1) Non-contingent future debts.

Where a debt is not contingent, but would have been payable at a date after the relevant date were it not for the insolvency proceedings—for example, where a debtor was sequestrated on 23rd May 1998 and in terms of a contract was due to make a payment to a creditor on 1st January 2000—the amount which the creditor may claim is reduced accordingly. The relevant date in sequestration is the date of sequestration;[54] in liquidation, the date of commencement of the liquidation;[55] in CVAs, the date of the meeting or, if the company is being wound up or is in administration, the date of its going into liquidation or the date of the administration order as appropriate;[56] in administration, the date of the administration order;[57] and in receivership, the date of appointment of the receiver.[58] The amount of the claim is calculated as at that date by deducting interest at the rate specified in s 51(7) of the 1985 Act[59] from the original sum due between that date and the original date of payment. This method of calculation may have a curious result: if the debt is due some considerable time after that date, in extreme cases, the value of the claim may be reduced to nothing.

(2) Aliment and periodical allowance.

Claims for unpaid aliment due by a living debtor prior to the date of sequestration will only be allowed if the aliment is due by virtue of a court decree or written agreement; where the aliment is due to a spouse or, in the case of aliment being paid to a divorced spouse for a child, an ex-spouse, the spouses or ex-spouses must also have been living apart during the period in respect of which the aliment is due.[60] Claims for aliment due after the date of sequestration are excluded altogether.[61] Similar rules apply

---

[53] 1985 Act, Sched 1, para 1(3).

[54] 1985 Act, Sched 1, para 1(2).

[55] Within the meaning of s 129 of the 1986 Act in the case of a compulsory liquidation (Scottish Rules, rule 4.16(2)) and s 88 of the 1986 Act in the case of a creditors' voluntary liquidation (Scottish Rules, rule 4.16(2), as modified by rule 5 and Sched 1, para 10, to the Scottish Rules).

[56] Scottish Rules, rule 4.16(2), as applied and modified by rules 7.9(3) and 7.9(4)(c)(i) of the Scottish Rules, respectively.

[57] Scottish Rules, rule 4.16(2), as applied and modified by rules 7.9(3) and 7.9(4)(c)(ii) of the Scottish Rules, respectively.

[58] Ibid.

[59] Which is the higher of the prescribed rate at the date of sequestration, commencement of liquidation, etc, as appropriate, or the rate otherwise due apart from the insolvency proceedings, if applicable.

[60] 1985 Act, Sched 1, para 2(1)(a).

[61] 1985 Act, Sched 1, para 2(1)(b).

where the claim is by an ex-spouse for periodical allowance.[62] Such claims are, of course, relevant only in the context of the sequestration of individual debtors.[63]

(3) Contingent debts.

In order to claim in respect of a contingent debt, a creditor must apply to the permanent trustee, liquidator, CVA supervisor, administrator or receiver (as appropriate) to have a value put on his claim.[64] Where there is no such office holder, the creditor may apply to the relevant court to determine the value of his claim.[65] The creditor's claim is limited to the value thus put on it.[66] A determination of the value of the claim made by a permanent trustee, liquidator, CVA supervisor, administrator or receiver may be appealed to the relevant court.[67]

(4) Debts due under composition contracts.

Where a sequestration has been brought to an end by a judicial composition under the 1985 Act[68] and is subsequently revived, a creditor may claim the amount of his original debt under deduction of any sums paid under the composition. By its nature, this provision is restricted to sequestration.[69]

(5) Secured debts.

A secured creditor must deduct the value of his security, as estimated by him, from the amount of his claim, unless he surrenders it, or undertakes in writing to surrender it, for the benefit of the debtor's estate.[70] The definitions of 'secured creditor' and 'security' have already been discussed.[71] It should be noted that as a result of these definitions, a creditor is only obliged to deduct from his claim the value of a security over the *assets* of the debtor: he is not obliged to deduct the value of any security which is not over the assets of the debtor—for example, where the security is over the assets of another or is in the form of a cautionary obligation. It has already been noted that, in sequestration, a creditor who has done certain types of diligence which is not cut down is treated as a secured creditor:[72] such a creditor will therefore be obliged to value the security created by the diligence and deduct it from the value of his claim. It has also been suggested that such a creditor must be regarded as a secured creditor in

---

[62] 1985 Act, Sched 1, para 2(2).

[63] The operation of para 2 of Sched 1 to the 1985 Act in relation to company insolvency proceedings under the 1986 Act is excluded by rule 4.16(1)(f) of the Scottish Rules (which applies to compulsory liquidations and thence to the other relevant proceedings under the 1986 Act: see the beginning of this section).

[64] 1985 Act, Sched 1, para 3.

[65] Ibid.

[66] Ibid.

[67] 1985 Act, Sched 1, para 3(3).

[68] Judicial compositions are discussed in Chapters 36 and 40.

[69] Its application to company insolvency proceedings under the 1986 Act is excluded by rule 4.16(1)(f) of the Scottish Rules (which applies to compulsory liquidations and thence to the other relevant proceedings under the 1986 Act: see the beginning of this section).

[70] 1985 Act, Sched 1, para 5(1). In relation to company insolvency proceedings, the phrase 'debtor's estate' should be read as 'company's assets': Scottish Rules, rule 4.16(2).

[71] See Chapter 22.

[72] *Gibson* v *Greig* (1853) 16 D 233; and see Chapter 31.

liquidation also[73] and accordingly should also be obliged to value the security created by the diligence and deduct it from the value of his claim, but whether such a creditor can be regarded as a secured creditor in other company insolvency proceedings, for this or any other purpose, is more problematic.[74]

In sequestration and liquidation, a secured creditor may be required to discharge his security or convey or assign it to the trustee or liquidator on payment of its value as estimated by the creditor and, where this has been done, the creditor must deduct the payment received by him from the amount of his claim.[75] Similarly, a creditor whose security has been realised must deduct the net proceeds of the security (ie, the proceeds of the security less the expenses of realisation) from his claim.[76]

(6) Claims against partners for debts of partnership.

Where a creditor claims in the sequestration of the estate of a partner of a firm for a debt due by the partnership, the creditor must estimate and then deduct the value of any claim against the partnership itself.[77] By its nature, this provision applies only to sequestration.[78]

In addition, it is specifically provided in relation to administration that, for the purposes of entitlement to vote, a creditor who has a retention of title must deduct from his claim the value of his rights arising under that agreement as estimated by him.[79] Creditors under hire-purchase, conditional sale and certain hiring agreements, however, are entitled to vote in respect of their debts under these agreements without deducting from their claims the value of any rights which have arisen under these agreements purely as a result of the administration.[80]

Liabilities and rights of co-obligants

A creditor may be entitled to look to someone other than the debtor for payment of his debt—for example, where the debtor is jointly and severally liable for the debt or a third party has given caution for the debt. Normally, where a cautioner or other person bound to the creditor along with the debtor (hereafter referred to as a co-obligant) has had to pay the creditor, he would have a right of relief against the debtor. In the case of a cautioner, his right of relief would be for the full amount paid to the creditor; in any other case, it would be for anything in excess of his proportionate share of the debt. Where the debtor is subject to insolvency proceedings, however, the normal rules are altered.

---

[73] See Chapter 31.

[74] Ibid.

[75] 1985 Act, Sched 1, para 5(2). This sub-paragraph does not apply to company insolvency proceedings other than liquidation as a result of the Scottish Rules, rule 7.9(5).

[76] 1985 Act, Sched 1, para 5(3). This sub-paragraph does not apply to company insolvency proceedings other than liquidation as a result of the Scottish Rules, rule 7.9(5).

[77] 1985 Act, Sched 1, para 6.

[78] Its application in company insolvency proceedings under the 1986 Act is excluded by rule 4.16(1)(f) of the Scottish Rules (which applies to compulsory liquidations and thence to the other relevant proceedings under the 1986 Act: see the beginning of this section).

[79] Scottish Rules, rule 2.11.

[80] Scottish Rules, rule 2.12.

First, the common law rule against double ranking applies: where a creditor has claimed payment of the debt in the relevant insolvency proceedings and also claimed against a co-obligant of the debtor, the co-obligant cannot exercise his right of relief by also claiming in the insolvency proceedings.[81] The rationale behind this rule is that the same debt (or part of it) would thereby be claimed twice in the same insolvency proceedings (once by the creditor and once by the co-obligant) to the prejudice of other creditors. It may be the case, however, that if the co-obligant has paid the whole amount of the debt, he will be entitled to receive payment from the creditor of any dividends which the creditor receives or, if he has paid the outstanding balance of the debt, any future dividends received by the creditor.[82] This would be equitable, since it would be unfair if the creditor received more than full payment while the co-obligant was excluded from claiming his right of relief. Where the creditor has not claimed in the insolvency proceedings and the co-obligant has paid the debt in full, he will be subrogated to the creditor's claim and may claim in his stead.[83]

Secondly, s 60 of the 1985 Act sets out a number of rules regarding co-obligants in sequestration. This section, subject to specified modifications, is applied directly to compulsory liquidation by rule 4.16(1) of the Scottish Rules and thence, subject to further specified and any other necessary modifications, to creditors' voluntary liquidation[84] and to CVAs, administration and receivership.[85] In the following discussion, references are to s 60 of the 1985 Act, as applied to the relevant company insolvency proceedings under the 1986 Act by the rules referred to, and references to liquidation are to compulsory and creditors' voluntary liquidation only.

In terms of s 60(1) of the 1985 Act, a co-obligant[86] is not freed from his liability for the debt as a result of *either* the debtor's discharge *or* certain actings of the creditor, namely voting, drawing a dividend, consenting to (or not opposing) the debtor's discharge or consenting to (or not opposing) any composition. This provision alters the previous common law regarding the ways in which a co-obligant can be freed from liability by the actings of the creditor.

Section 60(2) of the 1985 Act provides for the situation where the co-obligant has a security over any part of the debtor's estate. Such a situation poses a problem because where the creditor claims in the insolvency proceedings, there is a way round the rule against double ranking: the creditor is paid out of the debtor's assets to the extent of his dividend and the assets are also subject to the co-obligant's security. Section 60(2) of the 1985 Act deals with this by obliging the co-obligant to account for his security in a way which will put the debtor's estate in the same position as if the co-obligant had paid the debt and then had his claim accepted under deduction of the value of the security.

---

[81] See Goudy, *Bankruptcy*, p 561; see also *Mackinnon v Monkhouse* (1881) 9 R 393.

[82] See Gloag and Irvine, *Rights in Security*, pp 831–832, where old English authority is used to support these propositions: the writer is not aware of any modern Scottish authorities.

[83] Ibid.

[84] Rule 5 of the Scottish Rules, which applies the rules on compulsory liquidation subject to specified and other necessary modifications.

[85] Rule 7.9(3) of the Scottish Rules, which applies the rules on claims in compulsory liquidations, subject to the specified and any other necessary modifications, for the purposes of determining a creditor's right to vote at any creditors' meeting in any insolvency proceedings in the same way as they apply in a liquidation.

[86] For the purposes of s 60, 'co-obligant' is defined as including a cautioner: 1985 Act, s 60(4).

Finally, s 60(3) of the 1985 Act provides that without prejudice to any rule of law regarding the rights of a co-obligant who has paid the debt, such a co-obligant may require and obtain at his own expense an assignation of the debt from the creditor and thereafter submit a claim, vote and (where appropriate) draw a dividend in respect of it. This rule does not, however, affect the rule against double ranking, so it will only be relevant where the creditor has not submitted a claim in the relevant insolvency proceedings.

The balancing of accounts in bankruptcy

This section deals with the situation where a creditor of the insolvent is also a debtor to the insolvent.

In such a situation, a creditor will not wish to pay his debt to the insolvent in full and then have to submit a claim in the insolvency proceedings for the debt due by the debtor: he will wish to set the debts off against one another so that he can *either* contribute only the balance due by him to the debtor's estate *or* claim the balance due to him by the debtor in the relevant insolvency proceedings. Where one of the parties is insolvent, the statutory rules on set-off contained in the Compensation Act 1592 do not apply[87] and the position is governed by the common law rules on the balancing of accounts in bankruptcy.

Meaning of insolvency for the purposes of the balancing of accounts in bankruptcy

The rules on the balancing of accounts in bankruptcy apply where the debtor is 'insolvent'.

In the context of non-company insolvency, it was said in *Paul & Thain v Royal Bank of Scotland*[88] that the balancing of accounts in bankruptcy arose where debtors 'become bankrupt or insolvent, or were *vergentes ad inopiam*, or at least that their pecuniary responsibility and circumstances had materially altered to the worse'.[89] Professor McBryde takes the view that apparent insolvency under s 7 of the 1985 Act[90] or absolute insolvency would be sufficient to allow the application of the rules on balancing of accounts in bankruptcy[91] and it seems to be accepted that sequestration itself, or the granting of a trust deed for creditors, would amount to 'insolvency' for this purpose.[92]

In the context of company insolvency, it would appear that liquidation constitutes insolvency for the purpose of the rules on the balancing of accounts in bankruptcy, irrespective of whether the liquidation is solvent or insolvent: in *G & A (Hotels) Ltd v THB Marketing Services*,[93] the rules on balancing of accounts in bankruptcy were applied in a (solvent) members' voluntary liquidation. Receivership does not necessarily constitute insolvency for this purpose. In the case of *Taylor, Petnr*,[94] it was suggested that the rules on the balancing of accounts in bankruptcy would not apply in receivership at all, but it has since been held

---

[87] These rules are not, therefore discussed in any detail here, but for a detailed discussion, see Wilson, *The Scottish Law of Debt* (2nd edn), Chapter 13, and McBryde, *Contract*, p 531 et seq.

[88] (1869) 7 M 361.

[89] Ibid at 365.

[90] See Chapter 1.

[91] *Bankruptcy* (2nd edn), pp 372–373.

[92] See *Liquidators of Highland Engineering Ltd v Thomson* 1972 SC 87.

[93] 1983 SLT 497.

[94] 1981 SC 408.

that they will apply in receivership if the company is actually insolvent.[95] There is no judicial authority on whether CVAs or administration constitute insolvency for this purpose, but it is suggested that the rules should apply, at least where the company is actually insolvent. This will almost certainly be the case in relation to most administrations, because it is a requirement of the making of an administration order that the company is, or is likely to become, unable to pay its debts.[96] St Clair and Drummond Young[97] take the view that insofar as *G & A (Hotels) Ltd* v *THB Marketing Services*[98] applies the rules on the balancing of accounts in bankruptcy to solvent liquidations, it is based on a misunderstanding of earlier dicta[99] and is incorrect. They suggest that the rules on the balancing of accounts in bankruptcy should only apply where there has been a finding of insolvency as such. This approach concentrates on defining 'insolvency' for this purpose by reference to the financial state of the company rather than by reference to the fact that the company is subject to a particular type of procedure and would seem to be supported by the approach taken in *McPhail* v *Cunninghame District Council; William Louden & Son Ltd* v *Cunninghame District Council*[100] in relation to receivership. It is true that receivership is different from liquidation and bankruptcy (the reasoning behind the original stance on the application of the rules in receivership taken in *Taylor,* Petnr),[101] but it is thought that the approach taken by St Clair and Drummond Young is more logically correct and that they are correct in stating that *G & A (Hotels) Ltd* v *THB Marketing Services*[102] is wrongly decided insofar as it looks to the procedure (liquidation) rather than the question of insolvency in a financial sense as the determining factor in application of the rules on balancing of accounts in bankruptcy to companies.

The rules on the balancing of accounts in bankruptcy

The rules on the balancing of accounts in bankruptcy may be stated relatively briefly although in certain cases their application is not free from difficulty.

Debts arising prior to insolvency may be set off against each other, as may debts arising after insolvency,[103] but a debt arising before insolvency cannot be set off against a debt arising after insolvency.

> '[T]his principle of bankruptcy law presupposes reciprocal obligations which are both existing at the time of the declaration of insolvency, although only one of them is, it may be, immediately exigible. It has no application to the case of a new obligation arising after bankruptcy or declaration of insolvency when the rights of the parties are irrevocably fixed.'[104]

---

[95] *McPhail* v *Cunninghame District Council; William Louden & Son Ltd* v *Cunninghame District Council* 1985 SLT 149.
[96] See Chapter 10.
[97] At p 318 et seq.
[98] Note 93 above.
[99] Those of Lord Fraser in *Liquidators of Highland Engineering Ltd* v *Thomson*, note 92 above.
[100] Note 95 above.
[101] Note 94 above.
[102] Note 93 above.
[103] *Liquidators of Highland Engineering Ltd* v *Thomson*, note 92 above.
[104] Lord McLaren in *Asphaltic Limestone Co Ltd* v *Corporation of Glasgow* 1907 SC 463 at 474.

Whether the debts do both exist at the time of insolvency will depend on the circumstances in each case, and may not be easy to determine. In *Asphaltic Limestone Co Ltd* v *Corporation of Glasgow*,[105] which involved two contracts, one of which was adopted by the liquidator and completed by him, the other of which was refuted by him, leaving the other party with a claim for damages, the court held that the claim for the contract price and the claim for damages could not be set off against each other because they did not both arise prior to the liquidation. St Clair and Drummond Young accept this decision as straight-forward[106] but Professor Wilson regards it as suspect, suggesting that the claims should have been allowed to be set off against each other because they both arose from obligations which existed prior to the liquidation.[107]

So long as the debts arise from obligations existing prior to the insolvency, it does not matter whether only one of them is immediately exigible: illiquid claims may be set off against liquid claims.[108] This includes future and contingent debts[109] but may not include certain illiquid claims for damages.[110] In contrast to the position outwith insolvency, the debts need not be of the same nature: it has been held, for example, that a claim for the return of plant could be set off against a claim for breach of contract.[111] Nor need they arise from the same contract.[112] There must, however, be *concursus debiti and crediti*. So, for example, a creditor who was due a debt to the insolvent estate could not set off against it a debt being claimed by him from the insolvent estate in his capacity as executor.

The balancing of accounts in bankruptcy is excluded in a number of cases. A debtor to the insolvent may not set off against the debt due by him to the insolvent a claim which he has acquired after the insolvency.[113] A co-obligant of a debtor may not set off sums due by him to the debtor against any right of relief he may have against the debtor if the creditor in the obligation has also claimed in the debtor's insolvency, because this would violate the rule against double ranking.[114] A contributory cannot set off any debt due to him by the company against a call in a liquidation,[115] at least until all creditors have been paid in full (together with interest at the official rate).[116] Finally, it is thought that the balancing of accounts on bankruptcy is excluded if there is a specific agreement to exclude it:[117] this may be contrasted with the position in England and Wales, where set-off on insolvency is mandatory and cannot be excluded by agreement.[118]

---

[105] Ibid.

[106] *The Law of Corporate Insolvency in Scotland*, at p 322.

[107] *The Scottish Law of Debt*, p 165. See also *Myles J. Callaghan Ltd (In Receivership)* v *City of Glasgow District Council* 1988 SLT 227, where the court held that both claims in question did arise before receivership and could therefore be set off.

[108] See *Asphaltic Limestone Co Ltd* v *Corporation of Glasgow* (note 104), discussed above.

[109] See, for example, *Mill* v *Paul* (1825) 4 S 219; *Hannay & Sons' Tr* v *Armstrong Brothers & Co* (1875) 2 R 399; *Smith* v *Lord Advocate (No 2)* 1980 SC 227; *Powdrill* v *Murrayhead Ltd* 1997 SLT 1223.

[110] *The Scottish Law of Debt*, p 164, referring to Gloag, *The Law of Contract* (2nd edn), p 626.

[111] *Myles J. Callaghan Ltd (In Receivership)* v *City of Glasgow District Council*, note 107 above.

[112] Bell, *Commentaries*, ii, 122. Cf, however, *Niven* v *Clyde Fasteners Ltd* 1986 SLT 344, where it was said, in the context of liquidation, that the debts did need to arise from the same contract.

[113] *Smith* v *Lord Advocate (No 2)*, note 109 above.

[114] *Anderson* v *Mackinnon* (1876) 3 R 608; cf *Christie* v *Keith* (1838) 16 S 1224. For the rules in relation to co-obligants, see above.

[115] *Liquidators of Coustonholm Paper Mills Co Ltd* v *Law* (1891) 18 R 1076. This applies even where the call was made by the directors prior to the liquidation: see *Cowan* v *Gowans* (1878) 5 R 581.

[116] 1986 Act, s 149(3).

[117] McBryde, *Contract*, p 540.

[118] *National Westminster Bank Ltd* v *Halesowen Presswork & Assemblies Ltd* [1972] AC 785.

Where the balancing of accounts in bankruptcy is available, a creditor may choose to set off sums due to him by the insolvent against any non-preferential or unsecured element of his claim first.[119] This may be contrasted with the position in England and Wales where it has been held that debts should be set off rateably against preferential and non-preferential debts.[120]

Particular problems in receivership

Particular problems regarding set-off have arisen in receivership as a result of the fact that in relation to the company's book debts, the effect of the appointment of a receiver is that they are treated as if there had been an intimated assignation in security of them to the floating chargeholder. However, it now seems to be settled that set-off is available against the receiver and, where the company is insolvent, the rules on the balancing of accounts in bankruptcy will apply.[121]

The balancing of accounts in bankruptcy and the Crown

Where the Crown are involved, set-off generally, and the balancing of accounts in bankruptcy, in particular, is governed by the Crown Proceedings Act 1947, s 35(2), as applied to Scotland by s 50 of that Act. Set-off and the balancing of accounts in bankruptcy is not available in any claim by the Crown for taxes, duties or penalties; nor can any claim for the repayment of taxes, duties or penalties be set off against any other type of claim by the Crown.[122] In relation to other types of claim, although set-off and the balancing of accounts in bankruptcy is available without restriction where the debts in question relate to the same government department, the leave of the court must be sought where either the (insolvent) debtor or the Crown seek set-off or the balancing accounts in bankruptcy and the debts in question relate to different government departments.[123] Leave will normally be granted, however.[124] As indicated above, the Crown may set off any sums due to the debtor first against the non-preferential elements of their claim.[125]

---

[119] *Turner* v *IRC* 1994 SLT 811. That case concerned the Crown (for which see further below), but the principle is of general application. For preferred and preferential debts, see the following chapter.

[120] See *Re Unit 2 Windows Ltd (In Liquidation)* [1985] 1 WLR 1383.

[121] See above.

[122] Crown Proceedings Act 1947, s 35(2)(b).

[123] Crown Proceedings Act 1947, s 35(2)(c) and (d).

[124] *Smith* v *Lord Advocate (No 2)*, note 109 above.

[125] *Turner* v *IRC*, note 119 above. For preferred and preferential debts, see the following chapter.

33 : CREDITORS' CLAIMS: DISTRIBUTION OF THE DEBTOR'S ASSETS

In sequestration and liquidation, there is a mandatory statutory scheme for distribution of the debtor's assets which encompasses all creditors. In receivership, there is also a mandatory statutory scheme for distribution of the debtor's assets, but the receiver is only obliged to deal with certain specified creditors: once he has done so, any remaining balance of the company's assets is disposed of in accordance with the statutory provisions, and creditors whose debts have not been dealt with in the receivership must pursue these outwith it—usually in a subsequent liquidation. In administration, there is no provision for a general distribution of assets to creditors in the context of the administration itself, at least where the company is insolvent, although such a distribution may be achieved through a CVA or section 425 arrangement within the administration. In a CVA or section 425 arrangement, the distribution of the company's assets is determined by the terms of the arrangement itself.

This chapter deals with how the debtor's assets are distributed in each of these régimes.

Sequestration

It has been noted that it is a basic principle of insolvency law that all creditors should be treated equally,[1] but in practice this principle is imperfectly applied and some categories of creditors are given priority over others when it comes to the distribution of the debtor's assets. The order of priority for distribution of the debtor's estate in sequestration is set out in s 51(1) of the 1985 Act.[2] It is specifically provided, however, that this is without prejudice to (1) the rights of secured creditors which are preferable to those of the trustee and (2) any preference to be accorded to the holder of a lien over title deeds which had to be delivered to the trustee in terms of the 1985 Act.[3]

Secured creditors as defined by the 1985 Act have already been discussed.[4] In essence, a secured creditor may enforce his security without reference to the

---

[1] See Chapter 3.
[2] See further below.
[3] 1985 Act, s 51(6).
[4] See Chapters 22, 31 and 32.

sequestration, subject to the trustee's right to require him to discharge it or to convey or assign it to the trustee on payment of its value as estimated by the creditor[5] and the trustee's right to intimate his intention to sell heritable property subject to a security.[6] Where the property subject to the security is realised by the trustee, the secured creditor will have first claim on the proceeds of the property. A secured creditor may claim in the sequestration for the unsecured balance of his debt after deduction of either the value of his security or the proceeds thereof.[7] Alternatively, he may surrender his security and claim for the whole amount of his debt.[8]

Subject to these rights, s 51(1) of the 1985 Act states that the debtor's estate will be distributed to meet the following debts in the order mentioned.

(1) The interim trustee's outlays and remuneration.

(2) The permanent trustee's outlays and remuneration.

(3) In the case of a deceased debtor, reasonable deathbed and funeral expenses and reasonable expenses of administering the estate. Any such expenses which are unreasonable will rank as ordinary debts.

(4) Reasonable expenses of petitioning or concurring creditor.

(5) Preferred debts (excluding interest thereon up to the date of sequestration). Preferred debts are those listed in Part I of Sched 3 to the 1985 Act.[9] They are:

   (a) PAYE contributions which were or ought to have been deducted from the wages or salaries of employees during the 12 months prior to the relevant date;[10]

   (b) tax which was or should have been deductible from certain payments to sub-contractors in the construction industry during the 12 months prior to the relevant date;[11]

   (c) VAT in the six months prior to the relevant date;[12]

   (d) car tax which became due in the 12 months prior to the relevant date;[13]

   (e) general and pool betting duty, bingo duty and gaming licence duty due in the 12 months prior to the relevant date;[14]

   (f) excise duty on beer due in the 6 months prior to the relevant date;[15]

---

[5] See Chapter 22.
[6] Ibid and Chapter 24.
[7] See Chapter 32.
[8] Ibid.
[9] The categories of preferred debts are now considerably reduced, but there are many who advocate their abolition altogether. The government has indicated an intention to reassess the relative rights of creditors in insolvencies, including the Crown's status as a preferential creditor: White Paper on Competitiveness (1998).
[10] 1985 Act, Sched 3, para 1(1).
[11] 1985 Act, Sched 3, para 1(2).
[12] 1985 Act, Sched 3, para 2(1).
[13] 1985 Act, Sched 3, para 2(2).
[14] 1985 Act, Sched 3, para 2(3).
[15] 1985 Act, Sched 3, para 2(4).

(g) class 1 and 2 national insurance contributions due in the 12 months prior to the relevant date;[16]

(h) up to one year's class 4 national insurance contributions which have been assessed up to the 5th April preceding the relevant date;[17]

(i) certain contributions to occupational or other pension schemes;[18]

(j) certain levies and surcharges due under the European Coal and Steel Community Treaty;[19]

(k) certain sums connected with the remuneration of employees. These are:

   (i) arrears of wages due to an employee for a period of up to four months prior to the relevant date, subject to a prescribed limit;[20]

   (ii) accrued holiday pay due to an employee prior to the relevant date where the employee's employment has been terminated;[21]

   (iii) so much of any money advanced to the debtor as was used to pay wages which would otherwise have been preferential debts due to the employees: the lender is effectively substituted for the employees and has a preferential claim for such sums subject to the same limits as would apply in the case of the employees themselves (ie, four months' arrears up to the current prescribed limit).[22] The lender must, however, have advanced the money specifically for the purpose of paying the employees;[23]

   (iv) certain payments ordered under the Reserve Forces (Safeguard of Employment) Act 1985.[24]

Remuneration and holiday pay are defined in para 9 of Part II of Sched 3 to the 1985 Act.

The relevant date in each case is the date of sequestration or, in the case of a deceased debtor, the date of death.[25]

Interest on preferred debts which has accrued prior to the date of sequestration is *not* treated preferentially:[26] such interest is included within the category of ordinary debts.[27]

(6) Ordinary debts, ie, debts which are not secured and not mentioned in any of the other categories set out in s 51(1). These are the bulk of the debts in

---

[16] 1985 Act, Sched 3, para 3(1).

[17] 1985 Act, Sched 3, para 3(2).

[18] 1985 Act, Sched 3, para 4.

[19] 1985 Act, Sched 3 para 6A.

[20] 1985 Act, Sched 3, para 5(1). The current limit is £800: SI 1985/1925, reg 14, inserted by the Bankruptcy (Scotland) Amendment Regulations 1986 (SI 1986/1914).

[21] 1985 Act, Sched 3, para 5(2).

[22] 1985 Act, Sched 3, para 5(3).

[23] In practice, the monies will usually have been advanced by the debtor's bank, which will have opened a separate wages account in order to be able to demonstrate that the monies were advanced for that purpose.

[24] 1985 Act, Sched 3, para 6.

[25] 1985 Act, Sched 3, para 7.

[26] 1985 Act, s 51(1)(e).

[27] McBryde, *Bankruptcy* (2nd edn), p 359, mentions an alternative interpretation of the provisions which would result in interest on preferred debts accrued prior to the date of sequestration being excluded from the category of ordinary debts, but the author himself does not favour that interpretation and it seems unlikely to be correct.

any sequestration and, as noted above, include interest on preferred debts. In most cases, the ordinary creditors will be lucky to receive any payment at all in respect of their debts.

(7) Interest on preferred and ordinary debts between the date of sequestration and date of payment. Interest on preferred and ordinary debts between the date of sequestration and the date of payment is payable at the rate specified in s 51(7) of the 1985 Act,[28] which is the higher of the rate which would have applied but for the sequestration (for example, the contractual rate) or the rate prescribed by statutory instrument. Interest payable on preferred and ordinary debts ranks equally despite the fact that the debts themselves do not.[29]

(8) Postponed debts. These are loans made to the debtor which are postponed to the claims of other creditors under s 3 of the Partnership Act 1890, loans made to the debtor by the debtor's spouse and a creditor's right to anything vesting in the permanent trustee by virtue of a successful challenge under s 34 of the 1985 Act or the sale proceeds of such a thing.[30]

All debts falling within categories (3) to (8) have the same priority as any other debt falling within the same category, and where there are insufficient funds for payment of all the debts in any particular category, they abate equally.[31] This can be illustrated by the following example.

Sum remaining for distribution	£600

Creditors in category	amount of debt
Bill	£1,000
Ben	£500
Total debts in category	£1,500

There are insufficient funds to pay both creditors in full and so the debts abate equally. The sum which each creditor is to receive is calculated by working out the appropriate percentage to be paid to each creditor and then applying it to their individual debts.

$$\% \text{ payable to each creditor} = \frac{\text{sum available for distribution}}{\text{total debts in category}} \times 100$$

$$= \frac{600 \times 100}{1,500}$$

$$= 40\%$$

---

[28] 1985 Act, s 51(1)(g).
[29] 1985 Act, s 51(4).
[30] 1985 Act, s 51(3). The provisions of s 34 of the 1985 Act are discussed in Chapter 30.
[31] 1985 Act, s 51(4).

Apply this to the individual debts:

Bill	£1,000 × 40%	£400
Ben	£500 × 40%	£200
Total		£600

Bill and Ben have received the same percentage of their debt: the debts have abated equally. In the unlikely event of any surplus remaining after payment of all the debts specified, such surplus falls to be returned to the debtor.[32]

Accounting periods

The sequestration is divided into accounting periods. The initial accounting period is six months from the date of sequestration.[33] Subsequent accounting periods are also six months in length unless otherwise agreed or determined.[34] In a sequestration where the permanent trustee is not the Accountant in Bankruptcy, a variation in the length of an accounting period may be agreed by the permanent trustee and the commissioners or, if there are no commissioners, the Accountant in Bankruptcy.[35] In a sequestration where the Accountant in Bankruptcy is the permanent trustee, he may determine a variation in the length of any accounting period himself.[36]

Accounts for the sequestration will be made up by the trustee in respect of each accounting period[37] and, where appropriate, interim payments of dividend will be made to creditors in respect of each accounting period.[38] Final accounts are made up at the end of the sequestration once all the debtor's assets have been gathered in and realised and all distributions have been made.[39]

Liquidation

The distribution of a company's property in a voluntary liquidation is governed by s 107 of the 1986 Act which provides that, subject to the provisions of the 1986 Act relating to preferential payments,[40] the company's property is to be applied in settlement of its liabilities *pari passu*, any remaining balance being distributed to the members or otherwise as the articles may provide.[41] In a compulsory liquidation, the company's property is to be distributed to the company's creditors and, if there is a surplus, to the persons entitled to it.[42] The order of priority of distribution of the company's assets in a compulsory liquidation

---

[32] 1985 Act, s 51(5).
[33] 1985 Act, s 52(2)(a).
[34] 1985 Act, s 52(2)(b).
[35] 1985 Act, s 52(2)(b)(i).
[36] 1985 Act, s 52(2)(b)(ii).
[37] 1985 Act, s 52(1).
[38] 1985 Act, s 52(3).
[39] See Chapter 40.
[40] See further below.
[41] The section applies to both members' and creditors' voluntary liquidations, but as this book is concerned with insolvency law and a members' voluntary liquidation will generally be a solvent liquidation, the following discussion will be confined to creditors' voluntary liquidations.
[42] 1986 Act, s 143(1). A compulsory liquidation will not necessarily be an insolvent liquidation, although this book is primarily concerned with those which are.

is set out in rule 4.66(1) of the Scottish Rules,[43] which is applied, subject to s 107 of the 1986 Act, to creditors' voluntary liquidation by rule 5 of the Scottish Rules. It is specifically provided, however, that this is without prejudice to (1) the rights of secured creditors which are preferable to those of the liquidator or (2) any preference of the holder of a lien over title deeds which had to be delivered to the liquidator in terms of the Scottish Rules.[44]

The rights of secured creditors as defined by the 1986 Act have already been discussed.[45] In essence, a secured creditor may enforce his security without reference to the liquidation, subject to the liquidator's right to require him to discharge it or to convey or assign it to the liquidator on payment of its value as estimated by the creditor[46] and the liquidator's right to intimate his intention to sell heritable property subject to a heritable security.[47] Where property subject to a security is realised by the liquidator, the secured creditor will have first claim on the proceeds of the property. A secured creditor may claim in the liquidation for any unsecured balance of his debt after deduction of either the value of his security or the proceeds thereof.[48] Alternatively, he may surrender his security and claim for the whole amount of his debt.[49] It should be noted, however, that where the assets of the company available for the payment of general creditors are insufficient to pay the preferential creditors in full, the preferential creditors are given priority over the claims of any floating chargeholder and fall to be paid out of the assets secured by the charge.[50]

Subject to these rights, rule 4.66(1) provides that the funds of the company's assets are to be distributed by the liquidator to meet the following debts and expenses in the order mentioned.

(1) The expenses of the liquidation. In the event of there being insufficient assets to pay all the expenses of the liquidation, the court may make an order for their payment in such order of priority as the court thinks fit.[51] In the absence of such an order, the expenses are paid in the order set out in rule 4.67 of the Scottish Rules, which is as follows:

  (a) any outlays properly incurred by the provisional liquidator or liquidator, with the exception of those mentioned in the following paragraph and, where a compulsory liquidation follows on from a voluntary liquidation, such outlays and remuneration of the liquidator in the voluntary liquidation as the court allows;

  (b) the cost of caution provided by a provisional liquidator, liquidator or special manager;

  (c) the remuneration of any provisional liquidator;

  (d) the expenses of the petitioning creditor and, if allowed by the court, those of any other person appearing;

  (e) the remuneration of any special manager;

[43] The rule applies irrespective of whether the company is solvent or insolvent.
[44] 1986 Act, rule 4.66(6).
[45] See Chapters 22, 31 and 32.
[46] See Chapter 22.
[47] Ibid and Chapter 24.
[48] See Chapter 32.
[49] Ibid.
[50] 1986 Act, s 175(2)(b).
[51] 1986 Act, s 112 (creditors' voluntary liquidation) and s 156 (compulsory liquidation).

(f) the expenses of a deponent in a statement of affairs approved by the liquidator;

(g) the remuneration of any person employed by the liquidator to perform services for the company where this was required or authorised by the 1986 Act or the Scottish Rules;

(h) the remuneration of the liquidator;

(i) any corporation tax payable on chargeable gains resulting from the realisation of any asset of the company.

It may be noted that this provision sets out a slightly different order of priority to that pertaining in sequestration—for example, in liquidation, the expenses of the petitioning creditor take precedence over the remuneration (though not the outlays) of the liquidator while they rank behind both the outlays and remuneration of a permanent trustee in sequestration.

(2) The properly incurred expenses of any CVA which was in force at the time the petition for winding up was presented. These rank behind the expenses of the liquidation, whereas it might have been expected that they would rank before it as relating to a prior insolvency proceeding.

(3) Preferential debts. Preferential debts in a liquidation are those within the meaning of s 386 of the 1986 Act, excluding any interest thereon prior to the date of commencement of the liquidation.[52] Section 386 of the 1986 Act defines preferential debts as those listed in Sched 6 to the Act. With the addition of lottery duty due within the period of 12 months prior to the relevant date,[53] the categories of preferential debts are virtually identical to those in sequestration, which are set out in full above, subject to certain minor differences in detail reflecting the different type of debtor. The relevant date for the purpose of calculating preferential debts in a liquidation is governed by s 387 of the 1986 Act. This provides that where the liquidation is a compulsory liquidation which was immediately preceded by administration, the relevant date is the date of the administration order;[54] where it is a compulsory liquidation which has not been immediately preceded by a voluntary liquidation, it is the date of the first appointment of a provisional liquidator or, if no provisional liquidator was appointed, the date of the winding-up order;[55] and in any other case (ie, where the liquidation is a voluntary liquidation, or a compulsory liquidation which has been preceded by a voluntary liquidation) it is the date of the resolution to wind up.[56]

Interest on preferential debts which has accrued prior to the date of commencement of the liquidation is included within the category of ordinary debts.[57]

---

[52] Scottish Rules, rule 4.66(1)(b). See also note 9.

[53] 1986 Act, Sched 6, para 5B.

[54] 1986 Act, s 387(3)(a).

[55] 1986 Act, s 387(3)(b).

[56] 1986 Act, s 387(3)(c).

[57] It was noted above (note 27) that Professor McBryde mentions an alternative interpretation of the provisions on sequestration which would result in interest on preferred debts accrued prior to the date of sequestration being excluded from the category of ordinary debts. If correct, that interpretation would also be equally applicable to liquidation, but the author himself does not favour that interpretation and it seems unlikely to be correct.

(4) Ordinary debts, ie, debts which are not secured debts and not mentioned in any of the other categories in rule 4.66(1). These are the bulk of the debts in any liquidation and, as noted above, include interest on preferential debts accrued prior to the date of commencement of the liquidation. In most cases, the ordinary creditors will be lucky to receive any payment in respect of their debts.

(5) Interest at the official rate on preferential and ordinary debts between the date of commencement of the liquidation and the date of payment. 'Official rate' is to be construed in accordance with s 189(4) of the 1986 Act[58] which, as applied in Scotland by s 189(5) of the 1986 Act, provides that the official rate is the greater of the rate specified in the Scottish Rules or the rate otherwise applicable to the debt (for example, the contractual rate).[59] Interest payable on the preferential and ordinary debts ranks equally despite the fact that the debts themselves do not.[60]

(6) Postponed debts. These are a creditor's right to any alienation which has been reduced or restored to the company under s 242 of the 1986 Act or to the proceeds of sale of such an alienation.[61]

All debts falling within categories (3) to (6) have the same priority as any other debt falling within the same category, and where there are insufficient funds for payment of all the debts in any particular category, they abate equally.[62] The operation of this principle is illustrated in the discussion of sequestration above.

It must be noted that where a floating chargeholder chooses to enforce his security by appointing a receiver after the commencement of liquidation, this has an effect on the order of priority of payment of debts set out in rule 4.66(1). A receiver appointed after the commencement of liquidation takes precedence over the liquidator[63] and is responsible for the payment of the preferential and certain other secured creditors prior to payment of the holder of the floating charge under which he was appointed.[64] This has a curious effect in terms of the ranking of debts in the liquidation itself: the preferential creditors effectively gain priority over the expenses of the liquidation because the receiver has to pay the preferential creditors but has no obligation to pay the liquidation expenses or the expenses of any prior CVA.[65] The somewhat anomalous result is that the preferential creditors get paid by the receiver prior to the liquidation expenses, upsetting the normal order of priority set out in rule 4.66(1).

Any surplus remaining after payment of all the specified debts falls to be distributed among the members of the company or otherwise as the articles

---

[58] Scottish Rules, rule 4.66(2)(b).
[59] The rate specified in the Scottish Rules is currently 15 per cent: Scottish Rules, rule 4.66(2)(b).
[60] 1986 Act, s 189(3).
[61] Scottish Rules, rule 4.66(2)(a). The provisions of s 242 of the 1986 Act are discussed in Chapter 30.
[62] 1986 Act, rule 4.66(4).
[63] See Chapters 4 and 27.
[64] See further below.
[65] See further below.

provide.[66] However, certain claims by a contributory *qua* member are payable after the debts of the company as specified here but prior to any distribution to the members as such[67] and claims for payment of the sum due by the company in respect of the redemption or payment of its own shares are payable after all other debts and liabilities of the company except those due to members *qua* members but prior to any distribution to the members as such.[68]

Accounting periods

The liquidation is divided into accounting periods. The relevant provisions of the 1985 Act relating to sequestration are applied, subject to specified and other necessary modifications, to compulsory liquidation by rule 4.68 of the Scottish Rules and thence to creditors' voluntary liquidation by rule 5. References are therefore to the relevant provisions of the 1985 Act as so applied. The initial accounting period is six months from the date of liquidation.[69] Subsequent accounting periods are also six months in length unless otherwise agreed by the liquidator and the liquidation committee or the court.[70]

Accounts for the liquidation will be made up by the liquidator in respect of each accounting period[71] and, where appropriate, interim payments of dividend will be made to creditors in respect of each accounting period.[72] Final accounts are made up at the end of the liquidation.[73]

Receivership

Distribution of the company's property in receivership, insofar as it takes place, is principally governed by s 60 of the 1986 Act. In terms of s 60(1) of the 1986 Act, the receiver must pay any monies received by him to the holder of the floating charge under which he was appointed in satisfaction or partial satisfaction of that creditor's debt, after paying any sums due under s 61 of the 1986 Act and to the categories of persons listed in s 60(1).

Section 61 of the 1986 Act deals with the sale or disposal of property subject to a security or effectually executed diligence. Where the authority of the court is sought for the sale or disposal of any such property, it may, and in certain cases must, be made a condition of the court's consent to any such sale or disposal that the monies realised, and in certain circumstances any shortfall, be paid to the creditor concerned.[74] These sums are accordingly given priority over all other sums due.

The categories of persons listed in s 60(1) of the 1986 Act who have priority, subject to any ranking agreement, in the order listed, are as follows.

(1) The holder of any fixed security (for example, a standard security) over property which is subject to the floating charge, where the fixed security ranks prior to or *pari passu* with the charge.

---

[66] Scottish Rules, rule 4.66(5). In an insolvent liquidation, of course, this is unlikely.
[67] 1986 Act, s 74(2)(f).
[68] CA 1985, s 178(6).
[69] 1985 Act, s 52(2)(a).
[70] 1985 Act, s 52(2)(b), as modified by rule 4.16 of the Scottish Rules: the subsection does not read particularly happily as modified, but the author takes it to have the meaning narrated.
[71] 1985 Act, s 52(1).
[72] 1985 Act, s 52(3).
[73] See Chapter 44.
[74] See Chapter 27.

(2) Persons with effectually executed diligence over any of the property subject to the floating charge. Effectually executed diligence is discussed in Chapter 31.

(3) Creditors in respect of all liabilities, charges and expenses incurred by the receiver. This does not include liabilities under a contract of employment adopted by the receiver which are not qualifying liabilities.[75]

(4) The receiver, in respect of his own liabilities, expenses, remuneration and any indemnity to which he is entitled out of the company's assets. The circumstances in which a receiver is entitled to an indemnity from the company's assets is discussed in Chapter 27.

(5) Preferential creditors entitled to payment under s 59 of the 1986 Act. The preferential creditors so defined are those whose debts are preferential debts in terms of s 386 of the 1986 Act which have been intimated, or otherwise become known, to the receiver within six months of his advertising for claims.[76]

In the unlikely event of there being any surplus, the receiver must pay this to any other receiver, the holder of a fixed security over any of the property subject to the charge whose debt has not already been paid, the company or its liquidator.[77] He need not concern himself with payment of any other categories of creditors.[78]

It should be noted that the order of priority of payment of debts provided for in s 60(1) will result in certain circumstances in some creditors receiving a different ranking in a receivership than they would outwith it, ie, under the normal rules of the general law applicable to ranking, a result which has been criticised as unjustifiable, and the Scottish Law Commission has recommended that the section be amended accordingly.[79]

Administration

An administrator has power to make payments which are necessary or incidental to the performance of his functions, and this could include payments to pre-administration creditors—for example, to ensure future supplies.[80] The 1986 Act does not, however, seem to anticipate a general distribution of assets to creditors in the course of an administration, at least where the company is insolvent.

Fletcher, Higham and Trower refer to an unreported case in 1990 in which it was held that the administrator could pay off pre-administration creditors in full in order to ensure the future of the company as a going concern and as a prelude

---

[75] *Lindop v Stuart Noble & Sons* (OH), 7th April 1998 (unreported). For a discussion of contracts generally and contracts of employment in particular, and of qualifying liabilities under such a contract, see Chapter 27.

[76] 1986 Act, s 59(2). Preferential debts within the meaning of s 386 of the 1986 Act are discussed above in the context of liquidation.

[77] 1986 Act, s 60(2).

[78] That includes the expenses of the liquidation where the company is already in liquidation: see above.

[79] See the Scottish Law Commission Discussion Paper No 78 on Adjudication for Debt and Related Matters, 1988, and the Report on Diligence on the Dependence and Admiralty Arrestments (Scot Law Com No 164).

[80] See Chapter 26.

to discharge of the administration order.[81] However, it was held in *Re St Ives Windings Ltd*[82] that an administrator has no power to make a partial distribution of assets to creditors where the assets of the company, which the administrator had mostly realised, were less than its liabilities, except through the mechanism of a CVA or section 425 arrangement. This approach has been followed subsequently.[83] Fletcher, Higham and Trower also refer to another unreported case, *Re Mount Banking plc*,[84] in which it was held that the administrator did have power to make a payment on account to a bank's depositors, but that case seems to have been somewhat special in respect that, again, one of the purposes of the administration was survival of the company as a going concern and the payments did not exceed what would have been payable on a liquidation and were conditional on the depositors agreeing to bring them into account in any subsequent liquidation.

It might therefore be said that where there is a surplus of assets, even after taking into account the expenses of the administration and any priority claims incurred in the course of the administration,[85] it might be permissible for the administrator to pay the creditors in full, but as it has been held that an administrator is not entitled to make a distribution to members either,[86] he would be prevented from distributing any remaining assets to the members. The safest course, therefore, and probably the only course where the company's assets are less than its liabilities (again taking into account the expenses of the administration and any priority claims incurred in the course of the administration), is to make a distribution through the mechanism of a CVA or section 425 arrangement,[87] or through a subsequent liquidation, although this will involve further time and expense.

It should be noted that debts and liabilities incurred under contracts entered into by an administrator, and qualifying liabilities under contracts of employment adopted by an administrator, form a first charge on the company's property.[88] The administrator's remuneration and expenses are also a charge on the company's property: they rank behind the debts and liabilities just described, but take priority over any security which, as constituted, was a floating charge.[89]

Company voluntary arrangements and section 425 arrangements

CVAs and section 425 arrangements will generally provide for the payment of the company's debts through either the realisation of its assets or its continued trading. The terms of any arrangement will vary from case to case depending on the circumstances of the company and what the creditors are prepared to agree to, and the arrangement will usually specify in detail the mechanisms for submitting claims and the rights of the creditors in terms of the agreement, how

---

[81] *The Law and Practice of Corporate Administration*, p 190, referring to the case of *Re John Slack Ltd* (Scott J), 2nd July 1990 (unreported).

[82] (1987) 3 BCC 634.

[83] *Re British and Commonwealth Holdings plc (No 3)* [1992] 1 WLR 672.

[84] 25th January 1993, referred to in Fletcher, Higham and Trower (note 81 above), p 191.

[85] See further below.

[86] *Re Business Properties Ltd* (1988) 4 BCC 684.

[87] Where this is not already a purpose of the administration, the administration order can easily be varied to specify this as an additional purpose on application to the court: 1986 Act, s 18(1).

[88] 1986 Act, s 19(5) and (6), and see Chapter 42.

[89] 1986 Act, s 19(4), and see further Chapter 42.

the expenses of the arrangement are to be dealt with and so on. It will be recalled however, that in a CVA, the rights of secured and preferential creditors may not be varied without their specific consent.[90]

---

[90] See Chapter 8.

34 : CREDITORS' COMMITTEES

In sequestration, administration, receivership and liquidation, statutory provision is made for the election of a number of creditors to fulfil, as a body, specified functions in the administration of the insolvency proceedings in question. In sequestration, these creditors take the form of commissioners; in administration and receivership, they form creditors' committees; and in liquidation they form the liquidation committee. There is no statutory provision for a creditors' committee in a CVA, but the CVA itself may, and usually will, make provision for such a committee.

The functions of these bodies of creditors (hereafter referred to collectively, if in some cases slightly inaccurately, as 'creditors' committees') vary according to the insolvency proceedings involved. This chapter deals with the constitution and functions of statutory creditors' committees in each of the insolvency régimes in which they are applicable.

Sequestration

Election, resignation and removal of commissioners

Commissioners may be elected in any sequestration other than one to which Sched 2 to the 1985 Act applies.[1] They may be elected at the statutory meeting or any subsequent meeting of creditors.[2] There may be up to five commissioners at any one time, and new and additional commissioners may be elected at any subsequent meeting of creditors provided the total number does not exceed five.[3] Commissioners are, however, optional.[4]

Commissioners are elected by the creditors, other than creditors whose debts are postponed and creditors acquiring their debts after the date of sequestration (unless the debt was acquired by succession).[5] They are elected from among the

---

[1] 1985 Act, s 4. The circumstances in which Sched 2 applies are discussed in Chapter 35.
[2] 1985 Act, s 30(1).
[3] Ibid.
[4] Where there are no commissioners, the functions which they would carry out if they existed are normally devolved on the Accountant in Bankruptcy or the court: see further below.
[5] 1985 Act, s 30(1), referring to s 24(3). For creditors whose debts are postponed, see the 1985 Act, s 51(3), and Chapter 33.

creditors or their mandatories,[6] but the debtor, any person who has an interest contrary to the general interests of the creditors and any person who is an associate of either the debtor or the permanent trustee are ineligible for election as commissioners.[7]

A commissioner may not continue to act if he becomes, after he has been elected, a person who would have been ineligible for election as a commissioner.[8]

A commissioner may be removed from office, censured or made subject to any other order the court thinks fit following on a report to the court by the Accountant in Bankruptcy that he has failed without reasonable excuse to perform any legal duty imposed on him.[9] He may also be removed from office by the creditors at a meeting called for that purpose[10] and, where he is a mandatory of a creditor, by the creditor recalling his mandate and intimating its recall in writing to the permanent trustee.[11] He may resign at any time.[12]

Where a sequestration becomes a Schedule 2 case after commencing as an ordinary sequestration, any existing commissioners cease to hold office.[13]

Functions of commissioners

The general functions of the commissioners are to supervise the permanent trustee's administration of the estate and advise him.[14] The permanent trustee must have regard to any advice the commissioners give him[15] and must consult them about recovery, management and realisation of the debtor's estate.[16] The permanent trustee is not obliged to follow the commissioners' advice, but they may apply to the court to give him directions about the recovery, management and realisation of the debtor's estate and, if such directions are given by the court, he must follow them.[17] The commissioners may also apply to the sheriff if they are dissatisfied with any act, omission or decision of the permanent trustee generally, and the sheriff may confirm, annul or modify any such act or decision, give the permanent trustee directions or make any other order.[18] They may apply for the permanent trustee's removal.[19]

In addition, the consent of the commissioners is required for certain matters. Where the permanent trustee wishes to carry on the debtor's business, bring, defend or continue any legal proceedings relating to the debtor's estate, create a security over any part of the estate or make payments or incur liabilities with a view to obtaining property under any right, option or power which is part of the

---

[6] 1985 Act, s 30(1), referring to s 24(3). For creditors whose debts are postponed, see the 1985 Act, s 51(3), and Chapter 33.

[7] 1985 Act, s 30(2). 'Associate' is construed in accordance with s 74 of the 1985 Act: 1985 Act, s 73(1).

[8] 1985 Act, s 30(2).

[9] 1985 Act, s 1A(2).

[10] 1985 Act, s 30(4)(b).

[11] 1985 Act, s 30(4)(a).

[12] 1985 Act, Sched 2, para 6, and see Chapter 35.

[13] 1985 Act, s 30(3).

[14] 1985 Act, s 4.

[15] 1985 Act, s 3(2).

[16] 1985 Act, s 39(1).

[17] Ibid.

[18] 1985 Act, s 3(7). The subsection allows 'the debtor, a creditor or any other person having an interest' to make such an application: this would include commissioners.

[19] 1985 Act, s 29(1), (6), and see also Chapter 19.

estate, he must obtain the consent of the commissioners, the creditors or the court to do so.[20] The permanent trustee must also obtain the consent of the commissioners, the creditors or the court where he wishes to refer any claim or other issue arising in the sequestration to arbitration, or to compromise any claim by or against the estate.[21] The consent of the commissioners is also required where the permanent trustee wishes to dispense with the formal requirements for submitting a claim,[22] to alter the length of the accounting periods,[23] to pay preferred debts[24] or to defer payment of a dividend.[25]

Commissioners also have a variety of other functions. They must, in specified circumstances, call a meeting of creditors to replace a permanent trustee who has resigned, died or been removed by the court.[26] They must determine the amount of the trustee's outlays and remuneration.[27] They must consider any offer of composition made by the debtor and decide whether to recommend that it be placed before the creditors.[28]

Commissioners also have a number of other rights and powers. They have a right to inspect the trustee's accounts[29] and to see confidential documents held by the trustee.[30] They also have the power to require the trustee to apply for a public examination of the debtor or any other relevant person under s 45 of the 1985 Act[31] and to require him to call a meeting of the commissioners.[32]

Status of commissioners

Commissioners have a fiduciary duty to the creditors and the debtor.[33] This means that they must act in the best interests of the sequestration, and not for their own personal benefit. One aspect of this fiduciary duty is specifically enshrined in s 39(8) of the 1985 Act, which provides that commissioners may not purchase any of the debtor's estate. Commissioners also act gratuitously, and are not even entitled to expenses.

Administration and receivership

Creditors' committees in administration and receivership are considered together because they operate in a similar way to each other, but in a different way to the liquidation committee in a liquidation, which has a more extensive role to play in that régime than creditors' committees do in administration and receivership. The Scottish Rules, which contain many of the provisions relating to creditors' committees in administration, receivership and liquidation, apply

---

[20] 1985 Act, s 39(2).
[21] 1985 Act, s 65(1).
[22] 1985 Act, s 48(3).
[23] 1985 Act, s 52(2).
[24] 1985 Act, s 52(4).
[25] 1985 Act, s 52(5).
[26] 1985 Act, s 28(2)(a), 28(3) and s 29(5) and (6) respectively, and see further Chapter 19.
[27] 1985 Act, s 28(6) and s 53(3) and Sched 4, para 9.
[28] 1985 Act, Sched 4, para 3.
[29] 1985 Act, s 3(1)(f).
[30] 1985 Act, s 62(5).
[31] 1985 Act, s 45(1). For a discussion of public examinations, see Chapter 29.
[32] 1985 Act, Sched 6, para 17. If the permanent trustee fails to call the meeting within 14 days, any commissioner may call the meeting: 1985 Act, Sched 6, para 18.
[33] See *Campbell* v *Cullen* 1911, 1 SLT 258.

the relevant rules in receivership directly to administrations with very little modification.[34]

Establishment and membership of the committee

In administration, a creditors' committee may be established at the meeting of creditors called under s 23 of the 1986 Act to consider the administrator's proposals, provided that the meeting actually approves the proposals either with or without modifications.[35] In receivership, a creditors' committee may be established at the meeting of unsecured creditors called under s 67(2) of the 1986 Act to receive the receiver's report, if held.[36] The committee is, however, optional in both cases: it need only be established if the meeting thinks fit.[37]

The committee must have a minimum of three and a maximum of five members.[38] Any creditor who has lodged a claim which has not been rejected for the purposes of entitlement to vote is eligible for election to the committee.[39] This includes creditors who are partnerships or bodies corporate, although such creditors must act by a representative.[40]

A member of the committee may be removed by resolution at a meeting of creditors.[41] In addition, membership of the committee will be terminated automatically if the member ceases to be a creditor (or is found never to have been one) *or* he is not present or represented at three consecutive meetings of the committee (unless the contrary is resolved at the third meeting) *or* his estate is sequestrated, he becomes bankrupt, he grants a trust deed for creditors or makes a composition with his creditors.[42] A member of the committee may resign at any time by giving notice in writing.[43]

Where a vacancy arises on the committee, the administrator or receiver (as appropriate) and the majority of the remaining members may agree not to fill any such vacancy, provided that the number of members on the committee does not fall below the minimum.[44] Alternatively, a new member may be appointed either

---

[34] Scottish Rules, rule 2.15. In fact a number of the provisions of the rules relating to liquidation committees are also applied directly to receivership and thence to administration, but none the less the functions of the liquidation committee remain sufficiently different from those of the creditors' committees in receivership and administration to justify treating the liquidation committee separately.

[35] 1986 Act, s 26(1).

[36] 1986 Act, s 68(1). A meeting under s 67(2) of the 1986 Act will not always be called. The receiver may apply to the court for a direction that it not be held: see s 67(2), (3); and if the company has gone or goes into liquidation, it may not be necessary to call the meeting: see 1986 Act, s 67(4). On these points, see further Chapter 13.

[37] 1986 Act, s 26(1) (administration), and s 67(1) (receivership).

[38] Scottish Rules, rule 3.4(1), as applied to administrations by rule 2.15.

[39] Scottish Rules, rule 3.4(2), as applied to administrations by rule 2.15.

[40] Scottish Rules, rule 3.4(3), as applied to administrations by rule 2.15. Other members may act through a representative, subject to certain restrictions: rule 4.48, as applied to receiverships by rule 3.16 and to administrations by rule 2.15.

[41] Scottish Rules, rule 4.51, as applied to receiverships by rule 3.16 and to administrations by rule 2.15.

[42] Scottish Rules, rule 4.50, as applied to receiverships by rule 3.16 and to administrations by rule 2.15.

[43] Scottish Rules, rule 4.49, as applied to receiverships by rule 3.16 and to administrations by rule 2.15.

[44] Scottish Rules, rule 4.52(2), as applied to receiverships by rule 3.16 and to administrations by rule 2.15.

by the administrator or by the receiver with the agreement of the majority of the remaining members of the committee or by a meeting of creditors.[45]

The committee can only commence acting after a certificate of its due constitution has been issued by the administrator or receiver.[46]

Functions of the creditors' committee

In administration, the general functions of the creditors' committee are to assist the administrator in discharging his functions and to act in relation to him in such manner as may be agreed from time to time.[47] It also has the specific function of determining the administrator's remuneration[48] and reviewing from time to time the adequacy of his caution.[49]

The committee also has a number of rights and powers. It may require the administrator to appear before it to furnish it with such information relating to the carrying out of his functions as it may reasonably require.[50] It may receive the administrator's resignation if there is no continuing administrator to receive it,[51] and it has the power to apply to the court for the appointment of a new administrator where the administrator has died, resigned or otherwise vacated office and there is no continuing administrator to make such an application.[52] Members of the committee are also entitled to receive an abstract of the administrator's accounts of the receipts and payments of the company.[53] Although the committee is not entitled as of right to see confidential documents held by the administrator,[54] if he refuses them access to such documents, an application may be made to the court to overrule his decision.[55] The committee may give directions for the disposal of the books, papers and records of the company where the administration has terminated and no other proceedings have commenced within six months of the date specified in the Scottish Rules.[56]

In receivership, the general functions of the creditors' committee are more limited, being only to represent the views of the unsecured creditors to the receiver and otherwise to act in relation to the receiver in such manner as may be agreed from time to time.[57] These general functions are stated to be in addition to the functions conferred on the committee by the 1986 Act, but the Act itself does not confer any functions on the committee. The committee must, however, review from time to time the adequacy of the receiver's caution[58] and it has a number of rights and powers. It may require the receiver to appear before it to

---

[45] Scottish Rules, rule 4.52(3), (4), as applied to receiverships by rule 3.16 and to administrations by rule 2.15.
[46] Scottish Rules, rule 4.42, as applied to receiverships by rule 3.16 and to administrations by rule 2.15.
[47] Scottish Rules, rule 2.15(4).
[48] Scottish Rules, rule 2.16.
[49] Scottish Rules, rule 7.28.
[50] 1986 Act, s 26(2).
[51] Scottish Rules, rule 2.18.
[52] 1986 Act, s 13(3), and see Chapter 19.
[53] Scottish Rules, rule 2.17.
[54] Scottish Rules, rule 7.27(2).
[55] Scottish Rules, rule 7.27(3).
[56] Scottish Rules, rule 7.34(2).
[57] Scottish Rules, rule 3.5.
[58] Scottish Rules, rule 7.28.

furnish it with such information relating to the carrying out of his functions as it may reasonably require.[59] Members of the committee are entitled to receive an abstract of the receiver's accounts of the receipts and payments of the company.[60] Although the committee is not entitled as of right to see any confidential documents held by the receiver,[61] if he refuses them access to them, an application may be made to the court to overrule his decision.[62] The committee must be given notice of the receiver's resignation, his death or his vacation of office as a result of his ceasing to be qualified as an insolvency practitioner[63] and may give directions for the disposal of the books, papers and records of the company where the receivership has terminated and no other proceedings have commenced within six months of the date specified in the Scottish Rules.[64]

Status of committee members

Like commissioners in a sequestration, committee members are fiduciaries. Unlike commissioners, however, they are not prevented from dealing with the company during the administration or receivership provided that any such transaction is on normal commercial terms.[65] Where it appears to the court on the application of any interested person that a transaction was not entered into on normal commercial terms, the transaction may be set aside and the court may give any other directions for compensating the company for any loss caused to it.[66]

Members of the committee are also entitled to reimbursement of certain expenses: they or their representatives are entitled to reasonable travelling expenses incurred either in attending the meetings of the committee or otherwise on the committee's business, subject to certain limitations.[67]

Liquidation

Provision is made for a liquidation committee in creditors' voluntary and compulsory liquidations only. Most of the provisions relating to the liquidation committee are the same for both creditors' voluntary and compulsory liquidation,[68] and the following discussion should therefore be taken as applying to the liquidation committee in both types of liquidation unless otherwise stated. Only those provisions which are relevant to the liquidation committee in an insolvent liquidation are discussed: provisions which apply only to solvent liquidations are omitted. There are special rules where liquidation follows immediately on administration: these are discussed separately.

---

[59] 1986 Act, s 68(2).
[60] Scottish Rules, rule 3.9.
[61] Scottish Rules, rule 7.27(2).
[62] Scottish Rules, rule 7.27(3).
[63] Receivers (Scotland) Regulations 1986, reg 6, and the Scottish Rules, rules 3.10 and 3.11 respectively.
[64] Scottish Rules, rule 7.34(2).
[65] Scottish Rules, rule 3.8(1), as applied to administrations by rule 2.15.
[66] Scottish Rules, rule 3.8(2), as applied to administrations by rule 2.15.
[67] Scottish Rules, rule 4.57, as applied to receiverships by rule 3.16 and administrations by rule 2.15.
[68] The majority of the provisions in the Scottish Rules applicable to liquidation committees in compulsory liquidation are applied with specified and other necessary modifications to creditors' voluntary liquidations: Scottish Rules, rule 5 and Sched 1.

Establishment and membership of the committee

In a creditors' voluntary liquidation, a liquidation committee may be established at the creditors' meeting called under s 98 of the 1986 Act or any subsequent creditors' meeting.[69] In a compulsory liquidation, a liquidation committee may be established at the first meeting or meetings in the liquidation called under s 138 of the 1986 Act[70] or at general meetings of the creditors and contributories called by the liquidator for the purpose of deciding whether a liquidation committee should be established.[71] Where no liquidation committee is established by either of these methods, it may be established by a meeting of creditors or a meeting of contributories following the procedure laid down in rule 4.43 of the Scottish Rules.[72] A liquidation committee is not, however, compulsory in either a creditors' voluntary or a compulsory liquidation.

In the normal case, the committee must have a minimum of three and a maximum of five creditors as members.[73] Such members are known as creditor members.[74] Any creditor of the company who has lodged a claim which has not been wholly rejected for the purposes either of voting or for entitlement to claim a dividend is eligible to be a member of the committee, provided that he is not a fully secured creditor who has not agreed to surrender his security to the liquidator.[75] This includes creditors who are partnerships or bodies corporate, although such creditors must act by a representative.[76] Where the company is an authorised institution or former authorised institution, a duly authorised representative of the Deposit Protection Board is entitled to be a member of the committee,[77] but any such representative is an additional creditor member and is not counted for the purpose of calculating the minimum or maximum number of members otherwise allowed.[78]

In a creditors' voluntary winding up, the company may appoint up to five additional members to the committee,[79] but the creditors may resolve that any or

---

[69] 1986 Act, s 101(1). Where the liquidation commences as a members' voluntary liquidation and is subsequently converted to a creditors' voluntary liquidation, the meeting called under s 95 of the 1986 Act is treated as if it were the meeting under s 98 of the 1986 Act: 1986 Act, s 96(b).

[70] 1986 Act, s 142(1).

[71] 1986 Act, s 142(2). The liquidator may call such meetings at any time (1986 Act, s 142(2)) and, where he is a liquidator appointed by the court other than under s 139(4) of the 1986 Act, he must do so where requested to do so by one-tenth in value of the creditors: 1986 Act, s 142(3).

[72] The procedure in rule 4.43 is applicable only where the first meeting of creditors under s 138 of the 1986 Act or the creditors' meeting called by the liquidator under s 142(2) of the 1986 Act has either not decided or refused to establish a liquidation committee. In such a case, the meeting of contributories may appoint one of their number to apply to the court for an order to have a further creditors' meeting called for the purpose of establishing a liquidation committee. If the court so orders, the creditors' meeting will be duly called, and if it does not establish a liquidation committee, a meeting of contributories may do so.

[73] 1986 Act, s 101, and the Scottish Rules, rule 4.41(1), as modified in relation to creditors' voluntary liquidation by rule 5, Sched 1, para 21 (creditors' voluntary liquidation); Scottish Rules, rule 4.41(1)(a) (compulsory liquidation).

[74] Scottish Rules, rule 4.41(5).

[75] Scottish Rules, rule 4.41(2), applied to creditors' voluntary liquidation by rule 5 and Sched 2.

[76] Scottish Rules, rule 4.41(4), as applied to creditors' voluntary liquidation by rule 5 and Sched 2. Other members may act through a representative, subject to certain restrictions: rule 4.48, as applied to creditors' voluntary liquidation by rule 5 and Sched 2.

[77] Banking Act 1987, s 58(8)(iv).

[78] Scottish Rules, rule 4.41(6).

[79] 1986 Act, s 101(2).

all of such persons shall not in fact be members of the committee.[80] Where the creditors do so resolve, the persons appointed will not be members of the committee unless the court so directs.[81] Committee members appointed by the company are known as contributory members.[82] Contributory members are not applicable in an insolvent compulsory liquidation,[83] except in the case of a liquidation committee established by a meeting of contributories under rule 4.43(3), where the committee will consist of a minimum of three and a maximum of five contributories.[84]

A creditor member of the committee may be removed by resolution at a meeting of creditors and a contributory member may similarly be removed at a meeting of contributories.[85] In addition, membership of a creditor member will be terminated if he ceases to be a creditor (or is found never to have been one) and membership of any member of the committee will be terminated automatically if he is not present or represented at three consecutive meetings of the committee (unless the contrary is resolved at the third meeting) *or* his estate is sequestrated, he becomes bankrupt, he grants a trust deed for creditors or makes a composition with his creditors.[86] Any member of the committee may resign at any time by giving notice in writing.[87]

Where a vacancy on the committee arises, the liquidator and the majority of the remaining creditor or contributory members (whichever is appropriate to the type of vacancy) may agree not to fill it, provided that the number of members on the committee does not fall below the minimum.[88] Alternatively, a new member may be appointed either by the liquidator with the agreement of the majority of the remaining creditor or contributory members of the committee or by a meeting of creditors or contributories.[89] However, where a new contributory member is appointed by a meeting of contributories in a creditors' voluntary liquidation, the creditor members of the committee may resolve that that person shall not in fact be a member of the committee,[90] and where the creditors do so resolve, the person appointed will not be a member of the committee unless the court so directs.[91]

The committee can only commence acting after a certificate of its due constitution has been issued by the liquidator.[92]

---

[80] 1986 Act, s 101(3).

[81] Ibid. The court may appoint other persons to act in place of those appointed by the company: 1986 Act, s 101(3)(b).

[82] Scottish Rules, rule 4.41(5).

[83] Rule 4.41 of the Scottish Rules provides for the election of contributories to the committee only in the case of a solvent winding up: rule 4.41(1)(b).

[84] Scottish Rules, rule 4.43(4).

[85] Scottish Rules, rule 4.51, as applied to creditors' voluntary liquidation by rule 5 and Sched 2.

[86] Scottish Rules, rule 4.50, as applied to creditors' voluntary liquidation by rule 5 and Sched 2.

[87] Scottish Rules, rule 4.49, as applied to creditors' voluntary liquidation by rule 5 and Sched 2.

[88] Scottish Rules, rule 4.52(2) (creditor members) and rule 4.53(2) (contributory members), as applied to creditors' voluntary liquidation by rule 5 and Sched 2.

[89] Scottish Rules, rule 4.52(3) and (4) (creditor members) and rule 4.53(3) and (4) (contributory members), as applied to creditors' voluntary liquidation by rule 5 and Sched 2.

[90] Scottish Rules, rule 4.53(4A), as applied to creditors' voluntary liquidation by rule 5 and Sched 2, para 25.

[91] Ibid. Where an application is made to the court for a direction, it may alternatively appoint another contributory to fill the vacancy: Scottish Rules, rule 4.53(4A)(b).

[92] Scottish Rules, rule 4.42, as applied to creditors' voluntary liquidation by rule 5 and Sched 2.

Special rules apply to the way in which the liquidation committee is constituted, where liquidation follows immediately upon administration and the administrator is appointed as liquidator.[93] In such a case, if a creditors' committee was established in the administration, it becomes the liquidation committee unless the number of members of the committee had fallen below three at the time of the liquidator's appointment.[94] The liquidator must issue a certificate of continuance of the committee, and the committee is suspended until he does so.[95] Once the committee is established, the rules described above relating to changes in membership and the subsequent operation of the committee are the same as for a liquidation committee established in the normal way.

Functions of the liquidation committee

The legislation does not contain any general statement of the functions of the liquidation committee, but it has a number of specific functions, powers and duties which give it an important role in the administration of the liquidation process. Its role is much more extensive than that of the creditors' committees in administration and receivership, and is more akin to that of the commissioners in sequestration. Indeed, the 1986 Act provides that in addition to the powers and duties conferred under that Act, the liquidation committee will have such of the powers and duties of commissioners as may be conferred or imposed upon them by the rules,[96] although no additional provision of this nature is in fact made in the Scottish Rules.

In both creditors' voluntary and compulsory liquidation, the sanction of the liquidation committee or the court is required before the liquidator may exercise any of the powers contained in Part I of Sched 4 to the 1986 Act, namely the power to pay any class of creditors in full, the power to compromise claims and the power to compromise calls, debts and other claims of contributories and carry out other specified actions in relation thereto.[97] In a compulsory liquidation, the sanction of the liquidation committee or the court is also required before the liquidator may exercise either of the powers contained in Part II of Sched 4 to the 1986 Act, namely the power to bring or defend legal proceedings and the power to carry on the business of the company so far as may be necessary for its beneficial winding up.[98] In a creditors' voluntary liquidation, the sanction of the liquidation committee is also required where the liquidator proposes to sell or transfer the whole of the company's property to another company and to accept as whole or part payment for that sale or transfer *either* shares, policies or other like interests in the acquiring company for distribution among the members *or*, in lieu of or in addition to such shares, etc, some other scheme whereby the members may participate in the profits or receive some other benefit from the acquiring company.[99] In addition, in both creditors' voluntary liquidation and compulsory

---

[93] Scottish Rules, rule 4.60.
[94] Scottish Rules, rule 4.61. Where these special rules do not apply, of course, any committee will be established in the normal way, as discussed above.
[95] Scottish Rules, rule 4.63.
[96] 1986 Act, s 101(4) (creditors' voluntary liquidation) and s 142(6) (compulsory liquidation).
[97] 1986 Act, s 165(1) (creditors' voluntary liquidation) and s 167(1), (2) (compulsory liquidation). For further discussion of the liquidator's powers, see Chapter 28.
[98] 1986 Act, s 167(2), (3). For further discussion of the liquidator's powers, see Chapter 28.
[99] 1986 Act, s 110. This provision is discussed further in Chapter 28.

liquidation, the consent of the liquidation committee is required for any alteration in the length of accounting periods and for payment of preferential debts.[100]

The liquidation committee has other specific functions. It must determine the amount of the liquidator's outlays and remuneration,[101] and it must review from time to time the adequacy of his caution.[102]

It also has a number of rights and powers. In a creditors' voluntary liquidation, it may sanction the continuance of some or all of the powers of the directors after the liquidator's appointment.[103] In both creditors' voluntary and compulsory liquidation, it is entitled to receive reports from the liquidator of all matters relating to the liquidation which are of concern to it[104] and, where the committee has come into being more than 28 days after the liquidator's appointment, it is entitled to a summary report of the liquidator's actions since his appointment and to question the liquidator thereon.[105] This is without prejudice to its right to inspect the liquidator's cash and sederunt books and to seek an explanation of any matter within its competence from the liquidator.[106] The committee is also entitled to direct the liquidator to send it written reports regarding progress in the liquidation generally and any other matters which he feels should be drawn to their attention,[107] and even where it does not make any such direction, it is entitled to receive a written report at least once every six months.[108] It may require the liquidator to call a meeting of the committee;[109] it may, in appropriate circumstances, sanction transactions between members of the committee and other specified persons and the company;[110] it may give directions for the disposal of the books, papers and records of the company at the conclusion of the liquidation;[111] and although it is not entitled as of right to see any confidential documents held by the liquidator,[112] if he refuses access to such documents, an application may be made to the court to overrule his decision.[113] The committee is entitled to receive notice of the liquidator's disposal of any property to a person who is connected with the company.[114]

Status of committee members

Members of the committee are in a fiduciary position. Unlike commissioners in a sequestration, they are not prohibited entirely from dealing with the company in

---

[100] 1985 Act, s 52, as modified by rule 4.16(2) and rule 4.68 of the Scottish Rules and applied by the latter, and as applied to creditors' voluntary liquidation by rule 5.

[101] 1985 Act, s 53, as modified by rule 4.16(2) and rule 4.32 and applied by rule 4.68 of the Scottish Rules, and as applied to creditors' voluntary liquidation by rule 5.

[102] Scottish Rules, rule 7.28.

[103] 1986 Act, s 103, and see further Chapter 23.

[104] Scottish Rules, rule 4.44(1), as applied to creditors' voluntary liquidation by rule 5.

[105] Scottish Rules, rule 4.44(3), as applied to creditors' voluntary liquidation by rule 5.

[106] Scottish Rules, rule 4.44(5), as applied to creditors' voluntary liquidation by rule 5.

[107] Scottish Rules, rule 4.56(1), (3), as applied to creditors' voluntary liquidation by rule 5. The committee cannot require reports more often than once every two months.

[108] Scottish Rules, rule 4.56(2), as applied to creditors' voluntary liquidation by rule 5.

[109] Scottish Rules, rule 4.45(2)(a), as applied to creditors' voluntary liquidation by rule 5.

[110] Scottish Rules, rule 4.58(3), as applied to creditors' voluntary liquidations by rule 5, and see further below.

[111] Scottish Rules, rule 7.34(3)(a) (compulsory liquidation) and rule 7.34(3)(c) (creditors' voluntary liquidation).

[112] Scottish Rules, rule 7.27(2).

[113] Scottish Rules, rule 7.27(3).

[114] 1986 Act, s 165(6) (creditors' voluntary liquidation) and s 167(2) (compulsory liquidation). 'Connected with' has the meaning given to it by s 249 of the 1986 Act.

liquidation, but the Scottish Rules contain detailed provisions regulating such dealings which are considerably stricter than those applicable to members of the creditors' committee in administration or receivership. The restrictions also extend beyond current members of the committee to the representative of any committee member, any associate of *either* a member of the committee *or* the representative of a member of the committee, and any former member who was such a member within the 12 months preceding the transaction.[115] Such persons may not acquire any of the company's assets, receive payment for supplying goods or services in connection with the liquidation, or otherwise obtain any profit from the liquidation unless they have received *either* prior leave of the court *or* retrospective leave from the court, applied for without undue delay, where the transaction was urgent or involved a contract which was in force before the liquidation *or* the prior sanction of the liquidation committee, which must be satisfied that the transaction will be on normal commercial terms.[116] Where these provisions are not complied with, the court may set aside a transaction on the application of any interested person and may make consequential orders, including an order to account for any profit from the transaction and to compensate the company for any loss.[117]

As in administration and receivership, members of the committee are entitled to reimbursement of certain expenses: they or their representatives are entitled to reasonable travelling expenses incurred either in attending the meetings of the committee or otherwise on the committee's business, subject to certain limitations.[118]

---

[115] Scottish Rules, rule 4.58(1), as applied to creditors' voluntary liquidation by rule 5 and Sched 2.
[116] Scottish Rules, rule 4.58(2), (3), as applied to creditors' voluntary liquidation by rule 5 and Sched 2.
[117] Scottish Rules, rule 4.58(5), as applied to creditors' voluntary liquidation by rule 5 and Sched 2. The court will not, however, make an order if the person transacting with the company is an associate of a committee member or a committee member's representative and the court is satisfied that that person had no reason to suppose he was contravening the provisions: rule 4.58(6), as applied to creditors' voluntary liquidation by rule 5 and Sched 2.
[118] Scottish Rules, rule 4.57, as applied to creditors' voluntary liquidation by rule 5 and Sched 2.

35 : ABBREVIATED PROCEDURES IN SEQUESTRATION

In some cases the normal procedures in sequestration are modified with a view to enabling the sequestration to be completed more quickly and with less expense. There are two types of abbreviated procedure: that under Sched 2 to the 1985 Act (hereafter 'Schedule 2 procedure') and summary administration, which is dealt with in Sched 2A to the 1985 Act. In most summary administration cases, the modified procedures in Sched 2 apply as well as those in Sched 2A.

Schedule 2 procedure

Cases to which the modified procedures in Sched 2 apply are often referred to as small assets cases, but not all cases falling within the schedule are cases where there are few or no assets.

When Schedule 2 procedure applies

Schedule 2 procedure applies whenever the permanent trustee is not elected, that is, in the following circumstances.

(1) Where the Accountant in Bankruptcy is the interim trustee but does not call a statutory meeting and is therefore appointed permanent trustee.[1]

(2) Where the Accountant in Bankruptcy applies for and is granted a certificate of summary administration.[2]

(3) Where no creditor entitled to vote attends the statutory meeting or no permanent trustee is elected at the meeting for some other reason and the permanent trustee is therefore appointed by the court.[3]

(4) Where no permanent trustee is elected to replace one who has resigned,[4] died[5] or been removed.[6]

---

[1] 1985 Act, s 21B(2) and s 25A.
[2] 1985 Act, s 23A(4) and s 25A.
[3] 1985 Act, s 24(3A) and s 25A, where the interim trustee is the Accountant in Bankruptcy; s 24(4) and (5), where the interim trustee is a private insolvency practitioner.
[4] 1985 Act, s 28(5) and s 25A.
[5] Ibid.
[6] 1985 Act, s 29(8) and s 25A.

(5) In all summary administration cases *except* those where the permanent trustee has been elected.[7]

Modifications to the procedure

The main modifications to ordinary sequestration procedure are as follows.

(1) A modified Act and Warrant is issued.[8]

(2) There are simplified procedures for replacing the permanent trustee.[9]

(3) There are no commissioners.[10] Where a sequestration becomes a Schedule 2 case after commencing as an ordinary sequestration, any existing commissioners cease to hold office.[11]

(4) Where the permanent trustee is the Accountant in Bankruptcy, he need not consult with anyone regarding recovery, management and realisation of the estate and he does not need consent for any of the actions normally requiring it.[12] Where the permanent trustee is a private insolvency practitioner, he requires only the consent of the Accountant in Bankruptcy rather than the consents normally required.[13]

(5) A permanent trustee who is a private insolvency practitioner requires the consent of the Accountant in Bankruptcy to apply for a public or private examination.[14]

(6) There are modified procedures in relation to accounts where the permanent trustee is the Accountant in Bankruptcy.[15]

Summary administration

Summary administration was introduced by the 1993 Act to deal with cases where there are few or no assets.

When summary administration procedure applies

Summary administration procedure applies when a certificate of summary administration is granted by the court. It may be applied for in the following circumstances:

(1) Where the petition is by the debtor, the Accountant in Bankruptcy may apply for a certificate of summary administration within seven days of the award of sequestration,[16] but this will only be granted where he is the interim trustee.[17]

(2) Where the Accountant in Bankruptcy is the interim trustee and does not call a statutory meeting, he may apply.[18]

---

[7] 1985 Act, Sched 2A, para 5.
[8] 1985 Act, Sched 2, para 2(2).
[9] 1985 Act, Sched 2, paras 3, 4.
[10] 1985 Act, Sched 2, para 6.
[11] Ibid.
[12] 1985 Act, Sched 2, para 7.
[13] Ibid.
[14] 1985 Act, Sched 2, para 8.
[15] 1985 Act, Sched 2, para 9.
[16] 1985 Act, s 12(1A).
[17] See 1985 Act, s 23A(9).
[18] 1985 Act, s 21B(2).

(3) Where no creditor entitled to vote attends the statutory meeting or no permanent trustee is elected for some other reason.[19]

(4) Where the permanent trustee is elected.[20]

The court must grant the application where the debtor's liabilities (excluding secured liabilities) are less than £20,000 and his assets (excluding heritage and any property which would not vest in the permanent trustee) are less than £2,000.[21]

Withdrawal of certificate of summary administration

The debtor, a creditor, the permanent trustee or the Accountant in Bankruptcy may apply to the court for the withdrawal of the certificate of summary administration at any time.[22]

Modifications to procedure

The following are the main modifications to ordinary sequestration procedure.

(1) The permanent trustee is required to carry out his functions only to the extent that he thinks it would be of financial benefit and in the interests of the creditors to do so.[23] He need not, therefore, waste time and resources carrying out extensive investigations which he thinks would be fruitless or produce nothing of worth to the creditors.

(2) The permanent trustee must obtain from the debtor every six months a report of the debtor's current position.[24]

(3) A permanent trustee who is a private insolvency practitioner is subject to directions from the Accountant in Bankruptcy.[25]

As indicated above, in all summary administration cases except those where the permanent trustee has been elected, the modifications to normal procedure contained in Sched 2 also apply.[26]

---

[19] 1985 Act, s 24(4A) (private insolvency practitioner interim trustee) and s 24(3B) (Accountant in Bankruptcy interim trustee).
[20] 1985 Act, s 25(2A).
[21] 1985 Act, s 23A(1), (2). These limits are subject to alteration by regulation: s 72A.
[22] 1985 Act, s 23A(5). The procedure is specified in s 23A(6) – (8).
[23] 1985 Act, Sched 2A, para 1.
[24] 1985 Act, Sched 2A, para 2.
[25] 1985 Act, Sched 2A, para 3.
[26] 1985 Act, Sched 2A, para 5.

Part IV

THE EFFECT OF INSOLVENCY PROCEEDINGS ON A DEBTOR AND A COMPANY DEBTOR'S OFFICERS

36 : THE EFFECT OF INSOLVENCY PROCEEDINGS: SEQUESTRATION

S equestration does not only affect the debtor's estate. It affects the debtor and, in the case of a debtor other than an individual, the debtor's representatives, in consequence of the various duties and disabilities imposed by the legislation.[1]

This chapter considers the effect of sequestration from the debtor's point of view, including the debtor's eventual discharge.

Effects of sequestration generally

The consequences of insolvency as such for a debtor are less harsh than they were historically, where non-payment of debts might result, for example, in imprisonment or exile of an individual debtor,[2] but the consequences of sequestration for the debtor (and, in the case of an individual, his family) are still serious. Many of these have already been discussed in the preceding chapters: almost all of the debtor's existing assets and any assets acquired after sequestration and prior to discharge vest in the trustee to be distributed to creditors; where a debtor is earning, he may be required to contribute part of his earnings to the trustee; there are restrictions on the debtor's dealings; there are various obligations to be complied with under the 1985 Act and there is the possibility of a private or public examination. In addition, an undischarged bankrupt is disqualified from holding certain public offices (for example, Member of Parliament[3]) and other types of appointment (for example, director of a company[4]) and may be unable to carry on his trade or profession (for example, as a solicitor.[5][6]) There may also be long-term effects—for example, the debtor may have difficulty in obtaining credit in the future.

---

[1] Some of these duties and, in particular, disabilities will, of course, only be applicable to a debtor who is a living individual, as will become clear.

[2] See Chapter 2.

[3] See the 1986 Act, s 427, which details the extent of the disqualifications applicable to both Houses of Parliament.

[4] Company Directors (Disqualification) Act 1986, s 11(1).

[5] Solicitors (Scotland) Act 1980, s 18(1).

[6] There is a wide variety of disqualifications which it would be impractical to list: these few examples give only a brief flavour of the effects of sequestration. Further examples may be found particularly in McBryde, *Bankruptcy* (2nd edn), pp 407–408, but as the circumstances of individual cases will vary, further research may need to be done as to the effect of the sequestration in any given case.

Duty to co-operate with the permanent trustee and other duties

The 1985 Act imposes a number of specific duties on a debtor, many of which have already been considered in context, such as the duty to comply with the interim trustee's instructions regarding management of the estate under s 18[7] and the duty to provide a statement of assets and liabilities to the interim trustee under s 19.[8] There is also a general duty to co-operate with the permanent trustee: the debtor is required to take 'every practicable step' necessary to enable the permanent trustee to carry out his functions under the 1985 Act.[9] The subsection specifically refers to the debtor signing documents, but would cover a wide range of other things—for example, completing tax returns, instructing agents or carrying out the transfer of property (for example, property abroad which the trustee might not otherwise be able to recover.[10])

Offences

Bankruptcy or insolvency no longer renders a debtor liable to imprisonment of itself, but the 1985 Act creates a number of criminal offences. Some relate to failure to comply with specific provisions of the 1985 Act itself—for example, it is an offence for the debtor to fail without reasonable excuse to follow a direction of the interim trustee relating to the management of his estate[11] or to fail without reasonable excuse to provide the interim trustee with the statement of assets and liabilities required by s 19.[12] A number of general offences are also created by s 67 of the 1985 Act—for example, destroying, damaging, concealing or removing from Scotland any assets or relevant documents[13] and falsifying documents.[14] Some offences may be committed by persons other than the debtor. For example, the offence of destroying, damaging, concealing or removing from Scotland any assets or relevant documents may also be committed by anyone acting in the debtor's interests, with or without his authority.[15] There are also common law offences such as 'away-putting of assets'.

The permanent trustee has an obligation to report suspected offences to the Accountant in Bankruptcy,[16] who may in turn refer the matter to the Lord Advocate for prosecution. Penalties may be severe: in *Shelvin* v *Carmichael*[17] the debtor was sentenced to three months' imprisonment for concealing assets.

---

[7] See Chapter 20.
[8] See Chapter 7.
[9] 1985 Act, s 64(1).
[10] See further Chapter 22, dealing with property which raises special issues in insolvency generally, including foreign property, and Chapter 48, which deals with insolvencies with international aspects.
[11] 1985 Act, s 18(5)(a)(i).
[12] 1985 Act, s 19(3), (4).
[13] 1985 Act, s 67(2).
[14] 1985 Act, s 67(4).
[15] 1985 Act, s 67(2).
[16] 1985 Act, s 3(3).
[17] 1991 GWD 36–2173.

Discharge of debtor

Automatic discharge

Unless discharge is deferred, the debtor will be discharged automatically three years after the date of sequestration,[18] irrespective of whether the administration of the estate is still continuing or not.[19] The debtor may apply to the Accountant in Bankruptcy for a certificate of discharge as evidence of the discharge,[20] but the discharge is effective whether or not the debtor obtains the certificate. The effect of the discharge is that the debtor is discharged within the United Kingdom of all debts and obligations for which he/it was liable at the date of sequestration, with a few exceptions.[21] The exceptions are:

(1) Liability to pay fines or other penalties payable to the Crown.[22]

(2) Liability to forfeit money deposited in court under s 1(3) of the Bail (Scotland) Act 1980.[23]

(3) Liability for fraud or breach of trust.[24]

(4) Liability for aliment or periodical allowance which could not be claimed in the sequestration.[25]

(5) Liability for child support maintenance in respect of any period prior to the date of sequestration.[26]

(6) The obligation to co-operate with the permanent trustee under s 64.[27] This exception is necessary because, as noted, the debtor may be discharged before the administration of the estate is complete.

(7) Liability in respect of a student loan.[28]

Any property which the debtor acquires after discharge and which would have vested in the permanent trustee during the sequestration will now vest in the debtor, and cannot be attached by creditors for pre-sequestration debts.[29] Once discharged, a debtor may once more become eligible for public offices and other appointments from which he/it was previously disqualified by being an undischarged bankrupt.[30] The debtor's discharge does not, however, affect the

---

[18] 1985 Act, s 54(1).

[19] The debtor's discharge does not bring the sequestration to an end: see *Henderson* v *Bulley* (1849) 11 D 1470, and Chapter 40.

[20] 1985 Act, s 54(2).

[21] 1985 Act, s 55(1). The effect of the discharge in foreign law, as opposed to within the UK, is a matter for the foreign law applying its rules of domestic and private international law: see Chapter 48.

[22] 1985 Act, s 55(2)(a).

[23] 1985 Act, s 55(2)(b).

[24] 1985 Act, s 55(2)(c).

[25] 1985 Act, s 55(2)(d)(i).

[26] 1985 Act, s 55(2)(d)(ii).

[27] 1985 Act, s 55(2)(e).

[28] Education (Student Loans) Act 1990, Sched 2, para 6.

[29] Other than those which, as detailed above, are not affected by the discharge. It may, of course, be attached for debts which the debtor has incurred since the sequestration.

[30] Parliamentary disqualification, for example, ceases on discharge (or earlier annulment, recall or reduction of the sequestration): 1986 Act, s 427. But the terms of the provision containing the relevant disqualification will require to be consulted in each case to ascertain when it ceases.

right of a secured creditor to enforce his security in respect of any debt or obligation of which the debtor has been discharged.[31]

Deferment of automatic discharge

The debtor's automatic discharge may, in certain circumstances, be deferred. An application to have the discharge deferred may be made by the permanent trustee or any creditor, and should be made within two years and nine months of the date of sequestration.[32] The applicant will be ordered to serve a copy of the application on the debtor and, where the applicant is a creditor, on the permanent trustee,[33] and the debtor will be ordered to lodge in court a declaration that a full surrender of the estate has been made and that every relevant document relating to the estate and business and financial affairs of the debtor has been delivered to the trustee.[34] Where the debtor fails to lodge the declaration, the discharge is automatically deferred for up to two years.[35] Where it is lodged, a hearing is fixed and the permanent trustee (or, if the permanent trustee has already been discharged, the Accountant in Bankruptcy) lodges in court a report on the debtor's assets and liabilities and financial and business affairs, the sequestration generally and the debtor's conduct in relation to his/its affairs and the sequestration.[36] The debtor, the applicant or any creditor can make representations at the hearing.[37] The court may refuse the application or defer the discharge for a period of up to two years.[38]

Normally, the hearing will take place prior to the date for the debtor's automatic discharge, and so a decision on deferral will be taken before the debtor is automatically discharged. In some cases, however, it may not be possible to hold the hearing prior to the date when the debtor is automatically discharged. In *Clydesdale Bank plc v Davidson*[39] it was held that so long as the application was made timeously, it did not matter that it was not disposed of before the three-year period expired: the automatic discharge was effectively suspended pending the outcome of the application. Where the application is not presented timeously—for example, because the trustee has overlooked the time-limit—there will need to be an application to the court to extend the time-limit to allow late lodging of the application. In *Whittaker's Tr v Whittaker*[40] it was held that, in such cases, there is effectively a two-stage process: stage 1 is the decision on the request to be allowed to lodge the application late, stage 2 is the decision on the merits of the application itself. It was further held that even where neither stage could be dealt with before the three years expired, the automatic discharge was effectively suspended in the same way as in the circumstances of *Clydesdale Bank*

---

[31] 1985 Act, s 55(3).
[32] 1985 Act, s 54(3).
[33] 1985 Act, s 54(4). Service on the permanent trustee is only required if he is not discharged.
[34] 1985 Act, s 54(4).
[35] Ibid.
[36] 1985 Act, s 54(5).
[37] 1985 Act, s 54(6). Curiously, this would seem to exclude the permanent trustee if he is not the applicant. It is also unclear how 'any creditor' other than a creditor applicant would be in a position to make representations, since there is no provision for notification of creditors or advertisement, so that they would appear to be able to find out only by chance.
[38] Ibid.
[39] 1993 SC 307 .
[40] (Sh Ct) 1993 SCLR 718.

plc v Davidson. Earlier cases had taken the more cautious approach of interim deferment of the discharge if either or both stages could not be dealt with prior to the expiry of the three years.[41]

The Act does not give any guidance as to the grounds for deferring a discharge, but some good reason will be required. This was emphasised in *Crittal Warmlife Ltd v Flaherty*,[42] where deferment for four years to allow the trustee to claim the debtor's pension was refused. In *Watson v Henderson*[43] deferral was granted to allow the trustee to sist himself in an action for reparation by the debtor, although, in the light of recent case-law, it is not clear that such a step would now be necessary and thus a justifiable ground for a deferral of discharge.[44] It has been held that the debtor's conduct alone can justify deferral of the discharge,[45] but it is suggested that the better view is that although conduct is undoubtedly relevant, it is only one factor and ought not to be used as the sole ground for deferring a discharge. Whatever the reasons for which deferral of discharge is sought, they must be clearly set out in the application.[46]

If discharge is deferred, the debtor may apply at any time thereafter for a discharge.[47] Further applications for deferment may be made by the permanent trustee or a creditor.[48]

Discharge by composition

The debtor may also obtain his discharge by making an acceptable offer of composition. A composition is an agreement between the debtor and the debtor's creditors whereby the creditors agree to discharge the debtor on part payment of their debts. Compositions are competent at common law and may be used as an alternative to the sequestration process,[49] but they may also be used to bring a sequestration to an end.[50] In the latter case, the special procedure set out in Sched 4 to the 1985 Act must be followed, and the composition is known as a judicial composition.

The debtor may make an offer of composition at any time after the issue of the act and warrant to the permanent trustee.[51] The offer is put to the commissioners or, where there are no commissioners, the Accountant in Bankruptcy,[52] to decide whether the offer should be put to the creditors.[53] The composition must propose payment of at least 25 pence in the pound.[54] If it is submitted to the creditors, and if a majority in number and at least two-thirds in value of them

---

[41] *Pattison v Halliday* 1991 SLT 645.

[42] 1988 GWD 22–930. See also *Whittaker's Tr v Whittaker*, note 40 above.

[43] (Sh Ct) 1988 SCLR 439.

[44] See Chapter 22.

[45] *Nicol's Tr v Nicol* 1996 GWD 10–531. See also Jones, 'Deferral of Debtor's Discharge' (1995) 40 JLSS 388.

[46] *Chowdhury's Tr v Chowdhury* (Sh Ct) 1996 SCLR 948 (Notes).

[47] 1985 Act, s 54(8). A suitably modified version of the procedure for the original application for deferment is followed.

[48] 1985 Act, s 54(9). The same procedure applies as in the original application for deferment.

[49] See Chapter 45.

[50] 1985 Act, s 56.

[51] 1985 Act, Sched 4, para 1.

[52] 1985 Act, Sched 4, para 2.

[53] 1985 Act, Sched 4, para 3.

[54] Ibid.

accept it,[55] the offer goes to the sheriff for approval.[56] The sheriff fixes a hearing[57] and then decides whether to approve the composition. If he does approve it, further sundry procedure follows and the debtor and the permanent trustee are then discharged[58] and the sequestration is brought to an end.[59] The debtor is reinvested in his assets[60] and can use them to generate the income needed to make the payments agreed in the composition.

If the debtor defaults or for some other reason the composition cannot continue, the composition may be recalled and the sequestration revived.[61]

The attraction of this procedure for the debtor is that if the offer of composition is accepted, it is possible to obtain a discharge more quickly than is provided for in s 54 of the 1985 Act.[62]

---

[55] 1985 Act, Sched 4, para 5.
[56] 1985 Act, Sched 4, para 6.
[57] 1985 Act, Sched 4, para 7.
[58] 1985 Act, Sched 4, para 11.
[59] 1985 Act, Sched 4, para 13, and see further Chapter 40.
[60] 1985 Act, Sched 4, para 16(a).
[61] 1985 Act, Sched 4, para 17.
[62] It is a curious feature of the legislation that there does not seem to be a provision for the debtor to obtain a discharge less than three years from the date of sequestration other than by way of a discharge by composition, even if the administration of sequestration has been completed before that time, although this is unlikely to happen often.

37 : THE EFFECT OF INSOLVENCY PROCEEDINGS: COMPANY INSOLVENCY

This chapter examines the effect of the various company insolvency proceedings on the company and its officers.

Company voluntary arrangements

Status and corporate powers of the company

The company's status and corporate powers as such will remain unaffected by a CVA: the whole essence of CVAs is that they are arrangements between the company and its creditors and members.

Effect of company voluntary arrangements on officers of the company generally

The directors and other officers of the company will remain in office during the CVA. The directors' powers to act on behalf of the company, however, will depend on the terms of the CVA itself.[1]

Duties of the company's officers in relation to the company voluntary arrangement

Various specific duties are imposed on the current, and in some cases former, directors and other officers of the company in connection with the procedures leading up to the approval of the CVA. Some of these have already been considered in context, such as the duty of the directors where they have proposed the CVA to provide additional information to the nominee.[2] Generally, however, no sanctions are specified for failure to comply with these duties. During the currency of the CVA, the directors and other officers of the company will require to fulfil their statutory duties in the normal way.

Offences

The 1986 Act and the Scottish Rules create a variety of offences connected with the various company insolvency proceedings,[3] but there are very few connected specifically with CVAs. However, it is specifically provided that it is an offence

---

[1] See further Chapter 23.
[2] Scottish Rules, rule 1.16.
[3] Some of these are discussed further below. Sched 10 to the 1986 Act summarises the offences created under that Act itself.

for a past or present officer of the company, including a shadow director, to make any false representation or commit any fraud for the purposes of achieving the approval of a CVA.[4]

Discharge of the company

The approval of the CVA has the effect of discharging the original claims of creditors who are bound by the agreement and substituting whatever claims have been provided for in the agreement: the new obligations created by the CVA are legally substituted for the original obligations by virtue of the statutory provisions—a process known as statutory novation. Where the CVA is subsequently fully implemented, the company will be discharged of these debts by their payment; where the CVA is not fully implemented, the creditors will have a claim for any unpaid balance of the sums due to them in terms of the CVA.

Section 425 arrangements

Status and corporate powers of the company

The company's status and corporate powers as such will remain unaffected by a section 425 arrangement: as with CVAs, the essence of such arrangements is that they are arrangements between the company and those with whom it is concluded.

Effect of the section 425 arrangement on officers of the company generally

The directors and officers of the company will remain in office during the currency of the section 425 arrangement. The directors' powers to act on behalf of the company, however, will depend on the terms of the section 425 arrangement itself.[5]

Duties of the company's officers in relation to the section 425 arrangement

There are some specific duties imposed on the directors and other officers of the company in connection with the procedures leading up to the approval of the section 425 arrangement. Some of these have already been considered in context—for example, the duty of the directors to furnish the company with such information as needs to be included in the statement circulated with the notice summoning the required meetings.[6] During the currency of the section 425 arrangement, the directors and other officers of the company will require to fulfil their statutory duties in the normal way.

Offences

Failure to comply with specific duties in relation to the section 425 arrangement is an offence. For example, where the company fails to comply with the requirement to attach a copy of the court's order sanctioning the arrangement to all copies of its memorandum or other constituting instrument, all officers of the company who are in default are liable to a fine,[7] and directors who fail to furnish

---

[4] Scottish Rules, rule 1.24.
[5] See further Chapter 23.
[6] See Chapter 9.
[7] CA 1985, s 425(4).

the company with such information as needs to be included in the statement circulated with the notice summoning the required meetings are similarly liable to a fine.[8]

Discharge of the company

As with a CVA, the approval of a section 425 arrangement will discharge the original claims of creditors bound by the agreement and substitute whatever obligation has been provided for in the agreement by statutory novation. Where the section 425 arrangement is subsequently fully implemented, the company will be discharged of the obligations created by it by their payment. Where the section 425 arrangement is not fully implemented, the creditors will have a claim for any unpaid balance of the sums due to them in terms of the arrangement.

Administration

Status and corporate powers of the company

The status and corporate powers of the company as such are not affected by an administration order: the company continues although it is managed by the administrator and the exercise of its corporate powers is restricted.[9]

Effect of the administration order on officers of the company generally

Unless the administrator exercises his power to remove directors,[10] they and other officers of the company will remain in office during the administration. It has already been noted, however, that the administrator effectively supersedes the directors in the management of the company and any power of the company or its officers which could be exercised in such a way as to interfere with the administrator's powers may not be exercised except with the consent of the administrator.[11]

An administrator may bring proceedings on behalf of the company against any director for breach of his fiduciary or common law duties to the company.[12]

The administrator must in all cases submit a report on the directors' conduct to the Secretary of State so that he may determine whether disqualification proceedings should be brought against any or all of the directors.[13] Disqualification is discussed further in Chapter 39.

Duties of the company's officers in administration

There are various specific duties imposed on the current, and in some cases former, directors and other officers of the company—for example, there is an obligation to provide a statement of affairs if required.[14] There is also a duty to co-operate generally with the administrator.[15] During the currency of the

---

[8] CA 1985, s 426(7).
[9] See the next paragraph.
[10] 1986 Act, s 14(2)(a), and see further Chapter 26.
[11] See Chapter 23.
[12] See further Chapter 38.
[13] Company Directors (Disqualification) Act 1986 (hereafter 'CDDA 1986'), s 7.
[14] 1986 Act, s 22, and see generally Chapter 29, which deals with recovery of documents and other information.
[15] 1986 Act, s 235, and see generally Chapter 29, which deals with recovery of documents and other information.

administration, the directors and other officers of the company will require to fulfil their statutory duties in the normal way.

Offences

Failure to comply with specific duties in relation to the administration is generally an offence, as is failure to comply with the general duty to co-operate with the administrator under s 235 of the 1986 Act. Schedule 10 to the 1986 Act lists the various offences which may be committed under that Act, together with details of the mode of prosecution, the punishment and the daily default fine where applicable.

Discharge of the company

Whether the company's debts are discharged depends on the outcome of the administration. The administration may result in the conclusion of a CVA or section 425 arrangement and the effect of such arrangements, where concluded, is discussed above. In other cases, much depends on what has happened in the course of the administration. Where creditors are paid in full in the course of the administration, their debts will be discharged by such payment in the normal way; where creditors are not so paid, or receive only part payment, in the administration itself, they will be able to pursue their debts or any outstanding balance thereof after the discharge of the administration order, unless otherwise agreed.[16]

Receivership

Status and corporate powers of the company

The status and corporate powers of the company as such are not affected by the appointment of a receiver.

Effect of receivership on officers of the company generally

The directors and other officers of the company will remain in office during the receivership. It has already been noted, however, that the receiver effectively supersedes the directors in the management of that part of the company's property which is attached by the charge.[17]

A receiver may bring proceedings on behalf of the company against any director for breach of his fiduciary or common law duties to the company.[18]

A receiver must in all cases submit a report on the directors' conduct to the Secretary of State so that he may determine whether disqualification proceedings should be brought against any or all of the directors.[19] Disqualification is discussed further in Chapter 39.

Duties of the company's officers in receivership

Some specific duties are imposed on the current, and in some cases former, directors and other officers of the company—for example, there is an obligation

---

[16] Distributions to creditors in the context of administration are discussed further in Chapter 26; see also Chapter 33.

[17] See Chapter 23.

[18] See further Chapter 38.

[19] CDDA 1986, s 7.

to provide a statement of affairs if required.[20] There is also a duty to co-operate generally with an administrative receiver.[21] During the currency of the receivership, the directors and other officers of the company will require to fulfil their statutory duties in the normal way.

Offences

Failure to comply with specific duties imposed in relation to the receivership is generally an offence, as is failure to comply with the general duty to co-operate with an administrative receiver under s 235 of the 1986 Act. Schedule 10 to the 1986 Act lists the various offences which may be committed under the Act, together with details of the mode of prosecution, the punishment and the daily default fine where applicable.

Discharge of the company

The receiver is only obliged to deal with certain categories of claims in the course of the receivership.[22] Where such debts are paid in full by the receiver, they will be discharged by such payment in the normal way, but any outstanding balance may be pursued by the creditor—for example, by claiming in the liquidation of the company.[23] Creditors whose claims are not dealt with by the receiver will require to take action in the normal way to recover the sums due to them. Where the whole of the company's property is affected by the receivership, as is the usual case, creditors will generally only be able to take such action after the conclusion of the receivership, if indeed any assets remain against which they can enforce their claims; alternatively, they will be able to claim in any subsequent liquidation of the company.

Liquidation

Status and corporate powers of the company

It is specifically provided in relation to voluntary liquidation that, even though the company must cease to carry on business after the commencement of the liquidation except so far as necessary for the beneficial winding up, the corporate state and corporate powers of the company continue until it is dissolved, even where the articles provide otherwise.[24] There is no such specific statutory provision in relation to compulsory liquidation, but logically the corporate state and powers of the company must continue in a compulsory liquidation also until the company is finally dissolved.

---

[20] 1986 Act, s 66, and see generally Chapter 29, which deals with recovery of documents and other information.

[21] 1986 Act, s 235, and see generally Chapter 29, which deals with recovery of documents and other information. The section refers only to administrative receivers, and accordingly there would not seem to be a general duty to co-operate with a receiver who is not an administrative receiver.

[22] See Chapter 27.

[23] It is specifically provided in s 61 of the 1986 Act, which deals with the disposal of property subject to a security or effectually executed diligence, that nothing in the section prejudices the right of a creditor affected by the section to claim in a liquidation.

[24] 1986 Act, s 87.

Effect of liquidation on officers of the company generally

The directors and other officers of the company will remain in office during the liquidation. However, as has already been noted, in the case of a voluntary winding up, the directors' powers cease on the passing of the resolution to wind up except to the limited extent provided for in the 1986 Act, and in the case of a compulsory liquidation, they cease on the making of a winding-up order or, if applicable, the appointment of a provisional liquidator.[25]

In certain circumstances, a director may be personally liable for certain debts of the company in liquidation. In addition, a liquidator may in certain circumstances seek a contribution from directors or other specified persons to the assets of the company. These provisions are discussed further in Chapter 38, which deals with the personal liability of directors and others generally.

A liquidator must in all cases submit a report on the directors' conduct to the Secretary of State so that he may determine whether disqualification proceedings should be brought against any or all of the directors.[26] Disqualification is discussed further in Chapter 39.

Duties of the company's officers in liquidation

A number of specific duties are imposed on the current, and in some cases former, directors and other officers of the company, such as the obligation in a compulsory liquidation to provide a statement of affairs if required.[27] There is also a general duty in all liquidations to co-operate with the liquidator.[28] During the currency of the liquidation, the directors and other officers of the company will require to fulfil their statutory duties in the normal way.

Offences

Failure to comply with the duties imposed by the legislation is generally an offence, as is failure to comply with the general duty to co-operate with the liquidator under s 235 of the 1986 Act. Schedule 10 to the 1986 Act lists the various offences which may be committed under the Act, together with details of the mode of prosecution, the punishment and the daily default fine where applicable. Specific provision is made for the matter to be referred to the Lord Advocate where it appears that, *inter alia*, any past or present officer of the company has committed a criminal offence in relation to it.[29] There is also provision, in certain circumstances, for the matter to be referred to the Secretary of State for further investigation prior to any prosecution.[30]

---

[25] See Chapter 23.

[26] CDDA 1986, s 7.

[27] 1986 Act, s 131, and see generally Chapter 29, which deals with recovery of documents and other information.

[28] 1986 Act, s 235, and see generally Chapter 29, which deals with recovery of documents and other information.

[29] 1986 Act, s 218. In the case of a compulsory liquidation, the matter is referred by the liquidator on the direction of the court, which will be given either on the liquidator's application or of its own volition. In a voluntary liquidation, the matter is referred by the liquidator directly without intervention by the court, but the court may, of its own volition or on the application of an interested person, direct the liquidator to report the matter if it appears that an offence has been committed which should have been reported, but no such report has been made.

[30] 1986 Act, s 218(5). This applies where a report is made to the Lord Advocate by a liquidator in a voluntary liquidation.

Discharge of the company

Whether the company's debts are discharged in the liquidation depends on what happens in the context of the liquidation. A company in liquidation may conclude a CVA or a section 425 arrangement with all or some classes of its creditors, and the effect of such arrangements is discussed above. A liquidator in both a voluntary and compulsory liquidation also has power to enter into a compromise with creditors or any class of them. A compromise by the liquidator using his general powers will usually provide for discharge of the company by participating creditors. Unless a debt is discharged in one of these ways, however, any balance remaining unpaid following completion of the liquidation will continue to subsist even after the company has been dissolved.[31] Thus, creditors would be able to press their outstanding claims against the company where, for example, fresh assets came to light and the company was restored to the register to allow these to be distributed to the creditors.

---

[31] Subject to the normal rules of prescription and limitation.

38 : PERSONAL LIABILITY OF DIRECTORS AND OTHERS

Where debts and liabilities are incurred by a limited company it is normally only possible to look to the company itself for satisfaction of those debts and liabilities. Shareholders normally have no personal liability for the company's debts and other liabilities by virtue of the doctrine of limited liability itself,[1] and directors and others employed by or otherwise acting on behalf of the company normally incur no personal liability for its debts and other liabilities because they are acting as agents for the company which will normally be liable for their actions on its behalf.[2] The Cork Committee was concerned about abuse of the privilege of trading with limited liability by some company directors who, because they would have no personal liability if the company failed, were either indifferent to the consequences of such failure for others or took advantage of the fact that their liability was limited to walk away from the failed company, start a new company free from the debts of the old, and repeat the whole process over again.[3] It therefore recommended, *inter alia*, new and stricter provisions regulating the circumstances in which directors and others could become personally liable either for the actual debts of the company or to make an appropriate contribution to the assets of the company on its insolvency.[4]

This chapter examines the circumstances in which directors and certain other persons can become personally liable either for the actual debts of the company or to make an appropriate contribution to its assets. These can be divided into a number of broad, sometimes overlapping, categories: breach of duty, 'misfeasance',[5] fraudulent trading, wrongful trading, involvement in the management of

---

[1] There are, of course, certain circumstances where the corporate veil may be lifted and shareholders incur personal liability. A discussion of these circumstances is, however, beyond the scope of this book and reference should be made to relevant works on company law for a full discussion.

[2] It is possible for some directors or managers, or the managing director, to have unlimited liability if this is specifically provided for in the memorandum: see Companies Act 1985, s 306, but this would be unusual.

[3] A phenomenon known as 'the phoenix syndrome'.

[4] The other main recommendation for addressing this problem was reform of the provisions on disqualification of directors and others from further involvement with limited companies. The current provisions on disqualification are discussed in the following chapter.

[5] A slightly inaccurate, but, for this purpose, convenient, term: see further below.

a company while an undischarged bankrupt, use of a prohibited company name and acting in contravention of a disqualification order.

Breach of duty

Directors have certain fiduciary duties towards their company, including a statutory duty to have regard to the interests of its employees in general when performing their functions.[6] They also owe a common law duty to the company to exercise an appropriate degree of skill and care in the performance of their functions.[7] The classic definition of the standard of skill and care required at common law is that contained in the dicta of Romer J in *Re City Equitable Fire Insurance Co Ltd*.[8] While indicating that he found it difficult to derive from the authorities a clear answer to the question as to what particular degree of skill and care was required of a director, he none the less set out three general propositions which he regarded as warranted by the reported case-law.

> '(1) A director need not exhibit in the performance of his duties a greater degree of skill than may reasonably be expected from a person of his knowledge and experience. A director of a life insurance company does not guarantee that he has the skill of an actuary or a physician. In the words of Lindley MR: "If directors act within their powers, if they act with such care as is reasonably to be expected of them, having regard to their knowledge and experience, and if they act honestly for the benefit of the company they represent, they discharge both their equitable as well as their legal duty to the company."[9] It is perhaps only another way of stating the same proposition to say that directors are not liable for mere errors of judgement. (2) A director is not bound to give continuous attention to the affairs of his company. His duties are of an intermittent nature to be performed at periodical board meetings; and at meetings of any committee of the board upon which he happens to be placed. He is not, however, bound to attend at all such meetings, though he ought to attend whenever in the circumstances, he is reasonably able to do so. (3) In respect of all duties that, having regard to the exigencies of the business, and the articles of association, may properly be left to some other official, a director is, in the absence of grounds for suspicion, justified in trusting that official to perform such duties honestly.'[10]

The standard of care represented by these propositions is at a very basic level. In *Re D'Jan of London Ltd*[11] Lord Justice Hoffmann (as he then was) took the

---

[6] A detailed discussion of the fiduciary duties owed by directors to the company is beyond the scope of this book, but can be found in most company law texts: see also the Joint Consultation Paper issued by the Law Commission and the Scottish Law Commission, Company Directors: Regulating Conflicts of Interests and Formulating a Statement of Duties (LC Consultation Paper 153/SLC Discussion Paper 105 (1998)) which contains a good discussion of fiduciary duties. The statutory duty to have regard to the interests of the company's employees is set out in s 309 of CA 1985.

[7] *Re City Equitable Fire Insurance Co Ltd* [1925] Ch 407.

[8] Ibid.

[9] *Lagunas Nitrate Co v Lagunas Syndicate* [1899] 2 Ch 392 at 435.

[10] [1925] Ch 407 at 427.

[11] [1994] 1 BCLC 561.

view that the common law standard of care could now be equated with the standard of care owed by a director under s 214 of the Insolvency Act 1986,[12] a standard which, as will be seen below, is somewhat higher than that set out in *Re City Equitable Fire Insurance Co Ltd*. He did not, however, give any reasons for making this assertion, and it is not therefore clear on what basis this departure from previous authority is justified.[13]

Directors also have a duty to the company to consider the interests of the company's creditors—at least when the company is at or near insolvency—although there may be some doubt about the precise nature and extent of this duty.[14, 15]

If any of the duties owed to the company are breached, the company may take action against the directors with a view to recovering damages for the breach. In practice, such actions will rarely be taken while the company remains in the hands of the directors because the power to bring them rests primarily with the directors themselves, and they are generally unlikely to instruct such actions. However, where the directors have been superseded by an insolvency office holder on the commencement of formal insolvency proceedings such as administration, receivership or liquidation, an action may be brought by the office holder on behalf of the company. Where the company is in liquidation, the action should be brought under s 212 of the 1986 Act, which is discussed in the following section.

Summary remedy against delinquent directors and others

A summary remedy against delinquent directors and others, sometimes referred to, in England at least, as a 'misfeasance action', is provided for in s 212 of the 1986 Act. The section provides that on the application of the liquidator or any creditor or contributory of a company, the court may examine the conduct of specified persons where it appears that such a person has misapplied, retained or become accountable for any money or other property of the company, or has been guilty of any misfeasance or breach of any fiduciary or other duty in relation

---

[12] Discussed further below. See also *Norman v Theodore Goddard* (1992) BCC 14, where the same judge (then Hoffmann J) adopted part of the section 214 test in determining a director's duty at common law.

[13] The Law Commission and the Scottish Law Commission in their Joint Consultation Paper on Company Directors: Regulating Conflicts of Interests and Formulating a Statement of Duties (note 6 above) explore a number of options for reform in relation to the duty of care encompassing both the form of the duty itself and various mechanisms for its enforcement.

[14] The case-law is not always consistent. See, in particular, *Walker v Wimborne* (1976) 50 ALJR 446e; *Lonrho Ltd v Shell Petroleum Co Ltd* [1980] 1 WLR 627; *Re Horsley & Weight Ltd* [1982] 3 All ER 1045; *Multinational Gas and Petrochemical Co v Multinational Gas and Petrochemical Services Ltd* [1983] 3 WLR 492; *Nicholson v Permakraft (NZ) Ltd* [1985] 1 NZLR 242; *Winkworth v Edward Baron Development Co Ltd* [1986] 1 WLR 1512; *Kinsela v Russell Kinsela Pty Ltd (in liquidation)* (1986) 4 NSWLR 722; *West Mercia Safetywear Ltd v Dodd* [1988] BCLC 250; *Re Welfab Engineers Ltd* (1990) BCC 600; *Facia Footwear Ltd v Hincliffe* [1998] 1 BCLC 218; and *Yukong Line Ltd v Rendsburg Investments Corporation (No 2)* [1998] 1 WLR 294, which trace the history of this duty. See also Finch, 'Creditor's Interests and Director's Duties' 1990 OJLS 265; Grantham, 'Directors' Duties and Insolvent Companies' 54 MLR 576; MacCann, 'Directors' Duties: To Whom Are They Owed?' 1991 ILT 3, 30.

[15] A director might also owe a duty to a particular individual creditor on the normal principles of delict: see *Williams v Natural Life Health Foods Ltd* [1998] 1 WLR 830. This, however, is a different matter.

to the company.[16] The persons whose conduct may be examined are any person who is or has been an officer of the company, any person who has acted as liquidator, administrator or administrative receiver of the company, or any person who is or has been otherwise concerned in, or taken part in, the promotion, formation or management of the company.[17] Where such a person is found to have misapplied, retained or become accountable for money or property of the company, the court may order him to repay, restore or account for any such money or property (or any part of such money or property), with interest at such rate as the court thinks just;[18] where he is found to have been guilty of misfeasance or breach of duty, the court may order him to contribute such sum to the company's assets as the court thinks just.[19]

The section applies only on the winding up of the company.[20] It does not create any substantive rights, but provides a procedural mechanism for enforcing an existing claim.[21] It covers a wide variety of conduct.[22] For example, in *Re D'Jan of London Ltd*[23] a director signed a proposal form for fire insurance containing incorrect information without reading it, with the result that when a claim was made under the policy the insurance company was able to repudiate it. In an action brought under s 212 of the 1986 Act, it was held that the director had breached his common law duty of care and skill to the company. In *West Mercia Safetywear Ltd (in liquidation)* v *Dodd*[24] it was held that a director had breached his duty to a company by causing it to transfer funds to another company in order to reduce his liability under a guarantee granted in respect of the second company, even though the first company was actually indebted to the second company at the time of the transfer. The section cannot, however, be used as a means of obtaining information on which to base a claim,[25] nor is an application under the section an appropriate way of dealing with what is in effect a breach of interdict.[26]

Strict rules of pleading do not apply to actions brought under this section: all that is required is that the defender be given fair notice of the case against him.[27]

---

[16] 1986 Act, s 212(1), (3). A contributory's application requires leave of the court, but he need not show that he will benefit from any order made as a result of the application: 1986 Act, s 212(5).

[17] Where the application relates to a person who has acted as liquidator or administrator of a company and who has had his release, leave of the court is required: 1986 Act, s 212(4).

[18] 1986 Act, s 212(3)(a).

[19] 1986 Act, s 212(3)(b).

[20] 1986 Act, s 212(1).

[21] For a recent restatement of this principle, see *Ross* v *Davy* (OH) 1996 SCLR 369. One aspect of the fact that the claim must be actionable in the general law is that it must not have prescribed: this was the issue which arose in *Ross* v *Davy*. The court pointed out that the prescriptive period applicable to any particular claim depended on the nature of the claim, irrespective of the means adopted to enforce it (ie, s 212). In that particular case, the claim was essentially one based on fraudulent breach of trust and was therefore imprescriptible.

[22] In *Ross* v *Davy*, above, for example, it was said that 'breach of fiduciary or other duty' might at one end of the spectrum include simple carelessness and at the other extend to acts which were, on any view, criminal in the narrowest sense of the word, and there was scope for considerable overlap between such breach of duty and misapplication of funds.

[23] Note 11 above.

[24] [1988] BCLC 250.

[25] *Gray* v *Davidson* 1991 SLT (Sh Ct) 61.

[26] *Canon (Scotland) Business Machines Ltd* v *GA Business Systems Ltd (in liquidation)* 1993 SLT 386.

[27] *Blin* v *Johnstone* 1988 SLT 335; see also *Ross* v *Davy*, note 21 above.

Where an application under s 212 of the 1986 Act is made in respect of a person to whom s 727 of CA 1985 applies, that person may invoke the latter section in the section 212 proceedings. Section 727(1) of CA 1985 provides:

'If in any proceedings for negligence, default, breach of duty or breach of trust against an officer of a company or a person employed by a company as auditor (whether he is or is not an officer of the company) it appears to the court hearing the case that the officer or person is or may be liable in respect of the negligence, default, breach of duty or breach of trust, but that he has acted honestly and reasonably, and that having regard to all the circumstances of the case (including those connected with his appointment) he ought fairly to be excused for the negligence, default, breach of duty or breach of trust, the court may relieve him, either wholly or partly, from his liability on such terms as it thinks fit.'

Section 727(2) of CA 1985 provides that an application for relief may be made to the court in advance of any proceedings where these are reasonably apprehended.

Section 727 of CA 1985 was successfully invoked in *Re D'Jan of London Ltd.*[28] Although the director was found to be negligent in signing the insurance proposal without reading it, the court granted relief under s 727 of CA 1985 to the extent of limiting the amount of compensation to be paid to the company to an amount equivalent to future dividends which the director would have received from the liquidation. The court said that the breach of duty was not gross, and that although the company was of course a separate legal entity, the commercial reality of the situation was that it was effectively the director's own money that was being put at risk since he owned 99 per cent of the company's shares.

Where the court has ordered a defender to return money or property to the company, or has ordered him to make a contribution to the company's assets, the question will arise as to how any such property, money or contribution is to be dealt with in the context of the liquidation where there is a floating charge over the company's assets. It has been said that any such property, money or contribution should be regarded as being caught by an appropriately worded floating charge, since the substantive rights being vindicated in the proceedings are assets of the company even though they are being vindicated by the liquidator.[29] In this respect, the position under s 212 would appear to be different both from the position under ss 213 and 214 of the 1986 Act[30] and the position with regard to property or money which has been recovered as a result of gratuitous alienations or unfair or fraudulent preferences.[31]

Fraudulent trading

The current provisions on civil liability for fraudulent trading are contained in s 213 of the 1986 Act, which provides that where any business of the company has been carried on with intent to defraud creditors (whether creditors of the company or creditors of any other person) or for any fraudulent purpose, the liquidator

[28] Note 11 above.
[29] St Clair and Drummond Young, *The Law of Corporate Insolvency in Scotland* (2nd edn), p 141.
[30] See below.
[31] See Chapter 30.

may apply to the court for an order that any person who was knowingly a party to the carrying on of the business in that way make such contributions to the company's assets as the court thinks proper.[32] The section applies only on a winding up.[33] Essentially a re-enactment of the previous provisions on fraudulent trading,[34] it differs from them in that only the liquidator may bring an action under s 213 of the 1986 Act whereas, under the previous provisions, an action could be brought by a creditor or contributory as well as the liquidator.

There are no reported cases on s 213 of the 1986 Act itself, but the case-law on its statutory predecessors shows that in order to establish liability for fraudulent trading, there must be fraud in the criminal sense.[35] In *Re Patrick and Lyon Ltd*[36] Maughan J said that 'the words "defraud" and "fraudulent purpose" ... are words which connote actual dishonesty involving, according to current notions of fair trading amongst commercial men, real moral blame'.[37] It is up to the applicant (ie, the liquidator) to show the necessary dishonesty.[38] In *Re William C. Leitch Bros Ltd*[39] it was held that if a company continued to carry on business and incur debts at a time when there was, to the knowledge of the directors, no reasonable prospect of the creditors ever receiving payment of those debts, it would in general be a proper inference that the company was carrying on business with intent to defraud,[40] but other authorities recognised the so-called 'light at the end of the tunnel' defence, whereby fraudulent trading was held not to be established if the person against whom the action was brought demonstrated a genuine belief that creditors would be paid off one day, however unreasonable that belief actually was.[41]

Where an application under s 213 of the 1986 Act is made in respect of a person to whom s 727 of CA 1985 applies, the question arises as to whether that section may be invoked in the same way as it may be in relation to an action under s 212 of the 1986 Act.[42] It is thought that it cannot. The requirements for invoking s 727 of CA 1985 (honesty and reasonableness) seem to be completely incompatible with the intent necessary to establish fraudulent trading.

Where fraudulent trading is established, the court may order the person against whom liability has been established to make such contributions (if any) to the company's assets as the court thinks proper. In *Re Cyona Distributors Ltd*,[43] a case decided under s 332 of the Companies Act 1948, it was held that the sum ordered to be paid could include a penal element as well as a compensatory element, and this approach was followed in *Re a Company (No 001418 of 1988)*,[44] decided

---

[32] Fraudulent trading is also a criminal offence under s 458 of CA 1985.

[33] In contrast to the criminal provision ibid.

[34] Section 630 of CA 1985, derived with some amendments from s 332 of the Companies Act 1948, in turn derived from s 275 of the Companies Act 1929.

[35] *Rossleigh v Carlaw* 1986 SLT 204. Fraud in the criminal sense involves an intent to defraud, or at least a reckless indifference as to whether creditors are defrauded.

[36] [1933] Ch 786.

[37] Ibid at 790.

[38] *Re Patrick and Lyon Ltd*, note 36 above.

[39] [1932] 2 Ch 71.

[40] See also *R v Grantham* [1984] QB 675, where a similar view was taken in a criminal prosecution under the predecessor of s 458 of CA 1985.

[41] See, for example, *Re White and Osmond (Parkstone) Ltd*, 30th June 1960 (unreported), discussed in *Re Produce Marketing Consortium Ltd (No 2)* [1989] BCLC 520 at 549.

[42] The terms of s 727 of CA 1985 are set out above.

[43] [1967] Ch 889.

[44] (1990) BCC 526.

under s 630 of CA 1985.[45] It is thought that such an approach would also be open under s 213 of the 1986 Act given the wide discretion available to the court under that section. In *Re a Company (No 001418 of 1988)*[46] the view was also expressed that the compensatory element should be limited to the amount of the debts of the creditors proved to have been defrauded by the fraudulent trading,[47] and it was said that the usual order on an application by a liquidator was for any sum ordered to be paid to be dealt with as part of the general assets of the liquidation. Under the statutory predecessors of s 213 of the 1986 Act, which provided that a person who was knowingly party to fraudulent trading was liable for all or any of the debts of the company as the court might direct, it was open to the court to order payment direct to particular creditors,[48] but this would no longer seem to be an option under s 213 of the 1986 Act, since the provision is for a contribution to be made to the company's assets. However, a question may arise as to how any sum ordered to be paid under s 213 of the 1986 Act is to be dealt with in the context of the liquidation where there is a floating charge over the company's assets. In *Re Produce Marketing Consortium Ltd (No 2)*[49] it was assumed that contributions ordered to be paid under s 214 of the 1986 Act as a result of a finding of wrongful trading would be attached by any appropriately worded floating charge[50] and, if this were correct, it would seem logical that the same approach be taken in relation to contributions ordered under s 213 of the 1986 Act. The correctness of the assumption made in *Re Produce Marketing Consortium Ltd (No 2)* has, however, been doubted[51] and it has been suggested that in relation to both ss 213 and 214 of the 1986 Act, in contrast to the position in relation to s 212 of the 1986 Act, the better view is that any contribution ordered under either section should go into the general pool of assets available to meet the claims of all creditors and should not be regarded as being attached by a floating charge.[52]

Wrongful trading

The provisions on wrongful trading are contained in s 214 of the 1986 Act.[53] They were introduced on the recommendation of the Cork Committee, who felt that the provisions on fraudulent trading were inadequate to deal with directors who continued to trade when the company was insolvent. They felt that

[45] Cf the position in a claim for wrongful trading, below.
[46] Note 44 above.
[47] Cf the formulation in a claim for wrongful trading, below.
[48] See, for example, *Re Cyona Distributors Ltd*, note 43 above.
[49] Note 41 above.
[50] See further below.
[51] See St Clair and Drummond Young, *The Law of Corporate Insolvency in Scotland* (2nd edn), pp 141–142.
[52] Ibid. Part of their argument for this position is that any right under ss 213 and 214 (unlike a right under s 212 of the 1986 Act) does not, and never has done, inhere in the company, but arises only on liquidation and vests in the liquidator. This argument is strengthened by the decision in *Re Oasis Merchandising Services Ltd* (1995) BCC 911, in which it was held that an agreement to assign part of the benefit of a claim under s 214 of the 1986 Act was invalid because it was not property of the company but could only be pursued by the liquidator as part of his statutory duties. The position in relation to s 212 is discussed above.
[53] In fact, the term 'wrongful trading' is used only as the headnote to the section and does not appear in the section itself, but that term is commonly used to describe the provisions of s 214 and will be so used here.

irresponsible or unreasonable behaviour on the part of directors deserved sanction just as much as dishonest behaviour, but was inappropriately escaping it because of the strict requirements for establishing fraudulent trading.[54] Their original recommendation was for one all-embracing provision on 'wrongful trading' which would encompass the existing notion of fraudulent trading but be much wider. However, s 214 of the 1986 Act, which adopted a different formulation from that suggested by the Cork Committee, was ultimately enacted in addition to the provisions on fraudulent trading now contained in s 213 of the 1986 Act, although in practice the terms of s 214 of the 1986 Act are sufficiently wide to encompass conduct which would fall within s 213.

The liquidator of a company may apply to the court for an order that a past or present director of the company contribute such sums (if any) as the court thinks proper to the company's assets where the conditions specified in s 214(2) of the 1986 Act are satisfied.[55] These conditions are that the company has gone into insolvent liquidation[56] and that at some time prior to the commencement of the liquidation, the director, being a director at that time, either knew or ought to have known that there was no reasonable prospect of the company avoiding such insolvent liquidation.[57] The court has a discretion with regard to the making of an order under the section, but it must not make an order if it is satisfied that after the director knew or ought to have known that insolvent liquidation was not reasonably to be avoided, he took every step that he ought to have taken with a view to minimising the loss to the company's creditors.[58] Section 214(4) of the Act provides that, for the purposes of s 214(2) and (3), the facts which a director ought to know or ascertain, the conclusions which he ought to reach and the steps which he ought to take are those which would be known or ascertained, or reached or taken by a reasonably diligent person having both (a) the general knowledge, skill and experience that may reasonably be expected of a person carrying out the director's functions (including those with which he has been entrusted but has not carried out)[59] and (b) the general knowledge, skill and experience that the director has.

The section does not define the type of conduct which amounts to wrongful trading, but sets a qualitative standard against which the conduct of a director is to be measured. This standard is part objective (based on the general knowledge, skill and experience that may reasonably be expected of a person carrying out the director's functions) and part subjective (based on the general knowledge, skill and experience that the director has). If the objective part of the standard is not to be deprived of content, the subjective element must be interpreted as applying only where it results in a higher standard of conduct being expected from the

---

[54] These have already been discussed above.

[55] 1986 Act, s 214(1). 'Director' includes a shadow director: 1986 Act, s 214(7). A shadow director is a person in accordance with whose instructions the directors of the company are accustomed to act, although a person is not a shadow director by reason only that the directors act on advice given by him in a professional capacity: 1986 Act, s 251. Nor is a person a shadow director only because he is a director of another company which is a director of the company in liquidation: *Re Hydrodam (Corby) Ltd (in liquidation)* (1994) BCC 161.

[56] 1986 Act, s 214(2)(a). For the purposes of the section, a company goes into insolvent liquidation if it goes into liquidation at a time when it cannot pay its debts and other liabilities and the expenses of the winding up: 1986 Act, s 214(6).

[57] 1986 Act, s 214(2)(b).

[58] 1986 Act, s 214(3).

[59] 1986 Act, s 214(5).

particular director than would otherwise be indicated by the objective standard. This approach seems to be reflected in the (relatively few) cases under the section. The section therefore sets a minimum objective standard of conduct for directors.

The cases decided under the section provide some guidance as to the types of conduct which may result in liability under s 214 of the 1986 Act, but it is up to the court to decide precisely when a director has fallen short of the requisite standard of conduct and each case will turn on its own facts. Some general guidance on how the standard is to be interpreted was, however, given in the leading case on s 214 of the 1986 Act, *Re Produce Marketing Consortium Ltd (No 2)*.[60] In that case, Knox J said that the test to be applied under the section was one 'under which the director in question is to be judged by the standards of what can reasonably be expected of a person fulfilling his functions, and showing reasonable diligence in doing so'.[61] He went on to say that it was necessary to have regard to the particular company and its business, because the general knowledge, skill and experience expected will be much less in a small company in a modest way of business, with simple accounting procedures and equipment, than in a large company with sophisticated procedures.[62] Nevertheless, he continued, certain minimum standards would be assumed to be attained. Directors had statutory obligations in relation to accounts. These accounts were, in the instant case, woefully late, but the knowledge to be imputed to directors was not limited to documentary material which was actually available. The case would therefore proceed on the basis that the directors had had knowledge of what the relevant accounts would have disclosed had they been available at the time when they should have been, even though in fact they were not available until later. This was information which directors should have ascertained or been able to ascertain.

The pleadings should contain all the information necessary to allow the court to draw the relevant conclusions and to give sufficient notice to the defender of the case being made against him. They will usually specify the date on which it is alleged that he either knew that insolvent liquidation was unavoidable or ought to have concluded this. It is thought, however, that the liquidator is not bound to suggest specific dates for the court to consider and that even where he does so the court is not restricted to considering any particular date or dates suggested by the liquidator and is free to determine the matter itself.[63] A strict approach to pleadings in cases of this kind is not appropriate so long as fair notice is given.[64]

Given the objective standard set out in s 214 of the 1986 Act, it is irrelevant for the purposes of establishing liability under the section that the directors were honest and genuinely believed that they would be able to turn the company

---

[60] Note 41 above.

[61] At 550.

[62] Ibid. This statement is perhaps somewhat simplistic, but the important point is that the standard must be related to the particular circumstances of the company in question.

[63] Cf *Re Sherborne Associates Ltd* (1995) BCC 40, where the court held that the case was not made out in relation to the dates suggested by the liquidator and that the liquidator could not argue for another date not specified in the pleadings. It is thought this is incorrect: see McKenzie, 'Wrongful Trading - A Paper Tiger?' 1996 JR 519; *Palmer's Company Law*, para 15.723, n 41.1.

[64] See discussion on this point in relation to s 212 of the 1986 Act, above. As s 214 of the 1986 Act involves a similar type of action, the same reasoning applies.

round.[65] In *Re Produce Marketing Consortium Ltd (No 2)*[66] Knox J was careful to point out the difference between the provisions on fraudulent trading, where actual dishonesty was required,[67] and the new provisions on wrongful trading, which widened the circumstances in which a director might be found liable to contribute to the assets of a company on insolvency and in the context of which there was no need to show dishonesty.[68] The only defence which a director might put forward is that contained in s 214(3) of the 1986 Act, in terms of which the court is directed not to make an order if it is satisfied that after the director first knew or ought to have concluded that insolvent liquidation could not reasonably be avoided, he took all the steps he ought to have taken to minimise the loss to the company's creditors. It is up to the director to establish this,[69] but the test is very high and may be virtually impossible to establish in many cases.[70] The appropriate steps will vary with the circumstances of the company: in some circumstances, resignation may be appropriate, in others not; in some circumstances, ceasing trading may be appropriate, in others not. Directors may therefore find it difficult to know exactly what they should do. The question has arisen as to whether a director might utilise s 727 of CA 1985 in the context of an action against him under s 214 of the 1986 Act.[71] In *Re Produce Marketing Consortium Ltd*[72] Knox J held that as a matter of law relief under s 727 is not available in the context of an action under s 214 of the 1986 Act, on the basis that the tests involved in the two sections are entirely different and cannot be applied in the same case. In the later case of *Re DKG Contractors Ltd*,[73] although an argument on s 727 of CA 1985 was rejected on the facts (the court held that the directors had been honest, but they had not acted reasonably), the availability of relief under that section was not questioned. The matter was not the subject of argument, however, and there was no reference to the decision in *Re Produce Marketing Consortium Ltd*. It is suggested that the approach taken in the latter case is the correct one.

Where wrongful trading is established, the court may order payment of such contribution (if any) to the company's assets as the court thinks proper. The section contains no guidelines as to when a contribution should be ordered or the factors to be taken into account in determining its amount. In *Re Produce Marketing Consortium Ltd (No 2)*[74] Knox J took the view that the jurisdiction under the section was primarily compensatory rather than penal and stated that, prima facie, the appropriate contribution would be the amount by which the company's assets had been depleted by the conduct of the director which had

---

[65] Although this may be a factor to be taken into account in fixing the amount of the contribution: see below.
[66] Note 41 above.
[67] See above.
[68] See pp 549–550.
[69] For a contrary view, see Sealy and Milman, *Annotated Guide to the 1986 Insolvency Legislation* (4th edn), p 256. However, when the issue arose in *Re Produce Marketing Consortium Ltd (No 2)* (note 41 above) and *Re DKG Contractors Ltd* (1990) BCC 903, the way in which it was treated suggests that the onus is on the director to establish this if he wishes to do so.
[70] See the article by McKenzie, note 63 above.
[71] The terms of s 727 of CA 1985 are set out above.
[72] [1989] BCLC 513.
[73] Note 69 above.
[74] Note 41 above.

given rise to the liability under the section.[75] He was careful to emphasise, however, the width of the discretion under the section and the undesirability of seeking to spell out limits on that discretion. This would seem to indicate that a penal element to a contribution under this section cannot be ruled out on principle. In deciding the amount of the contribution in *Re Produce Marketing Consortium Ltd (No 2)*, Knox J took into account the nature of the conduct which had given rise to the liability; the fact that there was no fraudulent intent; there was no deliberate wrongdoing; actual lies counted against the director; ignoring a solemn warning by the company auditor; guarantees by the directors; and the fact that the contribution should benefit unsecured creditors. Clearly, the relevant factors will vary from case to case. The amount of the contribution may also be affected by any other liability which the director may have to contribute to the assets of the company: it would appear that, generally, the amount of the contribution will be adjusted in the light of any other contribution which the director is required to make to the company's assets—for example, under s 212 of the 1986 Act.[76]

It was specifically stated in *Re Purpoint Ltd* that the court had no jurisdiction to direct that payments be made to particular creditors or to direct that the contribution should be used to pay particular classes of creditors.[77] As to whether the contribution is attached by any floating charge, see the discussion in relation to s 213 of the 1986 Act above.

Procedural aspects of fraudulent and wrongful trading actions

The liquidator is entitled to give evidence himself in relation to the application and to call witnesses.[78] Where the court orders a contribution to be made, it may also give further directions to give effect to its ruling,[79] including providing for the liability of the person against whom the order has been made to be secured on specified assets of that person[80] and for enforcement of any such security.[81] In addition, it may direct that the whole or any part of any debt (including interest) owed by the company to the person held liable be postponed to all other debts and interest owed by the company.[82]

Liability under the sections is independent of (and may therefore arise in addition to) any (potential) criminal liability arising out of the conduct on which it is based.[83]

---

[75] This approach was specifically adopted in *Re Purpoint Ltd* (1991) BCC 121; see also *Re DKG Contractors Ltd*, note 69 above.

[76] See *Re Purpoint Ltd* and *Re DKG Contractors Ltd*.

[77] This is not inconsistent with Knox J's dictum in *Re Produce Marketing Consortium Ltd (No 2)* (note 41 above) that the contribution should benefit ordinary creditors, as this was said only in the context of fixing the amount of the contribution (presumably with a view to achieving that effect).

[78] 1986 Act, s 215(1).

[79] 1986 Act, s 215(2).

[80] 1986 Act, s 215(2)(a).

[81] 1986 Act, s 215(2)(b).

[82] 1986 Act, s 215(4).

[83] 1986 Act, s 215(5).

Involvement by an undischarged bankrupt in the management of a company

An undischarged bankrupt who is involved in the management of a company, in contravention of s 11 of the Company Directors (Disqualification) Act 1986 (hereafter 'CDDA 1986'), and any person involved in the management of the company who acts or is willing to act on his instructions, is personally liable for specified debts of the company.[84]

The relevant provisions are discussed in the context of disqualification in Chapter 39, to which reference should be made.

Use of prohibited company name

A person who is involved in the management of a company with a prohibited name, in contravention of s 216 of the 1986 Act, and any person involved in the management of the company who acts or is willing to act on his instructions, is personally liable for specified debts of the company.[85]

The relevant provisions are discussed in the context of disqualification in Chapter 39, to which reference should be made.

Acting in contravention of a disqualification order

A person who is involved in the management of a company in contravention of a disqualification order made under CDDA 1986, and any person involved in the management of the company who acts or is willing to act on his instructions, is personally liable for specified debts of the company.[86]

The relevant provisions are discussed in the context of disqualification in Chapter 39, to which reference should be made.

---

[84] CDDA 1986, s 15.
[85] 1986 Act, s 217.
[86] CDDA 1986, s 15.

39 : DISQUALIFICATION

It was noted in the previous chapter that the Cork Committee was concerned about abuse of the privilege of trading with limited liability by some company directors and that one of its principal recommendations for dealing with such abuse was wide-ranging reform of the then existing provisions on disqualification of persons from acting as directors of, or in certain other defined capacities in relation to, companies. Their recommendations were in the main accepted and the current, much-extended, provisions on disqualification are now contained principally in the Company Directors (Disqualification) Act 1986 (hereafter 'CDDA 1986'). This chapter examines the current provisions on disqualification.

The disqualification provisions can be divided into two types: those which automatically disqualify a person from acting as a director or engaging in other specified activities in relation to a company without the leave of the court, and those which provide for a person to be so disqualified only on the making of an order to that effect by an appropriate court. Provisions of the former type are contained in both CDDA 1986 and in the 1986 Act itself, and are described in the next section; provisions of the latter type are contained in CDDA 1986 and are described in the sections which follow thereafter.

CDDA 1986 applies to building societies and incorporated friendly societies in the same way as it applies to companies—references to companies, directors, officers of companies, etc, being amended accordingly in these cases.[1] Specified sections of CDDA 1986 also apply to European Economic Interest Groupings, again with references to companies, directors, officers of companies, etc, being amended accordingly.[2] For ease of reference, this chapter refers only to companies, directors, etc, when discussing CDDA 1986, but its extended application should be borne in mind.[3]

Circumstances in which a person may not act as director

This section deals with the circumstances where a person is automatically (ie, without any specific order being made) prohibited from acting as a director of, or participating in certain other activities in relation to, a company.

---

[1] CDDA 1986, ss 22A and 22B respectively.
[2] European Economic Interest Groupings Regulations 1989, reg 20.
[3] Reference should be made to the relevant provisions for the precise amendments which apply.

Undischarged bankrupts

It is an offence for an undischarged bankrupt to act as a director of a company, or to be concerned with or take part in the promotion, formation or management of a company, without the leave of the court.[4] 'Company' for this purpose includes an unregistered company and any company incorporated outside Great Britain which has an established place of business in Great Britain.[5] Any application for leave should be made to the court which awarded sequestration of the bankrupt's estates.[6] The court has unfettered discretion to grant or refuse such leave.

An undischarged bankrupt who acts in any of the ways described also incurs personal liability for specified debts of the company,[7] as does any person who is involved in the management of the company and who acts, or is willing to act, on his instructions knowing that he is an undischarged bankrupt acting without the leave of the court.[8] The undischarged bankrupt himself is personally liable for such debts and liabilities as were incurred by the company at any time when he was involved in its management,[9] and a person involved in the management of the company and acting or willing to act on the undischarged bankrupt's instructions is personally liable for those debts and liabilities incurred by the company at any time when he was acting or willing to act on the undischarged bankrupt's instructions.[10] In both cases, liability is joint and several with the company and any other person who is also liable for the specified debts, whether under s 15 of CDDA 1986 or otherwise.[11]

Companies with prohibited names

A person who was a director or shadow director of a company ('the liquidating company') within the 12 months preceding its going into insolvent liquidation is prohibited from engaging in a number of activities.[12] He is prohibited, without the leave of the court, from:

> (1) acting as a director of, or directly or indirectly being concerned with or taking part in the promotion, formation or management of, a company with a prohibited name and

> (2) directly or indirectly being concerned with or taking part in the carrying on of any business which, although not being carried on by a company, is being carried on under a prohibited name

---

[4] CDDA 1986, s 11(1). 'Director' includes a position which is effectively that of a director even if called by another name: see CDDA 1986, s 22(4).

[5] CDDA 1986, s 22(2)(a).

[6] CDDA 1986, s 11(2).

[7] CDDA 1986, s 15(1)(a).

[8] CDDA 1986, s 15(1)(b). A person is involved in the management of a company if he is a director or is directly or indirectly concerned in, or takes part in, the management of a company: CDDA 1986, s 15(4). Such a person is deemed to be willing to act on the instructions of an undischarged bankrupt at any time after he has actually done so, unless the contrary is proved: CDDA 1986, s 15(5).

[9] CDDA 1986, s 15(3)(a).

[10] CDDA 1986, s 15(3)(b).

[11] CDDA 1986, s 15(2).

[12] 1986 Act, s 216(1). 'Director' includes someone occupying the position of director however designed and 'shadow director' means someone in accordance with whose instructions the directors of the company are accustomed to act, except that a person will not be a shadow director where the directors are acting on his advice given in a professional capacity: 1986 Act, s 251.

for a period of five years from the time the liquidating company went into liquidation.[13]

For the purposes of the section, 'company' includes a company which may be wound up under Part V of the 1986 Act,[14] and a company goes into insolvent liquidation if it goes into liquidation at a time when its assets are insufficient for payment of its debts and liabilities and the expenses of the winding up.[15] A prohibited name is one by which the liquidating company was known at any time within the 12 months prior to the liquidation, or one which is so similar to any such name as to suggest an association with that company.[16]

An application for leave to engage in any of the otherwise prohibited activities may be made to any court with jurisdiction to wind up companies.[17] The court may call on the liquidator or any former liquidator of the liquidating company for a report of the circumstances in which that company became insolvent and, if applicable, the extent to which the applicant was responsible for the insolvency.[18] The court has unfettered discretion to grant or refuse such leave, but it has been held that since the purpose of the section is to protect both the creditors of the liquidating company (in particular against the risk of the assets being sold to the new company at an undervalue) and the creditors of the new company (in particular against the risk that they will be misled into thinking that the business is being carried on by the same company), where there is no risk of these things happening, leave should be granted.[19]

There are some circumstances in which a person may engage in activities which would otherwise be prohibited by s 216 of the 1986 Act without the leave of the court.

(1) Where a company (referred to as 'a successor company') acquires the whole or substantially the whole of an insolvent company's business under arrangements made by the latter's liquidator, administrator, receiver or supervisor of a company voluntary arrangement and it gives effective notice to the insolvent company's creditors in terms of rule 4.80 of the Scottish Rules, any person named in the notice with a view to being a proposed director of the successor company or otherwise associated with it may act in relation to it in any of the ways which would otherwise be prohibited by s 216 of the 1986 Act without the leave of the court.[20] To be effective, the notice must be given to all the creditors of the insolvent company of whose addresses the successor company is aware within 28 days of the completion of the relevant arrangements and must contain the name and registered number of the insolvent company, details of the circumstances in which the successor company acquired its business, the (prohibited) name which the successor company has assumed or proposes to assume for the purpose of the carrying on of the business and any change of name

---

[13] 1986 Act, s 216(3).
[14] 1986 Act, s 216(8). Part V of the 1986 Act deals with the winding up of unregistered companies.
[15] 1986 Act, s 216(7).
[16] 1986 Act, s 216(2).
[17] 1986 Act, s 216(5).
[18] Scottish Rules, rule 4.79.
[19] *Penrose* v *Official Receiver* [1996] 1 WLR 482. For a good discussion of leave and a review of the case-law, see Milman, 'Curbing the Phoenix System' 1997 JBL 224.
[20] Scottish Rules, rule 4.80(1),(4).

which it has made or proposes to make for that purpose.[21] It must also give details of the nature and duration of the named person's directorship of the insolvent company.[22]

(2) Where a director or shadow director of the liquidating company applies for leave of the court under s 216 of the 1986 Act within seven days of the date that the liquidating company went into liquidation, he may act in any of the ways which would otherwise be prohibited by s 216 of the 1986 Act for a prescribed period without leave of the court.[23] The pre-scribed period is the lesser of six weeks from the date on which the company went into liquidation or the period until the court determines the application.[24]

(3) Where the company with the prohibited name has been known by that name for the whole of the 12 months preceding the liquidation of the liquidating company and it has not at any time within that 12 months been dormant, leave to act in any of the ways which would otherwise be prohibited by s 216 of the 1986 Act is not required.[25]

A person acting in contravention of s 216 of the 1986 Act is liable to a fine or imprisonment[26] and the offence is a strict liability offence: no *mens rea* is required.[27] He will also incur personal liability for specified debts of the company,[28] as will any person who is involved in the management of the company and who acts, or is willing to act, on the instructions of a person whom he knows to be acting in contravention of s 216.[29] The person acting in contravention of s 216 is personally liable for such debts and liabilities as were incurred by the company at any time when he was involved in its management,[30] and a person involved in the management of the company and acting or willing to act on the instructions of the person in contravention of s 216 is personally liable for debts and liabilities incurred by the company at any time when he was acting or was willing to act on that person's instructions.[31] In both cases, liability is joint and several with the company and any other person who is also liable for the specified debts, whether under s 217 of the 1986 Act or otherwise.[32]

---

[21] Scottish Rules, rule 4.80(2).

[22] Scottish Rules, rule 4.80(3).

[23] Scottish Rules, rule 4.81.

[24] Scottish Rules, rule 4.81(2).

[25] Scottish Rules, rule 4.82. The rule defines 'dormant' by reference to s 252(2) of CA 1985, which no longer exists: the current provision of CA 1985 is s 250(3), which provides that a company is dormant during any period in which no significant accounting transaction (ie, one which requires to be entered in the company's accounting records by s 221 of CA 1985) occurs, disregarding specified share transactions. The lack of a consequential amendment was presumably an oversight.

[26] 1986 Act, s 216(4). It has been held that a community service order is also a competent disposal: *R v Cole* [1998] 2 BCLC 234.

[27] *R v Cole*.

[28] 1986 Act, s 217(1)(a).

[29] 1986 Act, s 217(1)(b). A person is involved in the management of a company if he is a director or is directly or indirectly concerned in, or takes part in, the management of a company: 1986 Act, s 217(4). Such a person is deemed to be willing to act on the instructions of an undischarged bankrupt at any time after he has actually done so, unless the contrary is proved: 1986 Act, s 217(5).

[30] 1986 Act, s 217(3)(a).

[31] 1986 Act, s 217(3)(b).

[32] 1986 Act, s 217(2).

Disqualification orders generally

This section and the following sections deal with the circumstances in which a person may be disqualified by an appropriate court from acting as a director of, or engaging in certain other activities in relation to, a company, and the procedural aspects of such disqualification. This section begins by dealing with disqualification orders generally.

A disqualification order is an order made by an appropriate court which disqualifies a person, without the leave of the court, from being a director, liquidator, administrator, receiver or manager of a company or being concerned, or taking part, in any way, directly or indirectly, in the promotion, formation or management of a company for a set period beginning with the date of the order.[33] 'Company' includes a company which may be wound up under Part V of the 1986 Act.[34] The use of the word 'person' in CDDA 1986 means that not only individuals but bodies corporate may be the subject of a disqualification order.

Maximum periods, and in the case of orders under s 6 of CDDA 1986 a minimum period, of disqualification are set out in relation to each ground on which a disqualification order may be made.[35]

An order may be made on grounds which consist of or include matters which have not yet been the subject of criminal proceedings but may be so at a later stage.[36] Where a disqualification order is made against a person who is already subject to a disqualification order, the periods of disqualification run concurrently.[37]

CDDA 1986 sets out six grounds on which a disqualification order may be made. Although not formally divided into parts, its provisions are grouped under various headings and the six grounds on which a disqualification order may be made are grouped under three such headings: disqualification for general misconduct in relation to companies; disqualification for unfitness; and other grounds for disqualification. The following three sections follow this classification and examine the various grounds on which a disqualification order may be made.

Disqualification for general misconduct in connection with companies

Disqualification on conviction of indictable offence

A disqualification order may be made against a person who has been convicted of an indictable offence in connection with the promotion, formation, management or liquidation of a company, or with the receivership of its property.[38]

So long as the offence was indictable, it does not matter whether the proceedings which gave rise to the conviction were actually on indictment or were summary proceedings.[39] The definition of an indictable offence is that

---

[33] CDDA 1986, s 1(1). 'Director' includes a position which is effectively that of a director, howsoever called: see CDDA 1986, s 22(4).
[34] CDDA s 22(2)(b). Part V of the 1986 Act deals with the winding up of unregistered companies.
[35] CDDA 1986, s 1(2).
[36] CDDA 1986, s 1(4).
[37] CDDA 1986, s 1(3).
[38] CDDA 1986, s 2(1).
[39] Ibid.

contained in Sched 1 to the Interpretation Act 1978, which is applied to Scotland for the purposes of this section.[40]

There is no minimum period of disqualification under this section. The maximum period is five years where the order is made by a court of summary jurisdiction and 15 years in any other case.[41]

Disqualification for persistent breaches of companies legislation

A disqualification order may be made against a person who has been persistently in default in relation to certain provisions of the companies legislation, namely those which require returns, accounts or documents to be filed with the Registrar of Companies, or notice of any matter to be given to him.[42]

Persistent default is not defined, but it is specifically provided that, without prejudice to its proof by any other means, it will be conclusively proved that a person has been persistently in default of such provisions if it is proved that, in the five years ending with the date of an application under this section, he has been guilty of three or more defaults in relation to them.[43] A person is guilty of a default in relation to the relevant provisions of the companies legislation where he is convicted of an offence consisting of a contravention of, or failure to comply with, such a provision[44] or a default order is made against him.[45] A default order is an order under any of the following provisions in respect of a contravention of, or failure to comply with, that provision:[46]

(1) Section 242(4) of CA 1985 (order requiring delivery of company accounts).

(2) Section 245B of CA 1985 (order requiring preparation of revised accounts).

(3) Section 713 of CA 1985 (enforcement of company's duty to make returns).

(4) Section 170 of the Insolvency Act 1986 (enforcement of liquidator's duty to make returns).

There is no minimum period of disqualification under this section. The maximum period is five years.[47]

Disqualification for fraud, etc, in a winding up

A disqualification order may be made against a person if, in the course of the winding up of a company, it appears that he has been guilty of fraudulent trading under s 458 of CA 1985, whether he has been convicted of that offence or not; that he has otherwise been guilty of fraud in relation to the company while an officer, liquidator or receiver of the company; or that he has been guilty of any breach of duty as such officer, liquidator or receiver of the company.[48] 'Officer' includes a shadow director.[49]

---

[40] CDDA 1986, s 2(2).
[41] CDDA 1986, s 2(3).
[42] CDDA 1986, s 3(1). 'Companies legislation' is defined in s 22(7) of CDDA 1986.
[43] CDDA 1986, s 3(2).
[44] CDDA 1986, s 3(3)(a).
[45] CDDA 1986, s 3(3)(b).
[46] Ibid.
[47] CDDA 1986, s 3(5).
[48] CDDA 1986, s 4(1).
[49] CDDA 1986, s 4(2).

There is no minimum period of disqualification under this section. The maximum period is 15 years.[50]

Disqualification on conviction of summary offences

A disqualification order may be made against a person who is convicted of a prescribed summary offence in specified circumstances.[51]

A prescribed summary offence for this purpose is one which involves a contravention of, or failure to comply with, provisions of the companies legislation which require returns, accounts or documents to be filed with the Registrar of Companies, or notice of any matter to be given to him.[52] 'Summary offence' is given the same meaning as in Sched 1 to the Interpretation Act 1978, which is applied to Scotland for the purposes of this section.[53] It does not matter whether the contravention or failure was on the part of the person himself or on that of the company.[54]

A disqualification order may be made where the person has been convicted of any such offence and, in the period of five years ending with the date of that conviction, he has accumulated not less than three convictions for such offences or three default orders or any combination of three such offences or default orders.[55] 'Default orders' in this context are the same as default orders in the context of s 3(3)(b) of CDDA 1986.[56] The offence giving rise to the disqualification order and any other offence of which he was convicted at the same time may count towards the required total.[57]

There is no minimum period of disqualification under this section. The maximum period is five years.[58]

Disqualification for unfitness

Disqualification of unfit directors of insolvent companies

A disqualification order must be made against a person if he is or has been a director of a company which has at any time become insolvent and the court is satisfied that his conduct as a director of that company, taken alone or in conjunction with his conduct as a director of any other company or companies, makes him unfit to be concerned in the management of a company.[59] 'Director' includes a shadow director[60] and any person occupying the position of director however designed,[61] and it is irrelevant that a director had ceased to be a director at the time the company actually became insolvent.[62] This is by far the most common ground of disqualification.

---

[50] CDDA 1986, s 4(3).
[51] CDDA 1986, s 5(1).
[52] Ibid.
[53] CDDA 1986, s 5(4)(a).
[54] CDDA 1986, s 5(1).
[55] CDDA 1986, s 5(3).
[56] CDDA 1986, s 5(4)(b). Default orders under that subsection are discussed above.
[57] CDDA 1986, s 5(3).
[58] CDDA 1986, s 5(5).
[59] CDDA 1986, s 6(1).
[60] CDDA 1986, ss 6(3) and 22(4).
[61] CDDA 1986, s 22(4).
[62] CDDA 1986, s 6(1).

For the purposes of disqualification on this ground, a company becomes insolvent where it goes into insolvent liquidation when its assets are insufficient for the payment of its debts, liabilities and the expenses of the winding up *or* an administration order is made *or* an administrative receiver is appointed.[63]

CDDA 1986 does not attempt to define what constitutes unfitness: the matter is one for the court. However, s 9(1) of CDDA 1986 provides that in determining unfitness, the court must have regard in particular to the matters set out in Part I of Sched 1 to CDDA 1986 and, where the company has become insolvent, to the matters mentioned in Part II of that Schedule also. 'Insolvent' has the same meaning as it does in s 6 itself;[64] in the context of disqualification under s 6 of CDDA 1986, therefore, the court will need to have regard to all the matters listed in Sched 1 to that Act. These are currently as follows.

Part I (All cases)

(1) Any misfeasance or breach of any fiduciary or other duty by the director in relation to the company.

(2) Any misapplication or retention by the director of, or any conduct by the director giving rise to an obligation by the director to account for, any money or other property of the company.

(3) The extent of the director's responsibility for the company entering any transaction which is liable to be set aside under Part XVI of the 1986 Act (provisions against debt avoidance).[65]

(4) The extent of the director's responsibility for any failure by the company to comply with any of the following provisions of CA 1985:
   (a) s 221 (companies to keep accounting records)
   (b) s 222 (where and for how long records to be kept)
   (c) s 288 (register of directors and secretaries)
   (d) s 352 (obligation to keep and enter up register of members)
   (e) s 353 (location of register of members)
   (f) s 363 (duty of company to make annual returns)
   (h) ss 399 and 415 (company's duty to register charges it creates).[66]

(5) The extent of the director's responsibility for any failure by the directors to comply with the following provisions of CA 1985:
   (a) s 226 or 227 (duty to prepare annual accounts)
   (b) s 233 (approval and signature of accounts).

Part II (Insolvency)

(6) The extent of the director's responsibility for the causes of the company becoming insolvent.

(7) The extent of the director's responsibility for any failure by the company to supply any goods or services which have been paid for in whole or in part.

---

[63] CDDA 1986, s 6(2).

[64] CDDA 1986, s 9(2), applying the definition contained in CDDA 1986, s 6(2): see above.

[65] It should be noted that the provisions of Part XVI of the 1986 Act apply to England and Wales only, and not to Scotland.

[66] Section 399 of the 1985 Act applies to England and Wales; s 415 applies to Scotland.

(8) The extent of the director's responsibility for the company entering into any transaction or giving any preference, being a transaction or preference

    (a) liable to be set aside under s 127 of the 1986 Act or ss 238 to 240 of the 1986 Act or

    (b) challengeable under s 242 or 243 of the 1986 Act or any rule of law in Scotland.[67]

(9) The extent of the director's responsibility for any failure by the directors of the company to comply with s 98 of the 1986 Act (duty to call creditors' meeting in voluntary winding up).

(10) Any failure by the director to comply with any obligation imposed on him by or under any of the following provisions of the 1986 Act:

    (a) s 22 (company's statement of affairs in administration)

    (b) s 47 (statement of affairs to administrative receiver)[68]

    (c) s 66 (statement of affairs in Scottish receivership)

    (d) s 99 (directors' duty to attend meeting; statement of affairs in creditors' voluntary winding up)

    (e) s 131 (statement of affairs in winding up by the court)

    (f) s 234 (duty of anyone with company property to deliver it up)

    (g) s 235 (duty to co-operate with liquidator, etc).

The provisions of Schedule 1 may be modified by statutory instrument.[69]

Since the court is only directed to have regard to these matters *in particular*, it is free to take other relevant matters into account[70] and, as noted, the director's conduct in relation to companies other than the insolvent company may also be taken into account. In *Re Godwin Warren Control Systems plc*[71] it was held that a director's conduct in relation to companies other than the insolvent company must have some nexus with the conduct complained of in relation to the insolvent company before it could be taken into account. Chadwick J said that if that were not so, a director whose conduct was blameless in relation to the insolvent company would be at risk of disqualification if his conduct in relation to other (unconnected and not insolvent) companies was not satisfactory, and that where conduct in relation to companies other than the insolvent company was quite independent of conduct in relation to the insolvent company, it could not be taken into account. In *Secretary of State for Trade and Industry v Ivens*,[72] however, the English Court of Appeal disagreed with this approach, holding that where there was evidence relating to companies, the only connection required was that the director was a director of all of the companies concerned, including the insolvent company, and that his conduct in relation to each showed that he was unfit to be concerned in the management of a company. The court said that to

---

[67] Sections 238–240 of the 1986 Act relate to transactions at an undervalue and preferences in England and Wales: though different in effect, they equate with the statutory Scottish provisions on gratuitous alienations and unfair preferences mentioned here. Such transactions are, however, challengeable at common law also in Scotland, hence the reference to any other rule of law in Scotland. For the Scottish rules on challengeable transactions generally, see Chapter 30.

[68] This section relates to England and Wales only.

[69] CDDA 1986, s 9(4), (5).

[70] See further below.

[71] (1992) BCC 557.

[72] (1997) BCC 396.

imply any further connection would be contrary to the purpose of CDDA 1986: there was no requirement in that Act that any of the other companies of which the director was a director should have become insolvent, and accordingly the fact that such a company was insolvent was neither a necessary nor a sufficient connection. The court also held that the conduct complained of in relation to the other companies need not be of the same type as that complained of in relation to the insolvent company. This represents a much broader approach to the role of conduct in relation to companies other than the insolvent company.

Previous cases under the section give some guidance as to the type of conduct which will result in disqualification, but the courts themselves have been careful to say that they cannot and will not limit the discretion of future courts by laying down guidelines as such, so previous cases should be treated as illustrative only. Subject to that caveat, some general guidance as to what will constitute unfitness can be gleaned from the cases, although the approaches taken are not always consistent. There seems to be no doubt that conduct which is actively dishonest will render a director unfit, but conduct falling short of actual dishonesty is more problematic. In one of the earliest cases, *Re Bath Glass Ltd*,[73] it was said that for unfitness to be established, there must have been a serious failure or failures on the part of director to perform those duties of directors attendant on the privilege of trading with limited liability and it did not matter whether the failures were deliberate or arose through incompetence. But the degree of incompetence required to render a director unfit has also proved to be problematic. In *Re Stanford Services Ltd*[74] the disqualification was based on the director's recklessness, a concept which actually seems to go beyond incompetence altogether. In *Re Lo-Line Electric Motors Ltd*[75] it was said that ordinary commercial misjudgment was insufficient to render a director unfit, and that there must be 'a lack of commercial probity' involved, although it was conceded that disqualification would be appropriate in extreme cases of 'gross negligence or total incompetence'. A similar approach was taken in *Re Dawson Print Group Ltd*,[76] where the court took the view that in order to be unfit, the director must have been guilty of conduct which, if not really dishonest, was at least in breach of standards of commercial morality, or of 'some really gross incompetence which persuades the court that it would be a danger to the public if he were to be allowed to continue to be involved in the management of companies'. In *Re Sevenoaks Stationers (Retail) Ltd*,[77] however, the court expressly disapproved the idea that incompetence had to be total, referring instead to 'incompetence or negligence of a very marked degree'. The exact degree of incompetence necessary to render a director unfit may therefore be regarded as in some doubt. Further, incompetence seems to be treated as distinct from conduct which breaches the standards of commercial morality, with the latter forming an alternative basis for a finding of unfitness. This also raises questions, however, about exactly what type of conduct will be held to fall below the expected standards of commercial morality and thereby render a director unfit. It has been said that not every falling off of standards which ought to be maintained by a company director will necessarily

---

[73] (1988) 4 BCC 130.
[74] [1987] BCLC 607.
[75] (1988) 4 BCC 415.
[76] (1987) BCC 322.
[77] [1991] Ch 164.

be 'of so blameworthy a character as to be stigmatised as a breach of commercial morality'.[78]

The uncertainty over exactly what constitutes unfitness is further complicated by two other factors. One is the fact that whereas under the previous law disqualification for unfitness was discretionary, under s 6 of CDDA 1986 disqualification is mandatory once unfitness is found. The courts may therefore be taking into account in deciding whether a director is unfit at all matters which previously would have been taken into account only in deciding whether or not to disqualify once unfitness had been established. The other is the purpose for which a disqualification order is made. It may be regarded as a penal sanction or as a protective measure to protect the public from the future actions of the unfit director. Both approaches may be found in the cases although the weight of authority tends to emphasise the latter. The perception of the purpose of the order may have a bearing on the court's view of unfitness as, for example, in the case of *Re Dawson Print Group Ltd*, where the court thought that in order to establish unfitness, the director's actions had to be so incompetent that they demonstrated a danger to the public if he were not disqualified.[79] On the other hand, in *Re Stanford Services Ltd*[80] the fact that the director did not intend to act as a director again in the future, so that it might have been said that there was no danger to the public in the future, did not prevent the making of a disqualification order.

A clear definition of unfitness therefore remains elusive. The cases do show, however, that specific types of conduct can generally be regarded as being indicative of sufficient incompetence or sufficient blameworthiness to result in a finding of unfitness. For example, in *Re Firedart Ltd*[81] Arden J identified a number of matters which he said, if proved, would generally lead to the conclusion that a director was unfit to be concerned in the management of a company. These included trading while insolvent, taking personal benefits over and above any proper remuneration and failing to keep proper accounting records. Trading at the expense of creditors will generally be regarded as a breach of commercial morality and therefore lead to a finding of unfitness.[82] It has also been held that remaining on the board of the company will not necessarily lead to a finding of unfitness if this is done in order to protest against continuing trading and to try to bring such trading to an end, but remaining for the purpose of collecting fees and for the status involved after it was clear that such protests would avail nothing would be regarded as unfitness.[83]

Relevant convictions may be taken into account in assessing unfitness even where they would otherwise be regarded as spent.[84]

---

[78] *Re ECM (Europe) Electronics Ltd* [1992] BCLC 814.

[79] The different approaches to the purpose of the order also impact on various other aspects of disqualification, notably the issue of the burden of proof which is discussed further below.

[80] Note 74 above.

[81] [1994] 2 BCLC 340.

[82] *Re Sevenoaks Stationers (Retail) Ltd*, note 77 above. Prior to this case, there had been conflicting decisions at first instance over whether trading at the expense of the Crown was even more blameworthy than trading at the expense of other creditors. This case clarified the position by confirming that trading at the expense of the Crown was no more blameworthy than trading at the expense of other creditors. Rather, the issue was whether the forbearance of creditors, whoever they were, had been taken advantage of.

[83] *Secretary of State for Trade and Industry v Taylor* [1997] 1 WLR 407.

[84] *Secretary of State for Trade and Industry v Queen* 1998 SLT 735.

The minimum period of disqualification under this section is two years, the maximum 15 years. In the case of *Re Sevenoaks Stationers (Retail) Ltd*,[85] the English Court of Appeal divided disqualification periods into three 'brackets' and set out guidelines for determining the appropriate period of disqualification as follows.

'(i) The top bracket of disqualification for periods over 10 years should be reserved for particularly serious cases. These may include cases where a director who has already had one period of disqualification imposed on him falls to be disqualified yet again. (ii) The minimum bracket of two to five years should be applied where, although disqualification is mandatory, the case is, relatively, not very serious. (iii) The middle bracket of disqualification from six to ten years should apply for serious cases which do not merit the top bracket.'[86]

This approach has also been adopted in Scotland.[87] Within those guidelines, however, the matter is still one for the discretion of the court. Again, the cases provide some illustrations of the factors which the court may take into account in determining the length of the disqualification period. For example, in *Re Rolus Properties Ltd*[88] the court reduced the disqualification from a four-to-six-year period to the minimum two years because the director had relied on professional advice. The court will not, however, take into account the length of time the director has effectively been prevented from acting as a director while the disqualification proceedings were pending in deciding on the length of the disqualification order.[89]

Disqualification after investigation of company

A disqualification order may be made against a person who is or has been a director or shadow director of any company in certain circumstances following investigation of a company.[90] Such an order may be made on the application of the Secretary of State where he deems that it is expedient to do so as a result of *either* a report made by inspectors under s 437 of CA 1985 *or* s 94 or 177 of the Financial Services Act 1986 *or* information or documents obtained under s 447 or 448 of CA 1985, s 105 of the Financial Services Act 1986, s 2 of the Criminal Justice Act 1987, s 28 of the Criminal Law (Consolidation) (Scotland) Act 1995 or s 83 of the Companies Act 1989.[91] It may be made where the court is satisfied that the conduct of the person in question in relation to that company is such as to make him unfit to be concerned in the management of a company.[92]

---

[85] Note 77 above.

[86] Dillon LJ, ibid, p 174.

[87] See, for example, *Secretary of State for Trade and Industry v Marshall* 1994 GWD 19–1151; *Secretary of State for Trade and Industry v Palfreman* 1995 SLT 156.

[88] (1988) 4 BCC 446.

[89] *Secretary of State for Trade and Industry v Arif* [1997] 1 BCLC 34.

[90] CDDA 1986, s 8. 'Director' includes someone occupying the position of director however designed and 'shadow director' means someone in accordance with whose instructions the directors of the company are accustomed to act, except that a person will not be a shadow director where the directors are acting on his advice given in a professional capacity: CDDA 1986, s 22(4) and (5) respectively.

[91] CDDA 1986, s 8(1).

[92] CDDA 1986, s 8(2).

As with disqualification for unfitness under s 6 of CDDA 1986, there is no definition of what constitutes unfitness: the matter is one for the court. However, the court must have regard in particular to the matters set out in Part I of Sched 1 to CDDA 1986 and, where the company has become insolvent, to the matters mentioned in Part II of that Schedule also.[93] The court may also take other relevant matters into account.

There is no minimum period of disqualification under this section. The maximum period is 15 years.[94] The guidelines set out in the *Sevenoaks* case as to the appropriate period of disqualification under s 6 of CDDA 1986 have been applied to disqualification under this section also.[95]

Other cases of disqualification

A disqualification order may be made against a person if he is found liable to contribute to the assets of a company under s 213 or 214 of the 1986 Act (fraudulent or wrongful trading respectively).[96]

Such an order may be made whether an application for disqualification was made or not.[97]

There is no minimum period of disqualification under this section. The maximum period is 15 years.[98]

Procedure for obtaining a disqualification order

In certain cases a disqualification order may be made by a court following on from its conviction of, or other finding of liability against, the person concerned; where a disqualification order is not considered by that court, and in all other cases, an application for a disqualification order on the appropriate ground or grounds must be made to the specified court. This section deals with the procedure for the making of applications for disqualification orders in appropriate cases.

Which court?

A disqualification order under s 2 of CDDA 1986 may be made by the court which convicted the person of the offence in question or, on application, by any court having jurisdiction to wind up the company in respect of which the relevant offence was committed.[99] A disqualification order under s 3 of CDDA 1986 may be made, on application, by any court having jurisdiction to wind up the company in relation to which the relevant offence or default was committed.[100] A

---

[93] CDDA 1986, s 9(1). 'Insolvent' has the same meaning as in s 6 of CDDA 1986: CDDA 1986, s 9(2), applying the definition contained in CDDA 1986, s 6(2), discussed above. The matters contained in Sched 1 are set out above in the context of disqualification under s 6 of CDDA 1986.

[94] CDDA 1986, s 8(4).

[95] *Re Samuel Sherman plc* (1991) BCC 699.

[96] CDDA 1986, s 10(1). The headnote refers only to wrongful trading, but the section clearly applies to both.

[97] Ibid.

[98] CDDA 1986, s 10(2).

[99] CDDA s 2(2).

[100] CDDA 1986, s 3(4).

disqualification order under s 4 of CDDA 1986 may be made, on application, by any court having jurisdiction to wind up the company in relation to which the relevant offence or breach of duty was committed.[101] A disqualification order under s 5 of CDDA 1986 may be made by the court which convicted the person of the relevant prescribed summary offence.[102] Section 16(2) of CDDA 1986,[103] in setting out who may make an application where that application is made to a court having jurisdiction to wind up the company, includes a reference to such an application being made under s 5 of CDDA 1986, but the latter section does not provide for an order to be made other than by the court which convicted the person of the relevant prescribed summary offence: there is therefore a discrepancy in these provisions.

A disqualification order under s 6 of CDDA 1986 is made, on application, where the insolvent company is being wound up by the court, by the court by which the company is being wound up;[104] where it is being wound up voluntarily, by any court having jurisdiction to wind up the company;[105] where it is in administration, by the court which made the administration order[106] and, in any other case, by the Court of Session.[107] The court to which the application should be made is determined at the time of the application. So, for example, where a company was being wound up by the court at the time the application for disqualification was made, but the winding up had been preceded by a receivership, the application should have been made to the court which was dealing with the winding-up proceedings, and not to the Court of Session.[108]

A disqualification order under s 8 of CDDA 1986 is made, on application, by the Court of Session.[109]

A disqualification order under s 10 of CDDA 1986 is made by the court which made the finding of liability under s 213 or 214 of the 1986 Act; it may be made whether or not an application for disqualification was made.[110]

Who may apply?

Applications under ss 2, 3, 4 or 5 of CDDA 1986 to a court having jurisdiction to wind up companies may be made by the Secretary of State *or* the liquidator (if applicable), any past or present member or any creditor of any company in relation to which the person against whom the disqualification order is sought committed or allegedly committed the relevant offences or defaults.[111]

---

[101] CDDA 1986, s 4(2).
[102] CDDA 1986, s 5(2).
[103] Discussed further below.
[104] CDDA 1986, s 6(3)(a).
[105] CDDA 1986, s 6(3)(b).
[106] CDDA 1986, s 6(3)(c).
[107] CDDA 1986, s 6(3)(d). See also further below in relation to procedure.
[108] See *Secretary of State for Trade and Industry* v *Barnett* 1998 SLT 63.
[109] CDDA 1986, s 8(3).
[110] CDDA 1986, s 10(1).
[111] CDDA 1986, s 16(2). It has already been noted that there is a discrepancy between this section and s 5 of CDDA 1986, because s 16(2) seems to imply that a disqualification order may be made on application to a court having jurisdiction to wind up companies, while s 5 appears to envisage disqualification only by the court which convicts of the relevant offence(s).

Applications under s 6 of CDDA 1986 may only be made by the Secretary of State[112] where he considers it expedient in the public interest.[113] Liquidators, administrators and administrative receivers are under an obligation to report cases where it appears to them that a person is unfit to be concerned in the management of a company to the Secretary of State[114] and the Secretary of State has power to seek information from the liquidator, administrator or administrative receiver about the conduct of any person as a director of the company in order to allow him to decide whether to apply for a disqualification order.[115] He may also require the liquidator, administrator or administrative receiver to produce for inspection relevant books, papers and other records for that purpose[116] and where the information, books, papers or other records sought are not forthcoming, he may apply for an order from the court requiring the office holder to comply with his request within such time as the court may direct.[117]

Applications under s 8 of CDDA 1986 may be made by the Secretary of State only, where he considers it expedient in the public interest.[118]

In practice, the administration of cases involving applications by the Secretary of State under s 6 of the CDDA 1986 is handled by the Insolvency Service (an executive agency of the Department of Trade and Industry) through its Disqualification Unit in Edinburgh.

Time-limits

An application under s 6 of CDDA 1986 must be made within two years of the company becoming insolvent, unless the leave of the court is obtained to present it outwith that time-limit.[119] The time-limit will be complied with where the application is presented to the court within that time: it is unnecessary for the application to have been served on the defender, or even the appropriate warrant for service to have been granted, within the two-year period.[120] Where the company is subject to successive insolvency régimes, the time-limit runs from the time the company first became insolvent within the meaning of s 6(2) of CDDA 1986, unless the company regained solvency in the meantime.[121] So where, for example, a receivership is followed immediately by a liquidation, the time-limit will run from the time the company went into receivership and not from the time it went into liquidation.

In considering whether to grant leave to allow an application to be made late, the court will take into account matters such as the length of the delay, the

---

[112] CDDA 1986, s 7(1). In England and Wales, where the order is being sought against a person who is or has been a director of a company being wound up in England and Wales, the application may alternatively be made by the official receiver on the Secretary of State's directions.

[113] CDDA 1986, s 7(1).

[114] CDDA 1986, s 7(3). The report is made on a prescribed form: see the Insolvent Companies (Reports on Conduct of Directors) (Scotland) Rules 1996 (SI 1996/1910), which also provided for certain returns to be made by the office holder in addition to the report under s 7.

[115] CDDA 1986, s 7(4).

[116] Ibid.

[117] Insolvent Companies (Reports on Conduct of Directors) (Scotland) Rules 1996, rule 6.

[118] CDDA 1986, s 8(1).

[119] CDDA 1986, s 7(2).

[120] *Secretary of State for Trade and Industry v Josolyne* 1990 SLT (Sh Ct) 48; *Secretary of State for Trade and Industry v Normand* 1994 SLT 1249.

[121] *Re Tasbian Ltd (No 1)* [1991] BCLC 54. For the meaning of insolvency under this subsection, see above.

reasons for the delay, the strength of the evidence against the director and the degree of prejudice to the director.[122] It would seem that where leave to present the application late is sought only after the two-year time-limit has expired, leave may be more difficult to obtain.[123]

Form of application

An application to the sheriff is made by way of a summary application[124] and to the Court of Session by petition.[125] Where the application is to a court with jurisdiction to wind up companies, the person intending to make the application must give 10 clear days' notice of his intention to do so to the person against whom the disqualification order is to be sought so that he may appear and be heard if he so wishes.[126] However, it has been held that this requirement is directory and not mandatory and the court may therefore waive it if appropriate.[127]

Hearing and standard of proof

Where the proceedings are in the sheriff court, affidavit evidence may be substituted for parole evidence where the application proceeds as unopposed[128] and in an unopposed application in the Court of Session the court may be satisfied without evidence. Otherwise, the hearing will proceed in the normal way. In England and Wales the Practice Direction (Companies Court: Directors Disqualification)[129] provides for a simplified procedure whereby the parties prepare an agreed schedule of facts, which also sets out areas of dispute which it is proposed not to pursue, and agree on the general level of disqualification appropriate. These matters are then placed before the court. If the court is satisfied that disqualification itself and the proposed length of the disqualification are appropriate, it may agree to proceed on the basis of those submissions. This procedure was first adopted in the case of *Re Carecraft Construction Co Ltd*[130] and has been given formal standing by the Practice Direction. There is no equivalent to the Practice Direction in Scotland although it would always be open to the parties to agree any facts which are not in dispute by joint minute.[131]

In England and Wales also, some cases have been dealt with by the court accepting from the person against whom the disqualification order is sought an undertaking not to act in any of the ways in which he would be prohibited from acting if he were actually disqualified, in lieu of making a disqualification order.[132] Acceptance of such an undertaking is, however, a matter for the discretion of the court: it has been held that it was not an abuse of process for the Secretary of State to continue with proceedings for disqualification where an undertaking had

---

[122] See *Secretary of State for Trade and Industry* v *Carmichael* (1995) BCC 679.
[123] See *Re Crestjoy Products Ltd* [1990] BCLC 677.
[124] Act of Sederunt (Company Directors Disqualification) 1986 (SI 1986/2296), para 3(1).
[125] Court of Session Rules, rule 74.33.
[126] CDDA 1986, s 16(1).
[127] *Secretary of State for Trade and Industry* v *Lovat* 1996 SC 32.
[128] Act of Sederunt (Company Directors Disqualification) 1986, para 3(2).
[129] [1996] 1 WLR 170.
[130] [1994] 1 WLR 172.
[131] See, for example, *Secretary of State for Trade & Industry* v *Brown* 1995 SLT 550.
[132] See, for example, *Re Homes Assured Corp plc* (1996) BCC 297 and *Secretary of State for Trade and Industry* v *Cleland* [1997] 1 BCLC 437.

been offered by the person facing disqualification.[133] There are no reported cases relating to such undertakings in Scotland. There are difficulties with such undertakings. One is that the undertaking, unlike an actual disqualification order, will not be registered.[134] Another is that although breach of an undertaking and any additional undertaking to be liable for the debts of the company if the primary undertaking is breached would be punishable as a contempt of court, this is not the same as the person breaching the undertaking being subject to the consequences of breaching an actual disqualification order. Further, Palmer points out that anyone involved in the management of a company who knowingly acts on the instructions of such a person would not be personally liable for the debts of the company under s 15 of CDDA 1986 as they would be if the person were actually disqualified.[135] There has been judicial support for the idea of amending the legislation to allow a person facing disqualification proceedings to give an appropriate undertaking in appropriate cases, such an undertaking being given the same force as a disqualification order itself, thus allowing lengthy and expensive proceedings to be avoided.[136]

The standard of proof in an application for disqualification is the balance of probabilities. It has been suggested that the case of *Re Dawson Print Group Ltd*[137] may imply that the standard required in fact varies according to the seriousness of the allegation,[138] and in the case of *Re Topglass Windows Ltd*[139] it seems to have been suggested that owing to the serious nature of a disqualification order, a higher degree of probability was required. It is thought, albeit that there is a lack of direct authority on the matter, that any suggestion of a higher burden of proof on account of the 'quasi-criminal' nature of disqualification cannot be correct, and that the standard is simply the balance of probabilities applied as in any other case.

Applications for leave to act

General considerations

Disqualification orders only prohibit the person affected from acting in the relevant capacities without leave of the court.[140] An application for leave to promote or form a company may be made to any court with jurisdiction to wind up companies, and an application for leave to act as a director, liquidator, administrator or receiver of a company, or otherwise take part in its management, should be made to any court having jurisdiction to wind up the particular company in question.[141] The application for leave may therefore be heard by a different court from the court which pronounced the original disqualification order, although this is partially alleviated by the provision that where the

---

[133] *Re Blackspur Group plc (No 2)* [1997] 1 WLR 710.
[134] See below.
[135] *Palmer's Company Law*, para 8.112. *Palmer* also takes the view that such a person would be liable for contempt of court, although it is not clear on exactly what basis.
[136] Ibid.
[137] Note 76 above.
[138] See Dine, 'The Disqualification of Company Directors' 1988 *Company Lawyer* 213 at 218.
[139] 26th September 1995 (unreported), discussed in Hoey, 'Disqualifying Delinquent Directors' 1997 *Company Lawyer* 130.
[140] See disqualification orders generally above.
[141] CDDA 1986, s 17.

disqualification order was made on the application of the liquidator or the Secretary of State, he is required to appear and call the attention of the court to any relevant matters.[142]

Form of application

An application for leave to act is made by way of summary application in the sheriff court[143] and by petition in the Court of Session.[144] Where such an application in the sheriff court is unopposed, affidavit evidence may be submitted in place of parole evidence.[145]

Grounds on which leave will be granted

In order not to destroy the whole purpose of the disqualification order, leave will only be granted if the court is satisfied that there will be no danger to the public in doing so, and then only to the extent necessary in the particular circumstances[146]—for example, to act in relation to a particular company. The court may impose conditions on the grant of leave. In *Re Chartmore Ltd*[147] the court accepted an undertaking that board meetings would be held monthly and would be attended by a representative of the company's auditors, and leave was granted on that basis despite the court's concerns about the viability of the company involved. In *Secretary of State for Trade and Industry v Palfreman*[148] the court expressed some doubt not only about the validity of imposing such conditions in view of the terms of CDDA 1986, but also about the efficacy of conditions such as requiring supervision by third parties of the person seeking leave to act. Having done so, however, the court none the less granted leave to act, on condition that a solicitor was appointed as an 'independent' director.

Register of disqualification orders, etc

A register of orders relating to disqualifications was first established under the Companies Act 1976. By virtue of 18(2) of CDDA 1986, the Secretary of State is obliged to continue to maintain the register from information supplied to him by officers of court. The Companies (Disqualification Orders) Regulations 1986[149] require the appropriate officers of court (in Scotland, the sheriff clerk and the Deputy Principal Clerk of Session[150]) to provide him with, in the prescribed form, certain prescribed particulars of disqualification orders and grants of leave[151] within 14 days of their being made.[152]

The Secretary of State is also obliged to delete from the register any order which ceases to be in force, and any particulars relating to it,[153] so that the register

---

[142] CDDA 1986, s 17(2).
[143] Act of Sederunt (Company Directors Disqualification) 1986, para 3(1).
[144] Court of Session Rules, rule 74.33.
[145] Act of Sederunt (Company Directors Disqualification) 1986, para 3(2).
[146] *Re Cargo Agency Ltd* (1992) BCC 388.
[147] [1990] BCLC 673.
[148] Note 87 above.
[149] SI 1986/2067.
[150] Companies (Disqualification Orders) Regulations 1986, reg 4.
[151] Companies (Disqualification Orders) Regulations 1986, reg 5. The prescribed forms, which set out the particulars which are required to be furnished, are set out in the schedules to the regulations.
[152] Companies (Disqualification Orders) Regulations 1986, reg 6.
[153] CDDA 1986, s 18(3).

remains up to date. The register is open for inspection on payment of a prescribed fee.[154]

Contravention of disqualification orders

This section deals with the consequences of contravening a disqualification order.

Criminal offences

Where an individual acts in contravention of a disqualification order, he is liable to imprisonment or a fine or both.[155] Where a body corporate acts in contravention of a disqualification order, it is also guilty of an offence,[156] although such a body obviously cannot be imprisoned. However, any director, secretary, manager or similar officer of such a body, or anyone purporting to act in such a capacity, who consented to or connived at it so acting, or who was responsible for it so acting as a result of his neglect, is also guilty of an offence and liable to be proceeded against and punished accordingly.[157] Similarly, a member of a body corporate whose affairs are managed by its members who, in the course of exercising management functions in relation to it, consented to or connived at it acting in contravention of a disqualification order, or who was responsible for it so acting as a result of his neglect, is guilty of an offence and liable to be proceeded against and punished accordingly.[158]

Personal liability for debts

A person who becomes involved in the management of a company in contravention of a disqualification order incurs personal liability for specified debts of the company,[159] as does any person who is involved in the management of the company and who acts, or is willing to act, on his instructions knowing that he is acting in contravention of a disqualification order.[160] The person acting in contravention of the disqualification order is personally liable for such debts and liabilities as were incurred by the company at any time when he was involved in its management,[161] and a person involved in the management of the company and acting or willing to act on his instructions is personally liable for debts and liabilities incurred by the company at any time when he was acting or was willing to act on that person's instructions.[162] In both cases, liability is joint and several with the company and any other person who is also liable for the specified debts, whether under s 15 of CDDA 1986 or otherwise.[163]

---

[154] CDDA 1986, s 18(4). It may now in fact be accessed free of charge via the Internet.

[155] CDDA 1986, s 13.

[156] See CDDA 1986, ss 13 and 14(1).

[157] CDDA 1986, s 14(1).

[158] CDDA 1986, s 14(2).

[159] CDDA 1986, s 15(1)(a).

[160] CDDA 1986, s 15(1)(b). A person is involved in the management of a company if he is a director or is directly or indirectly concerned in, or takes part in, the management of a company: CDDA 1986, s 15(4). Such a person is deemed to be willing to act on the instructions of an undischarged bankrupt at any time after he has actually done so, unless the contrary is proved: CDDA 1986, s 15(5).

[161] CDDA 1986, s 15(3)(a).

[162] CDDA 1986, s 15(3)(b).

[163] CDDA 1986, s 15(2).

Part V

THE END OF INSOLVENCY PROCEEDINGS

40 : THE END OF SEQUESTRATION

S equestration comes to an end following the approval of a judicial composition.[1] In any other case, it might be said that sequestration never ends: it has been held that sequestration continues even after the discharge of the debtor and the trustee,[2] and the sequestration process may be revived at a later date.[3] For practical purposes, however, a sequestration will come to an when the trustee's administration is complete.

This chapter deals with the end of the sequestration process.

The end of sequestration on approval of judicial composition

Where the court approves an offer of composition under s 56 of and Sched 4 to the 1986 Act (known as a judicial composition),[4] the sequestration is brought to an end after certain further procedure.

Where the permanent trustee is a private insolvency practitioner, he must submit his accounts of his intromissions with the debtor's estate to the commissioners or, if there are no commissioners, to the Accountant in Bankruptcy, for audit;[5] at the same time he must submit a claim for his outlays and remuneration.[6] Where he was not himself interim trustee, he must also take all reasonable steps to ensure that the interim trustee has submitted, or submits, his accounts and claim for outlays and remuneration to the Accountant in Bankruptcy.[7] His accounts and claim for remuneration and outlays are then dealt with in more or less the same way as the accounts and claim submitted at the end of every accounting period under s 53 of the 1985 Act.[8] Where the Accountant

---

[1] See further below.
[2] *Buchanan* v *McCulloch* (1865) 4 M 135.
[3] *Northern Heritable Securities Investment Co* v *Whyte* (1888) 16 R 100. A sequestration which has been brought to an end by a judicial composition may also be revived in certain circumstances: see further below.
[4] For this procedure generally, see Chapter 36, where the procedure is dealt with in the context of the debtor's discharge.
[5] 1985 Act, Sched 4, para 9(1)(a).
[6] Ibid. Where the accounts and claim are submitted to the commissioners, he must also send a copy of these to the Accountant in Bankruptcy.
[7] 1985 Act, Sched 4, para 9(1)(b).
[8] 1985 Act, Sched 4, para 9(2), which applies specified subsections of s 53 of the 1985 Act. Accounting periods are dealt with in Chapter 33.

in Bankruptcy is the permanent trustee, he must prepare accounts of his intromissions with the debtor's estate and make a determination of his fees and outlays calculated in accordance with the appropriate regulations.[9] His accounts and determination of remuneration and outlays are then dealt with in more or less the same way as they are under s 53 of the 1985 Act, as adapted by para 9(2) and (3) of Sched 2 to the 1985 Act.[10]

Following completion of the appropriate procedure, the permanent trustee must lodge with the sheriff clerk a declaration either that all necessary charges in the sequestration have been paid or that satisfactory provision has been made for the payment of such charges.[11] When that document, and the bond of caution or other security for payment of the composition which has to be lodged by or on behalf of the debtor,[12] have been lodged, the court will make an order discharging the debtor and the permanent trustee.[13]

On the debtor's discharge becoming effective, the sequestration ceases,[14] although it may subsequently be revived in certain circumstances.[15]

The end of sequestration otherwise than on approval of judicial composition

It was noted above that other than on a judicial composition, the sequestration does not come to an end even on the discharge of the debtor and the trustee,[16] but, for all practical purposes, the sequestration will come to an end when the permanent trustee completes the administration of the estate and obtains his own discharge. This may be before or after the debtor's discharge.[17]

Where the permanent trustee is a private insolvency practitioner, it is provided that after he has made a final division of the debtor's estate and has inserted his final audited accounts in the sederunt book, he must deposit any unclaimed dividends and any unapplied balances in an appropriate bank or institution and thereafter send a copy of the sederunt book, a copy of the audited accounts and a receipt for the deposit of the unclaimed dividends and unapplied balances to the Accountant in Bankruptcy.[18] He may then apply to the Accountant in Bankruptcy for his discharge.[19]

Where the permanent trustee is the Accountant in Bankruptcy, it is provided that after he has made a final division of the debtor's estate, he must insert in the sederunt book his final accounts of his intromissions with the estate, the scheme

---

[9] 1985 Act, Sched 4, para 9(1A). The regulations are those made under s 69A of the 1985 Act, that is the Bankruptcy Fees (Scotland) Regulations 1993 (SI 1993/486).

[10] 1985 Act, Sched 4, para 9(3), which applies specified subsections of s 53 of the 1985 Act, as so adapted. Accounting periods are dealt with in Chapter 33.

[11] 1985 Act, Sched 4, para 10(a).

[12] 1985 Act, Sched 4, para 10(b).

[13] 1985 Act, Sched 4, para 11. The debtor's discharge is dealt with in Chapter 36; the discharge of the permanent trustee is discussed below.

[14] 1985 Act, Sched 4, para 13.

[15] See 1985 Act, Sched 4, para 17.

[16] See above.

[17] The sequestration is not brought to an end by the discharge of the debtor: *Henderson* v *Bulley* (1849) 11 D 1470, and see Chapter 36. The administration of the estate may therefore continue after the debtor's discharge until everything has been completed.

[18] 1985 Act, s 57(1).

[19] Ibid. The procedure for obtaining his discharge is discussed below.

of division (if any) and a determination of his fees and outlays.[20] He must also deposit any unclaimed dividends and any unapplied balances in an appropriate bank or institution.[21] Thereafter, he must take the appropriate steps which will lead to his discharge.[22]

Discharge of permanent trustee

The discharge of the permanent trustee where the sequestration is brought to an end as a result of the approval of a judicial composition has already been discussed above as an integral part of the discussion on the end of sequestration following such approval.

In all other cases the procedure for the permanent trustee obtaining his discharge is set out in ss 57 and 58A of the 1985 Act: the former applies where the permanent trustee is a private insolvency practitioner, the latter where he is the Accountant in Bankruptcy.

Where the permanent trustee is a private insolvency practitioner, he must apply to the Accountant in Bankruptcy for his discharge.[23] The application is notified to the debtor and the creditors, who are given an opportunity to make representations to the Accountant in Bankruptcy.[24] The Accountant in Bankruptcy then decides whether or not to grant the discharge on the basis of the documents submitted by the permanent trustee and any representations made to him.[25] His decision is subject to appeal to the sheriff.[26]

Where the permanent trustee is the Accountant in Bankruptcy, he must send to the debtor and all creditors a copy of his determination of his fees and outlays and a notice informing them, *inter alia*, that he has put in motion the procedure for his discharge.[27] The debtor or any creditor may then appeal to the court against his discharge.[28] Where no appeal is made or an appeal is made and dismissed, the Accountant is duly discharged.[29]

The effect of the permanent trustee's discharge is to relieve him of any liability to the debtor or any of the creditors for any of his acts or omissions in carrying out his functions as permanent trustee except liability for fraud.[30] In relation to cases other than those where the sequestration is brought to an end on approval of a judicial composition, specific provision is made for the discharge to cover also his actings as interim trustee if he has not already obtained a discharge as interim trustee.[31]

---

[20] 1985 Act, s 58A(2).
[21] 1985 Act, s 58A(3).
[22] 1985 Act, s 58A(4). The procedure for obtaining his discharge is discussed below.
[23] 1985 Act, s 57(1)(c).
[24] 1985 Act, s 57(2).
[25] 1985 Act, s 57(3).
[26] 1985 Act, s 57(4). That appeal is final: 1985 Act, s 57(4A).
[27] 1985 Act, s 58A(4).
[28] 1985 Act, s 58A(5).
[29] 1985 Act, s 58A(7).
[30] 1985 Act, Sched 4, para 12 (discharge on approval of composition) and ss 57(5) and 58A(7) (private insolvency practitioner and Accountant in Bankruptcy respectively in all other cases).
[31] 1985 Act, s 57(5) (private insolvency practitioner), s 58A(9) (Accountant in Bankruptcy). The omission of a similar provision in relation to discharge on composition was presumably an oversight.

41 : THE END OF COMPANY VOLUNTARY
ARRANGEMENTS AND
SECTION 425 ARRANGEMENTS

This chapter considers the circumstances in which a CVA or section 425 arrangement may be brought to an end.

Company voluntary arrangements

Circumstances provided for in the company voluntary arrangement itself

The CVA itself may specify circumstances in which it will be brought to an end—for example, if no purchaser is found for specified assets within a specified time or if the company defaults. It will also generally provide that it will come to an end on its successful completion.[1]

Completion of a company voluntary arrangement

A CVA will come to an end on its successful completion. Where a CVA has been successfully completed, the supervisor must, within 28 days of the final completion, send to all creditors and members of the company who are bound by it a notice that the arrangement has been fully implemented.[2] The notice must be accompanied by a report from the supervisor containing a summary of the receipts and payments made in the course of the arrangement and an explanation of any differences in implementation of the CVA as compared with the proposals agreed by the creditors' and members' meetings.[3] The supervisor must also send a copy of the notice and report to the Registrar of Companies and to the court within that time-limit.[4]

Where the company is not subject to any other insolvency procedure, such as administration or liquidation, it will return to normal following completion of the CVA. Where the CVA was concluded during administration and the administration order was not discharged following the approval of the CVA, the

---

[1] See below.
[2] Scottish Rules, rule 1.23(1). The 28-day period may be extended by the court: Scottish Rules, rule 1.23(4).
[3] Scottish Rules, rule 1.23(2).
[4] Scottish Rules, rule 1.23(3). Again, the 28-day period may be extended by the court: Scottish Rules, rule 1.23(4).

administration will be completed in the normal way. Similarly, where the CVA was concluded during liquidation, the liquidation will be completed in the normal way after recall, where necessary, of any sist of the liquidation proceedings granted under s 5(3)(a) of the 1986 Act.

Application to the court under section 7 of the 1986 Act

Section 7(3) of the 1986 Act empowers any creditor or other person who is dissatisfied with any act, omission or decision of the supervisor to apply to the court, who may confirm, reverse or modify any act or decision of the supervisor, give him directions or make any other order which it thinks fit. This is wide enough to include an order bringing the CVA to an end. Alternatively, the court might give the supervisor directions to apply for the administration or liquidation of the company.[5]

Subsequent administration or liquidation of a company

There is nothing to prevent the subsequent administration or liquidation of a company which has concluded a CVA.[6] The CVA may constrain those bound by it from instigating such proceedings, at least where the CVA is progressing satisfactorily, but any creditor who is not bound by the CVA may be in a position to petition for the administration or liquidation of the company;[7] alternatively, such a petition may be presented by the supervisor of the CVA himself[8] or by anyone else who is entitled to do so,[9] and it has been held that a resolution to wind up voluntarily passed by the company while a CVA is in force is perfectly valid even where this breaches the terms of the CVA.[10] There is nothing explicit in the 1986 Act to indicate the effect of a subsequent administration or liquidation on an existing CVA. In *Re Arthur Rathbone Kitchens Ltd*[11] it was held that a CVA ceased operation on a resolution for the voluntary winding up of the company, although it continued in force for the purpose of allowing the supervisor to petition for the compulsory liquidation of the company, and that a winding-up order had the effect of discharging the CVA, the supervisor then being required to hand over the assets held by him for the purposes of the CVA to the liquidator.[12] In *Re Excalibur Airways Ltd (in liquidation)*,[13] however, it was held that a winding-up order did not bring the CVA in question to an end. In that case the petition had been presented by the directors and *Re Arthur Rathbone Kitchens Ltd* was distinguished on the basis that there was a difference between a petition presented

---

[5] The supervisor is included among those who may apply for administration or liquidation of the company: 1986 Act, s 7(4), and see further below.

[6] Indeed, it is specifically provided that where a winding-up order is made while a CVA is in force, the court may appoint the supervisor of the CVA to be the liquidator: 1986 Act, s 140(1).

[7] The CVA binds all creditors who, in accordance with the rules, had notice of, and were entitled to vote at, the creditors' meeting, whether or not they were present or represented at the meeting (1986 Act, s 5(2)), but some creditors might not be bound by it—for example, because they had not received the required notice or were not entitled to vote at the meeting: see also Chapter 8.

[8] 1986 Act, s 7(4).

[9] See Chapters 10 and 16 in relation to administration and liquidation respectively.

[10] *Re Arthur Rathbone Kitchens Ltd* [1997] 2 BCLC 280.

[11] Ibid.

[12] The decision in relation to the latter point turned partly on a provision of the English Insolvency Rules for which there is no direct equivalent in the Scottish Rules, but it is thought that this was not essential to the court's decision.

[13] [1998] 1 BCLC 436.

by the supervisor with the agreement of the CVA creditors, who were choosing to abandon the CVA (the situation in *Re Arthur Rathbone Kitchens Ltd*), and a petition by the directors or a non–CVA creditor.

The appointment of a receiver does *not* bring a CVA to an end although, depending on the terms of the CVA, it may in practice render it incapable of being implemented. A floating chargeholder's right to appoint a receiver is, of course, unimpaired by the approval of a CVA unless the CVA specifically provides otherwise.[14] But in the case of *Re Leisure Study Group Ltd*[15] it was held that an administrative receiver appointed while a CVA was in force in relation to the company had no right to sums received by the supervisor from the company for distribution to creditors or to restrain him from distributing the funds in terms of the agreement because the supervisor held the sums as trustee for the creditors. Where the terms of the CVA are such that the property and monies required for its implementation are in the hands of the supervisor, therefore, they will be unaffected by a subsequent receivership and the CVA may continue, not-withstanding the receivership. Where this is not the case, however, the CVA may be rendered incapable of implementation in practice. In such circumstances, the supervisor may petition for liquidation of the company.[16]

Discharge or release of supervisor

There are no statutory provisions for the release or discharge of the supervisor on termination of the CVA, but the CVA itself will usually provide that the supervisor, in the absence of bad faith or wilful misconduct, will incur no personal liability in connection with the administration of the CVA or in respect of any act or omission by him in carrying out his functions as supervisor.

Section 425 arrangements

Circumstances provided for in the arrangement itself

The arrangement itself may specify circumstances in which it will be brought to an end. It will generally provide at least that it will come to an end on its successful completion.[17]

Completion of a section 425 arrangement

A section 425 arrangement will come to an end on its successful completion. Where the company was not subject to any other insolvency procedure, such as adminis-tration, receivership or liquidation, it will return to normal following completion of the arrangement. Where the company was subject to any of these régimes, they will thereafter be completed and brought to an end in the normal way.

Subsequent administration, receivership or liquidation of the company

Although all creditors who are included in a section 425 arrangement will be bound by it, even if they did not attend and/or vote at the meeting called to

---

[14] The floating chargeholder would have had to consent specifically to any such interference with his rights: see further Chapter 8.

[15] [1994] 2 BCLC 65.

[16] It was held in *Re Leisure Study Group Ltd* that the administrative receiver had no locus to prevent the supervisor from doing so.

[17] See below.

consider it or voted against the arrangement,[18] there might still be a subsequent administration, receivership or liquidation of the company.[19] The effect of an administration order, receivership or winding–up order on an existing section 425 arrangement is not specified in CA 1985 or the 1986 Act, but it is thought that any of these must have the effect of bringing it to an end.

---

[18] See Chapter 9.

[19] For example, the terms of the arrangement might not prevent a floating chargeholder from appointing a receiver; the arrangement might be with some classes of creditors only, thereby allowing a creditor of a different class to petition for administration or liquidation; an administration or liquidation petition might be presented by any other person who is not bound by the arrangement and who has the right to do so.

42 : THE END OF ADMINISTRATION PROCEDURE

Administration is brought to an end by discharge of the administration order, which may happen for a variety of reasons.

This chapter describes the circumstances in which an administration may be brought to an end and the procedure involved.

Discharge on approval of a company voluntary arrangement

The court may discharge the administration order on approval of a CVA under Part I of the 1986 Act.[1] It will not do so, however, during the 28-day period within which an application to challenge the approval of the CVA under s 6 of the 1986 Act may be made; nor will it do so where any such challenge is pending, where an appeal from the court's decision on such an application is pending or where the time for bringing such an appeal has not yet expired.[2]

Discharge on application by administrator

In terms of s 18 of the 1986 Act the administrator may apply to the court for, *inter alia*, discharge of the administration order,[3] and he must do so where it appears to him that the purpose or purposes for which the administration order was granted have either been achieved or are incapable of being achieved, or where he is required to do so by a meeting of the company's creditors summoned for that purpose.[4]

The court has a wide discretion in dealing with the application, and where it discharges the administration order it may also make such consequential provision as it thinks fit.[5] On the discharge of the order, the administrator must immediately

---

[1] 1986 Act, s 5(3). Curiously, there do not appear to be any provisions for notification of the discharge of the administration order under this section, but the administrator will be required to vacate office on the discharge of the administration order and to notify his vacation of office to prescribed parties (see further below), so the discharge will be notified in this way.

[2] 1986 Act, s 5(4).

[3] 1986 Act, s 18(1).

[4] 1986 Act, s 18(2).

[5] 1986 Act, s 18(3).

send a copy of the order effecting the discharge to the Keeper of the Register of Inhibitions and Adjudications.[6] He must also within 14 days send a copy of it to the Registrar of Companies.[7]

Discharge on failure to secure approval of proposals

Where the report made to the court following the meeting of creditors called to consider the administrator's proposals under s 24 of the 1986 Act is to the effect that the meeting declined to approve the proposals, the court may, *inter alia*, discharge the administration order.[8]

Where the court decides to discharge the administration order, it may make such consequential provision as it thinks fit.[9] The administrator must immediately send a copy of the order effecting the discharge to the Keeper of the Register of Inhibitions and Adjudications.[10] He must also within 14 days send a copy of it to the Registrar of Companies.[11]

Discharge following application under section 27 of the 1986 Act

Section 27 of the 1986 Act allows any creditor or member of the company to apply to the court for an order on the basis that the administrator's conduct of the administration is or has been prejudicial to either the creditors or the members generally or to some part of them including himself, or on the basis that some proposed act or omission of the administrator is similarly prejudicial.[12] The court has a wide discretion in dealing with such an application, including the option of discharging the administration order.[13]

Where the court discharges the administration order, it may make such consequential provision as it thinks fit.[14] The administrator must send a copy of the court's order to the Registrar of Companies within 14 days.[15]

Vacation of office by administrator on discharge of administration order

On discharge of the administration order the administrator must vacate office.[16] Section 19 of the 1986 Act makes provision for payment of his remuneration and

---

[6] Scottish Rules, rule 2.3(4).

[7] 1986 Act, s 18(4). Rule 2.3(4)(b) of the Scottish Rules also requires the administrator to send, within 14 days of the making of the order, a notice with a certified copy of the order to the Registrar of Companies, and this requirement is stated to be without prejudice to the requirement of s 18(4): Scottish Rules, rule 2.3(5).

[8] 1986 Act, s 24(5). The procedure under section 24 is discussed in Chapter 11.

[9] Ibid.

[10] Scottish Rules, rule 2.3(4).

[11] 1986 Act, s 24(6). Rule 2.3(4)(b) of the Scottish Rules also requires the administrator to send, within 14 days of the making of the order, a notice with a certified copy of the order to the Registrar of Companies, and this requirement is stated to be without prejudice to the requirement of s 24(6): Scottish Rules, rule 2.3(5).

[12] This section is discussed in Chapter 23.

[13] 1986 Act, s 27(2).

[14] Ibid.

[15] 1986 Act, s 27(6).

[16] 1986 Act, s 19(2)(b).

expenses and specified debts and liabilities incurred by him on his ceasing to be administrator. The administrator's own remuneration and expenses are charged on and paid out of any property under his control, and payment of these takes priority over any security which, as constituted, was a floating charge.[17] Any debts and liabilities incurred under contracts entered into by the administrator or any predecessor of his, and any qualifying liabilities under contracts of employment adopted by himself or any predecessor of his, are also to be charged on and paid out of any property under the administrator's control, and payment of these sums takes priority over both the administrator's own remuneration and expenses and any security which, as constituted, was a floating charge.[18]

Release of the administrator

The administrator gains his release at such time as the court may determine.[19] The usual practice is for this to be granted at the same time as, and to take effect from, the discharge of the administration order.[20]

The administrator's release has the effect of relieving him of all liability for his acts and omissions in the administration and his conduct as administrator generally, but does not relieve him of any potential liability under s 212 of the 1986 Act.[21]

---

[17] 1986 Act, s 19(4).

[18] 1986 Act, s 19(5), (6). 'Qualifying liabilities' under a contract of employment are those sums representing wages or salary or contributions to an occupational pension scheme which are due in respect of services rendered wholly or partly after the adoption of the contract by the administrator, but excluding any part of such sum which represents payment for services rendered before the adoption of the contract: 1986 Act, s 19(7), (8), and see further Chapters 26 and 33.

[19] 1986 Act, s 20(1)(b).

[20] See Fletcher, Higham and Trower, *The Law and Practice of Corporate Administrations*, n 2 to para 14.25.

[21] 1986 Act, s 20(2), (3). Section 212 of the 1986 Act is discussed in Chapter 38, which deals with the personal liability of directors and others. It applies, *inter alia*, to administrators.

43 : THE END OF RECEIVERSHIP

O n completion of his administration of the assets attached by the floating charge, the receiver will resign office and thereby effectively bring the receivership to an end.

This chapter outlines the procedures which take place on completion of the receivership.

Procedure following completion of receivership

Once the receiver has realised the assets attached by the floating charge and applied the sums received by him in accordance with the rules laid out in the 1986 Act,[1] the receivership will be complete. Where there is a question as to the person entitled to a payment under s 60 of the 1986 Act, or a receipt or discharge of a security cannot be obtained in respect of a payment, the receiver must consign the amount of the payment in any joint stock bank of issue in Scotland in the name of the Accountant of Court for behoof of the person or persons entitled to the payment.[2]

Resignation of the receiver on completion of receivership

Once everything is complete, the receiver will resign office. He must give at least seven days' notice of his resignation to the holder of the floating charge under which he was appointed, the holder of any other floating charge, any other receiver, the members of the creditors' committee (if established) and the company or its liquidator, and the notice must specify the date from which his resignation will take effect.[3] Once he has ceased to act, the receiver must give notice of his ceasing to act to the Registrar of Companies within 14 days of the date of his resignation[4] and give further notice of his vacation of office to the holder of the floating charge under which he was appointed, the holder of any other floating

---

[1] See Chapter 33.
[2] 1986 Act, s 60(3).
[3] 1986 Act, s 62(1), and the Receivers (Scotland) Regulations 1986 (SI 1986/1917 (S 141)), reg 6.
[4] 1986 Act, s 62(5).

charge, any other receiver, the members of the creditors' committee (if established) and the company or its liquidator.[5]

On vacating office, the receiver is entitled to be paid his remuneration and any expenses properly incurred by him, and also any indemnity to which he is entitled, out of the property of the company which is subject to the floating charge.[6]

Re-floating of charge

Where a receiver has vacated office and no other receiver has been appointed within one month thereafter, the floating charge under which he was appointed ceases to attach to the property then subject to the charge and again subsists as a floating charge.[7] Where the receiver vacates office on completion of the receivership, no replacement will be appointed and so the charge will re-float in accordance with this provision. If the company subsequently acquired further property which was caught by the charge, a new receiver could be appointed and a new receivership commenced. Where the company goes into liquidation after the charge has re-floated, the charge will crystallise on the liquidation in the normal way, but where it goes into liquidation before the charge has re-floated, the charge will not re-float.[8]

---

[5] Scottish Rules, rule 3.11.
[6] 1986 Act, s 62(4). For the order of priority of payment, see Chapter 33.
[7] 1986 Act, s 62(6).
[8] Greene and Fletcher, *The Law and Practice of Receivership in Scotland* (2nd edn), para 11.10.

44 : THE END OF LIQUIDATION

O n completion of the liquidation process the liquidator will take the final
procedural steps for bringing the liquidation to an end and vacate office
and the company will thereafter be dissolved. There is provision for early
dissolution of the company in certain circumstances in a compulsory liquidation.

This chapter deals with the final procedural steps for bringing the liquidation
to an end and with dissolution of the company, including the provisions for early
dissolution in a compulsory liquidation.

Final procedural steps in liquidation

Voluntary liquidation

In both members' and creditors' voluntary liquidations, the liquidator must
prepare an account of the winding up showing how it has been conducted and
how the company's property has been disposed of as soon as the company's
affairs are fully wound up.[1] He must then call, in the case of a members' voluntary
liquidation, the final meeting of the company, and in the case of a creditors'
voluntary liquidation, final meetings of the company and the creditors, for the
purpose of receiving his account and his explanation of it.[2] At the final meeting
of creditors in a creditors' voluntary liquidation, the creditors may question the
liquidator about his account, and may resolve against the liquidator having his
release.[3]

Within a week of the meeting or meetings or, in the case of a creditors'
voluntary liquidation where the meetings were not held on the same day, the
later of them, the liquidator must send to the Registrar of Companies a copy of
his account and a return of the holding of the meeting or meetings and its/their

---

[1] 1986 Act, s 94(1) (members' voluntary liquidation), s 106(1) (creditors' voluntary liquidation).
[2] Ibid.
[3] Scottish Rules, rule 4.31(2), as substituted in its application to creditors' voluntary liquidations
by rule 5 and para 18 of Sched 1 to the Scottish Rules. The liquidator's release is discussed
further below.

date(s).[4] As soon as he has complied with this requirement and given notice to the Registrar of Companies that the meeting or meetings have been held and of the decisions (if any) taken at it or them, the liquidator vacates office.[5]

Compulsory liquidation

As soon as it appears to the liquidator that the winding up of the company is for all practical purposes complete, he must call a final general meeting of the company's creditors for the purpose of receiving his report of the liquidation and determining whether he should have his release.[6] The liquidator may give the notice summoning this meeting at the same time as giving notice of the final distribution of the company's property, but where the meeting so summoned takes place before the liquidation is for all practical purposes complete, the meeting will be adjourned, more than once if necessary, until the liquidator can report that this is the case.[7]

The liquidator's report must contain an account of his administration of the liquidation process and a summary of his receipts and payments.[8] At the meeting, the creditors may question the liquidator about any matter contained in the report, and may resolve against the liquidator having his release.[9]

Within seven days of the meeting, the liquidator must give notice to the court and to the Registrar of Companies that the final meeting has been held and the decisions, if any, of the meeting.[10] The notice must also state whether or not he has been released and be accompanied by a copy of the report laid before the meeting.[11] As soon as he has given notice of the holding of the final meeting and its decisions to the court, he vacates office.[12]

Dissolution of the company

Voluntary liquidation

When the Registrar of Companies receives the liquidator's final account of the liquidation and his report of the final meeting or meetings in the liquidation, he duly registers them, and three months after such registration the company is dissolved.[13] The dissolution may, however, be deferred by the court for such

---

[4] 1986 Act, s 94(3) (members' voluntary liquidation), s 106(3) (creditors' voluntary liquidation). If no quorum is present at the meeting(s), the liquidator submits his account with a return to the effect that the relevant meeting(s) took place and no quorum was present: 1986 Act, ss 94(5) and 106(5).

[5] 1986 Act, s 171(6). In a creditors' voluntary winding up, the liquidator must also state in the notice given to the Registrar of Companies under this subsection whether or not he has been released: Scottish Rules, rule 4.31(3), as substituted in its application to creditors' voluntary liquidations by rule 5 and para 18 of Sched 1 to the Scottish Rules.

[6] 1986 Act, s 146(1). The liquidator's release is discussed further below.

[7] 1986 Act, s 146(2).

[8] Scottish Rules, rule 4.31(2).

[9] Scottish Rules, rule 4.31(3).

[10] 1986 Act, s 172(8).

[11] Scottish Rules, rule 4.31(4). If no quorum was present at the meeting, the liquidator reports to the court that the final meeting was summoned but no quorum was present, and it is then deemed that the meeting was held and the creditors did not resolve against the liquidator's release: Scottish Rules, rule 4.31(5).

[12] 1986 Act, s 172(8).

[13] 1986 Act, s 201(2).

period as it thinks fit on the application of the liquidator or any other interested person.[14]

Compulsory liquidation

When the Registrar of Companies receives the liquidator's notice of the holding of the final meeting in the liquidation and its outcome and the liquidator's vacation of office, he duly registers it, and three months after such registration the company is dissolved.[15] The dissolution may, however, be deferred by the court for such period as it thinks fit on the application of any interested person.[16]

Early dissolution of the company in compulsory liquidation

Where the liquidator comes to the conclusion, after the first meetings in the liquidation, that the realisable assets of the company are insufficient to cover the expenses of the winding up, he may apply to the court for an order that the company be dissolved at that stage.[17] If the court is satisfied that the realisable assets of the company are indeed insufficient to cover the expenses of the liquidation, and that it is appropriate to do so in the circumstances, it will order the company to be dissolved.[18] The liquidator must send a copy of the order to the Registrar of Companies within 14 days; the Registrar will register the order and three months after registration the company is dissolved.[19] The dissolution may, however, be deferred by the court for such period as it thinks fit on the application of any interested person.[20]

Release of the liquidator

In a members' voluntary liquidation, the liquidator has his release from the time when he vacates office after the final meeting in the liquidation.[21] In a creditors' voluntary liquidation, where the final meeting of creditors has not resolved against his release, the liquidator has his release from the time he vacates office;[22] where the final meeting of creditors has resolved against his release, he has his release from the time determined by the Accountant of Court.[23]

In a compulsory liquidation, where the final meeting in the liquidation has not resolved against his release, the liquidator has his release from the time he

---

[14] 1986 Act, s 201(3). Where dissolution is so deferred, the person on whose application the order was made must deliver a copy of the order to the Registrar of Companies within seven days: 1986 Act, s 201(4).
[15] 1986 Act, s 205(1), (2).
[16] 1986 Act, s 205(5). Where dissolution is so deferred, the person on whose application the order was made must deliver a copy of the order to the Registrar of Companies within 7 days: 1986 Act, s 205(6).
[17] 1986 Act, s 204(2).
[18] 1986 Act, s 204(3).
[19] 1986 Act, s 204(4).
[20] 1986 Act, s 204(6). Where dissolution is so deferred, the person on whose application the order was made must deliver a copy of the order to the Registrar of Companies within seven days: 1986 Act, s 204(6).
[21] 1986 Act, s 173(2)(d).
[22] 1986 Act, s 173(2)(e)(i).
[23] 1986 Act, s 173(2)(e)(ii), as modified in its application to Scotland by s 173(3).

vacates office;[24] where the final meeting in the liquidation has resolved against his release, he has his release from the time determined by the Accountant of Court.[25]

The liquidator's release has the effect of relieving him of all liability for his acts and omissions in the liquidation and his conduct as liquidator generally, but does not relieve him of any potential liability under s 212 of the 1986 Act.[26]

---

[24] 1986 Act, s 174(4)(d)(ii).

[25] 1986 Act, s 174(4)(d)(i), as modified in its application to Scotland by s 174(7).

[26] 1986 Act, s 173(4) (voluntary liquidation), s 174(6) (compulsory liquidation). Section 212 of the 1986 Act is discussed in Chapter 37, which deals with the personal liability of directors and others. It applies to, *inter alia*, a liquidator.

Part VI

ALTERNATIVES TO
FORMAL INSOLVENCY PROCEEDINGS

45 : ALTERNATIVES TO FORMAL PROCEEDINGS

D ebtors may wish to avoid formal insolvency proceedings where possible because of the serious consequences which they may have.

This chapter describes a number of alternatives which may be open to a debtor to avoid formal insolvency proceedings.

Informal arrangements with creditors

Any type of debtor may enter into informal arrangements with creditors. Examples of such arrangements include instalment payments, a rescheduling of payments and a simple moratorium whereby creditors agree to postpone formal action against the debtor for an agreed period of time. Whether such arrangements are likely to be acceptable to creditors in the first place, or successful once embarked upon, will depend on a number of factors, including the number of creditors involved (generally, the fewer creditors involved, the easier it will be to obtain agreement); the stage at which the debtor approaches the creditors (in general, the earlier, the better); the manner in which the creditors are approached; the type of offer which the debtor is in a position to make; the nature and extent of the debtor's difficulties and the reason for them; and so on. The parties should consider whether any arrangement is likely to be subject to challenge either by other creditors or on any subsequent formal insolvency proceedings.[1]

Composition contracts

A composition contract is an agreement between a debtor and the debtor's creditors whereby the creditors agree to discharge the debtor in return for part payment of their debts in accordance with the terms of the agreement. Composition contracts have already been discussed in the context of sequestration, where they may be utilised, in the form of a judicial composition, to obtain the debtor's discharge and bring sequestration proceedings to an end.[2] It has also been noted that a liquidator (with the relevant sanction), an administrator and a

---

[1] For the circumstances in which transactions can subsequently be challenged, see Chapter 30.
[2] See Chapters 36 and 40.

receiver all have power to enter into arrangements or compromises with creditors in the context of liquidation, administration and receivership respectively.[3] Composition contracts may, however, be utilised by any form of debtor at common law outwith formal insolvency proceedings as an alternative to such proceedings. Typically, they provide for participating creditors to accept a lesser sum than the outstanding amount of their debts in exchange for granting a discharge of the debts. The agreed sum is usually to be paid in instalments, from income generated by the debtor, who is allowed to retain his/its assets for that purpose. All creditors participating in the agreement must be treated rateably.

It is competent at common law to have a composition with some creditors only, but because such agreements are purely contractual, any creditor who is not included in the agreement or does not agree to be bound by it remains free to proceed against the debtor or the debtor's assets in the normal way. In many cases, the result of such actions would be effectively to prevent the debtor from being able to fulfil his/its part of the contract. Whether or not creditors will be willing to agree to a composition and whether or not it is likely to be successful will depend on the same kinds of factors as discussed above in relation to more informal arrangements.

Where the debtor defaults—for example, by failing to pay agreed instalments in full or on time—creditors may pursue the debtor for payment of the full amount of the original debt less any sums paid under the composition contract.

Trust deeds for creditors

Trust deeds generally

A trust deed for creditors is a voluntary deed whereby a debtor conveys specified assets to a named trustee to be administered for the benefit of creditors and the settlement of debts.[4] Trust deeds are creatures of the common law and at common law any type of debtor may grant a trust deed for creditors, although in practice it would be unusual for a company debtor, for example, to do so. The assets to be conveyed to the trustee under the trust deed are a matter for the debtor, who may convey all or only part of his assets to the trustee. At common law, the trustee's powers are those, and only those, granted to him in the trust deed, and the trust deed must be carefully drawn in order to ensure that the trustee is given all the necessary powers.

The 1985 Act contains a number of provisions relating to trust deeds. These are defined for the purposes of the 1985 Act as 'voluntary trust deed[s] granted by or on behalf of the debtor whereby his estate (other than such of his estate as would not, under s 33(1) of this Act, vest in the permanent trustee if his estate were sequestrated) is conveyed to the trustee for the benefit of his creditors generally'.[5] The provisions of the 1985 Act do not apply to trust deeds which do not fall within this definition—for example, where the assets conveyed to the trustee under the trust deed do not correspond with the definition set out above. It is thought that trust deeds granted by companies (and other entities which cannot be sequestrated) will not come within this definition, principally because

---

[3] See Chapters 26 (administration), 27 (receivership) and 28 (liquidation).

[4] Trust deeds raise many complex issues and a full discussion of these is beyond the scope of this text, but see McBryde, *Bankruptcy* (2nd edn), ch 20, for a detailed discussion.

[5] 1985 Act, ss 73(1) and 5(4A).

of the reference to 'if his estate were sequestrated': the 'estate' of a company cannot, of course, be sequestrated.[6] Trust deeds which do not come within the definition in the 1985 Act will, however, be perfectly valid at common law and will be governed wholly by common law.

In terms of the 1985 Act, the granting of a trust deed is one of the events which renders a debtor apparently insolvent.[7] A trustee under a trust deed is one of the persons who may petition for sequestration of the debtor where specified conditions are satisfied[8] and a trustee under a trust deed which has become protected is given the same powers as a trustee in sequestration to challenge gratuitous alienations, orders on divorce and unfair preferences.[9] In addition, a number of general provisions relating to trust deeds are contained in Sched 5 to the 1985 Act.[10] In terms of that Schedule, the debtor, trustee or any creditor may insist on the trustee's accounts being audited and his remuneration fixed by the Accountant in Bankruptcy, whether the trust deed makes alternative provision for these matters or not;[11] the trustee is given rights and obligations regarding the recording of certain notices in the Register of Inhibitions and Adjudications;[12] the lodging of a claim by a creditor is the equivalent of an effective acknowledgement of a creditor's claim for the purpose of any enactment or rule of law relating to the limitation of actions in any part of the United Kingdom, with the exception of an enactment which implements or gives effect to an international agreement in the same way as it is in sequestration[13] and, unless the trust deed otherwise provides, the provisions of Sched 1 to the 1985 Act relating to the valuation of creditors' claims applies subject to certain specified modifications.[14] The Schedule also provides a mechanism for trust deeds to become protected.[15]

At common law, creditors who do not accede (agree) to a trust deed may carry on with independent action against the debtor. Prior diligence is not cut down by a trust deed, although where the granting of a trust deed renders a debtor apparently insolvent, this will result in equalisation of certain diligences within the relevant period.[16] Action by non-acceding creditors may include, where applicable, the institution of formal insolvency proceedings in relation to the debtor. One of the difficulties which then arises is the effect of any such subsequent proceedings on the trust deed itself. It has been held in relation to sequestration at least that the trustee under the trust deed must hand over the

---

[6] It might, of course, be argued that the definition could be read as applying to company debtors as if they could be sequestrated, but this seems rather strained. In any event, there are other reasons to support the conclusion reached above: the definition of 'debtor', the whole structure and terms of the provisions relating to trust deeds, especially Sched 5 to the 1985 Act (discussed further below) and the fact that where the provisions of the 1985 Act are extended to company debtors, this is usually expressly made clear, all tend to argue against the provisions of the 1985 Act relating to trust deeds applying to such deeds by companies or other entities which cannot be sequestrated.

[7] See Chapter 1.

[8] See Chapter 6.

[9] See Chapter 30. Protected trust deeds are discussed further below.

[10] 1985 Act, s 59. See also *Weir, Petnr* 1990 GWD 30–1714.

[11] 1985 Act, Sched 5, para 1.

[12] 1985 Act, Sched 5, para 2.

[13] 1985 Act, Sched 5, para 3. The lodging of a claim also interrupts the running of prescription: Prescription and Limitation (Scotland) Act 1973, s 9(1).

[14] 1985 Act, Sched 5, para 4. The valuation of claims in sequestration is dealt with in Chapter 32.

[15] See further below.

[16] See Chapter 31.

debtor's assets to the trustee in sequestration to be administered via the sequestration,[17] but the matter remains one of difficulty. It was in order to prevent action by non-acceding creditors where the majority of creditors did agree to the trust deed procedure that the concept of a protected trust deed was introduced by the 1985 Act.

Protected trust deeds

The 1985 Act originally provided for a trust deed to which it applied to become protected if a defined majority of the creditors acceded to it and certain other conditions were satisfied. However, few trust deeds became protected and the 1993 Act accordingly amended the procedure whereby a trust deed could become protected. The current provisions allow a trust deed which satisfies certain defined conditions to become protected if the trustee follows certain procedures and a defined percentage of the creditors *do not object* within a specified time-limit.

Schedule 5 to the 1985 Act sets out the conditions which must be satisfied for a trust deed to become protected. The trustee under the deed must be someone who would be able to act as trustee in the debtor's sequestration.[18] He must publish a notice in prescribed form[19] and thereafter send a copy of the trust deed, the notice and other prescribed information to all known creditors within a week of the publication of the notice.[20] If a majority in number, or at least a third in value, of the creditors notify the trustee in writing of their objection to the trust deed within five weeks,[21] the deed does not become protected. Otherwise, the trust deed becomes protected provided that the trustee sends a copy of the trust deed to the Accountant in Bankruptcy with a certificate endorsed on it stating that he has not received the required objections immediately on the expiry of the five-week period.[22] Creditors who do not object are effectively deemed to have acceded to the deed.

The effect of the trust deed becoming protected is, in simple terms, to prevent any creditor, even one who objected to it, from carrying on with independent action against the debtor or his assets. Paragraph 6(a)(i) of Sched 5 to the 1985 Act provides that any creditor who objected to the deed has no higher right to recover his debt than one acceding to it. Similarly, any creditor who did not receive the relevant notice from the trustee has no higher right to recover his debt than a creditor acceding to the deed.[23] However, an objecting creditor or one who did not receive the relevant notice has the right to apply for sequestration within six weeks of the original notice published by the trustee.[24] The court may award sequestration if it considers it is in the best interests of the creditors to do so.[25] Any such creditor may also apply for sequestration at any other time if he alleges that the distribution is or is likely to be unfairly prejudicial.[26] In such a case the court will only award sequestration if it is satisfied that this is true.[27]

---

[17] *Salaman v Rosslyn's Trs* (1900) 3 F 298.
[18] 1985 Act, Sched 5, para 5(1)(a).
[19] 1985 Act, Sched 5, para 5(1)(b).
[20] 1985 Act, Sched 5, para 5(1)(c).
[21] 1985 Act, Sched 5, para 5(1)(d).
[22] 1985 Act, Sched 5, para 5(1)(e).
[23] 1985 Act, Sched 5, para 6(a)(ii).
[24] 1985 Act, Sched 5, para 7(1)(a).
[25] 1985 Act, Sched 5, para 7(2).
[26] 1985 Act, Sched 5, para 7(1)(b).
[27] 1985 Act, Sched 5, para 7(3).

The debtor is also prevented from applying for sequestration during the currency of the trust deed.[28]

Proposed reforms in relation to trust deeds

The Scottish Office is currently consulting on a number of proposed reforms to trust deeds.[29]

---

[28] 1985 Act, Sched 5, para 6(b).
[29] See The Bankruptcy (Scotland) Act 1985, a Consultation Follow-up: Protected Trust Deeds and Other Issues, issued by the Scottish Office in July 1998.

46 : JUDICIAL FACTORS

In certain circumstances, a debtor's insolvency may result in the appointment of a judicial factor. A judicial factor may be appointed under specific statutory provisions or at common law. He is an officer of the court and is supervised in the carrying out of his functions by the Accountant of Court.

This chapter outlines the circumstances in which a judicial factor may be appointed, the procedure for obtaining the appointment of a judicial factor, the most important features of judicial factories and the relationship between a judicial factory and other insolvency procedures.

Circumstances in which a judicial factor may be appointed

Judicial factors may be appointed in a wide variety of circumstances, many of which have nothing to do with insolvency. This section considers the most common circumstances linked to insolvency where a judicial factor may be appointed.

Appointment under section 41 of the Solicitors (Scotland) Act 1980

In terms of the Solicitors (Scotland) Accounts Rules,[1] the Council of the Law Society of Scotland has power to investigate the books and accounts of any solicitor. Where the Council has carried out such an investigation and determined, first, that the solicitor has failed to comply with the provisions of the Accounts Rules and, secondly, that in connection with the solicitor's practice as such, any of the conditions specified in s 41 are satisfied, it may apply for the appointment of a judicial factor. The conditions specified in s 41 are:

(1) The solicitor's liabilities exceed the assets in the business.

(2) It is not reasonably practicable to ascertain from his books and accounts whether his liabilities exceed his assets.

(3) There is reasonable ground for apprehending that a claim on the Guarantee Fund may arise.

---

[1] That is, the rules made under s 35 of the Solicitors (Scotland) Act 1980.

Appointment on partnership estate

Although the primary responsibility for winding up the affairs of a dissolved partnership rests with the partners, in cases of difficulty, which may include insolvency or suspected insolvency, the court may appoint a judicial factor on the partnership estate.

A partnership will be dissolved in the circumstances specified in the partnership agreement itself (where there is one) or in any of the circumstances set out in the Partnership Act 1890 (hereafter 'the 1890 Act'). The circumstances therein include, subject to any contrary agreement between the partners, the bankruptcy of a partner,[2] although of course the bankruptcy of a partner need not mean that the partnership itself is insolvent. The partnership may also be dissolved on application to the court on any of the grounds set out in s 35 of the 1890 Act, which include that the partnership can only be carried on at a loss, and that it is just and equitable to wind up the partnership.

The court may appoint a judicial factor to the estate of a partnership which is already dissolved, or it may appoint one when it orders dissolution of the partnership on an application under s 35 of the 1890 Act.

Appointment under section 11A of the Judicial Factors (Scotland) Act 1889

Under this section, a judicial factor may be appointed to the estate of a deceased person where that person has *either* left no settlement appointing trustees or other persons having power to manage all or part of his estate *or* the trustees or other persons do not act.

The estate need not be insolvent for the appointment of a judicial factor under this section, but insolvency or doubtful solvency may be the reason for the application and where the estate is absolutely insolvent, certain provisions of the 1985 Act apply.[3]

Appointment on recall or reduction of orders relating to a composition under the 1985 Act

It has already been noted that sequestration may be brought to an end and the debtor and permanent trustee discharged by the approval of a judicial composition under the procedure provided for in s 56 of and Sched 4 to the 1985 Act,[4] but in certain circumstances a judicial factor may subsequently be appointed to the debtor's estate.

The Court of Session may, on the application of a creditor, recall the order of the sheriff approving the composition and discharging the debtor and the permanent trustee where it is satisfied that there has been or is likely to be default in payment or that the composition cannot proceed, either at all, or without undue delay or injustice to the creditors.[5] Where the order is recalled, the sequestration is revived and, where the permanent trustee has been discharged, the court may appoint a judicial factor to administer the debtor's estate.[6]

The Court of Session may also, on the application of a creditor, reduce the order of the sheriff discharging the debtor where it is satisfied that a payment or preference was given or promised for the purpose of facilitating the debtor

---

[2] 1890 Act, s 33.
[3] 1889 Act, s 11A(2), and see further below.
[4] See Chapters 36 and 40.
[5] 1985 Act, Sched 4, para 17(1).
[6] 1985 Act, Sched 4, para 17(3).

obtaining his discharge.[7] The court may then appoint a judicial factor to administer the debtor's estate.[8]

Appointment to a company

The appointment of a judicial factor to a company will usually be in circumstances other than insolvency, such as where there is deadlock between shareholders,[9] or where there has been illegal or dishonest conduct on the part of the directors[10] (although either of these situations may be combined with insolvency).

However, a factor may also be appointed to a company under various private Acts for the limited purpose of clearing secured creditors' debts[11] and, as the court has an unlimited discretion at common law to appoint a judicial factor, such a factor may be appointed to a company in any appropriate circumstances, involving insolvency. For example, it is thought that the appointment of a judicial factor might be sought in preference to other insolvency proceedings to avoid the consequences for contracts which might flow from such proceedings,[12] and a judicial factory might be more appropriate than a liquidation under Part V of the 1986 Act in the case of a foreign company.[13]

Other appointments at common law

An appointment of a judicial factor on a trust estate has been made at common law in circumstances where the trustees were insolvent and were mismanaging the trust estate.[14]

An executor may apply for the appointment of a judicial factor to the deceased's estate where that estate is insolvent as an alternative to applying for sequestration of the estate. Where the executor does not apply for either sequestration or the appointment of a judicial factor within a reasonable period after he knew or ought to have known that the estate was absolutely insolvent and likely to remain so, he will be regarded as intromitting with the estate without title if he continues to intromit with it.[15]

Appointments at common law have been made to the estates of chartered accountants in circumstances similar to those which would ground an application for the appointment of a judicial factor to a solicitor under s 41 of the Solicitors (Scotland) Act 1980.[16] Such appointments fall to be made at common law in the absence of specific statutory provisions to the same effect as s 41 of the Solicitors (Scotland) Act 1980.

---

[7] 1985 Act, Sched 4, para 18(1).

[8] 1985 Act, Sched 4, para 18(3).

[9] *McGuinness* v *Black (No 2)* 1990 SLT 461.

[10] *Fraser*, Petnr 1971 SLT 146. A judicial factor may be appointed as an alternative to a remedy under ss 459–461 of the Companies Act 1985 or any other minority shareholder remedy, or may be appointed under s 461 itself.

[11] See, for example, *Greenock Harbour Trs* v *Judicial Factor of Greenock Harbour Trust* 1910 SC (HL) 32.

[12] It was for this reason that an administration, rather than a liquidation, was sought in the case of *Re Dallhold Estates (UK) Ltd Pty* [1992] BCLC 621, discussed in Chapter 48; the circumstances there were different, but the principle is the same.

[13] For example, where the foreign company was already being wound up in another jurisdiction.

[14] See Walker, *Judicial Factors*, p 36.

[15] 1985 Act, s 8(4).

[16] Addison, *Judicial Factors*, p 62.

Procedure for obtaining the appointment of a judicial factor

Applications for the appointment of a judicial factor are by petition to the appropriate court.

In the case of an application for the appointment of a judicial factor under s 41 of the Solicitors (Scotland) Act 1980, the petition is presented by the Council of the Law Society of Scotland[17] to the Inner House of the Court of Session.[18]

In all other cases, the petition is to the Outer House of the Court of Session[19] or to the appropriate sheriff court, as defined by s 4(1A) of the Judicial Factors Act 1880.[20] The relevant procedure in each case is set out in the Court of Session Rules and the Act of Sederunt (Judicial Factors Rules) 1992[21] respectively. Applications for the appointment of a judicial factor under s 11A of the Judicial Factors (Scotland) Act 1889 may be made by one or more creditors of the deceased or any person having an interest in the succession.[22] There is no definitive list of those who may apply in other cases, but it seems clear that anyone who has a direct interest in the estate in question will be able to apply for the appointment of a judicial factor—for example, a partner in the case of a partnership, a shareholder or director in the case of a company.

The court may appoint a judicial factor *ad interim* in appropriate cases.

Important features of judicial factories

Sequestration of estate

The appointment of a judicial factor may be accompanied by sequestration of the estate which he is appointed to manage. Sequestration in this context means the taking of possession of the property in question by the court and its placement in the hands of the person appointed by the court to manage it—in this case the judicial factor.[23] Sequestration is necessary in order to deprive those with title to the property of the power to deal with it and confer that power on the judicial factor. Sequestration is not, however, invariable: it is only really necessary where there is likely to be a conflict of powers, so that although the estate will usually be sequestrated in the case, for example, of a partnership or trust, it will not always be sequestrated, for example, in the case of an individual.

Functions and powers of a judicial factor

The nature and extent of a judicial factor's duties and the scope of his powers depend on the circumstances of his appointment.[24] A judicial factor is generally thought of as an appointment to conserve property, and in some kinds of judicial

---

17 Solicitors (Scotland) Act 1980, s 41.
18 Court of Session Rules, rule 14.3(b).
19 Court of Session Rules, rule 14.2.
20 Section 4 of the 1889 Act, as amended, gives the sheriff court the same powers to appoint judicial factors as the Court of Session.
21 SI 1992/272.
22 Judicial Factors (Scotland) Act 1889, s 11A(1).
23 Although the term sequestration has come to be associated with the particular process of placing the estate of a debtor in the hands of a trustee in bankruptcy under the appropriate bankruptcy legislation (currently, of course, the 1985 Act), sequestration was originally a general term describing, as indicated, any process whereby the property of a person was taken into the possession of the court and placed in the hands of a person appointed to the court to manage it.
24 See *Council of the Law Society of Scotland* v *McKinnie (No 2)* 1995 SLT 880.

factory this is still the main purpose of the appointment. In many other cases, however, the factor will be appointed to realise and distribute the estate in respect of which he is appointed, and this is likely to be the case in judicial factories involving insolvency: it is certainly the case in relation to factors appointed on partnership estates and factors appointed under s 41 of the Solicitors (Scotland) Act 1980 and s 11A of the Judicial Factors (Scotland) Act 1889.

In the case of a judicial factor appointed on recall or reduction of orders relating to a composition under the 1985 Act, it is specifically provided that the court may give the judicial factor such order as it thinks fit as to the administration of the debtor's estate.[25] A judicial factor appointed to a company is usually appointed with the powers of a receiver under the 1986 Act.[26] Generally, a judicial factor will have the right and duty to gather in the property which is comprised in the factory estate and administer it. Where the factor is also appointed to realise and distribute the estate, he will also have powers to carry out these functions. It must be noted, however, that a judicial factor takes the estate subject to diligence and other legal rights,[27] although in the case of the estate of a deceased debtor where the estate was absolutely insolvent at the date of death and a judicial factor was appointed to the estate under s 11A of the Judicial Factors (Scotland) Act 1889 within 12 months of the death, the provisions of s 37 of the 1985 Act apply and any diligence affected by those provisions will therefore be of no effect in a question with the judicial factor.[28]

A factor appointed to the estate of a deceased debtor under s 11A of the Judicial Factors (Scotland) Act 1889 also has the power to challenge gratuitous alienations and unfair preferences and to apply for the recall of an order for financial provision on divorce if he was appointed within 12 months of the debtor's death and, in the case of gratuitous alienations and unfair preferences, the estate was absolutely insolvent at the date of death.[29]

A judicial factor may apply for special powers either at common law or under s 7 of the Judicial Factors (Scotland) Act 1849: such an application may be made in the petition itself or by subsequent note in the process.[30]

Distribution of the estate

In broad terms, where the factor is appointed to realise and distribute the estate, he must distribute it to those who have a right to it—for example, in the case of a partnership, the creditors and partners.[31]

In the case of a judicial factor appointed under s 11A of the Judicial Factors (Scotland) Act 1889, where the estate is absolutely insolvent, the scheme of distribution applicable on sequestration applies in the judicial factory, with claims being calculated to the date of the judicial factor's appointment.[32]

---

[25] 1985 Act, Sched 4, paras 17(3) and 18(3).

[26] The powers of a receiver under the 1986 Act are discussed in Chapter 27.

[27] For example, securities, leases, etc.

[28] 1985 Act, s 37(7). The provisions of s 37 of the 1986 Act are discussed in detail in Chapter 31. This is the only type of factory to which these provisions apply.

[29] See the 1985 Act, ss 34, 35 and 36. The challenge can be made under the appropriate statutory provisions or, where applicable, at common law. For a discussion of the relevant provisions, see Chapter 30.

[30] Court of Session Rules, rule 61.15(2); Act of Sederunt (Judicial Factors Rules) 1992, rule 5.

[31] *Armstrong, Petnr* 1988 SLT 255.

[32] Judicial Factors Act 1889, s 11A(2). The scheme of distribution applicable on sequestration is discussed in Chapter 33.

Relationship of a judicial factory with other insolvency procedures

Judicial factory and sequestration

The appointment of a judicial factor to a non-company debtor will not necessarily prevent a subsequent sequestration. In terms of s 10 of the 1985 Act, the petitioner in a sequestration petition, the debtor or any creditor concurring in a sequestration petition must advise the court as soon as they become aware of the fact, *inter alia*, that a judicial factor has been appointed to the estate in respect of which sequestration is sought or that there is a pending petition for the appointment of a judicial factor to that estate.[33] The court may then allow the sequestration petition to proceed or may sist or dismiss it[34] and, where the sequestration petition is (as is usual) being heard in the sheriff court, the Court of Session may direct the sheriff to sist or dismiss the sequestration petition or hear the sequestration petition and the petition for the appointment of a judicial factor together.[35] Either procedure may have particular advantages over the other in any given situation, and the court will take this into account in determining how best to proceed.[36]

Where sequestration is awarded, this brings the factory to an end,[37] but the respective rights of the judicial factor and the trustee in sequestration in the estate thereafter may not be easy to determine. The interrelationship of a judicial factory and a subsequent sequestration was discussed in the case of *Council of the Law Society of Scotland v McKinnie (No 2)*,[38] which involved a factor appointed under s 41 of the Solicitors (Scotland) Act 1980. In that case, the court held that since the factor in question was not merely a conservator, but had the power and duty to distribute the funds in his charge, all that vested in the trustee in sequestration on the subsequent sequestration of the solicitor was a right to an accounting from the judicial factor, rather than the actual assets of the solicitor in the hands of the factor. On this reasoning, the same would apply to any factory where the factor was appointed to realise and distribute the estate rather than simply to conserve it, which would be the usual situation where a judicial factor was appointed in circumstances involving insolvency. However, it is thought that the decision in *McKinnie* may be questioned on this point, as it is not consistent with the fact that the judicial factory comes to an end as a result of the subsequent sequestration.[39]

Judicial factory and company insolvency proceedings

It is thought that, in the same way as a judicial factory does not prevent a subsequent sequestration in relation to a non-company debtor, it would not prevent the subsequent administration or liquidation of a company. There is no direct

---

[33] 1985 Act, s 10(1).

[34] 1985 Act, s 10(3)(a).

[35] 1985 Act, s 19(3)(b).

[36] For example, it might be deemed appropriate to allow a sequestration under the 1985 Act to proceed in preference to a judicial factory in order to allow prior transactions to be challenged— a right which only a judicial factor appointed under s 11A of the 1889 Act where the estate was absolutely insolvent and the factor was appointed within 12 months of the debtor's death would otherwise have.

[37] *Mitchell v Scott* (1881) 8 R 875.

[38] Note 24 above.

[39] See McKenzie, 'Council of the Law Society of Scotland *v* McKinnie (No 2)' (1996) 1 SLPQ 252. Where the estate has been sequestrated on the appointment of the judicial factor, as appears not to have been the case in *McKinnie*, the matter is even more problematic.

equivalent of s 10 of the 1985 Act in either case, but the petitioner in an administration petition is required to disclose in the petition details of various matters and, although the appointment of a judicial factor is not specifically mentioned, the matters to be disclosed include 'other matters which, in the opinion of the petitioner, will assist the court in deciding whether to grant an administration order',[40] which would include any judicial factory. The court would then exercise its discretion in dealing with the administration petition in the light of the judicial factory.[41] It is suggested that where the court decides to make an administration order, this would, of necessity, have the effect of terminating the factory. In relation to liquidation, a petitioner seeking a winding-up order from the court is also obliged to disclose various matters in the petition, but the appointment of a judicial factor is not one of them and there is no provision equivalent to that relating to administration petitions to disclose other matters of relevance which would require disclosure of a judicial factory. It is suggested, however, that it would be a matter of good practice to disclose any such judicial factory if known to the petitioner, and it would probably come to light in any event following service, intimation and advertisement of the petition. Where the existence of a judicial factory was known to the court, it would then exercise its discretion to make a winding-up order in the light of the judicial factory.[42] Again, it is thought that where a winding-up order is made, this would of necessity have the effect of terminating the judicial factory. In the case of a voluntary liquidation, although there is no court involvement and therefore no opportunity for the exercise of a discretion as to whether to allow a liquidation to proceed in the light of the existence of a judicial factory, it is thought that the commencement of a voluntary liquidation would have the effect of terminating the judicial factory in the same way as a winding-up order.

Receivership raises more difficult issues. Where an application is made to the court for the appointment of a receiver, the petitioner is required to disclose in the petition details of various matters including, generally, matters which will assist the court in deciding whether to appoint a receiver.[43] This would include the existence of a judicial factory. The court would then exercise its discretion as to whether to appoint a receiver in the light of the judicial factory. However, court appointments are virtually unknown, and the most likely situation would be for a receiver to be appointed by the chargeholder. There seems to be nothing to prevent a chargeholder appointing a receiver during the course of a judicial factory and it is thought that a receiver would take precedence over a judicial factor in relation to the assets affected by the charge because the factor takes the property of the company subject to securities.[44] On the other hand, there may be difficulties with this approach, particularly where the estate of the company has been sequestrated into the hands of the factor.

Company voluntary arrangements under Part I of the 1986 Act and section 425 arrangements raise even more difficult issues. It is difficult to see how the company could propose a CVA during a judicial factory as it would not be in a

---

[40] Court of Session Rules, rule 74.10(1); Sheriff Court Rules, rule 10(1).

[41] It might, for example, sist the petition pending recall of the judicial factory.

[42] The court might, for example, sist the petition pending recall of the judicial factory.

[43] Court of Session Rules, rule 74.17(1); Sheriff Court Rules, rule 15(1).

[44] An analogy can be drawn with liquidation where the receiver takes precedence over the liquidator as a general office holder.

position to deal with its property, which would be under the control of the factor. For the same reason, it is difficult to see how the company could apply to the court for orders to call meetings for the purpose of agreeing a section 425 arrangement while a judicial factor was in office. Of course, a section 425 arrangement can be applied for by other persons—for example, creditors. In such a case it is thought that the court would have to exercise its discretion as to whether to allow the relevant meetings to be called in the light of the judicial factory. It is thought that where any section 425 arrangement was ultimately sanctioned by the court, this would logically require to be regarded as superseding the judicial factory.

Part VII

CROSS-BORDER INSOLVENCY

47 : CROSS-BORDER INSOLVENCY:
INTRODUCTION AND THEORY

Insolvencies where the law of more than one jurisdiction comes into play cause special problems. This is not just a matter of academic interest for those concerned with 'domestic' insolvency law in Scotland; many domestic insolvencies may have international or cross-border (the terms are interchangeable) aspects. Nor are such cases necessarily confined to the obvious example of multinational companies because, for these purposes, not only jurisdictions outwith the United Kingdom, but both England and Wales and Northern Ireland are foreign jurisdictions. Businesses, whether companies, sole traders or partnerships, may trade with other jurisdictions within the United Kingdom or increasingly commonly, even for small businesses, outwith it, especially within the European Union. Even non-trading insolvencies may involve international aspects—for example, a contract for the supply of new furniture by a firm outwith Scotland, the ownership of a holiday timeshare in another part of the United Kingdom or abroad. In addition, questions may arise as to the effect of foreign insolvency proceedings in Scotland, whether or not there are also insolvency proceedings ongoing in Scotland.

Where such cross-border insolvency issues arise, these are dealt with according to the rules of Scots law, including its rules of private international law. These rules are discussed further in the next chapter. This chapter provides a context for the rules by examining further some of the typical cross-border issues which can arise on insolvency and by considering the need for international rules in this field, the theoretical approaches to dealing with the problems of cross-border insolvency and the various national and international initiatives aimed at establishing international rules on cross-border insolvency.

Some typical cross-border insolvency issues

Typical cross-border insolvency issues, or problems, include the following.

(1) Issues related to jurisdiction. For example, does a Scottish court have jurisdiction to commence insolvency proceedings in relation to a particular debtor—say, a foreign company with a branch in Scotland or a foreign national residing and/or trading in Scotland? Can foreign debtors and creditors avail themselves of Scottish insolvency procedures?

(2) Issues related to the effect of Scottish insolvency proceedings outwith Scotland. For example, will foreign jurisdictions recognise Scottish insolvency proceedings and give effect to them? What effect will that recognition have? Can an insolvency office holder sell the debtor's timeshare in Spain or insist on delivery of goods the debtor has ordered from the United States?

(3) Other issues related to administration of Scottish insolvency proceedings. For example, can foreign creditors claim in the insolvency proceedings? Will their securities be recognised? What if one particular creditor is a foreign government seeking recovery of taxes?

(4) Issues related to insolvency proceedings in another jurisdiction. What effect will concurrent proceedings in another jurisdiction have on existing Scottish insolvency proceedings or any subsequent attempt to commence insolvency proceedings in Scotland? On what grounds will Scots law recognise insolvency proceedings in another jurisdiction and what effect will recognition (if granted) have?

(5) Issues related to co-operation between jurisdictions where more than one set of insolvency proceedings exist in relation to the same debtor. For example, in what circumstances, and to what extent, does the law permit co-operation and in what form—directly between the office holders in the proceedings concerned or through the courts or through some other mechanism?

The need for international solutions to cross-border insolvency problems

The types of issue identified above can give rise to significant problems in practice. Further, in the absence of agreed international solutions, the solutions which may be reached may differ widely from case to case as a result of the application of different rules of law—the result, in turn, of the operation of different rules of private international law. These facts speak for themselves in demonstrating a need for a framework of international co-operation in relation to cross-border insolvency cases. They also give rise, however, to important questions of principle, in particular, the appropriate approach to dealing with cross-border insolvency problems.

Theoretical approaches to the problems of cross-border insolvency

There are essentially two theoretical approaches to the problems of cross-border insolvency: unity and universality, and plurality and territoriality.

Unity and universality

This approach advocates that there should be only one set of insolvency proceedings in relation to a particular debtor (unity) and that it should have effect in every other jurisdiction (universality).

This is conceptually attractive, but is not without difficulties. The domestic insolvency laws of different jurisdictions can vary widely, so there may be practical difficulties in giving effect to one set of proceedings in every other jurisdiction. Perhaps even more importantly, doing so will almost inevitably upset settled rights and expectations about their enforcement on insolvency. There may also be debate as to the proper location for the 'universal' proceedings. Should it be the debtor's domicile, centre of activity, location of the majority of assets, etc?

Plurality and territoriality

This approach allows a plurality of proceedings but confines the effect of each set of proceedings to the assets within the jurisdiction.

This also has attractions, particularly the fact that it is much more likely that settled expectations based on existing rights will be preserved. However, there are disadvantages with this approach also. The costs of administering a number of separate proceedings may use up much of the assets, and because the location of assets and creditors may be entirely fortuitous, failure to pool assets and allow all creditors to claim in respect of that pool may result in substantial injustice.

These two approaches are, essentially, mutually exclusive and one of the main reasons for the lack of success in achieving international agreement(s) on rules for dealing with cross-border insolvency problems to date is the difficulty in getting agreement on the theoretical basis for such rules. The next section outlines briefly the various initiatives aimed at achieving international agreement on rules for dealing with cross-border insolvencies.

Initiatives on cross-border insolvency

It has been stated that there are essentially four levels at which action can be taken to improve international co-operation in cross-border insolvencies: multi-lateral treaties, bilateral treaties, facilitative provisions in domestic legislation and use of protocols at an individual level.[1] Harmonisation of national insolvency laws—the ultimate solution to cross-border insolvency problems and the goal of some of the earlier initiatives in this field—has largely been abandoned by those involved in current initiatives on the basis that it is not realistically capable of achievement in anything but the long term, if then.[2]

A limited number of bilateral and localised multilateral treaties exist,[3] and a number of countries have also incorporated facilitative provisions in domestic legislation.[4] Similarly, there are instances of protocols being used in individual cases.[5] A more wide-ranging solution, however, remains elusive despite a number

---

[1] Bruce Leonard at the first Vienna Colloquium on International Insolvency. The edited proceedings are contained in the special Conference issue of 1995 4 *International Insolvency Review*.

[2] Ron Harmer at the first Vienna Colloquium, above. National pride apart, one of the main reasons for this is that insolvency law is so interlinked with almost every other area of law (see the Preface) that any major changes to the principles on which it is based would have massive ramifications for the entire legal system.

[3] See Wood, *Principles of International Insolvency Law*, ch 17.

[4] The longest standing of these is s 304 of the United States Bankruptcy Code, which came into force in 1978. The United Kingdom introduced legislation in 1986 in the form of s 426 of the 1986 Act (discussed further in Chapter 48). Australia also has provisions similar to those contained in s 426 of the 1986 Act.

[5] The most famous example is probably that of the *Maxwell* case, where the US and UK proceedings were co-ordinated by means of such a protocol drawn up by the examiner appointed by the US court and approved by the US and UK courts. Such protocols have also been used in cases involving the US and Canada: see, for example, the case of *Everfresh Beverages Inc*, discussed in Leonard, 'Committee J's Initiatives in Cross-Border Insolvencies and Reorgani-sations: The Experience of the *Everfresh* Case' 1997 6 IIR 127.

of international initiatives. This section details the most important current initiatives in this field.

The International Bar Association's Cross-Border Insolvency Concordat

The Cross-Border Insolvency Concordat produced by the International Bar Association (hereafter 'the IBA') provides a statement of principles to be followed in drawing up protocols for use in individual cases. The principles contained in the Cross-Border Insolvency Concordat were utilised in drawing up the protocol in the *Everfresh Beverages* case (see note 5 above).

The International Bar Association's Model International Insolvency Co-operation Act

The IBA's Model International Insolvency Co-operation Act ('MIICA') provides model legislation which can be adopted by countries into their own domestic legislation. The provisions of the model legislation provide for recognition of the foreign representative in insolvency proceedings and mandatory assistance to the foreign proceedings if either the foreign jurisdiction has substantially similar legislation or the foreign forum is a proper and convenient one and it is in the overall interest of the creditors to administer the estate there. They provide further that the foreign representative may commence ancillary proceedings for the purposes of obtaining prescribed reliefs or, if such ancillary proceedings are unavailable or denied, a full insolvency proceeding in accordance with the provisions of the local law. In the former case, they provide for application of the foreign substantive law in the normal case, with local law applying in the latter. They also provide for supersession of the provisions where any treaty is applicable. The model legislation has not, however, been adopted by any country as yet, perhaps because it relies on or contains concepts which may be unacceptable to some countries.

The UNCITRAL Model Law on Cross-Border Insolvency

Under the auspices of the United Nations Commission on International Trade Law (hereafter 'UNCITRAL'), a draft model law has been produced which, like MIICA, provides model legislation which can be adopted into each country's domestic legislation. It is longer and more detailed than MIICA, but none the less essentially restricts itself to dealing with the issues surrounding the recognition of foreign proceedings, access to the courts of the country in which recognition is sought, either through the foreign court or directly by the foreign representative, and the kinds of relief necessary to protect businesses and assets. However, some provisions are more far-reaching—for example, a distinction is drawn between foreign 'main' proceedings and others, with certain consequences following on the recognition of such 'main' proceedings. An important provision is that which allows and encourages direct co-operation between courts and provides a non-exhaustive list of means by which this might be achieved. This would be a major facilitating provision where courts do not have inherent power to achieve this. It is thought that the United States is currently taking steps to adopt the model law, but there do not appear to be any immediate plans to do so in the United Kingdom.

The Council of Europe Convention on Certain Aspects of International Insolvency

This Convention applies only to proceedings involving disinvestment (*sic*) of the debtor. Initially, it was intended to make provision only for the exercise of certain powers of office holders in such proceedings outside their own jurisdiction, but ultimately its scope was expanded to cover three areas: exercise of an office holder's powers outside his home jurisdiction; the opening of secondary proceedings in other jurisdictions; and matters relating to creditors' claims. It allows for a plurality of proceedings in different jurisdictions, but provides for only one of these to have universal effect, the others being limited in effect. Signatories may choose to disapply the provisions relating to the exercise of the office holder's powers outside his own jurisdiction and/or the provisions relating to the opening of secondary proceedings. However, the Convention has not yet come into force. It was opened for signature on 5th June 1990, but few member countries have signed it and none have ratified it: a minimum of three ratifications would be necessary to bring it into force between ratifying states.

The EU Convention on Insolvency Proceedings

This also is restricted to proceedings which entail the partial or total divestment of the debtor and the appointment of a liquidator.[6] The proceedings which are specified in Annex A to the Convention as meeting that definition for the United Kingdom include administration and CVAs, but some of the important provisions are restricted to winding-up proceedings,[7] which exclude these rescue-oriented procedures. It is a direct Convention which imposes mandatory rules of jurisdiction in relation to the insolvency proceedings to which it applies, and these override national rules. Like the Council of Europe Convention, which actually formed the basis for it, the Convention allows for a plurality of proceedings, and determines the effect of the proceedings according to the jurisdictional basis on which the proceedings are opened. All proceedings opened in accordance with the grounds of jurisdiction specified in the Convention are accorded automatic recognition throughout the European Union, but proceedings opened in the debtor's 'centre of main interests' are given universal effect throughout it, the liquidator being able to exercise his powers with few restrictions in any other member state. Any other proceedings opened on the alternative basis of the presence of an 'establishment' of the debtor have only territorial effect. The Convention provides a number of choice of law rules by which questions arising in the insolvency will be determined, some of which are qualified or may be disapplied in certain circumstances. The Convention does not, however, attempt to deal with the difficulties caused by the situation where there are some proceedings within the European Union and some outwith it—a situation which is potentially fraught with disaster.

Like the Council of Europe Convention, the EU Convention is not yet in force. It was opened for signature on 23rd November 1995 and stipulated that it remained open for signature until 23rd May 1996.[8] It was signed within that time period by all the member states except the United Kingdom, who refused to sign it as part of its policy of non-cooperation resulting from the BSE crisis. Since

---

[6] That term is used in the Convention as a generic term: the Convention is not restricted to liquidation of companies.

[7] Again, that term is used in the Convention as a generic term: the provisions of the Convention which are restricted to winding-up proceedings are not restricted to the winding up of companies, but rather the term is used to mean those procedures which make a final distribution of the debtor's assets to creditors. In a United Kingdom context, this would include, for example, a Scottish sequestration.

[8] Article 49.2 of the Convention.

the legal basis for the Convention is art 220 of the Treaty of Rome, all member states must sign it before it can come into force. The United Kingdom's failure to sign before the stipulated date therefore effectively means that the Convention cannot progress any further. It would still be possible for it to be revived, but at the time of writing there do not appear to be any immediate plans to do so.

The International Bar Association's Model Insolvency Code

This aims to develop a set of model provisions relating to each of the major concepts of insolvency law—for example, grounds of challenge of prior transactions, priority claims, tests for insolvency and, importantly, recognition of foreign proceedings and assistance to foreign insolvency office holders. The intention is that the provisions be considered by countries reforming (or indeed forming) their domestic insolvency laws and adopted by them into their new domestic legislation. Its goal is to promote harmonisation of insolvency laws world wide and thereby facilitate the proper and fair treatment of creditors' claims in international insolvencies.

Other initiatives

There are a number of other initiatives currently being considered by various domestic bodies in different countries, particularly the United States. For example, the American Law Institute has embarked on a project to explore the possibility of harmonisation of the insolvency laws of the North Atlantic Free Trade Association states.

48 : CROSS-BORDER INSOLVENCY: SCOTS LAW

The law of Scotland pertaining to cross-border insolvency is found partly in statute and partly in case-law. The 1985 and 1986 Acts set out the jurisdictional and other criteria for commencing insolvency proceedings in relation to non-company and company debtors respectively, and the 1985 Act contains specific provisions relating to concurrent insolvency proceedings, including foreign proceedings.[1] The 1985 and 1986 Acts also set out the effect claimed for Scottish non-company and company insolvency proceedings respectively where relevant, and the 1985 Act contains various procedural provisions relating to foreign claims which are also applied to the relevant company insolvency proceedings by the Scottish Rules. The substantive rules relating to claims are found in the common law. Recognition of, and co-operation with, insolvency proceedings taking place in the different jurisdictions within the United Kingdom itself is governed by the 1986 Act, part of the provisions of which extend to certain other designated jurisdictions, while recognition of, and co-operation with, insolvency proceedings outwith those jurisdictions is a matter for the common law. Finally, the 1985 Act also regulates the international effect of the debtor's discharge, although this question is again a matter for the common law where applicable in relation to company debtors.

This chapter outlines the relevant provisions in relation to the above matters.

Jurisdiction

This section considers the effect of the relevant rules of jurisdiction in relation to non-Scottish debtors and applications for the commencement of insolvency proceedings by non-Scottish debtors and creditors generally.

Non-company debtors

Jurisdiction in sequestration proceedings is outlined in detail in Chapter 6. It will be recalled that in the case of a living or deceased debtor, jurisdiction will be established if the debtor *either* had an established place of business *or* was habitually

---

[1] Concurrent foreign proceedings relating to company debtors are regulated not by the 1986 Act but by the common law.

resident in Scotland at any time within the year immediately preceding the date of presentation of the petition for sequestration, or the date of death, as the case may be.[2] In addition, jurisdiction exists in relation to any partner of a firm, whether alive or deceased, even where these requirements are not satisfied in relation to that partner, if the firm of which he is or was a partner is the subject of current sequestration proceedings before the Scottish court.[3] Sequestration is not, therefore, restricted to 'Scottish' debtors, or even debtors present in Scotland at the time the proceedings are raised.

Similarly, it will be recalled that in the case of trusts, partnerships, limited partnerships, bodies corporate and unincorporated bodies, jurisdiction is established if *either* the entity had an established place of business in Scotland at any time within the year immediately preceding the date of presentation of the petition for sequestration *or* it was constituted or formed under Scots law and at any time carried on business in Scotland.[4] Sequestration is not therefore restricted to Scottish entities (ie, entities constituted or formed under Scots law) so long as the entity has or has had within the relevant time period an established place of business in Scotland.

Company debtors

In the case of companies, jurisdiction varies according to a number of factors, including the type of insolvency proceedings to be invoked. Jurisdiction in relation to each type of insolvency proceeding is set out in detail in previous chapters[5] and although the main provisions are summarised here, reference should be made to the appropriate chapters for further detail.

It will be recalled that it is thought that the CVA procedure is not open to a company which is not registered in Scotland, other than one which is in liquidation.[6] A section 425 arrangement, however, is open to any company liable to be wound up in Scotland[7] and, since companies other than Scottish companies may, in certain circumstances, be wound up in Scotland, such an arrangement would be open to any such company.

It is thought that administration is not open to a company which is not registered in Scotland other than pursuant to a request for assistance under s 426 of the 1986 Act.[8]

A receiver may be appointed by, or by the court on the application of, the holder of a floating charge granted by an incorporated company which the Court of Session has jurisdiction to wind up.[9] Since the Court of Session may, in certain circumstances, wind up companies other than Scottish companies, a foreign incorporated company which has granted an appropriate floating charge may go into receivership in Scotland.

---

[2] 1985 Act, s 9.

[3] Ibid.

[4] Ibid.

[5] Chapter 8 (CVAs); Chapter 9 (section 425 arrangements); Chapter 10 (administration); Chapter 12 (receivership); Chapter 14 (voluntary liquidation); Chapter 16 (compulsory liquidation: registered companies); and Chapter 17 (compulsory liquidation: unregistered companies).

[6] 1986 Act, ss 1(3) and 251, and CA 1985, s 735.

[7] Companies Act 1985, s 425(6)(a).

[8] 1986 Act, ss 8(1) and 251, and CA 1985, s 735, and *Re Dallhold Estates (UK) Pty Ltd* [1992] BCLC 621.

[9] 1986 Act, s 51.

Voluntary liquidation is available only to companies registered in Scotland.[10] With respect to compulsory liquidation, the Scottish courts do not have jurisdiction to wind up companies registered in England and Wales, or Northern Ireland. They do, however, have jurisdiction to wind up unregistered companies, which includes other foreign companies, where the company is dissolved, or has ceased to carry on business, or is carrying on business only for the purpose of winding up its affairs; where the company is unable to pay its debts; where the court is of the opinion that it is just and equitable that the company should be wound up or where there is a subsisting floating charge over the company's property, and the security of the creditor is in jeopardy. There is no additional requirement for the company to be doing business in Scotland or to have a place of business or assets in Scotland,[11] although in practice, the court might very well exercise its discretion to decline to make a winding-up order if there was no sufficient connection with Scotland. In addition, a company incorporated outside Great Britain which has been carrying on business in Great Britain and then ceases to do so may be wound up as an unregistered company, notwithstanding that it has been dissolved or otherwise ceased to exist as a company under or by virtue of the laws of the country under which it was incorporated[12] and the Scottish court also has jurisdiction to wind up an 'oversea company' as defined in s 744 of CA 1985.[13]

Applications by non-Scottish debtors and creditors for the commencement of insolvency proceedings generally

A non-Scottish debtor may apply for the commencement of appropriate insolvency proceedings in Scotland where these allow for an application by the debtor and the appropriate jurisdictional and any other relevant criteria are satisfied. Similarly, a non-Scottish creditor may apply for the commencement of any appropriate insolvency proceedings in Scotland where these allow for applications by creditors and the appropriate jurisdictional and any other relevant criteria are satisfied. Section 11 of the 1985 Act contains provisions facilitating the making of the oath by creditor required in relation to a creditor petition for sequestration where the creditor concerned is outwith the jurisdiction.[14]

Concurrent proceedings

The 1985 Act contains specific provisions relating to concurrent insolvency proceedings, including foreign proceedings. In the case of company insolvency proceedings, the position with regard to concurrent foreign proceedings is governed by common law.

Sequestration

Section 10 of the 1985 Act provides, *inter alia*, that where a petition for seques-tration is pending before a Scottish court, and it is brought to the court's attention

---

[10] 1986 Act, s 73, and the Companies Act 1985, s 735; see also the 1986 Act, s 221.
[11] *Inland Revenue* v *Highland Engineering Ltd* 1975 SLT 203.
[12] 1986 Act, s 225.
[13] An oversea company as defined by that section is one which is incorporated outside Great Britain but has an established place of business inside Great Britain.
[14] Such an oath is not necessary in any company insolvency proceedings.

that an application for an 'analogous remedy' is proceeding or is in force, the court may allow the Scottish sequestration to proceed or sist or dismiss it.[15] An analogous remedy is defined as including, broadly, bankruptcy or administration proceedings in England and Wales or any like proceeding in Northern Ireland, or any remedy analogous to those proceedings or to sequestration in any other country.[16] The court has complete discretion in the matter, and may allow Scottish proceedings to continue, notwithstanding that there are prior foreign proceedings.

If sequestration has already been granted in Scotland and it is then discovered that there are analogous foreign proceedings pending or in force, the court, on the application of an interested person, may recall the Scottish sequestration.[17] Again, however, the court has complete discretion as to whether it will do so. There have been no cases under the present statutory provisions, but under the previous common law the court has generally considered the matter from the point of view of what constitutes the most appropriate forum.[18]

Company insolvency proceedings

A foreign liquidation or similar insolvency proceeding is no bar to a Scottish liquidation, although the court may exercise its discretion to refuse to grant a winding-up order in appropriate circumstances. Alternatively, the court may direct that the Scottish liquidation be ancillary to the foreign liquidation in appropriate circumstances.[19]

It is thought that foreign proceedings would not be a bar to a CVA, a section 425 arrangement or an administration. In the latter two cases, however, the court again has discretion in dealing with the relevant applications and it might refuse to allow the calling of the appropriate meetings in relation to a section 425 arrangement or to make an administration order in appropriate circumstances. Indeed, in relation to administration, the court might not be satisfied that the administration would be likely to achieve the purposes for which it is sought in the first place in the light of the existence of foreign proceedings.[20] Much would depend on the nature of the proceedings and whether they fell to be recognised. Foreign proceedings would be no bar to the appointment of a receiver.

The extra-territorial effect of Scottish insolvency proceedings

Sequestration

Section 31 of the 1985 Act states that the whole estate of the debtor 'wherever situated' vests in the permanent trustee. Sequestration therefore claims to affect property located abroad. In practice, however, it is recognised that the *lex situs* of any such property will in fact determine the effect, if any, to be given to the Scottish sequestration and the ability of the trustee to deal with foreign assets. A

---

[15] 1985 Act, s 10(4).
[16] 1985 Act, s 10(5).
[17] 1985 Act, s 17.
[18] *Cooper* v *Baillie and Ors* (1878) 5 R 564.
[19] *Marshall*, Petnr (1895) 22 R 697. The designation of proceedings as ancillary is discussed further below.
[20] If the court was not so satisfied, it would not be in a position to make an administration order: see Chapter 10.

debtor is under an obligation to co-operate with the permanent trustee, however, and to do everything necessary, including executing documents, to allow the trustee to carry out his functions, so the trustee may be able to enforce his claim to foreign assets through the debtor. In relation to the other jurisdictions within the United Kingdom, s 426 of the 1986 Act provides that an order of a court exercising its insolvency jurisdiction in one part of the United Kingdom will be enforced in the other parts as if it was made by a court exercising insolvency jurisdiction in that part,[21] but it is specifically provided that the section does not require a court in one part of the United Kingdom to enforce an order relating to property situated in that part which is made by a court in another part.[22]

Company insolvency proceedings

Company insolvency proceedings differ from sequestration to the extent that none of the proceedings claim to vest the company's assets in the insolvency office holder: although insolvency office holders are given extensive powers to deal with the company's property,[23] title to the company's property remains with the company except where an order is made vesting specific property in a liquidator.[24] There is no territorial restriction on the assets which can be included in a CVA inherent in the legislation itself, so an appropriately drafted arrangement can extend to assets outwith Scotland. Similarly, there is no territorial restriction on the assets which may be included in a section 425 arrangement and an appropriately drafted arrangement can therefore extend to assets outwith Scotland. An appropriately worded floating charge can also extend to property outwith Scotland and administration and liquidation affect the company's property 'wherever situated'.[25] CVAs, section 425 arrangements and receiverships may, therefore, claim to extend to the company's property outwith Scotland, and administration and liquidation claim to do so as a result of the definition of property contained in s 436 of the 1986 Act. However, as in relation to sequestration, it is recognised that, in practice, the ability of a supervisor of a CVA, an administrator, a receiver or a liquidator to enforce this claim will ultimately depend on the *lex situs*.[26] With respect to the other jurisdictions within the United Kingdom, it is specifically provided in relation to receivership that a receiver appointed under a floating charge in either part of Great Britain may exercise his powers in the other part of Great Britain insofar as they are not inconsistent with the law there.[27] In addition, the provisions of s 426 discussed in

---

[21] 1986 Act, s 426(1).

[22] 1986 Act, s 426(2). Subsection (3) of the section allows provision to be made by order for an insolvency office holder in one part of the UK to have, with any specified modifications, the same rights in relation to property in another part of the UK as if he was an office holder in that part, but no such order has ever been made.

[23] See also Chapter 21 and the discussion of foreign property in Chapter 22. In the case of a section 425 arrangement, where the company is not in administration, receivership or liquidation, there will not in fact be any office holder at all.

[24] 1986 Act, s 145. The section applies to compulsory liquidations, but is available in voluntary liquidations by virtue of s 112 of the 1986 Act.

[25] See 1986 Act, s 436, and Chapter 21.

[26] Section 425 arrangements, as already noted, do not involve an office holder unless the company is also in administration, receivership or liquidation. Where the arrangement is being implemented by the company itself, therefore, it is unlikely that the company would even be regarded as being subject to insolvency proceedings by a foreign jurisdiction.

[27] 1986 Act, s 72.

the preceding paragraph in the context of sequestration also apply to company insolvency proceedings, and the comments made apply *mutatis mutandis.*

Claims

With some limited exceptions, all creditors may claim in Scottish insolvency proceedings irrespective of whether they are Scottish or not, and irrespective of whether the claim is governed by Scots law or not. This section discusses a number of important issues in relation to claims with a foreign element.

Administrative provisions relating to the submission of claims

The 1985 Act makes provision for creditors who neither reside nor have a place of business within the United Kingdom to be allowed to submit informal claims in writing,[28] and for the claim to be stated in foreign currency in prescribed circumstances.[29] In relation to company insolvency proceedings, there is no specific provision relating to informal claims by foreign creditors, but there is a general provision allowing the insolvency office holder to dispense with the usual requirements in relation to any debt or class of debt which would allow him to dispense with such formalities in the case of foreign creditors.[30] Claims may also be stated in foreign currency in specified circumstances.[31]

Determination of claims

The subsistence and validity of claims is determined by the proper law applicable to them.[32] Such questions are determined by the insolvency office holder, subject to an appeal to the appropriate court.[33]

Classification and ranking of claims

The classification and ranking of claims in Scottish insolvency proceedings is exclusively a matter for Scots law (the *lex fori*),[34] except where foreign assets have been transmitted to Scotland for distribution in the Scottish insolvency proceedings on the condition that certain foreign priorities are preserved in relation to these assets.

Foreign and domestic claims will be ranked alongside each other according to their classification under the Scottish rules. If, therefore, a foreign claim is recognised as a secured claim, it will be ranked with other secured claims; if it is an ordinary debt, it will be ranked with other ordinary debts and so on. Some particular types of claim raise special problems. These are as follows.

   (1) Claims by foreign public authorities. Revenue claims by foreign public
        authorities are not admitted in any Scottish insolvency proceedings.[35]

---

[28] 1985 Act, ss 22(3) and 48(3).

[29] 1985 Act, ss 22(6) and 48(7), and SI 1985/1925, reg 6.

[30] Scottish Rules, rule 4.15(3). The rule applies to claims in a compulsory liquidation and is applied to creditors' voluntary liquidations by rule 5 and Sched 1 and to CVAs, administrations and receiverships by rule 7.9(3) of the Scottish Rules.

[31] Scottish Rules, rule 4.17(1). The rule applies to claims in a compulsory liquidation and is applied to creditors' voluntary liquidations by rule 5 and Sched 1 and to CVAs, administrations and receiverships by rule 7.9(3) of the Scottish Rules.

[32] *Williamson* v *Taylor* (1845) 8 D 156.

[33] See further Chapter 32.

[34] *Lusk* v *Elder* (1843) 5 D 1279.

[35] *Government of India* v *Taylor* [1955] AC 491.

'Revenue' in this context has a wide meaning, including not only taxes, but other non-contractual payments to the state or public authorities, such as estate, customs, stamp and gambling duties, local rates and state health insurance schemes.[36] The rationale for this rule is that the courts will in no circumstances directly or indirectly enforce the revenue laws of a foreign country. Similarly, claims by foreign public authorities based on the foreign criminal or penal law (for example, unpaid fines) are not admitted in Scottish proceedings, for the same reasons.

(2) Security interests created abroad. The general principle is that if the security claimed is valid according to the *lex situs* of the property at the time of the creation of the security (including any conflicts rule of the *lex situs* which may in turn refer the matter to some other law such as the *lex loci actus*), effect will be given to the security in the Scottish proceedings, even if it is a type of security which is not known to domestic law. The court will, however, require to classify the nature of any such security interest, which may cause difficulty if it is not of a type known to domestic law.[37] Once the security has been classified, the extent and ranking of the security will be determined by reference to the normal rules of Scots law.[38]

(3) Claims where the creditor has been partially satisfied abroad out of foreign assets of the debtor or has also claimed in foreign insolvency proceedings. Where a creditor has been partially satisfied abroad out of foreign assets of the debtor, the hotchpot rule applies in any domestic proceedings. The effect is that where any creditor[39] makes a claim for the purposes of receiving payment in Scottish insolvency proceedings, he must account for any property or monies recovered by virtue of private diligence or proceedings abroad to which the Scottish insolvency office holder would otherwise have been entitled[40] and he may be required to surrender the fruits of his diligence or the foreign proceedings to the said office holder before his claim will be admitted. The hotchpot rule also applies to any sums which a creditor may have received in foreign insolvency proceedings.[41] Such a creditor will not be paid any dividend in the Scottish proceedings until the other creditors have received dividend at the same rate as he has received abroad. If the Scottish proceedings are more advanced than the foreign proceedings, it is possible that the creditor will be made to account for future dividends received in the foreign proceedings after payment of the Scottish dividend. Where property or monies recovered by a creditor are recovered by virtue of the enforcement of a valid security, however, it is thought that the creditor will not need to account for them, but may claim the outstanding balance due to him in full in the Scottish proceedings, in the same way that a Scottish secured creditor may enforce his security without reference to any Scottish

---

[36] See, for instance, *Metal Industries (Salvage) Ltd* v *Owners of ST 'Harle'* 1962 SLT 114.

[37] The security may be classified by analogy to the types of security which are known to domestic law.

[38] See above.

[39] The rule applies equally to Scottish and foreign creditors.

[40] See, for instance, *Lindsay* v *Paterson* (1840) 2 D 1373; *Clydesdale Bank* v *Anderson* (1890) 27 SLR 493.

[41] *Stewart* v *Auld* (1851) 13 D 1337.

insolvency proceedings and claim any unsecured balance in those proceedings. Similarly, if the private diligence or proceedings abroad were completed prior to the Scottish proceedings, the creditor will not need to account for property or monies recovered thereby, because they ceased to be part of the debtor's estate before the commencement of the insolvency proceedings and the insolvency office holder accordingly has no right to them.

Recognition of, and co-operation with, foreign insolvency proceedings

Scots law adopts a fairly generous approach to recognition of foreign insolvency proceedings and the corresponding right of the foreign office holder, and to co-operation with foreign office holders where proceedings fall to be recognised.

Recognition of foreign insolvency proceedings

No formal application for recognition of foreign insolvency proceedings is necessary.[42] In certain circumstances, a foreign office holder may act without taking any formal steps in Scotland at all.[43] Where a foreign office holder raises any action in Scotland in connection with the insolvency or otherwise seeks the assistance of the court either directly or at the request of his own insolvency courts under the procedure set out in s 426 of the 1986 Act,[44] recognition will be granted informally within those proceedings.

In considering the rules for recognition of foreign insolvency proceedings, two separate distinctions must be borne in mind: first, that between non-company insolvency proceedings (ie, sequestration or its equivalent) and company insolvency proceedings; and, secondly, that between insolvency proceedings taking place within parts of the United Kingdom, the Channel Islands, the Isle of Man and certain other designated countries or territories and insolvency proceedings taking place in any other jurisdiction.[45]

In relation to non-company insolvency proceedings, the common law rule is that recognition will be afforded to a foreign sequestration or its equivalent[46] if it is regular according to the law of the country in which it is made and the ground

---

[42] This may be contrasted with the position in many other jurisdictions where a formal exequatur is necessary.

[43] See further below. Of course, if his title was challenged, the matter might then come before the court, who would decide on the matter, but if not, there may be no formal acknowledgement of the recognition of the proceedings and his right to act at all.

[44] Discussed further below.

[45] Recognition (and enforcement, which is dealt with further below) of insolvency proceedings taking place within parts of the UK, the Channel Islands, the Isle of Man and certain other designated countries or territories is regulated by s 426 of the 1986 Act. The countries which have been designated to date are Anguilla, Australia, the Bahamas, Bermuda, Botswana, Canada, Cayman Islands, Falkland Islands, Gibraltar, Guernsey, Hong Kong, Republic of Ireland, Malaysia, Montserrat, New Zealand, St Helena, Republic of South Africa, Turks and Caicos Islands, Tuvalu and the Virgin Islands: see Co-operation of Insolvency Courts (Designation of Relevant Countries and Territories) Order 1986, (SI 1986/2123); Insolvency Act 1986 (Guernsey) Order 1989 (SI 1989/2409); and the Co-operation of Insolvency Courts (Designation of Relevant Countries and Territories) Order 1996 (SI 1996/253). Recognition and enforcement of insolvency proceedings in any other country is regulated at common law.

[46] The types of proceeding which qualify as insolvency proceedings for this purpose are discussed further below.

of jurisdiction in the foreign court is regarded as valid.[47] What exactly will be accepted as a valid ground of jurisdiction is not entirely clear. In *Obers* v *Paton's Tr*,[48] the court took the view that it could hardly refuse to recognise if done abroad what the court itself would do at home: this suggests that if jurisdiction in the foreign proceedings was based on any ground which was the same as or similar to that available in Scots law,[49] recognition would be granted. By the same reasoning, grounds of jurisdiction based on a lesser connection with the forum state than that provided for in Scots law would probably result in recognition being refused. Where sequestration proceedings in Scotland have already been commenced, the question of recognition of foreign proceedings is more problematic. Historically, Scots law took a unitary approach to this issue, holding that since sequestration or its equivalent acts as a transfer of the debtor's assets to the trustee, there cannot be more than one sequestration.[50] This would suggest that prior Scottish proceedings would be a bar to recognition of a subsequent foreign award. However, as discussed above, the 1985 Act now allows the court a discretion in dealing with a Scottish sequestration petition where analogous foreign proceedings already exist, and a Scottish award of sequestration can be recalled at the discretion of the Scottish court on the basis, *inter alia*, that one or more awards of sequestration or analogous remedies has also been granted. Accordingly, it is suggested that on principle, if the foreign proceedings would otherwise fall to be recognised, the existence of prior Scottish proceedings would not necessarily act as an absolute bar to recognition.

In relation to company insolvency proceedings, the common law rule regarding foreign liquidations or their equivalent[51] is that such liquidations will generally be recognised if they take place in the place of incorporation, on the basis that it is for the law of the country which brought the company into being to determine its fate. A Scottish court may also recognise a liquidation which does not take place in the place of incorporation in appropriate circumstances. For example, in *Queensland Mercantile and Agency Co Ltd* v *Australasian Investment Co Ltd*[52] the Scottish court recognised English liquidation proceedings relating to a company incorporated in Australia where the company was also being wound up in Australia and the English winding up was declared to be ancillary to the Australian one. The court took the view that the proceedings, although not in the place of incorporation, were competent and proper. As there is in general no transfer of assets to the liquidator, the problems of principle encountered in cases where there is more than one sequestration do not arise in the context of liquidation, and consequently the fact that proceedings may have been commenced in this country prior to or after the beginning of foreign proceedings will not bar recognition of the foreign proceedings if they would otherwise fall to be recognised. The Scottish court may, in appropriate circumstances, declare

---

[47] *Araya* v *Coghill* 1921 SC 462.

[48] (1897) 24 R 719.

[49] The grounds of jurisdiction in the 1985 Act are discussed in Chapter 6 and summarised above.

[50] It was said in *Queensland Mercantile and Agency Co Ltd* v *Australasian Investment Co Ltd* (1888) 15 R 935 that where a sequestration has taken place in Scotland, title to the debtor's property has passed to the trustee, and it is impossible for there to be another sequestration either in the same country or in another country from that in which the first took place.

[51] The types of proceeding which qualify as company insolvency proceedings generally for this purpose are discussed further below.

[52] Note 50 above.

Scottish liquidation proceedings to be ancillary to liquidation proceedings abroad or take other appropriate steps for the purposes of facilitating or sanctioning agreements between foreign and domestic liquidators with regard to distribution of the company's assets. It is thought that recognition of foreign insolvency proceedings other than liquidation or its equivalent will be based on similar principles. In the case of *Marshall*, Petnr,[53] for example, the Scottish court recognised a receivership in Iowa on the basis that the receivers were appointed by a competent United States court and were administering the assets for the benefit of the debenture holders and other creditors, and made the Scottish liquidation ancillary to that receivership.

Notwithstanding that the conditions for recognition outlined above appear to be fulfilled, recognition may still be denied on a number of grounds. These are:

(1) Where the insolvency proceedings offend against some fundamental principle of public policy.

(2) Where there has been a breach of natural justice.[54]

(3) Where the insolvency proceedings have been obtained by fraud[55] or amount to a fraud upon the other creditors, as where they have been invoked to avoid Scottish proceedings.[56]

(4) Where the insolvency proceedings are to enforce the penal laws of another country.

(5) Where the insolvency proceedings are *solely* to enforce the revenue laws of another country (as opposed to where there are claims other than that of the foreign revenue authorities: recognition will not be denied only because there is such a claim among others).[57]

Where the proceedings in question are taking place in another jurisdiction within the United Kingdom, the common law rules described above are superseded by the provisions of s 426 of the 1986 Act. These provisions ensure that insolvency proceedings in other jurisdictions within the United Kingdom will always be recognised by a Scottish court.[58] Where assistance is rendered to the courts of the Channel Islands, the Isle of Man or any other country or territory designated under s 426 of the 1986 Act in pursuance of the obligation in that section to assist the courts of those jurisdictions in relation to insolvency law matters,[59] recognition of the relevant proceedings will be implicit. It cannot be said that proceedings in those jurisdictions will automatically be recognised, however, because despite the mandatory terms of the obligation to render assistance to the courts of those jurisdictions, assistance may in some circumstances be refused.[60]

---

[53] Note 19 above.

[54] See, for instance, *Det Norske Bjergnings og Dykkercompagni v McLaren* (1885) 22 SLR 861.

[55] *Boe v Anderson* (1857) 20 D 11.

[56] *Geddes v Mowat* (1824) 2 Shaw's App Cas 230.

[57] *Scottish National Orchestra Society Ltd v Thomson's Exor* 1969 SLT 325.

[58] It is thought that this would be the case even if there might be grounds for refusing to recognise the proceedings were they proceedings not within the compass of s 426—for example, where the grounds of jurisdiction in an English bankruptcy did not coincide with the grounds for a Scottish sequestration.

[59] See further below.

[60] This is considered further below.

There remains the question of what foreign proceedings qualify as insolvency proceedings for the purpose of recognition. With regard to proceedings in other parts of the United Kingdom and the other jurisdictions within the compass of s 426 of the 1986 Act, 'insolvency law' is defined in s 426(10). The effect of this is that CVAs, administration, receivership, liquidation, individual voluntary arrangements, bankruptcy and certain other proceedings relating to disqualification of directors in England and Wales, the equivalent proceedings under the Insolvency (Northern Ireland) Order 1989 or Part II of the Companies (Northern Ireland) Order 1989 in Northern Ireland, and any proceedings which are the equivalent of those proceedings or their counterparts in Scotland,[61] are insolvency proceedings for this purpose. With regard to other jurisdictions, there is no comprehensive definition of what qualifies as insolvency proceedings for the purposes of recognition. Particularly in company proceedings, there may be a plethora of foreign proceedings of a type unknown to Scots law, but the fact that the proceedings are of a type not known to Scots law will not necessarily bar recognition. American proceedings under Chapter 11 have been recognised in England as insolvency proceedings[62] and it is thought that a Scottish court would adopt the same approach. In the context of non–company insolvency, it has been held that where a foreign trustee or his equivalent is claiming property in Scotland, this will only be recognised if the proceedings claim to extend to assets outwith the jurisdiction and to vest those in the office holder.[63]

Effects of recognition

There are a number of important effects which will flow automatically from recognition of foreign insolvency proceedings.

In certain limited circumstances, some insolvency proceedings in England and Wales will automatically affect court actions or other proceedings in Scotland. Presentation of a petition for administration in England or Wales will automatically impose the restrictions contained in s 10 of the 1986 Act[64] in Scotland as well as in England and Wales; similarly, the granting of an administration order in England or Wales will automatically have the effect provided for in s 11 of the 1986 Act[65] in Scotland as well as in England and Wales. In a compulsory liquidation, s 130(2) of the 1986 Act provides that where a winding-up order has been made or a provisional liquidator appointed, no action or proceeding against the company or its property shall be commenced or continued without leave of the court and on such terms as it may impose. Thus, actions in Scotland would be automatically stayed where a winding-up order was granted in England or Wales.[66] The subsection applies to any company being wound up by the court in England and Wales, not only to companies registered in England and Wales being wound up by the court.

An order of a foreign court purporting to stay automatically all proceedings world wide has not been recognised as directly achieving that effect in England,[67]

---

[61] That is, company voluntary arrangements, administration, receivership, liquidation, sequestration and certain other proceedings relating to disqualification of directors.

[62] *Felixstowe Dock & Railway Co v United States Lines Inc* [1989] QB 360.

[63] *Colville v James* (1862) 1 M 41.

[64] See Chapter 10.

[65] Ibid.

[66] *Martin v Port of Manchester Insurance Co Ltd* 1934 SC 143, a case involving a previous legislative provision identical in its terms to s 130(2).

[67] *Felixstowe Dock & Railway Co v United States Lines Inc*, note 62 above.

and the same decision would probably be reached in Scotland. An order made by a court in another part of the United Kingdom restraining a creditor from proceeding with an action or diligence against the debtor or the debtor's property would, however, be enforced in Scotland as a result of the provisions of s 426 of the 1986 Act.[68] In cases involving proceedings other than those in another part of the United Kingdom, the Scottish court could sist court proceedings or interdict a creditor from taking action against the debtor or the debtor's property *either* in response to a request for assistance by a court under s 426 of the 1986 Act *or*, where this did not apply, by exercising on request its inherent discretion to control proceedings or diligence. The court may sist Scottish proceedings if the matter could more appropriately be resolved in the context of the foreign insolvency[69] and may interdict the carrying out of diligence by creditors in Scotland in the face of foreign insolvency proceedings.[70]

At common law, a trustee or equivalent office holder in foreign bankruptcy proceedings may claim the debtor's moveable property situated in Scotland without further procedure in Scotland,[71] provided that the foreign proceedings claim to extend to such property and to vest it in the foreign office holder.[72] Heritable property situated in Scotland does not automatically vest in the foreign office holder,[73] but he may apply to the court for assistance in realising this.[74] In relation to company insolvency proceedings, where there is usually no question of the property of the company vesting in the insolvency office holder, recognition will allow the foreign office holder to administer the company's assets and to seek the assistance of the court in this connection if required. However, it should be noted that foreign proceedings will affect only those assets which could have been assigned by the debtor at the date of the foreign order.[75] So prior attachments will not be affected by a later foreign insolvency even where this is recognised, but equally, where the foreign proceedings are recognised, diligence carried out after the commencement of the foreign proceedings will not prevail in competition with such foreign proceedings. This applies equally to bankruptcy and company insolvency proceedings. In certain specialised cases, prior foreign insolvency proceedings which are recognised may also have an effect on prior diligence carried out in Scotland: in terms of s 185 of the 1986 Act, certain diligences carried out in Scotland within certain periods will be cut down by the subsequent winding up of a company registered in England and Wales.

It has already been noted that although proceedings taking place within the other jurisdictions in the United Kingdom will be recognised and the orders of the relevant court enforced in Scotland, the Scottish court is not required to enforce any orders relating to property situated in Scotland.[76]

---

[68] 1986 Act, s 426(1), discussed above.

[69] *Okell* v *Foden* (1884) 11 R 906; *Edinburgh & Glasgow Bank* v *Ewan* (1852) 14 D 547.

[70] *Strother* v *Read and Others* July 1, 1803 FC; *Selkrig* v *Davies* (1814) 2 Dow 230.

[71] *Araya* v *Coghill*, note 47 above.

[72] See above.

[73] Although it has been held that a trustee in bankruptcy in England, where the relevant legislation purported to vest the bankrupt's whole property, including land, in England or elsewhere, in the trustee, had a real right to heritage in Scotland on recording a title to it in the Register of Sasines: *Rattray* v *White* (1842) 4 D 880.

[74] Ibid.

[75] *Galbraith* v *Grimshaw* [1910] AC 508.

[76] 1986 Act, s 426(2), and see above.

Recognition carries with it standing to apply to the Scottish court for assistance and, where appropriate, to institute proceedings in Scotland and appear in existing proceedings.[77] This leads on to the question of co-operation with the foreign insolvency proceedings.

Co-operation with foreign insolvency proceedings

As in relation to recognition of foreign insolvency proceedings, it is necessary to distinguish between insolvency proceedings taking place within parts of the United Kingdom, the Channel Islands, the Isle of Man and the other countries and territories designated under s 426 of the 1986 Act and insolvency proceedings taking place in any other jurisdiction.

Section 426 of the 1986 Act, as well as providing for automatic recognition and enforcement of court orders in insolvency proceedings between the different jurisdictions within the United Kingdom,[78] provides for mandatory assistance between the insolvency courts of the separate jurisdictions of the United Kingdom, the Channel Islands, the Isle of Man and those countries or territories designated under the section.[79] Requests for assistance are made direct from one court to another. The section has been used with success. For example, in the case of *Dallhold Estates (United Kingdom) Pty Ltd*[80] an administration order under the 1986 Act was made in the United Kingdom in relation to an Australian company already in liquidation in Queensland, thereby allowing the preservation of assets which would otherwise have been lost, and in one of the many proceedings relating to the collapse of BCCI, the Scottish court appointed liquidators to a company in pursuance of a request from the English court under the section.[81] However, although the wording of the section is mandatory (the court 'shall' assist the foreign court), in the case of *In Re Focus Insurance Ltd*[82] the English court refused an application for assistance under the section on behalf of the liquidator of a Bermudan company on the basis that the relief sought was in relation to a person subject to a bankruptcy order in England and was inconsistent with the scheme imposed by the English insolvency legislation for recovery of the assets of a bankrupt. The court took the view that it was entitled to refuse assistance, notwithstanding the mandatory wording of the statute, if there were sufficiently strong reasons for doing so. This decision has been confirmed by the decision in *Hughes v Hannover Ruckversicherungs AG*,[83] in which the English Court of Appeal held that the court had power, in the exercise of its general discretion, to refuse an application under the section and that the grounds for doing so were not restricted to public policy.[84] Where the court grants assistance, it may apply its own insolvency law or the law of the foreign jurisdiction.[85]

Where s 426 of the 1986 Act is not applicable, reference must be made to the common law. The Scottish courts have generally shown themselves to be

---

[77] Although caution may be required.
[78] See the preceding section.
[79] The countries and territories so designated are listed at n 45; and see further above.
[80] Note 8 above.
[81] 1991 and 1992 (unreported).
[82] [1997] 1 BCLC 219.
[83] [1997] 1 BCLC 497.
[84] The decision contains a useful review of the existing authorities on s 426. See also *Purves v England, The Times*, 29th January 1998, where a request for assistance was again refused.
[85] 1986 Act, s 426(5), and see also *Hughes v Hannover Ruckversicherungs AG*, note 83 above.

willing to assist foreign office holders, and in appropriate cases have declared Scottish proceedings to be ancillary to foreign proceedings[86] and sanctioned a reasonable scheme of co-operation between Scottish and foreign office holders.[87] The foreign office holder may apply directly to the court for assistance at common law.

The full implications of designating Scottish proceedings as ancillary to foreign proceedings have not yet been worked out in the case-law, but the nature of ancillary proceedings was discussed in some detail in the English case of *Re Bank of Credit and Commerce International SA (in liq) No 11*,[88] where an English liquidation of the company had been designated as ancillary to the principal liquidation of the company taking place in Luxembourg. The issue which arose in that case was whether or to what extent the English court could disapply the relevant English statutory provisions relating to set-off which provided for automatic and mandatory set-off. The court said that an English winding up which was ancillary was so in the sense that the English liquidators would not have the power to get in and realise the property of the company world wide but would have to concentrate on getting in and realising the English assets, and that since the pooling of assets and the declaration of a dividend from that pool would be necessary to achieve a *pari passu* distribution of the company's assets world wide, the English liquidation was also ancillary in the sense that it would be the liquidators in the principal liquidation who would declare that dividend and distribute the assets in the pool. It also recognised that it was inherent in the concept of the English liquidation being ancillary that the court could direct the English liquidator to transmit funds from the English ancillary liquidation to the foreign principal liquidation for the purpose of enabling a *pari passu* distribution to be made to creditors world wide. It also said, however, that the ancillary character of an English liquidation did not relieve the English court of an obligation to apply English law, including English insolvency law, to the resolution of any issue in the liquidation which was brought before the court and that the court had no inherent or statutory power to disapply at its discretion the substantive rules of the statutory insolvency scheme. It is thought that a Scottish court would be likely to take a similar approach and that the scope of Scottish ancillary proceedings would therefore generally be restricted to ingathering the Scottish assets to be remitted to the foreign principal proceedings. It is also thought, however, that secured and preferential creditors and the expenses of the ancillary proceedings would have to be paid first and only the balance of the funds then remitted to the office holder in the principal proceedings, all remaining creditors, Scottish or otherwise, then entering their claims in the principal proceedings[89] and conflicts with the principal proceedings being avoided by restricting the scope of the ancillary proceedings and by the court regulating the proceedings as necessary to avoid conflict. Where there is more than one set of

---

[86] See, for example, *Marshall*, Petnr, note 19 above. The court will only designate the Scottish proceedings as ancillary, however, if it is satisfied that all creditors will be treated appropriately in the foreign proceedings and there will be no prejudice to domestic creditors.

[87] See *Stewart v Auld*, note 41 above.

[88] [1997] 1 BCLC 80.

[89] Any further claim by secured or preferential creditors—for example, for any unpaid balance of their debts—would be a matter for the law of the principal proceedings on the basis, discussed above in relation to claims, that the *lex fori* governs claims.

foreign proceedings and the Scottish proceedings are designated as ancillary proceedings, the matter is even more complicated.[90] It is thought that the correct course to be followed would be for any surplus in the Scottish proceedings to be transmitted to the office holder in the other ancillary proceedings prior to onward transmission to the office holder in the principal proceedings.[91]

It should be noted that the mere existence of foreign proceedings is not of itself sufficient grounds for opening insolvency proceedings in Scotland, although the fact that foreign proceedings have been opened may be used in some cases as evidence of a ground for the opening of proceedings in domestic law being satisfied—for instance, that it was just and equitable to wind up a company. It may be possible for Scottish proceedings to be opened at the instance of the foreign office holder under s 426 of the 1986 Act where this applies. It was noted above that in *Re Dallhold Estates (UK) Pty Ltd*,[92] an administration order was made in pursuance of a request by the Federal Court of Australia under s 426 of the 1986 Act in respect of a company incorporated in Australia to which provisional liquidators had been appointed in both Australia and England. However, the court required the statutory conditions contained in the 1986 Act for an administration order to be satisfied before making the order.

Discharge of the debtor

Non-company insolvency proceedings

The effect of the debtor's discharge in a Scottish sequestration is governed by s 55(1) of the 1985 Act, which provides that, with certain specified exceptions, the debtor will be discharged of his debts *within the United Kingdom*.[93] No further action to recover a pre-sequestration debt can therefore be taken in the United Kingdom, but the discharge does not purport to extend to foreign jurisdictions and the effect of a discharge outwith the United Kingdom is a matter for the foreign law.

The effect in Scotland of a debtor's discharge in foreign proceedings is regulated by the common law. With respect to a bankruptcy in England and Wales, there is no statutory provision similar to s 55(1) of the 1986 Act, but because a discharge in such a bankruptcy claims, under English law, to discharge all debts, it is thought that Scots law would recognise the effect of a discharge in such a bankruptcy.[94] In relation to other foreign bankruptcies, the foreign discharge will be regarded as effective in Scotland if it has the effect of discharging the debt under the proper law of the debt,[95] and where a creditor has taken part in the foreign insolvency proceedings, he may be personally barred from taking further action in Scotland in relation to the debt for which he has claimed in the foreign proceedings.[96]

---

[90] It is (relatively) less complicated where the Scottish proceedings are the principal proceedings, because ultimately any surplus from the foreign ancillary proceedings will be remitted to the Scottish proceedings.

[91] *Queensland Mercantile and Agency Co Ltd* v *Australasian Investment Co Lt,* note 50 above.

[92] Note 8 above.

[93] See Chapter 36.

[94] Anton, *Private International Law* (2nd edn), pp 739–740.

[95] *Rochead* v *Scot* (1724) Mor 4566. The same approach has been taken in subsequent cases.

[96] See, for example, *Rose* v *McLeod* (1825) 4 S 311.

Company insolvency proceedings

With regard to company insolvency proceedings in Scotland, the effect of the proceedings on the company's debts depends on the proceedings in question.[97] Where the proceedings result in the discharge of the company, it is suggested that the position would be the same as for sequestration, at least insofar as no further action could be taken to recover the debt so discharged in Scotland. The effect of the discharge outwith Scotland would be a matter for the foreign law.

With respect to the effect of a foreign discharge on liquidation, the position is similar to that in sequestration insofar as the foreign discharge will not be regarded as effective in Scotland unless the law of the liquidation is the proper law of the debt.[98] It is thought that the rule that where a creditor has taken part in foreign insolvency proceedings he may be personally barred from taking further action in Scotland in relation to the debt for which he has claimed in the foreign proceedings[99] will apply equally in liquidations. Equally, it is thought that the effect of a foreign discharge in any other type of company insolvency proceedings will be judged by the same test, ie, whether it is effective under the proper law of the debt.

---

[97] See Chapter 37.
[98] *Adams v National Bank of Greece* [1961] AC 255.
[99] See above.

INDEX